Prostitution and Sexuality in Shanghai

A Social History, 1849–1949

Shanghai's night life, from the mid-nineteenth century until the victory of the Communist Party in 1949 was dominated by the world of prostitution. Henriot portrays the Chinese sex trade, from the sophisticated life of the courtesan to the day-to-day travails of the common prostitutes. He examines the extent to which these worlds were integral to Chinese social and business life, mores and sexuality. Henriot portrays a sector that was sensitive to economic and social conditions, and thus accurately reflected Shanghai's changing social structure, societal attitudes, and commercial development. This is the most comprehensive treatment available of a social phenomenon that has been much discussed in studies of Chinese culture, but largely neglected as a subject of serious historical concern. At the crossroads of social and intellectual history, this study goes behind the curtain of exoticism and takes a realistic look at a vibrant sector of Shanghai's economic and cultural life.

Christian Henriot is Director of the Institute of East Asian Studies and Professor of Chinese History at the Lumière-Lyon 2 University in France. He is the author and editor of several books on modern Chinese history, including *Shanghai 1927–1937: Municipal Power, Locality, and Modernization.*

Prostitution and Sexuality in Shanghai

A Social History, 1849–1949

CHRISTIAN HENRIOT
Lumière-Lyon 2 University

Translated by Noël Castelino

CAMBRIDGE
UNIVERSITY PRESS

PUBLISHED BY THE PRESS SYNDICATE OF THE UNIVERSITY OF CAMBRIDGE
The Pitt Building, Trumpington Street, Cambridge, United Kingdom

CAMBRIDGE UNIVERSITY PRESS
The Edinburgh Building, Cambridge CB2 2RU, UK
40 West 20th Street, New York, NY 10011-4211, USA
10 Stamford Road, Oakleigh, VIC 3166, Australia
Ruiz de Alarcón 13, 28014 Madrid, Spain
Dock House, The Waterfront, Cape Town 8001, South Africa

http:www.cambridge.org

Belles de Shanghai: Prostitution et secaulité en Chine aux XIXe–XXe siècles
© CNRS Editions 1997

English translation © CNRS Editions 2001

First English translation published 2001

Printed in the United States of America

Typeface Times Roman 10/12 pt.   *System* QuarkXPress™ [BTS]

A catalog record for this book is available from the British Library.

Library of Congress Cataloging in Publication data
Henriot, Christian.
    [Belles de Shanghai. English]
    Prostitution and sexuality in Shanghai: a social history (1849–1949) / Christian Henriot.
        p.   cm.
    Includes bibliographical references (p.   ) and index.
    ISBN 0-521-57165-0 (hbk)
    1. Prostitution – China – Shanghai – History.   2. Prostitutes – China – Shanghai – History.   I. Title.

    HQ250.S52 H4613   2000
    306.74′0951′132 – dc21

ISBN   0 521 57165 0   hardback

For Kevin, Axel, and Feng Yi

It is through their encounter with officialdom that they are wrested from the night in which they could – and perhaps always should – have stayed [. . .]. These lives, fated to vanish from the realm of discourse without finding voice, have left nothing but fleeting, incisive and often enigmatic traces at their immediate point of contact with the State. So that they will probably never be understood for themselves, for what they may have been in their own world.

Michel Foucault, La vie des hommes infames

Where the trail [of the lives of women] is missing, it is not because of the nature of their experience. Rather, it is because the very social modalities through which the trail is made, by groups or by individuals, testify to relationships of force that are not to the advantage of women.

Christine Planté,
Ecrire des vies de femmes, Les cahiers du Grif, spring 1988

The historian of modern times must make do with invasive middlemen. The forms of discourse at his disposal interpret reality according to their own rules and ends. They reveal the observer far more surely than the object of observation.

M. Baulant and R. Chartier,
Les marginaux et les exclus de l'histoire

Contents

Tables, Figures, Plates, and Maps

Figures

Author's Preface

In 1985, when I started this research, the history of prostitution in China was virtually *terra incognita*. It took me seven years to complete this project and turn it into a *thèse d'État*, the inescapable exercise imposed on French academics, especially historians, after the Ph.D., to make sure they have internalized the norms of the profession. Fortunately, like the Chinese traditional examinations, this great but cumbersome tradition has now been abolished. By the time I published this text in France – it took another few years to trim down the original 1,200-page dissertation – prostitution had emerged as a subfield of the thriving Chinese urban history, at a point of intersection with women's studies.

The present book does not fit into the current mainstream of postmodern approaches to Chinese women's history, especially the more recent studies of prostitution in China. This research is firmly rooted in the belief that a history of prostitution cannot be reduced to a critical examination of the forms of discourse this phenomenon has generated, that history is not simply a "fiction-making operation" (Hayden White), that the historian has the ability and the duty to "provide an adequate and controlled knowledge on this population of dead – characters, mentalities, prices – which form his object" (Roger Chartier). To give up all "intention of truth" in historical research would be tantamount to letting the door open to all kinds of falsifications and, consequently, treasons of memory.

This study of prostitution in Shanghai was written with the explicit purpose of retelling the history of Chinese prostitutes for themselves, though rarely by themselves and most often through the "voice" of others. Yet, I kept an unwavering commitment not to lose track of the fact that I was dealing with real lives, not merely with historical figures or images. These lives had been part of a larger historical process, from which they could – and should – not be detached, of overwhelming and changing power relations within Chinese urban society. Prostitution was a prominent reflection of these changes. This English edition was revised in the light of the new historiography produced in the United States on Chinese prostitution and with a view to taking issue with the interpretations it offers. Through this book, I hope to contribute both to a better understanding of the "margins" of Chinese urban society and to the stimulating debates on the historical rendering of women's lives in modern China.

Christian Henriot
Lyons, April 2000

Acknowledgments

Historical research is a solitary form of intellectual activity. At the same time, it draws sustenance from many sources whose contributions cannot be fully measured and accounted for. This work is based on a Doctorat d'État thesis prepared under the direction of Professor Marie-Claire Bergère. In these pages, she will find an expression of gratitude for the keen sense of history that she passed on to all who were privileged to work under her direction.

The documents that I was allowed to consult in China for this study would have been far smaller in number had it not been for the help of a historian and friend. Bao Xiaoqun cleared a path for me into the arcane world of the historical archives extant in Shanghai, and he pinpointed numerous sources and files hitherto unavailable to foreign research workers. His unfailing support and skill made it possible for me to consult many essential documents.

I have made extensive use of a wide variety of collections of documents, including those of the Hoover Institution on Peace, War, and Revolution in Stanford, California, in the United States. I am heavily indebted to this institution. In particular, I must thank Ramon Myers, Chen Fu-mei, and Julia Tung for the facilities that they placed at my disposal during each of my visits to the Institution. At the Archives diplomatiques in Nantes, France, Claude Even, Conservator of the Archives, and Mr. Blanchard were immensely helpful. The Shanghai Municipal Archives hold the most remarkable collection on the history of that great city, and I would like especially to thank the Department of Consultation and its successive directors. I am grateful to the Franco-American Commission for the grant of a Fulbright scholarship, which enabled me to do some very fruitful research in the United States.

At Cambridge University Press, Elizabeth Neal and Mary Child offered unwavering support in steering the manuscript through to completion and, in the final stretch, Regina Paleski performed expert production editing. Finally, in the preparation of the English edition, I owe a special word of thanks to Noël Castelino. I was blessed to rely on a most remarkable translator and friend who relentlessly reviewed the most minute details of the translation and helped me correct many inconsistencies in the original version.

Christian Henriot
Lyons, April 28, 2000

Introduction:
Prostitution and Sexuality –
a Historiographical Review

The study of prostitution provides a unique vantage point from which to observe society, even if the view that it offers might appear to be a singular one. Of all the so-called fringe groups, the prostitutes are closest to the point of linkage (the "interface" in today's vernacular) between "respectable society" and its deviant communities. Prostitutes straddle the shifting boundary between the world of the castoffs and the society that rejects them or that they have rejected. Prostitution is of course also related to sexuality. And although historians have long neglected it or banned it from their works, sexuality is an essential dimension of human societies. As such, prostitution can furnish a unique and sometimes distorting mirror of both sexual behavior and its underlying sensibilities. Besides, the prostitutes' world is eminently sensitive to economic and social change, to which it responds and adapts more speedily than do other groups in society. In the case of Shanghai, prostitution may serve as a barometer of the accelerated process of modernization that the city experienced between 1842 and 1949.

The idea for the present work came originally from a fascinating book, *Laboring Classes and Dangerous Classes*, by Louis Chevalier.[1] It was tempting to try and transpose Louis Chevalier's thinking to the case of Shanghai. An earlier study that I had made of this city, based on a scrutiny of its press, had already opened a few windows into a rather special type of society and urban space. My reading of the Chinese sources made it clear that the notion of "dangerous classes" does not really correspond to the reality of Shanghai. However, it is by reference to this primary idea, although unrelated, that I conceived the idea of studying Shanghai's "fringe" groups in the nineteenth and twentieth centuries. I very soon came up against an imbalance in my source materials. Although I had gathered large quantities of data on prostitution, I was unable to obtain equally varied and reliable materials on which to base a study of the other groups. Besides, it seemed that the milieu of prostitution might itself provide new insights into Chinese society. It was another work, *Women for Hire: Prostitution and Sexuality in France after 1850*, by Alain Corbin, that converted me to this point of view.[2] Alain Corbin's work is a superb example of the extent to which the histor-

ical approach to prostitution can make a vital contribution to an understanding of social change and of the evolution of group sensibilities.

It appeared then that a monographic approach, limited to the city of
Shanghai, was preferable to a vain attempt to deal with the entire phenomenon of "Chinese prostitution." In this attempt to penetrate the arcane
realms of a singular world about which (notwithstanding what I have said
earlier) the available information is often fragmentary, the fact of choosing
one city alone made it easier to demarcate the world of prostitution, identify the individuals, groups, and institutions involved in this activity, and
search for the documents and traces that they might have left behind.
Besides, the city of Shanghai had the particular feature of being divided
into three territories (the French and International Settlements and the
area of the Chinese Municipality), each endowed with an autonomous
organ of power[3] (see Map 1). This division into three distinct jurisdictions
and the lack of collaboration between the administrative structures and the
police of the different parts of the city created a fertile breeding ground for
all kinds of criminal activity. The growth of prostitution also benefited from
this administratively polycentric character that hindered the adoption of
common policies both for the repression of the criminals implicated in this
activity and for the rescue of the prostitutes. The present study begins with
the year 1849, at a time when prostitution, as practiced in a traditional
Chinese city, had not yet experienced the effects of the Western presence.
It ends in 1949, when the Chinese Communist Party took power in a
metropolis that had long been part of the "other China" (M.-C. Bergère),
a modern, cosmopolitan city open to the world.

My approach seeks to address two main questions. The first part of this
work relates to the activity of prostitution itself and the hugely varied
reality covered by the term. First of all, I have tried to identify the various
forms of prostitution, from the kind practiced in the most notorious brothels to that of the upper-class houses, while trying at the same time to locate
possible cases of interpenetration between the different levels and chart the
pathways that linked the different categories of prostitutes. I have also tried
to determine the extent to which there was a "hierarchy of prostitution" in
Shanghai. Shanghai underwent tremendous changes during the period
under study, and my aim has been to examine the effects of these changes
on the world of the prostitutes and find out especially if any reclassification
took place and, if so, in what form. Secondly, I have attempted to find out
who the prostitutes were, how they came to prostitution, how they got out
of it, and what their working and living conditions were. In particular, I have
tried to compare the pictures and glimpses available in many contemporary
studies and in the literature of the period with the reality as it might be
apprehended through a cross-examination of the available sources. The
third aspect, included in this general topic, relates to the organization of
prostitution in the broad sense of the term. The question is how the huge

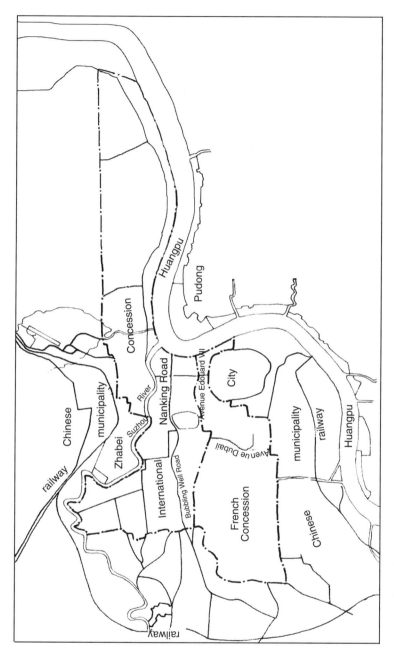

Map 1. Shanghai in the 1920s. *Source:* Feetham, Richard, *Report*, p. 356.

traffic in women supplied to the houses of prostitution was organized. What place did these women occupy in the urban space? How did the brothels function? What sort of clientele did they receive? How was what we might call the economy of sex constructed? Beyond the "prostitutional" reality, this approach might lead us to reflect on the place of women in Chinese society, the evolution of Shanghai's social structure, and the ways in which the Chinese relate to sexuality.

A good part of the work done by historians of prostitution in the West deals with (a) the different systems of control set up by government authorities with the support or cooperation of certain professional groups (such as doctors) or social groups and (b) the movements of opposition and resistance aroused by these systems. I was therefore curious about the place of prostitution in the public sphere in China and about the measures that might have been taken to manage prostitution, contain it, or repress it. The question was whether the Chinese and foreign authorities in China followed comparable or even coordinated policies in this field. Was there ever, as in the West, an intense and public debate on this subject, and, if so, who were its protagonists? Was there any significant change in the attitudes of the different authorities of the city during the century under study? The first level of my study is therefore devoted to an examination of the institutions, authorities, and organizations involved in the "administration of prostitution," the reasons for and the modalities of their action, the goals pursued, and the effects of the measures taken.

One clarification needs to be made regarding the scope of this research. Only Chinese female prostitutes have been taken into account. This means that two categories will not be studied here: foreign female prostitutes and homosexual prostitutes. They have been left out for two main reasons. At the time when I was conducting this research, the available documents on these aspects of prostitution in China were very incomplete and consisted of only secondhand sources. The materials I was then able to gather were far too disparate and vague. The situation regarding homosexual prostitution is even more difficult. This topic was a source of obvious embarrassment among the Chinese authorities as well as in Chinese society and among its elites. The silence on the subject is almost total even though the existence of this type of prostitution is proven.[4] The second reason for leaving these two groups out is that they are not relevant to my general approach, which is centered on female prostitution in Chinese society. Homosexuals represented only a very minor and peripheral fringe group in prostitution and catered to a very specific demand. Western and Japanese prostitutes were visited by an almost exclusively foreign clientele even if an "opening out" to Chinese customers can be seen toward the end of the 1930s.

The way in which this book has been organized only partially corresponds to the two questions evoked above, which are present in varying degrees throughout the book. This short introduction reviewing the historiography of prostitution in China is followed by the first part, "The Courtesans: Prostitutes to the Elite and the Elite of the Prostitutes," dealing with the upper stratum of prostitutes. The first chapter seeks to draw a portrait of this group and focuses on its particular form of integration into local society, its highly formalistic modes of relationship with customers, and the reasons for its very sharp decline starting from about the end of the nineteenth century. The second chapter describes the different stages in the life of the courtesans, starting with their entry into the trade, as well as their religious practices and even their "civic" activities. It ends with an analysis of the culture (and its forms of expression) common to the elites who patronized these Chinese "hetaerae."

Four chapters deal with common prostitution ("The Market of Prostitution and Mass Sexuality"), which included that of intermediate groups located on the edges of the world of the courtesans. The first chapter traces the evolution of the different forms of common prostitution between 1849 and 1949, a period that saw a real explosion in the number of prostitutes and their increasingly visible presence in the city. Apart from the "professionals," there were women whose jobs made for contact with male customers and who sometimes fell into prostitution. It is to these "auxiliary" groups of prostitutes that the second chapter is devoted. This chapter is followed by an essay seeking to identify prostitutes in the twentieth century and specify their numbers, geographical and social origins, and ultimate fate. Finally, this part ends with a study of the condition of the prostitute. I shall examine sexual practices for the light that they might shed on customer "demand" and sexual behavior; I shall also study one of the effects of this trade, namely the frightful ravages of venereal disease. These diseases were, however, only one aspect of the suffering endured by prostitutes. Violence, sometimes in extreme form, was their daily lot. This unavoidable aspect of the prostitutes' existence needs to be clearly brought out.

The geographical space of the world of prostitutes consisted of a series of concentric circles centered on the house of prostitution. The outermost circle included all the zones forming the reservoir from which came all the women to be found in the brothels of Shanghai. There were numerous ways of entering the trade, but the constant replenishment of the prostitutes' ranks relied on a vast traffic in women whose organization, while complex in appearance, actually masked an undeveloped mode of integration. The first chapter of the part entitled "The Space and Economy of Prostitution" therefore begins with a study of the many and varied channels by which women went into prostitution.

The intermediate concentric circle was that of the urban space. Shanghai underwent massive transformation. This meant that the places of prostitution had a certain unsettled character before they became almost permanently established in clearly demarcated areas. The second chapter of this section is therefore devoted to the development of the geography of prostitution in relation to changes in the urban fabric. The last (or first) circle was naturally formed by the house of prostitution itself. I shall examine the organization and functioning of these houses, including their different categories of staff. Moreover, because money lies at the very heart of venal sexuality, I shall devote a chapter to the economic organization of the courtesans' houses as well as to the highly sophisticated forms of monetary circulation that characterized them.

Finally, the part entitled "Abortive Attempts to Regulate Prostitution in Shanghai" consists of four chapters on policies and modes of control of prostitution between 1869 and 1949. This section first of all plots the boundaries of the political and administrative machinery that was set up to try to lay down rules and constraints in a milieu that was particularly difficult to come to grips with. The chronological subdivisions mark the three great periods of regulationism in Shanghai and correspond to major stages in the development of prostitution in the city. One chapter is devoted to institutions for the uplift of prostitutes.

This history of prostitution in Shanghai in the nineteenth and twentieth centuries has not been conceived as a history of women, particularly not as a history of the Chinese woman. This is not to say that I am uneasy with the concept, but the fact is that the term "women's history" leads to a dead end if it means looking at women as a separate object of the historical discourse. The following research seeks above all to examine the social history of a phenomenon of society – that is, prostitution – through the forms that it took in the particular context of the Chinese world. The concept of gender has offered a valuable tool of analysis because it enables women to be looked at in terms of the relationships between the sexes. The study of prostitution is specifically a field where the historian cannot reflect on women without being constantly reminded of the other sex even if, almost paradoxically, there is little evidence of the latter in the sources. The important work that has been done in "women's studies" has not always skirted the danger of raising such studies to the status of an independent field of historical knowledge. For my part, I have striven to avoid this obstacle and integrate the study of prostitution into a comprehensive historical examination of Chinese society.

Shanghai's reputation as the "Paris of Asia" deservedly went side by side with the title of "brothel of Asia." No local government, whether foreign or Chinese, was capable of stemming the phenomenon of prostitution and local government was even less capable of eradicating it. In May 1949, this city was taken by the Communist armies, which immediately condemned prostitution as one of the most degrading forms of female exploitation. Their violent rhetoric apart, the new authorities were faced with a formidable challenge: that of eliminating prostitution in a recalcitrant city where the women engaged in this activity could be counted in the tens of thousands. The "closure" effected between 1950 and 1958 formed an epilogue to the history of prostitution in Shanghai (although it was a temporary one, as can be seen from present-day developments). It led to the total disappearance of the sex trade but also to a tragic fate for the "liberated" prostitutes.[5]

To the specialists of China, and especially to the historian, the study of prostitution might still appear to be a "minor" subject, an aside as it were in a historiographical discourse that has long dwelt chiefly on the great events (revolutions) and on certain social groups (such as the scholar-bureaucrats, the peasants, and to a lesser extent the merchants and the proletariat). A good part of the research on China has been overdetermined by the country's political history and especially the Communist Revolution. Attempts have been made to search ever further back into the past for the causes and modalities of the sudden collapse of a bimillenial empire and its passage to communism within the space of half a century. The following study forms part of a relatively new trend, that of Chinese urban history understood as the social history of the cities. The work done in the context of this trend has been presented elsewhere, and I shall now try to examine the current state of the historiography of prostitution in China.[6]

The present study of prostitution seeks to add to our knowledge about the Chinese social fabric, especially in Shanghai, which has already been the subject of research covering almost the entire range of the social spectrum.[7] The prostitutes in many ways formed a fringe world, and we might ask to what extent research on this particular milieu might shed light on the general development of society. This study is an addition to a body of historical work on prostitution that is rich and varied, yet not abundant. It must be said that this work is the result of progress that did not come of its own accord, as Alain Corbin points out in the preface to the American edition of his book *Women for Hire: Prostitution and Sexuality in France after 1850*. Prostitution and, more generally, sexuality were new fields that few historians had as yet touched upon.[8] The historians had a demeaning view of the matter and were clearly uneasy about dealing with a topic that might seem to be anecdotal or indelicate.

Historical work on prostitution in China is not wholly nonexistent, although it includes all sorts of studies that, strictly speaking, should not be placed in this category. Some of them might almost be regarded as "first-hand source material." However, it would be useful to briefly trace the different stages in the Western perception of prostitution in China since the nineteenth century.[9] The subject is mentioned in general encyclopedic works on the history of world prostitution, such as those produced up to the beginning of the twentieth century. In these studies that attempt to describe prostitution and its forms in all societies, in some cases "since time immemorial," China and the Far East generally receive only a few pages that only highlight their authors' lack of knowledge and the strength of their prejudices. At best, they bring out only one dimension, that of the courtesans whom they compare to the hetaerae of classical Greece.[10]

Although more modest in their ambitions, the articles written by Western physicians living or traveling in China have long been considered to be authoritative and have helped convey a singular and at times astonishing picture of prostitution in China. These documents are of little value. They are motley collections of experiences in the field, unverifiable quotations from Chinese documents (without the least attention to chronology), and moral considerations. This is material that is interesting more in what it tells us about its authors than in the picture that it gives of prostitution in China.[11] During the same period, two travelers provided a slightly more precise view of a particular mode of prostitution, that of the "flower boats" of the Canton region. The first of these narratives is a rather amusing and superficial account of a brief escapade in these boats.[12] The second, although it bears the imprint of very deep prejudice, is a more methodical description of a world to which Westerners rarely had access. However, it merely touches on the reality of prostitution in China.[13] In the twentieth century, it was the white slave trade that gave rise to a fairly similar genre of works of low credibility, describing the fate of Western women in Asia.[14] However, there is one book in which the author sought to encompass every aspect of sexual life in the Far East. The fact is that his work is based solely on indirect sources written in Western languages and focuses on only limited aspects of prostitution in China.[15]

It is only in the work of Robert Van Gulik and Howard Levy that sexual topics and prostitution in China begin to be dealt with from an academic perspective, although these writers take very different approaches. Thirty years after its appearance, *Sexual Life in Ancient China* is still the only reference work on sexuality in Chinese society.[16] It followed a limited edition of an annotated collection of erotic engravings from the Ming period (1368–1644).[17] Van Gulik's study is certainly a unique compendium that has been neither continued nor added to. This is so because of the quality of the research, carried out by a cultivated individual with a passionate interest in China, that led him to write even detective novels that he set in the world of the Empire and its mandarins.

Sexual Life supports the idea that sexuality was lived as a normal part of the life of individuals, who were free of any particular inhibition at least until the Song period (960–1279). The young in the upper classes were educated with the help of freely circulating "manuals" that gave a very positive view of sexuality. While, by the time of the Song, Neo-Confucianism had begun to throw a veil of puritanism over sexual life, it was the women who were its targets rather than the men. The latter continued to have access to information. Above all, they continued to live relatively unfettered lives that were distinguished, especially among the elites, by diligent attendance at the houses of courtesans. The women, on the contrary, especially among the elites, were the victims of a system whose purpose was to protect them (against the Mongol invaders) but actually led to their confinement. Finally, under the Qing (1644–1911), an atmosphere of prudishness gradually enveloped Chinese society and snuffed out the forms (the erotic and pornographic engravings, poetry and novels, manuals, erotic objets d'art, and the like) through which Chinese sexual culture had found expression.

Despite its great qualities, Van Gulik's study has two limitations in regard to the subject of my study. First of all, prostitution takes up only a minor part of his work and is dealt with exclusively in relation to the status and role of the courtesans. This point nevertheless underlines the extent to which high-class prostitution was not only accepted within Chinese society but also integrated into the various essential aspects of social and political life. The courtesans had their acknowledged place in ceremonies, both private (such as marriages and anniversaries) and official. It will be seen that, while this status fell into rapid decline at the end of the nineteenth century, it had endured unchallenged up to the arrival of the Westerners. Van Gulik makes little mention of common prostitution, but the women who practiced it were apparently despised as much for their activities as for the fact that they had been forced into their trade, having been sentenced to it, most usually as part of a collective punishment inflicted on their male relatives (fathers, husbands, etc.). However, it is impossible to know how prostitution and prostitutes were regarded by the Chinese population in general.

The other limitation of Van Gulik's work is the fact that it stops precisely at the end of the Ming period (1644). Thus, between his study and my research, there is a gulf of more three centuries for which practically nothing is known about the evolution of Chinese society in the matter of sexuality and prostitution. We cannot be satisfied merely with the notion that a shroud of puritanism was cast over the field of sexuality, smothering all forms of change and novel expression. A recent study, limited to the field of erotic art, shows that despite taboos and even repression, the Chinese continued to favor these forms of expression, even if they were obliged to be secretive about it.[18] My own feeling, based on the study of prostitution in the nineteenth and twentieth centuries, is that Chinese society (and men in particular) were subjected to a "social" inhibition of sexuality (which was entirely and strictly excluded from the public sphere). However, this did not militate against a positive perception of sexuality and of matters related to sexuality in the life of the individual and in his day-to-day experiences.

Another important part of the historiography of sexuality and prostitution in China consists of the works of Howard Levy, who dealt almost exclusively with the Tang (618–907) and Ming (1368–1644) periods, from which he translated several documents on the courtesans.[19] Once again, the perspective is distorted by its exclusive focus on the upper stratum of prostitutes. These documents are valuable in that they shed light on the way in which the Chinese elites perceived prostitution, or at least its most sophisticated stratum that they tried to depict. These writings convey an eminently favorable view that happens to correspond to Van Gulik's observations. Howard Levy, however, did not seek to make a study of prostitution. All his efforts and interest were directed toward furnishing English translations of a part of this literature that otherwise would have remained inaccessible to Western readers. He appends notes and sometimes commentaries to his translations, but there is very little analysis. For equivalent or earlier periods, we might add Robert de Rotours's translation of a classic from the Tang period (618–907) and Arthur Waley's short article on the Qinglouji (*The Green Bower Collection*) from the Yuan dynasty (1271–1368).[20] These documents, in my view, complement *Sexual Life in Ancient China* in that they illustrate an aspect of the social habits of the Chinese before the Qing.

Historical works on prostitution in China are as yet very rare even if there has been some progress here in recent years. An early work (1929) by James H. Willey cannot go unmentioned. The author attempts to apply sociological analysis to the state of prostitution in China at the end of 1920s. He explains the "causes" of prostitution, its organization, and its various modes, as well as the attempts made by the authorities to control it. His conclusions are sometimes astonishing. For example, he suggests that prostitution was not very widespread in China and also that the courtesans were threatened in their status by the Chinese "new woman" or modern woman. If the courtesans did come under threat, it was not so much because of the very relative emancipation of the female population as because of the general change that Chinese society underwent and the growing commercialization of leisure activities.[21] James H. Willey's study suffers from two major weaknesses. First of all, the sheer scale of his subject actually means that his book is a patchwork of examples and pieces of collected information of unequal value about different cities in China. The other drawback is that the author uses only secondary sources, written in English, which singularly limit his possibilities of analyzing and understanding the phenomenon of prostitution in China.

Another historian, Sue Gronewold, has also studied prostitution in China from the opening to the West up to 1936.[22] Although here again her approach appears to me to be far too ambitious, the author has striven to take a fresh look, illuminated by the methods of social sciences, at a field that has been neglected by the historians of China. Sue Gronewold's standpoint is set in the feminist perspective that has profoundly renewed the historical approach (and the approach in other disciplines) in the United States by reintroducing the notion of gender into the analysis and interpretation of social phenomena.

In *Beautiful Merchandise*, Sue Gronewold presents women above all as objects of transaction. Seen from this viewpoint, prostitution appears to be only one of many modes of traffic in women, such as marriage, the making over of adopted daughters, and the purchase of concubines. Naturally, the author does not place all these modes on the same level, although she emphasizes the continuum that exists between these forms of exchange. There is a reality here that, according to Gronewold, reflects the inferior status of women, which is related to the persistence of the conservative ideology of Confucianism, the absence of women in the public domain, and a lack of interest, and even complicity, on the part of the authorities. This interpretation is not unfounded. However, it appears to be excessive for two reasons. First of all, women were not the only victims of what was a real trade in human beings. Men and children also were objects of this active commerce of which we know neither the history nor the development. In the nineteenth century, it is clear that women formed the great majority of human beings sold in what was actually a slave market.

However, the reality needs to be set in historical perspective and fleshed out with an examination of the other factors that determined the nature of this market. The socioeconomic context is of essential importance, because the sale of women was conditioned by a type of demand that was very different from what it had been, for example, in the seventeenth century, when serfdom and slavery were still very much a reality. Secondly, prostitution cannot be likened to a mere extension of the other forms of transaction in women. It may shock Western sensibilities, but marriage as the *de facto* sale of a woman to her future husband was considered, even by the parties themselves, to be a normal given fact of social life. This was not questioned until the beginning of the twentieth century. However, in every period, the prospect of being made over as a prostitute was always lived as a fall from grace, a blemish that compromised a person's future. For a family, the sale of a woman to a house of prostitution was generally the last resort in a critical situation.

The biggest weakness of *Beautiful Merchandise* lies not so much in the author's approach as in the fragmentary and dubious character of the sources used. Sue Gronewold's study is based solely on an analysis of Western-language sources. Chinese sources are quoted only when they exist in an English version. Some of the documents quoted (e.g., missionary literature and archives) are interesting and at times original, but it appears to be difficult to deal with a subject of social history of this magnitude without making use of the Chinese sources. The prostitutes do not reveal themselves of their own accord. The historian can study them only through "intermediaries" (the police, the legal profession, doctors, etc.). And yet these sources should be as close as possible to the milieu that they describe. In the case of China, the use of Western sources adds a cultural prism to the filter created by social barriers. Limited as she is by her sources, the author has pieced together a history of prostitution consisting of information gleaned from documents whose value is at times questionable. Her work therefore does not take account of the evolution of prostitution in China. Literary works, for example, arc yoked to her purpose, even as sources of quantitative data. These serious gaps contribute to making *Beautiful Merchandise* an ahistorical work.

The history of prostitution in Shanghai has received contributions from two directions: on the one hand, from the Chinese historians, especially Sun Guoqun, and, on the other, from two Western historians, Renate Scherer (in an unpublished dissertation completed in 1983) and Gail Hershatter (in various overlapping articles and in her more recent book).[23] In China, prostitution is not a subject deemed to be interesting or even truly respectable. The revival of the phenomenon in the past few years and the questions that it raises explain the relatively greater attention that is being paid to the study of this subject. They also explain the publication of a series of works that, *inter alia*, describe the process by which prostitution was eliminated after 1949.[24] The research done to date falls within the perspective of anecdotal history, as can be seen from the titles published.[25] These studies provide a static description of the state of prostitution in nineteenth- and twentieth-century Shanghai, and they lack any genuine issue-oriented analysis. Furthermore, these studies are often overlapping in their contents, even when they appear in the same volume.[26]

There is only one author, Sun Guoqun, who, in a little work on prostitution in Shanghai, has brought together all the characteristic features of Chinese works on prostitution – although the title, *Jiu Shanghai changji mishi* (*A Secret History of Prostitution in Old Shanghai*), indicates that she has established a clear distance between herself and her work. Apart from its lack of any issue-oriented analysis, the work's fundamental weakness lies in its total neglect of the archival documents. Sun Guoqun uses secondhand sources, often lifted without quotes and without any preliminary criticism and presented as a sort of compilation. The work seeks to bring out only the negative aspects of prostitution and demonstrate its features involving exploitation by the capitalists, the nationalist regime, and the authorities of the settlements. This leads the author at times to use catchphrases that are either (at best) factual inexactitudes or (at worst) falsifications of history. It is obvious that the Chinese political context imposes limits and directions on historical research, but, apart from this aspect of the matter, it would appear that, as far as prostitution is concerned, the force of prejudice has prevailed over the historical method.

Among works by Western historians, there is Renate Scherer's thesis, which seeks to examine the "Chinese prostitutional system" in the light of the case of Shanghai.[27] In fact, the title of her thesis encompasses a field that is far broader than the one actually dealt with. Basically, the author draws up a sort of catalogue of prostitution in Shanghai, from its most sophisticated to its most wretched forms, without paying any notable attention to chronology. Another section, forming the essential part of her research, is devoted solely to the courtesans and their modes of relationship with their customers. The author describes prostitution as an institution complementary to marriage, central to the social life of the elites, enabling men to fill the sentimental void enforced on them by the dominant values and the extreme formalism of social etiquette. The interpretation is on the whole accurate, but Renate Scherer describes only a very narrow segment of the world of prostitutes and provides a completely static view of it. Time does not seem to exist, and what is not clear is whether these courtesans continued to enjoy the same degree of social prestige between 1840 and 1949. The ahistorical nature of this study can be explained once again by the paucity of the sources used (about 30 Chinese works), which even the use of Western archives does not remedy.

Gail Hershatter's work appears as one of the most ambitious attempts to examine the history of prostitution in the twentieth century. From her first published articles to her more recent book, the author has followed a fairly consistent thread, basing herself on a few central ideas about Shanghai prostitution.[28] Gail Hershatter supports the view that there was a formal hierarchy of prostitutes, one that reflected social structure and demand, even if this hierarchy was partly imaginary. She considers this hierarchy to have had an impact on the actual structure of prostitution. She also describes the modes by which the girls were recruited. Women were the objects of a massive trade based on a regional distribution that, to some extent, determined their place and future in the milieu of prostitution. The entry of a woman into prostitution was often marked by a situation of crisis (possibly an economic or family crisis) or by acts of violence that wrenched her out of her original environment and removed her from its protection.

Another major point is the evolution of the market of prostitution in Shanghai in the first half of the twentieth century. Gail Hershatter states that, from a luxury market dominated by a small group of courtesans meeting the demand of the urban elites in the nineteenth century, it became a market providing sexual services to the growing number of unattached men belonging to the city's working and business classes. The author also describes the condition of the prostitutes, the rules governing visits to courtesans, and the ways of getting out of the profession. In the development of prostitution, she perceives a deterioration in women's living conditions while, at the same time, noting that they did not spend all their lives in this trade and that even the most underprivileged of them managed to maintain a certain degree of control over their existence.

Although Gail Hershatter's analysis and interpretation of the structure and working of prostitution in Shanghai are sound in many respects, I must disagree on a number of points that mark a difference in terms of both historical knowledge and historical method. Gail Hershatter's book can be described as a study in the representations of prostitution by Republican-era writers and literati rather than as an attempt to provide a social history of this phenomenon. From her perspective, this distinction may not be relevant at all; but even for a historian familiar with a post-Foucault vision of history, it does seem necessary to distinguish between "representations" as a set of discourses – in the present case by Chinese writers on prostitution – and "representations" as a construct applying to all historical documents. I would argue that Chinese sources must be used with the utmost care, and, above all, I would emphasize the need to base research as far as possible on a close comparative study and analysis of the archives.

In relying on secondary sources alone, the historian runs the risk of mistaking what ultimately is merely a "discourse" on prostitution for a source of raw data. If we look at the issue of a "hierarchy" as delineated by Gail Hershatter, her reconstruction takes account of various categories of prostitutes that are not all located on the same chronological plane. The persistence of certain forms of appellation sometimes masks profound changes in the realities that they describe. This leads the author to set up a hierarchy that, by adopting the terms used to designate different "categories" of prostitutes in their immense variety, actually mixes up elements of the nineteenth and twentieth centuries and falsifies her perspective on the evolution of the market of prostitution throughout this period.

Contemporary historians dealing with the study of prostitution in China have all come up against the problem of sources. The following study is no exception to this rule, although it is based on a range of documents that have enabled intensive reflection on the history of the phenomenon of prostitution in Shanghai, from the middle of the nineteenth century up to 1949. Naturally, I am not trying to say that the historians who have looked at prostitution in Europe or in the United States have had an easy task. No historical topic lends itself willingly, and it is even more difficult when the groups being studied lie on the "fringes" of society. Nevertheless, it would seem to me that two major differences can be highlighted between the West and China as regards the study of prostitution. The first difference lies in the attention paid to this form of activity by all kinds of "authorities" in Western culture: the police, the judicial system, hospitals, citizens' leagues, religious organizations, and the like. This concern, which is an old one, is linked to particular ways of looking at sexuality, associated with notions of sin and fornication in Judeo-Christian civilization. Sex is seen to be a dirty thing; and prostitution, which makes a commerce of it, requires particular surveillance. The spread of venereal diseases, especially syphilis, has buttressed the tendency of the "authorities" to manage, regulate, and suppress prostitution.

I am aware at this point that I am making an arbitrary simplification of very complex phenomena. Yet these phenomena are underpinned by this constant factor, and nothing of the kind can be found in traditional Chinese culture where sexuality was felt and lived as something normal, conforming to the natural order. It is not possible, for the period being studied here, to rule out the effects of Neo-Confucianism and of an entire range of religious and popular literature seeking to "standardize" the behavior of individuals.[29] This factor has thrown up a constant hurdle against my efforts to shed light, through the phenomenon of prostitution, on certain aspects of the sexuality of the Chinese. This said, it would not be an exaggeration to suggest that in those predominant values that contribute to the shaping of social behavior, China has not known that dark anguish over sexuality that has been predominant in the West and that, therefore, China has not experienced that social or administrative "investing" of prostitution that is the hallmark of the societies belonging to Judeo-Christian culture.

The second difference of note lies in China's political and administrative organization and in the Chinese conception of the role of the state. Although known for its bureaucracy and its mandarinal system – whether deemed to be exemplary and autocratic (for a premodern state) or overmanned, corrupt, and inefficient (for a modern state) – China has never been endowed with a political and administrative machinery with which to exert the powers that would make it a despotic police state. In fact, the traditional Chinese state may be seen as a "minimal" state based on a limited bureaucracy and relying on the numerous linkages formed by the scholar and merchant elites within society. Its vocation was to regulate economic and social life while limiting direct action and leaving the responsibility for day-to-day management to the elites. Hence, before the 1911 revolution and the remodeling of institutions that followed, there never was any jurisdiction (such as the police or a judicial authority) comparable to the French law courts and constabulary. As a result, there never was that huge accumulation of archives generated elsewhere by these institutions, providing the material for the above-mentioned studies of prostitution in Europe and in the United States.

Finally, a word on the nature of the sources on which this study is based. Of the archives, I had envisaged two possible sources, namely, the law courts and the police. In fact, I did not succeed in consulting the judicial archives. However, I was allowed access to the police archives, albeit in very unequal fashion. It must be said that, whatever the materials consulted (those of the police in the settlements or of the Chinese police), my reading was neither exhaustive nor based on any rationale in the choice of material selected by sampling or by some other method. All that I could examine was what was given to me by the staff in charge of the archives, and I was unable to take any part in the search for files. It is from these documents that I have drawn the major part of my information. The French diplomatic archives, especially those of the consular station in Shanghai, shed light on an entire aspect of the municipal policy of the French Settlement on prostitution, especially the way in which it was regulated, and also on the institutional background (the organization of the services, the role of the police, and links with other local authorities).

Another set of archives proved to be useful, although it would appear to be unrelated to the subject of prostitution in China. These were the archives of the League of Nations, which spent many years from the mid-1920s onward studying the problem of traffic in women and children, especially in the Far East. Two private organizations also left extensive archives. One was the *Zhongguo furu jiuji zonghui* (Anti-Kidnapping Society), which combated traffic in women from 1912 up to an unspecified date (at least up to 1941). The second group was less important but interesting all the same: the Sisters of Charity of the Good Shepherd from the city of Angers in France, who set up an establishment in Shanghai where they took in, among others, "repentant" prostitutes. Finally, although they cannot be counted as archives, I have made extensive use of the annual reports and published pamphlets of the other main rescue organization, the Door of Hope.[30]

Apart from the archives, this study has made extensive use of the press, which is an indispensable source, not only because it partially fills in the gaps in the archives, but also because it gives a better account of the state of public opinion and of social evolution in Shanghai. I have carefully examined, among others, the English-language newspapers such as the *North China Daily News* and the *North China Herald*, which comprehensively covered the years 1850–1941, as well as the major national and local daily *Shen Bao* for the period 1872–1949. In addition, there are a large number of miscellaneous periodicals whose references, along with the reasons for their use, are given in the footnotes and in the bibliography. Apart from the articles, I have made abundant use, for the nineteenth century, of the etchings and rare photographs published in the press or in other media. A part of this iconographic material, which is indispensable to an understanding of the reality of prostitution in Shanghai's society of the period, will appear in the course of this book.

A third major field of investigation consists of the many works on prostitution, written in many very different genres by Chinese scholars and intellectuals. This category, especially for the nineteenth century, comprises memoirs and recollections of youth as well as collected "biographies" of courtesans. In the following century, when these modes of literature were no longer in fashion, there were on the contrary what the Chinese called "compasses of the world of gallantry" (*piaojie zhinan*), namely works whose purpose was to inform readers about places of prostitution and the rules to be followed, especially with courtesans. Among works in the same vein that I have used, there are also the general guides to the city that almost always included a section on prostitution (dealing with places, categories, rates, etc.). Finally, to conclude on the main sources, my reading includes a portion of the vast number of novels, especially those from the turn of the century, written from a very specific viewpoint (as "discourses" on prostitution). I have used them at times to illustrate an aspect of prostitution.

The above presentation is not intended to justify gaps or errors in this study. Historians of contemporary China have long known about the difficulties that have to be faced in any attempt to consult the archives. These clarifications have been necessary to better define the context of my research and illuminate its general direction. The issues and problems raised by the historiography of prostitution in the West were in my mind throughout the quest and work of reflection that led to this book. Although I have drawn much inspiration from this Western historiography, the nature of the sources, the conditions of their accessibility, and above all the special place of prostitution in Chinese society and culture have led me to move away from it and try to chart a clear and consistent path through Shanghai's "world of flowers."

Part 1

The Courtesans: Prostitutes to the Elite and the Elite of the Prostitutes

1

The Courtesans from the Nineteenth to the Twentieth Centuries: The End of a World

For nearly a century, the world of prostitution in Shanghai was dominated by the courtesans. The term "courtesans" covers several originally distinct categories. The evolution of this group, like that of the prostitutes as a whole, reflects the profound transformations of Chinese society, especially in Shanghai, from 1849 to 1949. This period saw a change from a society dominated by status to one dominated by money. The commercialization of the local economy, combined with the restructuring of the various social strata, typified by the emergence of the middle classes, led to the decline of the courtesans and fostered the emergence of forms of prostitution that were more diversified, even if they were also more homogeneous in their function. This chapter presents the milieu of the courtesans who, more closely than any other group, represent an essential dimension of Chinese sexual culture and its development. It will also strive to explore the reasons for the inevitable decline of this group and its assimilation into the ranks of ordinary prostitutes.

In the "world of flowers" in the nineteenth century, two groups of courtesans formed the apex of what a historian has misleadingly called the "hierarchy of prostitution."[1] These courtesans indeed were patronized by male elite members of society, but also by a wider range of people not from the elites. Actually, the notion of a hierarchy corresponding to the social hierarchy is only partially true. Chinese society in this period was indeed more rigidly stratified than it would be in the following century. But this does not mean that it was a strictly ordered society in which all possibility of social mobility was ruled out. A great deal of research has shown that, on the contrary, there was a fairly high degree of fluidity as far as individuals were concerned, thanks to the existence of a special route open to all: the imperial examinations. This well-known point needs little explanation.[2] That said, its consequence was the domination of society by a small stratum of scholar-administrators who, even if their ranks constantly received newcomers, never faced any threat to their power as a group. It was a stratum that possessed knowledge, power, and, although they did not have exclusive possession of it, money.[3] Above all, the literati enjoyed status and prestige that no other social group shared or enjoyed in equal measure. Finally, it was they who defined the forms of Chinese culture, if we take "culture" in the broad sense of the term.

Shanghai was not a city of literati. Well before 1840, it had been above all a commercial port where merchants formed the largest elite. Yet, there was also a community of literati that was associated with the various administrative bodies set up in the city (the *xian* [district], the administration, the circuit intendant[4] [*daotai*], the examinations, etc.) or had come from the surrounding smaller towns. The merchants themselves were eager, as elsewhere in China, to join this privileged group, whether through the purchase of titles or by proxy, by preparing their offspring for the imperial examinations. It was the scholar-administrators who set the tone and served as a model for the other social groups.[5] Finally, it must be accepted that the opposition between merchants and literati was an artificial one, both socially and culturally. William Rowe's work has conclusively demonstrated the fact that many passageways existed between the two groups.[6] At the higher levels, they shared the same lifestyle, social *habitus*, and culture. In Shanghai, as in other cities in the last two decades of the nineteenth century, the two groups had begun largely to merge with each other.[7]

The predominant social tone in Shanghai changed rapidly under the effect of the opening to the West and of modernization, and it did so faster than elsewhere in China. This change was reflected in the world of prostitution, especially among the courtesans. At the risk of simplifying the picture, we might take up William Rowe's idea that there was a specific corps of prostitutes for each major social group in the city.[8] The reality, as we shall see, was slightly more complex and less clear-cut. And yet, there can be no doubt that clear divisions existed within each world. Members of the elites did not patronize the same places as did the poorer members of society, and the courtesans had no relations with their sisters working in the opium dens and lower-class brothel houses. This stratification came to be altered by the emergence of new social groups who were less educated than the literati and the wealthy merchant-patrons. These new groups, to be sure, were eager to flaunt the status that set them apart from the common people but nevertheless looked for the kind of easy sexual gratification that the courtesans did not necessarily provide. This change in behavior led to the disappearance of a refined form of entertainment for males that had become obsolete.

The Changing Nature of Courtesans and Prostitutes

Before 1821, according to Chinese sources, all activities of prostitution were conducted on boats moored along the Huangpu River. Afterward, the most sophisticated class of prostitutes, the courtesans, began to settle in the walled city with the rest of the population. None of the available documents uses any special name to designate the courtesans during this period. In fact, the term *shuyu*, which actually refers to the courtesan's apartments or the place where stories are told or read, is said to have made an official appearance only in 1851 in Shanghai, following its use by a courtesan, Zhu Sulan, but it did not come into widespread use until 1860, when this class of courtesans established its predominant status in the world of prostitution.[9] Strictly speaking, the courtesans were storytellers. By extension, the girls themselves came to be called *shuyu*. Of course, 1851 is an inaccurate date. By this name or another, the *shuyu* had existed before this time and were heirs to a long tradition of educated and even highly cultivated courtesans of the kind described in numerous works of the Song (960–1279) and Ming (1368–1644) dynasties, some of which have been translated and commented upon by Western sinologists.[10] The *shuyu* of Shanghai originated in Suzhou, the chief commercial metropolis of the Lower Yangzi area before 1821 and a center famed for the beauty of its women.

The *shuyu* defined themselves as artists whose vocation was to entertain their customers at festive occasions and banquets in the customer's home, in the city's traditional places of entertainment, or in their own apartments. In principle, they did not prostitute themselves: "they sell their art, not their body."[11] At any rate, it was impossible to purchase their favors or obtain them by means of simple presents. They provided company at banquets, served wine, and entertained customers with their songs.[12] This was not an absolute rule, but, as with the Japanese geisha in the same period, a would-be customer had to court the courtesan in order to have his way with her. The *shuyu* of the early nineteenth century were therefore quite independent, again if the rare surviving accounts are to be believed. Wang Tao, best known as one of the earliest Chinese reformers,[13] but less so as an assiduous customer of the houses of prostitution, reports that when a customer invited courtesans of an inferior rank – for example, a *changsan* – to a banquet or celebration, the *shuyu* would immediately set themselves apart in order to avoid mixing with the rest. If the customer invited the *changsan* to sit next to him, the *shuyu* would leave the table.[14] Although Wang Tao's text is difficult to date, it would seem that he is referring to the 1860s.[15] This means that, at that time, there were at least two categories of courtesans, one of which, the *shuyu*, still sought to be distinguished from girls whom they considered to be prostitutes. The *changsan* later adopted the same discriminatory attitude toward the next lower ranking category of prostitutes, the *yao'er*. The customers of the courtesans patronized this category too, which means that the dividing line between the various categories became increasingly blurred in the course of time. The *changsan* would absolutely refrain from meeting a customer in a *yao'er*'s house except during one period of the year, at the chrysanthemum festival (*juhuajie*) that these houses organized in the autumn. However, the *changsan* did not sing at these festivities.[16]

The *shuyu* formed a very small community (although no statistical data are available on them). Wang Tao says that there were around 50 girls of great fame in Shanghai.[17] Their total number can be estimated to have been 200 to 300 at most in the mid-nineteenth century and 400 around 1896.[18] Strict rules governed entry into the profession. All candidates had to meet a certain number of qualifications that were examined once a year at a sort of festival. In the seventh lunar month (corresponding roughly to the month of August), all the male and female storytellers of the city met at the east gate. Each person had to sing a melody and recite a piece of opera. There could be no repetition. But only the last one to sing was required to repeat the same melodies as the first participant. This was one way to verify the range of each participant's repertory. Those who did not take part in the festival or were unable to meet these standards were not allowed to appear in the traditional music halls (*shuchang*).[19] Later, the rules became less strict. Two categories were introduced: those who could play a full role – that is, both sing and perform opera – and those who could only sing. The purpose of the competition was to set limits on the number of courtesans.[20]

The courtesans were trained from childhood by music teachers who, as masters of musical knowledge, had *de facto* control over entry into the profession. To open a *shuyu* house, a substantial sum of 30 taels (about one month's earnings) had to be paid to the musicians' guild (*gongsuo*). This practice seems to have disappeared around the years 1870–1880.[21] Because the courtesans increasingly opted for pieces from the Peking opera instead of *kunqu* and even preferred to play the *pipa*, the role of the musicians declined. The *shuyu* appear therefore to have been originally closer to the storytellers (Wang Tao compares them to the women who used to tell *tanci* [storytelling, accompanied by an instrument] in bygone days[22]) than to prostitutes. They were ladies of entertainment whom customers addressed by the respectful term of *xiansheng* (sir), which was normally reserved for males. Within their own community, this was a sign of social recognition. It goes without saying that, outside this context, in the street for example, this honorific term was not used. The *changsan* were called *jiaoshu*, a term that was perhaps less distinguished but denoted respect.[23]

It appears that there was always one or more groups of courtesans who were sexually more accessible than the *shuyu*. The emergence of other categories of courtesans cannot be easily dated, because there are no accounts for the period 1821–1850 that might serve as a reference and there is little more for the next period, 1850–1875, when the landscape of prostitution was transformed. The courtesans formed a community in which the *shuyu* emerged as first among equals. The other groups split up as a result of reclassification wrought by social change in Shanghai that created a "downward movement" – in other words, a trend toward a greater "sexualization" of the courtesans. These groups were designated by the amount of money that had to be paid for their services. This was so for the *changsan*, whose name was derived from a piece in Chinese *majiang* (mah-jong) known as the "long three" or "double three," meaning that she would charge three yuan to go out on call (*tangchai*) with a customer and three yuan to spend the night with him.[24] There were also the *er'er* (double-two), *ersan* (two-three), and *yao'er* (one-two) classes of women. The first two categories were ephemeral and were later assimilated into the *changsan* or the *yao'er*.

In the earliest documents – those of Wang Tao – the *changsan* were called *changsan shuyu*, which suggests that they belonged to the same community, but they were characterized by greater accessibility and a fixed tariff that did not exist among the "genuine" *shuyu*. This is also true for the *yao'er*, who were initially called *pipa jiaoshu* to indicate the fact that they could only play the *pipa* (but possessed no theatrical repertory). What can we infer from this? The courtesans' customers, especially those who patronized the *shuyu*, did appreciate their artistic talents, but they also expected or hoped for sexual gratification, even if they had to go through a subtle game of seduction and courtship in order to obtain it. The fact was that they had to be patient, and, given the limited numbers of *shuyu*, success was far from certain. It was natural then that there should appear other categories of individuals who offered comparable artistic qualities but were at the same time more accessible.

At the beginning of the 1860s, the Taiping revolt brought a mass of people of urban origin to Shanghai, many of whom were well-off and cultivated. This population included many members of the gentry from Suzhou as well as many refugees who were not as highly educated and who attracted the interest of those courtesans who were not as selective as the *shuyu*. In purely economic terms, this large influx of population greatly increased the demand for courtesans at a time when their supply was limited. There were nearly 500 *changsan* around 1875.[25] The girls who came into the profession at this time did not have the same qualifications as their predecessors, all the more so as many of them came in by force of circumstance. Many girls from good families got stranded in the houses of courtesans and of prostitution.[26] In the 1860s, the distinction between *shuyu* and *changsan* still undoubtedly meant something. Then, gradually, a process of downward assimilation prevailed. From 1875 onward, the term *shuyu*, even if it was still used, was increasingly losing any real significance.[27] Thereafter, there remained only one group of courtesans, the *changsan*, whose numbers increased considerably. Around 1918, there were 1,281 according to various sources.[28]

A Portrait of the Courtesans

The following portrait of the courtesans in the nineteenth century relies on fragmentary sources, namely the "biographies" of courtesans written by literati such as Wang Tao in the nineteenth century and Wang Jimen in the 1920s. Rather than being true biographies, they are actually personal reminiscences of encounters with courtesans, most usually describing their character, appearance, talents, and skills and particular episodes in their lives. This is an old literary genre in China, but one that is of little use to the historian. The details given in these biographies are presented in unmethodical fashion and are extremely sketchy. They reflect the subjectivity of their authors and, at a more fundamental level, the superficiality of the relations that the courtesans actually maintained with their customers. In fact, in most instances these "biographies" very usually do no more than relate an event that came to the author's knowledge at a time when he himself patronized the courtesan in question or the milieu in general, or they recount rumors and anecdotes that were widespread among the community of courtesans.[29]

The sources therefore are rare, but explicit enough to provide a profile of the courtesans and bring a certain number of myths into question. In the first two books that he devoted to this topic, *Haizou Yeyou Lu* (*The Tale of a Libertine at the Seaside*) and *Huaguo Jutan* (*A Chat about the [Theatre of the] Realm of Flowers*), Wang Tao mentions altogether 155 women whom he patronized in varying degrees.[30] I have methodically examined these memoirs for any information that might help identify the courtesans.

In the middle of the nineteenth century, the courtesans formed several groups constituted according to regional origin. According to Wang Tao, who listed them in order of quality, there were courtesans from Suzhou, Nanjing, Yangzhou, Ningbo, Huzhou, Hubei, and Jiangxi. The diversity of provincial origins is without doubt a reflection of the heterogeneity of Shanghai's population up to the beginning of the 1870s.[31] Each group had its courtesans. Later on, although this heterogeneity remained, the Jiangsu-Zhejiang communities grew considerably while the other provincial groups became small minorities. Most of the regional groups of courtesans disappeared, and their place was taken by courtesans originating from Jiangsu and, secondarily, from Zhejiang.[32] The largest group, that of women from Suzhou, ultimately came to supplant all its rivals and dominate the world of the *shuyu*.

In all Chinese cities, whatever the region (except perhaps in Guangdong), the world of prostitution was divided into regional groups, and it was almost always the women of southern Jiangsu who were to be found in the upper strata.[33] In his memoirs, Wang Tao mentions the geographical origin of 106 courtesans, a key element of the identity of an individual in China. Wang is able to identify the native village of most of the women, but the fact that it is a village makes it paradoxically difficult for the historian to identify these places. My own incomplete reconstruction shows that 54 courtesans were born in Jiangsu. Among them, 16 came from the Suzhou area, 10 from Jiangnan (the south of the province), and 8 from Jiangbei (half of them

Table 1.1. *Origin by province of a group of 77 courtesans (1923)*

Place of birth	Number	Percentages
Suzhou	63	82
Changzhou	5	7
Shanghai	3	4
Ningbo	2	3
Hangzhou	1	1
Wuxi	1	1
Yangzhou	1	1
Jiaqing	1	1
Total:	77	100

Sources: Archives de la direction des services adminis-tratifs, French Concession, Archives municipales de Shanghai, Dossier 1934 25 MS 1554.2, "Maisons des chanteuses: demandes de licence" (1922–1924).

from Yangzhou). Eight of the courtesans came from Zhejiang. The rest (7) originated in various parts of China (Guangdong, Hunan, Hubei, and South Shandong). Thirteen came from villages that I have been unable to locate. It can be assumed that these villages were located in nearby provinces (Jiangsu, Zhejiang); otherwise, Wang Tao would have noted the name of the province. These figures hardly have any statistical value. Yet they highlight the predominance of Jiangsu women in the world of courtesans, a pre-dominance that was noted by every observer of the time. Even courtesans from other regions of China adopted the Suzhou dialect, whose mellifluous character was considered to have been an essential part of the success of its speakers.[34] In Shanghai, only one "outsider" group of courtesans remained. They were the Cantonese established in three or four houses near Nanking Road around 1890, and later further to the north, in Hongkou, where the Cantonese population was concentrated.[35]

This predominance remained unchallenged well into the twentieth century and even became more pronounced. An author writing in the early 1920s noted that the *shuyu* group was composed exclusively of women orig-inating from Suzhou.[36] This statement is corroborated by a police report on applications by courtesans to set up shop in the French Concession in 1923.[37] Eighty-two percent of these women came from Suzhou (see Table 1.1). By adding this figure to those originating from Shanghai, Wuxi, and Changzhou, we arrive at a total of 93% as the proportion of the cour-tesans who were natives of Jiangnan.

A majority of the courtesans were very young. Wang Tao mentions

Table 1.2. *Age structure of a sample of courtesans (nineteenth century)*

Age	Number
13	6
14	4
15	24
16	5
17	6
18	3
19	2
20	4
24	1
28	1
30+	2
Total:	58

the ages (probably their ages when he knew them) of fifty-eight women (see Table 1.2).[38]

The courtesans began their careers at a very early age and usually left quite soon, after five to ten years at most for those who were lucky enough to find a husband. We have confirmation here of a reality that is never mentioned in the Chinese sources: the great partiality of nineteenth-century Chinese men for "young sprouts." The extreme youth of the courtesans was seen as something natural; and no author, in any period whatsoever, was outraged by it. This phenomenon was not as widespread after 1911, partly because of the penalties laid down in successive penal codes. Still, all that the youngest courtesans did was to provide company for customers at table. It was usually around the age of fifteen that they were deflowered. On the other hand (although there was no formal rule in the matter, and some famous courtesans were able to practice their craft well into their fifties), it was difficult for a courtesan to keep working after the age of twenty. By then, she would already be considered to be "old." Wang Tao expresses this sentiment twice: "Although she was more than twenty years of age,"[39] and "although she was already twenty years old." It may be concluded from this that the twenty-year age limit was an almost physiological boundary beyond which a courtesan would be expected to find a husband. Otherwise, she ran the risk of losing her charm and beauty and seeing her house deserted by her customers (a condition in which, as Wang writes many times, "*chema leng luo men qian*" – the carriages seldom stop at her doorstep).

Wang Tao also sheds some light on a very little known dimension, namely, the social origin of the prostitutes. I have managed to retrieve information on only forty-two of them. The definition is often very vague. Twelve of these women came from "good families" (*liangjia*), two came from "great families," eight came from "modest" (*xiaojia*) or poor families, six were adopted daughters (*yangnü*), and fourteen were daughters of persons belonging to the following categories: madam (one), peasant (three), fisherman (one), butcher (one), clerk (one), merchant (two), literati (five). If we exclude the literati and the "good families" (though this term does not exactly refer to a high socioeconomic level),[40] this distribution gives the impression of a generally modest social background. This is not surprising in itself, but we shall see below that it challenges the traditional image of the courtesans *qua* learned women. The reasons for entry into prostitution are also given for forty women. Four were coerced into the trade by poverty, thirteen were sold to a madam or a courtesan (three of them by their own parents), fourteen were orphans, and one was the natural daughter of a madam. Of the others, three fell into prostitution after losing a husband, two after being kidnapped, one after being expelled by her parents, and two as a result of war. The general cause was undoubtedly poverty, whether as a lasting condition or the consequence of an accident. The death of parents, especially of the father, is frequently cited as a cause. Troubles associated with the Taiping rebellion are also mentioned eight times in relation to the death of parents. This tends to confirm the generally lowly origin of these girls, who appear to have been sold at a young age to a madam who took care of their training as courtesans.

Wang Tao is not very forthcoming about the talents and skills of the courtesans. Their physical appearance is always described in conventional language, with little variation on the same theme[41]:

> She was as beautiful as the morning dew, her skin glistened like the almond, her bones were light and her body could be held in one hand, her gait was like a willow tree in the wind.

Writers tended to focus on clothing more than on the person herself and expressed first of all their own subjective reaction, either as admirers or as critics of the courtesans.[42] It is simply impossible to know from such descriptions what any particular courtesan actually looked like and what distinguished her from another. Even the literature sheds only a little light on this aspect of the matter. With regard to their artistic skills, we learn from Wang Tao that nineteen of them were famous for their singing, playing the *pipa* (six), the Chinese lute (six), and the flute (two), singing and playing an instrument (two), telling *tanci* (two), and the art of hospitality (three). Wang Tao provides some rare though valuable clues to the courtesans' level of education, which seems to have been fairly limited (see Table 1.3).

The vision of the well-educated courtesan is a myth that does not stand up to a close examination of the facts or to simple logic. Wang Tao gives us an idea of the reality as he perceived it in the nineteenth century. Wang Tao

Table 1.3. *Educational level of a sample of 25 courtesans (nineteenth century)*

Educational level	Number in sample
Able to read and write calligraphy	9
Able to read poetry	2
Able to read	5
Able to write poetry	1
Private education	1
Able to talk about poetry	1
Able to write letters	1
Some reading ability	4
Illiterate	1

Sources: Yu Baosheng (one of Wang Tao's pseudonyms), *Haizou yeyou lu*; *Haizou yeyou fulu*; *Haizou yeyou yulu*; Wang Tao, *Songbin suohua*.

specifically mentions a "literary" education for only 17 out of 155 courtesans. The others seem to have had a more superficial knowledge of Chinese writing. This is a very small proportion, even if we allow for the subjective and random nature of Wang Tao's selection. Did it conform to reality? Many more courtesans doubtless had a certain level of education, but that is not the point. Wang Tao recorded only those whose literary knowledge made an impression on him. We cannot deny the fact that few actually had any command of the written language (poetry and calligraphy). Most of them had only a rather elementary knowledge of Chinese characters that allowed them to read and write ordinary documents, such as letters. This is a far cry from the image of the learned courtesan, wittily engaging in intellectual games such as the improvising of poems, as described in late nineteenth-century and early twentieth-century[43] novels or in travel accounts by Westerners[44] and subsequently included by all those who wrote about the courtesans. In the following century, the level of education of prostitutes was extremely low, no matter what category they belonged to.

In fact, it is not surprising that the level should have been low even among the courtesans. Most came from families with modest incomes or even poor families and had therefore received no formal education. Only a minority, probably those from better-off families, could have received a more advanced education before joining the ranks of the courtesans. Raised from an early age by a madam, the girls were given lessons in singing, playing music, and performing opera. These were all skills directed toward making them professional entertainers, not intellectuals. The madams, who considered the girls as "money trees" (*yaoqianshu*), had no financial interest in having them receive a formal education from a private tutor, and they preferred to limit their investment to the minimum: "Within a few months, she had learned her art and could go around singing and serving at table."[45] Finally, given the early age at which the courtesans began to exercise their trade and the difficulties that they faced in learning the Chinese classical language, it was practically impossible for the vast majority of courtesans to have been learned women. More prosaically, they played the role of ladies of company, from whom customers expected wit and lively conversation, but above all entertainment – that is, singing and music. One of the first initiatives taken by a group of "politicized" courtesans after 1911 was to set up a school to provide the girls with a way out through education.[46]

Whatever the weakness of the statistical data presented here, there is no reason to think that the examples chosen by Wang Tao – an active and assiduous patron of courtesans' houses for more than four decades – present an excessively biased picture of reality. It is true that his writings offer an insufficiently clear view of Chinese courtesans at a time when Western influence was still small (from the dates given here and there in the texts, it can be inferred that these girls were active between 1860 and 1872), but they are one of the very rare direct testimonies available on this topic. The general impression given by these accounts is that the courtesans were a group of women who lived by selling sexual favors and that most of them were basically hardly better off than those who ended up in the common houses of prostitution. What made the difference in the paths that they took was circumstance, occasionally outstanding beauty or more simply luck.

Several authors, including Wang Tao himself, emphasized the decline in the level of education of the courtesans. A book published in 1891 stated that it was not easy to find courtesans who could sing and play an instrument, and it was even rarer to find girls who knew how to receive and treat their customers properly or who were able to write.[47] One account in 1923 noted that ever fewer girls knew how to play the *huqin* (two-string violin), though a small minority was still able to handle the *pipa* (Chinese mandolin). The majority of them could only sing pieces from the Peking opera, which made for a noisy and not very refined ambiance when several courtesans happened to be in the same place.[48] A short biography of a courtesan published in 1926 notes that after losing both her parents at the age of thirteen, she had taken singing lessons arranged for by her aunt. After a year, she had mastered thirty songs and was farmed out to a madam as a courtesan.[49] This apparent "decline in quality," which was a perception that must be ascribed partly to nostalgia on the part of these authors for an idealized past, was also observed in the courtesans of Beijing at the turn of the century.[50]

The fact, however, is that the available data on courtesans in the twentieth century is paradoxically much scantier than the admittedly limited information given by Wang Tao for the nineteenth century. This points to a greater homogenization of the different categories of prostitutes. The nature of the social demand changed and determined a different profile for the courtesans. Ironically, the demand for sexual services overshadowed the function of entertainment that had been the primary feature of this particular group of prostitutes up to the nineteenth century. Depending on their status, the courtesans enjoyed varying degrees of freedom and of control over their life. Yet, their capacity for autonomous action remained somewhat curtailed.

The Status of the Courtesans

The status of the courtesans depended on the circumstances in which they entered the trade. There was no correspondence between the socioeconomic condition of the women, which could be privileged, and their "legal" status, which, in most cases, was characterized by servitude.

Entry into the courtesans' milieu came at an early age, as we have seen. This meant that it was very exceptional for the girls reduced to this condition to have entered it of their own accord. The courtesans came from families who had deliberately given them up to a madam or placed them as "adopted daughters" (*yangnü*) without really worrying about their fate. Sometimes, the girls had lost their families and were orphans or dependent on relatives (uncles or aunts) who had no wish to be burdened with additional mouths to feed. In a later chapter, I shall examine the question of the traffic in women in China. It will suffice here to note that in the nineteenth century and up to the 1920s, most of the courtesans came from the immense market in human beings during that period, namely, China.

Whether purchased or kidnapped, the young girls trained in the courtesans' trade became *de facto* slaves of their madams. Ordinary prostitutes as well as courtesans were subjected to strict surveillance. They lost all freedom over their person and their goods. They could not go out without being accompanied by their madam or a maidservant. And the only outings allowed to them had to be within the ambit of their professional activity. Nor did the courtesans freely dispose of their earnings. The entire amount of a girl's official earnings, if she was a "slave," went into the madam's pouch. All that the courtesan actually kept was the gifts that were directly given to her by her customers. Only the famous courtesans could ensure the favors of rich customers, obtain many gifts, and save enough money to escape from the madam's clutches. Unlike other prostitutes, the courtesans could emancipate themselves, namely buy back their bodies (*shushen*), enfranchise themselves rather in the manner of slaves and recover their freedom from the madam. Jin Cai'e, a famous courtesan, herself the adopted daughter of a renowned prostitute, paid off her debt at the age of seventeen and set herself up in her own right.[51] Yue Fang, another famous courtesan at the beginning of the 1890s, paid 2,000 taels for her freedom and then set herself up as an independent courtesan.[52] The madam was able to "reinvest" the sum that she received in the purchase of another young girl, who may or may not have been trained, in order to turn her into a courtesan and live off her earnings. As a rule, a madam found it worthwhile after a few years to negotiate a girl's departure, whether through self-enfranchisement or by marriage, because a courtesan's career could not last for very long. It was therefore necessary to ensure a turnover of staff in order to stay in the market. A proportion of the courtesans were hired. Some were mortgaged by their families for specified periods at the end of which they could, if they wished, remain in the trade. They were recruited by madams who paid them an agreed sum as well as a part of the earnings. These courtesans had greater freedom of movement and could leave the world of prostitution more easily.

Rules of Etiquette and Games of Seduction

The practice of patronizing courtesans was regulated by a sort of unspoken but strict code that applied both to the customers and to the girls, and the relationship entailed far more than a mere exchange of money or gifts. Up to the end of the nineteenth century, courtesans did not give themselves to the first comer, whatever his degree of wealth, and the customers themselves were certainly looking for something other than immediate sexual gratification, which was easily available elsewhere. In this respect, the modes of relationship between the prostitutes and their customers quite clearly point to a form of culture that had no equivalent in the West, except perhaps in ancient Greece. They shed light on the state of Chinese society on the eve of the great upheaval caused by the intrusion of Westerners. They shed light especially on (a) the strict separation between the sexes, to which the world of the courtesans was an exception, and (b) the force of rituals, etiquette, and rules of reciprocity – related to *ganqing* (sentiments) – among the Chinese elite. Although the construction of a subtle code was in itself the expression of a cultural form peculiar to China, it also responded to commercial considerations inasmuch as the services provided by courtesans, which were always paid for at the end of the season, were based on trust. This trust was obtained only at the end of an "initiatory" stage in which the courtesan and her madam could gauge the customer as candidate.

The first contact was an important step. A customer could not visit a courtesan whom he did not know or even call her out (*jiao ju*). In order to make her acquaintance, he had to have her invited to a restaurant or to the theater by a friend who was already patronizing her. Only then, after having been personally introduced by this go-between, could the customer in turn invite the courtesan to come out with him. If he had no friend to offer his services, there remained the solution of going to a *shuchang* and asking a courtesan of his choice to sing a few melodies. When she had finished singing, the courtesan would go up to the men who had, so to speak, honored her and also given proof of means. After this first contact, she would agree to be called out.

This first stage clearly shows the importance given to face-to-face contact. Such contact was a constant in Chinese society, which was particularly marked by the culture of the go-between. Implicitly, the person who made the introductions was a guarantor for the two parties, and, as far as the courtesan was concerned, he was a guarantor of the new customer's status and solvency. Some people aspiring to become customers would mention a friend's name in his absence. The courtesans did not appreciate this style of behavior and cold-shouldered those who resorted to it. It would appear that from the 1920s onward, when the courtesans had become more like high-class prostitutes, the rules were less strict. For example, customers could consult a restaurant's register of invitations (*tangchai dengjibu*) and copy out a courtesan's name and address.[53] Similarly, there were directories (*huajie dianhuabu*) that listed courtesans with their particulars, especially their phone numbers.[54] All that had to be done then was to send a message or ask for the girl to be called out.

Starting with the first meeting, the courtesan embarked on a process in which she made an advance installment," so to speak, of her person and her talents. The customer had to invite her out to dinner in order to entertain his friends. In this way, he helped nurture a more trusting relationship. The first invitation was not recorded in any accounts. After two or three invitations, the customer was registered in the "book of outings," and each invitation was written down and invoiced at the end of the season along with the customer's other expenses. In the beginning, the courtesans kept their service to the minimum and left as soon as they had made an appearance, considering the invitation to be a chance call that would not necessarily be repeated. Thereafter, if the customer displayed his interest by successive invitations, they would take time to converse and dally with him and his guests.

After several regular invitations, the customer was permitted to go to the courtesan's house. This was a sort of courtesy visit (*da chawei*) that cost nothing.[55] The courtesan served tea and delicacies and offered a pipe. In a later period, the pipes were replaced by cigarettes. This visit, unlike invitations to go out, could be repeated only once or twice, after which the courtesan had to be "compensated " (*baoxiao*) for her work and hospitality.

Moreover, the visits had to be within certain times – that is, from the beginning of the afternoon to 6:00 P.M. Before this time, it was inconvenient because the women were either asleep or getting ready. Afterward, they were busy responding to the invitations to go out (*tangchai*) that started coming in at that point.

The third and last step awaited by the courtesans was that of the *huatou*. It is not at all easy to render this expression with its ambiguity. *Huatou* literally means "flower chief." It goes with a verb, *zuo* (to make), which does not have the meaning of "to become, to be, to embody" in Chinese but rather designates the facet of acting as in "to make a feast," which corresponds to a reality: "to make a *huatou*" is to organize a dinner or a gambling party. The expression therefore designates the maker and what is made. A *huatou* was also a unit of account corresponding to either a meal or a gambling party. When a customer wished to be accepted as a "habitué" and win over a courtesan, he could not confine his gestures to "calls." The houses earned most of their income from activities ancillary to prostitution, such as dinners and gambling, which brought in people and also helped them attract new customers.

If the customer met all these conditions, he might hope to sleep with the courtesan, who could then be sure of his interest in her. There was no fixed rate. The only constant expenditure lay in the inevitable tips to the house staff. This does not mean that the customer could limit himself to *huatou*. He had to give the courtesans gifts in order to maintain their regard. At the same time, it was highly ill-advised to push for sexual relations with a courtesan by giving her money, especially by putting pressure through the madam, who would be generally less particular in these matters. Except in their descriptions of the *shuyu* in the nineteenth century who, it would seem, were not easily available sexually, it is likely that Chinese authors tended to idealize the condition of the courtesans and to tone down their increasing sexualization.

Up to the First World War, the *changsan* were not simple prostitutes. However, the latitude that they could enjoy in the face of a determined customer and a madam who was mainly interested in money was probably very small. The relationship between these three actors consisted of a subtle game where each tried to use his or her power to draw the greatest advantage from the situation. One author writing around 1920 felt that about one or two dozen *huatou* were necessary in order to be able to sleep with a courtesan, although another suggested that half a dozen was already a basis for claiming a night.[56] The sentimental and even formal aspect totally disappeared. In 1940, one author said that girls were no longer interested in anything but money and that the rest was just play-acting.[57] All the signs are that the *changsan* then joined the populous ranks of the common prostitutes, even if they continued to receive a more selective type of customer.

The Courtesans in the Public Space: Being Called Out

Being called out (*tangchai*) corresponded to an essential activity of courtesans, both financially and for their reputation. The women never went
out alone. They were always chaperoned either by a maidservant or by
the madam herself. Up to the end of the nineteenth century, they sometimes also came with a musician. The well-known courtesans could have
up to fifty to sixty outings in an evening, but a woman of average reputation could easily go on twenty to thirty outings.[58] Because they
stayed only for a very short time, a wealthy customer could call out
about ten of them in the course of an evening. The outings began toward
6:00 P.M. and continued up till midnight, that is for six hours during
which a courtesan enjoyed hardly any respite. The courtesans most in
demand stayed with a customer for barely more than five minutes. This
pace was possible only because the distances to be traveled were often
very small. This was because the courtesans' houses, the restaurants, and
the teahouses were concentrated within a defined perimeter in the foreign
settlement that I have called "the golden circle of prostitution" (see
Chapter 8).

It was impossible for a courtesan to refuse an invitation from an already-
known customer. The atmosphere of the evening organized by the customer
but also his reputation depended on her arrival. The absence of a courtesan whom he had invited would make him lose face before his friends,
and this was a mistake to be avoided at all costs. Thus, whatever the circumstances and the weather, a courtesan had to respond to invitations
posthaste. Some customers were extremely sensitive. A minor delay could
arouse their anger and lead them to insult a courtesan. A customer might
also retaliate against a slight by having a nasty article printed in one of the
small newspapers that reported the activities of these circles.[59] The most
irascible would even go to the house where the woman lived to protest and
cause trouble or provoke a quarrel.[60]

On their outings, the courtesans would travel in sedan chairs. Although
the distances traveled were relatively small, their bound feet prevented
them from any walking, apart from short spells in a park. Besides, they had
to respond to several invitations in a single evening, especially the most
famed courtesans. And then, the roads and alleys of Shanghai of the period
were still mud roads. This ruled out walking on rainy days because the courtesans could not soil their fine clothes. Thus, the sedan chairs that could go
anywhere (as rickshaws did later) proved to be the most rapid and convenient mode of transport. Each house generally had its own sedan chair and
later its own rickshaw. In the evening, it was not rare to see a large number
of these chairs around a big restaurant or a *shuchang*. Bystanders gathered
around to admire these chairs and try to get a glimpse of the girls.[61] The
courtesans, who were inaccessible to the majority of the population, were

part of the street scene, especially in the evening, when, before the introduction of gas and then electricity, most work came to a halt and was
replaced by activity in a few lively areas concentrated in the same district.
The sedan chairs gradually disappeared, first of all because of the introduction of a tax on these vehicles by the authorities of the International
Settlement around 1915. To avoid paying this tax, the houses decided to
have the women carried on men's backs.[62] This practice, which was prohibited by the police as disreputable, is a significant indication of the way in
which the standing of the courtesans declined.[63] The sedan chairs were later
replaced by rickshaws, which were more comfortable. The use of rickshaws
became widespread after 1920.

The Leisure Space of the Urban Elites

The life of the courtesans was not limited to the confines of their establishments. Their activity extended considerably beyond this framework
and hinged upon what I would call the "four cardinal points of the world
of the courtesans." These four points, along with the courtesans' houses,
formed the leisure space of the Chinese elites even if these elites did not
enjoy a monopoly over them. These points can be assembled in pairs. One
pair corresponded to entertainment and consisted of the *shuchang* and
the theater, and the other pair corresponded to the pleasures of the table
and consisted of the restaurants and the teahouses. Some of these institutions did not survive the "long nineteenth century" as places of entertainment for the elites.[64] The *shuchang* disappeared while the theater became
an ordinary place for performances, a place that was open to all and was
more anonymous. The teahouses, which were numerous even in 1949,
lost their status as places of recreation for the elites to the benefit of the
coffee houses and open-air cafes (*huayuan*) opened by the amusement
centers and the big stores.[65] Only the restaurants, those inevitable centers
of Chinese sociability, withstood the changes that came about in manners
and customs.

The general trend that encompassed all these changes saw a shrinking
of the space within which the courtesans moved. Paradoxically, as they
gradually became "public girls," the courtesans became ever less present
in the public places. The decline of this group and its gradual assimilation
into the ranks of prostitutes (a process that was completed after 1920)
was accompanied by a shrinking of the courtesans' role until it became
limited to the sexual function. A revealing aspect of this trend is the fact
that a new institution, the hotel, began to assume central importance in
this period and replaced other places as a trysting point between courtesans and their customers. These courtesans thereafter became mere
"high-class call girls" whose company gave a certain social status to those
who had the means to pay for them, but they were no longer the thread

that linked the different points of the leisure space of the elites. The culture in which they had participated no longer existed, having gone under with the collapse of the old regime and the disappearance of the traditional elites.

The "Shuchang": An Intermediate Space

The *shuchang* were big halls that provided music-hall shows in the Chinese musical tradition. They could receive up to a hundred spectators seated around a platform on which the courtesans were placed individually or in groups. The first establishment of this type is supposed to have opened in Shangrenli, a little lane off Fuzhou Road, at the beginning of the 1860s. Thereafter, they mushroomed very rapidly, always in the courtesans' district, and reached a high point in the years 1890–1892. The most famous *shuchang* were Tianlewo ("The Nest of Celestial Bliss"), Jiaolou ("The Pavilion of Relations"), Xiaoguanghan, and a few others.[66] Some remained at the end of the Qing Dynasty, but they were supplanted by amusement centers such as the Great World. The last *shuchang* closed in 1916.[67] In 1919, a Shanghai guidebook stated that there were still sixteen of them, but, while the name had not changed, the reality no longer bore any relationship to the establishments of the past.[68]

Plate 1 gives an idea of what these establishments were like toward the end of the nineteenth century. At this time, the girls appeared alone, without musicians. They had already opted for the Peking opera and for ballads that they sang to the accompaniment of the ubiquitous *pipa*. In the illustration, the stage is a sort of richly decorated platform with a table around which the courtesans are seated. In the background, there is a group of maidservants who accompany the courtesans on all their trips. The maids who are attending to customers already known to the girl or to those who have asked her to sing a song are preparing their water pipes and conversing with them. The customers are seated around tables that provide a frame for the stage. Some are drinking while others are smoking the water pipe while listening to music.

The *shuchang* would invite three or four courtesans whose names, date, and time of presence were displayed outside on long strips of red paper.[69] Later, it was in the press (the small newspapers or *xiao bao*) that the *shuchang* published lists of the women that it would be receiving.[70] The price of entry was 0.20 to 0.70 yuan, depending on the number of girls present. In addition, the spectators paid only for the tea that they consumed, and they paid the courtesans for the songs that they had specially requested.[71] The customers could ask a courtesan to sing one or more special melodies. This was one way of honoring her or making first contact for anyone who wished to be received at her house. Each song cost one yuan. When the girl had finished her turn, she could join the customer

Plate 1. Performance in a *shuchang* (music hall).

outside and depart with him. A *shuchang* could also be requested to bring in a particular courtesan.[72]

The *shuchang* provided the musicians. The *shuyu* themselves did not have any qualified musicians with them, unlike the *changsan*. Very often, they accompanied themselves on an instrument.[73] At the turn of every season (*jie*), the musicians would organize a show. The establishment was decorated with bouquets of real flowers and multicolored lanterns. Each courtesan invited a faithful customer, seated in the first row, who naturally had to request several songs. The girls received no part of the takings, which were shared between the musicians and the owner of the *shuchang*. The earnings from this show provided the musicians with their salary for the entire season.[74] Every courtesan's "turn to sing" was organized on the same lines. It began with ballads followed by a piece of opera and ended with songs.

In these establishments, the pieces played were originally melodies from the theater (*chuanqi*) and *kunqu*, as well as ballads with instrumental accompaniment. It was fairly difficult to learn the *kunqu*. According to Wang Tao, this is why the girls went in for the Peking opera. Wang did not conceal his distaste for the latter: ("the girls' necks turn red and their faces crimson"), preferring the softer strains of music from Changzhou and Suzhou.[75] More prosaically, this was probably a fashion-related phenomenon leading in the 1870s to the growth of a craze for the Peking opera that persisted thereafter.[76] The *shuchang*, along with the theater, the tea houses, and the brothels, were among the favored places of diversion for the scholars. Leisure activities took fairly limited forms in the Chinese cities, and in the *shuchang* the scholars found an atmosphere of friendship that was propitious to discussion and to listening to music, away from the rest of the populace.

The Theater

In the nineteenth century, the theater was one of the places where courtesans frequently could be met. There was a close link between this milieu and that of the courtesans, as can be seen in a number of older writings. Actors and courtesans had long been relegated by law to the fringes of society. They belonged to the category of "mean people " (*jianmin*), a status that was officially lifted only in the eighteenth century. Apart from this discrimination dictated by the establishment, it was the art of music and rhetoric that brought these two groups together. Courtesans who did not manage to marry young sometimes ended up in a theatrical troupe. In the modern period, the link between the two groups was getting tenuous, but it was still solid at the beginning of the period being studied here. Spectators often invited a courtesan to keep them company for the space of a melody on the stage. The courtesans themselves were keen on the theater and attended it very regularly, especially when a famous actor was playing. Many a courtesan took a lover from among the actors.

There were about ten theaters in Shanghai.[77] They performed mainly Peking opera and, to a lesser extent, *kunqu*. To understand the way in which courtesans organized their visits to their customers during a theatrical performance, we must of course discard images based on contemporary Western theater. Chinese theaters in the nineteenth century were rather like those of the eighteenth century in France, although they were more comfortable. Plate 2 is a faithful representation of such a theater. These establishments were actually similar to the *shuchang*, but they surpassed the *shuchang* in size and internal disposition. The organization of the hall, as shown, provided for greater conviviality and remarkable ease of exchange among the spectators, who sat in groups at round tables where

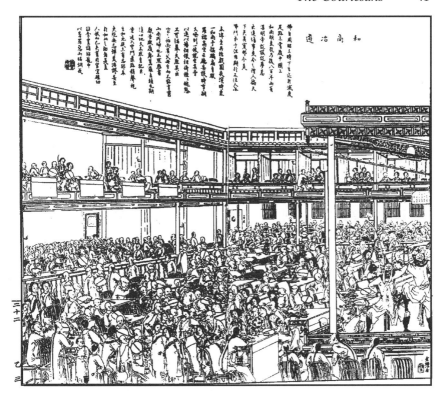

Plate 2. Interior of the Dan'gui theater in Shanghai, nineteenth century.

they were served food and drink. They could thus follow the course of
the play while discussing, judging, uttering exclamations, or complaining,
depending on the talent of the troupe. It was more common for theatrical
performances to take place in the daytime.

The courtesans could come and sit beside those who had sent for them
without disturbing the performance. This was an opportunity for them to
be seen and for the customer to make a public display of his social status,
especially when the courtesan was famous. The girls generally did not stop
by for more than one or two melodies. It was not uncommon for the most
celebrated courtesans to go from one customer to another in the same
theater, and one author claimed to have seen this happen six times in the
course of the same evening.[78] From time to time, there could be an incident
of rivalry that arose when a spectator called over a courtesan who was with
another member of the audience. When this happened, and depending on
the financial means of the rivals, there would be a sort of tournament waged

with invitations that followed one another, with the courtesan going from one to the other as she received notes inviting her to come over. One courtesan is thus said to have made several dozens of trips in one evening, thereby earning the tidy sum of 2,000 yuan.[79]

Restaurants and Teahouses

In the mid-nineteenth century, and probably even before that, Shanghai had a large variety of restaurants offering all of China's regional cuisines. It was possible to dine very late in the Cantonese restaurants, where it was customary to take a meal toward midnight.[80] A customer could have a courtesan of his choice brought to the restaurant provided that he was known to her. In the beginning, a courier would be sent with a large piece of red paper that had no particular shape. Then, restaurants introduced little cards of red printed paper with the name and address of the establishment that customers filled in with the courtesan's name and address. Each establishment (restaurant or theater) had an employee whose sole function was to carry the invitation cards to the courtesans' houses. They were paid directly by the houses in proportion to the number of cards carried.[81] Toward 1893, the courtesans' houses adopted the same system when they invited customers to a particular occasion.[82]

When the courtesans were invited to accompany a few guests at a restaurant, they did not sing any pieces from the opera and came without musicians. The customer generally stated his wishes in advance on his card. The word *pipa* was enough to tell the courtesan what he wanted from her.[83] The courtesans never took part in the meal, whether in restaurants or in their own establishments. They would remain seated behind the customers who had invited them and would offer them drinks in the Chinese fashion. They usually sang while the dishes were being served, and then they would invite the customers to a game of finger-guessing (*caiquan*).[84] Each game consisted of five successive turns at the end of which the loser had to drink a glass of liquor. The courtesans drank only half a glass and often asked their maidservants to swallow the liquor for them.[85]

The teahouses were another much favored and convivial meetingplace, both in the towns and in the rural townships. They were the equivalent of the French bistros, vectors *par excellence* of popular culture and places for the exchange of information, places for friendly or professional meetings, or relaxation and diversion.[86] There were famous houses such as Yidongtian, Songfengge, and Lisuitai in the north of the old city or again Qingliange in the International Settlement that provided an appropriate setting for inviting courtesans.[87] These houses were richly decorated with etchings and works of calligraphy by well-known painters. The interior of Qingliange was furnished with black lacquered tables and seats covered with white linen cushions delicately interwoven with red thread.

When the teahouse moved to a new three-story building, the furniture was replaced by redwood chairs and marble tables. In 1884, the house employed waiters (who were then known as *nütangguan*) and a number of vendors of several varieties of hot dumplings (*dianxin*) who worked throughout the day.[88]

The presence of courtesans in these establishments made for a particularly lively atmosphere. Their constant coming and going was in addition to the bustling movements of waiters and vendors of all kinds. A visitor from outside remarked in 1891 that the scholars went to these establishments as much to take tea as for their atmosphere.[89] Wang Tao observed that certain houses, located near the temple of the city god (Chenghuangmiao), had become havens for the courtesans who came there to take tea after burning incense before their guardian deity. It was an opportunity for them to be seen. The less sophisticated prostitutes were far more direct and solicited the exclusively male customers of the teahouses by making eyes at them.[90] At the turn of the century, the teahouses were often places where prostitutes met and solicited customers.

Outings in the Country

The courtesans liked to flaunt themselves outdoors. It was probably a way of escaping from their confinement in the restricted space of the house and the chamber, as well as an opportunity to attract the attention of new customers. The fact that they frequented certain places is hardly surprising. These places included the gardens attached to the temple of the city deity to which the courtesans went frequently. These gardens, known as the Western Gardens (*xiyuan*, today's Yuyuan), were visited by the populace seeking to escape from Shanghai's already congested habitat. The gardens also contained many pavilions that had been built or were occupied by certain merchant guilds for their daily meetings. There were also some very lively teahouses where the courtesans liked to enjoy the fresh air and chat. In the International Settlement, the Bund also became a very highly regarded place.

The courtesans and their customers always looked for places where they could find some greenery and escape from the overcrowding that characterized the old city. Thus, the Temple of Jing'ansi, located in the west of the city, which was still right in the country at the end of the century, attracted many walkers who came there to look at the hot springs. The Longhua pagoda in the southwest was also a place of peace and quiet. People traveled there by wheeled carts, by sedan chairs, and, for comfort and speed, by horse carriage, which by the end of the century became the mode of transport most commonly used by the elite for traveling in the city.[91] An expedition of this kind counted as an invitation to go out (*tangchai*), requiring remuneration by the customer. It was also an occasion

Plate 3. Various modes of transportation in the old city about 1890.

for the girls to receive gifts (jewelry and money) that would escape the madam's vigilant eye.[92]

The arrival of Westerners created new locations and new opportunities for outings. The most important of them was the race course where every year, whatever the circumstances, there was a whole set of events connected with the horse races. Gradually, what had been an annual event became more frequent with the organization of races and betting, which drew large crowds. The well-to-do Chinese who went to the races, especially in the nineteenth century when this event was as yet highly elitist in character, were accompanied by the courtesans of whom they were the official customers. The more famous the girl in these circles, the greater was the advantage to the customer in terms of social prestige. And the courtesan herself boosted her position and aroused interest on the part of potential customers. The tradition of taking walks did not survive the shrinking of the leisure space of the Chinese elites. No source mentions these outings after 1911.

The Chinese courtesans belonged to a cultural tradition and a social structure that did not withstand the onslaught of modernity. As in ancient Greece or modern Japan, the existence of a group of women especially devoted to the entertainment of male members of the elites – who enjoyed full freedom to have several wives and concubines in their homes – could be imagined only in a society characterized by a rigid separation of the sexes and a very restrictive definition of the role of women. China, unlike the West, continued to live in this mode until late into the nineteenth century. The opening of Shanghai to foreign trade, the slow but growing externalization of Chinese women, and changes in the composition of local society gradually undermined the status and role of the courtesans, to the benefit of a system in which there now existed only common prostitutes. This change was initiated very quickly under the combined effect of foreign influence and social upheaval caused by internal rebellion, but it reached completion only half a century later with the economic take-off of the city.

The fact that this transformation was gradual points to the profound entrenchment of the courtesans in the social habitus of the Chinese upper classes. Our image of this milieu is undoubtedly idealized, as I have tried to show in the first part of this chapter. Nevertheless, the fact that this reality differed from the representations that the literati made of it is ultimately of only relative importance. What matters above all is the discourse that was elaborated about this community. This discourse dominated the perception that the literati and the population in general had of the courtesans. The myth thus created permeated the collective consciousness to such a degree that the notion of the courtesan endured well after her actual disappearance in the twentieth century. I shall return to this point because it was decisive in the vision that might be had of the place of prostitution in China. The idealization of courtesans helped mask the contempt in which the Chinese elites actually held the common prostitute and therefore contributed to projecting a distorted image of the attitude of the Chinese toward prostitution.

In nineteenth-century Shanghai, courtesans enjoyed a socially recognized status that the poorest sections of the city's population probably envied. The patronizing of courtesans was governed by relatively strict rules that emphasized the respect in which they were held by their customers. These were not mere rituals aimed at masking a squalid sex-for-money relationship. The men who went to these houses looked for something other than mere sexual gratification. The courtesans provided company, vivacity, and diversion in a context of relaxation and conviviality. The leisure space of the elites comprised the four cardinal points referred to earlier, and the courtesan's house clearly represented the center or focal point of this space. It was the only place where the merchants and literati found the peace and quiet as well as the intimacy in which to enjoy themselves among friends, in pleasant company. The most important events in an individual's life – birthdays, success in examinations, business deals, and so on – were celebrated in these places. Patronizing a courtesan's house was a normal part of social life for the Chinese urban elites, and it could be done on a regular and sometimes daily basis.

In Shanghai, there was a leisure space and a leisure time proper to the elites, and the courtesans were the Ariadne's clew (i.e., the unifying thread) that unified this time and space. If we make an exception for women from the more popular classes, courtesans were the only women who moved in a male-dominated public space. We must keep in mind this particular structure of urban society in nineteenth-century China – which differed radically from that of cities in the West where women practiced various small crafts and trades that took them daily into the streets – to appreciate the very special role of courtesans. The kind of privileged status that resulted from this situation was undermined by the increasing entry of women into the labor market and the public space. Other modes of entertainment emerged that eliminated or modified the traditional places of leisure of the elites. The courtesans withdrew into their proper domain – their own houses – and went out only in order to entertain customers in restaurants. The movements of courtesans in the public space was limited to these brief "to-and-fro trips," and this fact signaled the decline in their function. From being artists praised for their vivacity, talents, and sense of sociability, the courtesans saw their role drop to that of luxury prostitutes who could still be taken out publicly as objects of social status, but whose services were henceforth limited to the sexual domain.

2
Lives of Splendor and Wretchedness

The writings of the Chinese scholars convey a positive and much idealized – even mythical – image of the courtesans. Our perception of this group is thereby necessarily biased, all the more so as the sources, by their very silence, conceal a part of the reality that the scholars would not see. It is therefore through the prism of an exclusively male viewpoint that we must try to detect a more complex and less benign reality behind "the perfume and the powder."[1] To be sure, these hetaerae of traditional Chinese society had a higher social status than their sisters struggling in the opium dens and brothels of the Huangpu docks, and they enjoyed far better living conditions. And yet we have seen that in the nineteenth century many, if not most, of them lived in conditions of virtual (albeit gilded) servitude from which their only hope of escape was to buy their own freedom (and this was a privilege reserved for a minority) or be redeemed by a wealthy customer. In this chapter, I shall first of all touch on the condition of the courtesans and the essential stages in their careers and then explore a dimension peculiar to this milieu in China, the "culture of the courtesans" that was shared by the Chinese urban elites up to the First World War.

Keeping Up Appearances and the Illusion of Appearances

Beauty and elegance were two qualities that set the courtesans apart from most other women. It was their richly decorated robes that drew attention at first sight. The courtesans took extremely great care of their physical appearance, which was an essential attribute of their success. A critical view expressed at the end of the nineteenth century deemed them to be capable of little else but self-adornment.[2] But further reflection would suggest that it is not really easy to get an idea of what a Chinese courtesan looked like at this time. The written testimony is often couched in a conventional language that does not give a full account of physical appearance in precise terms related to specific individuals. The Chinese scholars were very particularly fond of the subtle game of using literary quotations from ancient writings. These quotations were of course powerfully evocative in the minds of those who used them but are a source of frustration to the historian seeking to "see" these courtesans and perceive changes, if any, both in their appearance and in the male perception of beauty. This may be the rational viewpoint of a Westerner; and perhaps it makes no sense to the aesthetic sensibility of the Chinese scholars, who were concerned with the "essence" of beauty rather than with its "externals." In their eyes, true beauty lay in the spirit (*qi*) that gave life to a woman and not in her external physical appearance.[3]

All that remain, therefore, apart from a few stray jottings, is the iconography. Unfortunately, the iconography is not really wide-ranging. The Chinese do not have the tradition of the portrait, which, in the West, has given us valuable sources for the study of dress, hairstyles, and so on. It is almost impossible, in Chinese art, to find the quasi-ethnographic curiosity of a painter like Toulouse-Lautrec, who was able to assemble both the externals and the atmosphere of the Parisian houses of vice in one and the same painting. There is one exception, although it is not comparable and is limited in time: It consists of the remarkable etchings published by the illustrative supplement (*Dianshizhai huabao*) of the newspaper *Shen Bao*.[4] Nor did the introduction of photography into China make any major contribution toward this type of portraiture. A good number of photographs of courtesans can be found, but these were generally meant for self-advertisement. A courtesan would have her photograph taken in order to display it at home or present it to a good customer. Some courtesans had their visiting cards printed along with a photograph. Others were even more businesslike and put up their portraits for sale.[5] These photographs showed the courtesans at their best, but in conventional attire. In this field, too, photography lacked the ethnographic eye that, in the West, has given us superb glimpses of the interior of brothels, the behavior of prostitutes and their customers, and so on.

It is hard for the Western sense of aesthetics to reconcile the excessively bland and impersonal image of the Chinese courtesans with the idea of beauty. Just like the Japanese geishas today, the Chinese courtesans plastered their faces with white rice powder. All that could be distinguished were the lips, painted with bright carmine red, and the eyebrows, which were shaven and then penciled over with a black line. It would seem rather that the courtesans went in for uniformity of appearance. This also applies to height and size, which are never mentioned. In this respect, the variety that the nineteenth-century French brothels looked for in their prostitutes was not much favored in China.[6] The very silence of the sources reveals a special kind of aesthetic sensibility that was little concerned with "appearances."

The clothing of the courtesans was flamboyant, according to the memoirs of the customers and the literary descriptions. They were made of luxurious materials (mostly silk) dyed in bright colors and delicately embroidered. The classic dress consisted of trousers and a succession of silken vests

Plate 4. Portrait of a courtesan in the nineteenth century.

and bodices covered with a very long tunic. Two written portraits depict courtesans who actually existed even if the description given of them is partly the product of the author's imagination[7]:

> Zhang Shuyu was one of the four diamonds. . . . She wore a coat padded with pale green silk gauze on a robe of the same material, but colored purple. Her tiny feet wore little boots of violet brocade.
>
> Lu Lanfen came in walking with slow steps. She had on a pair of trousers and a tunic made of light white silk and wore pale blue boots. . . . In her carefully combed hair, there was only one hairpin studded with emeralds while her chignon was adorned with a row of jasmine flowers.

It was only in the twentieth century that the courtesans began to wear dresses inspired by Western styles, such as the formless long dress with the split side that is still worn in Taiwan and Hong Kong today. At the beginning of the 1920s, there was a craze for men's clothing, and it became particularly fashionable to wear a jacket over a dress.[8] Fashions changed every year, even if it was only in the details. The influence of the courtesans on dress was great. It was they who innovated and gave the tone for fashions in women's clothing. They were in the forefront, as they had been in the great cities of Jiangnan under the Ming dynasty.[9] Their sense of novelty could take astonishing forms. At the beginning of the revolution, after 1911, there was a fashion for wearing trousers in the colors of the national flag (five horizontal red, yellow, blue, white, and black stripes) as a symbol of newfound liberty. There was no trace of mockery in this dress, which the courtesans wore as a way of expressing their patriotism. This fashion did not last more than a year, because the most "politically conscious" courtesans spread the word that this dress might be misunderstood, especially by foreigners.[10]

The beauty of the Chinese courtesans drew constant praise from Chinese scholars, even if they couched their praise in conventional literary language. In these women who were professionals of diversion and amusement, they found qualities that were lacking in their wives, or at least more discreetly expressed: elegance and charm, a lively and mischievous nature, a sharp sense of repartee, and a spirit of independence that was socially forbidden to women of good standing. There can be no doubt that the Chinese elites had a regard for these women who enlivened their leisure activities and in whom they found real partners, even friends and lovers. But the relationship was unbalanced. The courtesans were basically consumer articles. They were a pool from which pretty concubines could be drawn. They were a group of women particularly exposed to social upheavals. The restructuring of the Chinese elites, which was marked by the disappearance of the scholar classes, removed the veneer of appearances to which the scholar culture had appended its seal, and it paved the way for a purely commercial and sexual relationship.

Defloration

Defloration sanctioned the entry of young girls into the world of prostitution. It was a crucial step for the party concerned, both physically and psychologically, because it was a sort of initiatory step. In the world of the courtesans, defloration was the equivalent of marriage for a girl from a good family. An interested customer first of all had to negotiate with the brothel madam. This was an arduous task, given that the occasion was unique and offered her a way to recover, at one stroke, a good portion of the money invested in the girl. Very often, it was the madam herself who picked out and encouraged a faithful and wealthy customer to avail himself of this "privilege." Defloration was accompanied by a set of rituals designed to make the experience more solemn and provide a semblance of marriage. These rituals also had the effect of masking the rather sordid nature of the role that the girl was being made to play and the very materialistic aspect of an operation whose importance, for the madam, was above all financial. The defloration took place around the age of fifteen or sixteen because Chinese girls often had their first menstrual periods at about this age.[11]

On the appointed evening, the courtesan wore her best clothes and offered prayers before the altar of the household deity. The customer organized a banquet with friends before retiring to the room where two big red candles had been lit.[12] On the next day, the employees and other courtesans of the house came to congratulate the girl and the customer. As it happened, this was also an opportunity for them to get some additional tips.[13] From this day onward, the girl no longer wore the pigtail that set her apart from the other courtesans. The defloration itself was not limited to one night. The customer could come back three or four nights in succession or even for one or two weeks. This was a form of privilege designed to reinforce the quasi-nuptial character of this step.[14]

The financial cost that the customer paid for such an experience could be fairly high. Although the information given by the sources, especially the literary ones, is often very general, it is possible to identify the amounts spent and put this partiality for virgins in perspective. For the 1870s, Wang Tao mentions two examples of customers, one of whom paid 300 taels while the other paid a "large sum" (*zhongjin*).[15] Around 1920, one author estimated that a customer had to expect to pay 400 to 500 taels. This figure included the cost of a series of *huatou*, gifts of jewelry and clothing for the girl and tips amounting to 80 to 100 yuan. Another author speaks of several hundreds of yuan and a pair of gold bars.[16] The cost also varied according to the girl's fame: It could be 400 to 500 yuan for a courtesan of ordinary repute but 2,000 to 3,000 yuan for a celebrity.[17]

The authors of works on prostitution assert that the "old hands" in the brothels abstained from the practice of defloration, which they left to the naive or to novices.[18] However, this is an assertion that dates from the 1920s at a time when this practice was in fact tending to disappear and when it could not be guaranteed that a girl was truly a virgin. Given the major financial stakes that it represented, certain madams did of course try to vend the virginity of their charges to several customers in succession, using various artifices to dress up the previous defloration. By the end of the century, works on prostitution were warning customers about these practices, which, it must be said, are not exclusive to Chinese madams.[19] Increasingly, the Shanghai guidebooks made it a point to ask potential customers to reject all such propositions, not out of any consideration for the concerned parties but in the name of business ethics: The madams were trying to sell adulterated merchandise.

The practice of defloration tended to disappear, and, above all, it came to lose its symbolic significance. It no longer corresponded to the demand that, in the twentieth century, was first and foremost a sexual demand. The idea of virgin courtesans could be imagined in a context where there were customers to appreciate their artistic talents and their wit. With the growing "sexualization" of their trade, the courtesans were no longer seen as anything other than sexual objects. The supply of sexual services grew considerably, and the customers no longer felt any interest in defloration, which did not appear to them to be a source of gratification. In 1940, one author stated the problem very crudely when he compared virgin courtesans to fish in an aquarium: "good to look at but not to eat." He pointed out that very often it was homosexuals who patronized these girls. This gave them a social "alibi" while sparing them the need to engage in sexual relations.[20]

The Sexual Conduct of the Elites

Sexual conduct is a subject about which the Chinese were discreet in the nineteenth century, surprisingly so because there were no religious taboos attached to it as there were in the West. Here, there is a real gulf between the perceived view of very great freedom of expression in sexual matters, as in Van Gulik's description of ancient China up to the Ming Dynasty (1368–1644), and the weighty silence of the Qing, especially in the nineteenth century, with which we are concerned. Van Gulik notes this change without really explaining it. He attributes it to the adoption of a prudish morality by the Manchu emperors, whose concern was to be seen by their new subjects as models of virtue.[21] My own research on a far later period, at a time when this puritanical attitude became prevalent in Chinese society as a whole, does not make for a new interpretation of the phenomenon. All I can do is to take note of a profound silence that is difficult to penetrate.

In Wang Tao's book *Huaguo jutan*, there is only one explicit reference to sexual relations between a customer and a courtesan[22] ("he spent the night with the girl"). And the literary documents are never more precise than this. One author mentions the sexual aspect of relationships with courtesans but only to complain that the courtesans had forgotten the intimacies of the bedchamber. The old tradition of the *ars amandis* (*fang zhong miaojue*) had been lost. Only one or two girls were renowned in this sphere; but because everybody visited them, there was a risk of "catching a bad illness and, in return for a brief instant of pleasure, of being infected for life."[23] It was only in the second decade of the twentieth century that the sexual dimension was evoked, albeit in terms that were still metaphorical. One expression that recurs frequently is *song kuzidai* ("loosening the [courtesan's] trouser belt"). There can be no ambiguity about this image. Another expression encountered is [*guo*] *yi du chunfeng* ("[taking] a breath of spring air"). "Spring" has a clear sexual connotation in Chinese. It was often employed in literary expressions.

Because the Chinese sources are practically silent on sexual behavior, it is only by reading between the lines that we can get an occasional glimpse of a few details of sexual behavior, even if they are scanty and need to be treated with caution. One author mentions two Chinese ideograms not found in the dictionaries. In one, the radical for woman is between the radical for man placed to the right and to the left. The second ideogram is composed in exactly the same way except that it is the man in the middle. All that the author says is that if the ideograms exist, then it means that they correspond to reality. He does mention the first ideogram but states that in Shanghai it is not rare for a customer to sleep with two girls at a time. All that is needed, he says, is to find two girls who do not hate each other, adding however that a well-born person would not go in for such practices.[24] It is unlikely that the courtesans would have agreed to play this role very often, given the nature of the relationships that they maintained with their customers.

The Chinese elites had a pronounced distaste for sexual promiscuity. This can be seen in the way in which the courtesans' houses were organized. These houses saw to it that regular customers did not meet each other and above all that they did not ever feel that they were sleeping with the same girl. This attitude was related partly to the Chinese view of sexual relations, which was heavily permeated with Taoism, seeing the sex act as a means of regeneration and, at the same time, as entailing a possible loss of vital energy. The resolution of this contradiction lay in the conditions in which sexual relations took place, namely in a state of exclusiveness that avoided the mixing of essences. One author states that certain customers who were far too closely watched by their wives were unable to spend the night in a house of prostitution. They preferred to come in the small hours. If a girl had received a customer on the previous day, it was a very serious matter because the consequent mingling (of sperm) could be an essential cause of illness.[25] Beyond the obvious risk of transmission of an infection, what motivated the author and shocked the Chinese mind was the fact that two men could follow each another with the same prostitute. This possibility naturally formed part of the logic of prostitution; but it was something that was rejected by the elites, who had the illusion, in visiting the courtesans, of having a special relationship with one girl alone.

Within the courtesans' houses, attitudes were rather reserved even under the warming effect of alcohol. Neither the etchings of the mid-nineteenth to the early twentieth century nor the literature of the period give any indication of any ostensibly ribald behavior (be it in attitude or in language). Bodies stayed out of contact; the courtesans remained seated, at a small distance behind their customers; and crudity had to be avoided in speech. It appears that it was acceptable to exchange glances or hold hands, but this was a boundary not to be crossed.[26] In the 1920s, it is less certain that these rules of etiquette were followed, even in places that were more public than the courtesans' houses. One newspaper reports an incident where a certain Fang tried to surreptitiously caress a courtesan he had invited by putting his hand into her sleeve.[27] Although Fang was deemed to be lacking in manners, his behavior clearly points to a shift in the status of the courtesan to that of a high-class prostitute. Ten years earlier, a courtesan would never have accepted this type of advance.

The particular and highly selective mode by which these high-class prostitutes received visitors shielded them from excessively frequent sexual contact. There were no more than one or two good customers in a single season with whom they had physical relations.[28] Given the times at which they were available, these relations had to be relatively spaced out. If a girl became pregnant, the madam would be able to determine the father's identity. This is an indirect (and extremely tenuous) clue suggesting that it was infrequent for the courtesans to have sexual relations. Besides, these courtesans deliberately sought to avoid physical relations. In 1934, a guidebook warned potential customers against the forms of evasion practiced by the girls, who would pretend, for example, that they were having their menstrual periods when a customer became too demanding.[29] This practice of evasion is a sign that the courtesans were facing greater demand from customers for sexual services. Before 1914 and to an even greater extent in the nineteenth century, they did not need to resort to these stratagems because the customers were more dependent in their relationship with the courtesans.

The question of venereal disease is completely avoided in the nineteenth-century sources. The apparently low frequency of sexual relationships between courtesans and their customers, along with the fact that they received a smaller number of men, probably shielded this category of prostitutes from repeated infection. However, it is also known that venereal disease was very widespread in nineteenth-century China.[30] Thus, there is no reason to believe that the courtesans and their customers could have escaped this problem entirely. Yet, it does not seem to have caused any particular concern among the literati. Wang Tao, who wrote three works on the world of the courtesans, mentioned the topic of venereal disease only once when referring to a Chinese doctor who specialized in the treatment of such diseases. An author at the end of the century wrote in passing that girls who were sexually in great demand were often ill.[31] It was only in the years following the First World War that cases of venereal sickness among courtesans were made public, usually in the small newspapers. The reports were sometimes in the category of rumor or even defamation. However, they show that no category of prostitutes was spared.[32] In the 1930s, the problem of venereal disease was raised in very explicit fashion. The courtesans were no longer considered separately. Like their colleagues, they were seen as "the source and point of transmission of venereal diseases."[33]

The courtesans were also exposed to the risk of unwanted pregnancy. This aspect is only exceptionally touched on in the works or novels that dealt with prostitution. Once a girl announced that she was pregnant, the madam would seek to identify the father so that, if possible, she could try to extort money from him as compensation for time lost during the pregnancy. If the infant was a boy and the customer wanted to adopt it, the madam would naturally raise the stakes. However, if the customer refused to pay, the madam had no means of exerting pressure. One author mentioning this topic says that if two customers had slept with a girl in the same month, then the madam would begin by approaching the wealthier of the two.[34] This information is anecdotal per se but confirms the fact that the courtesans slept with only a very small number of customers and that sexual relations were probably quite spaced out.

The risk of repeated pregnancy was a practically unavoidable reality. Given the absence of contraceptives, even of the makeshift kind used by French prostitutes, there can be no doubt that this was a problem that the courtesans had to face. The madams made the courtesans take medicines from the Chinese pharmacopoeia to prevent pregnancies. If these medicines failed (which was likely), they would use every means to make the girl abort through other medicines or even more brutal means.[35] Although the written sources totally conceal this side of things, the iconographic documents frequently show the presence of children in the houses of courtesans (cf. *Dianshizhai huabao*). It was not rare for a courtesan to be herself the daughter of a courtesan. The total avoidance of this reality in the written sources, memoirs, and literature forms part of the same logic that led Chinese scholars to idealize the world of courtesans and retain only the positive aspects conforming to the image that they wished to give of this world and of themselves. Thus, "minor details" such as pregnancies, venereal disease, and the condition of the girls were wholly concealed.

Relationships of Affection and Love

The relationship between a courtesan and a customer had a special character that needs to be briefly evoked. It was based in part on purely material interest, but there can be no doubt that feelings also came into it. Naturally it is difficult, for want of direct testimony on the part of the courtesans, to apportion these two aspects of the relationship. All that I can do, therefore, is to infer the nature and quality of these liaisons from the modes of relationship of Shanghai's courtesans.

From the customer's point of view, establishing a relationship with a courtesan in the nineteenth century was not a simple matter of money: It entailed an operation of conquest and seduction. In the world of the courtesans, the members of the Chinese elite found a space in which they could set up "normal" contacts with women – that is, contacts that were unencumbered by the weighty code of Confucian etiquette with its strict regulation of relationships between men and women. Women of good family were in fact often recluses in their apartments and had no contact with men apart from members of their families. For these men, the quality of the marital relationship was often not the ideal because, in almost every case, the marriage would have been arranged. The ties between husband and wife were marked by a certain distance and a certain degree of formality, especially on social occasions.

With the courtesans, men could experience sensations and feelings that were not accepted outside this context. If they were intrigued by a courtesan whom they had happened to meet by chance or who was particularly renowned, they were required to play a subtle game in which seduction and remuneration were intermingled without the latter aspect being brought into the open. Customers were required, so to speak, to embark on a courtship in order to win a courtesan's favors. This was a unique experience made possible only in this context. Moreover, the highly informal atmosphere of these exchanges needs to be emphasized. The courtesans were women trained as "ladies of entertainment." They possessed a degree of culture. They knew how to entertain. They had a sense of repartee and could play a whole range of indoor games to enliven their customers' evenings.

Of course, this environment must not be idealized in the manner of the Chinese scholars. And yet their writings, however biased, bear testimony to a world where the relationships between men and women could attain a special intensity and a special quality. Wang Tao mentions several cases of severe disappointment, and even suicide, on the part of men who had lost the courtesans that they patronized, either through death or because of marriage to a wealthier customer. The growing commercialization of this milieu and its sexualization very probably impaired the nature of the ties between the courtesans and their customers. It is also difficult to imagine that the courtesans could have stood up to the insistent demands of a determined customer. However, up to the 1940s, the customers were continually advised to be patient: The girls had to be courted and won over and not merely bought.[36]

From the courtesan's point of view, the relationship with the customer was not a simple matter of money either. First of all, there were barely more than one or two good customers with whom she had a close, and especially sexual, relationship. These customers practically provided for her upkeep by their regular and assiduous presence. The others only revolved around her world: They would invite her out, hold occasional dinners in her home, and so on. Not all the customers of the courtesans' houses were necessarily looking for sexual gratification. There were those who were looking more simply for a space of conviviality and diversion. Good customers were not permanent customers or those who did not stay for long. They changed over time, although the pace of the change cannot be defined. It depended on the state of their fortune, their interest in the girl, and their patronizing of other houses. However, it must be emphasized that, at any given time, there was a limited number of customers who could offer the possibility of a more intense relationship. The courtesans also knew that there was only a limited amount of time available to them and that they had to find a husband in order to escape from their condition. The affective dimension was therefore not absent from their concerns even if other criteria (such as fortune and age) came into the equation.

The courtesan–customer relationship had an undoubtedly exclusive and almost conjugal character. A courtesan expected a certain degree of fidelity from a customer. If he began to visit another girl, this was an act of straying experienced as a form of betrayal that could provoke outbursts of anger between the girls concerned or between the customer and the girls (the press frequently reported these cases).[37] These altercations could sometimes take a very aggressive turn. Even for a permanent separation, the "compasses of the world of gallantry," those works designed to guide a man's first steps in the world of courtesans, recommended that sharp breaks should be avoided. It was preferable that the customer should reduce the frequency of his visits using the pretext of trips abroad, and so on.[38] Where sentiment was lacking, what was at stake was of course money but also considerations of prestige. This aspect of the matter is clearly present in the sometimes violent reactions of the courtesans when a customer betrayed their trust.

This mode of relationship can be imagined only in a society where there was strict separation between the sexes and an almost absolute segregation of women, at least among the elites. As and when Chinese society (and, as far as we are concerned, Shanghai society) opened out, giving women increasingly wider scope for action in the public space, the courtesans began to lose their *raison d'être*. The process was slow because, despite change, no "sexual revolution" took place in China. The emergence of intermediate social strata, the development of new forms of venal sexuality, and the appearance of a different sensibility with regard to sex helped undermine the courtesan's function. Although it would be somewhat arbitrary to lay down precise chronological markers, it would seem to me that the main divide can be located at around 1914–1915. After that, for about ten years, the illusion of the existence of the "world of flowers" persisted, but it no longer corresponded to reality.

Although the relationships between a courtesan and one of her customers could be tinged with sentiment and even love, this was not generally the case. The courtesans who were independent of their madams therefore looked elsewhere for a genuine sentimental relationship. It was frequent for the *changsan* to take lovers, at least in the twentieth century. I have little information on this subject for the preceding period – the nineteenth century – where it is mentioned only once.[39] This phenomenon could be related to the fact that a greater number of courtesans gained their freedom in the first and second decades of the century. A courtesan had to refrain from disclosing a love relationship because the customers would not be pleased to learn of it, especially if the other man was an actor. For it was in the world of the theater, which they patronized by profession and taste, that the courtesans most usually found their lovers. There were affinities between the two worlds (a love of music, singing, the actor's play) that explain this mutual attraction. Both groups, actors and courtesans, led a fairly similar, essentially nocturnal, lifestyle and occupied a position somewhat on the fringes of society. Finally, and this is not a negligible point, the actors were often young, handsome, and full of life, which distinguished them from the girls' habitual customers.

It is difficult to assess the scale of this phenomenon was widespread. An author who gave a list in 1922 of thirty-eight courtesans having one or more lovers added that this figure represented only a small proportion of the real number.[40] Indeed, he only listed the most famous courtesans, who led very independent lives. In reality, it was probably difficult to keep a love relationship hidden for long. The courtesans generally had little opportunity for regular contact with men outside the circle of their clientele. The close watch that the madam kept over them, the physical limits dictated by the fact that they had bound feet, and their fairly short working hours were all factors that worked against an independent love life. Certain courtesans married actors or musicians. One of them was Lin Daiyu, a leading figure among the courtesans at the turn of the century. But her marriage to an actor was a sign of her failure. Once she had passed a certain age, a courtesan lost almost any chance of getting married to a scholar or merchant.

Marriage

Marriage was the second major step in a courtesan's life because it meant the possibility of making an honorable exit from their profession. As such, it was the object of intense preparation and festivities equivalent to those of a real marriage even if these festivities were limited to the courtesans' house. Wang Tao frequently mentions this topic and, more broadly, refers to love relationships between courtesans and customers. According to him, only two-thirds of the girls managed to get married, but he does not say what happened to the others.[41] It must be emphasized at the outset that these were marriages in low key. The courtesans who married members of the gentry in this way never acceded to the rank of wife but only to the more modest one of concubine. Some of them could be only the umpteenth concubine of a rich merchant.

Just as in the case of defloration, a courtesan's marriage was preceded by negotiations between the customer and the madam, because everything depended on the madam who decided the fate of the girls in her charge. Because, as a rule, a madam had only one or two girls in her charge, she had to negotiate the best terms, because the girl's marriage would mean the end of her business, unless she could buy another courtesan. The customer would also sometimes seek guarantees. Certain customers sought to test the sincerity of their concubine-to-be so as to avert any risk of a subsequent flight with money and jewelry.[42]

Buying a courtesan her freedom was a particularly expensive operation for the customer. To the "body price" (*shenjia*) proper, which could amount to a considerable sum, there had to be added the costs of the ceremony and all various gifts and tips that were demanded in return for the courtesan's departure. On the financial aspects of the marriage, the sources are rather imaginative. In *Huaguo jutan*, Wang Tao explicitly mentions the cases of eleven courtesans who were purchased as concubines, and he gives their price as 1,000 taels. Clearly, these are nonrepresentative figures because it is difficult to imagine that there was a fixed rate or that the market remained steady to such an extent. Besides, Wang writes that in one case, after discussion, the price was set at 800 taels and that in another case, it was set at 1,500 taels, which was a considerable sum in the nineteenth century. The negotiations between the madam, the customer, and the courtesan were sometimes strenuous.[43] In *Songbin suohua*, Wang Tao mentions Lu Daiyu, who was repurchased for 2,000 taels, and Zhou Fenglin, who was repurchased for 8,000 or 9,000 taels. A reader's letter in the *Shen Bao* refers to the repurchase of Xiao Guizhu for 8,000 taels and of Wu Yue's for 10,000 taels.[44] Wang Wenhua, a chief of general staff in 1920, repurchased the courtesan Ling Juxian for 5,000 yuan.[45] There was an inflationary trend according to a 1923 guidebook, which indicates an average price of 7,000 to 8,000 yuan in that year. However, the most renowned courtesans were sometimes taken for much greater sums: Bei Jin was bought for 10,000 yuan, and Guan Fang was purchased for 20,000 yuan.[46]

In 1920, one source gives a more detailed account of the expenditure involved. The customer paid the madam money in compensation for the cost of educating and supporting the courtesan up to the time of her marriage. This was the price of her freedom, but it was also the form in which the transaction for the marriage of any woman in China was conceived. The parents were "indemnified" for their expenditure on education by the bridegroom's family. The customer also had to pay off the girl's debts, if any. Accessory expenditure included the purchase of a pair of silver food sticks for the banquet, which was not returned. All categories of personnel took advantage of this opportunity to obtain tips.[47] To avoid this expenditure, Yang Diguang, chief of staff of the Chinese Army, used the pretext of a journey to take away the courtesan he was patronizing and make her his concubine without paying any money to the madam. When he next passed through Shanghai, the madam had his hotel room surrounded by a gang of thugs. To get out of his predicament, Yang had to call for help from Du Yuesheng, the infamous boss of Shanghai's secret societies, and promise to pay the madam 3,000 yuan.[48]

Almost all the ingredients of a traditional marriage can be found in the organization of a courtesan's marriage ceremony. The customer would invite his friends and acquaintances to a banquet. Because a courtesan could not always receive large numbers of guests together in her house, she would organize a banquet lasting several days. The ceremony was accompanied by religious rites, most usually in the presence of a Taoist priest. The courtesan was visited by other girls who came to congratulate her, all of which caused a constant flow of sedan chairs and rickshaws. The courtesan's habitual customers also came to congratulate her. A courtesan's marriage was a major affair that created much excitement in the *lilong* (lane) on which the house was located. When everything was over, the customer arranged for the courtesan to be fetched from her home to his house like a young bride.

A marriage concluded in this way was not always a success. The husband could become aloof from his new partner and seek his pleasure elsewhere. The courtesans also found it difficult to adjust to their new mode of living, where they were confined to a restricted area in the women's apartments, having no contact with the outside world. Wu Peixiang, who married a "man from the countryside" (*xiangren*), soon got bored with the rural life and returned to her former trade.[49] In 1872, the *Shen Bao* recounted the story of a courtesan who continued to see her former lover after getting married. The husband got angry when he learned of this and threw the lover out. The courtesan preferred to return to her former trade.[50] Most usually, the courtesan was badly received in her new family, especially by the wife who saw her as a rival. The premature death of a husband often meant the rejection of a courtesan by the family, sometimes at an age when her beauty was already a thing of the past.[51]

Despite all that, there was hardly any way out for courtesans other than marriage, which alone could ensure a decent retirement. The inevitable sequel to a courtesan's career was for her to be resold to a lower-class brothel until, having become old and ugly, she would be reduced to beggary. In one case, a courtesan who did not attract customers and bring in enough money was resold by her madam for 200 yuan to another establishment, very probably a lower-class brothel.[52] Marriage, whatever the hardships and sorrows that it brought to the courtesans, was actually their only salvation. "The world of prostitution is an empty world," wrote Wang Tao in his last work on prostitution; the courtesans had to leave that world before it was too late.[53]

Leaving the Trade

A sword of Damocles was poised permanently over a courtesan's head: It was the sword of old age and physical decline. Beauty was an essential advantage, even for courtesans who had been able to develop other charms less vulnerable to the ravages of time. Wang Tao frequently referred to the fact that the courtesans, when they reached an "advanced age," would be deserted by their customers for newcomers.[54]

Apart from marriage or entry into lower-class brothels, the courtesans had hardly any choice except to turn to begging or to die. Death could also come in the course of their working lives, through sickness or sometimes because of profound disappointment. Wang Tao mentions five deaths, two of them suicides and three from fatal illness. A fatal illness, generally appeared in connection with a disappointment in love or a conflict with a madam over the choice of a husband. The particular feature of these illnesses (the symptoms were lassitude, loss of appetite, and coldness in the body: "she was affected by weakness, her hands were as cold as ice and could not be warmed even when they were held tightly"[55]) was the speed with which they took effect.[56] The girl would succumb within a few months or even a few weeks or days. Conversely, the death of the cause of the annoyance could produce a miraculous effect and bring about the patient's almost immediate recovery. These descriptions parallel the way in which women were depicted in nineteenth-century European painting and literature.[57]

Suicide was very much present in reports about courtesans. In Wang Tao's works, the suicides were always caused by a sentimental mishap. Often, it was the courtesan's refusal to accept a marriage arranged by the madam that pushed her to this act. One girl committed suicide in order to avoid marrying some ordinary man when she would have preferred a scholar.[58] Again, the death or sudden disappearance of a man she had in mind could lead to suicide;[59] the most common method of committing suicide was to swallow crude opium. This interpretation of the courtesan's behavior might be questioned and seen as yet another way of mystifying the issue by reference to an idealized reality. But this was not at all the case, as can be seen from the press.

In 1872, Yu Mei and her lover took their own lives because they were no longer able to live together.[60] A young man who had a love affair with a courtesan found himself to be short of money, whereupon his father, a strict man, refused to help. The courtesan swallowed opium.[61] The *Shen Bao* also reports the sad tale of a Hubei merchant who had met a courtesan named Jin Mei on a boat in the Pearl River delta (in Guangdong). They had a passionate love affair, but the merchant died shortly thereafter. When his family found evidence in his papers of the commitments he had made to the courtesan, they sought her out and gave her the sad news. Despite all the precautions of her entourage, Jin Mei committed suicide. The merchant's family decided to bury them together.[62] Sometimes, the suicide resulted from an argument between two lovers, especially when the man suspected the courtesan of cheating on him. Suicide here provided postmortem proof of the courtesan's honesty.[63]

The Courtesans and Politics

The world of prostitution formed a space and a community in which the principal activity was designed to divert customers, far from the serious topics that usually took up their time. Furthermore, the condition of the courtesans and, to an even greater extent, the condition of other prostitutes hardly allowed them any possibility of expressing their views on major national issues and organizing themselves to participate in these issues. There were exceptions, however, apart from the fact that the houses of prostitution could have involuntarily contributed to political action. The world of prostitution reacted to the major political and social crises of China in the twentieth century. The courtesans were in the forefront of spontaneous action forming part of broader collective movements. It was their level of political consciousness and knowledge, derived from their familiarity with the elites who were preoccupied with these problems, that explains their political stances, which shall be outlined here.

The courtesans' sphere of action was twofold, encompassing the political and the humanitarian fields. In the political field, the *changsan* reacted to Japan's repeated attempts to encroach on China. In 1915, the twenty-one demands that placed strategic sectors of China's economy and defense under Japanese control aroused a movement of mobilization. Several organizations began to set up a "national salvation fund" (*jiuguo chujinhui*). A courtesan from Shanghai, Zang Chunge, then proposed that the money earned from invitations to go out (*tangchai*) should be paid into this fund.

She published a declaration in the city's newspapers that deserves to be quoted:

> Although [we] belong to the world of the green pavilions [the world of prostitution], [we] [too] have families. If [we] have families, [we] should have a country, and our duty therefore is to support the country. . . . There is a certain country that is demanding unfair privileges in order to turn our country into a second India or a second Korea. Although [we] are only prostitutes, [we] too are citizens [*guomin yi fenzi*] and we have been greatly affected by this news. Our country cannot consider the possibility of war for lack of resources. There are courageous patriots who are proposing to set up a national salvation fund. [We] do not have the means to do as much but we would like to set aside half of the earnings from our outings for the national salvation fund. . . .

This appeal was heard, and other courtesans followed suit. In all, 300 yuan were paid into the fund.[64]

Like the majority of Chinese, the courtesans were shocked by the outcome of the Conference of Versailles in 1919. The huge wave of protests and patriotic mobilization provoked by the terms laid down at the conference are known. The courtesans made their contribution to the nationalistic upsurge. On the 9th of May 1919, Lin Daiyu and ten other well-known *changsan* appealed to their colleagues to join in commemorating the day of national shame (*guochi jinian*) by refusing to sing and by posting notices on doors of their establishments to explain their strike action. They also called on the people to buy only domestically produced goods.[65] Jian Bing organized tea parties with political discussion in her establishment. Others, like Miao Lian, published messages in the press, demanding the resignation of the Peking government.[66]

In the humanitarian field, it was during major natural catastrophes that the courtesans made individual and collective contributions to fund collection campaigns. In December [1920, twelve Cantonese prostitutes decided to hand over their day's earnings (176 yuan) in aid of the drought-affected northern provinces.[67] In March 1921, a group of courtesans led by Lin Daiyu met in a big Western-style restaurant. They decided to write a play describing the state of the drought-affected population. The piece was written in a few days. The play, which was planned to last for an entire season, called for about a hundred actors. After each song, the courtesans went into the audience to collect contributions.[68] This was not the only case of mobilization for humanitarian purposes. A print in the *Dianshizhai huabao*, the *Shen Bao*'s illustrated supplement, shows a courtesan handing over her earnings in order to aid the famine-hit populations of the same region in 1878–1879.

Political upheavals and crises also provided the circumstances for courtesans to become aware of their own condition and try to organize themselves. Even though these efforts were short-lived, the fact that they occurred at specific periods is significant. The democratic spirit and the thrust toward emancipation that marked the 1911 revolution found an echo among the courtesans. In Shanghai, Zhu Ruchun came together with eight other *changsan* in 1912 to create an association designed to help girls get out of the prostitute's trade. This association, the "Circle for the Advancement of the Green Pavilions" (*Qinglou jinhuatuan*), adopted a charter that was published in the press. The charter declared: "Under the republic, social classes will disappear. [We] have founded the Circle for the Advancement of the Green Pavilions by joining forces to foster education in order to create conditions for the rehabilitation [*congliang*] [of the courtesans (*yiji*)]."[69]

A school was opened under Liu Rushi's direction, using money collected at a special performance. The classes began in August with about fifty girls. However, many dropped out after a few months. The school had to close, for want of regular funds but also because of the particular lifestyle of the courtesans.[70] In 1919, a similar initiative was launched by another courtesan, Jian Bing, in the wake of the May 4th movement. The school worked for four months before it closed.[71] All of these attempts at providing an exit through education ended in failure. It was unrealistic to seek some sort of salvation given the circumstances under which most courtesans lived and worked. Furthermore, even if they were public figures in their own right, they could hardly be reached beyond the world to which they belonged.

The "Culture of the Courtesans": Window Dressing or Reality?

In the nineteenth century, and to some extent up to the First World War, the courtesans and their customers formed a sort of community governed by common codes and practices and a common language. There existed a particular form of culture, engendered by the practice of paying visits to courtesans. I shall present the constituent elements of this culture and examine its social significance and scope.

The "culture of the courtesans" was expressed above all in the composition, by scholars, of various pieces of writing dedicated to a girl in order to enchant her or celebrate a special day (New Year's, a birthday, and so on). The "parallel sentences" consisting of eight ideograms generally derived from a particular courtesan's name were the most widespread form. Most were fairly humdrum, although they were based on a sound knowledge of classical literature. Not all, however, were innocent. Some included a touch of humor, while others included a critical judgment or even an element of teasing, although they were couched in elegant language with a double meaning that is impossible to render in English. Other forms of composition in the same vein included simple poems (*ci*) and various pieces of composition offered to courtesans by their most assiduous, and on occasion most love-smitten, customers. This tradition, which is of limited interest to the historian, was swept away by developments in the twentieth century.[72]

There was another genre affected by the customers of the courtesans: the writing of *huabang*, in which lists were drawn up of courtesans who excelled (*huabang*) in a particular field, such as music, singing, and so on. The "descriptions" of courtesans in these documents are limited to a sequence of a few ideograms composed by the author or taken from classical works. These lists would be made at the initiative of an assiduous customer who was well informed about this milieu and whose judgment could be taken as a reference. They were printed and circulated among the customers. This was a very old tradition because one work reports that a certain Shen from Songjiang (Jiangsu) had prepared a list as early as 1656.[73] Some examples of this genre have been reproduced in various works.[74] Wang Tao mentions one such list in the second collection of his work, probably dating from around the 1870s.[75] The different sources give several dates: 1877 with twenty-three girls listed, 1878 with sixteen girls, 1882 with three girls, 1888 with sixteen, and 1890.[76] Not much is known about this genre, of which no trace remains. One Chinese scholar writing in 1922 confessed that he himself did not know how the *huabang* of this period were produced.[77]

After having practically fallen into disuse, the tradition of the *huabang* was revived at the end of the nineteenth century by a great champion of the courtesans' cause, the writer-journalist Li Boyuan (1867–1906). In 1896, Li organized the first "public" *huabang* in which the courtesans were selected according to opinions expressed by the customers. The newspaper founded by Li, the *Youxibao* (*The Journal of Leisure*), was used as a mailbox to collect these opinions. The courtesans were required to declare their candidacy "with a flourish" by publicly placing a tablet on the lines of an ancestor's tablet at the newspaper's offices.[78] The girls were classified according to the titles of the degrees awarded to successful candidates in the metropolitan exams. A second competition was organized in the summer of 1897 and then another in the winter. There were two categories in these competitions: beauty (*yanbang*) and artistic qualities (*yibang*). A third category that did not correspond to any particular quality (*huabang*) was added in the next competition.[79] This way of creating news was a means of sales promotion for these newspapers. It also served the interest of courtesans, whose business increased manifold when they were selected among the winners.

Although the *Youxibao* abandoned this practice after Li Boyuan's departure, the contest itself was maintained at the rate of practically one election a year, except in 1900 and 1901. Elections were organized by the other small journals interested in the world of courtesans, in 1902, 1903 (*Huatian ribao*), 1904 (*Yuxian ribao*), and 1906. In 1906, there were even three elections organized by three rival newspapers (*Tianduobao, Canghai yizhubao*, and

Guohunbao). However, there seems to have been a loss of interest in this election, which did not occur again until 1909 when it was organized for the last time (by the *Caifengbao*).

One author reports that, after the abolition of the traditional exams in 1905, the organization of the *huabang* lost its significance. This explanation appears to me to be doubtful.[80] The link was fictitious, and the "electors" were enthusiastic above all about the respective merits of the courtesans. On the day that voting began for the first *huabang*, all the 5,000 voting slips printed were sold out before midday. Several thousands more had to be printed in order to satisfy customers who continued to flood in. The *Youxibao* received more than two hundred letters from readers approving, criticizing, and vilifying its initiative and its choices.[81] This indicates a definite interest. However, the *huabang* had an artificial character, with a tinge of favoritism and corruption, and this might have caused a loss of interest among the elites who patronized the courtesans. This loss of the initial enthusiasm probably also resulted from the decline in the status of the courtesans, who increasingly came to be seen as prostitutes. Besides, the years 1910–1911 were a period of intense political agitation that perhaps moved the elites away from these forms of superficial diversion. It was only in 1917 that this tradition was revived temporarily, although in another form.

In the winter of that year, the New World (*Xin Shijie*), one of Shanghai's amusement centers, organized an election that resembled a beauty context, although it involved only courtesans.[82] However, unlike in the *huabang* of the past, most courtesans of some renown could receive ratings in this contest even if they only received consolation prizes. It was no longer the traditional examinations but Chinese political organization that was taken as the model. The New World elected the representatives of the Kingdom of Flowers (*Huaguo*), from its president (*Huaguo Zongtong*) to its deputies and senators with a good measure of ministers and vice ministers. There was a sufficient number of positions to satisfy a large number of courtesans. This was a parody of the Peking national government. As in real life, the vote was based on property qualifications. A customer could put in as many voting slips as he was willing to purchase for a courtesan.

The operation was a success and was repeated a year later. In March 1920, a British dairy company organized a similar election to the Kingdom of Perfumes (*Xiangguo*). The New World, which was having a dispute with this company, organized its third election a month later.[83] However, neither of these elections accomplished anything. They were prestige operations that enhanced the image and status of the *changsan*, and, at the same time, they were business operations by virtue of the results they yielded for the successful candidates. This confirms the irreversible transformation of the condition of the courtesans and the change in the sensibility of the elites. It was possible to conceive of the *huabang* in the context of an elitist culture dominated by men of letters, not that of a society where money and the wish to consume took precedence over culture.

Wang Tao says that being ranked had the effect of making a girl immediately famous and of increasing her value tenfold. Conversely, those who were not selected saw it as a form of disgrace or discredit.[84] In the twentieth century, the courtesans made good use of the fact that they had been selected in one or other of the "flower" elections by placing advertisements in the small newspapers.[85] The Qin Lou became very busy when one of its inmates was elected "president" of the Kingdom of Perfumes (*Xiangguo*) in 1920. Every evening, its two courtesans had to reply to forty or fifty calls (*tangchai*). The "president's" value grew tenfold, and this caused a dispute with the madam, who refused to increase the sum she was paying the girl for her services.[86] Although these elections helped the courtesans find good matches, they nevertheless had to find a way to get married quickly because the glamour derived from their ranking did not last forever. Suzhen, who came first in a *huabang* in 1882, had her freedom purchased by a rice merchant for the modest sum of 200 taels.[87]

The development of new media, especially the press, contributed to making the world of courtesans a place of increasingly numerous and varied exchanges. It was at a very early date that Shanghai saw the birth of a press designed first of all for religious information produced by the missionaries and then for general information, namely, the spread of scientific and technical knowledge, and so on. A wide range of newspapers appeared. This phenomenon was linked especially to the political crises that shook China in this period.[88] In the context of this development, small newspapers (*xiao bao*) were created. These were intended rather for mass readers and were sensational in nature. Some of these newspapers made it their specialty to report gossip from the world of courtesans.[89] Li Boyuan founded the first newspaper of this type, the *Zhinanbao* ("The Guide") in 1896. It did not last long but was followed, under the leadership of the same individual, by the *Youxibao* ("The Journal of Leisure"), published from 1897 to 1910. Li Boyuan, however, left after three years to found a new paper, the *[Shijie] Fanhuabao* ("The [World's] Splendors"), which he directed for five years.[90]

Li Boyuan had many imitators, as can be seen from the following incomplete list of small newspapers. Their titles generally left no doubt about their preferred field: *Xiaolinbao* ("The Forest of the Smile"), *Huaguo Bao* ("The Flower Kingdom"), *Hua Shijie Mingbao* ("The Voice of the Flower World"), *Huaguo Ribao* ("The Flower Kingdom Daily"), *Huabao* ("The Flowers"), *Huahua Shijie* ("The World of Flowers"), and so on. It was after the appearance of the *Haishang Fanhuabao* in 1901 that the phenomenon of small newspapers began to take off.[91] I have found a few of them, covering very short periods, and they have given me an idea of the special role played by this press in the formation of a culture of courtesans. These newspapers took the form of a single page printed on both sides in a rather unusual rectangular format with the text arranged in columns. The back page was taken up essentially by advertisements. It was the front page that published announcements, serials, stories, and various items of news about courtesans. They were generally published every three days. This press appears to have reached its high point between the turn of the century and 1920. All of Shanghai's amusement centers (Great World, New World, etc.) also launched their own newspapers. However, the transformation of the courtesans' milieu, along with the measures of prohibition taken by the International Settlement authorities, put an end to this form of activity. In 1926, there were still newspapers being published by the amusement centers, but their contents tended to reflect all the activities of these centers.

What appear to me to be significant are the types of exchanges that took place through this press. The courtesans made use of them when they wished to take revenge on a rival. Often, this took the form of rumors about the state of health (infection with venereal disease) of the person to be discredited or by an announcement of her marriage.[92] Sometimes, a heated debate would break out between two courtesans and would last for several issues. Finally, the press could be a means to remind tardy payers to pay up. The method was unbeatable because the concerned parties were far too afraid of losing face if the press came to know that they were no longer able to pay their expenses. Thus, Zhang Shuyu announced that she would disclose the name of a customer who owed her money if he did not pay up within ten days. Three days later, she repeated the warning.[93] The details given were precise enough for the concerned party to recognize himself without in any way enabling him to be identified by others. This practice points to the fact that the circle of those who patronized the courtesans was a restricted one, consisting of persons who more or less knew one another, at least by name.

The journalists who wrote in these newspapers reported all the tittle-tattle and incidents that gave spice to Shanghai's nightlife. Their favorite topics included disputes between courtesans, especially when one courtesan took a customer from another. Inasmuch as certain courtesans lived in the same house, it was not rare for serious conflicts to break out with insults, brawling, and the destruction of objects belonging to the rival, especially her external signboard[94] (Plate 5). The customers also contributed to the columns of the newspapers. They frequently wrote pieces (poems, "parallel sentences," criticisms) referring to a particular courtesan. At the beginning of the century, one customer criticized a courtesan, Jin Hanxiang, in rather disagreeable terms for not having replied to an invitation to a restaurant and thus provoking the mockery of his friends. The affront that he had suffered explains his anger. Jin replied by the same channel, saying that she had actually responded to the invitation, even if she had been late. She criticized the customer for not having discussed matters with her before

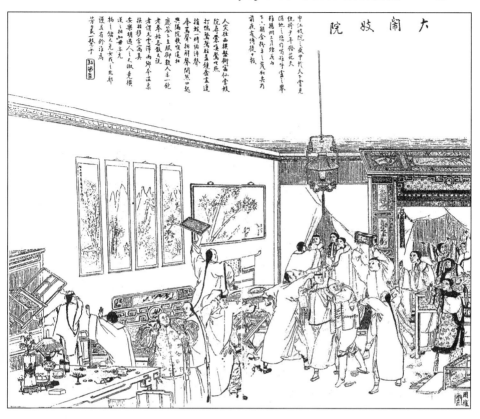

Plate 5. A brawl in a brothel.

writing an article in the press.[95] In 1926, one customer praised a girl with whom he claimed to have spent a wonderful night, while another asserted that she was still a virgin. A third confirmed the statement of the first customer and poked fun at the second one for having been hoodwinked.[96] The authors always used pen names, which makes it impossible to identify them. In general, the articles written by the customers of the courtesans' houses tended to praise this institution.[97] All these exchanges implied a good knowledge of the milieu.

Documents of another type helped sustain this particular form of culture: These were the nineteenth-century "compasses of the world of gallantry" (*piaojie zhinan*) and the many other guidebooks that followed. These "compasses" included a large number of works that were presented as literary works. These works, on the pretext of describing or even denouncing the world of courtesans, gave the reader all the rules and tricks needed to patronize this milieu without being taken for a peasant or a fool. This genre contains many works of very unequal quality published up to the 1940s. Their effect was to help perpetuate standards that were probably less rigid in reality and conceal the profound changes in the status of the courtesans. Even when they were outwardly aimed at denouncing the wiles and tricks of the prostitutes and dissuading youth from patronizing their houses, these works actually imparted knowledge of all the ropes supposed to enable a neophyte to get the best out of a courtesan.[98]

The twentieth century saw the appearance of the first Shanghai guidebooks (*zhinan*) in Chinese. One of the classics, the *Shanghai Zhinan* ("Guide to Shanghai, A Chinese Directory to the Port"), appeared for the first time in 1909. It was published several times successively up to the 1930s. The market for guidebooks was naturally a very lucrative one given the very large number of visitors who came to Shanghai. Many works were therefore published by different authors, furnishing clear examples of reciprocal plagiarism. In addition, there were the guidebooks published in English, which were fewer in number and different in their contents.[99] The Chinese guidebooks always had a part on prostitution giving information, for example, on the location of the prostitution district, the various categories of prostitutes, the rules for visiting the elegant houses (of the courtesans), and the price scales. This information was given on the same basis as information on the different types and places of entertainment and leisure, transport, or local administration. They contain no moral discourse and no particular reservations apart from a few warnings about venereal disease. However, certain well-established works, like the *Shanghai Zhinan* or the guidebooks published after 1927 under the auspices of the Chinese municipal government – which officially banned prostitution – omit this category of information. The editions of the *Shanghai Zhinan* after 1924–1925 no longer speak of prostitution.

The life cycle of the courtesans was very short, even if some of them managed to keep themselves in the running for more than ten years. It is true that the cycle began "upstream," as soon as the girl was taken in hand by a madam who began to train her, first in the arts and then in the wiles indispensable to the courtesan's function. This was a step that I have only mentioned briefly in this study. This cycle then was punctuated with a few great moments, experiences similar to those of other women but lived in a far different context. I do not share the interpretation of some women historians who tend to liken prostitution to a variant of the trade in women within Chinese society. That marriage in general was accompanied by a financial transaction and that it set up a tie between two persons who were unknown to each other without the least preparation is an incontestable fact. However, this union, whatever the conditions and effects on the concerned parties, was contracted in an enhancing, legitimate, and recognized framework. For the women who were forced to become courtesans, the same experiences, especially that of defloration, meant the irreparable loss of their integrity and set in motion a process of both social and psychological impairment. Even in the best of circumstances, namely when they got married, the courtesans could enter the house of their husband only by the back door.

The prostitute's existence was not necessarily an unhappy one. She enjoyed living conditions that would have been the envy of a majority of women in China. Apart from the common prostitutes who lived lives of great hardship, no one could dare suggest that the life of a peasant woman was more comfortable. In general, the prostitutes lacked nothing in material terms even if not all of them lived the same lives of ease. In the circles in which they moved, the courtesans were valued, praised, and admired. Better still, they were courted, and they received repeated attention from their customers. They were not exposed to the harsh and even brutal treatment meted out to their sisters in misery in the low-class brothels. In the nineteenth century, genuine love relationships could arise between a girl and a customer or, failing this, a lover of her own. And yet, their fate was ruled by precariousness, transitoriness, and illusion. They knew that the customers who admired them would not even give them a second glance later on if they made the mistake of staying too long in this profession.

The proportion of courtesans who managed to achieve their ends is not known and will never be known, even if marriage was indeed their main goal. The frequency with which courtesans were separated from their partners and returned to the trade would suggest that this solution did not always bring the desired serenity and security. It must be said that many courtesans quite simply never attained the married state. And these girls had hardly any alternative other than to pass into a lower category or a lower-level house, recycle themselves as procurers, join a theatrical troupe, or "descend into hell." However, such a view often leads commentators to false pity. The example of the prostitutes in the twentieth century shows that decline after their prime was not inevitable. Otherwise, we would have to accept the improbable idea that thousands or tens of thousands of women ended up on the pavement or in homes for beggars. All the research so far shows that prostitution was only a stage in a prostitute's life and that it was generally followed by reintegration into society. Without putting an excessive gloss on matters, I would believe that most courtesans found a way to get out of prostitution, even if it was at the cost of social demotion.

This chapter has also thrown light on the extraordinary proliferation of activities and initiatives that the world of courtesans provoked in Shanghai. This variety of activities drew its source and strength from the existence within the Chinese elites of a very strong common culture and common *habitus*. The courtesans represented a sort of reserved space, with codes and a language that were shared by initiates alone. It is not surprising that the scholar's pronounced taste for word games should find expression here. Poetry, parallel sentences, and *huabang* were types of diversion among men of learning. All these writings were addressed as much to the courtesans for whom they were composed as to the individuals who patronized this milieu as a whole. This frame of mind has no equivalent in the West, no matter what the period. Chinese society engendered the particular phenomenon of a "culture of courtesans" at the end of the nineteenth century. This culture resulted from the conjunction of a long tradition of intertwined relationships between the elites and the courtesans with the emergence, in a new environment (namely, the open port of Shanghai), of tools – the small newspapers – that fostered communications and the flow of information.

In my view, it would be futile to try to force this phenomenon into a framework of tradition or modernity. It was but a straw in the wind, an ephemeral and nostalgic movement corresponding to a final unconscious and involuntary burst of energy on the part of an elite that was already profoundly destructured and had reached the threshold of a more radical and even more brutal transformation. The unquestionable success of the *huabang* between 1897 and 1905 reflects a state of society that still had one foot in the past. However, the movement ran out of steam, enthusiasm waned, and indifference prevailed. Other, more immediate and more important factors might perhaps explain this growing lack of interest. The Chinese elites had other, more vital issues on their minds, such as reform, foreign encroachment, and the emergence of active political organizations and currents. However, the pressure was not yet strong enough to take the elites away from their preferred leisure activities.

The change was more fundamental. During the six decades that followed the opening of Shanghai to foreign trade, there was a major restructuring of the local elites to the detriment of the scholars and the benefit of the merchants. The commercialization of the economy grew apace, and the courtesans, like those in the other service professions, were drawn into this spiral that was to turn them into mere objects of consumption. The beauty contests organized between 1917 and 1920 can tell us a great deal here. It was no longer art or beauty that was judged as in the past. It was the wealthiest who won by throwing their yuan about. Although there was still some relation to the *huabang*, what the competition between the customers expressed was a concern with prestige and social status. This factor apart, the courtesans may be said to have fallen once and for all into the ranks of the prostitutes.

Part 2
The Market of Prostitution and Mass Sexuality

3
From the High-Class Brothel to Mass Sexuality: The Explosion of Common Prostitution from 1849 to 1949

Prostitution in Shanghai between 1849 and 1949 was far from limited to the courtesans. And it would be an illusion if not the effect of an incomplete reading of the sources to imagine that, even in the nineteenth century alone, prostitution was "essentially a luxury market in courtesans."[1] Although the literature on the lower categories of prostitutes is not abundant, the fact remains that they always were the most numerous category because their clientele was much bigger than the privileged stratum of the merchant and scholar elites. This is an obvious fact. Naturally, insofar as the rare testimony left by the Chinese on this milieu comes from the elites, the vision conveyed by their writings is completely skewed. First of all, as mentioned earlier, the courtesans as a group are highly idealized and even enshrined in myth. Secondly, the other categories are almost always concealed.

The first trap to be avoided is that of being taken in by what is above all a "discourse" on prostitution. This discourse was repeated by the succession of authors who wrote on this subject. Wang Jimen, in 1922, drew his information from Wang Tao, who wrote between 1853 and 1880, while works written in the 1930s and 1940s were based on Wing Jimen's writings and other accounts from the early 1920s. An uncritical reading of the sources would lead to serious confusion about the types of prostitutes and the chronology. I will therefore seek in this chapter to present the various groups of prostitutes to whom I hesitate to assign any precise labels. I have assembled them all under the heading of "common" prostitutes, although I am aware that, at least until the beginning of the twentieth century, some of them existed at the interface between the world of the courtesans and that of truly common prostitution. It will be seen that this choice is not fortuitous. In this chapter I shall examine the state of common prostitution in the nineteenth and then the twentieth centuries. This chronological presentation intersects with the description of the different categories of prostitutes and sheds light on the lines of continuity and points of transition as well as the fundamental transformation that was wrought by the development of the city in the twentieth century.

Intermediate Forms of Prostitution

The structure of prostitution in mid-nineteenth century Shanghai was not very complex, even though it contained categories that are hard to define. Wang Tao has painted a fairly complete and utterly fascinating picture of this singular world, although the details that he gives are not sufficient to determine the classes of prostitutes and pinpoint the social origins of the customers in each category. This probably points to the fact that this world was marked by a degree of fluidity and the absence of a rigid hierarchy. The idea of a pyramid might be attractive to the historian's mind, but we cannot be certain that it provides a very exact reflection of the realities of society as they were lived by the Shanghainese in the last century. What is quite striking about Shanghai before the turning point that came with the First World War is the wide range of prostitution on offer, depending on the place, purse, time, and type of customer. The fondness of the Chinese authors for classification, grading, and hierarchical organization tends to magnify distinctions that were often purely formal. It would be more appropriate here to think in terms of types of prostitutes, rather than of rungs on an imaginary ladder. Up to the First World War, there were undoubtedly different levels, but also intermediate groups – or bridges – that succumbed to a phenomenon of downward standardization to the level of the ordinary categories of prostitutes and even underwent a process of elimination. It is these bridges that I shall now discuss.

In the mid-nineteenth century, even before the opening of Shanghai to foreign trade, the old city already had a very lively nightlife and a flourishing sex market. Wang mentions a number of houses, barely a dozen in number, all located in the walled city and known to the local population as *tangming* (lodges). These were establishments that he called "deep and obscure" places whose luxury impressed first-time visitors. In their most prosperous period – probably from the end of the 1850s to the 1860s – a *tangming* housed thirty to forty women in individual rooms. Wang unequivocally places them in the category of *jiyuan* (literally "house of prostitution"), a term that he never uses for the courtesans' houses. All the same, there is no special condemnation or criticism on his part, which means that these houses could be (and probably were) visited by persons of good society.[2]

Later sources suggest that the term *tangming* fell into disuse and that the prostitutes of these establishments made way for the *yao'er* (one–two) prostitutes, a category slightly below that of the *changsan*.[3] Through a growing process of assimilation, the number of *yao'er* dropped to the point where there were no more than about ten of them around 1874–1875.[4] Wang Tao mentions the *yao'er* only in the second volume of *Notes of a Libertine from the Seaside* (*Haizou yeyou lu*), adding that they were set up on one street in the International Settlement, where they had initially formed a group with a part of the *changsan*. At the same time, he notes the existence of a group of twenty-four *ersan* (two–three) establishments that he implicitly links with the *tangming*. The *yao'er* and *ersan* establishments were qualified as second-category houses.[5] Up to the beginning of the twentieth century, some of them competed with the *changsan* houses.[6] These few records clearly indicate the intermediate status of these establishments.

Wang Tao mentions another type of establishment constituting a similar though more broad-based genre: the *caotai* (straw platform), which was like a kind of cabaret. The *caotai* were said to have appeared at the beginning of the Daoguang era (1821). Their chief attraction was provided by actresses from the popular theater who were less refined than those patronized by the elites. The number of women in each house was also thirty to forty. When a customer entered, he was served tea, fruit, and melon seeds while the women came down to present themselves. Once the customer had made his choice, he went up to the prostitute's room. According to Wang Tao, these places provided the same services as the *tangming*, but for less money. Those who went to houses of prostitution looking for sex preferred to patronize these establishments.[7]

Finally, among the establishments explicitly intended for prostitution, Wang lists a large category, that of the *siju* (the "private residence"), which offered a more intimate and quieter atmosphere than the *caotai*. The *siju* usually had bigger apartments in which it was possible to hold banquets for which the madam would call in outside staff as waiters. Wang Tao notes that the decor was refined and dwells on the cleanliness of the sheets and curtains. The *siju* appeared around 1875, and there were no fewer than 300 of them in the walled city. This is an impressive figure, although it does not mean that a great many women were involved. Initially, each establishment had only one or two women. By the end of the century, some had up to four or five inmates.[8]

This already diversified range also included "independent" and occasional prostitutes. The smartest were the *zhujia* ("single families"), who rented rooms in discreet places. They would receive small numbers of carefully selected customers who were rich enough to maintain them.[9] Some of them joined the *changsan* when the latter replaced the *shuyu* and dominated the world of prostitution. The twentieth-century sources also mention the *zhujia yeji*, who became a substitute for the former *zhujia* prostitutes (see below). According to Wang, there were also around a dozen or so houses where the girls were maintained by men from wealthy families who would spend tens of thousands of yuan on them. When their "protectors" were absent, these women would solicit other customers through their maidservants. This form of conduct was roundly condemned by Wang Tao.[10]

There remains a new genre of prostitute whose appearance is not easy to date. This new genre considerably troubled the local ruling elites. Wang

Tao refers twice to this type of prostitute. In one context, he speaks of women acting as intermediaries to set up contacts between women from "good families" (*liangjia*) and prospective customers. They rented out dwellings in retired spots where they could carry out their business on the quiet. They were nothing more and nothing less than *maisons de rendez-vous* offering greater privacy than the more easily controllable hotels of the city. These establishments, called *taiji* (corridors), appear to have functioned, at least initially, as genuine *maisons de rendez-vous* for lovers. These places later evolved into houses of prostitution, although they continued to draw customers by presenting their inmates as respectable young girls and women. Wang Tao also makes it clear that customers could not spend the night in these places because the girls had to return to their own homes.[11]

The *taiji* were severely condemned by the authorities. For Wang, these places were "from the moral standpoint the most detestable in Shanghai."[12] They existed in the old city up to the 1880s and were then banned and suppressed by the authorities. They moved to the settlements, especially the French Concession, where the police, under pressure from the circuit intendant (*daotai*), would sometimes make arrests when the existence of an establishment was reported to them.[13] These were not high-class houses. We shall see below that, in the 1940s, they even became "meat factories." Their emergence, however, probably reveals a change in sensibility and a search for novelty. The customers who patronized these houses hankered after novel sensations that could not be found in the ordinary establishments of prostitution. It was the illusion of a relationship with a decent woman that gave piquancy to this experience, even if the experience was false. On the supply side, the subject is equally interesting even if it is difficult to identify these women. They probably came from the lower-class sections and were seeking a kind of freedom of movement.

The patrons of these establishments in the nineteenth century probably came from strata that were less well off than the elites, less demanding as regards artistic qualities, yet looking for prostitutes who would give them the illusion of relative intimacy and a certain status. Some members of the elites themselves patronized these establishments for the immediate sexual services that were available. Wang Tao's discourse is particularly clear in this respect: His condemnation of common prostitution is very harsh, and he always specifies the categories that no decent person should patronize. We may conclude that the intermediate establishment, on the contrary, could be patronized by the elites. These prostitutes were not related to a specific social group, even broadly defined. Again, this type of establishment was symptomatic of a transitional stage where the lifestyles and consumer habits of the elites were expressed in a debased and simplified form among certain segments of society.

Well before the arrival of the Westerners, therefore, there was an exceptional variety of choices offered in the world of prostitution. The question is, What was the course of development taken by these establishments, which are no longer mentioned after the turn of the century? My own guess, based on an analysis of changes in the designation of these houses in the sources, is that there was a contraction and simplification of the fabric of prostitution. Whatever the names used, these were approximately equivalent categories that were by and large "pulled downward" and assimilated into the houses of common prostitution that sprang up in the settlements at the end of the century. Some of them, like the *yao'er* establishments, maintained a separate identity, while the others lost all specificity and joined the mainstream of prostitution.

Common Prostitution in the Nineteenth Century

It is possible, when looking at the nineteenth century, to obtain a glimpse of some aspects of common prostitution that then already accounted for the largest contingent of the prostitutes. Here, Wang Tao's testimony provides a vision that departs from the conventional images that may be obtained of Chinese urban society. This vision is not one of a well-ordered and controlled society, but rather that of a heterogeneous population containing groups of people who were indigent or living in precarious conditions. Wang especially notes the presence of many *youmin* (literally "floating population") without employment or identifiable sources of income who spent their evenings drinking and making the rounds of the houses of prostitution. Although these men had not a penny on them, the madams had no choice but to let them in and serve them tea and fruit as with any customer. Otherwise, they would create scenes and provoke brawls.[14] This was a discredited category of persons known as *wulaizi* or layabouts, who inspired fear also among the elites. William Rowe has described these rootless populations, as yet poorly integrated into the local population and often relegated to petty precarious jobs, who were a cause of disturbances in Hankou in the same period.[15]

In Shanghai, according to Wang Tao, these populations included Cantonese, Fujianese, and Ningbonese – in other words, immigrant communities *par excellence*. They formed gangs who made actual raids into the prostitutes' houses, which, for self-protection, were required to pay them bribes or a percentage of their income.[16] In a very recent work, Bryna Goodman provides an extremely good description of this "new frontier" atmosphere that characterized the city during the first decades after the arrival of Westerners. The presence of various regional groups, at times in a state of rivalry with one another, was a repeated source of trouble.[17] Even if they were still a far cry from Louis Chevalier's "dangerous classes" as described in his masterly treatment of nineteenth-century Paris, Shanghai's fringe populations did include recently established and sometimes temporary groups of young and unmarried men who were no doubt hard-working but also fond of drink and women and quick to brawl.[18]

As might be expected in a port city, it was near the docks that many houses of prostitution could be found. They were located outside the city wall, in the suburbs that had seen the growth of many commercial activities related to the river and maritime trade. These districts contained a large floating population consisting especially of sailors.[19] Wang Tao reports that in the wetlands along the river, going from north to east, there were many houses made of "mud and woven bamboo."[20] There were also prostitutes' boats, moored in the middle of the Huangpu River, which, in the evening, would come close to the *bang* or "groups of boatmen" whose sampans were anchored along the riverside. Wang Tao speaks with great distaste of these women, who, he felt, would inspire disgust even among sedan-chair carriers.[21] This form of prostitution on boats, referred to in the French sources as "junk boats of tolerance," probably disappeared around the middle of the 1860s.[22] The old city housed other forms of prostitution. Xuexiang Lane, in a relatively central area that was quiet in the daytime, underwent a radical transformation in the evening. According to Wang Tao, an unbelievably large number of prostitutes gathered on the doorsteps, calling passersby and making eyes at them.[23] Common prostitution was not limited to the specialized establishments. In the hotels of the old city, there were also women – known as the "ten thousand flowers" (*wanhua*) – who would solicit customers in the streets and take them back to a hotel.[24] The prostitutes were undoubtedly the precursors of the *yeji* (pheasants), a category whose ranks swelled significantly after 1890.[25] It cannot be denied that this group was firmly rooted in the nineteenth century. And yet it was eminently representative of the development of prostitution in the century that followed. Houses of prostitutes could also be found close to Nanking Road, but this was a later development (1860–1870). These were "not very recommendable" establishments where, every evening, "when the sun set in the West and the moon rose in the East, powdered women stood in their doorways and solicited merchants from country towns with winks and hand signs." Wang Tao gives a very unfavorable description of it.[26]

At the end of the century, the walled city also had a large number of opium dens where customers were attended by young women who also provided sexual services.[27] Originally, these places were just opium dens that, in order to compete with each other and attract customers, recruited or simply purchased young girls to replace male waiters.[28] Very soon, these girls were pushed into prostitution, whence the name of their establishments *huayanjian* or *yanhuajian* (literally "chambers of smoke and flowers"). The Chinese authorities sought in vain to prohibit this practice by means of regular police raids.[29] This was undoubtedly the most prevalent form of common prostitution at the time. Almost all the press reports on prostitution are about this category of establishment. By the end of the century, the majority of them were located in the suburbs of Nanshi, along the Huangpu docks – that is, close to the Northern and Eastern Gates.[30]

The *huayanjian* gradually moved into the foreign settlements, along Yangjingbang, the channel between the two settlements, near the bridge that spans this channel. In the evening, seen from the bridge, their lanterns resembled myriad stars. This was the spot used by the Jiangbei prostitutes.[31] The *Shen Bao* notes that the *huayanjian* were the most numerous of the establishments near Yangjingbang.[32] After the prohibition of opium in the settlements, these establishments were transformed into full-scale houses of prostitution, although their designation remained in vogue until the beginning of the 1920s. By this time, they had become a residual form of prostitution employing aging and sick women who were unable to escape their condition.

In addition to these recognized forms of prostitution, Wang Tao mentions fairly unusual forms of behavior that were unconventional by Confucian norms. They represent perhaps a small window on popular culture that, to a great extent, is unknown to us. Close to the South Gate – an area that was somewhat out of the way and covered with wild peach trees – a district grew up where it was not unusual to see men roaming the streets and knocking on doors in search of women. Wang does not explicitly say that the women involved were prostitutes. He speaks of young girls (*qing nüzi*).[33] Were they occasional prostitutes taking advantage of the absence of husbands or family to make a bit of money on the side? We cannot be certain. There were also female fruit sellers who plied their merchandise in the teahouses of the Western Garden (today's Yuyuan). Among them, there were pretty girls who would sometimes be pulled over and have their arms and breasts fondled by layabouts (*wulaizi*). When their fruit was all sold out, these girls went home, sometimes accompanied by a man. This was also the case with the female servants from poor families who worked in the teahouses. They came and left in groups, but the prettier ones stayed in the evening and allowed themselves to work as prostitutes.[34] This testimony is obviously very partial, but it sheds some light on the lower-class sections that were characterized perhaps by a more direct and more brutal relationship between the sexes.

On the whole, Wang Tao passes very harsh judgment on the lower categories of prostitutes. In his view, their quality declined with their position on the ladder. Also, these were girls patronized by rickshaw drivers and servants, and there was nothing to be said about them.[35] Whenever he referred to these groups, he took care to state that no self-respecting individual would step into their premises for risk of losing his integrity, both physical and moral. What shows through this uncompromising judgment is the arrogance peculiar to the scholar elites who felt little but contempt for the lower sections of society and their leisure activities. This attitude meant the almost total masking of a social reality (Wang Tao was all the same an exception here) that to a great extent eludes the historian. There can be no doubt, however, that among the lower classes there existed a wide variety of forms of behavior and activity in the field of prostitution that was completely opposite to Confucian morality. Perhaps we should modify this judgment by stating that the increasing stabilization of Shanghai's society from the 1870s onward probably contributed to a reinforcement of the social control and values of the elites.

The Regional Groups of Prostitutes

Almost all Chinese writers on the subject have reported the existence of regional groups of courtesans and prostitutes, especially from Canton and Zhejiang. Western historians have generally concluded that this was the result of a type of recruitment that reflected the specific demand of one regional community or another in the Shanghai population.[36] This interpretation is not incorrect, but has been given more importance than it deserves. We have seen that among the courtesans there were various regional groups that gradually disappeared, leaving only one group, that of the Suzhou courtesans whose songs, dialect, and so on, came to prevail as the *lingua franca* of their milieu. Even if this diversity originally corresponded, in part, to the variety of ethnic groups in the city, it also corresponded to a variety in the supply of distraction. Each group of courtesans was renowned for one or more particular qualities, and their members offered their services not only to customers from the same regional group, but more broadly to customers in search of varied forms of diversion. The thinning out of the ranks of these regional groups tends to underline the fact that the Chinese elites were not so much attached to a particular group of courtesans as to a style, that of the women of Suzhou, heirs to a long tradition, many of them having settled in Shanghai after the Taiping destroyed their city. Certain groups, however, lasted longer than the others, especially those hailing from Guangdong and Zhejiang.

For the nineteenth century, Wang Tao mentions only the courtesans originally from Zhejiang in his writings, and he gives no other details. Whether they maintained a separate identity or not, most of them appear to have adopted the Suzhou style. What is evident is that they never managed to establish their own identity and survive as a specific group in spite of the power of the community of Zhejiang natives in Shanghai. Although dominant in the financial sectors and defended by the city's most influential guild, the members of this regional group, especially its elites, do not seem to have provided a demand sufficient to create and maintain a geographically corresponding corps of prostitutes. For the twentieth century, the sources mention Ningbo prostitutes in the small hotels of Daxin Road and Zhejiang Road. Would-be customers had to be introduced first – although this rule was not strictly enforced.[37] The girls received their customers for dinners (only Ningbo specialties were served) and gambling sessions. They also accepted invitations to go out with known customers.[38] There was no fixed rate to spend the night with them.[39] They belonged to the "upper layer" of the *yeji* (the *zhujia yeji*), forming an intermediate stratum between the prostitutes and the courtesans. They were patronized by Zhejiang natives who appreciated their cuisine and their singing. Conversely, the Shanghainese unanimously found them to be loud with a nasal twang and thought their songs vulgar.[40]

Does this mean that there was a pronounced regional segmentation of prostitutes and courtesans? Were there specific networks of recruitment supplying each provincial group? The answer would appear to be no. These Ningbo courtesans in the twentieth century were too small in number. Although they did correspond to a specific demand, it was small and did not generate any significant recruitment. In other words, Zhejiang members of the elite satisfied their need for female company with women hailing from places other than Zhejiang. Conversely, there was a large number of Zhejiang women among the prostitutes who were assimilated into the ranks of the *yeji* or other categories of prostitutes but served no community in particular. The phenomenon was confirmed in the 1940s by the fact that it was common to find a madam and prostitutes of extremely varied origins in one and the same house. It was sexual desire and not regional identity that determined demand. There may have been one exception to this fluidity of supply and demand. These were the Cantonese prostitutes. They belonged to a community that had settled very early in Shanghai and been reinforced by the massive influx of new members in the wake of the Westerners after the Treaty of Nanking (1842). More than the other groups, these women from Canton met a specific demand. This was related to lifestyles and to a language far removed from those prevailing in the lower Yangzi region. It was also related to the economic power of the Cantonese merchants, at least until the end of the nineteenth century. Wang Tao mentions prostitutes from eastern Guangdong who had settled in the International Settlement (then the British Settlement). Wang was struck by their large – eight-inch long – feet, which made a marked contrast with the tiny bound feet of other Chinese women.[41] In the twentieth century, they all formed a group in the Hongkou quarter in which a major part of Shanghai's Cantonese community was concentrated.

In the 1920s, Cantonese prostitutes appear to have been relatively accessible and, along with the Zhejiang prostitutes, appear to have occupied an intermediate level between the courtesans and the ordinary prostitutes. Their mode of operation was rather similar to that of the *changsan*, but with some differences. The Cantonese women did not organize banquets in their apartments but rather in restaurants and hotels. They came accompanied by musicians and would stay throughout a meal, but for a period of time that could not exceed four hours. Beyond this limit, the customer had to make extra payment. They also organized late suppers – this was a specifically Cantonese practice – for small groups of guests. They sang fishermen's songs rather than opera. When they accepted an invitation to go out, they would sing two songs.[42] They were easier to visit than the courtesans from Jiangsu.[43]

The sources of the 1930s and 1940s indicate a fairly marked change in quality in the practices of the Cantonese prostitutes. While they continued to operate in the hotels and restaurants of Hongkou, they no longer accepted invitations to go out with unknown customers. It was necessary to be introduced. Their prices also went up from 1 to 2 yuan and had to be paid on the spot.[44] Some had their nameplates hung outside the restaurant. Moreover, it would seem that there was no longer any fixed rate for the night. The customer had to organize a few *huatou* and negotiate a price with the girl.[45] It can be seen, therefore, that there was a change whereby this group of prostitutes rose in status – unless this view of reality has been distorted by the sources. The fact, however, is that these sources are consistent with each other for each period. The phenomenon is perhaps linked to the relative scarcity of Cantonese prostitutes in Shanghai, as well as to the infatuation of the customers with a group of girls who offered a different repertory of songs and were reputed for their cleanliness.

The "sailor's girls," on the contrary, belonged exclusively to the ranks of common prostitution. They formed a small and fairly stable group of 200 to 250 prostitutes until the 1920s. These Cantonese women came to Shanghai in the wake of the foreigners. They were practically the only prostitutes to welcome Westerners in the nineteenth century. As a group, they were called *xianshuimei* ("salt-water sisters"), a term that refers to the fact that they had originated among the wives and daughters of the boatmen who occasionally ferried the foreigners in the Pearl River delta, especially near Hong Kong. Some of these wives and daughters had started prostituting themselves with foreign customers.[46] Like other groups of Cantonese (compradors, translators, cooks, servants, etc.) accustomed to working with Westerners, these women were brought to Shanghai after the opening of the city to foreign trade. The local prostitutes feared contact with the foreigners and did not receive them.

The *xianshuimei* were despised by the local populace, especially the elites, because they prostituted themselves with Westerners while refusing to receive Chinese customers. The *xianshuimei* establishments were set up mainly in Hongkou, then a poorly controlled district located near the docks where the ships were anchored. The girls differed from the other Chinese prostitutes in their clothing and hairstyles, which were more Westernized, and in the fact that they possessed a rudimentary knowledge of English. They did not have bound feet and were often even barefooted.[47] Apart from their specific provincial origin, the *xianshuimei* were similar in their practices and prices to the *yeji*, who are described below.

Whether it was for prostitutes hailing from Zhejiang or for those from Guangdong, it cannot be seriously maintained that there was a system of recruitment corresponding to a community-related structure of the population. If we set aside the specific case of the *xianshuimei* who served the foreigners, the total number of individuals belonging to each regional group was too small – barely a few dozen girls – in comparison with the great mass of the prostitutes to permit any conclusions to be drawn about the existence of a "regional" organization of prostitution. Although it is obvious that these prostitutes almost exclusively received members of their own native community (this was not completely true in the case of the Cantonese women) who, in this form of visiting, were looking for an atmosphere, a *habitus* (cuisine, music, language) that briefly took them back to their native province. And yet they were but a tiny part of the very wide variety of prostitution on offer. At best, they brought in an "exotic" dimension. The organization and regulation of the market of prostitution responded to criteria – sexual demand, economic and political factors – other than that of regional identity.

The Twentieth Century: Downgrading and Standardization

The multiplicity of terms used to designate the various categories of prostitutes actually masks the general downgrading of the intermediate groups that might have existed before the First World War. It also masks the general standardization of practices that were now reduced to the provision of sexual services only, even if brothels still served as meeting places for friends to play cards and mahjong. The twentieth century in Shanghai saw the development of a modern consumer society in which the circulation of persons and goods grew with increasing rapidity. The prostitutes, who were individuals as much as chattels having no control over their fate, were swept along by the mainstream of commercialization of leisure activities. The sex trade, a venal occupation *par excellence*, became standardized in its practices even if new forms of prostitution came into existence.

The *yao'er* houses had left the old city for the settlements in the 1870s. Only about ten establishments remained in the International Settlement at the beginning of the 1920s when the Shanghai Municipal Council implemented its policy of abolishing brothels.[48] Clearly, even if they housed about ten girls each, the *yao'er* establishments represented a very small minority in the world of prostitution, and it must be said that they were headed for extinction. Some Chinese authors did continue to speak of the *yao'er* in the 1930s; but, in my view, this is a mistaken term resulting plagiarized from earlier works.[49] The authors of the 1920s are agreed that the *yao'er* as such did not survive the Shanghai Municipal Council's policy of abolition and were replaced by another category, the *xianrouzhuang* ("salt meat shop").

The *yao'er* houses were unable to maintain a foothold in the face of competition from the *changsan*. Although some of the rules of visiting – for example, the practice of the *da chawei* – were maintained in a formal way, any customer could in fact make an appearance without being specially introduced. When he crossed the door, a waiter would cry out: "Yicha" ("bring the tea"), and all the girls of the house would come forward. Once his choice had been made, the customer would go up to the room with one of the girls. If he did not find any girl to his liking, he could go away after leaving a tip. The *yao'er* were sometimes former *changsan* who had not managed to make a timely exit through marriage or had been resold by the madam because of illness or low earnings. They also included maidservants (*ajie*) and *yeji* for whom this work represented a form of upward mobility.[50] One author notes their advanced age, meaning that they were around 30 years old.[51] This condition was the logical outcome of a status that, after the merger of the *changsan* and the *shuyu*, made them the group that was best qualified and at the same time most accessible to men with "urgent sexual needs."[52]

Certain authors give a very unfavorable description of this group of prostitutes. Zhang Qiugu depicts their premises as being filthy and foul-smelling, with the air worsened by the fact there were no windows that could be opened. The girls were old and often ill. For eating and playing, it was better to go to a *changsan* house, which was not more expensive and where the service and food were better.[53] A 1923 guide says these houses were like "hen coops" and describes the girls' faces as resembling those of demons (*niugui sheshen*).[54] The *yao'er* houses of this period were hardly different from the *yeji* houses. They did not offer any particular entertainment to their customers and engaged primarily in the sex trade.[55] Their decline was linked to the general debasement of the houses patronized by the urban elites. Caught between the level of the courtesans – who were themselves swept along by a process of "sexualization" – and common prostitution, the *yao'er* were unable to maintain a specific identity. The case of the *yao'er* is representative of a social transformation that no longer left a niche for sophisticated forms of prostitution: With the relative exception of the *changsan*, all other categories of venal women became mere prostitutes.

The *xianrouzhuang*, another intermediate category of houses of prostitution, sprang directly from the *taiji* or *maisons de rendez-vous* that had been prohibited in the old city and had moved to the settlements. The *taiji* gradually became genuine houses of prostitution. The term *xianrouzhuang*, which appeared at the beginning of the Republican era, literally means "salt-meat shop," an establishment where a customer could get himself a cut of "salted meat" and enjoy its flavor, to quote some of the cynical expressions used by the Shanghai guides.[56] This term was abandoned in 1924 and replaced by *hanzhuang*, which was suggested by the *Jingbao (The Crystal)*, a mosquito newspaper seeking to expunge what it considered to be a particularly sordid expression.[57] What distinguished the *xianrouzhuang* from the *yeji* houses was that they functioned like true brothels, whereas the *yeji* solicited in the street.

These establishments fell victim to the Shanghai Municipal Council's policy of abolition in 1920–1925 (see Chapter 12) and moved to the French Concession, all around the Grand Monde and in rue Palikao. A 1921 guide said there were thirty to forty of them, and a 1934 guide counted about fifty.[58] While the majority of the girls were permanent prostitutes who had generally been pledged, the *xianrouzhuang* also made use of women who prostituted themselves on an occasional basis. They also took in dancers, cast-off concubines, and even employees who had turned to prostitution to earn quick money.[59] The price for a night could be raised twofold or threefold depending on the girl.[60] It would appear from the guides that, around the beginning of the 1920s, not all the *xianrouzhuang* were truly establishments for all classes. The prices indicated and the amounts of money (several hundreds of yuan per month) earned by certain well-known girls tended to differentiate the *xianrouzhuang* from the *yeji* houses. This distinction was completely wiped out in the 1930s.

The "Legions" of Prostitution: The *Yeji*

The vast legions of prostitutes, however, were to be found elsewhere in a very huge category: the *yeji* (pheasants), who were themselves subdivided by Chinese authors, for their own pleasure, into myriad subdivisions that did not correspond to any significant differences. It was their modes of soliciting custom rather than their level that distinguished them from one another. The *yeji* existed well before the term attached to them came into use. We have seen that, as early as the 1870s, Wang Tao mentioned groups of prostitutes soliciting in the streets. He even noted what he called "the Jiangbei prostitutes' corner," describing these girls as *liuji* ("mobile prostitutes"), which was very precisely what they were. The illustrated supplement of the *Shen Bao* also gives numerous examples of lanes where prostitutes could be seen soliciting in the open. In fact, it was probably in the 1900s that the phenomenon of the *yeji* really took off.[61] Its use was then extended to include poor women who prostituted themselves occasionally and then to the prostitutes who could be seen every evening trying to attract customers from their doorsteps or on the sidewalks.

Within this group, there were indeed many categories depending on the elegance of the houses, dwelling places, and modes of soliciting. Very often, the Chinese authors distinguished two classes. There was first of all an upper class, the *zhujia yeji* ("lone pheasants"), who formed a minority, often living alone with a madam and working rather like the earlier courtesans, although they sold only sex. They offered relatively elegant and clean surroundings where friends could get together to eat and play. These prostitutes were designated by other evocative terms, such as *ban kaimen* ("half-opened doors"), *si mentou* ("private doors"), or *penghe taizi* ("scenes of play and feasting"). They got their customers by recommendation from one to the next and were to some extent the forerunners of the call girls.[62] In the 1930s, however, some of them could be found near the large stores (Wing, On, Sincere, etc.), especially in the coffee terraces (*huayuan*) installed on top of these stores. There was a specific term applied to prostitutes soliciting in the amusement centers, cinemas, and theaters: *tangpai*, which referred to the rafts on the water edge that floated here and there and could be taken hold of by all and sundry.[63]

The lower class (*xiaji*) or ordinary class (*putong*) of prostitutes consisted of all the others, attached to a house and forced to actively seek customers in the street. These houses provided sordid surroundings and sold nothing but sex, although it was possible to come and play there for a moderate price (2 to 4 yuan). The sources indicate that, in the 1920s and 1930s, the majority of the *yeji* girls were natives of Jiangbei. Some sources state that the *zhujia yeji* were Suzhou natives; but there is nothing to confirm this view, which, as will be seen in Chapter 5, could be based on prejudice.[64] The situation was less clear-cut in the 1940s when the war brought many refugees from all over the lower Yangzi region. Many authors mention the *yeji* with the greatest contempt: They use terms like *Jiangbei chan* ("Jiangbei produce") or *Jiangbei huo* ("Jiangbei goods").[65] It must be recognized, however, that this contempt extended to the other lower categories of prostitutes as well.

Girls on Call: The *Xiangdaoshe*

The extreme commercialization of venal sexuality in the twentieth century found its ultimate expression in a form of prostitution that is now very common in Hong Kong and Taiwan but actually took off in Shanghai in the 1940s. This was a form of organization capable of providing girls à la carte and around the clock. We would call them "escorts." In pre-1949 Shanghai they were known as "guides." The guide agencies (*xiangdaoshe*) appeared originally as genuine organizations proposing female guides to tourists. The first agency set up shop in 1922–1923 but soon went out of business. It is at the beginning of the 1930s that the idea was resumed in a different form, seeking to provide visitors to Shanghai with female companions, hostesses of a kind, to take them to the city's interesting places while at the same time catering to other needs of a nontouristic nature.[66] In the 1940s, because most of these escorts were refugees from the war zones, they barely knew Shanghai and their role was limited to accompanying customers to hotels, restaurants, and amusement centers.[67]

The recipe is a modern one and was symptomatic of changing lifestyles in the great business metropolis. The initial investment called for no more than a room, simply furnished with a sofa and a few chairs, a telephone, an operator, and a dozen or so girls. The agencies were set up in the center of town or even in the hotels themselves.[68] They made themselves known through paper napkins printed with their names that they distributed to the restaurants. A directory was also published. Around 1937 there were about a hundred such agencies in the International Settlement.[69] The madam's responsibility was reduced to the minimum. She no longer had to worry about finding a dwelling to shelter her charges, take out licenses for all of them, and see to their upkeep. All she had to do was to take her share (50%) of the receipts. The clients paid the agency one yuan per hour for hire, and they remunerated the girl directly for her sexual services.

This mode of organization, which relied on the presence of large numbers of single or poverty-stricken women, helped dissolve the sometimes close relationships that united a madam with her "daughters." Although it did not make these girls free, the *xiangdaoshe* system no longer possessed the means of surveillance traditionally used by the brothels to maintain prostitutes in slavery or quasi-slavery. In this respect, there was a change that contributed to an enfranchisement of the prostitutes. This enfranchisement was relative because these women were in a situation of economic dependence that was in some cases total. Yet their condition no longer included the sordid and detestable feature of total and unremitting submission to the madam. The ranks of the *xiangdaoshe* consisted of women such as *yeji* who came from the world of prostitution, dancers from the dancing halls seeking to make ends meet, and even girls from good families (students, office workers, and teachers) who had taken refuge in Shanghai, like the tens of thousands of their sisters during the Taiping Rebellion, and had been suddenly thrust into prostitution by the necessity of survival.

The 1940s saw the "high noon" of this system, especially during the Civil War, when the city, despite economic hardship, resumed life after the lifting of the heavy lid clamped down by the Japanese occupying forces. The police files abound with reports of arrests of members of these guide agencies. In October 1945, a police raid led to the arrest of thirty-one male and female proprietors of agencies, including a number of repeated offenders. Only forty-five girls were taken in for questioning.[70] It goes without saying that these establishments to a great extent worked in tandem with the hotel attendants who were entrusted with propositioning the customers and plying them with girls. Some customers did not appreciate their proposals and the disturbance and nuisance caused by the activities of these girls in the hotels. In August 1946, a customer in the *Zhongyang lüshe* (Central

Hotel) wrote to the police complaining about the thirty or forty prostitutes who were active in the hotel. After an inquiry, the police station wrote to headquarters to say that almost all the hotels in the district had guide agencies on their premises.[71]

Although they did not declare themselves to be such, the guide agencies were indeed houses of prostitution. They represented one of the most significant responses to the increasingly intensive commercialization of sex and to a more varied demand that called for greater flexibility and speed. In 1946, the police did not hesitate to classify them as establishments of prostitution and force them to undergo registration. Despite a small show of resistance at a general assembly meeting of agency proprietors that was called to define a common position, most of them accepted the decision of the municipal administration that had the advantage of giving them a clear-cut status and sparing them police repression.[72]

The Castoffs of Prostitution

The landscape of prostitution would not be complete without a reference to either (a) those who were unable to leave the trade in time and return to their villages or find a new occupation or (b) those who came late into the trade. These were women who were relatively old, at least to be able to ply the prostitute's trade in a society where a girl was already considered to be an "old tart" at thirty. The sources always refer to these women, but it is clear that those who wrote about them never dared approach them. There is therefore a lack of precision here that is difficult to surmount.

This group is collectively called *dingpeng* ("nail shed"). The term appears to designate their dwellings, which consisted of boards held together by nails. I am not sure that the reality corresponded exactly to this image that appeared in the guides in the 1820s. The press sometimes used the term, although very rarely. The nineteenth-century sources do not mention them. They were found close to the Western Gate, near the Fangbangqiao Bridge and in the French Concession, in the prostitution quarters (see Chapter 8).[73] In the twentieth century, this category included the *huayanjian* mentioned earlier, of which there remained a few establishments near the Small Eastern Gate and the Northern Gate as well as along Avenue Edward VII in the French Concession and in Pentang Lane (*Pentanglong*), in the International Settlement.[74] All the descriptions are agreed in classifying these prostitutes among the castoffs of prostitution. They were patronized by a clientele consisting of coolies and beggars.[75] The girls were old and reduced to tugging at their customers' sleeves as if to beg for their favors. They were sick, suffering from advanced stages of syphilis to the point of being treated as pariahs.[76]

There is hesitation among the various authors on the way to classify common prostitution, especially in the 1920s and 1930s. There are several reasons for this. On the one hand, there was a great variety in the supply, as can be seen from the large number of terms used to designate the categories of prostitutes. However, this abundance resulted from the fact that terms from the past were superimposed on terms in current use. New names appeared all the time to qualify new forms of behavior and new modes of prostitution rather than new types of prostitute. This was the case, for example, with the "semiclandestine" prostitutes, such as the *tangpai* and the *zhujia yeji*. On the other hand, the biases and illusions of Chinese authors sometimes masked reality. In the intermediate categories (for example, the *tangpai* and the *taiji-xianrouzhuang*), they saw women from a very great variety of backgrounds: textile workers, castoff concubines or wives, bond servants on the run (*beinü*), Cantonese servants, students, and so on. In other words, they saw them as honest women forced by circumstances to undertake occasional prostitution. This was an effect of self-mystification, a distortion of reality corresponding to a flight from reality in a society that was in the throes of upheaval. It was the nostalgic image of the "lost flower" in nineteenth-century writings reappearing forcefully in an age when prostitution had become a real sex industry.

The Invasion of the Streets

The practice of soliciting on the public highway was not new, although it did not correspond to Chinese tradition. It is probably necessary to qualify this "tradition." Wang Tao's notes on the walled city in the mid-nineteenth century testify to the existence of soliciting; but the example of Shanghai, which was a business center and port city, is perhaps not typical. To be sure of this point, it would be necessary to have other studies available on popular culture in the Chinese cities under the emperors. Nevertheless, I tend to believe that, even in Shanghai, soliciting in the streets was a recent phenomenon related to the expansion of the city after its enforced opening to Western trade. All the indirect, iconographical testimony (such as the etchings in the *Dianshizhai huabao*) or the textual testimony (such as the press articles) is from the 1890s.[77] The *Shen Bao* does not mention any cases of soliciting in the previous decades. My interpretation is based on limited and scanty documentation, but it is nevertheless a singular fact that nothing was written on this subject during the newspaper's first twenty years. Even if the phenomenon existed, it had not yet reached the scale at which it could be perceived as a social problem.

Figure 3.1 shows that soliciting as a phenomenon really began to take off during the First World War. Although the average number of arrests was 400 to 500 per year from 1909 to 1916, the figures rose to more than 1,200 in 1917 and then dropped to 639 in 1918.[78] The figures can be linked partly to a substantial enfeeblement of the police forces in both settlements, with a large proportion of the European officers having decided to return

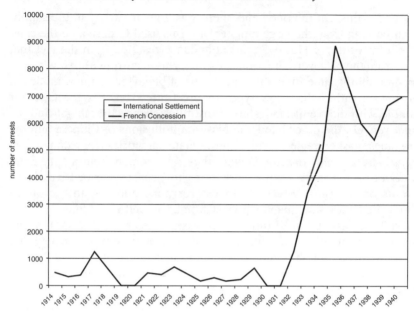

Figure 3.1. Arrests for soliciting in the International Settlement (1914–1940) and in the French Concession (1933–1934). *Sources*: Shanghai Municipal Council, *Report for the Year 1914*, p. 50A; *1915*, p. 43A; *1916*, p. 41A; *1917*, p. 43A; *1918*, p. 47A; *1921*, p. 67A; *1922*, p. 72A; *1923*, p. 41; *1924*, p. 48; *1925*, p. 42; *1926*, p. 41; *1927*, p. 62; *1928*, p. 67; *1929*, p. 86; *1932*, p. 125; *1933*, p. 132; *1934*, p. 96; *1935*, p. 124; *1936*, p. 104; *1937*, p. 113; *1938*, p. 134; *1939*, p. 121; *1940*, p. 147; *Shanghai shi tongji [di'er ci] buchong cailiao*, 1936, p. 127.

to their countries and enlist.[79] Then, up to 1928, the variations were small and the number of arrests relatively low.[80] These variations probably should be linked with varying degrees of zeal on the part of police. In this respect, the figures for 1917 and 1925 may indicate a sterner policy at a time when several Protestant mission organizations were campaigning for the abolition of prostitution. In certain streets, the activity was at a level where it became a real nuisance in the eyes of the businessmen who protested.[81]

Perhaps again, the authorities became aware of a qualitative and quantitative change in the practices of prostitution and made an initial attempt to react to it but then gave up before the huge scale of the task. A second upturn on an unprecedented scale began in 1929. What was new was that, this time, the phenomenon affected both settlements, as can be seen in the number of arrests in the French Concession in 1933 and 1934. This new wave undoubtedly reflected the phenomenal scale of the practice of soliciting on the public roads of Shanghai. It is probably also necessary to take account of the pressure from the Chinese authorities who pushed for greater severity. In the previous year, the Nationalist government had banned houses of prostitution in the capital, Nanking, and ordered that this measure be implemented throughout Chinese territory.

The prostitutes who most frequently solicited customers on the public roads were the *yeji*. Of the 115 prostitutes arrested according to the *Shen Bao* in 1909–1910 and in 1919–1920, only two were *huayanjian* and six were Cantonese. Although there is no information available on 38 of them, there is every reason to believe that they were *yeji*: "Conspicuous everywhere are the Chinese 'Women of the street,' or rather the girls and children, because nearly all are pitifully young. Bedecked and bejeweled, they stand sometimes in the bright glare, but more often within the shadow of a closed doorway, or at the entrance to a lane, usually in groups under the care of an older woman who acts as 'business agent.' "[82] They were *par excellence*, "night beauties" who participated in the myth of Shanghai as the city of delights.

The prostitutes were exposed to the whims of the police. One of them was surprised in the act of simpering and smirking to attract a Western customer.[83] Another girl named Wang Zhen was arrested while arguing with a Cantonese man. The Cantonese, named Lu, accused Wang of having tried to draw his attention by provocative gestures as he passed by. The girl replied that it was Lu who had engaged in small talk with her. It is quite likely that it was the price of the encounter that was the cause of the altercation.[84] Most usually, however, it was when they were trying to pull a client by the arm that the girls were caught and arrested, as shall be seen below.[85] More rarely, soliciting was done in the daytime and very boldly. Huang Heshang and Ma Rongsheng, two notorious hooligans, were arrested while trying to attract the attention of a group of masons by undressing a girl.[86]

The girls also solicited in teahouses, standing before the doorways, strolling up and down on the sidewalks, or even walking among the customers. They had their favorite places like Qingliange (a famous teahouse on Fuzhou Road), Changle, Yi'an, or Sihai Shengpinglou.[87] A female American resident has left an account of these processions of young prostitutes walking through the teahouses under the watchful eye of a madam: "In and out among the square tables, filling the brilliantly lighted rooms, trail slowly little processions of young girls. . . . Clad in silk and satin, adorned with jewelry, their faces unnatural with paint and powder, they follow the lead of the women in charge of each group. She stops often to draw attention ingratiatingly to her charges and expatiates on their good points. When one is chosen she leaves her to her fate and passes on to dispose of others."[88] The prostitutes were led like real cattle that customers could look at, assess, and purchase in the lively atmosphere of these establishments.

Plate 6. Fuzhou Road.

The girls worked singly or in company. For fear that they might run away, the prostitutes were chaperoned by a maidservant or by the madam. In groups of two or three, they would try to seize a passerby and pull him into their establishment.[89] These methods of soliciting could also take a muscular turn. One passerby who resisted was violently struck by the two *yeji* who were trying to drag him along with them.[90] In 1910, the police arrested thirteen people: a madam, two waiters, and ten girls.[91] The Shanghai guides all warned visitors against the risks of going to certain streets and responding even in the most circumspect manner to the advances of prostitutes, because the smallest expression could be interpreted as a sign of assent. Indeed, if their glances and hand signs were not enough, the girls would go so far as to draw the customer by the arm or grab his personal effects (umbrella, cigarettes, raincoat, etc.).[92] They would try to convince an unwilling customer to stay or at least to give them a small tip, tea money (*chaqian*), for their pains.[93]

The warnings of the guides, which may seem to be part of the local folklore, were not empty. The press and the police archives attest to the reality of these practices. A Hangzhou merchant was forcibly introduced into a house with the help of a servant who gripped his neck. The prostitute took advantage of the situation to divest him of 40 yuan.[94] I have also found picturesque complaints by city dwellers about "kidnapping" in a brothel. One passer-by who was going through the rue de Saigon in the French Concession at about 8:00 P.M. was set upon by several women who pushed him into their house at the end of a lane: "As I was alone, I could not resist and I was hardly seated in their room when they searched me and undressed me." The man was able to get away but noted that they had removed 12 yuan from his pockets.[95]

The same mishap occurred to another absentminded or unwitting passer-by who wandered into the rue de Hué at around 11:00 P.M.: "More than ten prostitutes leaped on me, surrounded me despite my defensive action and my shouts . . . , there was no policeman on the beat, the passers-by did not want to help me, I was taken by force into a dark passageway . . . , and I was robbed."[96] One anecdote reported by the press shows that the strong-arm tactics of the girls could have unexpected consequences. A *huayanjian* who was unable to force a customer to make up his mind gave a vigorous tug at his trousers. The poor man, who was probably in an advanced stage of syphilis, started bleeding heavily and began to scream and call for help. The police had to take him to a hospital.[97]

The practice of soliciting was harshly suppressed at the turn of the century. Then, as Western law came to prevail and the phenomenon of solic-iting tended to become commonplace, the punishments became increas-ingly benign. Before the 1911 Revolution, when cases involving Chinese residents were still being dealt with by the Chinese magistrate, the offense of soliciting was sanctioned by physical punishment. Ultimately, the prosti-tute was condemned to caning by twenty strokes on the palm of the hand.[98] It may or may not mean that her role was held in lower esteem, but a maid-servant caught helping a prostitute to draw a customer by force received harsher punishment: a hundred strokes on the palm.[99] It would appear that the scale of the punishments varied according to the indulgence of the Chinese magistrate: In 1899, two prostitutes were sentenced to a mere fine of 10 yuan (a few days' earnings) (see Table 3.1).[100]

In the twentieth century, physical punishment was abolished. It was replaced by fines whose amount varied little: It was generally 5 yuan in 1909 as well as in 1919. This was also the case in the 1930s. A comparison between the punishment meted out for simple soliciting and for soliciting with vio-lence does not show any significant difference. The madams were sentenced more strictly but less frequently. This is because they were sentenced only when they were caught red-handed in the act of soliciting. Their punish-ment, which consisted of fines or imprisonment, was usually twice that meted out to the prostitutes.

The case of the French Concession deserves closer scrutiny. The author-ities were careful to maintain order on the public roads for which the con-cession was renowned. In 1914, the police chief proposed that licenses should no longer be granted to houses located on the boulevard des Deux-Républiques, where there had often been abuses: "The girls come out of the houses; they annoy and pursue passers-by and remove their hats." There were sometimes also traffic problems. When a road that the prostitutes were

Table 3.1. *Record of sentences handed out to prostitutes and madams for soliciting on the public roadways*

Sentences	1909–1910		1919–1920	
	Prostitutes	Madams	Prostitutes	Madams
Fines				
2–3 yuan	1	—	4	—
5 yuan	14	—	10	—
10 yuan	—	4	—	2
20–25 yuan	1	2	—	1
Prison				
7 days	4	1	2	—
10 days	3	—	—	—
14 days	3	4	—	—
21 days	1	—	—	—
30+ days	—	1	—	1

Sources: *SB*, 19 Jan. 1909 (CF); 21 Jan. 1909; 29 Jan. 1909; 1 Feb. 1909; 20 Feb. 1909; 18 Feb. 1909; 17 March 1909; 22 March 1909; 26 March 1909; 4 April 1909; 17 April 1909; 21 April 1909; 14 May 1909; 21 May 1909; 2 July 1909; 3 August 1909; 20 Sept. 1909; 26 Sept. 1909; 7 Oct. 1909; 3 Nov. 1909; 12 Nov. 1909; 10 Dec. 1909; 21 Dec. 1909; 21 Dec. 1909; 25 Dec. 1909; 12 April 1910; 24 June 1910; 13 Oct. 1910; 24 Nov. 1910; 13 Dec. 1910; 13 March 1919; 14 March 1919; 27 July 1919; 29 July 1919; 19 August 1919; 1 Sept. 1919; 6 Oct. 1919; 21 Oct. 1919; 12 Nov. 1919; 13 Nov. 1919; 18 Nov. 1919; 20 Nov. 1919; 28 Nov. 1919; 27 Dec. 1919; 5 Jan. 1920.

obstructing by their trade had to be opened to traffic, the police suspended the renewal of licenses in order to force the houses of tolerance to move.[101] On the other hand, certain roads were *de facto* reserved for the activities of prostitution. People were afraid to pass through certain main roads, such as the Rue des Pères, the Rue de Hué, the Rue du Moulin, and so on. The police were criticized for their inaction.[102] In fact, despite complaints from city dwellers, the police defended these "reserved districts."

When a group of merchants asked that the prostitutes' houses in the rue du Marché be shut down, the police informed the council that their eviction would mean their moving to other more visible districts: "[la Rue du Marché] is the only place concealed from the view of people passing through the major roads, and there are many Shanghai dwellers who are even unaware of the location of this street and of the type of trade that goes on therein."[103] The French policy showed a certain degree of tolerance, undoubtedly because they were faced with the inevitable. In 1921, a regulation laid down by the vice squad tolerated the presence of girls outdoors in certain streets, although they were forbidden to carry out active soliciting.[104]

In the twentieth century, most of the Chinese authors criticized and even severely condemned these groups of prostitutes. Their apparent motive was the disorder created by their presence in the street and, secondarily, the danger that they posed to public health, even if this notion was never explicitly stated. I have found only one author who defended the *yeji* in arguing that, without them, those who had a wish to "open their hearts" (*kai xin*) would not know where to go. The *yeji* were not expensive and were accessible to all social classes. As such, they played an irreplaceable role.[105] The argument of the sexual outlet was of course neither new nor soundly based, but this was the only author, at a time when prostitution came under repression in Shanghai, to express these views in a positive fashion. In 1934, Wang Dingjiu specifically referred to the *yeji* as a "sexual outlet" (*xieyuqi*) but with a frankly pejorative connotation.[106]

The market of prostitution in nineteenth-century Shanghai cannot be reduced to the elitist world of the courtesans. The courtesans were only the cream of a trade that encompassed a very wide range of establishments where males of all social classes could find what they were looking for. In a city where the demographic imbalance was pronounced to such a degree, it would have been surprising for prostitution to have concentrated on serving the elites. It is actually the opposite that is true even if, through an effect of concealment by the sources, it seems as if only the courtesans were on the scene and that they dominated this market. In fact, if it is possible to speak of a "hierarchy of prostitution," it is really during this period that there was a grading of establishments along a continuum that stretched from the knocking shops for sailors to the courtesans' establishments with a series of intermediate, undefinable levels, such as those of the *caotai* and the *siju*, the *yao'er* and the *ersan*, the *maisons de rendez-vous*, and so on. What needs to be done is to simply take note of this diversity that reflects the fact that there was a substantial demand in society for these services. It seems to me to be futile, given the lack of the tiniest amount of information about the nature of the customers, to try to establish any real classification.

The transformation of the urban landscape, the shifting of economic activity, and the growth of the population led to corresponding changes in the market of prostitution. I shall not refer here to the geographical dimension that is dealt with in Chapter 8. The most significant phenomenon in the development of prostitution in Shanghai was the leveling out of these different types of establishments that lost their specific features – especially the fact that they appeared to offer places of conviviality and entertainment – to the benefit of an activity that was centered exclusively on the sex trade. In the course of this process of leveling out, all the intermediate categories of prostitutes were pulled "downward," inasmuch as prostitution was dragged along by the growing commercialization of the local economy. The fact that prostitution always was a venal activity goes without saying. But its forms varied. In the case of Shanghai, between 1849 and the 1920s, there was a change of scale, with an expansion of the range of economic activity and the increasingly rapid circulation of goods and services. The prostitutes – this "beautiful merchandise," to use Sue Gronewold's apt expression – did not escape this irreversible cycle.

Shanghai in the first half of the twentieth century deserved its name of "the Paris of Asia," with its flourishing economy, its cosmopolitan population, its lively cultural life, and the diversity of its leisure activities, but it also deserved its less glorious name of "the brothel of Asia." Not only was this twofold reputation well deserved, but, as far as the latter title is concerned, it cannot be doubted that, within its walls, the city contained a number and variety of leisure establishments without equal in Asia. Prostitution was omnipresent in the city. Soliciting on the public roadways, which the authorities were unable to control, added to the impression of an invasion. Sex occupied a major place in the male collective psyche, as can be seen in the many forms through which preoccupation was manifested.

The daily press, with its numerous advertisements for medicines, treatments, doctors, clinics, and nursing homes dealing with sexual problems, especially venereal disease and problems related to virility, reveals this phenomenon in an explicit though indirect manner.[107] The market of prostitution was marked (and this might appear to be paradoxical) by growing sexualization. The paradox is only apparent because it relates here to the passage to a money-dominated consumer society where customers sought immediate and direct returns for payment. The amazing development of prostitution in Shanghai, apart from the fact that it took place in an international port city, resulted from the conjunction of this remarkable economic modernization and a culture where patronizing prostitutes was not an abnormal act in social life.

4
Ancillary Forms of Prostitution (1920s–1940s)

The commercialization of prostitution and the emergence of new forms of leisure and relaxation after World War I gave birth to novel modes of prostitution. Because these modes were not originally intended to be places of prostitution and because they never did become so in full measure, I have chosen to present them separately and to deal with them as ancillary forms of prostitution. The sex trade could be one of the activities involved in these modes, but not the only one. By order of involvement with prostitution, three occupations can be listed in this section: waitresses belonging to a profession that was not new but underwent extraordinary expansion, masseuses who appeared in the 1920s, and professional dancers or taxi dancers who appeared after the First World War and whose activity reached its zenith in the 1930s and 1940s. The latter even became a major feature of Shanghai nightlife, taking over *mutatis mutandis* the role played by courtesans in the past. As time went on, the Chinese authorities became very much concerned by this new institution and its impact on society, and they tried to curb it but with limited success.

Masseuses and Waitresses: Ancillary Workers of Prostitution

The association in Asia between massage parlors and prostitution would surprise no one today. Several countries in the region have made a reputation for themselves in this field. One of the chief images that cling to Thailand today is that of its masseuses. Hong Kong and Taiwan are not lagging behind. The number of road signs for *mashaji* (the Chinese transliteration of "massage") is quite instructive. Although there can be no doubt today that these massage parlors are actually houses of prostitution, historically their status long remained ambiguous. Having been in the vanguard of modernity in every field, Shanghai was Asia's first city to experience this disguised form of prostitution.

Massage parlors (translated at the time by the term *anmoyuan*) were introduced into Shanghai by Russian émigrés.[1] The 1917 Revolution and the Civil War in Russia made tens of thousands of people take to the road, especially women who sought refuge in the big cities of Northeast China in which many Russian communities had been established. Some of these refugees then went to Shanghai seeking employment, but in vain, given their general lack of qualifications and the obstacle of language. Forced to survive in a highly competitive and pitiless environment, some of the women went into professions that required no special training or took up trades that could be learned on the job.

This was the case with the massage parlors, a form of activity that was monopolized at its beginnings by Russian emigré women. The first massage parlor is thought to have opened on Hongjiang Road in Zhabei in the early 1920s. It was followed by a second one in the French settlement on rue Lafayette. To draw customers, these parlors hired young girls whose work was actually limited to massage.[2] In 1933, two other establishments opened close to the Great World in the French Concession. Chinese girls soon realized all the advantages that could be derived from this apparently respectable activity. Those of them who had been employed in the Russian-run parlors set up on their own as soon as they had learned the rudiments of the trade.[3] The Chinese massage parlors then mushroomed. Around 1935, there were parlors in both settlements.[4] The Russian parlors managed to hold on at least up to the war with Japan and at least in the French Concession as can be seen from the official records of permission granted by the municipality to open these establishments.[5] The Chinese parlors followed them into the settlements but gradually moved toward the downtown area of Shanghai where there were many more customers. One source reports that, by the end of the 1930s, there were 105 parlors in Shanghai employing 2,800 masseuses.[6]

The emergence of large numbers of these establishments led to rather sharp competition. To draw customers, the massage parlors advertised in the press. They took names that left hardly any doubt about their calling, unless we prefer to believe that the Chinese predilection for certain ideograms evoking spring and revitalization are not common to parlors and houses of prostitution. The advertisements drew attention to the presence of young girls (*nianqing nüzi*). In the 1940s, the parlors even offered room service to hotel guests.[7] There can be no doubt that the services offered by a good many of these establishments went beyond massage. Some of them were even houses of prostitution disguised under the name of massage parlors. Their development followed the prohibition of prostitution by the Shanghai Municipal Council. Setting up a massage parlor was a way to circumvent this prohibition temporarily or partially.

The parlors were open all day, from nine in the morning to one o'clock in the small hours of the next day. They were not all alike, even if the differences lay mainly in the degree of comfort and luxury offered to the patron. On his arrival, the patron would select a masseuse from a book of photographs or directly from among the girls who were brought in.[8] Certain masseuses even took on professional names that would be displayed at the entrance to the parlor.[9] In the Russian parlors, the proprietress offered coffee and cigarettes and negotiated the price with the patrons. If the patron did not speak English, it was the Chinese employees who translated for him.[10] The masseuses did not wear any specific professional garb. In certain low-level parlors, the customer was brought straight to the point as the girls welcomed him bare-breasted.[11] The authorities introduced regulations requiring them to wear white blouses.[12] The patron was led by the masseuse into a room adjoining a bath. He was bathed by the girl, then placed on a table where he received his massage. The parlors had a convivial touch: A patron could take tea and order a few *dianxin* (snack dumplings). After the massage, he could simply go away without "taking any extras." However, even if the customer did not take the initiative, the masseuse would lead him to understand that she could provide him with other services.

Prices varied according to the establishments. According to a source from the 1930s, a customer could expect to pay 5 yuan for a massage, by the lowest-priced girls and 10 to 20 yuan for the others. This was so in the Russian parlors. In the Chinese houses, the price was 1 to 2 yuan for a massage, but it continued to drop with the opening of new parlors. In 1942, a few *mao* (dimes) were enough.[13] This money went to the proprietress. The masseuses received no fixed salary and kept only the tips they received from their customers.[14] This was one of the reasons that pushed them into prostitution. When tips were insufficient, theft was a means to make up the amount. The guidebooks advised visitors not go to a massage parlor with money or wristwatches. The girls would take advantage of the fact that a customer had undressed for a bath to rifle his pockets.[15]

The authorities had hardly any illusions about the real purpose of the massage parlor trade even if they did not take any genuinely repressive measures. I have not come across any special regulations for the International Settlement. In the French zone on the other hand, the municipality adopted a set of regulations aimed at setting up a degree of control similar in certain ways to that imposed on the houses of prostitution. Apart from being required to register and apply for authorization documents, the proprietresses of the parlors had to report all staff members as well as all departures along with the reasons thereof. She had to inform the authorities of any contagious illnesses suffered by masseuses or members of their families. There was a compulsory medical inspection when making the application. It was forbidden to employ minors under eighteen.[16] These rules were nevertheless limited in their scope. Above all, they reflected the authorities' concern to overlook no possible source of revenue.

Although the massage parlors, by the very nature of their activity, provided a framework that was propitious to the growth of prostitution, they nevertheless represented only one of the forms of work in which the women of Shanghai found employment, generally related to their sex. In the pre-

1949 period, the proliferation of a wide variety of places where male patrons could relax or have a drink created a considerable number of occupations for women. In the 1940s, although the position of women in urban society had improved (by then, female work was no longer seen as something exceptional or disturbing), the fact remained that they were confined to trades in which their status as sex objects was particularly pronounced. Whether they were taxi dancers or waitresses and singers, it was their "pretty faces" that were used to bait customers.

One occupation that employed large numbers of women was that of the waitress. In the 1920s, women even began to supplant men in this traditionally male preserve. Wherever they worked (dance halls, teahouses, cafes, cabarets, etc.), these women often received no fixed salary and depended on tips from patrons for their remuneration. In the open-air cafes of the amusement centers, in addition to the tips, they would receive a commission on the drinks that they persuaded patrons to order.[17] They could earn up to 3 to 4 yuan per day, but their average monthly earnings around 1934 amounted to 50 yuan. This was quite a sum when compared with the salaries paid to workers in industry, who earned four times less. Still, their business outlay on clothing and makeup was higher. They moved in circles where it was not rare for them to fall victim to protection rackets by gangsters who were constantly harassing lone women.[18]

The waitresses were often hired to keep company with patrons. This practice was introduced by an amusement center, the World of Immortals (*Shenxian shijie*), which replaced men by women in its hairdresser's establishment. All the amusement centers followed suit. Women then took the place of the waiters in the open-air cafes. Around 1937, there were more than 800 waitresses in the different amusement centers.[19] Their main role was to bring in tea to welcome arriving customers and converse with them. The price for their service was very small: It ranged from 2 to 4 *mao*, depending on the generosity of the patron, who was able in this way to relax, chat, and enjoy the cool of the evening.[20] So closely was the image of these waitresses associated with this role of serving tea that the populace nicknamed them *bolibei* (tea glasses). This was not a profession that paid well, nor was it well-esteemed, but it enabled young women to earn a little money without greatly compromising themselves.

It was widely known that some of them did go in for prostitution. The reasons for this were many and varied. A primary reason of course was the desire to earn more money or make ends meet. Many were married and sometimes had to pay for their husbands' misadventures (related to gambling, drugs, indebtedness, etc.). Their work brought them into permanent contact with men who often made passes at them. Finally, the proprietors often put pressure on the waitresses to make them submit to their patrons' wishes – for example, by allowing themselves to be fondled. If they rejected their customers' advances or objected to such behavior, they would lose their jobs.[21] Even if all waitresses did not come under such pressure, many were led into prostitution in this way. They were similar to the *yeji*, who were associated with a clientele from the middle and lower levels, and they sometimes joined the ranks of the women (*tangpai*) who went in for occasional soliciting in the public amusement centers.

Masseuses and waitresses represented two new categories of prostitution whose emergence was related to developments in the twentieth century. Although the former were quite a novelty, this was not entirely true for the waitresses. We have seen that, from the 1850s onward, women had been employed in the teahouses and that some of them had turned to prostitution. However, they had formed an extremely small group as compared with the number of prostitutes as well as with the number of females employed in general. Female employment in Shanghai really began to take off after the First World War. It was related to the economic boom and to the profound social transformation that came about in the city. The job market expanded, especially in industry and in offices. However, it was in the services sector, and especially in the leisure sector, that the change was most radical. It is not necessary here to dwell again on the discriminatory nature of these forms of employment. Women in these occupations were valued only as females if not purely for sex, moving as they did in a public domain that was essentially masculine. The fact that some jobs served as a passageway toward prostitution can be explained by the precarious nature of the income that they provided.

The Dance Halls: Between Sensuality and Sexuality

The dance halls (*wuting* or *wuchang*) formed a part of this development in Shanghai toward a modern consumer and leisure-oriented society. This phenomenon presented an opportunity for a Chinese sociologist to examine social change in large urban settings. It is unfortunate that no Chinese sociologist has come up with an equivalent study that even approximately approaches Paul Cressey's classic work on the dance halls of Chicago in the 1930s, because it is an established fact that this institution was the very expression of a major movement toward the commercialization of leisure activities.[22] Dance halls appeared in China in the aftermath of the First World War. They were practically contemporary – give or take a few years – with their American counterparts. The first dance halls were opened by the foreigners in the city's big hotels. These establishments were rather selective, and they laid down very formal dress requirements.[23] This recipe was taken up by the Chinese with growing success. In the 1920s, about ten establishments were opened throughout the city, as the fashion gradually spread to the middle sections of society.[24] The dance halls engaged in fierce competition for customers.

The situation became stabilized in the 1930s when the number of establishments remained relatively constant. However, the dance halls went through a difficult period marked by decline during the Sino-Japanese War. During the fighting, many of them were converted into reception centers for the sick, the wounded, and refugees. After the withdrawal of Chinese troops, the halls were reopened, but the curfew imposed by the Japanese army forced them to close at 9:30 P.M., especially after 1941 when the Japanese occupied the International Settlement. At this time, the dance halls would open every morning to compensate for this reduction in working hours. It was only in 1943 that Zhou Fohai, the mayor of Shanghai, yielded to a request from a taxi dancer who had become his mistress and changed the closing time to midnight.[25] At the end of the war, the dance halls came back into vogue more than ever in spite of the economic difficulties created by inflation.

Dancing, Power, and Morality

Chinese officials always looked with disfavor on the dance hall. They objected not so much to the practice of dancing (even if they judged Western dancing to be decadent) as to the promiscuity between the sexes that was fostered by these establishments. Besides, the dance halls were accused of having a corrupting effect on Chinese youth, who represented the majority of their patrons. In 1928, the public security bureau of the Chinese municipality prohibited cabarets and dance halls throughout its territory. This prohibition was made primarily on the grounds that the taxi dancers wore indecent clothing. The dance halls were likened to houses of ill-fame, having detrimental effects on the morals of the young.[26]

The authorities proved to be incapable of implementing this prohibition that people could, in any case, circumvent by setting up shop in the settlements. They therefore tried to regulate them – for example, in the French Concession. In 1933, a regulation required taxi dancers as well as dance-hall proprietors to register with the police. The taxi dancers had to be more than 16 years old, always carry professional cards on their person, and refrain from indecent behavior. Any change in establishment or profession had to be reported to the police.[27] Penalties were inflicted for infringement of these rules, but they were too light to act as genuine deterrents. The lines that delineated the taxi dancers' profession were far too blurred and shifting to be controlled with the resources available to the police.

The Chinese authorities also tried to tackle the problem at the customers' end by limiting their access to the dance halls. As it turned out, it was the students who were the target of these measures. The executive committee of a "Group of Ten" representing Chinese Protestants wrote to the Chancellors of Shanghai's universities and to the city's three municipal administrations, asking that students be prohibited from visiting dance halls.[28] Only the Chinese municipal government followed this advice, although it pointed

out that it was powerless in the settlements, adding that it would be difficult to distinguish between students and other categories of patrons.[29] The
students themselves were not very keen on the idea and asked that the
leaders of society should begin by setting an example.[30]

The association of university teachers also spoke out for prohibition and
said that the universities themselves would be sending investigators to the
dance halls at the same time as the police did their rounds. This was one
way of getting around the fact that it was impossible to take action against
establishments located in the settlements. Students caught red-handed were
threatened with serious punishment, including expulsion from school.[31]
However, the professors themselves were not beyond reproach, and some
of them patronized the dance halls. An association of "teachers against
dancing" was therefore set up to raise the moral standards of the teaching
profession. The students of Fudan, Dongwu, Daxia, and Wujiang universities organized groups of investigators to track down students and teachers
who went to dance halls.[32] In addition, the municipal government instructed
university chancellors to make it compulsory for students to wear uniforms
and punish those who did not comply with the prohibition, including
teachers.[33] The Guomindang asked for a ban on advertisements for dance
halls in the press.[34]

After the war, the authorities did not prohibit the dance halls but sought
to put an end to the abuses resulting from the functioning and organization
of these establishments.[35] A new and more detailed set of regulations was
adopted to set up standards in the profession and protect women.[36] The new
regulations added clauses to the provisions of 1928. These new clauses
required the signing of contracts between the parties and the apportioning
of fixed shares in profits (with 70% going to the taxi dancers). The new law
also prohibited the employment of girls suffering from contagious diseases
or, quite simply, in feeble condition and also girls who were far too young
for the job, possessed no identity papers, or had been kidnapped and forced
to ply this trade. The employers had to make monthly reports to the police
and obtain permission from the parents or guardians of minors. The penalties laid down included fines (of 100 to 1,000 yuan) and imprisonment (from
one to seven days). The waitresses came under similar regulations. In particular, it was forbidden for them to wear outlandish clothing (*qizhuang
yifu*), adopt indecent postures, and go out with customers.[37]

In 1947, when the negotiations between the Nationalists and the Communists gave way to war, the Central Government considered it improper
that there should be dance halls in the rear while soldiers were sacrificing
their lives on the front. A decree ordered their immediate closure. In Shanghai, which had the largest number of establishments, the authorities were
in a quandary. The Social Affairs Bureau, after indirect negotiations with
the association of dance halls, decided to keep the prohibition in abeyance
until the Chinese New Year and eliminate them gradually, starting with the

small dance halls. However, the bureau then went back on its word and drew lots in which forty major establishments were actually eliminated at one stroke. This change in policy aroused the anger of the dance-hall proprietors, who had no difficulty in mobilizing their taxi dancers and other employees.[38] On January 31, more than 2,000 taxi dancers and employees marched through the streets to protest in front of the Social Affairs Bureau. When Wu Kaixian refused to come out and discuss matters, the assembly turned into a riot.

The police were sent to the spot to clear the premises and the district that had been blocked for more than six hours. The confrontation was violent as testified to by the press photographs. More than 40 policemen were injured, along with 31 taxi dancers. Several hundreds of demonstrators (797 according to the police) were arrested, while warrants were taken out against the leaders of the unions involved. They were jailed shortly afterward and their organizations dissolved.[39] The authorities appear to have believed in the existence of a plot and were shocked by the scale of the violence during the demonstration.[40] According to the press reports, the movement was initiated by dance-hall proprietors and dance-hall supervisors. A number of girls said that they had been forced by the threat of financial consequences to participate in three meetings that had preceded the demonstration and then in the demonstration itself.[41] Several groups of people were released in successive waves (the dance halls went on strike to protest against the arrests); but on February 3, there were still 116 persons in jail, 85 of them employees.[42] The police pressed charges against only about 50 individuals.[43] The plan to eliminate the dance halls was indefinitely postponed.[44] However, the municipal government prohibited the presence of taxi dancers in the bars and cabarets, where their activities most often constituted a form of disguised prostitution.[45]

This "legislating" zeal formed part of a broader movement by the Nationalist authorities to regain control over society in a city from which they had been cut off for seven years and that was greatly shaken by the effects of the Civil War, especially the massive arrival of refugees. The authorities especially targeted women who, in the social context of the day, were more exposed than men to exploitation in all its forms. There was a legitimate and sincere desire on the part of the authorities to protect all these women as far as was possible by laying down the minimum rules in the industries in which they worked. Beyond this determination, there was also the desire to establish close-range or even long-range control over all matters that concerned sexuality. Now Shanghai had become a huge market in women in which every form of venal sexuality proliferated. Since the 1930s, women had made a massive entry into the lower-grade jobs in establishments such as bars, cabarets, cafes, and so on, whose numbers grew considerably. The municipal government took care to limit excesses and restrict prostitution to the houses intended for this purpose, but its aim of raising moral standards was illusory so long as these activities remained tenuous and so long as their participants were being constantly replaced and the means of surveillance remained scanty.[46]

The Phenomenon of the Dance Halls

The principle of the dance halls was fairly simple. When a hall opened, it would recruit professional dancers to accompany the customers. Because the recruiting ground was small, many dancing schools grew up to supply this new market by providing accelerated training programs. Because most of the customers did not know how to dance, the level of qualification required was not very high. Besides, by dint of practice, the taxi dancers soon learned the necessary techniques. It is difficult to estimate the number of dance halls because it all depends on the way in which they are defined. The guidebooks listed only the best-known establishments. There were fifteen dance halls in 1933 and thirty-three in 1937, fourteen of which were run by Chinese.[47] The official yearbook of the municipality listed twenty-eight establishments in 1946, while a police report listed thirty of them.[48] To these dance halls, we must add all the coffee houses, nightclubs, and cabarets that had a small dancing stage, always with a few taxi dancers.

It is even more difficult to estimate the number of taxi dancers (*wunü*). The activity of the dancer was most usually a transitory one, and the training was often done on the job. There was a high rate of turnover among this group of women. Besides, the official statistics counted only those who were registered with the authorities, and a large number of dancers escaped registration. Those who worked in the numerous cabarets and other night establishments that made up Shanghai's night life slipped entirely through the net of the administration. Nevertheless, there are said to have been 300 professional dancers around 1932.[49] In 1937, an official document estimated a number ranging from 2,300 to 5,000 individuals.[50] About ten years later, the municipality yearbook put the number of taxi dancers at 1,588, while the annual statistical report of the police departments put them at 1,622.[51] These figures greatly underestimate the reality. The press reported the presence of 2,000 demonstrators during the protest in 1948 against the municipality.[52] The dance halls were a leisure industry that provided many jobs in addition to those of the taxi dancers. In the 1940s, they employed more than 200 musicians and more than 2,000 waiters and waitresses as well as 200 supervisors (*daban*).[53]

The taxi dancers came from fairly varied backgrounds. According to the Shanghai guidebooks, they were from every walk of life: students gone astray, recycled prostitutes of all kinds (*yeji, xianshuimei*), waitresses, courtesans, and so on.[54] They seem in fact to have come from the same circles as the prostitutes (poor families and war-zone refugees) but had had the possibility or luck to be able to choose another way of life. The taxi dancers

Table 4.1. *Structure by age: taxi dancers in 1946*

Age range	Number	Percentage	Cumulative percentage
15–20 years	745	45.9	45.9
21–25 years	660	40.7	86.6
26–30 years	156	9.6	96.2
31+ years	61	3.8	100.0
Total:	1,622	100.0	

Source: Shanghai shi jingchaju sanshiwu nian tongji nianbao, 1947, p. 76.

were rather young, as can be seen from Table 4.1. Nearly half of them were below twenty, and most of them were no more than twenty-five. This was a profession in which no careers could be made and that sometimes served to supplement an insufficient income earned in a regular job. It was above all a stopgap activity for thousands of young refugee girls pending their return to their village or a better situation.[55]

Most of the dancers were Chinese, although there were about sixty foreigners, chiefly of Russian origin.[56] A preponderant majority of the Chinese dancers (64% in 1946) came from the two provinces of Jiangsu and Zhejiang. This point supports the view that they had come to Shanghai to escape the difficult economic conditions of the war. Unlike the prostitutes, the proportion of dancers describing themselves as Shanghai natives was very high (24%). This means that the urban context was more propitious to learning to dance and gave city girls the advantage over peasants who went straight into prostitution. Most of the dancers had no education. Fifty-eight dancers had had a secondary education, 537 had been to primary school, and the great majority (1,027) were completely illiterate.[57]

Life in the Dance Halls

Not all the dance-hall establishments resembled one another. Although there was no explicit grading, there were two major categories of dance halls. On the one hand, there were the dance halls patronized by foreigners and the wealthier Chinese residents that were sometimes set up in the big hotels. Some tried to create a special atmosphere. In one of them, the hall was decorated so that it resembled a beach. The dancers wore bathing suits with a number on the front so that the customers could single them out more easily.[58] The biggest dance halls generally provided a full range of entertainment. In July 1933, a new establishment, the Majestic Garden, opened on avenue Haig in the French settlement. It was set in a large two-hectare field with a miniature golf course as well as facilities for boating and even fishing. The dance hall offered three sessions, from 2:00 P.M. to the early hours of the morning.[59] It had two orchestras and could receive 2,500 people.[60] On the other hand, most of the dance halls were more modestly sized, and some were little more than cabarets with a little space set aside for dancing.

The principle of the dance halls was to provide dancers to patrons who would pay a girl by handing her a ticket before each dance. She would collect the tickets and exchange them for money with the proprietor of the establishment. Although the patrons were required to buy only one ticket per dance, those who wished to win a dancer's goodwill, either in order to keep her to themselves or in the hope of winning her favors, had to be more generous and hand out additional tickets even if they did not "avail themselves" of all the dances. Up to 1937, the principle was to leave matters to the patrons' free choice, even if the dancing supervisors (*daban*) acted as middlemen between the patrons and the dancers. After 1937, the proprietors of the dance halls introduced a system of automatic assignment (*zuo taizi*). As soon as a patron entered, a girl would keep him company for a series of dances. Later on, the dance halls set up another procedure, that of "going around the tables" (*zhuan tai*). A girl would come to a table for a quarter of an hour and then go to another table.[61]

Going to dance halls was not a particularly costly affair. This is one of the reasons why they were successful with customers from all social groups. For those who were satisfied with simple beverages, a cup of tea or coffee would cost no more than 4 mao. But those who let themselves go and ordered alcohol – especially champagne, which the dancers would encourage them to imbibe – risked having to pay a rather heavy bill. All the guidebooks advised potential patrons of dance halls to be cautious.[62] As for the dancing itself, which was the customers' main purpose, it all depended on their enthusiasm. Around 1919, a ticket cost only 3 mao for a dance lasting about five minutes.[63] The prices had barely changed by the beginning of the 1930s when it cost 1 yuan for three dances in the most expensive dance halls and 1 yuan for ten dances in the smaller establishments.[64] These smaller establishments were patronized by customers who came for the pleasure of dancing. The dance halls proposed ticket books for 5, 10, 20, 50, or 100 yuan, carefully printed with golden characters and tied together with red ribbon.[65]

Although most customers saw a dance hall as a place of entertainment, visiting certain establishments and patronizing "red" dancers gave the elite an element of social status of the kind derived from visiting the courtesans' houses. Even if they did not know how to dance, the members of the political, military, and merchant elite flaunted themselves in the company of these young dancers. Du Yuesheng, the boss of Shanghai's secret societies, was a regular patron of these dance halls, which he visited especially in the company of Wang Xiaolai, an influential member of the local bourgeoisie. Du always received special treatment. When he entered, the orchestra would immediately stop playing and then start a tune of welcome.[66] Neither Du nor Wang knew how to dance, but they would take one or two turns, walking around the dance hall. The patrons were essentially local and came from Shanghai's emerging middle classes: service employees, students, bureaucrats, journalists, and so on.

One of the goals of the dancers was to secure the loyalty of some of their customers. By establishing a stable relationship with a few good customers, they could ensure higher and more regular incomes without having to accept every invitation to dance. The establishment of a special relationship did not necessarily imply the existence of sexual relations. Instead, it meant a system of mutual obligation, just as the courtesans used to maintain special relationships with some of their customers. In the jargon of the dance halls, a dancer's "accredited" patrons were known as *tuoche* ("wagons") because they were tugged by their engine (*longtou*, literally dragon's head), who was the female dancer.[67] One of the difficulties of the taxi dancers' trade, however, was to manage several special relationships at a time. The life of the dance halls was punctuated by the quarrels that would sometimes break out between rivals vying for the same girl. Similarly, the taxi dancers often came to blows when a customer decided to change a favorite partner.

The taxi dancers received a salary calculated according to the number of tickets that they collected. In addition, they received a commission on the drinks that they persuaded their patrons to order. However, they received only a small part of the commission. The earnings from the tickets were divided in a proportion of 40% for the dancers and 60% for the proprietor. However, the supervisors (*daban*) who saw to it that the customers handed over tickets to the dancers were themselves remunerated out of the girl's share. There was no fixed price. The amount depended on the dancer's status (that is, her reputation). The better-known dancers paid only 15%, while the others had to hand over 30% of their earnings.[68] There was therefore a great temptation for the dancers to ask patrons to pay them cash directly so that they did not have to share it with a supervisor.

The taxi dancers also had obligations toward the dance hall in which they worked. They had to somehow get a minimum number of tickets daily. This minimum was equivalent to a value of 1,000 yuan in the 1940s. If they fell ill or needed to be absent themselves, they were required to purchase a minimum number of tickets with which to pay the supervisors.[69] It was therefore important for a taxi dancer to obtain a good place in the hall. For this, they were dependent on their *daban*. The way in which the dance halls were organized was not left to chance. The dancers were placed in the room according to seniority and their reputation, namely the income that they brought to the establishment. In return, a favorable place naturally increased their chances of being approached and of increasing their customers. The girls most in demand (the "reddest" of them) were placed in the most visible positions on either side of the orchestra.[70]

The fact that there were large numbers of taxi dancers and, at the same time, an insufficient number of patrons in the smaller establishments (cabarets, cafes, etc.) meant that the girls were not always able to make a livelihood and cope with the professional expenses on which their success partially depended. Many dancers turned to prostitution. Unlike professional prostitutes, the dancers did not accept all comers. They were entirely free in their choice of partners and enjoyed the former status of the courtesans in another form. As it turned out, the emergence of the dance halls helped undermine the function of the courtesans. During the Sino-Japanese War, many *changsan* turned to dancing.[71] There was a relative correspondence in time between the emergence of this new group of prostitutes and the accelerated decline of the courtesans.

The rate was not a fixed one when taxi dancers prostituted themselves. The price for a night was negotiated with the customer. Around 1919, it was about 30 to 50 yuan.[72] However, agreement on the part of the girl was generally preceded by various gifts in the form of additional tickets or even invitations to restaurants or amusement centers. The more a girl was in demand, the more demanding she became. In this respect, there was a situation that, all things considered, recalls the custom of the *huatou* that a courtesan imposed before she would allow a customer into her bed. For many, the status of the taxi dancers appeared to be similar to that of the prostitutes. In a society where separation between the sexes was the rule and where bodily contact (a necessity in dancing) was quite inconceivable, the dancers were seen to be girls of loose morals. It was probably exaggerated and unfair to liken them to prostitutes even if many of them did indeed prostitute themselves. However, the negative image attached to their profession only reinforced the general trend toward increasing debasement and "prostitutionalization."

The Condition of the Female Dancers: Taxi Dancers and Supervisors

Although the dancers had great freedom with regard to their customers, they came under strict discipline within the establishment. The proprietors of the dance halls were concerned with profit. This led them, on the one hand, to pressure the girls to dance with greater numbers of customers and, on the other hand, to ensure vigorously that the girls would not dance with customers *gratis* or pocket the money received for their services. Because they could not keep an eye on everything, the proprietors of the dance halls had supervisory staff officially known as "managers" (*guanliyuan*) – in fact, they were supervisors or *daban* in the jargon of the dance halls. These supervisors had originally been recruited to entice well-known dancers in the earlier days of unbridled competition between dance halls.[73] Around 1946, there were about two hundred of them in Shanghai's dance halls.[74] The *daban* had powers that enabled them to take advantage of the dancers, especially the little-known ones. They took a major share of the girls' earnings and also subjected them to threats and various forms of sexual harassment. The well-known dancers escaped this type of constraint because of the income that they brought in and the indirect protection that they got from their influential customers. Apart from their supervisory function, the *daban* played the role of middlemen by introducing customers to dancers. The police generally considered them to be hoodlums. The police reports of the 1940s noted that the individuals who performed these jobs were very mobile and went from one dance hall to another.[75]

The press reported their misdeeds on several occasions and especially highlighted the fact that they pushed dancers into prostitution.[76] This is probably why the Police Bureau decided to promulgate a decree banning their activities.[77] On August 7, 1946, a regulation prohibited the presence of this category of staff in the dance halls.[78] The proprietors of the dance halls reacted badly and put forward two arguments against the regulation: first, the fact that employees with their dependents (i.e., their families), amounting to several thousand individuals, were going to be thrown out of work and, second, the prospect of the financial loss to the dance halls if there was no one to supervise the customers, including the loss to the government that levied a tax on each ticket sold.[79] However, the Police Bureau had made a methodical inquiry in each district and consulted every police station. They therefore did not budge from their position, asserting that the *daban*'s trade was not an upright one (*bu zhengdang zhiye*) and could not be authorized.[80]

The supervisors themselves formed an association and argued in defense of their profession. They contested the charge that they were exploiters and pointed out their role in collecting taxes by preventing customers from evading the ticket system. They even sent a delegation to plead their cause at the town hall. They found a defender in the person of Wu Kaixian, director of the Social Affairs Bureau. In a letter sent to the police prior to the official prohibition, Wu Kaixian reproached them for their haste, repeating precisely the arguments employed by the dance-hall proprietors.[81] The dancing halls had argued that the *daban* had many dependents who relied on their labor. However, it is difficult to imagine that the elimination of the supervisors could have had very profound social effects in terms of employment.

All these arguments shook the mayor's conviction. On August 22, he asked the police to reconsider the matter and draft a new rule enabling the individuals concerned to preserve their jobs while at the same time bringing them under stricter controls. The police chief was intransigent and refused to yield to another order from the mayor a week later.[82] The proprietors of the dance halls, however, decided to circumvent the police decision.[83] They formally dismissed their "managers" and then recruited them again under a new designation.[84] The taxi dancers now came out in their own defense. The announcement of the prohibition of *daban* had been a cause for rejoicing on their part, especially with the prospect of having their incomes doubled. But the fact was that these women now actually came under the authority of these same supervisors employed under other names. Some of them did not resign themselves to this situation and even had the courage to publicly report irregularities. A group of girls working in Yezonghui, a small dance hall in Hongkou, reported the presence of a supervisor after the ban. The police made an inquiry, punished the proprietor of the dance hall with a fine of 1,000 yuan, and forced him to dismiss the supervisor. The police reports nevertheless state that the dance halls appear to have complied with the rules. An investigation of seven establishments revealed only two infringements, but the number of dance halls visited is not sufficiently representative for any general conclusions to be drawn.[85]

The three professions examined here are symptomatic of modernity on the march affecting all fields of economic and social life. The rise of the forms of entertainment with which these professions were associated was an expression, in everyday life, of the intense social ferment that Shanghai experienced in the course of fifty years.[86] The social changes that had occurred since the nineteenth century had been radical in this respect. The public space (except for that of prostitution), which had been totally reserved for men occupying all the jobs in the different services, was literally invaded by women in the aftermath of the First World War (i.e., from 1919 onward). The social scene was thereby profoundly transformed, but this in no way changed the status and real condition of women. The public space continued to be dominated by men who merely permitted a greater female presence to assert (if not impose) itself in the sphere of services and desires. Nevertheless, this was a definite step forward in the slow march toward emancipation and toward the conquest of an image and status for women in the process of overturning tradition.

The phenomenon of the dance halls appears to reflect a profound change in sensibilities regarding sexuality. Although the relationship between the sexes was marked by a certain degree of formality and a fairly rigid segregation, the dance halls provided the experience of a special contact with a woman. There was undoubtedly a large measure of sensuality in the atmosphere of these establishments. Dancing made for a contact that was wholly forbidden and inconceivable outside this context. Furthermore, it provided immediate and instantaneous gratification by which an individual could entertain illusions and remove himself from reality while at the same time avoiding the stumbling block represented by the obligation to engage in sexual relations in the houses of prostitution. Apart from the aspect of cost, which was very moderate in the dance halls, this was, I believe, one of the keys to the success of these establishments. A patron could invite a girl without feeling oppressed by the kind of pressure that he might encounter in the other modes of entertainment: Nobody knew him, he did not have to worry about what the girl might think of him, and he was free to enjoy himself. Only customers who tried to set up special relationships with a taxi dancer had to give up this freedom.

The dance halls were a sort of in-between place, midway between social diversion and prostitution. They corresponded to a transformation of social life related especially to the emergence of middle classes and marked by a growing commercialization of leisure. The dance halls provided an intermediate space in which it was possible to express and satisfy a sensibility centered on sensuality rather than on raw sexuality. In a radically different context, these establishments created an environment where patrons could, as with the courtesans of the past, sleep with a girl after going through a process of conquest, albeit largely fictitious, and not merely by paying a madam her due. This experience was not limited to the elites. It was shared by a majority of customers who could thus momentarily remove themselves from a social order in which it was impossible for the two sexes to meet outside any formal framework or without the prospect of a commitment to marriage. In the United States, the success of the dance halls in the 1920s was related to the fact that they made it possible to break the isolation of migrants who were still poorly integrated into American society. This achievement found an unexpected transposition in China where these establishments, all things being equal, fulfilled the same function for males in a society that limited contact between men and women.

5
The Prostitute in the Twentieth Century: An Essay in Social Anthropology

Who were the prostitutes? This chapter attempts to address the question of the identity of the prostitutes, what social scientists call their sociological profile. The reconstruction of this crucial aspect of the sex trade often falters because of the fluidity of this milieu, its anonymity, and the clichés that blurred a complex reality. We have seen that there is a paucity of data on the origins of the women who were cast into the world of the courtesans. In the case of ordinary prostitutes, the documentation is even scantier. However, by collating various sources, I have been able to marshal a sufficient amount of evidence with which to attempt a portrait of this group in the twentieth century and, when the data permit it, to make excursions to the last decades of the last century. As it turned out, it is the press that has provided me with fairly interesting material here. This chapter will also question a few widely held assumptions about prostitution in China, especially some biases introduced by the sense of pity that many texts by contemporaries conveyed to the public. It will discuss the issue of agency, which Western historians have been keen to attribute to prostitutes in China. The first part of this chapter will consist of an attempt to quantify the prostitutes of Shanghai between 1871 and 1949. This issue needs to be elucidated, even if it be in small measure, in order to contrast this reality with the set of discourses and policies it generated. The second part will present various factors of identity, culminating in an essay on the modes by which girls entered and left the trade.

The Numbers Game: The Ranks of the Prostitutes

One of the questions that spring to mind in any study of the phenomenon of prostitution is that of their numbers – especially in Shanghai, where I have referred several times to the idea of an explosion of prostitution in the twentieth century. The truth is that this is a question to which it is practically impossible to furnish an answer. All historians of prostitution, even when they study countries with the most heavily regulated and bureaucratically controlled systems, have come up against the same difficulty: the extremely fluctuating and elusive nature of the sex trade. The statistics of the official registers have never been able to account for more than a section of the prostitutes. There was a more or less large fringe group of clandestine or so-called "sly" prostitutes whose numbers the police tried to estimate (with a view to putting an end to their activities), but their estimates were usually very approximate. There was also a population of casual prostitutes who were never (or rarely) included in the figures. Certain official reports in Shanghai count dancers, waitresses, and so on in the category of prostitutes. I have not included them here because, strictly speaking, they were not prostitutes (see Chapter 4). It might be added that the terminology changed as and when certain categories changed or disappeared. All the figures available on this subject therefore correspond to orders of magnitude.

In the case of Shanghai, these statistics are rather of the "less" precise variety. This is so first of all because the city was divided into three different administrations (International Settlement, French Concession, Chinese Municipality). There was no single census of prostitutes taken for the entire city. Inasmuch as the girls, to a certain extent, were geographically mobile within the city, it might be assumed that a proportion of them could have been counted twice. The second type of explanation for the absence of relatively reliable statistics is that, except in the French Concession, the authorities showed a lack of interest in the issue of prostitution. The Chinese authorities made no attempt to register the houses of prostitution for purposes of control. It may be that these girls were entered in the tax registers, but I have been unable to find any trace of even the smallest mention of them in the primary and secondary sources. The police in the International Settlement had a vice squad that monitored prostitution-related activities without trying to regulate prostitution. It was only between 1920 and 1925 that there was an operation to register the houses of prostitution and the girls (see Chapter 12).

The most promising archives are undoubtedly those of the French Concession, which have the advantage of duration. However, the municipal police were probably no more efficient than police departments elsewhere. It would seem, however, that the way in which the municipal police controlled activities of prostitution from the end of the nineteenth century to the 1920s was relatively sound and that its statistics were a fairly accurate reflection of reality. However, I would be less certain for the 1930s and 1940s when a real upward surge can be observed in clandestine prostitution. Thus, all that I have available are a few fragments of information from these archives. The figures that I shall present should therefore be viewed with a degree of skepticism.

I shall first of all paint a general picture of the nineteenth century, for which there is a source that is remarkable because it remains unique to this day, even if its range does not equal that of works by writers like Parent-Duchatelet for Paris or Lord Acton for London. It is a survey by Dr.

Henderson, the doctor who initiated an attempt to carry out health checks on prostitutes in the 1870s (see Chapter 11). In 1869, Dr. Henderson set about looking for information to back up his cause with the authorities. In the International Settlement, he identified a total of 463 establishments containing 1,612 prostitutes. In the French Concession, a survey by Dr. Massais, quoted by Henderson, counted 250 houses with 2,600 girls.[1]

By contrast, the category of common and intermediate prostitution comprised a very large number of establishments and girls. The data are very fragmentary. Wang Tao mentions several categories of establishments, some containing 30 to 40 prostitutes, but does not mention even approximate numbers of establishments. It is only when referring to the *siju* (private residences) that he puts forward the figure of 300 (see Chapter 3). A Chinese historian also mentions a figure of 200 *huayanjian* prostitutes around 1875, an estimate that appears to me to be too low.[2] If we take account of the different categories of establishments existing in the old city and in the suburbs (*siju, taiji, zhujia, caotai, huayanjian*, etc.), even on the basis of a hypothetically low figure of 400 establishments, we would obtain a minimum of 1,000 to 1,500 prostitutes around 1875. Toward the end of the century, one *traveler* estimated that there were 1,500 brothels in the entire city.[3] This would mean that the city of Shanghai as a whole had between 5,500 and 6,500 prostitutes.[4] This assessment is admittedly subjective. However, it is based on tangible elements. Given that there were 4,200 prostitutes counted in both settlements and that the count was probably incomplete, it would not be unreasonable to imagine that there were at least a good thousand prostitutes in the walled city and its suburbs, which had several hundreds of thousands of inhabitants in 1875.

The number of prostitutes in 1915 is known with greater precision, although there is no definite information on the way in which they were counted. These data come from an article in the press, written after inquiries with the vice squad of the International Settlement[5]; it therefore does not cover the French zone. According to this article, there were around 10,000 prostitutes (9,791) in the settlement. The number of *changsan* was estimated with a certain degree of precision because the author had personally made the rounds of the houses. There were 1,229 of them. The *yao'er* accounted for 505 individuals, the *huayanjian* establishments accounted for 1,080, the *yeji* accounted for 4,727, the Cantonese prostitutes (*xianshuimei*) accounted for 250, and the *dingpeng* accounted for 30.[6] Up until 1918–1919, these figures were repeated constantly and at times even attributed to the year 1918. A population of 10,000 prostitutes for the International Settlement alone does not appear to be unusual. It was probably greater inasmuch as the numbers of *yeji* were estimated by a rough count. As for the French zone, I do not have the tiniest scrap of information for the period between 1869 (250 houses) and 1920 (114 houses).

Between 1920 and 1925, the policy of abolition at least had the effect of "revealing" the scale of the phenomenon of prostitution in Shanghai. The different estimates available lend further weight to the view that none of the surveys made was exhaustive. The Vice Committee set up by the Shanghai Municipal Council on the initiative of the Moral Welfare League counted 633 houses with 4,575 girls in 1920. According to the same report, the French Concession had 114 establishments with 478 prostitutes. These figures are far removed from reality. When the registration procedure was implemented in 1920, the police counted 1,771 houses (the fact is that not all of them had applied for registration), while the French archives gave a figure of 222.[7] If the same average ratio of prostitutes as that established by the Vice Committee's inquiry (7 girls per establishment) is applied to the number of establishments, we obtain 12,400 and 1,550 prostitutes, respectively giving a total of nearly 14,000 individuals. Here again, these are figures that need to be revised upward as a large number of "sly" prostitutes evaded registration, especially among the *yeji*. The total probably ranged from 15,000 to 20,000.[8]

For the next three decades, it becomes even more difficult to assess the number of prostitutes except in the French Concession. In 1928, a Chinese student wrote in his master's dissertation that the two settlements contained 805 establishments of prostitution with 5,100 prostitutes.[9] The figure appears to me to be low, because two years earlier another source gave 4,000 to 5,000 prostitutes for the French Concession alone.[10] In this source, the number of houses of prostitution dropped continually until 1936. Their numbers fell from 196 in 1922 to 108 in 1930, 90 in 1933, 50 in 1936, 51 in 1937, and 43 in 1938.[11] As for the number of girls, it was 1,200 in 1931 and 434 in 1937. However, for 1937, the number of sly prostitutes was assessed at 1,370.[12] For the International Settlement, there are the most whimsical estimates. For example, there was Luo Qiong, who very roughly put the number of prostitutes at 100,000 in 1935.[13] The Shanghai Municipal Council gave a low estimate of 5,000 prostitutes to the delegates of the League of Nations in 1931.[14] In 1937, the Chinese representative at the conference of central governments in Asia gave the figure of 20,000 girls, while a report by several feminine organizations in Shanghai estimated the number of prostitutes in the International Settlement alone at 25,000.[15]

These figures are probably underestimated. If they are compared with the number of arrests for soliciting, which amounted to thousands for the International Settlement alone (see Chapter 3), it would mean that, in the case of the former figure (of 5,000), there were more arrests than there were prostitutes in the city and that in the case of the latter figure (of 20,000), an average of only one girl in three was arraigned by the police. Arrests for soliciting or unlicensed prostitution also went into the thousands in the French Concession in 1933–1934.[16] Official and unofficial statistics actually show their limits and offer a very confused view of "reality." On the basis of accounts in the press and guidebooks and of what is known elsewhere about Shanghai's economic and social context in the 1930s, I would think that the number of prostitutes was in the region of 30,000. Here again, this is a piece of information that remains subjective.

The waters are muddied once again in the period of the Japanese occupation by the upheavals provoked by war and the sudden changes in the city's administrative organization. War conditions had a negative effect on prostitution even if the special deleterious climate created by the local puppet governments provided new opportunities in certain zones such as Western Shanghai. In 1939, the annual report of the Shanghai Municipal Council put the number of *shuyu* at 4,617. This amounts to an incredible leap when compared with the 562 prostitutes counted in 1931, even if it is assumed that increasing numbers of prostitutes were acquiring a legal right to exercise their trade by this means.[17] Two Japanese reports give figures of 5,232 and 7,028 prostitutes, respectively, for 1942 and 1943. These figures represent only girls registered with the authorities.[18] It is difficult to imagine such a substantial drop in the number of prostitutes, but the fact is that living conditions in Shanghai deteriorated terribly after 1941. However, I would give little credence to the idea that the numbers had ebbed to such a low level, even if I am unable to make even a rough guess here.

The years of the civil war were marked in Shanghai by an unprecedented growth of prostitution. The conflict between the Communists and the Nationalists pushed millions of persons out of their homes. They generally sought refuge in the big cities, hoping to find greater security and job opportunities. These refugees included many women, by themselves as well as accompanied, who discovered that nothing and nobody awaited them. The ranks of the prostitutes were therefore singularly swelled by these successive waves of refugees. The Chinese authorities, which tried to impose a system of regulation, managed at best to register 10,000 women in 1948. According to a doctor who was well aware of local conditions because he was in charge of the local venereal disease clinic for prostitutes, this figure had to be put at 50,000, or even 100,000 if casual prostitutes were included.[19] It is clear that while the official census does not reflect the reality, the figures given by Yu Wei, chief doctor of the Venereal Disease Center, appear to be excessively high. In January 1949, when the city came under the Communist rule, the Public Security Bureau estimated that there were still 30,000 women living by prostitution.[20]

On the general trend of prostitution, I would adopt the figures of Table 5.1, which give an idea of the scale of the phenomenon during different periods.

Although it might appear to be a futile exercise, many authors have sought to emphasize the seriousness of the situation by relating the number of prostitutes to the number of inhabitants. No observer of the period has mentioned a reality that nevertheless was obvious: the major imbalance between the sexes within the population. The way in which

Table 5.1. *Approximate numbers of prostitutes (1875–1948)*

Year	Numbers
1875	5,500 6,500
1915	10,000–15,000
1920	15,000–20,000
1930	30,000
1940	Undetermined
1948	50,000

prostitution prospered was closely linked to this factor, which was peculiar to the Chinese cities and hardly existed on the same scale in Western cities. It was common, up to the 1940s, for men to work in the city as bachelors and return to their village to get married. They would then come back to the city, leaving their women and children in the country. The censuses taken by the Shanghai Municipal Council in the International Settlement show that, between 1870 and 1900, there were twice as many men as women. The gap gradually narrowed, but in 1935 there were still 156 men for every 100 women. In the French Concession, the trend was similar in every respect. No information is available for the Chinese-administered part of the city, which was the largest sector in the nineteenth century. Nevertheless, it is likely that the same imbalance existed there because, from 1929 to 1936, there were still 130 men for 100 women in this zone.[21]

The presence of a large population of prostitutes in Shanghai can be explained partly by this demographic factor. However, it may be asked if the ratio between prostitutes and the population actually changed during this period. The report by the Vice Committee in 1920 established the fact that Shanghai had one of the world's highest levels of density, with one prostitute per 147 inhabitants in the settlements and one per 300 inhabitants for the city as a whole.[22] It is more relevant to relate the numbers of prostitutes to the size of the adult female population and of the adult male population.[23] According to these calculations, there was one prostitute per 30 women in 1875, one per 43 in 1915, one per 35 in 1920, and one per 28 in 1947, giving a rate of 2.3% to 3.6% of the female adult population. If we take a number of 100,000 for 1947, we get an even higher rate: one prostitute per 14 women, or 7.1%. In any case, prostitutes represented only a minute and relatively stable percentage of the population. As for their ratio to the male adult population, there was one prostitute per 45 men in 1875, one per 48 in 1915, one per 45 in 1920, and one per 34 in 1947. There was no real appreciable change except in 1947. The population of prostitutes followed the trends for the population as a whole.

Table 5.2. *Native province of the prostitutes (1941–1948)*

Province	1941	1942	1946	1946–1948
Jiangsu	94	71	530	41
Shanghai	30	14	202	15
Zhejiang	56	46	384	37
Guangdong	8	11	59	3
Shandong	2	7	2	—
Anhui	2	0	5	3
Sichuan	—	2	0	—
Fujian	—	—	3	—
Hunan	—	—	2	—
Hubei	—	—	7	—
Hebei	—	—	22	2
Guizhou	—	—	—	2
Foreigners	3	10	91	—
Total:	195	161	1,307	103
Percentage				
Jiangsu	48.2	44.1	40.5	39.8
Shanghai	15.4	8.7	15.4	14.6
Zhejiang	28.7	28.6	29.4	36.0
Guangdong	4.1	6.9	4.5	2.9
Shandong	1.0	4.3	0.2	—
Anhui	1.0	0.0	0.4	2.9
Sichuan	—	1.2	—	—
Fujian	—	—	0.2	—
Hunan	—	—	0.2	—
Hubei	—	—	0.5	—
Hebei	—	—	1.7	1.9
Guizhou	—	—	—	—
Foreigners	1.6	6.2	7.0	—
Total:	100.0	100.0	100.0	100.0

Sources: (1941 and 1942) Weekly reports, August 1941 and March 1943, police archives, file 1-4-125; (1946) Shanghai shi jingchaju sanshiwu nian tongji nianbao, 1947, p. 76; (1946–1948) analysis of police reports, police archives, 1945–1949; (1950) He Wannan and Yang Jiezeng, *Shanghai changji gaizao shihua*, p. 64.

The Geographical Origins of the Prostitutes

In terms of provincial origin, there is relative homogeneity between the different existing surveys that cover the 1920s–1940s. They show, however, that a large majority of the prostitutes were natives of the provinces of the lower Yangzi (see Table 5.2). Jiangsu topped the list, with an average of 40% to

50% of the prostitutes. Zhejiang accounted for around 30%, while Shanghai took third place with 15%. The other provinces taken individually had low representation. Only Guangdong stands out with 5% of the girls. Shanghai therefore was a central pole of attraction for women from the surrounding region. The market of prostitution was a veritable maw that was fed with external inputs. These data also belie the idea that there was a traffic in women from distant regions, even if it often turned out to be the case that women from the lower Yangzi were sold in places as far away as Manchuria (see Chapter 7).

My samples on the respective contribution of the southern (Jiangnan) and northern (Jiangbei) regions of Jiangsu to the ranks of the prostitutes are not as complete. I have the results of analyses (by Chinese research workers) of 220 files on prostitutes arrested after 1950 as well as police reports on 72 cases listed between 1946 and 1948. Both these sources show that the proportion of girls from Jiangnan was far higher than that of the natives of Jiangbei. These samples are very limited, but they corroborate my conclusions after studying the traffic in women where women from Jiangnan were always to be found in a larger proportion. The idea that Jiangbei women were predominant among the lower-class prostitutes, especially the *yeji* – an idea that was in vogue among most observers of the period and is being repeated by historians today – needs to be reconsidered.[24] Contemporary observers tend to greatly despise this lower category of prostitutes, and it is not surprising that it was included in the Jiangbei group or that this label was attached to it.[25]

The Age Groups

The prostitutes formed a particularly young age group. In the twentieth century, after 1915–1920, there are no longer any cases, as there had been earlier, of prostitutes who had barely reached puberty. Even among the courtesans, because the sexual function now took priority over other matters, the average age was higher (see Table 5.3). My data relate to the 1940s except for the *changsan*, for whom the French archives contain material from the 1920s. Nearly three-fourths of the courtesans were aged sixteen to eighteen. Very precisely half of them were not older than seventeen. This is exceptional as shall be seen below even if the *changsan* were, on average, older than their counterparts in the previous century (see Chapter 1).

The presence of very young girls in the houses of prostitution is a proven fact up to around 1925. This does not mean that the phenomenon totally disappeared after this date, but the press no longer mentioned it. After 1906, the presence in brothels of "minors" under fifteen (the threshold that was later raised to sixteen) became illegal in the two foreign settlements. I have noted twenty-seven cases that came before the courts between 1909 and 1924. In all, forty-one minor girls (including twenty-seven for whom the age

Table 5.3. *Age structure of a group of 77 courtesans (1923)*

Age	Number	Percentage
16	16	21
17	22	29
18	18	23
19	9	12
20	4	5
21	2	3
22	1	1
23	1	1
24	1	1
25	2	3
27	1	1
Total:	77	100

Source: Archives of the Director of Administrative Services. File 1934 25 MS 1554.2.

is given) were taken out of these establishments and placed in charitable institutions, the majority of them with the Door of Hope.

All the prostitutes belonged to age groups well above the sixteen-year legal limit. I have taken five counts, which were very different in terms of numbers and years considered (see Table 5.4). The 15–20 age group represented about a fifth to a quarter of the numbers of prostitutes except in 1946. These were girls registered with the police, and the oldest and most experienced among them were probably skilled in the art of evading the eye of the authorities. The 21–25 age group comprised practically half of the population of prostitutes in almost every case except in the figures for 1950, which were based on statements made by prostitutes arrested between 1951 and 1957 about their age of entry into prostitution. The figures undoubtedly include a higher proportion of female refugees who had become prostitutes at an advanced age. It is quite surprising to note that more than 18% of these women were aged 36 to 50+, whereas in the other counts this age group accounted for only 5% to 8% of the total. There is the same difference for the 26–30 age group, which accounted for 10% to 14% of the total number of prostitutes, except in the 1950–1958 survey. On the whole, the population of prostitutes was young and even very young even if there were no longer any girls under fifteen to be found in the 1940s. A repressive policy, changes in moral standards, and an increase in demand contributed to raising the average age of this population.

Given the young age of the prostitutes, the majority of them were unmarried. However, my data probably do not reflect the conditions of the prewar

Table 5.4. *Age structure of prostitutes in Shanghai*

Age	1941	1942	1946	1946–1948	1950–1958
Below 15	—	—	—	1	24
16–20	51	49	518	43	1,551
21–25	97	84	612	50	2,083
26–30	25	22	129	16	1,558
31–35	7	8	48	2	994
36–40	3	3	—	—	553
41–45	12	6	—	—	419
46–50	—	—	—	—	259
Over 50	—	—	—	—	72
Total:	195	172	1,307	112	7,513
Percentage					
Below 15	—	—	—	0.9	0.3
16–20	26.2	28.5	39.6	38.4	20.6
21–25	49.7	48.8	46.8	44.6	27.7
26–30	12.8	12.8	9.9	14.3	20.7
31–35	3.6	4.7	3.7	1.8	13.2
36–40	1.5	1.7	—	—	7.4
41–45	6.2	3.5	—	—	5.6
46–50	—	—	—	—	3.5
Over 50	—	—	—	—	1.0
Total:	100.0	100.0	100.0	100.0	100.0

Sources: (1941 and 1942) Half-yearly reports, August 1941 and March 1943, police archives, file 1-4-125; (1946) Shanghai shi jingchaju sanshiwu nian tongji nianbao, 1947, p. 76; (1946–1948) analysis of police reports, police archives, 1945–1949; (1950) He Wannan and Yang Jieceng, *Shanghai changji gaizao shihua*, p. 64.

years. In 1948, out of a sample of 500 prostitutes, 65% said they were unmarried, 32% married, and 3% divorced.[26] The high proportion of married women can be explained by the particular circumstances created by the civil war when there was a massive influx of population and many refugee women became prostitutes. The statistics prepared between 1951 and 1958 lend greater weight to this view. Out of 7,513 prostitutes questioned, 35% said they were unmarried, 54% married, and 11% divorced.[27] The proportion of married women is surprising, but we need to be able to consult the archives in order to be sure of this figure. The fact that these women had married status does not mean that they had husbands. Sixty-five percent of the married women (that is, 20% of the sample) were widows.[28] A more limited survey of 272 prostitutes interned after 1951 shows that 64 (23%) of them were orphans, including 49 who were fatherless or had lost both parents, and 77 (28%) were divorced.[29] The great majority of the prostitutes

Table 5.5. *Educational levels of Shanghai
prostitutes*

Level	1946	1949	1950
Illiterate	1,125	1,161	6,874
Primary	182	163	413
Secondary	—	20	225
University	—	—	1
Total:	1,307	1,344	7,513
Percentage			
Illiterate	86	86.4	91.5
Primary	14	12.1	5.5
Secondary	—	1.5	3.0
University	—	—	0.0
Total:	100.0	100.0	100.0

Sources: (1946) Shanghai shi jingchaju sanshiwu nian
tongji nianbao, 1947, p. 76; (1949) Zhou Yijun et al., "Xin
shehui ba gui biancheng ren: shanghai gaizao changji
shihua," p. 46; (1950) He Wannan and Yang Jieceng,"
Shanghai changji gaizao shihua, p. 87.

were single women, who were more vulnerable and more unsettled. Before
entering the trade, 57% of the 272 prostitutes mentioned above had lived
with one to three partners, which was very unusual in the Chinese social
context.

Whatever their origin, whether rural or urban, the prostitutes came from
the lower classes, as can be seen from their low level of education (see Table
5.5). In the 1940s, when education for girls was no longer the exception as
in the past, 86% to 90.5% of the prostitutes were illiterate. The proportion
of those who had been to primary school varied to a greater extent,
although only one census – the one for 1950–1958 – underestimates the
number of girls who had been to primary school and increases the proportion of those who had been to secondary school.

The prostitutes as a rule had had no professional activity before their
entry into prostitution. According to a 1948 survey, 64% stated that they
had never been employed in jobs. Those who had worked could be divided
into peasants (14%), household servants (8%), and workers (9%).[30] A
majority of prostitutes passed, without transition, from the status of women
attached to families (parents or husbands) to that of prostitutes. It was
therefore not life in the city or the experience of trades making for greater
contact with street life that brought these women into prostitution. The

passage was swift and even sudden. Many women came to Shanghai in the 1940s with the illusion of being able to find jobs, and then they found after some months or weeks that they had to prostitute themselves in order to survive. There is abundant testimony to this effect in the police archives. The usual cliché of the poor peasant forced into prostitution must be modified. Unfortunately, the percentages given in my source are mutilated, probably by a printer's devil. Only 37% of the prostitutes are said to have come from peasant families, while 28% came from merchant families. The proportion of girls from working class families is estimated at 5%, and that of girls whose parents had no profession is estimated at 8%.[31]

Reasons for Entry into Prostitution

The causes of prostitution were the central issue in all discussions on this subject from 1919 to 1949. Almost every author of this period who wrote on the subject provided his own explanations, which revolved around a few stereotyped images, especially poverty in the countryside or the absence of professional alternatives, lack of education, and so on. Contemporary historians have often adopted these notions, especially the view that there were no professions open to women before the industrialization that came about in the second decade of the twentieth century.[32] In my view, this is a false problem or at least a wrong way of stating the problem. Poverty apart, contemporary Chinese historians point to the role of foreigners, especially to the "abnormal" growth of Shanghai after Western imperialistic aggression as well as reactionary republican regimes such as the Nationalist government.[33] Prostitution has even been seen by some as a deliberate means of weakening the people's capacity to resist.[34] In this respect I would agree with Kingsley's long-standing but still relevant view that the search for "causes" of prostitution is irrelevant.[35]

The question of the absence of an alternative does not appear to me to be truly relevant. The trades open to women were certainly not numerous, and they were poorly paid: servants, nurses, household employees, waitresses in bars, and so on. Prostitution, on the contrary, made for higher earnings, at least for those who were not bonded. However, given the choice, most women would have probably chosen a less well-paid occupation rather than enter prostitution. It was therefore not a question of money that prevented a girl from going from an honorable occupation or from a state of unemployment into prostitution but a question of morality. If indeed prostitution was economically so advantageous, then we might ask why so few women became prostitutes, given the real or supposed poverty of the Chinese countryside. What were the specific reasons and circumstances of their entry into prostitution? Whatever the method used, the answers here can only be full of gaps. In the Tables 5.6 and 5.7, I have marshaled data from four different sources.

Table 5.6. *The causes of entry into prostitution*

(a)	1941		1942	
Causes and Circumstances	Number	Percentage	Number	Percentage
Poverty	177	90	172	79
Death of husband	11	6	4	2
Divorce	1	1	5	2
Orphaned without family	6	3	—	—
Economic difficulties	—	—	36	17
Total:	195	100	217	100

(b)	
Causes and Circumstances	1948 Percentage
Poverty	60
Loss of job, sudden ruin	18
Deliberate choice	13
Family presssure	5
Deceived, abused	4
Total:	100

(c)	Post–1949					
Causes and Circumstances	Number	Average	Peasants	Servants	Laborers	Jobless
Forced by life circumstances	113	41.7%	42.4%	54.6%	45.6%	35.4%
Deceived	46	16.9%	20.3%	30.3%	8.5%	11.5%
Sold	21	7.9%	3.4%	0.0%	0.0%	14.6%
Deliberate choice	91	33.5%	33.9%	15.1%	45.9%	38.5%
Total:	271	100.0%	100.0%	100.0%	100.0%	100.0%

(d)	1951	
Causes and Circumstances	Number	Percentage
Sold or pledged by family or husband	56	11.2
Family or husband deceased, jobless	199	39.7
No income	16	3.2
Ill treatment by family or husband	49	9.8
Deceived, kidnapped	47	9.4
Unhappy marriage, divorce, separation	88	17.5
Deliberate choice	17	3.4
Other causes	29	5.8
Total:	501	100.0

Sources: Police archives. Special Municipality of Shanghai (1937–1945), file 1-4-125; Yu Wei, "Shanghai changji wu bai ge an diaocha," p. 12; Lu Feiyun, Zhang Zhongru, "Shanghai jiefang chuqi de jinü gaizao gongzuo", p. 128; He Wannan, Yang Jieceng, *Shanghai changji gaizao shihua*, p. 61.

The data relate above all to the 1940s. Table 5.6(a) indicates that, in the case of more than 90%, it was poverty that brought them into prostitution. The other factors given throw light instead on the specific modalities of impoverishment and descent into conditions of economic precariousness. Table 5.6(b) also to a very great extent emphasizes the economic causes, although it begins to suggest the role of external circumstances or factors (such as family reasons or deception). The category of "deliberate choice" is ambiguous because it could mean "choice without external violence" as well as "deliberate choice" without economic reasons. Table 5.6(c) is based on an analysis of the files of 272 prostitutes arrested after 1949. It is closer to reality even if the nature of the categories is different. Poverty is the major reason here, too, if the term "forced by life circumstances" is inter- preted in this way. In this respect it may be noted that there is no differ- ence between the different categories of women. There are variations in the other reasons cited. Many, especially among peasants and servants, had been deceived. Few of them had been sold except in the "unemployed" cat- egory, which appears to be very vague.

Table 5.6(d) is based on files on the first group of 501 girls interned in 1951. It has the advantage of spelling out the factors covered by the heading "forced by life circumstances." More than half pertains to poverty (to which the first three categories correspond). Girls who had been deceived form a smaller proportion than in Table 5.6(c). However, a survey of 1,259 girls gave a rate of 17.5%, which was perhaps closer to reality.[36] The number of girls who had been sold or pledged is small. This lends credence to the idea that this practice had greatly diminished in the 1940s, at least in Shanghai. By contrast, it may be noted that there was a large contingent of women who had experienced unhappy marriages (entailing divorce, separation, or ill treatment) forcing them to lead solitary lives and encouraging their passage into prostitution. The notion of a deliberate choice expressed in Tables 5.6(c) and 5.6(d) remains ambiguous. The question is whether it must be interpreted as a choice "for want of alternatives in a critical economic situation." Inasmuch as we do not know how the questions were asked or how the Chinese authorities constructed their categories, it is hardly possi- ble to carry this analysis any further. Naturally, we cannot be satisfied with these explanations, although they provide some clues. There do not really exist any adequate sources to study this question. What Tables 5.6(a) to 5.6(d) show, however, is that the passage into prostitution was a phenome- non more complex than is generally seen in simplistic views of the subject. In the 1940s, the circumstances were many and varied. They resulted more often from accidents of fate than from any specific external intervention.

The economic crisis could have direct effects. A former temporary worker in a textile factory became a prostitute when the factory closed down.[37] A worker pledged his wife when he lost his job in a spinning mill.[38] A nineteen-year-old female worker in a textile factory in Hangzhou came to Shanghai with her husband's assent in the expectation of a better-paid job. She stayed in a small hotel with a friend, also a female worker from Hangzhou. There, a servant offered to find them housing, which turned out to be in a brothel.[39] Two girls from Huzhou, apprehended in a clandestine house, said they had had been led into prostitution by the proprietor of this house after having come to Shanghai in search of work.[40] A seventeen-year-old girl from Jinhua resolved to enter prostitution with the connivance of hotel waiters when she failed to find a job.[41] Many women came with the idea of taking jobs as servants with families. When they had used up their meager funds and found themselves to be all alone, they allowed themselves to be pressured into taking up residence in one place or another where they would be propositioned into becoming prostitutes.[42]

The time spent as a prostitute could range from some months to some years. There are no specific details on this subject for the 1940s, which are not the most representative period. This decade was characterized by a major influx of females and a very significant increase in the number of prostitutes. According to a survey in 1948, more than half (56%) of the prostitutes had been in the trade for less than a year. As for the rest, most of them (42%) had had less than five years' experience. Only 2% admitted that they had been prostitutes for more than five years. In fact, more than 80% of the girls said they had come to Shanghai less than four years earlier.[43] The author explains the large number of novices by wartime conditions, economic crisis, and the resulting social instability. Because the girls did not know how to protect themselves against venereal disease, they were physical wrecks within one or two years of entering prostitution.

It would be interesting to know how the girls perceived their condition as prostitutes. There can be no doubt that there were great differences between the courtesans and the ordinary prostitutes and between those who exercised this activity freely and those who had been sold into it. It is also certain that there were great changes in the course of time, resulting in an increasing debasement of the image and status of the prostitute. The only "direct" testimony we have comes from the answers given by 500 prostitutes in 1948. A majority of them (56%) said they were satisfied with their condition. Nearly a quarter of the girls (23%) expressed their dissatisfaction in clear terms, while the others had no opinion. Half of the prostitutes were not thinking of changing their line of activity, although they did hope to meet a rich man, marry him, and start a family. The prospects of working in a factory hardly aroused any enthusiasm, especially because factory wages were low. They preferred the lives that they were leading and were rather apprehensive of prohibitory measures that might deprive them of their sole means of subsistence.[44]

The Fate of the Prostitutes

What ultimately happens to prostitutes is a question that intrigues the historian. In the case of the Chinese, it was not easy to escape the prostitute's condition, especially for those girls, whether pledged or sold, whose earnings were expropriated by the madam, the brothel owner, and servants. Just as in the case of the courtesans, marriage was not an impossible dream, although it occurred less frequently and did not always offer the same prospects of a comfortable life. In any case, money had to be paid to the madam. If the prostitute (or her customer) could not find the wherewithal, their only way out was to take flight with whatever clothing and jewelry they could carry. Assuming that the prostitutes did not remain active for more than ten years, the question must be asked as to what became of them. I shall first of all examine the different modalities possible. Then, with the customary reservations, I shall present some information of a more general nature that might shed light on the way in which women made their exit from the cycle of prostitution.

Making an exit from the trade by purchasing one's own way out is not mentioned in my sources except for the nineteenth century. The articles that relate these facts are unfortunately very brief. It is known, however, that the women involved were really prostitutes and not courtesans. The sums of money that were paid out leave no doubt here. In September 1872, two prostitutes bought their freedom for 30 and 100 yuan, respectively.[45] In 1879, Yan Youzhen tried to negotiate her departure for 100 yuan. She reckoned that, in five years of work, she had brought in more than 3,000 yuan.[46] The madams would put obstacles in the way of the girls' departure (whether it was when they tried to buy their freedom or when a customer wanted to marry one of them), or they would try to raise the price, which would occasionally provoke loud quarrels.[47] It always came down to a question of money because the madams would try to exploit their charges to the fullest possible extent, especially when they were young and able to attract many customers.

Fleeing was another way out, although it was not always recognized as a legitimate means of escaping prostitution by the Chinese authorities in the nineteenth century. The girls would escape alone – like Zhao Lingshi, who took advantage of a moment of distraction to slip out of the brothel where she had been held and run to the station. She was chased in the street by the madam, who was finally arrested by the police.[48] Girls who fled would turn toward the authorities, especially the police or the Door of Hope, a rescue organization for prostitutes (see Chapter 14).[49] More frequently, the prostitutes had an accomplice, generally a customer with whom they hoped to get married or take up residence. This was a risky venture because the madams, aided by their employees and their husbands or lovers, would institute searches among the girls' habitual customers. Very often, they even went to the extent of seeking help from the authorities. Two sisters who had been pledged to a *huayanjian* took advantage of a trip to the temple to run away with two former customers. The *guinu* of the establishment found them and informed the police.[50] Because these two girls were being held against their will, the Chinese magistrate sentenced the brothel owner to have her establishment shut down, but the two customers each received 200 bamboo lashes.[51] In another case, the judges were more lenient toward the customer. A prostitute who had escaped after eight years in an establishment was recognized a few months later in the street, in the company of her partner, by the *guinu* of her former house. An argument broke out and led to the arrest of the three parties concerned. This time it was the *guinu* who was condemned to 200 bamboo lashes, while the girl was placed in a charitable institution pending marriage.[52]

The attitude of the Chinese judges was ambiguous, although they seem to have adopted the principle of upholding respect for mutual obligations. Running away in order to get married without paying compensation to the madam, or as a means of escaping indebtedness, was not accepted by the Chinese magistrates. In 1879, a prostitute who had fled with a man she wished to marry was arrested en route, probably following a complaint by the madam, and sentenced to return to the house of prostitution after being given 40 slaps. Her companion received the heavy punishment of 700 bamboo lashes.[53] In 1910, it was a hairdresser who hid a *huayanjian* in his home. The *guinu* discovered them and appealed to the law. The hairdresser was sentenced to 200 bamboo lashes.[54] I have found several cases where the police arrested prostitutes attempting to flee with customers.[55]

The madams themselves would appeal to the law in order to get back a girl who had fled or to obtain payment from a customer who had not met his commitments.[56] Zhang Shaoqing married a prostitute, promising to pay the madam 300 yuan on the Chinese New Year. On the promised day, while the couple was already living together, the madam came to ask for her due. As Zhang could not (or did not wish to) pay, the madam took the matter to the police who arrested Zhang. The court released the madam, sentenced Zhang to pay 40 yuan, and placed the prostitute in a charitable institution. In this case, ultimately each party got satisfaction, even if it was partial.[57]

Xu Xiaobao, who had been a prostitute for six years in a house to which she had been pledged, initiated legal proceedings against a madam who barred her departure even after a customer wishing to marry her had repaid the sums that she owed. The judge gave his approval to the marriage and ordered the customer to hand over 20 yuan in full and final payment of all debts in order to get Xu Xiaobao back.[58] One Jin Fengyao accused a madam of not letting her go even when her time of bondage had ended and of demanding money to compensate for her training. Jin had wanted to marry a former customer after eight years of prostitution.[59] Another prostitute, Li

Fengxian, was able to get married against payment of a sum of 100 yuan to the madam, while the latter asked for four times more from the customer who was hoping to marry Li.[60] It was not rare for a girl to ask the courts for permission to "mend her ways" (*congliang*) in order to marry a customer when her status (as an enslaved prostitute) left her with little hope, or on the grounds that she had been forced into prostitution.[61]

The prostitutes were considered as individuals without rights, as perhaps was the case with women in general, and they had to submit to the power of the magistrates. Hua Liqing, a sixteen-year-old prostitute, appealed to the courts to be allowed to marry a customer who had agreed to pay her debts. The judge dealing with the case decided to call in another customer who also wished to marry the girl (but had been rejected by her).[62] How this case ended is not known, but it illustrates the range of the powers that a magistrate had over the lives of prostitutes in the nineteenth century. Very often a magistrate would place a prostitute seeking to leave her trade in a charitable institution (whether she had a suitor or not).[63] Whatever the outcome of the trial, the women concerned never recovered their individual freedom. They were always handed over to a person (a husband, parents,[64] etc.) or to an institution (a place of refuge or the very establishment from which she had escaped).

Marriage, as can be seen from most of the cases seen here, offered the prostitutes an exit. In Chinese cities, the members of certain social classes were far too poor to hope to find wives. Others had professional occupations that were socially despised. It was in these classes that the prostitutes, who had hardly any long-term prospects other than old age, illness, and beggary, found a potential market of men who were less demanding and accepted their past. It was generally in the houses of prostitution that these men made the acquaintance of those whom they would decide to marry. There are a number of court cases that occasionally suggest that the range of professions involved was fairly wide and included categories that were not at the bottom of the social scale. An admittedly limited list reported in the press gives the following professions: merchant, cart-man, slaughter-house worker, rent collector, carpenter, hairdresser, and policeman.[65] This list is indeed short but provides a glimpse of the range of individuals who could take wives from the world of the prostitutes.

This said, marriage could prove to be an unpleasant surprise. Some customers would purchase a girl from an establishment of prostitution to obtain a temporary companion or a concubine, and this could happen even in social groups that did not form part of the elite. In one case that was brought to the police, a prostitute and her mother asked that a search be made for an individual who, having taken a prostitute as his concubine and promised to repay her 1,000-yuan debt to her former establishment, had suddenly disappeared a few months later after paying only 350 yuan. The mother and daughter appealed to the authorities as the brothel was trying

Table 5.7. *Reasons for leaving prostitution*

Reason	Number
Return to the village	4
Return to the village because of illness	2
Return to the village to care for a sick relative	7
Unexplained departure	2
Marriage (*congliang*)	8
Deliberate departure	3
Total:	26

Source: Report by the Taishan district police station, undated, police archives. Municipality of Shanghai (*Shanghai shi jingchaju*) 1945–1949, file 011-4-270, December 1946–December 1948.

to force the girl to return to prostitution in order to pay the outstanding amount.[66] For others, it was the possibility of returning to the village that gave them the possibility of regaining an honorable social status. In 1899, Lan Xian, who had become a prostitute of her own accord, returned to her village with an uncle who found her a husband.[67]

If we can rely on the above data, the modalities of leaving the profession that were open to prostitutes in the nineteenth century were hardly any different from those available in the following century. An undated report (from around 1946 to 1948) by the Taishan district police station on cases of individuals voluntarily turning in their licenses provides a glimpse of the fate of the prostitutes. They were required to furnish reasons for giving up their professional activity. Half of the women in this report were returning to their villages for a variety of reasons, in particular to look after a father or mother who was ill (see Table 5.7). One-third of them gave marriage as the reason. Although the term used, *congliang*, is ambiguous, it generally designates an exit from the trade through marriage. These particulars cannot be taken literally because they are vague and also because they might have masked a passage into clandestine prostitution.

From the above information, it may be inferred that the prostitutes did not practice their trade throughout their lives. This is a self-evident fact, but I believe that it must be borne in mind. A great many books on prostitution in China bewail the condition of women who had been sold to madams without any hope of getting out of prostitution. In fact, they had market value only so long as they possessed some measure of beauty. Beyond a certain age, this value would crumble and the madam would have no further interest in keeping them with her. On the contrary, she could turn them over to customers in search of wives or concubines and thus get rid of them and replenish her workforce. This logic was applicable to the prostitutes as a group. But it did not rule out the possibility that, at the individual level, the *desiderata* of a girl or customer could come into conflict with the interests of a madam who might feel that a girl had not yet yielded a sufficient "return" to be able to leave by purchase or by marriage. This explains the conflicts that arose and the way in which they erupted into the domain of law.

Given the very large number of women who came to swell the ranks of prostitution in Shanghai, things could not have been otherwise. Even if our analysis is based on average figures of the numbers of prostitutes such as those given in Table 5.1 and on age groups where the over-thirties formed an insignificant proportion, it is clear that the world of prostitution was always being constantly and extensively replenished. It will never be possible to obtain a precise estimate because of the lack of clarity in the available quantitative data. If we imagine, for argument's sake, that the same girls continued to be active throughout the period going from 1875 to 1948, then there would have had to be 610 new recruits every year to make the numbers of prostitutes rise from 5,500 to 50,000. But as we have seen, they remained in the trade for no more than ten years, and sometimes for even shorter periods. This means that thousands of women took to prostitution every year in Shanghai. It was also thousands of women who got out of prostitution in different ways.

The turnover of prostitutes was due partly to illness, both venereal and general, contracted in the course of a job that left little possibility of rest, was irregular, and most usually performed without the least recourse to hygiene, even in its most elementary forms. Illness is often mentioned in my sources. For lack of treatment, venereal diseases such as syphilis could have serious consequences, but I do not believe that it caused many deaths. On the other hand, many prostitutes had to leave the profession because of the ravages wrought by these illnesses, whose consequences they probably suffered to the very end of their lives. It must be added that, like the rest of the population, they were exposed to all the infectious (and often deadly) illnesses resulting from the absence of hygiene, vaccination, or proper diet. Death must also be considered as a factor in the disappearance of a proportion of the prostitutes. They were quite frequently at the receiving end of violence from the madams and clumsy or dissatisfied customers (some even went to the extent of using firearms). They were exposed to attacks by ruffians. Some chose to commit suicide (see Chapter 6). As for beggary, the numbers of those who lived by this activity would have probably been far greater if most of the prostitutes had ended their careers therein. Even if we take into account the numbers of deaths in service, it would seem that a good many prostitutes managed to get reintegrated into society, especially through marriage.

Shanghai, from the end of the nineteenth century to 1949, contained a very large population of prostitutes. Nevertheless, their numbers remained relatively constant in relation to the changing numbers of its inhabitants, except for the particular period of the civil war. The perception that contemporary observers had of the phenomenon of prostitution hardly matches this observation. In fact, there is no real contradiction. The absolute number of prostitutes is less important than (a) their concentration in certain districts up to the end of the 1930s, which made them more conspicuous, and (b) the changes that came about in their working practices, especially the rise of active soliciting in the streets. Seen from this angle, prostitution gave the impression of being an ubiquitous presence in the city and of being constantly on the increase. If the Civil War gave an indirect boost to the sex trade in Shanghai, the return to peace had the opposite effect. Within a few months of the Communist takeover in Shanghai in 1949, the number of prostitutes spontaneously returned to its low level of the 1930s. The effect of official warnings and exhortations cannot be ruled out, but the CCP did not act with any particular speed to adopt specific measures prohibiting prostitution. The years 1945–1949 were an aberration in the development of prostitution in Shanghai.

The portrait that emerges from the analysis of the above data does not diverge from commonly held view of prostitutes. They came from modest or poor origins. They were young but belonged to age groups normally encountered in this type of activity. Their educational level was low but hardly diverged from what might be seen in any general portrait of China's female population. On two points, however, my conclusions differ from those commonly put forward concerning Shanghai prostitutes. The first point relates to their geographical origin. My samples clearly show that the prostitutes came from the two provinces closest to Shanghai, namely, Zhejiang and Jiangsu. In this respect, they confirm the fact that the women who dwelt in the city's houses of prostitution were rootless and had, in most cases unwillingly, broken their ties with their native places. A closer examination has also shown that girls from Jiangsu were more numerous than those from Zhejiang, and especially that Jiangnan supplied a greater number of prostitutes than Jiangbei. This observation calls for two comments. The attraction that Shanghai might have exerted was probably stronger in this more commercialized part of the province where the means of communication were more numerous and efficient and encouraged movement by people. Besides, it is in this region that the population had the highest expectations and were more strongly motivated to try their luck in Shanghai. My second comment relates to the misrepresentation of reality that led observers in this period to identify those prostitutes most despised for their behavior, the *yeji*, with Shanghai's most despised population group, the natives of Jiangbei. If my conclusions on the geographical origin of the prostitutes are grounded, then we have a good example here of distortion through the dissemination of a dominant stereotyped discourse.

As for the prostitutes' social origins, my observations diverge sharply from the commonplace notions put out both in the press of the day and in current studies. Whatever the statistical series used, it appears that the peasants never formed the overwhelming majority of the prostitutes. There is perhaps a distortion here that is derived from the sources and the period being considered. I must acknowledge that my documentation is very meager in this respect. However, Chapter 7, which examines the traffic in women in China and in the lower Yangzi, notes the same overrepresentation of girls from a milieu that was more likely to be urban. Such a conclusion is not wholly surprising. In nineteenth-century France, prostitutes tended to come from the towns and small cities rather than the countryside.[68] If we leave out the girls who were kidnapped and sold against their will to the houses of prostitution, it is difficult to imagine that peasant girls who had sometimes come from very far places could have gone of their own accord, and without transition, from their thatched cottages to the bustling metropolis that was Shanghai in that age.

The fate of the prostitutes in many respects remains an enigma. The conditions and modes of entry into the trade were highly varied. This chapter has given only a glimpse, based on accounts by the prostitutes themselves, that will be amplified by a study of the traffic in women and children. The questionable quality of the answers given by the concerned parties itself results from the way in which the questions were asked (it would be no exaggeration to say that they were questions along the lines of "What made you become a prostitute"?). It confirms the idea that what we need to look for is not so much the causes as the circumstances that obliged tens of thousands of women in Shanghai alone to sell themselves in the market of prostitution.

For my part, I would emphasize two often complementary dimensions of this problem. Setting aside the place that can be assigned to kidnapping and the role of families in placing girls in the establishments of prostitution, entry into the trade was made rather by deliberate choice (this was true for a minority before the 1940s) or (as was most frequent) by chance. By this I mean that these women had initially aimed at a goal (they had been in search of employment or simply betterment) that they were subsequently unable to attain. They had limited resources available to them and were hardly equipped to cope with the pressures that were very soon exerted on them. Then they fell into prostitution. This said, and here we come to the second dimension, chance did not strike at random. Its victims tended to be lone and isolated women, widows and orphans, women looking for employment, and unemployed women, namely, women without ties. It cannot be denied that, well into the twentieth century, well after the inception of the emancipation movements in 1919, the Chinese woman remained a legal nonentity who could have no status or social recognition unless she was attached to a man, a family, or an institution. If she lost this protection through accident, illness, or any other circumstance, even a temporary one, then she became potential prey, liable to supply the stupendous "market in women," taken in the broad sense of the term, that flowed into Chinese society and of which prostitution formed the lower stratum.

Prostitutes did not remain irrevocably in their trade. Whatever the constraints placed on them and the exploitation to which they fell victim, they could not go beyond a certain "biological horizon." The madams had to be aware of this even if their logic required them to use the girls, when the latter were bonded to them, up to the last extremity. Although it is impossible to quantify this phenomenon (it would be necessary first of all to take into account those who died in "service" and those who came out of it in such a physical state that they had hardly any future other than in a home or as beggars), I believe that there was a movement of prostitutes out of the brothels that led to their reintegration into society. Even if their experience left its mark (especially in the aftereffects of venereal disease), the prostitutes, because they originally came from areas outside Shanghai, could return and become reintegrated into their local communities by remaining vague about the nature of their previous activities. Besides, the marriages that took place between prostitutes and men who were fully (and with good reason) in the know about their profession show that here, too, there was an exit. Even if there was a very significant difference in social level between the prostitutes and the courtesans, the former, like the latter, did benefit from the relative tolerance of the Chinese toward prostitution. Free of religious connotations, the Chinese view accepted the idea of full and complete "redemption" by virtue of the simple fact that a prostitute had stopped her activity. This did not make her an excellent match, but she could hope for a suitor from among those who had been left behind in the marriage race.

6
Sex, Suffering, and Violence

Up to a late period, and even up to 1949, Chinese prostitutes lived and worked in conditions that were quite unimaginable for the twentieth century. In Shanghai, which was in the vanguard of modernity in China, the prostitutes gradually gained freedom from the conditions of near servitude in which many of them, probably the majority, were trapped. In the preceding period, the girls had suffered often harsh conditions of surveillance, exploitation, and punishment. The courtesans had generally escaped this state of persecution and enjoyed favorable living conditions, although there had been exceptions. The ordinary prostitutes, on the contrary, had been obliged to yield to the demands of the madam and of the customer. When they did not provide satisfaction or if they tried to refuse certain requests, it was not rare for their refusal to result in various forms of violence.

Demands were made on the prostitutes for a variety of sexual services about which the sources, although limited, are slightly more precise than in the case of the courtesans. The information that I have been able to put together does not make for a clear picture of the sexual behavior of the Chinese in Shanghai in the twentieth century, but it does give a glimpse of the changing sexual culture of this huge cosmopolitan metropolis crisscrossed by numerous and varied currents. In the sexual field, it is impossible to determine the sources of influence at work. We can only confine ourselves to noting the emergence of new forms of behavior, at least in the sources. I shall return to this point. The girls were also exposed to a risk inherent in their trade, namely that of venereal disease. This is an important dimension because, as we shall see, neither the prostitutes nor their customers received treatment when they got infected. It is only in the 1940s that an effort was made to educate the girls and the customers regarding treatment for venereal infections. The consequences of this policy of *wuwei* for the Chinese population were particularly serious.

This chapter is about the darkest aspects of the prostitutes' condition. Whatever the angle of approach, I have not sought to exaggerate the picture but to give as clear an account as possible of the extreme harshness of life for the majority of prostitutes in Shanghai from the middle of the nineteenth century up to the 1940s. The prostitutes' trade was a highly risky activity, and few girls came out of it physically unscathed. This dimension, which is often emphasized by various authors in present-day China to underline the oppressive nature of capitalism and imperialism, deserves to be clarified in order to place the other facets of the world of prostitution in Shanghai in perspective.

Sexual Practices

The sexual practices of the prostitutes in the nineteenth century are hardly better known than are those of the courtesans. Wang Tao refers to them from time to time, but his remarks reveal above all his disdain for the girls of this category. The next century, especially in the period from the 1920s to the 1940s, saw the development of forms of conduct that appear to have been hitherto unknown. This said, the silence of the sources makes it rather difficult be quite sure about the novelty of these forms of behavior.

About the prostitutes who received sailors in the houses along the Huangpu, in the city's suburbs, Wang Tao notes that there were hardly any techniques that they did not practice.[1] This is obviously a vague way of putting it, but it sheds light, albeit weakly, on the varied nature of the supply and demand in the realm of sex. The question is what these "techniques" might have been. The twentieth century furnishes a few dertails. Around 1920, they were *xianrouzhuang* houses where the girls practiced the "*san mentou*"; that is, they agreed to receive customers by all "three doors".[2] These practices are confirmed by another source, which states that these houses tried to meet the demand from their customers. Each establishment thus had one or two girls who proposed special services – that is, fellatio and sodomy. These girls were often older than the others and agreed to these practices in order to get customers who otherwise would hardly come to them. They earned proportionately more out of it because these services cost more.[3] What this information indicates, if we read between the lines, is that prostitutes ordinarily would not comply with these requests.

These are accounts dating from the 1920s, at a time when it could be imagined that there was a change in moral attitudes in Shanghai, although the practices just mentioned do not appear to be truly novel when compared with the traditional erotic iconography.[4] Nowhere in the nineteenth-century sources have I found the slightest reference to "off standard" sexual behavior as can be found so often in works on prostitution in the West. In a case brought before the courts in 1921, it was reported that a man had made his wife submit to anal relations.[5] I would be hard put to cite the smallest instance of sadomasochism or any perversion. I feel as if I am on very shaky ground here because there is no way to prove that the silence of the sources did not result from a profound form of self-censorship on the part of those who controlled the written word. It is surprising, however, that absolutely nothing is mentioned in the literature or in the press.[6] Does this mean that the Chinese males who visited the houses of prostitution practiced a form of sexuality that, all things said and done, was quite simple and free of even minor perversions? I would tend toward this conclusion, although I am aware of the narrow confines of the documents available to me on which to base my interpretation.

However, there were clearly established cases of deviant behavior before 1949. Certain *xianrouzhuang* houses offered other special services, such as the organization of nude and live sex shows for voyeuristic customers sitting behind a glass. These shows could also be organized in hotel rooms for special customers, but then the fee was double.[7] In 1941, the police arrested five girls taking part in nude shows in a hotel at the corner between Hubei Road and Jiujiang Road right in the red-light district. They were being paid a daily wage of 3 to 8 yuan for participating in twelve shows. These girls were sentenced to fifty-nine days' imprisonment.[8] A police report in 1946 states that two minors under sixteen were made to perform with men in shows at which there were from one to five spectators who would pay 10,000 to 20,000 yuan each for the privilege.[9]

Another source reports the opening of three establishments called "theaters" (*xiyuan*) that offered striptease shows. One of them was in the old city, while the other two were on Yidingpan Road and Jing'an Road, to the west of the International Settlement. The girls who appeared in these shows were *yeji* whom the author describes as being neither beautiful nor artistic. All they were capable of doing was to make obscene movements on the stage.[10] When a customer arrived, he would choose one or more girls who would walk by in turn to the strains of three musical melodies. The house presented Chinese and Russian girls.[11] The customer could also sleep with a girl for a further payment of half the price of the show. It was even possible in Shanghai to attend shows involving bestiality (between women and dogs). A certain Zheng Xinzhai was arrested around 1926–1927, when he used underage girls to perform sex acts with dogs. He was sentenced to five years' imprisonment. The donkey was also called into play at shows arranged in a private house.[12] Usually, these shows were organized in hotel rooms after lengthy precautions had been taken against being caught by the police. Everything was arranged by telephone and by recommendation. In 1933, the entrance fee to a show of this kind would be 20 yuan.[13]

The frequency of sexual relations by prostitutes was extremely variable. A survey of 500 girls in 1948 indicates that about 12 customers a month was a mediocre figure. In fact, 212 prostitutes said that they received 10 to 30 customers a month, and 78 mentioned 30 to 60 encounters. A few of them worked at an even more sustained pace: Eleven girls said that they received 60 to 90 customers a month, while even placed themselves in the 90 to 120 bracket. It must also be noted that 63 prostitutes said that they had received no customers.[14] This makes for a fairly small number of sex acts on average.

It is not possible to generalize from these figures that relate to a fairly small sample of girls at a troubled time, namely the period of the Civil War, which was also marked by a major increase in the number of prostitutes. A police report on fifty-nine houses states that the girls began working at two or three in the afternoon and continued to solicit customers up to midnight. They received three to six customers in the daytime and one customer a night.[15] In 1947, a girl wrote the police to complain of ill treatment. She said that the madam had been asking her to receive at least four or five customers in the daytime and one every night.[16]

Venereal Disease

Venereal disease is indissociably linked with prostitution, although the nature of the link is a complex one. We shall see in Chapter 11 that a growing awareness by Western doctors in nineteenth-century Shanghai of the spread of venereal diseases led the authorities in the settlements to adopt measures of health regulation and inspection. Similarly, in the 1920s, the spread of venereal disease by prostitution was a point raised in the abolition campaign of the Moral Welfare League. The Chinese authorities embraced this outlook after the Second World War and tried to set up a highly regulated system to control the activity of prostitution and reduce the spread of venereal diseases among the population. The information presented here relates essentially to the period that followed the 1911 revolution. Before dealing with the problem of venereal disease in Shanghai and among the city's prostitutes, it is necessary to define the general context of health in China (to avoid presenting an excessively distorted view of reality in Shanghai) and the steps taken by the authorities of the settlements and the Chinese authorities to combat venereal disease.

This section does not set out to give a historical account of venereal disease in China. The history of illnesses, epidemics, and health in China is as yet uncharted territory. In a previous study, I used medical publications in China and various accounts by foreign doctors to try to assess the spread of venereal disease in the country and analyze the type of discourse that this phenomenon engendered within the medical community.[17] These sources revealed the very great extent to which these illnesses had spread in China from the nineteenth century onward. What immediately struck foreign doctors throughout the country was the fact that they were not really equipped to diagnose all the cases that came up before them.[18] As new tools such as the Wasserman and Kahn serum tests appeared, doctors carried out a variety of surveys that confirmed the scale of the phenomenon. Starting with the mid-1920s, which is the period of my sources although the reality that they describe may antedate it, every region, including the most peripheral provinces, came to be affected. Venereal disease became a major problem of public health at a time when the organization of health in China was in its infancy because of the weakness of the state and its lack of interest in the question.[19]

The case of Shanghai, in this context, was therefore not exceptional even if, as in all big cities (and even more so in an international port city), venereal disease was particularly prevalent. What distinguished this city was the effort made in the field of public health, especially to set up a system for the medical surveillance of prostitutes. Elsewhere in China, the authorities generally refrained from setting up such systems of control. The few examples that I have come across are concentrated in Manchuria (Andong, Daheihe), where these measures were enforced by the Japanese Army.[20] Of the big cities, only Peking made it obligatory for prostitutes to undergo medical checks with, in the event of illness, compulsory quarantine until recovery. However, this rule was not vigorously applied.[21]

In Shanghai, the Shanghai Municipal Council followed a hesitant policy that was oriented exclusively toward foreign residents and visitors. Specific measures were adopted for the foreign community as of the 1920s. They followed a debate on the abolition of prostitution and the arrival in Shanghai, in 1920, of a delegation of the National Council for Combating Venereal Diseases (NCCVD), an association responsible for combating venereal disease in Great Britain.[22] Following the recommendations of the NCCVD delegation, the Shanghai Municipal Council appointed a deputy health officer, specially responsible for the problem of venereal diseases, but he was unable to devote himself to this task because of other more pressing problems that had to be tackled. The Shanghai Municipal Council, moreover, deemed the subject to be highly controversial—especially because in Great Britain, the Department of Health had appointed an inquiry commission to study ways and means to curb venereal disease. The authorities therefore waited for the results of this inquiry before committing themselves to any particular policy.[23]

In 1923, the authorities of the International Settlement decided to open an evening clinic for venereal disease in the General Hospital. Advertisements in English, Japanese, and Russian were placed in the press to make the new establishment known to the public. Patients soon came in very large numbers. During its first six months of activity, the VD clinic received 1,170 visits (from 191 patients). Thereafter, as can be seen in Table 6.1 (a & b), the number of patients was fairly stable despite a drop due to the circumstances of the war in 1937–1938.[24] Very soon, the demand outstripped the resources of the clinic. Fifty to sixty persons came every evening. Although the head of the clinic emphasized the services rendered to foreigners passing through, especially sailors, the statistics tend to show that the customers were essentially local and especially of Russian origin. The Shanghai Municipal Council also envisaged the opening of a clinic reserved for women but did not have the will to surmount the hostile reactions aroused by this project among a section of foreign public opinion.[25] In 1934, the same

Table 6.1. *Record of venereal diseases treated in the dispensary of the International Settlement (1923–1940)*

(a)	Number						
Year	Patients	Visits	Gonorrhea	Syphilis	Soft Chancre	More than One Infection	Miscellaneous Diseases
1923	191	1,170	88	42	22	8	4
1924	551	9,316	178	120	102	17	69
1925	580	15,902	192	120	172	28	68
1926	—	21,194	240	68	114	23	—
1927	701	—	—	—	—	—	—
1928	—	—	—	—	—	—	—
1929	817	24,648	311	101	242	18	145
1930	834	22,243	259	134	247	12	182
1931	1,046	25,035	396	248	208	28	166
1932	1,213	30,703	534	185	320	28	146
1933	1,279	38,637	580	337	134	42	186
1934	1,225	36,546	533	374	26	33	310
1935	1,232	38,314	482	239	72	21	—
1936	1,041	41,095	459	38	107	50	287
1937	766	24,684	—	—	—	—	—
1938	656	21,825	209	99	155	37	156
1939	891	24,385	238	188	210	44	213
1940	1,620	44,005	423	64	52	781	300
Total:	14,643	41,9702	5,122	2,357	2,183	1,170	2,232

(b)	Percentages				
Year	Gonorrhea	Syphilis	Soft Chancre	More than One Infection	Miscellanesus Discases
1923	53.7	25.6	13.4	4.9	2.4
1924	36.6	24.7	21.0	3.5	14.2
1925	33.1	20.7	29.7	4.8	11.7
1926	53.9	15.3	25.6	5.2	—
1927	—	—	—	—	—
1928	—	—	—	—	—
1929	38.1	12.4	29.6	2.2	17.7
1930	31.1	16.1	29.6	1.4	21.8
1931	37.9	23.7	19.9	2.7	15.9
1932	44.0	15.3	26.4	2.3	12.0
1933	45.3	26.3	10.5	3.3	14.5
1934	41.8	29.3	2.0	2.6	24.3
1935	59.2	29.4	8.8	2.6	—
1936	48.8	4.0	11.4	5.3	30.5
1937	—	—	—	—	—
1938	31.9	15.1	23.6	5.6	23.8
1939	26.7	21.1	23.5	4.9	23.9
1940	26.1	4.0	3.2	48.2	18.5
Average:	40.5	18.9	18.6	6.6	15.4

Source: Shanghai Municipal Council, *Report for the Year 1923*, p. 123; 1924, p. 148; 1925, p. 134; 1926, p. 196; 1927, p. 182; 1929, p. 150; 1930, p. 166; 1931, p. 148; 1932, p. 175; 1933, p. 170; 1934, p. 137; 1935, p. 116; 1936, p. 144; 1937, p. 153; 1938, p. 174; 1939, p. 152, 1940, p. 178.

officials felt that the work of the clinic was purely palliative. The Shanghai Municipal Council's annual report for 1937 announced that the clinic had closed down at the outset of the hostilities between China and Japan, but it appears to have subsequently resumed activity because I have found data for up to 1940.[26]

In 1931, the Municipal Council of the French Concession opened a new municipal dispensary, but it was intended to give free treatment to people in need and did not specially treat venereal diseases.[27] However, Dr. Rabaute, director of the hygiene and assistance departments, was not satisfied with this arrangement. In 1934, he presented a lengthy report in which he emphasized the spread of venereal disease in Shanghai and the fact that it was impossible to count on the Chinese State or on mere education to solve the problem. He recommended the creation of a venereal disease dispensary, integrated with the municipal dispensary, that would open outside regular working hours so that larger numbers of people could come there.[28] Dr. Rabaute's recommendations do not seem to have been accepted by the Municipal Council.

In the territory under Chinese jurisdiction, no initiative was taken during the period that has been referred to. At the beginning of the Sino-Japanese War, the Health Bureau was even dissolved. It was re-established after 1941, but I am in no position to assess its activities, because I have had no access to the archives.[29] A major change came about when the Nationalist authorities retook the city in 1945. An important part of the policy of strict regulation set up in the following year comprised measures to curb venereal disease, especially among prostitutes. One of the instruments of this policy was the dispensary set up in February 1946.[30] In 1948, this dispensary had a staff of twenty-five, including six doctors and six nurses.[31] To promote treatment in the population as a whole, the Health Bureau ordered hospitals to open VD units. In 1948, there were sixteen of these units.[32]

The prostitutes underwent monthly medical checks and, if infected, could choose between treatment in the dispensary or outside by a doctor approved by the authorities.[33] The police station in the Tilanqiao district even procured medicine for sick girls, which it supplied to them either free of charge or at prices related to their earnings. It would seem that this was an isolated initiative because I have not found any other traces of such a policy.[34] Prostitutes with syphilis lost the right to ply their trade for two years. Because this prohibition had unwanted countereffects, the Health Bureau proposed that the prohibition should be waived as soon as the blood tests were negative. The bureau hoped that this provision would oblige prostitutes to come for treatment without any fear of losing their means of subsistence.[35]

The original plan was to have 200 girls examined per day.[36] In fact, the numbers that came to the dispensary fell far short of this target. The documents prepared by the dispensary are not a basis for reckoning the number

Table 6.2. *Number of medical visits and examinations in the municipal dispensary (1946–1948)*

Year	Prostitutes		Number of cards distributed		
	First Visit	Visit Repeated	First Examination	Examination Repeated	Total Number of Examinations
1946	1,310	6,988	1,022	2,096	9,749
1947	1,439	9,426	1,639	6,689	17,865
1948	1,955	12,382	1,192	11,170	26,502

Source: *Shanghai shi weishengju san nian lai gongzuo gaikuang*, 1949, p. 9.

of prostitutes examined because only actual visits were counted. Furthermore, the dispensary made a distinction between visits designed to obtain treatment and examination that corresponded to regular health checks on the prostitutes. Table 6.2 gives an idea of the number of visits and examinations in the establishment from 1946 to 1948. There was an appreciable rise in the figures, but it cannot be known if this corresponds to a larger number of girls or to a larger number of examinations per individual. For 1946 and 1947, the dispensary examined 1,420 and 3,550 girls, respectively. These figures are smaller than those for the prostitutes officially registered with the police. The police archives confirm the fact that the rules were not followed even in the big establishments of prostitution.[37]

Despite the facilities proposed to prostitutes, especially low-cost treatment, the dispensary noted that it was unable to attract more than a quarter of the prostitutes registered. These were lower-category prostitutes who were often ill.[38] The Health Bureau planned to set up mobile teams to visit the houses of prostitution that had been registered in the early years to accelerate the process of examination and medical treatment. However, the financial problems of the municipal government forced it to shelve this plan.[39] One of the difficulties encountered was the problem of coordination among the different departments involved in the health administration, especially because the Health Bureau did not have a laboratory of its own.[40] The most serious problem, however, was the absence of any liaison with the police. It was the police that were responsible for the administration of the prostitutes, but they were incapable of forwarding documents in time. This meant that the girls would sometimes be summoned too late, when they were going through their menstrual periods, making it impossible to examine them.[41]

One of the major causes of the spread of venereal disease in China was undoubtedly the absence of proper treatment and the taking of wholly ineffective medicines. In 1925, a gynecologist established the fact that at least a quarter of the 2,837 patients whom she had received in eight years were or had been suffering from venereal diseases. Sixty percent of the cases of sterility that she had treated had been caused by untreated gonorrhea.[42] Two years later, another medical survey of 1,500 patients showed that 90% of syphilis patients had received no treatment whatsoever.[43] According to these doctors' records and the scattered reports occasionally found in the press or in the archives, it would seem that the population, especially the prostitutes, went to traditional doctors rather than to those trained in Western methods.[44] This choice could probably be explained by cost considerations. Traditional doctors prescribed treatment that cost less than treatment using medicines imported from the West. The traditional treatment consisted of inhalations and the ingestion of mercury or calomel.[45]

The spread of venereal diseases created a real market for all sorts of physicians and medicines. The Shanghai press is full of advertisements for private medical clinics that specialized in these diseases (*hualiuke*) and for medicines that were always described as miracle cures. In fact, certain doctors earned their living solely by administering injections of "606" or "914," which were the two main preparations used to treat syphilis before the introduction of antibiotics.[46] Wu Lien-teh, writing about Harbin, a city with 300,000 inhabitants, says that there were more than 200 doctors in the city who had opened venereal disease "clinics."[47] The medicines, too, were relatively dear. In 1948, Heisidian, described by the advertisements as a new product from Germany, cost 3 yuan a box. A full course of treatment required three boxes. A bottle of "606" for two injections was sold for 7 yuan.[48] At the beginning of the 1940s, a full course of treatment cost 70 yuan to several hundred yuan.[49]

The case of Shanghai, from this viewpoint, was perhaps a special one if we follow the conclusions of a Chinese historian who has made a study of medical advertisements in the *Shen Bao* from 1912 to 1927.[50] Although all notions of sex were concealed or even repressed in public and during social intercourse, the subject manifested itself in several ways by pressure on the individual, especially the male, through a sort of latent anxiety about everything that concerned sex. The medicine merchants took advantage of this anxiety to make it the central factor in illnesses. Many ordinary ailments were attributed to a weakness of the genitals or to an excess of sexual activity.[51] The profusion of advertisements for medicines to cure venereal disease, which formed the greatest proportion of medical advertisements, was therefore only one aspect of a wider obsession with sexual revitalization. The period chosen by the author of the study is an arbitrary one because its bounds are demarcated by two dates of political history. The chronological scope of a study of this kind needs extending. From the very end of the 1890s, the *Shen Bao* published advertisements for pills to treat gonorrhea. The same brand of pills was also available in the 1920s.[52] These advertisements took a form in which they played on the sentiment of fear aroused by venereal diseases. They explicitly associated these diseases with prostitution. In the context of Shanghai at this time, these advertisements were effective because they touched on a sensitive point in the collective psychology.

The authorities tried to exert a certain degree of control over the sale of these medicines. In the police archives, I have several times come across bundles of newspapers in which all the advertisements for these medicines have been carefully marked with pencil.[53] The police had to carry out investigations on the manufacturers of these medicines at regular intervals whose frequency is not known. The following is a record of advertisements for VD treatment published on the 27th of April 1930:

> *Xinwenbao* ("The News"):   46
> *Shishi xinwen* ("China Times"):   7
> *Shen Bao*:   16

The large number of advertisements certainly reflects the extent of the demand.[54] Many patients preferred to treat themselves for reasons of discretion or economy. Certain companies even proposed mail-order sales.[55] The patients had a wide choice, but they also risked being the victims of their own credulity. Quacks were not rare, despite surveillance by the authorities.[56] It must be pointed out that these advertisements did not necessarily convey an unfavorable image of prostitution. Patronizing prostitutes was seen to be an activity that was normal but occasionally brought consequences that had to be accepted. This said, it was really prostitutes that the advertisements implicated in the transmission of venereal disease.

What might appear to be surprising is the total absence, up to 1945, of recommendations for the use of condoms. This absence must be set against the fact that I have not had access, for example, to the little pamphlets that were distributed to sailors when they came to Shanghai or to the documents distributed by the Shanghai Municipal Council for the benefit of the foreign population. Nevertheless, unless we assume that it was not appropriate to mention the topic in public, none of the articles published by foreign or Chinese doctors in the two major medical journals mentions the possibility of using condoms, even when the author is dealing with the problem of the spread of venereal diseases. In the less technical genres, none of the Shanghai guides or even the "compasses of the world of gallantry" recommends the use of condoms, although they warned against the serious risks of infection entailed in contact with the most common categories of prostitute.[57] It was only after 1945 that the police explicitly ordered the houses of prostitution to purchase prophylactic preparations and devices for girls and to oblige customers to use condoms. This rule was not complied with.[58]

The most prevalent venereal diseases at this time were syphilis, gonorrhea, and soft chancre. Cases of gonorrhea were the most numerous in all the statistical samples that I have found. At the Shantung Hospital, gonorrhea accounted for 48.5% of new cases in 1923. Syphilis and soft chancre together accounted for the remainder, with 33.8% and 17.7%, respectively.[59] Table 6.1 contains the information given by the VD clinic of the Shanghai Municipal Council from 1923 to 1940. Gonorrhea was always at the top of the list, with an average of 40% of cases, followed by syphilis (18.8%), and soft chancre (18.5%).[60] It is difficult to have any precise idea about the prevalence of venereal disease within the population. The registers of the General Hospital for the period 1875 to 1922 give an average rate of 9% of patients affected with venereal infections. The Shantung Road hospital recorded an even lower rate of 6.6% from 1870 to 1922. These figures probably underestimate the real situation because there were no serum tests during the greater part of this period.[61]

The director of the municipal dispensary, Yu Wei, estimated the number of syphilis victims at 10% of the population in 1938 and 15% in 1945, while gonorrhea affected half of the adults. He derived these figures from a study of the statistics maintained by the city's hospitals.[62] The methodical examinations carried out on the population after 1949 were not as alarming in their results.[63] Out of 31,861 persons examined in three hospitals from 1945 to 1950, only 9% reacted positively to the VD blood tests.[64] Even if the conclusions of the prewar doctors were, as I believe, biased by the role of the imaginary in society's reaction to prostitution, the prevalence of venereal diseases in Shanghai was probably greater than is suggested by the hospital registers.

What can be said about the prostitutes who are generally accused of being the source of all these ills? A Chinese doctor, Daniel Lai, wrote several articles about syphilis in China. In 1930, he published the results of a survey of 137 prostitutes from Shanghai (104), Nanking (22), and Suzhou (11). These were girls who had left the trade and who were living in refuges for prostitutes. On average, 49% had syphilis; the girls from Shanghai had the lowest rate, with 40.4%.[65] These samples, however, are limited and random. There are two series of complementary health data on the prostitutes of Shanghai. The first series, presented in Table 6.3, was prepared by the municipal VD dispensary and relates to 1946 and 1947. It shows that more than 80% of the girls examined were suffering from venereal disease. Syphilis accounted for about 80% of the cases, but the director of the dispensary deemed that the smear test method used was unreliable.[66] According to him, 95% of the girls had contracted gonorrhea.[67]

It will be noted that the total number of cases of infection was greater than the total number of girls who were sick. This means that certain pros-

Table 6.3. *Prevalence of venereal disease among prostitutes examined in the dispensary (1946–1947)*

	1946	1946	1947	1947
Number of girls examined	1,420		3,550	
Total number of infections	1,062		2,611	
Number of girls infected	931	87.7%	2,205	84.5%
Syphilis	885	83.3%	2,069	79.2%
Gonorrhea	174	16.4%	533	20.4%
Soft chancre	1	0.1%	5	0.2%
Other illnesses	2	0.2%	4	0.2%
Primary syphilis	32	4%	24	1%
Secondary syphilis	21	2%	46	2%
Tertiary syphilis	832	94%	1,999	97%

Source: Yu Wei, "Shanghai changji wu bai ge an diaocha," p. 13.

titutes were suffering from two illnesses at the same time.[68] It would also appear that almost all the prostitutes suffering from syphilis were in the third stage of the disease. These data may be biased by the fact that the dispensaries received mostly prostitutes from the lower categories who had been in the trade for a long time and were more frequently ill.[69] The second series comes from the first group of 501 prostitutes who were arrested by the police in 1951 and underwent serum tests. Girls without venereal disease formed only 10.9% of the total. The others were suffering from syphilis (11.5%), gonorrhea (30%), or both illnesses together (47.6%). As in the sample given by the dispensary, a very large percentage of them (73.7%) had reached the third stage of syphilis.[70]

Surveys conducted in different forms in other Chinese cities confirmed the prevalence of venereal disease among the prostitutes. A medical survey conducted in 1948 among 576 prostitutes and 95 dancers in Qingdao (Shandong) revealed that 80% and 60%, respectively, of these women were suffering from syphilis.[71] In the same year, two doctors conducted an inquiry among prostitutes registered with the Peking municipal dispensary. Their study covered 876 girls who had been receiving treatment under their supervision for forty-one days. This special monitoring revealed that 89% of the girls were infected during the period of the survey itself.[72] In 1950, 96% of the 1,303 Peking prostitutes arrested in a roundup by the police were ill, with 1,107 of them having contracted syphilis.[73] The conclusion is inescapable: The very large majority of Chinese prostitutes suffered from venereal diseases that, in most cases, were hardly, infrequently, or wrongly treated.

The practices of the Chinese prostitutes partly explains the extent to which they were infected, even if some establishments took certain precautions. In the Taotao, a doctor was employed full-time to treat the girls.[74] The hygiene followed, however, was very basic. The prostitutes washed their sexual organs only once a day and do not appear to have used condoms.[75] In most houses, even this minimum was not ensured. Certain girls regularly got injections of salvarsan (the famous "606"). In 1947, a prostitute said that she received two injections daily, for a cost of 20 American dollars each (200,000 yuan), whereas they actually cost no more than 1 dollar in the municipal VD center.[76] One sick prostitute who was treated in June 1948 by a doctor called in by the madam paid 80 U.S. dollars (800,000 yuan) for her first injection of neosalvarsan. The next two injections cost her 40 dollars each.[77]

A document from the Health Bureau noted that more than 60% of the doctors and private hospitals did not use the medicines most effective in the treatment of venereal diseases. Although antibiotics were available, they continued to use earlier preparations based on arsenic.[78] The municipal dispensary itself lacked money to procure the most efficient treatment that could have cured gonorrhea patients within a few hours and syphilis patients within a few days. Instead, months of treatment were needed. This discouraged prostitutes from coming to the dispensary because they knew that their licenses would be revoked.[79]

The fate of the girls who contracted venereal diseases was sometimes tragic. The discomfort and pain that these ailments caused during sexual intercourse made them unwilling to receive customers. The madams would make no allowances for the girls' state of health and, at the same time, would not allow them the possibility of seeking treatment. Nevertheless, it is not known what proportion of the girls were free enough to be able to obtain treatment. Actually, in every period, the press reported cases of a few prostitutes who had been exploited to the extreme. In 1899, a *yeji* in an advanced stage of syphilis was sent by the madam to a private nursing home in the French Concession. After ten days in hospital, her condition worsened. The doctor refused to keep her any longer because of the other patients and had her taken to the house of prostitution. The madam had no wish to take her back and threw her into the street, where a policeman found her shortly afterward.[80] In 1909, the police, during an inspection, discovered the corpse of a prostitute who had died from the aftereffects of an illness and whose death had not been reported.[81] In 1921, the municipal police found a girl seriously ill in a brothel because the madam had not allowed the girl to receive treatment.[82] Three years later, a sick *huayanjian* girl was thrown onto the streets by the madam of the establishment where she was working, and she later died in a small hotel.[83] The press reports refer to isolated cases, but the question is how many other girls suffered the same fate.

Prostitutes as Scapegoats and Objects of Torment

Violence is a theme that was often at the center of all that was said on the issue of prostitution after 1919. Ever since a public discussion on the conditions of the prostitutes had sprung up in the wake of the May 4th Movement, most authors brought up this issue. After 1949, the Communist authorities vigorously denounced all forms of violence practiced by the madams and their employees. Many accounts by prostitutes were published in the press at this time. Contemporary Chinese authors on this subject also stressed this essential dimension of the condition of prostitutes. The question is what was the reality?

At the beginning of my research, all I was able to find was second-hand accounts that repeat the same examples. This gives the impression that actions that were at times brutal and even cruel, but nevertheless exceptional, were magnified and above all generalized to include all prostitutes. The prostitutes are said to have been beaten and even made to kneel on bamboo rods or on washing boards with their hands tied behind their backs. In winter, the punishments went to the extent of perversity when the girls would be left outdoors naked. Another story often reported was that of the madam putting a cat into the prostitute's trousers and beating it vigorously. To close this list, the madams would have no qualms about using scissors to cut out sores in the genitals caused by untreated syphilis and cauterizing the wounds with hot irons. It is difficult to imagine cruelty on this scale.[84]

I have no firsthand information to confirm these accounts of barbarity. The story of the cat, which a journalist attributes to one of the prostitutes interned by the authorities after 1951, was already mentioned in prior sources. The bamboo torture is attested to in the press in the 1920s.[85] As for the last story, it was reported in accounts by prostitutes after 1951.[86] In other words, while I am quite ready to accept the idea that there was a certain degree of violence, I nevertheless have doubts about the frequency and the scale of these acts. Logically, it would seem that the madams had no interest in crossing the boundary beyond which their "working tools" could have been destroyed. The press sheds new light on the question and provides a measure of certitude.

It must be said, at the outset, that violence was the daily lot of a good many prostitutes. I shall not deal here with external violence by ruffians or violence by customers, which shall be studied below. I shall examine the violence suffered by prostitutes in their daily relationship with the madams and staff of the houses of prostitution. They did not necessarily experience acts of great cruelty such as those reported above, but their effect, by dint of repetition, was practically the same, leading them to despair and even to death. The information is sometimes brief: "A prostitute Lin Sibao accused the son of the proprietor of the house of prostitution of having ill-treated her."[87] Nothing more is stated, but it can be imagined that in 1889 a prostitute would have had to have good reasons to complain before the local magistrate.

One form of persecution that was common because it was related to the very work of the prostitutes was to force sick girls to receive customers. This is what a madam forced a girl (whom she had purchased for 200 yuan) to do in 1872. The girl died shortly afterward. The newspaper bewailed the fact that a human life was not even worth 200 pieces of cash.[88] A man who had placed his wife in a brothel got 200 yuan in compensation when she committed suicide because the madam had refused to let her go even though she was ailing.[89] Wang Jingzhu, who was sold at the age of ten to a *huayanjian*, started working when she was thirteen. Although she was sick, the madam ill-treated her and forced her to receive customers. Yielding to Wang's entreaties, the madam decided to take her to a doctor. They were hardly out in the street when Wang Jingzhu ran to a police station.[90] Another prostitute, Zhang Yuehong, was very severely beaten by the madam and her son because she refused to resume work immediately after childbirth.[91]

Blows were the most common form of punishment meted out to prostitutes who did not work satisfactorily or who resisted.[92] Fan Yubao, who was fifteen years old, was severely beaten by the madam because a customer had gone away dissatisfied. She was saved by the intervention of the neighbors and the police.[93] A *huayanjian* prostitute who had been sold four years earlier by her husband fled in order to escape the blows meted out to her. A young girl from Shandong, sold by her father at the age of nineteen to a *huayanjian* in Shanghai, took refuge in a heavily bruised state with the police. The madam came to protest about her rights, brandishing the contract that the father had signed. She was fined 30 yuan.[94] A girl purchased by a *yeji* house refused to receive customers. The madam beat her in order to break her resistance.[95]

In most of the cases reported by the press, the forms of violence are not indicated. The most common expression used is "ill-treatment" (*nüedai*). It is not through morbid curiosity that this topic is being raised here. Even at a century's distance, we cannot be indifferent to the wretched condition of the Chinese prostitute, but the reason for my interest lies elsewhere. Cases of extreme violence were generally spelled out in detail when they came before the judges. Where no precise details are given, I would conclude that the cases entailed "ordinary" violence, a form of daily violence that left no way out other than flight.[96] I would add, without seeking to diminish the importance of this reality, that "ill-treatment" was the argument routinely put forward by prostitutes to the police or to the judge to justify flight and to get away from their madams. They knew that this was the way to obtain judgment in their favor. Apart from action in cases that, thanks to various circumstances, came to the knowledge of the authorities, the latter took no active steps to put an end to the violence meted out in the houses of prostitution.[97]

Violence could also take more extreme forms. A brothel manager was arrested following a complaint by a prostitute whom he had mercilessly beaten and jabbed with needles.[98] Yuehong, a young girl of fifteen, was beaten by the madam with an iron bar because no customer had stayed for the night. Yuehong was seriously wounded and was saved only by the arrival of the neighbors.[99] In another house, a prostitute was whipped to death.[100] Zhao Ahuan took refuge with the Door of Hope because she could no longer stand the caning that the madam used to inflict on her.[101] Hua Yuxian, who had been sold to a house on Fuzhou Road, received customers badly. She was beaten frequently. Having contracted a painful venereal disease, she refused to take customers. The madam burned her face and kept her chained in a room.[102] Even in 1936, there was a case, according to the archives, of a girl who was forced to solicit in the street under threat of being whipped.[103]

When cases of violence came before the judges, the prostitutes generally obtained justice. The magistrates placed them in charitable institutions, which meant escape from the clutches of the madams.[104] Ill treatment could be grounds for releasing a prostitute even if she had been pledged. A prostitute, A Si, pledged by her husband, thus obtained a decision by a judge returning her to her spouse.[105] Such cases would come to light when a girl escaped (but this was probably only the tip of the iceberg). Many, probably the majority, could not escape. They just submitted to their fate. For some, the situation became far too intolerable. Li Guibao, who lived with one Mrs. Zhu Gu, was forced into prostitution. She put an end to her life by swallowing opium.[106] In 1910, a Cantonese prostitute did the same, while another hanged herself.[107] Death was the ultimate way out. Not all deaths, even if they were not common occurrences, were included in the official records. The madams arranged for corpses to disappear and took steps to avoid visits by the police.

The penalties handed out to the madams or the individuals guilty of violence against prostitutes are difficult to assess without precise knowledge of the facts. All that can be seen is that the penalties grew heavier after 1920. In one case of suicide by a prostitute, the madam was imprisoned pending a sentence. No further details are given.[108] A *guinu* and a madam were, respectively, fined 40 yuan and 50 yuan for ill treatment.[109] The other fines noted ranged from 30 to 100 yuan.[110] Prison sentences also varied greatly. One madam was sentenced to three days in prison.[111] I have found two sentences that were heavier, one for three months (in 1910) and one for six months (in 1923).[112] The heaviest sentence, of three years, was given against a madam and her son who had beaten a prostitute to force her to resume work after childbirth (1921).[113] These few examples give the impression that the penalties were relatively light. I have no information on the sentences handed down in the cases of extreme violence referred to above. In most of the cases of ill treatment, the madams did not get into trouble, even when the case came before the courts. Their punishment was the loss represented by the departure of the girl and her being placed in a charitable institution.

All these examples show that the Chinese prostitutes were subjected to extremely trying conditions. Violence was ubiquitous in their world. They were treated like cattle or slaves liable to forced labor at will with little hope, for some, of coming out alive from the trade. For the madams, the prostitutes were nothing but "money trees" (*yaoqianshu*) to be shaken until every last coin had dropped. Even the courtesans were sometimes beaten, although this was rare and came at a later date.[114] It is unnecessary to try to measure the extent and frequency of the phenomenon. Human suffering cannot be quantified. The prostitutes lived lives of wretchedness and pain for as long as they remained in the houses of prostitution. The only note of optimism that I can bring to this tragic story is that a change began to take place at the turn of the 1920s, with the gradual disappearance of the sale and crude enslavement of women for prostitution. Thereafter, the press hardly reported any cases of violence.[115] Conditions of absolute servitude and cases of girls being pledged no longer appear in the archives for 1945 to 1949. The transition very probably took place before this date.

Crime in the Houses of Prostitution

The world of prostitution lay at the interface between the society of decent people and that of the fringe elements, the ruffians, and the secret societies. This was also a world where there was a lot of money in circulation, where wealth – that of the customers as well as the, at times fictitious, wealth of the courtesans – was flaunted. It is therefore not surprising that such wealth aroused cupidity. Theft and racketeering were two unavoidable risks of the prostitute's profession. However, they were not the only risks. Violence could spring up in more brutal forms, whether it came from customers or from the girls themselves. It is these two aspects that I shall examine here, in stressing at the very outset that, in an essential dimension, namely the presence and role of the secret societies, the available documents are extremely scanty and even nonexistent.

The courtesans and the prostitutes were not exposed to exactly the same forms of crime, at least in the nineteenth century. The courtesans were above all concerned with the problem of theft, given the luxurious articles with which they surrounded themselves in their establishments and the luxurious ornaments that they wore. The prostitutes were more frequently victims of physical violence on the part of customers, ruffians, and, as we have seen, madams. However, both categories ran the same risk, even if it was higher among the prostitutes, of having quarrels break out between customers. They also shared a tendency to squabble as rivals. Shanghai in the twentieth century became a city in which there was a huge increase in criminal activities. A precise study of the phenomenon of criminality needs to be made in order to assess the place to be given to the real and to the imaginary in the social discourse. With regard to the prostitutes, it does not appear that during the period studied here, there was an aggravation in the level of violence or an increase in its frequency.

Theft was without doubt the worst problem in the houses of prostitution, especially for the courtesans. Certain thieves made a specialty of robbing these houses. Two natives of Jiangxi got into an establishment one evening around 10:00 P.M. and made off with a silver pipe. Following two other complaints, the police made a tour of various lodgings and arrested two suspects without finding any trace of the stolen pipes. The newspaper notes that this type of theft was constantly on the increase.[116] Some were more cunning: Several individuals passed themselves off as customers in order to steal the silver pipes and silk finery, which, along with the pipes, jewels, and, to a lesser degree, other clothing and tobacco pouches, were much coveted items.[117]

Other articles, all made of gold, appear in the complaints: watches, earrings, bracelets, hairpins, and snuffboxes.[118] The reports reveal the extent of the luxury that existed in the courtesan's houses. The amounts given are in hundreds of yuan: 400, 500, 800, 1,200, and 1,500.[119]

Robbery was sometimes organized as a real escapade. In March 1909, six ruffians disguised as policemen and armed with knives burst into a *huayanjian* on the pretext that they were there to make an inspection.[120] The same technique was used at a New Year's Eve party in 1921 by two individuals who made off with 600 yuan.[121] The guilty parties were severely punished. Again, in 1938, three individuals turned up claiming to be vice squad inspectors and obtained money by blackmailing the madam who was in illegal possession of an opium pipe.[122] In 1924, a well-informed group burst into a house where a lively evening had just come to an end, and the customer had just placed his money on the table. They pocketed 950 yuan.[123] These acts by ruffians could have serious consequences because the intruders would be armed. One *huayanjian* was wounded in the neck with a knife.[124]

Thieves, when they were caught in the days of the empire, would sometimes receive severe punishment. In 1899, the perpetrator of a theft in a brothel was sentenced to three months' imprisonment.[125] This was a light penalty. A customer who had deceived a courtesan by refusing to pay her for the night and stealing a pair of earrings from her was sentenced to 200 bamboo lashes.[126] A servant who had stolen a gold watch and snuffbox in a courtesan's house was sentenced to 300 bamboo lashes and one year's imprisonment.[127] Another servant who was unemployed and had been guilty of the same offense got off with 300 bamboo lashes, while a thief who had stolen hairpins received 100 lashes.[128] It can be seen that the range of penalties was fairly small even if it varied substantially for comparable offenses.

The physical penalties that were imposed on Chinese residents by the *xian* magistrate or his representative were replaced after 1911 by imprisonment and expulsion. Western magistrates loathed these methods, which, they deemed to be barbaric.[129] Nevertheless, severity was not always the rule. For stealing 1,200 yuan from a brothel, one individual was sentenced to four years' imprisonment followed by expulsion from the settlement.[130] The ringleaders of a group of ten individuals involved in an armed attack in the French Concession were sentenced to three months' imprisonment, while the others received one month. They were expelled for life from the concession.[131] In a case of theft and kidnapping, the penalties were six months to one year's imprisonment.[132]

Another risk that prostitutes ran was that of being kidnapped. This was a means used by ruffians to obtain money from a madam. Wang Tao says that layabouts (*wulaizi*) from Guangdong, Fujian, or Ningbo would sometimes break into a house and kidnap a courtesan.[133] One source from 1891 also reports this practice,[134] which was often a means used by local ruffians to extort money.[135] The police would not give the establishments sufficient protection unless they agreed to pay a bribe. In 1889, a group of ruffians obtained entry into a *huayanjian* in the evening and kidnapped two girls. The madam who tried to oppose them was wounded in the hand.[136] A courtesan was kidnapped by two individuals who sought a ransom for her. The two kidnappers were arrested and respectively sentenced to 100 and 300 bamboo lashes. The adventure turned to the courtesan's advantage because, at her request, she was placed in a charitable institution.[137]

The very expensive ornaments that the courtesans wore when they went out would sometimes also bring them into trouble. They would go out from 6:00 P.M. up to about midnight. Even if their routes were within a relatively limited perimeter, they were exposed to the risk of attack once nightfall came (Plate 7). The darkness that hung over the streets was propitious to attacks on courtesans, who were easy to identify in their sedan chairs illuminated by lanterns bearing the names of their establishments. In the twentieth century, street lighting had only a limited deterrent effect on the ruffians who came into action later in the evening, when the streets were deserted. In January 1920, a courtesan was divested of her headgear, estimated to have cost 3,000 to 4,000 yuan, while returning at midnight from a late outing.[138] The same misadventure befell another courtesan. In both cases, a servant was with the girl, not to mention a rickshaw puller. The ruffians also modernized their methods: Four individuals kidnapped a prostitute in broad daylight and took her away in a car.[139]

These attacks sometimes ended in tragedy. In 1922, a courtesan who was returning from an outing to which she had been invited was killed in front

Plate 7. A courtesan being attacked in the street.

of her house as she got out of her car. The attackers went away with her jewelry, whose cost was estimated at 1,500 yuan.[140] The most extreme case, however, was that of a murder that took place two years earlier and made the headlines. The victim, a famous courtesan named Lian Ying, had been drawn into a real trap by a customer who, having not a penny to his name, needed to settle his debts in another courtesan's house. After inviting her out a few times, he suggested a car drive. Although she had some doubts, Lian allowed herself to be taken in by appearances. Two of the customer's accomplices thereupon strangled her with her silken scarf to steal her jewelry and left her body in a rice field. After this murder, the Shanghai Municipal Council prohibited the practice of accepting invitations to go out after midnight.[141]

The houses were often the scene of another form of violence, namely, quarrels between customers. The causes of these quarrels are not always known, but they were often related to rivalry between two customers fighting for the same girl. In the courtesans' houses, such quarrels were seen to be misplaced. The customers were usually groups of friends who had come to spend some time together. The fairly strict ground rules followed in these houses generally prevented the risk of meetings between two customers of one and the same courtesan. However, it was not rare in Shanghai for quarrels to take place in a house and for furniture to be wrecked, as an author reported in 1891.[142] The iconography also testifies to the occurrence of brawls in the courtesans' houses.

The quarrels between customers that were reported in the newspapers generally took place in the lower-class brothels. Two customers of a *huayanjian* got into an argument because they wanted the same girl. One of them went and fetched a few friends who roundly beat up the rival.[143] In another case, it appears that a group of four persons who had come together to a *yeji* house started fighting with one another, breaking furniture and pipes and tearing open several tobacco pouches.[144] The fisticuffs may have arisen out of a gambling quarrel. Several individuals broke into a Cantonese brothel and began to argue with one of the customers. The free fight that followed caused heavy damage in the establishment.[145] This was very probably a case of people settling scores or conducting reprisals after a dispute.

In one case of rivalry over a girl, the dispute took an even more tragic turn. On the 8th of January 1910, a certain Liang Asi was in a Cantonese house of prostitution in the company of a girl when an individual, who happened to be a local gang leader and the girl's partner, burst into the room and struck Liang in the face. Two days later, while the gang leader was with the girl along with a few friends, four men armed with axes entered the house and started fighting with him and his guests. A Cantonese carpenter, who had recently become a regular visitor to the house, was stabbed to death. The law-enforcement authorities were unable to shed light on the circumstances in which the Cantonese carpenter had been killed. Even with the arrest of ten prostitutes and employees of the house, it was not possible to apportion responsibility to the different individuals involved. The courts suspected Liang Asi of being responsible in the matter and sentenced him provisionally to fifty lashes in order to make him confess. The press did not report the conclusion of the inquiry.[146]

The prostitutes were also exposed to risks of violence on the part of customers because of dissatisfaction or for reasons that were not always made clear. Ding Aibao was stabbed several times by a customer. Very fortunately, she escaped with minor wounds. The customer who had attacked her was sentenced to two weeks' imprisonment.[147] A Russian prostitute accused a Cantonese man of committing violence against her. The accused man was released for want of proof.[148] Another Russian prostitute in a Hongkou house had worse luck. She was knifed to death by two of her compatriots.[149] The cause of a dispute could be a minor matter: A *yao'er* had been trying to persuade four customers who had come for a mere visit (*da chawei*) to stay for a gaming session. The main guest was not happy about the idea and began arguing with the girl. The other three joined in the quarrel, which degenerated into an extremely violent affair according to the prostitute making the complaint.[150]

Sometimes it was an unhappy male partner who came armed with a knife. Xu Zhaodi, a *yeji*, was thus stabbed several times.[151] Another, similar case throws some light on the relations between the sexes in the lower classes. Zhu Qiaoliang had been living for a long time with Zhang Sibao, a man of little means who had placed her in a house of prostitution. Zhang appears to have continued to squeeze money out of the girl, who finally got fed up. When he came yet again to ask for money, the prostitute refused. Zhang got angry and stabbed her several times but only managed to hit her in the hands. The man was arrested and sentenced to one year's imprisonment.[152]

Sources of violence also included cases of gate-crashers who would try to sleep with prostitutes for free. In one case, a Cantonese man who had just spent the night with a prostitute had only 9 *mao* to hand over to the girl. She protested because the sum was far below the required amount. The man got enraged and hit her hard in the face, giving her a huge pair of black eyes.[153] Prostitutes were also victims of sexual violence, although this was rarer. In 1909, a customer dissatisfied with the services of a *yeji* hit her and inserted a bamboo rod into her vagina, causing her to hemorrhage. Several maids had to intervene to pacify the angry customer and take him to the police station.[154] During the same period, there was a *huayanjian* girl who also suffered sexual ill treatment (whether it was rape or sodomy is not known) from a customer. She had to be taken to the hospital.[155] Certain customers could turn vengeful. Two individuals who had not been pleased with the service in a *huayanjian* came back with about ten friends who broke everything in the establishment.[156]

Houses of prostitution, like all establishments of leisure (cabarets, night-clubs, etc.), came under the protection rackets by the secret societies. These houses thus ensured peace for themselves as well as a means of seeking assistance in the event of trouble with petty ruffians or with the police. Although it is difficult to reach any conclusions here, the practice was accepted and the establishments submitted to it knowing that they had no choice in the matter. The press therefore hardly mentions any cases of violence against recalcitrant houses. We must of course be careful not to make any definitive judgment, but it might be said that attacks by gangs of ruffi-ans (which could have been punitive expeditions) and of course cases of the kidnapping of prostitutes could fall into this category of violence. However, the cases reported date from before 1911, when the secret soci-eties had not yet gained the power, influence, and level of organization that they would acquire under Du Yuesheng's leadership. There are no

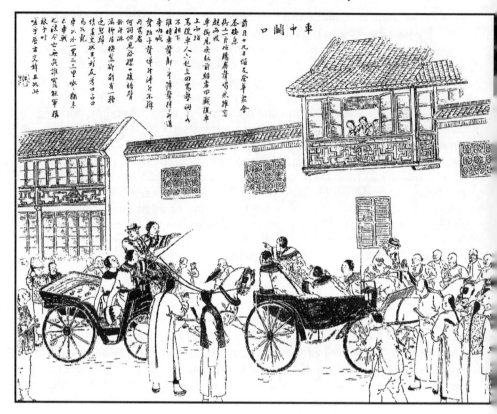

Plate 8. Two courtesans exchanging insults.

examples of violence explicitly directed against the establishments except during the Japanese occupation.[157] The special climate created by conflicts between the secret services and rival gangs for the control of all these lucrative activities probably explains these acts of violence.

Among the various little incidents that studded the Shanghai social scene, we must include the disputes that arose between courtesans or between prostitutes. As in the case of the customers, it was the jealousy or rivalry for the same man that was often the cause of the squabbles. The courtesans considered certain customers (the regulars who spent a lot of money) as personal possessions. Sentimental factors could also come into play in a relationship between a courtesan and one of her customers. A girl would therefore react very badly if such a customer left her for another girl, and the latter would immediately be accused of enticement. It is an incident of this kind that is reported by the *Dianshizhai huabao* in Plate 8, which shows two courtesans standing up in their rickshaws and unrestrainedly insulting each other in the street to the delectation of the passersby. Quarrels of this kind, however, were unusual in the world of the courtesans.[158]

Money was sometimes at the heart of violent disputes. A *huayanjian* girl borrowed 100 yuan from a colleague to pay the costs of moving to a new house. The loan was recorded in a document that the girl took back when she paid her debt. Her creditor, however, accused her of still owing money. The argument turned into a fistfight right in the middle of the road. This again led to intervention by the police.[159] The press reported a dispute between courtesans that is quite piquant in its very Chinese flavor. Two madams had together engaged a *changsan* named Lin Huanhuan. In the course of the season, the madams quarreled and decided to separate. One of them remained with Lin Huanhuan, while the other went to live a few blocks away with a new girl to whom she gave the same name. The two madams started fighting again for exclusive rights over the name. The madam who had remained with the first Lin Huanhuan got a few colleagues together to beat up her rival, who was four months pregnant and suffered a miscarriage from the blows that she received.[160]

This study of prostitution in Shanghai failed to shed light on sexual behavior in China and on its development during the period studied here. Whether it is in the nineteenth century or in the twentieth century and whether the historian is considering the courtesans or the common prostitutes, he or she constantly comes up against the silence of the sources. It is not certain that this silence will be permanent. Access to the legal or police archives will perhaps open new perspectives on this subject. The only provisional conclusion that I can draw from the few details that have been assembled in this chapter is that the demand for sex was rather ordinary as far as the customers were concerned. The Chinese do not seem to have been in search of particular services. Whether they were bachelors or married men, they visited the brothels as spontaneously as they did other centers of leisure.

The fact that prostitutes were visited by customers who cared little about their own health resulted in a massive spread of venereal disease. Around 1937, China probably had 30 to 35 million syphilis victims, a figure that only increased in the years that followed.[161] This situation was principally the result of a lack of health infrastructures, whether for prostitutes or for the population as a whole. Public hygiene, a concept that had been imported relatively late from the West, was never among the highest priorities of Chinese governments. When the authorities in Shanghai strove to curb the spread of venereal disease, they focused on very narrow segments of the population (the foreign community in the International Settlement and above all those who appeared to be responsible for the spread of the diseases, namely the prostitutes). These efforts were quite useless because they tackled only a part of the problem. Venereal diseases remained a scourge that added to the sufferings to which prostitutes were exposed.

Almost all of the cases of violence that I have found date from the years 1872–1910 and 1919–1920. The absence of violence on an equal scale after this period in no way means that it disappeared or even that it diminished. This absence was merely a consequence of changes in my source, the *Shen Bao*, which stopped reporting these miscellaneous incidents and the judgments handed down by the mixed courts in the settlements. The few examples for the 1930s and 1940s confirm the fact that violence continued to exist in the world of prostitution and more generally in all activities in which women were involved as sex objects. Taxi dancers, who are not discussed here, were sometimes subjected to the same torments.[162] All these examples have hardly any statistical value. Nevertheless, they are, I believe, representative of the climate that existed during this period. With variations that relate to changes in the profession itself, violence surrounded the lives of the prostitutes. Although this violence was not meted out on a daily basis and although it did not affect every single individual, it was a constant and unpredictable hazard.

Part 3
The Space and Economy
of Prostitution

7

The Female Market in Shanghai and China

The houses of prostitution were supplied through a vast traffic in human beings, most of whom were women. This traffic meant that China remained, well into the twentieth century, what an anthropologist has justifiably called "the world's greatest market in human beings."[1] Up to 1949, women and children were the victims of an almost ordinary trade to which the Chinese authorities began to pay attention only belatedly.[2] The laws and policies conceived to eliminate this scourge were hardly ever applied on the ground, and, at times, official neglect was compounded by the local authorities. The sale of women and children is attested to in many varied accounts. It is impossible to measure the full scale of the phenomenon. Its victims throughout China can be numbered in the millions. The question of female traffic for purposes of prostitution has received very little attention in contemporary historiography. This is linked to the relative paucity of works of social history devoted to Chinese women. We are still at the beginning of a quest whose thrust can only intensify with the vigorous currents of gender-based studies by historians.

The subject of this chapter will take me somewhat away from Shanghai. In part, it is the sources that dictate this choice, but the subject matter itself requires us to look beyond the city and even beyond its surrounding provinces. Naturally, the prostitutes of Shanghai will remain at the center of the picture. This picture will serve to support and sometimes correct the very general assertions made in works on the feminine condition. This chapter consists of three major parts dealing with the three dimensions of traffic in human beings. The first part relates to the way in which the phenomenon was perceived by contemporaries, especially the authorities. The second part deals with the traffickers themselves and with the organization of this trade. The third part examines the victims, the circumstances in which they were abducted and distributed throughout the country, and the ways by which they were sometimes able to escape from the spiral.

The subject of the female trade has been approached from a standpoint of prejudice and with preconceived notions that have resulted in guesswork and a vision also distorted by the use of limited sources. In *Beautiful Merchandise*, Sue Gronewold has written that "Brothels were usually supplied

with women by men whose major income came from trading in humans."
She adds that these men formed an undefined group having emerged
mainly from the ranks of unattached and unemployed individuals, even if
certain traffickers did have regular employment. Further on, Gronewold
mentions the existence of "networks of kidnappers, often roving bandits or
unemployed city men looking for an easy source of income." The role of
women here appears to have been limited to making contacts with potential victims.[3]

In the specific case of Shanghai, another perspective is provided by Emily
Honig, although the main theme of her work is not prostitution but female
textile workers. The fate of female workers sometimes intersected with that
of the prostitutes: A job termination, an unfortunate encounter, or an
abduction was all that was needed for an individual to fall into prostitution.[4] However, it was at the starting point itself that the paths began to
cross and overlap one another: "Some enterprising criminals used the
pretext of introducing village women to a factory to lure them to Shanghai,
only to sell them on arrival to brothels." Honig also notes that working
women, like prostitutes, were routinely recruited in the country and that
perhaps there was no real distinction between those who recruited prostitutes and those who recruited working women. The picture given here is
that of a rather formal organization of professional recruiters who went
around the villages looking for sufficiently naive or interested families who
would believe their fine talk and let their daughters go to the city. Women,
too, are seen in a more active role, especially in the kidnappings.[5]

I agree with the facts reported by these two authors, but their findings
need to be revised or modified. While Gronewold's statements are not false,
they tend toward a degree of generality that makes them quite meaningless. Her depiction neither looks at the chronology and the changes that
came about in the feminine condition between the nineteenth and twentieth centuries (for example, the ending of female segregation) nor allows for
the levels of involvement that might have existed in the female trade. The
essential weakness of her analysis lies, as often in the rest of her work, in
its ahistorical nature. Honig is far closer to reality because her study
is based on well-defined local sources and on a rigorous analysis of the
modes of recruitment of working women. Nevertheless, with regard to the
prostitutes, her vision is far too narrow. The question is whether we must
accept the idea that there was an organized trade. What is the role to be
attributed to "contractors" in the recruitment of prostitutes? In what circumstances did the girls become prostitutes? All these questions deserve
careful examination.

The most realistic approach is Gail Hershatter's. She distinguishes
between several types of traffickers: those who took advantage of the dis-
tressed condition of populations hit by natural calamity, those who preyed
on recent immigrants, those who recruited women ostensibly for proper

jobs, and those who abducted, raped, and brutalized lone women.[6] In another article, Hershatter places emphasis, almost in the same terms, on the essential role of the traffickers, although she never really mentions the idea of networks or of any structured organization. She also refers to the major road to prostitution in which girls were sold by their own families.[7] In my view, this was an essential dimension that has not been sufficiently highlighted. Hershatter's depiction is sometimes far too impressionistic to be fully satisfying.

The various accounts garnered from the press and from official police documents attest to the reality of the trade in human beings. The existence of this trade appears to have been more evident in the nineteenth century and up to the middle of the 1920s. Nevertheless, cases can be found up to the eve of the Communist victory in 1949. The city of Fuzhou was mentioned in 1870 as a place of exchange where several hundred women were sold every year.[8] Twenty years later, a reader reported that in Shanghai "there is going on every day traffic in young girls and women sold and bought for immoral purposes."[9] In 1930, a Western observer noted that in the aftermath of a famine that had raged for two years in Shaanxi, women were being taken to neighboring provinces by the cartload. So great was the supply that a mere 2 to 3 yuan was enough to buy a woman. Twelve cartloads of women left the province on the 12th of April 1930, with their occupants destined for prostitution. The authorities themselves, when strapped for money, would readily levy taxes on each individual "exported" out of the province.[10] In the same year, 70,000 women were sold in the province of Suiyuan, which had been affected by the same drought.[11]

Shanghai: A Focal Point of the Trade in Women

The female traffic in China is thus an established fact, and we must examine Shanghai's place in it. The police statistics show that the city was not only a center of prostitution but also a hub of the trade in women. The data in Table 7.1, taken from the French municipality's reports, pertain to convictions handed down for the abduction of women between 1908 and 1930. The data show a jagged development, with a peak in 1922–1926. This peak might have corresponded to greater severity on the part of the police at a time when prostitution and the traffic related to it were the focus of a public debate. The information provided by the Mixed Court in the International Settlement gives a rather similar picture marked by major fluctuations in the number of persons convicted of abduction. The number of persons brought before the courts was not necessarily proportional to the number of cases discovered by the police. The total number of persons sentenced for rape, abduction of women, and the sale of women into prostitution in 1933 and 1934, years for which statistics are available for all three sectors of the city, was 1,191 and 461, respectively.[12] Without doubt,

Table 7.1. *Number of sentences for abduction of women in the Mixed Court of the French Concession*

Year	Total Number of Cases	Discharged
1908	71	—
1909	83	—
1910	177	49
1911	83	28
1912	63	20
1913	86	23
1914	102	25
1915	84	19
1916	65	19
1917	79	23
1918	39	7
1919	31	10
1920	32	—
1921	74	14
1922	159	28
1923	295	64
1924	210	64
1926	126	49
1927	70	15
1928	66	11
1929	76	—
1930	115	28

Sources: Conseil d'administration municipale de la Concession française, *Compte rendu de la gestion pour l'exercice 1908*, p. 126; *1909*, p. 132; *1910*, p. 124; *1911*, p. 175; *1912*, p. 202; *1913*, p. 163; *1914*, p. 146; *1915*, p. 108; *1916*, p. 141; *1917*, p. 168; *1918*, p. 156; *1919*, p. 169; *1920*, p. 260; *1921*, p. 225; *1922*, p. 319; *1923*, p. 330; *1924*, p. 303; *1926*, p. 328; *1927*, p. 222; *1928*, p. 251; *1929*, p. 308; *1930*, p. 335.

Shanghai was the pole in the traffic in human beings, especially the traffic in women.

Shanghai provided traffickers with an easy field, not only because of the expanding market of prostitution but also because the metropolis, by its politically and administratively polycentric nature, encouraged all manner of illegal activities. The fact that the city was divided into three autonomous jurisdictions controlled by police departments that were ill disposed to collaborate and exchange information with one another was a godsend for the traffickers. In 1932, the League of Nations Far Eastern Inquiry Commission concluded that this absence of cooperation between the different police forces was having detrimental effects. There was little subsequent improvement in the situation, despite pressure from the League of Nations.[13] Table 7.2 brings together the very scanty information available on cases of abduction and traffic in women in the International Settlement between 1914 and 1940. This table also includes some data on the French Concession for the years 1929–1934.

Without doubt, there was hardly any letup in the incidence of kidnapping and abduction of women in China and in the Shanghai region during this period, although major fluctuations can be seen. However, it cannot be definitely known if this was due to variations in the volume of traffic or to a somewhat greater efficiency on the part of the police. These statistics give a very rough idea of the phenomenon. This is because the category termed "abduction" covers both women and children.

The Organization of the Traffic

The introduction to this chapter cites references to an organized traffic of women organized by groups of male and female recruiters of labor proposing city jobs to women in the villages. It is suggested that these individuals were integrated into a much larger network dominated by the secret societies, structured in order to provide for the distribution of girls throughout the country up to their final destination, namely, a house of prostitution. It appears to me that such an elaborate organization of the trade in women never really existed. At the local level, even if we allow for the activities of the "Green Gang" (*Qingbang*), it is probable that networks of traffickers and pimps formed an exception.[14] This does not negate the fact that individuals did earn money by devoting themselves entirely to this traffic.

The structure of the trade in women closely reflected that of trade in China in general. It was highly decentralized. It was characterized by the interconnection of a succession of middlemen who made contact with one another only occasionally when the opportunities arose. In the cities, there was a large number of individuals (*guinu*, brothel servants, hoodlums, etc.) located midway between delinquency and normal life or whose work (as coffee shop, hotel, and teahouse waiters, rickshaw pullers, etc.) brought them into contact with a great many people who were aware of one another's occupations. The extent to which they were involved in this huge traffic could vary, but rarely were they members of a particular network.

A few examples might be mentioned before a more precise analysis is attempted of the organization of the traffic in women. The traffickers generally worked on a small scale. In 1899, a Shanghai resident, Yuan Zhengtong, was arrested for trafficking in women. He had negotiated a purchase of girls from Jiangbei whom he concealed in an accomplice's house

Table 7.2. *Cases of abduction and traffic in women tried by the Shanghai courts (1914–1940)*

Year	Mixed Court Abduction — Arrested and Discharged	Mixed Court Abduction — Number of Individuals Sentenced	Mixed Court Abduction — Number of Cases	Mixed Court Trafficking — Arrested and Discharged	Mixed Court Trafficking — Number of Individuals Sentenced	Mixed Court Trafficking — Number of Cases	Chinese Court Abduction — Number of Individuals Sentenced	Chinese Court Trafficking — Number of Individuals Sentenced	French Concession[a] Abduction — Number of Individuals Sentenced	French Concession[a] Trafficking — Number of Individuals Sentenced
1914	—	133	—	—	122	—	—	—	—	—
1915	—	112	—	—	91	—	—	—	—	—
1916	—	68	—	—	54	—	—	—	—	—
1917	—	106	—	—	56	—	—	—	—	—
1918	—	95	—	—	13	—	—	—	—	—
1919	—	—	—	—	—	—	—	—	—	—
1920	—		—	—		—	—	—	—	—
1921	—	91	—	—	14	—	—	—	—	—
1922	—	63	—	—	9	—	—	—	—	—
1923	75	71	—	21	23	—	—	—	—	—
1924	66	84	—	—	29	—	—	—	—	—
1925	—	115	—	1	16	—	—	—	—	—
1926	—	80	—	4	20	—	—	—	—	—
1927	—	92	—	4	11	—	—	—	—	—
1928	—	231	—	7	33	—	—	—	—	32
1929	—	219	—	19	33	—	—	—	—	32
1930	—	52	45	—	31	11	—	—	—	9
1931	—	138	90	—	58	22	—	—	—	—
1932	—	149	76	—	66	32	208	115	—	—
1933	—	128	75	—	46	31	273	171	731	59
1934	—	90	65	—	46	21	257	75	124	15
1935	—	75	62	—	52	31	192	74	—	—
1936	—	71	54	—	49	29	214	45	—	—
1937	—	70	42	—	33	15	—	—	—	—
1938	—	39	42	—	44	18	—	—	—	—
1939	—	79	66	—	37	17	—	—	—	—
1940	—	66	51	—	22	13	—	—	—	—

a For purposes of prostitution.

Sources: Shanghai Municipal Council, *Report for the Year 1914*, pp. 48–51A; *1915*, pp. 41–44A; *1916*, pp. 39–42A; *1917*, pp. 41–44A; *1918*, pp. 45–48A; *1921*, pp. 65–68A; *1922*, pp. 72–73A; *1923*, pp. 41–42/51–54; *1924*, pp. 48–49/59–61; *1925*, pp. 42–43/56–57; *1926*, pp. 41–42/55–56; *1927*, pp. 58–62; *1928*, pp. 64–68; *1929*, pp. 83–87; *1930*, pp. 103–105; *1931*, pp. 73–75; *1932*, pp. 111–113/124–125; *1933*, pp. 117–119/131–132; *1934*, pp. 84–86/95–96; *1935*, pp.

pending their resale to houses of prostitution.[15] Another man was arrested immediately upon selling two women.[16] In 1912, three women were arrested and convicted of having kidnapped two girls from their grandparents. These girls had passed into the possession of five different persons before being sold to Cantonese purchasers.[17] In 1915, a girl abducted in Shanghai was rescued from her abductors in Manchuria shortly before she could be placed in a brothel. The individual arrested on this occasion was the third man to whom the girl had been transferred since her abduction.[18]

It is clear that the original abductor was very often not a professional trafficker. Our perception needs to be tempered in the case of women abductors. They were often lone women whose only means of earning a living was to carry out a variety of activities that were not always quite legal. Abducting minors or young women in distress (girls who were lost, widows, etc.) was one of their occupations. Once the abduction had been done, a way had to be found to sell one's prize, and it is always at this precise point that we find those middlemen who formed a bridge between the abductor and the houses of prostitution. A woman who had brought a young girl from Chaozhou to Shanghai sought the help of two ladies, whom she had met perhaps by chance while going around the teahouses, to sell her "goods" to a brothel.[19] A young girl of seventeen, who was "lured to Shanghai by an unknown person," was sold to another woman hailing from the same province, who was prepared to take her to a brothel in Xiamen (Fujian).[20] Some cases involved concerted and premeditated action. Two women, having targeted a sixteen-year-old girl, abducted her with the help of two accomplices Xu Guirong and Wang Ajie and sent her to Manchuria, where she was sold to a brothel.[21]

The press confirms the existence of professional recruiters making the rounds of the villages in their native regions. One peasant woman whose husband had died two years earlier entrusted her daughter to a woman who had visited the village. On arriving in Shanghai, the young girl had to prostitute herself.[22] In 1930, the police arrested two women from Shaoxing who had enlisted the help of a bandit (*guaifei*, or literally an abductor) to bring eight young girls to Shanghai, where they were destined for houses of prostitution.[23] These girls probably had no inkling at all of what lay in store for them. The traffickers were able to sell them off one by one by informing the girls, whenever one of their companions left, that a job had been found for her. The girls had no reason for concern when their companions failed to reappear because it was usual for young unmarried female workers to be given accommodation in factory dormitories.[24]

These examples suggest that it is possible to establish a schematic picture of the organization of the traffic of women in China. The first point to be stressed is that there were two major categories of traffickers. There were the "amateurs" who would grasp an opportunity or sometimes even provoke it. These individuals constituted the largest category at the beginning of the road that took a woman to prostitution. Then came the "professionals" who took charge of marketing the girls – that is, selling them to a house and exploiting them. In Shanghai, they came to be known at a very early stage as "white ants" (*bai maiyi*), a term found in Wang Tao's writings and in the press.[25] However, there was no clear-cut or permanent boundary between these two levels. There were other personalities and other levels of intervention whose role was essential, and here the individuals involved could belong to either category.

The world of the kidnappers and their accomplices in the abduction and sequestration of women in safe places belonged essentially to the category that I would call "amateurs" or "casual" kidnappers, even if they could at times be repeat offenders. Under the term "professionals," I would include traffickers proper, namely those who, in any particular city, would be on the lookout for women brought in by the kidnappers and who knew the requirements of the market. The term would also cover those who took delivery of the girls on their arrival at the city of destination and undertook to place them in the houses of prostitution. Some of these individuals were highly localized, while others were involved in long-distance trade.

The traffic in women was without doubt remarkably well organized in China. Nevertheless, it was organized in a "premodern" mode and followed a Chinese pattern of business transactions. There was no single, specific, strong, and easily identifiable organization. Rather, this trade had a pyramidal structure with a very wide and thinly spread out base and a succession of intermediate levels and various informers ensuring the flow of information and women according to demand. In Shanghai, reference has often been made to the role of the secret societies in the traffic in women. However, there is nothing to prove or disprove this possibility. Secret societies were undoubtedly implicated in this lucrative trade, but it was in the mode that I have just described, and this mode made it particularly difficult for the authorities to try and control or eliminate it.

The Identity of the Traffickers

There is little information on the social origins or professional occupations of the traffickers. Three individuals convicted of abduction in 1920 had close links with the world of prostitution, two of them being brothel owners. The third was a former shopkeeper, aged sixty-three.[26] In a work on criminality in Peking in the 1920s, a Chinese sociologist states that 40% of the women convicted of abduction were unmarried or widowed. A very great majority of them (70%) were aged fifty or more.[27] In 1936, out of a sample of 521 individuals, 56% were men and 44% were women.[28] In Shanghai, out of twenty-nine traffickers caught red-handed in 1936, thirteen (45%) were women and sixteen (55%) were men. It would therefore seem that the role of women, at a later date and in a more developed region, was not as crucial

Table 7.3. *Professions of persons convicted of trafficking in human beings in Peking*

Profession	Men	Percentage (men)	Women	Percentage (women)	Total	Percentage of Total Sample
Laborer	44	37.9	26	49.1	70	41.4
Factory worker	19	16.4	9	17.0	28	16.6
Itinerant merchant	22	19.0	3	5.7	25	14.8
Peasant	13	11.2	6	11.3	19	11.2
Shop employee	7	6.0	1	1.9	8	4.7
Brothel owner	3	2.6	4	7.5	7	4.2
Soldier	5	4.3	0	0	5	3.0
Various	3	2.6	4	7.5	7	4.1
Total:	116	100.0	53	100.00	169	100.00

Source: Report with Regard to the Traffic in Women and Children, Conf./Orient/25 (4 February 1937), archives of the League of Nations, File No. R3047, p. 6.

as it was in Northern China. These traffickers correspond in fact to eighteen cases of abduction. In seven of them, the traffickers formed a pair or a team of three. Most of the teams included both men and women.[29]

There is an interesting work on Peking and its region that will serve, for want of data on Shanghai, to draw a picture of these individuals who traded in human beings.[30] They were generally people with jobs. Nearly three-fourths (156) of the men and nearly half (116) of the women questioned in the study said that they had a job. Those without jobs amounted to only a third of the traffickers jailed.[31] If we take only those with professions or jobs, we obtain Table 7.3.

The table illustrates two points. Although the range of professions is slightly wider, there can be no doubt that the traffickers came from the same circles as those from which they drew their victims. Furthermore, a majority of the traffickers were of urban origin. The category corresponding to the term "worker" is certainly unclear, but it very probably refers to urban workers. Peasants formed only a small proportion of individuals convicted of trafficking in women.

Table 7.4 provides only limited information on the native provinces of the traffickers arrested in Shanghai in 1936. Natives of Jiangsu head the list, with 41%. Contrary to what might be expected, natives of the South Jiangsu (Jiangnan) were almost twice as numerous as those from the north. Anhui was very well represented, which is not at all surprising. A great many women were abducted in this poverty-stricken province. Zhejiang took third place. In all, the provinces of the lower Yangzi were predominant. This finding, in my view, corresponds fairly closely to reality. Even if the order might be completely changed in a bigger sample, it would not basically bring this predominance of Jiangnan into question. The other provinces repre-

Table 7.4. *Native province of 29 traffickers arrested in Shanghai (1936)*

Province	Number	Percentage
Anhui	7	24.1
Guangdong	2	7.0
Jiangbei	4	13.8
Jiangnan	7	24.1
Jiangxi	1	3.4
Shandong	2	7.0
Shanghai	1	3.4
Zhejiang	5	17.2
Total:	29	100.0

Source: Archives of the *Zhongguo jiuji fu ru zonghui*, file 113-1-9.

sented include, in particular, Guangdong, which, as we have seen, was the native region of a whole community of prostitutes in Shanghai.

The Victims of the Trade

Figure 7.1 is based on data taken from a large document prepared by the Anti-Kidnapping Society (AKS) in 1936 on its activities since its inception.[32] The document is not presented in a methodical way, but it contains lists of names of women, girls, and boys rescued between 1913 and 1920. The particulars set down in these lists are very scanty because they cover only age, place of birth, and the circumstances in which the person left the AKS (marriage, return to parents, etc.). In all, 410 women and girls were listed.

Among the women, it was the adolescents (aged thirteen to eighteen) who formed the largest contingent, representing 50% of the total. If the girls aged nineteen to twenty-two are added, we get a group covering almost three-quarters (72.9%) of the population under study. There were not many girls below thirteen and very few cases (2%) of girls below seven. I believe that it is the intended fate of these young girls that explains why the traffickers abducted them only at a relatively late age. This meant that they could enter rapidly into the trade – that is, as soon they had learned music, singing, and the basic etiquette of courtesans. For prostitutes, it was puberty, around fourteen or fifteen, that determined the start of their career. Logically, women over twenty-two were hardly represented in this sample. In the market of prostitution, the value of an older girl was inversely proportional to her age. The youngest girls were undoubtedly more pliant and vulnerable than women of ripe age.[33]

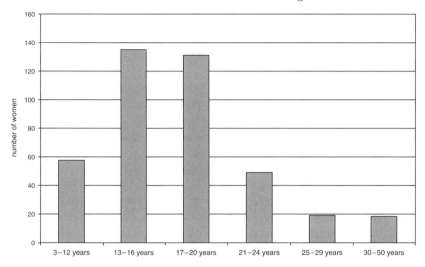

Figure 7.1. Ages of women and girls rescued by the AKS (1913–1920). *Source*: Archives of the *Zhongguo jiuji fu ru zonghui*, file 113-1-2: 1936.

These figures may be compared with those for prostitutes whose cases were reported in the *Shen Bao* during the same period – that is, between 1879 and 1923 (see Table 7.5). The two sets of figures are not very different. The members of the earlier population were on the whole younger than the prostitutes. This is a logical conclusion based on the difference between these two types of population, the former being women who had just been abducted and the latter being prostitutes. I have noted and taken account of the age at which the prostitutes were sold whenever this detail is specified. This explains the presence of a "6–12" age group. The little girls concerned became prostitutes only at puberty. In the other cases, I have chosen the age of the individual at the time of the facts leading to a newspaper report. At the other end of the scale, there is a total absence of women over twenty-nine. Among Chinese prostitutes, those over thirty were completely on the fringe. It must also be pointed out (and this fact does not appear here) that a classification in chronological order does not reveal any major differences, even if the age of girls can be seen to have increased slightly with the approach of the 1930s.

A comparison of data from the files of the AKS with those given in a study conducted in Peking in 1936 shows that, whatever the region, it is young women or even very young women who were the principal targets. Leaving aside some minor differences relating to age groups of little relevance, there is an almost perfect symmetry in the data. This confirms my interpretation about the predominant age groups among the women who fell victim to abduction (see Table 7.6).

Table 7.5. *Age of prostitutes as reported in Shen Bao (1879–1923)*

Age	Number	Percentage
6–12 years	9	15
13–16	9	15
17–20	20	33
21–24	15	25
25–29	7	12
Total:	60	100

Source: *SB*, 11 April 1879; 28 April 1879; 9 May 1879; 9 March 1889; 20 March 1899; 26 May 1899; 13 June 1899; 14 June 1899; 1 October 1899; 27 December 1899; 12 April 1909; 21 June 1909; 9 May 1910; 11 September 1910 [2]; 2 December 1910; 22 December 1910; 18 February 1919; 17 December 1919; 31 December 1921; 27 June 1922; 16 September 1922; 24 September 1923.

Table 7.6. *Age of the victims of trafficking in human beings in Shanghai and in Peking*

Age	Shanghai		Peking	
	Number	Percentage	Number	Percentage
0–4	5	0.8	2	1.2
5–9	15	6.6	16	3.7
10–14	91	20.6	50	22.2
15–19	185	41.2	100	45.1
20–24	77	18.1	44	18.8
25–29	20	7.0	17	4.9
30–34	12	4.1	10	2.9
35–39	1	0.4	1	0.2
40+	4	1.2	3	1.0
Total:	410	100.0	243	100.0

Sources: Archives of the *Zhongguo jiuji fu ru zonghui*, file 113-1-2: 1936.

An overwhelming proportion of the abducted women were natives of the lower Yangzi provinces, especially Jiangsu and Zhejiang (see Figure 7.2). These two provinces, respectively, provided 60.5% and 19.9% of the women. In a wider radius, the traffickers were active in Anhui and, to a lesser extent, in Hubei. This might relate to an effect of proximity and especially ease of transport. Sichuan provided a considerable quota of women.

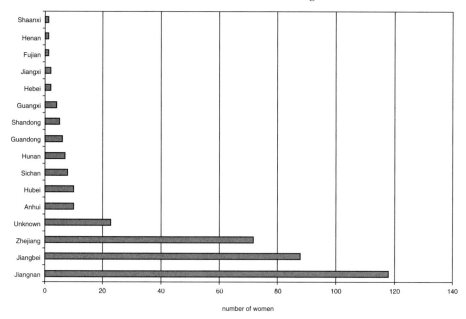

Figure 7.2. Geographical origins of women and girls rescued by the AKS (1913–1920). *Sources*: Archives of the *Zhongguo jiuji fu ru zonghui*, file 113-1-2: 1936; Report with Regard to the Traffic in Women and Children, Conf./Orient/25 (4 February 1937), archives of the League of Nations, File no. R3047, p. 4.

This was also related to the transportation route offered by the Yangzi, a long-used channel for the trade in women as attested to in an article published in 1882.[34] Guangdong does not appear to have been a province that contributed greatly to the trade passing through Shanghai, despite the city's permanent community of Cantonese prostitutes.

Naturally, in view of what has been written on immigration into Shanghai and the geographical distribution of the city's prostitutes, I have paid special attention to Jiangsu and Zhejiang. For Jiangsu, it is necessary to divide the province into north and south.[35] Women from Jiangnan (32.6%) were substantially more numerous than those from the north of the province (24.3%).

This observation contradicts the most common assertions about the predominance of Jiangbei girls among the prostitutes of Shanghai. However, the picture needs to be adjusted. The girls represented in Figure 7.3 were intended for sale into prostitution. Their destination, as will be seen below, was not necessarily Shanghai but instead the cities of the north and the northeast. The girls of Jiangnan were traditionally more sought after for their beauty and talents than those of Jiangbei. This is undoubtedly only a

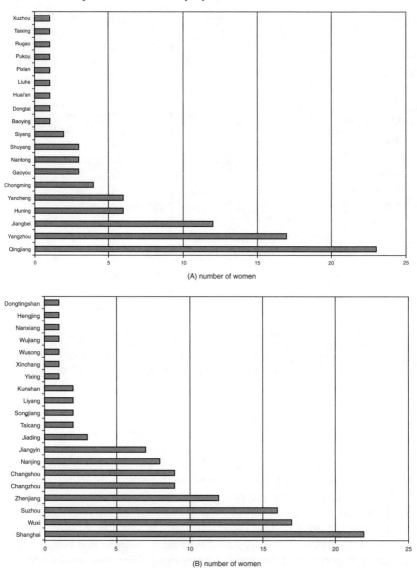

Figure 7.3. Contribution by the *xian* of (A) Jiangbei and (B) Jiangnan to the traffic in women (1913–1920). *Sources*: Archives de la *Zhongguo jiuji fu ru zonghui*, file 113-1-2: 1936.

part of the explanation. In Zhejiang, it was the north of the province (which can be considered to belong to Jiangnan) that was the area of recruitment even though it was not the poorest part of the province. The fact is that the trade in human beings had the same constraints, related to the means of transportation, as other forms of trade.

Map 2 clearly shows that there was a geography of the trade in women based on the main communication routes. In Jiangsu, the Great Canal appears to have been a preferred route. The line running through Pixian, Siyang, Qingjiang, Baoying, Gaoyou, Yangzhou, Changzhou, Wuxi, and Suzhou emerges very clearly. This was the original site of the "Green Gang" (*Qingbang*).[36] There was also a secondary route from Huning to Nantong. The Yangzi was the third route from this province. The case of Zhejiang was slightly different. If we leave out a few *xian* in the interior, which provided only a small number of victims, most of the areas from which the women came were on the coast and provided the same means of transport as the rivers of Jiangsu. Within the provinces themselves, certain cities and their surrounding *xian* made a considerable contribution. Jiangbei, Qingjiang and Yangzhou accounted for nearly half of the girls kidnapped in the region. Jiangnan, Changzhou, Changshou, Suzhou, and Zhenjiang accounted for about 40% of the total and Shanghai for 18.5%.

There can be no doubt that the girls who were sold or pledged by members of their own families generally came from very underprivileged and even destitute sections for whom the sale of a girl or a spouse could bring temporary relief or help pay some debt or other. But, on the contrary, it is far more difficult to be certain about the social origins of the abducted women because the data are extremely fragmentary. From time to time, the police and AKS reports provide some details that suggest that most of the girls came from lowly origins and were more exposed to contact with the street and to the risk of abduction. For the period 1915 to 1930, I have found fifteen references to the profession of the victim's father or mother (see Table 7.7).

It is clear that the women and girls who were victims of this trade came from the common classes, although they were not necessarily poor. Naturally, these fifteen cases cannot be used to draw any general conclusions. It can be seen, however, that these women were probably natives of urban areas rather than from the country. It may be assumed that profession was an important detail in identifying the parents of victims in the cities and towns but had no meaning for people from the country. This may explain the total absence of peasants in Table 7.7. What is striking, however, is the low degree of importance attached to this item of identification of an individual. It is a piece of information that hardly appears in the documents of the AKS. A study covering a hundred women abducted in the Peking region also reveals a fairly marked predominance of individuals from the urban lower classes[37] (see Table 7.8).

The idea that the prostitutes were overwhelmingly of peasant origin perhaps needs to be reconsidered. The information given about their birthplace is hardly useful in this respect because there is confusion, at the administrative level, between a city or town and its surrounding *xian*. A woman who was a native of Wuxi could equally well have come from a

Map 2. The geography of kidnapping: the main sites. Data taken from archives of the *Zhongguo jiuji fu ru zonghui*, file 113-1-2: 1936.

Table 7.7. *Social origin of female victims of abduction*

Social Origin	Number
Barber	1
Cobbler	1
Servant	2
Shop worker	1
Box merchant	1
Charcoal seller	1
Fruit vendor	1
Dumpling vendor	1
Worker	1
Small craftsman	1
Tailor	1
Dyer	2
Cigarette vendor	1

Sources: Archives of the *Zhongguo jiuji fu ru zonghui*, file 113-1-2: 1936, p. 14, p. 24, p. 111, p. 113, p. 114; file 113-1-4, p. 50 (1927), p. 62 (1927), p. 75 (1927), p. 85 (1926), p. 86 (1926); *SB*, 14 December 1921; 26 May 1930.

Table 7.8. *Social origin of 100 women abducted in the Peking region*

Occupation (of Father)	Number	Percentage
Jobless	25	25
Peasant	12	12
Rickshaw puller	12	12
Servant	11	11
Itinerant merchant	10	10
Shop worker	9	9
Policeman	6	6
Worker	5	5
Actor	5	5
Carpenter	2	2
Gas-lamp lighter	1	1
Postman	1	1
Road-mender	1	1
Total:	100	100

Source: Report with Regard to the Traffic in Women and Children, Conf./Orient/25 (4 February 1937), archives of the League of Nations, File No. R3047, p. 4.

village in the *xian* of Wuxi. A large number of these women perhaps took a route that led them from their village to one or more towns and then to Shanghai or Peking.

In the towns, it is clear that the main victims in the twentieth century were women who had to go outdoors. I have referred to examples of working women. These examples appear to have been more typical of the second half of the 1920s and the 1930s, as indicated by the cases that I have found. The double twelve-hour-shift system prevailing in the Chinese factories meant that women were obliged to move about in the dark when there were few people in the streets. Many went about in groups for self-protection against attacks by layabouts, but this was not always possible or adequate. The traffickers were often ready to tackle several girls at a time. In 1926, two women workers aged twenty-three and thirteen were abducted together while on the way to their factory.[38] In May 1930, two working women aged seventeen were lured by a woman who then held them prisoner in her home with her son's help.[39]

A seventeen-year-old working woman met a neighbor who offered her a job as a waitress earning five times more for lighter work. She followed him into his establishment, which turned out to be a brothel where she was raped and forced to prostitute herself.[40] Even if, as Emily Honig points out, many cases can be found of working women who became prostitutes, I do not think that the working women of Shanghai constituted a major hunting ground for the abductors.[41] The working women of Shanghai were used to the lifestyles of the big cities. They had more ways of coping in the event of abduction and were less likely to be pliant than the young girls from the villages and surrounding small towns. It also happened that prostitutes themselves were abducted and resold.[42]

The Price of a Woman

Most of the authors agree that what a woman was worth in the Chinese market of prostitution depended on her beauty and her age, and even on her talents if she had received a musical education. Table 7.9 lists fifty-four examples of sums paid for the sale of women. They are for the same period as earlier (1879–1930). A chronological classification indicates that the time variable was not very relevant to price fluctuations. What are the conclusions to be drawn from this scanty data?

The smallest sums correspond to the sale of little girls. Two little girls were sold for 28 and 32 yuan after having passed through several middlemen. However, adolescent girls, too, were sold for derisory prices. The average was 281 yuan. This figure is not of great significance. The mode was between 100 and 300 yuan, covering 50% of the cases. At the two extremes, one-fifth of the sums were smaller than 100 yuan and a good one-fourth ranged from 301 to 1,000 yuan. A woman's life really had little worth. Some

Table 7.9. *Purchase price of women destined for prostitution*

Amount (yuan)	Number	Percentages
20–50	6	11.1
51–100	6	11.1
101–200	14	25.9
201–300	13	24.1
301–500	6	11.1
501–1,000	9	16.7
Total:	54	100.0

Sources: *SB*, 28 April 1879; 9 June 1879; 9 March 1889; 19 January 1899; 20 January 1899; 26 May 1899; 13 June 1899; 14 June 1899; 13 December 1899; 13 January 1909; 8 May 1909; 15 April 1910; 9 September 1910; 21 October 1910; 22 December 1910; 20 February 1919; 22 May 1919; 9 June 1920; 17 July 1920; 19 February 1921; 19 August 1921; 28 October 1921; 31 December 1921; 17 May 1922; 27 June 1922; 3 July 1922; 6 July 1923; 24 September 1923; 28 November 1923; 9 July 1924; 20 October 1938; *North China Herald*, 1 June 1912 [2]; Archives of the *Zhongguo furu jiuji zonghui*, file 113-1-4 [5]; file 113-1-2: 1936, p. 13, p. 110, p. 112, p. 115 [2], p. 122; file 2-311-2; Archives of the Secretariat, International Settlement, file 3-00445.

hundreds of yuan were enough to acquire a "working tool" that would yield far more than the capital invested. Even among the *yeji* and the *huayanjian*, where the fees were low, a girl's price could be "recouped" within two to three months depending on her success with her customers.

Their Destination

The women who were abducted or sold were the object of a trade conducted over very great distances. First of all, it was necessary to meet the demand in areas that were demographically deficient in members of the fairer sex. Secondly, the traffickers' goal was to isolate the victims as far as possible by sending them far away to regions where they did not speak the local language. This meant that they were unable to lodge complaints, call out for help, or quite simply make themselves understood in any street altercation. The impact was also psychological. A woman outside her family, wholly without means in a strange land, became more vulnerable and more pliant. It must be specified that not all girls were sold as prostitutes. Some of them were sold as wives, concubines, daughters-in-law, adopted daugh-

Table 7.10. *The fate of 130 women abducted in the Peking region (around 1936)*

Fate	Number	Percentage
Prostitute	99	76
Wife	16	12
Concubine	5	4
Daughter-in-law	1	1
Adopted daughter	8	6
Bondservant	1	1
Total:	130	100

Source: Report with regard to Traffic in Women and Children, Conf./Orient/25 (4 February 1937), archives of the League of Nations, file No. R3047, p. 3.

ters, or bondservants (*beinü*) (see Table 7.10). I do not have quantitative data about the proportion of each category for Shanghai and the lower Yangzi. If we go by the young Chinese sociologist's study quoted above, the very great majority of the women went into prostitution.

In general, the trade in women flowed toward the north and northeast. Women who were natives of the lower Yangzi provinces were sold throughout China. A proportion of them came to Shanghai itself. They included especially natives of Jiangbei, although excessive generalization must be avoided here because there are no statistical data to prove this point. The women of Jiangnan were as much victims of this trade as their neighbors in the northern part of the province, and all we have as "proof" of the overrepresentation of the latter among the prostitutes of Shanghai is the testimony of contemporaries (journalists, authors of guides, etc.) whose viewpoint was strongly biased. In a facile generalization, the *yeji* were identified with the girls of Jiangbei and vice versa. This notion remains to be proven. There was no need to look very far for women incapable of making themselves understood by Shanghai's local population. The peasants of Jiangbei and Zhejiang spoke languages that were incomprehensible to the people of Shanghai. Hankou was also a frequent terminal point for girls abducted in Shanghai.[43]

A good number of them were also dispatched to the northern provinces and especially to the northeast. All the accounts that I have found point to Manchuria, which was a new region. It was China's last frontier, where hundreds of thousands of peasants came and settled throughout the twentieth century. The region was characterized by a heavy imbalance between the sexes, leading to a huge traffic in women destined for the brothels of its cities and towns. When the AKS opened sections in Manchuria (see Chapter

14), it was not by chance but rather because it discovered a close correlation between the abduction of women in the lower Yangzi and the flourishing market of prostitutes in northeast China. This said, the traffic went in all directions, depending on the place of abduction. The press reports the existence of traffic in women from Harbin (Manchuria) to Qingdao (Shandong).[44] In 1930, women purchased in the province of Shaanxi were sold in the neighboring provinces of Henan and Shanxi.[45]

The Procurers

Almost all those who became prostitutes did so under duress. In other words, they did not have any choice in the matter, because entry into prostitution was forced upon them by one or more outside individuals. Entry into the circuit of prostitution generally came about as a result of economic difficulties suffered by the concerned party or her family circle or following an abduction. I shall try to shed light here on an essential aspect of the traffic in women, on the basis of data on some hundred women whose circumstances of entry into prostitution are known. This sample is small as compared with the huge numbers of prostitutes for the period considered (1879–1930). However, it includes prostitutes rescued "by chance" and others whose fate surfaced in the press, often in connection with some trivial incident. The sample includes *yeji* as well as *huayanjian*, Cantonese prostitutes and courtesans of all kinds. It therefore does not form any special group. Rather it corresponds to a set of individuals who appeared fleetingly (for no more than the brief instant needed to register an identity) in the course of a half century of history.

Two main modes of action can be seen: (a) kidnapping, which includes deceit, and (b) intervention by individuals who were sometimes very close acquaintances. Kidnapping seems to have been the most common experience for half the prostitutes in my sample. This is a large proportion and not limited to any specific period. A classification that takes the chronology into account shows that kidnapping was a common mode of action in every period. However, this first impression needs to be modified. My data include a good number of cases drawn from the archives of the AKS whose vocation was to rescue kidnapped women or girls. The statistics that I have prepared from these cases tend to raise the proportion of cases of abduction. The last two columns of Table 7.11 therefore give only data taken from *Shen Bao*. The proportion of abductions fell very significantly, although it bottomed out at a fairly high level. Although it is hardly possible to calculate any average between the two sets of figures, it would seem that they are close to the reality of the female trade in China.

The other less brutal mode of kidnapping involved deceit followed or accompanied by abduction. Deceit is an ambiguous term that recurs very often in the statements by prostitutes. The corresponding verb actually con-

Table 7.11. *Persons responsible for entry into prostitution*

Person responsible for abduction	Shen Bao and AKS		Shen Bao	
	Number	Percentage	Number	Percentage
Kidnapper	47	35.6	15	17.0
Deceiver	17	12.9	10	11.4
Husband	20	15.1	19	21.6
Mother	19	14.4	18	20.4
Father	8	6.1	8	9.1
Parents	6	4.5	6	6.8
Relatives	10	7.6	8	9.1
Adoptive mother	3	2.3	2	2.3
Policeman	2	1.5	2	2.3
Total:	132	100.0	88	100.0

Sources: *SB*, 30 October 1879; 11 April 1879; 28 April 1879; 19 January 1899; 22 February 1899; 25 February 1899; 17 March 1899; 20 March 1899; 14 June 1899; 26 June 1899; 1 October 1899; 8 November 1899; 13 December 1899; 27 December 1899; 13 January 1909; 2 February 1909; 4 February 1909; 16 February 1909; 25 February 1909; 12 April 1909; 8 May 1909; 2 June 1909; 4 September 1909 [2]; 21 June 1909; 13 October 1909; 17 November 1909; 15 April 1910; 9 May 1910; 4 June 1910; 11 September 1910; 2 December 1910; 9 December 1910; 22 December 1910; 4 January 1919; 18 February 1919; 19 February 1919; 2 April 1919; 22 May 1919; 30 July 1919; 15 December 1919; 17 December 1919; 29 January 1920; 11 February 1920; 11 April 1920; 9 June 1920; 17 July 1920; 24 July 1920; 4 October 1920; 24 November 1920; 1 January 1921; 3 February 1921; 19 February 1921; 2 April 1921; 15 June 1921; 19 August 1921; 16 September 1921; 12 October 1921; 28 October 1921; 14 December 1921; 31 December 1921; 17 May 1922; 27 June 1922; 3 July 1922; 27 August 1922; 29 August 1922; 1 August 1922; 16 September 1922; 13 December 1922; 22 December 1922; 24 March 1923; 18 May 1923; 27 June 1923; 9 July 1923; 16 July 1923; 14 August 1923; 16 August 1923; 24 September 1923; 28 November 1923; 7 December 1923; 9 December 1923; 21 March 1924; 6 July 1924; 9 July 1924; 14 December 1924; 3 July 1928; 21 June 1930; 20 November 1930; *North China Herald*, 1 June 1912 [2]; archives of the *Zhongguo jiuji fu ru zonghui*, files 113-1-2 and 113-1-4.

sists of two complementary verbs: *you*, which means "to seduce" or "to deceive," and *guai*, which means "to abduct." The former term raises a problem because the precise nature of the seduction in question was never explicitly stated. It can be understood in the sense of amorous seduction or in a more day-to-day sense of deceiving someone about one's real intentions whatever they may be. It is in the latter sense that the word must be understood. The majority of the girls were deceived by other women rather than by men. The strict separation of the sexes in China prevented men from playing a major role in initiating contact with the girls. In the two percentage columns of Table 7.11, the proportion of women deceived and abducted into prostitution is very similar (11.4% and 12.9%). Although we must be cautious about extrapolating these figures to all the prostitutes in Shanghai, it would appear that about a third of them were sold like cattle and experienced conditions that were tantamount to slavery.[46]

The others were victims of their own parents or, if orphaned, of their relatives. They fell prey to acquaintances or to family friends. Parents weighed heavily (between 25% and 36%) among those who caused a girl to be placed in a brothel. While fathers are infrequently referred to by name, mothers appear to have been the major procuresses for the market. In most cases, they were poor women, very often with no means to bring up a daughter or not enough to support all of their children. When the girls were sold off at a very young age, the parents did not know what lay in store for them. In all likelihood, they preferred not to know. Despite all that has been said on the inferior condition of women in China, it is difficult to imagine that a peasant man or woman would light-heartedly accept separation from his or her daughter. It was poverty, hunger, and sometimes the most extreme destitution that pushed families to sell off their daughters, sometimes with full knowledge of their fate. On the contrary, a stable but poor family would sometimes go to any lengths to retrieve an abducted daughter, even if she had spent several weeks, months, or years in an establishment of prostitution.

After the parents, it was husbands who most frequently prostituted their wives. They amount to one-fifth of the individuals mentioned in the press, although they appear to have been far less numerous in the AKS figures. Poverty, gambling, opium, and delinquency were often the cause of their action. It would seem that being placed in a house of prostitution was looked upon as a temporary solution to difficult economic circumstances. Indeed, husbands would pledge their wives rather than sell them. In most cases, the women accepted a fate that was dictated to them by their husbands or families. This point is difficult to clarify for want of testimony on the part of the concerned parties. What can be seen, however, is that when women escaped or made complaints, they did so because of ill treatment on the part of the madam or *guinu* rather than because they had become prostitutes under duress. In other words, women were willing to abide by the terms of their contracts so long as their working conditions did not become unbearable or so long as they did not get a chance to quit (through the courts). The group that I have called "relations" and "acquaintances" encompasses almost the full range of possibilities within the Chinese family and even beyond it: uncles, elderly clan members, cousins, brothers, sisters, neighbors, local shopkeepers, working colleagues, policemen, and so on. We shall see, when examining the circumstances of abduction, that there were no limits to the varieties of "traffickers" in operation.

Kidnapping and Abduction: The Circumstances

The notion of a female trade evokes the idea of shady and cynical flesh merchants nourishing their sordid commerce with easy prey in the form of lone young women in the cities and villages. No such clear-cut picture emerges from a study of the facts. Actually, any Chinese woman was potentially exposed to the risk of an abduction or a kidnapping that could take her into a house of prostitution. Naturally, not all the social classes were equally affected. However, apart from the daughters and wives of the elites who were protected except in the case of accidental circumstances (such as war, the death of a husband, etc.), no women could be assured of even her relative safety. The main reason for this is that abduction and kidnapping often came about by chance or through a combination of special circumstances.

One of the classic methods was to propose a regular job to a woman in order to lure her to Shanghai. Once she arrived, a middleman would make contact with the house of prostitution and sell the girl. In this situation, women were hardly able to react. Cut off from their families, lost in the anonymity of the city, often illiterate, and above all threatened with violence or having become victims of violence, they were incapable of offering resistance. Wang Jinyi entrusted his wife to a recruiter who had offered her a servant's job in Shanghai and then discovered to his surprise that she had been sold into a house on rue Qipan.[47] Li Jing, a thirty-eight-year-old widow, placed her daughter as a servant in a family in return for a sum of 40 yuan. The girl worked for two years and then, being unable to pay off her debt, was sold to a house of prostitution by the mistress of the house.[48] In 1920, a young seventeen-year-old working girl went to the railway station to accompany a friend who had been promised a servant's job in Dalian. Both ended up in a house of prostitution in this city.[49]

It is not always easy to ascertain the truth. A girl from Ningbo said she had lost her husband and had been raped by an individual who had pledged her to a brothel. The accused replied that he had married the girl after having paid out 160 yuan but that she had taken to prostitution of her own accord. Not wishing to make a decision in the matter, the judge decided to set them both free.[50] A female resident of the old city accused her partner of having sold her to a brothel. After inquiry, the police concluded that the man and woman were individuals of low morals. They were given 200 and 100 bamboo lashes, respectively.[51] A woman who had pledged a young girl to a brothel owned by her uncle defended herself against the charge of abduction by blaming the girl's mother.[52]

Even if it was not always done explicitly, cases were often reported of women claiming to have been "lured" to Shanghai. This generally meant that they had been tempted by the dazzling prospect of a well-paid job.[53] It was women who most usually played the role of "seductress." These were especially women from the same region (*tongxiang*) as the victim, and they played on the trust inspired by this relationship. The wife of a carpenter from Hunan was lured to Hankou by a *tongxiang* who then took her up to Shanghai.[54] A young girl from Chaozhou (Guangdong) was lured to Shanghai by a *tongxiang* who promised her a job in a mill. In fact, she was sold for 700 yuan to a house of prostitution in the French Concession.[55] The role of *tongxiang* is mentioned in many other cases.[56]

In fact, anybody could go in for kidnapping, whether alone, in pairs, or in groups. A couple kidnapped a woman in Hankou and sold her to a house in Shanghai.[57] In a Shanghai family, the wife and her sister-in-law were kidnapped successively by four friends of their neighbors who often came to play mahjong. They invited the younger of the two women to a dance hall. When she did not return, they suggested to the other girl that she should go and look for her sister-in-law in the dance hall and then kidnapped her too.[58] In Hangzhou, a policeman and an old lady took advantage of the trust and naiveté of the female employee of a small noodle shop to take her to Shanghai. There she was handed over to two other women who placed her in a house of prostitution.[59]

A seventeen-year-old girl living with her family in a straw hut was urged several times by women in the region to go to Yangzhou and look for a job. She made up her mind to do so on the 25th of December 1920 and was later found in a house of prostitution in the city. Some days later, she was taken to Zhenjiang by another woman and an elderly man. From there, the trio went to Shanghai, where the girl was sold to a *huayanjian*.[60] In a similar case, a mother received an offer from a friend to take her daughter to Hankou on a pleasure trip. The friend actually took the girl to Tianjin and then Peking and Manchuria, where she sold her for 740 yuan.[61] In Wuhu, a man, abetted by his wife, seduced a friend's daughter, made her go to Shanghai, and sold her to a madam who, in turn, sold her to an establishment in Fuzhou.[62] These examples show that the culprits were often acquaintances and even friends of the family.[63] One also gets the impression that an opportunity was all that it took for an honest man to suddenly turn into a kidnapper. A sixteen-year-old girl was abducted by a shoemaker to whom she had brought some shoes for repair.[64] The daughter of an itinerant merchant tradesman of Wuxi, residing in Yangshupu, Shanghai's big industrial district, was kidnapped by a metal craftsman.[65]

The absence of men in a family could heighten a woman's risk of ending up in a house of prostitution. In 1910, a hotel servant informed the police of the presence of suspicious-looking couples in the establishment. An investigation revealed that two men had come from Jiangbei with two women, a mother and daughter, whom they were trying to sell to a *huayanjian* in Shanghai. The woman had lost her husband three years earlier. She and her daughter had followed the two individuals to Shanghai and then discovered their true intentions.[66] A girl, having lost her whole family, was lured to Shanghai by an old man (*lao touzi*) who sold her to a brothel in July 1919. As of October, she had not yet been prostituted and was sold as a daughter-in-law in a neighboring village. She was then taken to Shanghai for resale. This is when the police arrested the abductors.[67] No details are provided, but the impression given by this incident is that of a girl being used as a mere piece of goods to be sold and resold whenever there was any profit to be got out of her. Many cases of abducted orphaned girls are mentioned in the press.[68] To this, we must add the category of bondservants (*beinü*), who often had to go out of the house and were exposed to the risks of abduction.[69]

Abducted women were sometimes victims of sexual violence. Even if, as we have seen, it would be in the interest of a trafficker or abductor to preserve a girl's virginity in order to obtain greater profit from her, this was true only of the youngest and those destined for a courtesan's house. Most of the cases mentioned in this chapter are of girls sold to ordinary houses of prostitution where virginity was hardly of any value. The sources are rarely explicit on the subject of sexual violence. However, it is difficult to say if this means that rape was infrequently resorted to for the reason that it could have provoked a girl to resist more vigorously and draw outside attention before she reached the brothel or if it was a result of self-censorship by the press or by victims before the authorities.

The reality of sexual violence, however, is proven. Two maidservants of a merchant were lured to a small hotel by one Pan Quansheng with his concubine's connivance. One of the girls was raped thrice by Pan while the other managed to resist him. The cries of the girls alerted the hotelkeeper, who brought in the police. When arrested, Pan already had a boat ticket for Yingkou (Manchuria) and the visiting card of a house of prostitution where he was planning to sell the girls.[70] The daughter of a peasant from Nanhui (Pudong) was raped and sequestered for four days by a neighbor's lover, who had taken her to the city. She was then put on board a ship heading for Manchuria.[71] Shi Arong, a young girl from Changzhou, was lured to Shanghai by a *tongxiang* who entrusted her to two layabouts, also from Changzhou. The men took her to a small hotel where they raped her several times, having decided to sell her to a brothel.[72] The purpose of the rape was to psychologically destabilize the young girls and demean them in the eyes of society, and especially in the marriage market, by depriving them of their virginity.

To this list of victims who came into prostitution under duress, we must add women who were forced by circumstances to make this choice, not that they suffered any specific violence or constraint. Many came to Shanghai looking for jobs. Once their meager resources were gone, they had no choice but to give themselves up to prostitution.[73] Living as they did in small sheds inhabited by a population of pittance-earners, destitute individuals, and prostitutes, it is not surprising that they were dragged down the slope toward prostitution. Although cases of abduction can be found in recent times in Shanghai,[74] it would seem to me that the Sino-Japanese War caused an interruption in this phenomenon, at least locally. First, the Japanese occupation resulted in a profound economic crisis whose effects did not spare the world of prostitution. Demand fell considerably, and the market in women collapsed. At liberation in 1945, Shanghai was overwhelmed by millions of refugees, especially single women, widows, orphans, and women separated from their families by the haphazard circumstances of migratory movements. It was no longer necessary or economically profitable to look for women from outside when the city itself had such a "pool of labor."

The Suppression and Punishment of Traffickers

The traffickers, both men and women, were rarely caught, because most of them were able to sink into the anonymity of China's itinerant masses. However, when a victim resisted and drew the attention of the authorities or, in the case of Shanghai, when an inspector of the AKS pinpointed a suspicious traveler, then professional traffickers could be arrested. Still, it was not always easy to establish proof of an offense. A 1911 report by the head of the municipal police states that although the number of individuals discharged might appear to be great, it "results from the difficulty we are experiencing in finding proof of thefts (kidnappings) committed outside Shanghai as well as proof of practices involving the trade in children [and women] that is being carried out openly in China and against which we are powerless."[75] The statistics of the Mixed Court of the International Settlement also point to a fairly high proportion of acquittals.

When the accused were judged to be guilty, the punishments were relatively heavy. In the nineteenth century, when the Chinese authorities were still inflicting corporal punishment, traffickers would be given a severe volley of bamboo strokes and were sometimes also made to wear a cangue. In 1879, a certain Zhang who had promised a married woman a servant's job and then sold her to a house of prostitution was sentenced to 100 bamboo lashes.[76] An indelicate husband who had pledged his wife also received 100 lashes.[77] A housewife who had sold a girl who had been placed in her charge as a servant was sentenced to 40 slaps. The judge's relative clemency can be explained by the fact that the girl's own mother had previously pledged her as a prostitute.[78] In another case, all the persons implicated in the pledging of a girl were punished. Mrs. Xi Lu had pledged her daughter for 40 yuan through a lady named Qin Tang. It is not clear to what extent the girl had been a consenting party. The judge sentenced the prostitute to 200 slaps. Her mother and the middlemen received 100 slaps each, while the proprietor of the house and the girl's father were sentenced to 50 lashes. The proprietor's wife was not let off and got 40 slaps.[79] In 1909, two hairdressers who had kidnapped a prostitute for resale were punished with 400 bamboo lashes.[80]

Corporal punishment was gradually replaced by imprisonment whose severity seems to have depended on whether the trafficking was casual or done on a professional basis.[81] In 1909, a man who had sold his fiancée was sentenced to two weeks' imprisonment.[82] Two layabouts who had abducted a woman were imprisoned without any specific period being indicated, while the madam who had accepted the "goods" was fined 50 yuan.[83] In the same month, four gangsters were sentenced to three months' imprisonment for the same offense, and the madam was sentenced to two months' imprisonment.[84] In another case of kidnapping, the *guinu* of the house who had purchased a girl was sentenced to three months in prison. The two intermediaries, both women, were sentenced to two months' imprisonment. When the judges felt that they were dealing with real professional abductors, the sentences were heavier. In 1909, three layabouts, found accompanying a Ningbo woman whom they had abducted, were each sentenced to one year's imprisonment.[85] In the following year, a kidnapper and a madam were sentenced to nine months and two months of imprisonment, respectively.[86]

The adoption of a modern penal code in China made for greater efficiency in the punishment of acts of sequestration and trade in human beings, especially for purposes of prostitution. In 1920, a man from Huzhou (Zhejiang) who had sold his wife to a house of prostitution in Shanghai with the help of a pair of middlemen was sentenced to four years' imprisonment, while a sentence of nine months was handed down against the pair.[87] In the following year, two women who had taken part in the abduction of a sixteen-year-old girl and in her sale in Manchuria were sentenced to five years' imprisonment.[88] The court took note of aggravating circumstances. A kidnapper who had raped his victim several times was sentenced to ten years in prison, and his accomplice was sentenced to five years.[89] The courts began handing down severe punishments against the madams when they were found to be housing girls against their will.[90]

Table 7.12 confirms a trend toward increasingly heavy punishment, with sentences of more than five years' imprisonment in the 1920s and a larger number of cases where offenders were sent to prison for periods of more than two years.

In a limited sample (covering twenty-nine persons arrested through the offices of AKS inspectors between March and September 1936), the sentences handed down were limited to a narrow bracket, with more than half (55%) of the individuals having been sentenced to imprisonment for a year and a half or less. It is true that a good third (34%) of them received far heavier sentences (of five to eight years). These may have been traffickers known to be repeated offenders or professionals.[91]

The proprietors of the houses of prostitution defended themselves in the

Table 7.12. *Sentences handed down by the Mixed Court of the French Concession for the abduction of women (1910–1930)*

Sentence	1910	1911	1912	1913	1914	1915	1916	1917	1918	1919
Fines	10	2	1	—	9	3	2	10	7	2
1–3 months	8	7	8	18	8	13	14	14	7	9
3–6 months	6	4	5	7	12	11	5	8	3	1
6 months–1 year	4	1	3	5	6	18	12	6	2	2
1–2 years	7	5	4	3	5	4	6	1	3	2
2–5 years	1	—	2	3	3	3	1	3	—	—
5–10 years	—	—	—	—	—	2	—	5	—	—
10–20 years	—	—	—	—	—	—	—	—	—	—

Sentence	1920	1921	1922	1923	1924	1926	1927	1928	1929	1930
Fines	1	8	26	51	23	7	10	—	—	1
1–3 months	2	8	18	43	17	25	8	18	24	22
3–6 months	4	7	16	24	12	4	8	11	12	24
6 months–1 year	3	3	11	13	11	1	1	5	5	12
1–2 years	4	4	2	7	9	3	2	6	4	11
2–5 years	2	8	9	2	7	—	—	6	—	8
5–10 years	—	—	—	—	1	—	—	—	—	2
10–20 years	—	—	—	—	2	—	—	—	—	—

Sources: Conseil d'administration municipale de la Concession française, *Compte rendu de la gestion pour l'exercice 1908*, p. 126; *1909*, p. 132; *1910*, p. 124; *1911*, p. 175; *1912*, p. 202; *1913*, p. 163; *1914*, p. 146; *1915*, p. 108; *1916*, p. 141; *1917*, p. 168; *1918*, p. 156; *1919*, p. 169; *1920*, p. 260; *1921*, p. 225; *1922*, p. 319; *1923*, p. 330; *1924*, p. 303; *1926*, p. 328; *1927*, p. 222; *1928*, p. 251; *1929*, p. 308; *1930*, p. 335.

courts by protesting their good faith. They would generally say that a girl had been sold to them by persons purporting to be her parents, and they would go so far as to furnish proof that the girls in their care had been honestly purchased. Sometimes they were acquitted.[92] The sale of a girl was often covered by a properly drafted contract.[93] The courts, however, were not always taken in by these statements and would punish the brothel owners for lodging women whose "origins were unclear" (*lai li bu ming*).[94] The brothel proprietors themselves were sometimes victims of fraud: A madam brought a complaint against a man who had sold her his daughter for 175 yuan and who then returned to abduct the girl. This said, it must be pointed out that the madam, who had a certificate of sale, sued the father as if the girl had become her lawful possession.[95]

The Chinese magistrates in the nineteenth century and even up to 1911 did not question a madam's right to own a prostitute when the sale had been made with the agreement of the parents or legal guardians. They punished ill treatment but did not take action against brothel owners deemed to have acted in good faith. However, it would happen that a madam would of her own accord ask the police to find a prostitute who had taken flight. A madam, who had had one of her girls abducted by two hairdressers, complained to the authorities and was able to recover her property.[96] The madam of a Cantonese establishment informed the police about the escape of one of her inmates, and she asked for a search to be made.[97] Another prostitute was arrested upon a complaint by her madam, but then claimed to have been the victim of a sale to the house from which she was trying to escape. The court placed her in a charitable institution.[98]

The Way Out

For a prostitute or a victim of abduction, to find escape was in most cases a matter of chance: It could come about during an argument in the establishment, an arrest for soliciting, altercations in the street or in a hotel where girls were often locked up to be presented to potential buyers, and so on. All these incidents would enable a girl to draw attention and be brought before a judge, where she could state that she had been sold and had no desire to continue.[99] Other circumstances could sometimes serve as a raft to a drowning soul. In particular, they included investigations by families or by the AKS in Shanghai. However, it was not easy to look for abducted women because they were, to a certain extent, mobile. This mobility could come about in three ways: Either the madam would find it profitable to resell the girl elsewhere, in a place where her value was higher (for example, in Shanghai if she came from a small city)[100]; or the madam would get wind of an inquiry in progress that risked placing her in an awkward position[101]; or again the madam would try to get rid of a girl who was not yielding sufficient profit. In all these cases, the prostitute would be required to move from one house to another or from one city to another, and so it would become difficult to find any trace of her.

Although it was sometimes families that initiated the sales of young girls into the circuit of prostitution, they could also play the opposite role. A certain Wu tried to sell his seven-year-old stepdaughter as a prostitute. The mother discovered this and immediately complained to the authorities.[102] A young woman from Wuxi had been deceived and sold into a Shanghai house with the help of a prostitute. Her parents complained and got her back.[103] One woman informed the police when her niece sent word to her that she had been abducted.[104] A young girl of eighteen was sold by her own mother, an inveterate gambler who needed to settle her gambling debts. It was the father's intervention that got the girl out of the house of prostitution.[105] A woman who had been pledged to a brothel by her husband was rescued by her own family, who took the matter to court.[106]

Another very common method was to put out an announcement in the press with the victim's photo. I have not found any indications about the effectiveness of this method, but it must be pointed out that advertisements of this nature abounded in the Shanghai dailies. Some people relied on their own resources. A brother searched for his sister, starting in Hangzhou, where she had first been sold, and going up to Shanghai, where the madam had sold her again.[107] Some degree of stubbornness was needed to carry out these investigations all alone and bear the considerable costs of making a search. Complainants sometimes had to cope with indifference on the part of the authorities. A dumpling seller in Yangshupu learned from a friend returning from Fuzhou that his daughter, who had been missing for five months, had been sold as a prostitute into a house in that city. When the father and his friend went to Fuzhou to rescue the girl, they came up against the madam, who claimed that she had purchased the girl from persons purporting to be her parents. The local police station sent the complainants to the police headquarters, but there was no redress available there either. Finally, despairing of a solution, the man went to his native-place association (*Xijin gongsuo*) in Shanghai, which took the matter in hand and forwarded his request to the AKS.[108]

Customers would sometimes agree to help (Plate 9). A girl who had been kidnapped and placed in a Shanghai *huayanjian* managed to alert her sister through a sympathetic customer.[109] This kind of situation was more frequent when the prostitute and the customer were natives of the same region. First of all, geographical proximity created a special bond, and then the prostitute could explain her fate to the customer in a language that her guardians did not understand. A Hangzhou merchant, returning from Xi'an, agreed to inform a prostitute's mother that she was in a house in that city.[110] A prostitute from Pudong persuaded one of her customers, a native of the same region, to take a letter to her parents.[111] However, customers were probably not always the best recourse for getting out of prostitution. A girl who had managed to escape knocked on the door of a frequent customer, but he refused to welcome her. She then went to the police.[112]

Some girls got out because they knew how to write.[113] Despite generally close surveillance, they managed to send letters outside, especially through customers. The wife of a charcoal merchant, who had been abducted on her way to the market, managed to slip a missive to a sailor on a boat taking her to be sold in Qingdao.[114] Two women, one from Jiangbei and the other from Ningbo, wrote to their husbands, informing them that they had been abducted and giving them the address of the establishment in which they were located.[115] The period that elapsed between the abduction and the time when the girl managed to send word about her location could sometimes be very long. One girl abducted on April 4, 1925 was able to write to her family only a year later.[116] Another girl who had been abducted in Shanghai and then sold successively in Hankou and Tianjin had to wait four years for an opportunity to inform her family through a passing ship's engineer, in all probability a *tongxiang*.[117]

In Shanghai, the AKS played an essential role through its inspectors who monitored the places of transit for travelers, especially the wharves. Other institutions played a role. These included the police, the Mixed Courts, the

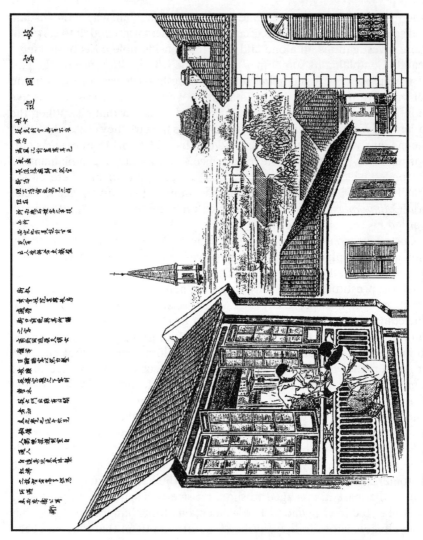

Plate 9. A prostitute trying to elope with a customer.

Table 7.13. *Institutions sending girls for admission to the Anti-Kidnapping Society (1913–1915)*

Institution	Number	Percentages
AKS inspectors	54	14.4
Native-place association	17	4.5
Police or outside AKS sections	50	13.3
Mixed Courts	31	8.3
Boats (presumably AKS inspectors)	41	10.9
Shanghai police	82	21.9
Outside Xian	24	6.4
Private individuals	42	11.2
Door of Hope	24	6.4
Various	10	2.7
Total:	375	100.0

Source: Archives of the *Zhongguo fu ru jiuji zonghui*, file 113-1-2.

authorities, and the police of the *xian* outside Shanghai. Table 7.13 provides a breakdown of the entities that sent girls for admission to the AKS between 1913 and 1915. The role of the AKS is preponderant but is still underestimated. Indeed, a few examples will show that the AKS never took direct action through its inspectors except in Shanghai. However, even here, it was for the police to arrest the wrongdoers. Outside Shanghai, the AKS relied on its various local branches, and it was the local authorities who took action and had the girl returned to a representative of the AKS. In general, if the information given by the complainants was precise enough, the victims would be recovered and repatriated.

The native-place associations played a very major role. The AKS was set up because the leaders of the Shaoxing-Ningbo community in Shanghai wanted it. It was the native-place association of this community that often acted as a go-between for the AKS and people looking for abducted girls or boys. The Zhejiang native-place associations often sought help for their members from the AKS. The Shaoxing native-place association asked the AKS to search for a girl who had been abducted in Shaoxing and sold as a prostitute in Shanghai.[118] On another occasion, it was a girl diverted from a servant's job in Shanghai who was found a few months later in a Xi'an brothel.[119] The Ningbo native-place association wrote to ask that a search be made for a sixteen-year-old girl who had been sent to Manchuria.[120]

The other associations also acted as intermediaries. The Pudong native-place association intervened on behalf of one of its members, whose twenty-one-year-old daughter had been sold in Jilin. In another case, it backed a request by a worker whose wife had been abducted in his absence and who lacked the means to bring her back in person from Hebei, where she had been found.[121] The Wuxi native-place association gave the AKS the address of a house of prostitution in Peking where the wife of one of its members had been sold.[122] The Changzhou native-place association asked the AKS to get back a nineteen-year-old girl sold in Manchuria.[123] The importance of a community would be essential in a country with a multitude of regional tongues. Members of the Taizhou native-place association (Zhejiang) intercepted an old prostitute living close to the association head office when they found her taking a young girl in tears to her house. They were able to understand the situation immediately because the girl's cries were being expressed in the Taizhou dialect.[124] This dimension must be emphasized because it points to the Chinese attachment to strong community-based forms of identity. When faced with a serious problem, such as the abduction of a girl, families would go more readily to their native-place association than to the police. When people ran into difficulties with the authorities and deemed them to be incompetent, powerless, or remote, it was again the native-place association that they would approach with their complaints.

Women abducted under these circumstances had, on the whole, little hope of escaping their fate. We need only look at the hundreds of thousands of women who were thrown into prostitution in Shanghai and compare their numbers with the ten thousand or so, both boys and girls, that the AKS and the Door of Hope were able to rescue in the course of their history. Even if we add those who managed to escape and return to their families by their own means and those who were rescued by other institutions, the fact remains that the gap is immense. There can be no doubt that in the twentieth century, especially in the 1920s, more lifelines were thrown out to the prostitutes. The Penal Code became sterner. The perception of the right to individual liberty, fostered by greater mobility and a greater externalization of women in the city, meant that people were increasingly willing to go to the courts to settle differences.

We might cite an example that is certainly atypical but nevertheless points to this trend. In the spring of 1936, Song Xiaodi brought her own father before the Mixed Court in the French Concession for having pledged her to a courtesan's house. The court sentenced the father to four months' imprisonment plus two months' probation. The madam was sentenced to six months in prison.[125] Although this case did combine fairly exceptional ingredients, it underlines the rise of an awareness, albeit imperfect, wherein a prostitute's fate was not regarded as being inexorably foreordained. It became increasingly known that the judges were showing clemency toward prostitutes who wished to leave a profession that they had entered under duress. In Shanghai, the prostitutes gradually learned to place their trust in the courts, the police, and the authorities in general.

The trade in women was a highly lucrative activity that affected hundreds of thousands of women during the century under study. However, as we have seen, it is necessary to avoid lumping together all the different forms of this trade, which ranged from the pledging of a girl by a close relative to abduction and sale into a house of prostitution with various forms of seduction and deceit in between. Even if it is true that for the individuals involved, this ultimately meant the sale of their bodies, there are distinctions that must be made if we are to avoid hasty generalizations and dubious assertions.[126] The female trade in China relied not so much on the existence of organized networks of traffickers that, even if they existed, played but a fairly peripheral role, as on the reality of the inferior social status of women considered as mere chattels. It is here that we must look for the prime cause of this huge traffic that drew the participation of individuals belonging to almost every layer of society and from every condition.

The Chinese State, as in other fields, did practically nothing that could have enhanced the status of women and nothing to curb the trade to which they were subjected. The Chinese government adopted modern penal codes prohibiting attacks on personal liberty but did not give itself the means to implement them. In the case of Shanghai, the local authorities were generally severe in their sentences even if they did not do much to actively combat the traffic. The division of the city into three rival entities bears a major share of the responsibility for this state of affairs. Moreover, it was only vigorous intervention by associations such as the Door of Hope that led to the establishment of a system of genuine protection for prostitutes who came before the Mixed Courts. Finally, it was private initiative that created the only organization that existed for the rescue of women and children who were victims of traffic, making use solely of networks that could partially compensate for the failings of the state, namely the community networks built up by the different native-place associations throughout Chinese territory.

The trade in women, which was totally eradicated after 1949, is now returning to the foreground in China. The ingredients that existed before 1949 can be seen again: regional demographic imbalances, local authorities that either act as accomplices or are impotent, an inferior status of women, and the existence of a market. From November 1989 to October 1990, 54,000 criminals were arrested for trafficking in women and children.[127] Most of the "abducted" persons in a study on a *xian* in Hebei were of peasant origin. A very large majority of them (63%) were illiterate. Their ages ranged from seventeen to twenty-five.[128] The areas from which they were procured include the *xian* of north Jiangsu.[129] Although, at present, the victims of this trade are intended for marriage, the press since 1991 has been reporting an increasing number of cases of women forced into prostitution.[130] In 1989, the Chinese government declared a ruthless war against the abduction and sale of human beings. However, in the context of the collapse of the Party-State and the social fragmentation that characterizes China today, it would appear, unfortunately, that female servitude is in for a revival that will be difficult to stem in the short term.

8
Houses of Prostitution in the Urban Space

Like every great metropolis, Shanghai secreted its own geography of prostitution. During the century being studied here, the "sex market" underwent constant change that was reflected especially in the itinerancy of the places of prostitution up to the turn of the twentieth century. The migration of prostitutes to the city was related to various factors. It was a natural result of the very transformation of the urban space and, in the case of Shanghai, of its massive expansion between 1849 and 1949. It was also a product of the growth in population that sometimes occurred in sudden spurts – for example, when waves of refugees poured into the city – and of movement by the activities and actors of Shanghai's socioeconomic life. Finally, we must also take account of accidents – such as fires – and action by different local authorities, such as the abolitionist policy of 1920–1925. In the twentieth century, the main areas in which the brothels were concentrated remained stable. The general phenomenon to be noted during the period starting from the second half of the 1920s, with a substantial acceleration at the beginning of the 1940s, was the spread of prostitution to the entire city even if certain traditional areas were still invested to a greater extent than the more peripheral districts.

This chapter seeks to shed light on the characteristics of the geography of prostitution in Shanghai and analyze the factors of its development. Prostitution, as we have seen in the earlier chapters, was extremely sensitive to modifications in the social and economic order. In turn, prostitution affected the way in which the city was perceived by its inhabitants, and it also affected their habits and the world of their imagination. Certain areas in Shanghai have become synonymous with prostitution in literature, in the press, and even in the political discourse, and this is true up to this very day.[1]

Reconstructing the Geography of Prostitution

To project the activities of prostitution on a map, at least two sets of particulars are needed: first, lists of addresses of the houses of prostitution or, failing this, information on the places of prostitution, and, second, sufficiently detailed maps with information that identifies these places. Inasmuch as this work relies on sources that are often very precise and highly disparate at the same time and even, for the nineteenth century, on mere testimony, the approach that has been followed needs to be explained in such a way as to define both its reliability and its limits. The methodological problems raised by this exercise shall not be developed here.[2] But first, the sources on which this study is based need to be briefly described.

For the nineteenth century, this study is guided by the writings of Wang Tao, already referred to in the chapters on the courtesans.[3] Like almost every scholar of his generation, Wang patronized the courtesans' houses and was a very assiduous patron. In his first work, *Haizou yeyou lu*, written in several stages from 1853 onward, Wang describes the condition of prostitution between 1849, when he arrived in Shanghai, and the beginning of the 1860s.[4] His testimony is particularly relevant because it corresponds to a time just before the beginning of the transition phase when the prostitutes moved from the old city to the settlements. Wang indicates the different places and types of prostitution in the city and settlements with sufficient precision to enable a map to be drawn of the "world of flowers" around 1850 and at the turn of the 1860s and 1870s.[5]

For want of suitable sources, there will be a gap between the nineteenth century and 1918 and 1920–1924. The date 1918 corresponds to a count made by a Chinese scholar and published in a book of reminiscences, *Lao Shanghai* ("Old Shanghai"). Here again, this is a census of the courtesans alone and refers only to the "golden circle" of prostitution, namely, the district near the race course. It is based apparently on the famous directories that were available at this time. This list provides a view in perspective of the major changes brought about by the Shanghai Municipal Council's abolitionist policy. The other two sources for this period are, first, the lists of the houses that were chosen by lot between 1920 and 1924 as well as those that went out of existence between each draw, all very painstakingly counted up by the police, and, second, a very full list of the houses of courtesans prepared in 1922 in a book narrating sixty years of the history of prostitution in Shanghai.[6]

For the French Concession, I have used two different series. The most complete series is a census of brothels taken by the municipal police in 1925.[7] This list, however, does not include singsong houses, which were classified separately. In addition, the consular orders promulgated between 1930 and 1938 have been methodically examined.[8] The deliberations of the works committee were appended to these orders. It was the works committee that authorized the opening (or moving) of classified establishments, including brothels. These data have been cross-checked with a list drawn up by the police departments in 1936.[9] The essential difference between the 1920s and the 1930s lies in the fact that some houses of prostitution opened in the western part of the settlement, although the main localities of prostitution remained unchanged. Finally, for the 1940s, all I have is a list made in 1947 by the Laozha district police station, whose area included the "golden circle" of prostitution. This list provides a view in perspective of this location.

The sources of this study are therefore limited, full of gaps, and sometimes inconsistent. However, they reflect the partial, scanty, and inconsistent character of every municipal administration that governed Shanghai up to 1945. All the same, this set of data provides sufficient material to project a geography of prostitution in the city on a map. What was still to be found were appropriate cartographic documents for the period under question, namely, maps indicating not only the roads but also the lanes (*lilong*). Indeed, the addresses of the houses of prostitution are often indicated in this form, rather than as mere numbers on a bigger street. This is one of the charming features of Shanghai's urban structure. I therefore had to use maps taken from the *Shanghai Local Gazetteer* (*Shanghai xian zhi*) or secondary reproductions drawn from this source for the nineteenth century.[10] For 1918–1924 and 1947, I have used the extremely detailed drawings published in the *Shanghai Street Directory*.[11] The main difficulty was to identify roads and lanes whose names changed in the course of time, not to mention the problems of conversion between English, French, and Chinese names and transcriptions from the Shanghai dialect. Using different editions of *Shanghai zhinan* (*The Shanghai Guide*), I have tried to identify all the streets and lanes in which prostitutes lived in the twentieth century.[12] Apart from the simple question of localization, it was interesting, in the case of Shanghai, to try to pinpoint the integration of prostitution into the city's specific urban fabric.

The Space of Prostitution in the Nineteenth Century

Up to the beginning of the nineteenth century, prostitution was an activity practiced on water, namely on the "flower boats" (*huachuan*) that were characteristic of Southern China. The few accounts available are unanimous: Before 1821, there was no other mode of prostitution in Shanghai.[13] These boats were moored on the Huangpu, along its banks, and they were lit up at night to receive customers. For Shanghai, I have not found any more precise description of these floating establishments, which could still be found in Nanking and Canton in the 1930s.

After 1821, when Shanghai experienced an unprecedented economic boom, the courtesans' houses were set up in the Walled City, where there was a huge increase in business activity along with a growing population.[14] The Chinese city, enclosed by a heavy wall since the fifteenth century, had been built without any specific plan. It was crisscrossed by a fine network of lanes that barely managed to separate the dwellings from one another.

In addition, there were canals that crossed the city and were increasingly used as open-air drains. Map 3, dating from 1860, gives a clear view of the structure of the city. The map shows the very tortuous nature of the streets, which are always curved, growing out of the interstices left between the houses that determined the path taken by these streets. Like all ancient Chinese cities, the Walled City was organized around primordial centers, especially the places of power, namely, the *yamen* of the *xian* magistrate, the Temple of Confucius, the Temple of the City God (*Chenghuangmiao*), and other ritual and official buildings.

The northeastern area of the city was set apart mainly for business. It contained especially the principal merchant organizations, namely, the different guilds that structured the local community. Some of them had their quarters in the Western Garden Pavilions (belonging to the temple of the city deity [*Chenghuangmiao*]). The members of the guilds carried out their business in the pavilions, which were built in these gardens. The southern half of the city consisted of residential areas that were more heterogeneous, where private houses, shops, and workshops all jostled together. In the northwest, near the French Concession, there was an extended lower-class locality close to the areas in which the guilds traditionally had their burial grounds and coffin repositories. It was inhabited by people from the humbler sections, including carpenters, weavers, dyers, and so on, most of them natives of Ningbo. Their guild set up its headquarters in a lavish building, not far from this area, outside the city walls. Outside the wall, along the river, there grew up a large number of suburbs. In the nineteenth century, these suburbs formed a continuous and highly dense urban fabric running from north to south. These areas contained workshops, shipyards, warehouses, wholesale shops of all kinds, oil merchants, furniture merchants, temples, and residences.[15]

This brief description of the Walled City gives a view in perspective of the special geography of prostitution in Shanghai. Map 3 shows the layout of the houses of prostitution in the Walled City and its surroundings in the mid-nineteenth century. Within the old city there were mainly the houses of the courtesans, except for a few *yao'er* establishments in the northeastern districts. The very high-class houses were near the Hongqiao Bridge straddling the main canal that ran through the city from one side to the other. The courtesans living in this district were natives of Suzhou, Changzhou, and Yangzhou. Some were of local extraction (*tu*). This was a locality that remained lively throughout the night. Further to the east, without leaving a central north–south axis, there was another famous lane, the Tang family lane (*Tangjia xiang*) with a large number of houses. There it was possible at all times to hear the sound of flutes and harps denoting, here again, intense activity throughout the night. Wang Tao provides no information on the residents of these establishments but speaks of their customers. These appear to have been mostly merchants from Guangdong and

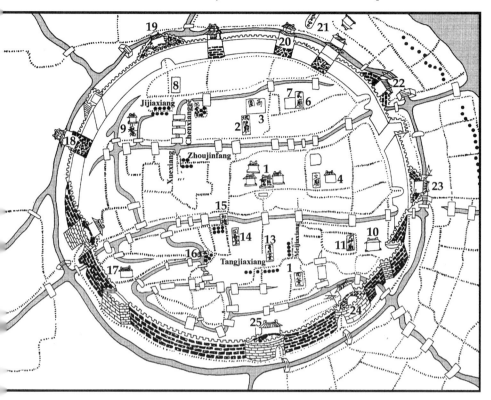

Map 3. The Walled City in the mid-nineteenth century. **1**, Shanghai *xian* magistrate's *yamen*; **2**, Temple of the City God (*Chenghuangmiao*); **3**, West Garden; **4**, school; **5**, examination hall; **6**, Temple of the God of War; **7**, Scholars' Institute; **8**, Temple of the Spirit of Fortune; **9**, small military ground; **10**, circuit intendant's (*daotai's*) *yamen*; **11**, Temple of the Spirit of Fire; **12**, *Tongdetang* (charitable institution); **13**, *Yingyutang* (orphanage); **14**, *Tongrentang* (charitable institution); **15**, Hongqiao Bridge; **16**, Western Granary Bridge (*Xicangqiao*); **17**, garrison commander's residence; **18**, Temple of Guan De, the God of War; **19**, North Gate; **20**, Tianma Temple; **21**, Chinese internal customs; **22**, Small East Gate; **23**, Great East Gate; **24**, Great South Gate; **25**, Small South Gate. Map based on an original in *Shanghai xianzhi* ("Local Gazette of the *Xian* of Shanghai"), Shanghai, Nanyuan zhiju, 1871 (reprint, Taibei, Chengwen chubanshe, 4 volumes).

Fujian who formed two of the major "foreign" communities at this time. A quick northward jump brings us to the *Meijia xiang*, a "peaceful and remote" lane renowned for the famous courtesan Mei Xuanshi. There were also other establishments.[16]

Wang Tao also refers to another group of houses between the Western Granary Bridge (*Xicangqiao*) and the Zhang family lane (*Zhangjia xiang*) slightly further to the south. These lanes were home to a good number of famous girls, although some of them did not have bound feet, which would appear to be surprising for courtesans hailing from the Suzhou region. It would seem that there were no other courtesans' houses in the walled city. However, there were other establishments intended for a less select variety of customers. There were three areas of settlement: one to the east of *Chenxiangge*, the second to the west of the *Houjia bang* canal, in the Ji family lane (*Jijia xiang*), and the third slightly further to the south in the *Xuexiang* lane, at the edge of *Zhoujinfang*, about which Wang Tao wrote: "At nightfall, large number of girls can be seen gathered on the doorstep, making eyes at potential customers."[17] One might ask if this was an *ersan* or a *yao'er* house.

It can be seen that the houses of prostitution of the old city were extremely concentrated in the way that artisans belonging to the same corporation usually were in premodern Chinese cities. This tendency toward heavy concentration in certain areas and even certain lanes is a constant that prevailed up to 1949. It was related to the nature of the courtesans' establishments, which, as we have seen, generally housed one or two girls each. This meant that the only way for these establishments to offer their customers a certain degree of variety was for them to be set up in groups. Being gathered together in one and the same place might also be seen to have brought other advantages such as a feeling of security, the possibility of collective bargaining (over rents and taxes), and the availability of the ancillary services (restaurants) that were indispensable to the work of the prostitutes. These places of diversion were not to be found in the city's political center, although they were hardly at a distance from it. What may be surprising is their absence from the business districts. Prostitutes could be found in the residential areas of the Walled City, which were characterized by a mixture of types of dwelling.

Common prostitution was localized near the river. Some of the prostitutes set themselves up on the boats. These were heirs to the "flower boats" of bygone days but appear to have shed all their luster. The prostitutes were no longer courtesans but girls vending their charms to the first comer, especially to sailors and dockworkers. Their junks were anchored in the middle of the river; as evening approached, they came closer to the groups (*bang*) of boats moored along the wharves.[18] Up to the 1860s, the authorities of the French Concession also referred to them as "junks of tolerance" anchored near the banks (which later became known as the "quai de France"). The girls clearly belonged to a category that was despised by the elites.

This common prostitution was, in part, also practiced in very makeshift houses "made of braided bamboo and mud walls" all along the river from the north to the southeast. However, this was a lower category of prostitute "that no self-respecting person would visit." People of rank would very rarely step inside, according to Wang. What this means, however, is that there were certain merchants or scholars who were quite willing to go whoring in the more common type of "dive" where every desire could be satisfied.[19] This group of establishments corresponded especially to the *huayanjian*, which were opium dens as well as brothels. Their appearance dates back to the 1860s.

This is the general picture that can be drawn of the geography of prostitution in Shanghai around 1850. There was hardly any further major development in the following decade even if certain houses began to be set up in the settlements around 1853 following the substantial destruction that came in the wake of the Small Sword Rebellion.[20] The northern and eastern suburbs were entirely burned down by the imperial troops, which furthermore proceeded to massacre the population.[21] The possibilities of moving away were limited. The settlements at this time had barely grown beyond a few blocks behind the Bund even if the first refugees driven by the onward march of the Taiping were beginning to settle in Shanghai. Besides, there was as yet no bridge over the Yangjingbang Canal, which separated the two settlements.

The first major turning point came in 1861–1862, following the upheavals created by the Taiping revolt in the lower Yangzi region. Hundreds of thousands of refugees from the big cities, such as Suzhou and even Hankou, fled the violence and destruction, seeking refuge in Shanghai.[22] Their arrival, which led to major economic growth, had two consequences for the houses of prostitution. It considerably increased pressure on available housing in the Walled City, where the population grew by two and a half times. This new presence stimulated the development of new districts built outside the settlements, providing new possibilities of setting up dwellings (see Map 4).[23]

Many refugee families were from the wealthy strata of society and brought capital and various goods with them.[24] Their presence created a new demand to which certain prostitutes adapted by moving to a new house. Two groups of courtesans chose to move. The *shuyu* houses came to the new lanes, such as *Zhoujingfang, Rixinli, Zhaoguili, Zhaorongli*, and so on, just to the north of the Yangjingbang Canal.[25] The *changsan* set themselves up further to the north in Fuzhou Road. Gradually, as the International Settlement took shape toward the west, there was a movement in this direction. In particular, after the race course was demolished and transferred to the west in 1861–1862, the area that developed in its vicinity drew a large number of houses of prostitution, first of all on Beihai Road and Guangdong Road between 1870 and 1875 and later, further to the north, on Fuzhou Road, which around 1890 became the center of prostitution in Shanghai.[26] The sudden drop in real estate prices at the beginning of 1864,

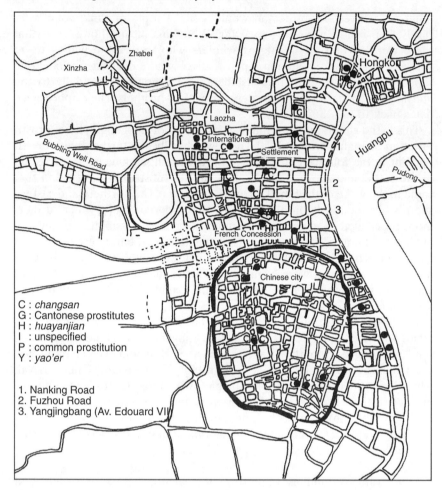

Map 4. The districts of prostitution around 1860.

which was related to the return by the majority of the refugees to their homes, certainly made it easier for the prostitutes to set up house in the deserted districts.

Those Cantonese prostitutes (*laoju*) who were patronized by the Chinese settled rather in the north, in the two lanes *Laoqichang* and *Wuchangli* at the crossing point between Nanking Road and Sichuan Road.[27] The others moved to Hongkou, a barely developed boundary area between the International Settlement and the Chinese sector. Very soon, especially after the building of the bridge in 1856 linking this area to the International Settlement (then known as the British Settlement), Hongkou acquired an unfortunate reputation as a place of brawling and depravity.[28] It was here that the first foreign prostitutes set up house. To this group, we must add the establishments of the French Concession. Their exact location is unknown to me, although it was probably in the same areas as in the 1920s. The concession housed a rather common type of prostitution. The northern gate area (especially Palikao Road, which was the former Baxianqiao) and some new roads to the south of the former race course had already been occupied by the prostitutes while the east continued to receive establishments for sailors.[29]

However, prostitution at this time was not to be found only in the brothels. There were other areas of recreation where it was usual to meet prostitutes, especially the *shuyu*, *changsan*, and *yao'er*. One of these favorite places within the Walled City was the huge garden surrounding the Temple of the City God (*Chenghuangmiao*). There were some ten teahouses for sipping *biluo*, the tea of Suzhou. They received very large numbers of customers with whom the prostitutes gladly intermingled.[30] Two other areas, the Longhua pagoda to the southeast of the city and the Jing'ansi Temple, were places for taking walks. In the nineteenth century, there were still stretches of countryside outside the city that had to be reached by horse carriage. The Chinese courtesans liked to show themselves off in these places, wearing their best finery and accompanied by their regular customers, to compete with others and attract the attention of new customers.

The general geography of prostitution acquired its almost definitive features at the end of the nineteenth century, faithfully reflecting the condition of the city in its demographic and social dimensions and in its physical fabric. The picture painted here is incomplete. For example, it does not include the *maisons de rendez-vous* (*taiji*) that were in the Walled City until they were banned by the Imperial authorities and emigrated into the French Concession. Nor does it include other subgroups of the kind that the Chinese were fond of distinguishing, even when the differences involved were minute. The sources on the whole reflect the image of prostitution as having been organized within the urban space in a manner that was clearly hierarchical, even segregated on the basis of the different groups of customers that they served, with contours that are fairly easy to delineate, unlike those in the twentieth century, which saw an intermingling of more varied and more numerous types of prostitution.

The Expansion of the Phenomenon of Prostitution in the Twentieth Century

The early years of the twentieth century were marked by a substantial increase in the numbers involved in prostitution. Many hitherto residential and business districts came to be occupied by prostitutes. Some areas even came to be wholly monopolized by this activity. The

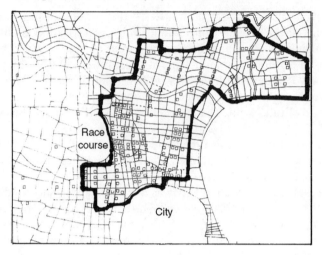

Map 5. The main roads and boundaries of the market of prostitution.

geography of prostitution became more complex as this activity split up into a greater number of forms, each having (to various degrees) its own preferred districts.

Let us begin with a general overview of this geography of venal sexuality. Map 5 shows the main routes occupied by the prostitutes, along with the boundaries of the market of prostitution. Two entities stand out clearly: (i) a central block including the southern part of the International Settlement and the western part of the French Concession and (ii) a northern block centered in the Hongkou district. The map probably does not reflect the full reality. Only the houses of prostitution have been shown, but the fact is that there were a number of girls working in the various bars and cabarets of the district. The central block, on the contrary, contained a very large number of streets of prostitution with a medium-sized settlement to the east, one or two blocks behind the Bund along a north–south axis. Most of the houses were along the same axis in the district lying on the back of the race course.

This situation, corresponding to data from 1920–1925, did not change in its essentials up to 1949. The Chinese municipality established in 1927 prohibited prostitution on its territory. In the 1930s, many massage parlors and prostitution houses were set up in the western part of the French Concession. They catered above all to foreign customers and did not transform the general geography of prostitution in the concession (see Map 6). In addition, there were the many dancing halls along the Avenue Edouard VII, even if these were not brothels in the strict sense of the term. With the Japanese occupation, the western area of the International Settlement,

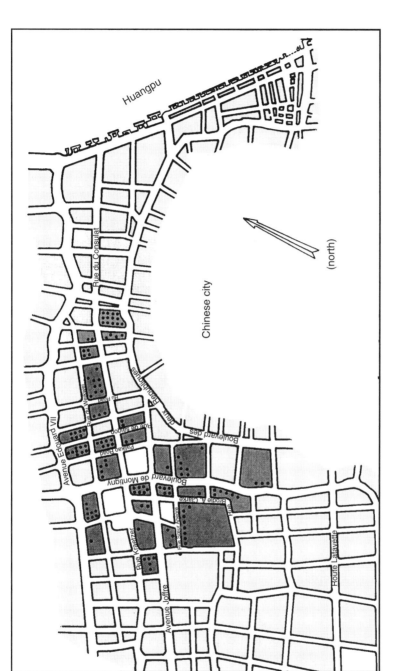

Map 6. The areas of prostitution in the French Concession (1925). *Source: Shanghai shi hanghao lutulu, 1947.*

Huxi, became a haven for gambling houses and brothels. However, this situation came to an end after 1941, following pressure by the Japanese army.

Conversely, certain districts were totally spared, whereas it might have been imagined that they would receive a more active form of prostitution. The western areas of the two settlements, essentially residential and affluent areas that were rather off-centered and sparsely populated, had practically no establishments of prostitution. But, paradoxically, the popular Yangshupu area too seems to have had few prostitutes, despite the existence of a few houses. It was located just behind the Huangpu wharves and contained a large working population. This is a situation that prevailed throughout the twentieth century. The very low purchasing power of the population in this area partly explains the absence of prostitutes. However, this explanation is inadequate because there were establishments of prostitution in other very low-class districts (in the eastern part of the old city, for example). It is the very nature of the Yangshupu district that bears a part of the explanation. Essentially, the area contained only factories and warehouses. This was a bleak and soulless locality that was hardly likely to attract customers. Besides, the workers probably preferred to go out of it in search of diversion.[31]

The most outstanding feature of prostitution in Shanghai was its extreme concentration. The report of the Vice Committee indicates that in 1919 almost 98% of Chinese prostitutes were located in three of the eleven police districts that comprised the International Settlement, namely, the Center, Laozha, and Hongkou. Almost two-thirds were concentrated in the Laozha district alone, which formed the "golden circle" of prostitution (see Map 7).[32] A similar phenomenon, though not as pronounced, could be found at the end of the 1940s. Yu Wei, the chief doctor of the Venereal Disease Center, was able to determine, in 1948, that 63% of the girls were working in the Laozha district, 11% in Hongkou, 13% in Gaoshan, and the remainder in the city's six other districts.[33] The essential difference as compared with the 1920s lay in the fact that the perimeter of prostitution had widened.

Table 8.1 gives the places of activity of the different categories of prostitutes in Shanghai around 1941–1942 and 1946–1947. It is obvious from this table that prostitution was present throughout the city. The names and boundaries of the districts have been changed, but it is still possible to find one's way. The Laozha district still heads all the categories, with two-thirds of the prostitutes. The sector that comes second is Taishan, which is none other than a part of the former French Concession. The other areas of concentration correspond to traditional areas of prostitution such as Hongkou and Tilanqiao. However, there is an extension to the west of Laozha into the Xincheng area, which, until then, was little represented.

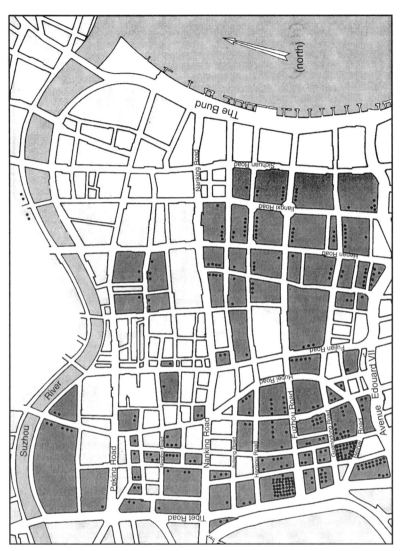

Map 7 The areas of prostitution in the central district of the International Settlement (1920–1924). *Source: Shanghai shi hanghao lutulu, 1947.*

Table 8.1. *Distribution of the houses of prostitution by district (1942–1947)*

	1941–1942								December 1946	1946		1947	
	Changsan		Xiangdaoshe		Houses of Prostitution		Massage Parlors		House of Prostitution	Prostitutes		Prostitutes	
District	Owners	Girls	Owners	Girls	Owners	Girls	Owners	Girls		Houses	Girls	Houses	Girls
Huangpu	—	—	—	—	3	18	1	13	37	3	7	4	7
Laozha	213	644	109	2,731	184	553	15	252	524	569	846	572	1,047
Xincheng	1	1	1	5	59	212	4	31	43	57	84	58	96
Jing'ansi	—	—	—	—	6	22	3	17	—	7	12	7	18
Putuo	—	—	—	—	1	5	—	—	—	1	2	1	3
Hongkou	—	—	1	4	27	96	3	44	71	49	86	51	102
Tilanqiao	—	—	—	—	42	174	—	—	10	54	108	55	152
Yulin	—	—	—	—	4	9	—	—	—	—	—	—	—
Huashan	—	—	—	—	1	9	—	—	—	—	—	—	—
Taishan	69	154	1	2	48	229	1	4	82	121	159	122	182
Lujiawan	—	—	—	—	—	—	5	24	22	1	3	1	5
Total:	283	799	112	2,742	375	1,327	32	385	789	862	1,307	871	1,612

Percentages by District

District	Changsan Owners	Changsan Girls	Xiangdaoshe Owners	Xiangdaoshe Girls	Houses of Prostitution Owners	Houses of Prostitution Girls	Massage Parlors Owners	Massage Parlors Girls	December 1946 House of Prostitution	1946 Houses	1946 Girls	1947 Houses	1947 Girls
Huangpu	—	—	—	—	1%	1%	3%	3%	5%	—	1%	—	—
Laozha	75%	81%	97%	100%	49%	42%	47%	65%	66%	66%	65%	66%	65%
Xincheng	—	—	1%	—	16%	16%	13%	8%	5%	7%	6%	7%	6%
Jing'ansi	—	—	—	—	2%	2%	9%	4%	—	1%	1%	1%	1%
Putuo	—	—	—	—	—	—	—	—	—	—	—	—	—
Hongkou	—	—	1%	—	7%	7%	9%	11%	9%	6%	7%	6%	6%
Tilanqiao	—	—	—	—	11%	13%	—	—	1%	6%	8%	6%	9%
Yulin	—	—	—	—	1%	1%	—	—	—	—	—	—	—
Huashan	—	—	—	—	—	1%	—	—	—	—	—	—	—
Taishan	24%	19%	1%	—	13%	17%	3%	1%	10%	14%	12%	14%	11%
Lujiawan	—	—	—	—	—	—	16%	6%	3%	—	—	—	—

Sources: [1941–1942] Police Archives (1945–1949), file 1-62-44; [Dec. 1946] Shanghai shi jingchaju tongji nianbao, 1947; [1946–1947] Yu Wei, "Jin chang yu xingbing fangzhi," p. 18.

The "Golden Circle" of Prostitution

The elite among the prostitutes, the *changsan*, were highly concentrated in what I have called the "golden circle" of prostitution. This was the district that grew on the former race course. Its shape matched the outlines of the track on which the horses used to run. A brief look at a map of Shanghai reveals this apparent anomaly of a grid of streets made of regular squares, on two mutually perpendicular axes running north–south and east–west, from which there emerges a sort of oblong circle encompassing almost all the courtesans' houses and a good number of other houses of prostitution, as can be seen in Maps 8 (1918) and 9 (1920–1922). According to the 1918 survey, 90.2% of the 1,167 courtesans were within the "golden circle." No doubt these figures have to be revised downward because not all the houses were counted. Indeed there were a few courtesans' houses on Bubbling-Well Road in the west and on Dixon Road in Hongkou.[34] According to Wang Jimen's fuller work dating from 1922, the percentage of courtesans in the "golden circle" was 81.8% out of a total of 763 girls. Now half the courtesans left the district. Although we cannot be sure about the reliability of the surveys, there can be no doubt about the massive presence of courtesans. For their night outings, they did not have to move beyond a radius of 1.2 kilometers.

The *changsan* practically never left this district, as is proved by the 1939 and 1947 *Street Directories*, although there was a temporary emigration at the time of the abolitionist policy of the Shanghai Municipal Council. To escape closure, many houses moved to the neighboring settlement or to another city.[35] The magnitude of the phenomenon can be envisaged by comparing the two census reports available, that of 1918 and that of 1920–1922. Certain districts or blocks of dwellings were literally deserted between 1918 and 1920. In particular, the *Huileli* lane, built in 1917 off Fuzhou Road, which housed seventy-nine courtesans in 1918, does not appear at all in the 1920–1924 lists. According to the 1918 census, there were more than 1,100 *changsan* in this locality, whereas Wang Jimen found only 763 in 1922. Nearly half of the girls had emigrated. Despite the movements of the 1920–1925 period, luxury prostitution generally remained concentrated in the International Settlement. When the Shanghai Municipal Council restored official permission in 1924 for the establishment of singers' houses under their old name of *shuyu*, they returned to their preferred localities from which they never moved again.

The immediately lower category of prostitute, namely the *ersan* and the *yao'er*, experienced a series of ups and downs. While there were no more than about ten of them in the walled city, most of these women formed a group near the small eastern gate (*xiao dongmen*) where a fire destroyed their entire locality.[36] In the mid-1870s, they began to come together with the *changsan* in the International Settlement, especially in the eastern

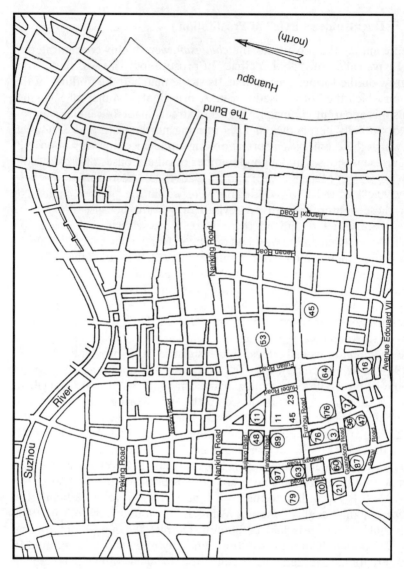

Map 8. The areas of prostitution in the central district of the International Settlement (1918). *Source: Shanghai shi hanghao lutulu, 1947.*

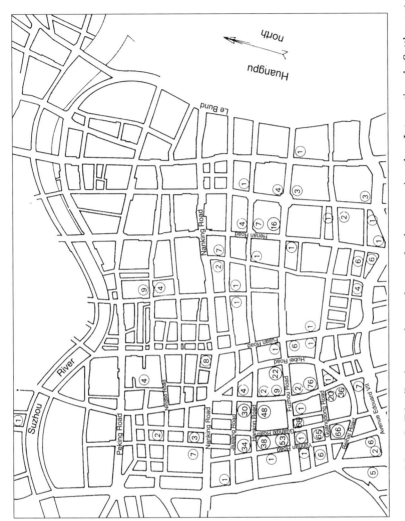

Map 9. Distribution and numbers of *changsan* in the International Settlement (1921–1922). *Source: Shanghai shi hanghao lutulu, 1947.*

section of Qipanjie. Between 1894 and 1904, the *yao'er* gradually replaced their rivals, who preferred to move further to the north. The development of business activity in this road forced them to move again. This time, the journey was shorter because the *yao'er* set themselves up in the western section of Qipanjie on the other side of Henan Road.[37] The number of these establishments considerably diminished with time, and they did not survive the abolitionist policy of the Shanghai Municipal Council.

The *yeji*, representing the most numerous group, are the most difficult to localize inasmuch as they were present somewhat everywhere in the city. Nevertheless, toward 1919, the greatest concentrations were near Nanking Road, in the west, in the aptly named *Xiangfen* ("perfumed powder") lane off Hankou Road, and in the *lilong* that intersected Fuzhou Road, Guangxi Road, and Yunnan Road.[38] The prostitutes found a large number of tea-houses in this area, where they went looking for customers. In the French Concession, they had their areas around the Great World, at the crossing between Avenue Edouard VII and Boulevard de Montigny, especially in Palikao Road, Rue des Pères, Rue de Saigon, and Weikwei Road. Similarly, the sector formed by the Rue de la Soeur-Allègre, Rue Brodie A. Clarke, Rue Marco Polo, with, further to the west, Rue Kraetzer and Rue Wagner, was a focal point of the *yeji* houses. Finally, along the Rue du Consulat, in the two small roads, Rue de Tourane and Rue du Moulin, there were a number of *yeji* houses and probably other even less patronized categories. During the period of prohibition by the Shanghai Municipal Council, many prostitutes set themselves up in the small hotels that flourished along the Yangjingbang when the canal between the two settlements was filled and was replaced by Avenue Edouard VII.[39]

The proletarians of prostitution, namely the opium-den girls (*huayanjian*), were numerous in the French Concession, where their establishments were tolerated up to 1919. Most of them were set up in the north and east of the old city. In the International Settlement, they were gradually eliminated after the prohibition of the opium traffic and opium consumption. However, the term *huayanjian* stayed in use even if it no longer designated anything more than prostitution. Another group, the *dingpeng*, hardly different from the previous groups, can be associated with the *huayanjian*. These establishments, which housed older women, were intended for a very poor class of customer. They were therefore to be found in the economically more peripheral areas of the city. Some of them were located in the old city, either to the east, near the small eastern gate or in the Sun family lane (*Sunjialong*), or to the north in the Rue de la Mission. The others were concentrated on the edge of the International Settlement, along Avenue Edouard VII, in the small roads (Songjiang, Pentanglong, the southern part of the rue du Shanxi, Qipanjie).[40] The other great temple of prostitution, although it was less densely occupied than the "golden circle," was Hongkou in the northeast of the city. On the main route leading to this quarter, *Bei*

Plate 10. Pentang Road at the intersection of Nanking Road.

sichuanlu, there were first of all the high-class Cantonese brothels that were sometimes ensconced in the small *lilong* (*Qingyun, Renzhi*, and *Tongde* lanes) off a parallel road, *Wuchanglu*.[41] This particular settlement is linked to the traditional presence of a large Cantonese community in this district. The houses of the Cantonese prostitutes gradually disappeared and were replaced by a few hotels in which the girls had their quarters. More to the east, on the boundaries of Yangshupu, the major industrial and harbor zone of eastern Shanghai contained houses of prostitution intended for foreigners. These were the Cantonese *xianshuimei* dives as well as cheap parlors containing destitute Western prostitutes, mainly Russians in the 1920s and Jews from Eastern Europe at the end of the 1930s. Four roads formed this locality, which Western residents knew as the "Trenches": Dixwell, Fearon, Yalu, and Yuhang (*Youheng*) roads.[42] All these establishments were in the vicinity of the wharves and residences of passing sailors who formed the major proportion of their clientele.

The Hongkou district contained another group of prostitutes, the Japanese (who were most usually of Korean origin). They were to be found in prostitution houses and in the many small Japanese restaurants in the Hongkou quarter that became Shanghai's "Little Tokyo." The majority of the Japanese community lived in this quarter. The other houses of Western prostitutes patronized by the foreign social elite were located to the north of the International Settlement on the other side of the Suzhou River in the Zilaishui Bridge area.[43]

The *Lilong*, a Haven of Prostitution

Despite what might have been expected, practically nothing of the massive presence of prostitutes could have been detected from a stroll in the streets, except in those streets that were actually reserved for this activity. To get a glimpse of this world, it was necessary to cross the threshold of the many *lilong* (lanes) that ran through the blocks of dwellings and housed the brothels, away from the noise and bustle of the street and the curiosity of passersby.[44] Two maps illustrate this phenomenon and give a precise idea of the particular grip that the houses of prostitution had over certain localities. Maps 10 and 11 show an area of prostitution within the "golden circle" in 1921 and 1947.

Not all the houses of prostitution were located within the *lilong*. A number of them directly opened onto the main road, but these were roads with a rather exceptional character. This was the case especially in roads such as Shantou Road where there were practically no establishments other than brothels. The other houses were cast in the specific mold of the lanes, which was a typical feature of Shanghai. Each block was closely surrounded by an alignment of premises that were either dwellings or, more usually, shops of all kinds. The rest of the dwellings were laid out within this peripheral ring that was pierced at several points to give access to the *lilong*. These *lilong* were barely distinguishable from other types of premises. On the contrary, the entrance was often framed by a stone arch (which gave the name of the lane), thus preventing the smallest break in the facade that gave onto the street.[45]

The layout of the *lilong* could vary a great deal. Some of them would go right through a block of dwellings from one end to the other like the *Leyuli*, which was also connected to the left with the cross-lanes of *Qunyufang* (Map 11). All that was needed to make the connection was to cross Yunnan Road. The most common form, however, had a main *lilong*, with one or two access points, feeding the interior of the block through little cross-lanes. The model for this type of layout is the *Huileli* (Map 11), but there were others that could be likened to it – for example, *Qunyufang, Fuyuli, Fuxiangli*, and so on. This network of lanes, which originated in a form of traditional rural architecture, facilitates rapid mobility without necessitating main-road detours around large blocks. This form of layout meant that activities that might have disturbed the sensitivities of the inhabitants could be carried out in peace and quiet.

In the French Concession, the concealment of prostitution in the *lilong* was a decisive criterion for the tolerant attitude of the administration toward these establishments. When neighbors and passersby protested, the

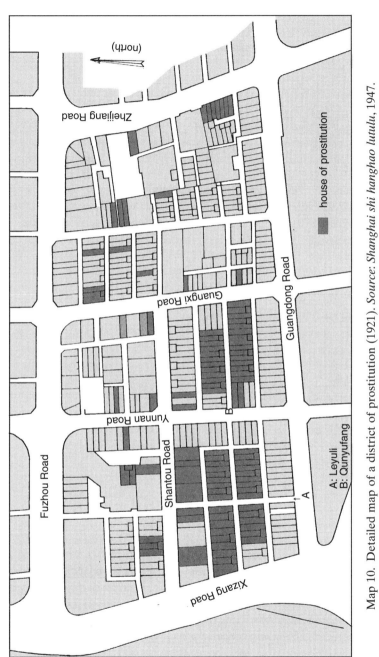

Map 10. Detailed map of a district of prostitution (1921). *Source: Shanghai shi hanghao lutulu, 1947.*

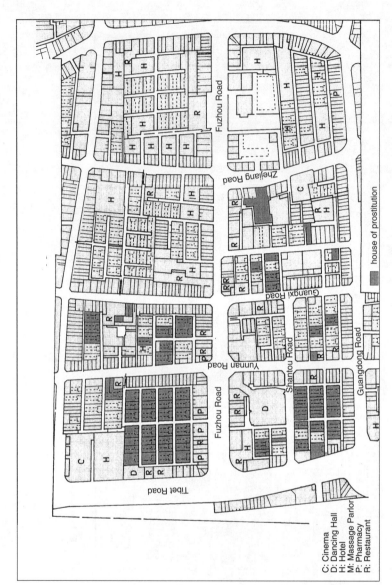

Map 11. Detailed map of a district of prostitution (1947). *Source: Shanghai shi hanghao lutulu, 1947.*

C: Cinema
D: Dancing Hall
H: Hotel
M: Massage Parlor
P: Pharmacy
R: Restaurant

■ house of prostitution

Plate 11. A prostitution lane (*lilong*).

police generally opposed expulsion: "[With regard to the Rue du Marché] [it] is a place concealed from individuals travelling through the major routes: many residents of Shanghai are not even aware of the location of this road and the type of commerce practiced therein."[46] On the contrary, the police emphasized the discretion with which this trade was conducted in a concealed manner within the *lilong*, out of the sight of respectable people. On the contrary, any house of prostitution opening directly onto the street would be automatically closed down, as can be seen from handwritten notes in the police memoranda.

What is absolutely fascinating is the network of services that formed around prostitution, especially in the courtesans' areas, where the demand was more varied and more exacting on the part of both girls and customers. In 1919, there was a whole string of establishments more or less linked with the activities of prostitution. The role of the hotels (*keyu*), especially after 1920, has been seen above. There were 111 of them (44% of the total number of establishments surveyed) in the wide perimeter of the "golden circle" and 7 in the streets of prostitution in the French Concession. As for the tea houses (*chaguan*), places where the prostitutes solicited customers and could be met, there were twenty-two in the "golden circle" and five in the French Concession. Another type of establishment that was indispensable consisted of the restaurants, which supplied provisions to the houses and served as places to which the courtesans could be invited in the evening. Shanghai had thirty-four big restaurants (*fanguan*) and eighty-nine smaller establishments (*jiuguan*) of which a third and nearly half (48%), respectively, were located within the famous perimeter.[47] The inventory of these establishments is very probably incomplete, but it points to the relative concentration of certain activities that made this locality a center of leisure and nighttime diversion.

Shanghai's urban development came about "abnormally" – that is, through extension along four different axes (Nanshi, Zhabei, the International Settlement, and the French Concession) starting from the city as it existed before the arrival of the Westerners. This metropolitan expansion occurred without the smallest degree of concerted planning between the concerned administrative authorities and, in the case of the area under Chinese jurisdiction, without the smallest degree of official control before 1927. Shanghai's urban landscape was modeled by the development of economic activities, which moved from the walled city to the International Settlement, especially its eastern part. The geography of prostitution followed the same development that, while it might have been encouraged by the effects of the Taiping revolt, was conditioned above all by the transformation of the local economic fabric. The French Concession did always harbor a large number of singsong houses and brothels, but these places were far more oriented toward the neighboring settlement.

The urban structure proper to Shanghai undoubtedly promoted the development of activities of prostitution. The very tightly packed network of *lilong* enabled a limited territory to take a high concentration of establishments capable of offering customers a wide choice of not only brothels but also ancillary services such as restaurants, teahouses, the service of various tradesmen, and so on. The second advantage of the *lilong* was that they created an intermediate space between private dwellings and public roads. In this intermediate space, activities that could have been a source of disturbance both morally and materially (in terms of noise, safety, etc.) were brought together, away from the gaze of ordinary passersby. Prostitution could very easily cohabit with other forms of business activity and even residential areas through this division of space. This special geography implied a certain knowledge of the terrain on the part of the customers so that they could find the type of establishment that they wished to patronize. Failing this, they could refer to the "compasses of the world of gallantry" or to the many guidebooks that identified the city's areas of prostitution with varying degrees of precision. This spatial organization of prostitution, which it is rather impossible to fully understand, might explain the fairly long period (of more than two years) that elapsed before the new authorities took measures to prohibit prostitution after 1949.

9
The Organization and Management of the Houses of Prostitution

The houses of prostitution were highly hierarchical institutions organized according to fairly strict rules. Of course, the extent of the formalism depended on the type of prostitute involved. The courtesans' establishments were far more complex than the rest and were governed by strict norms. They provided a wider range of services. This led them to employ very large numbers of individuals living off the girls' work. The houses were also the core of the economy of prostitution. All the money generated by this trade passed through the hands of their managers and madams. This chapter will describe how the houses were equipped and internally organized. Given their special role, and also because the available sources are abundant, I shall examine the courtesans' houses in greater detail. Then, I shall attempt briefly to shed some light on the type of customer who visited the prostitutes. Finally, I shall take a more specific look at the different categories of staff, as well as the owners of the houses.

An Inventory

The houses of prostitution were hardly distinguishable per se from other urban dwellings. And yet it was not difficult to single them out. Their location in the city, especially the manner in which they were "hidden away" in Shanghai's *lilong* (little lanes), was discussed in the last chapter. From the outside, the establishments could immediately be identified by the lanterns hanging over the entrance.[1] These lanterns, which were compulsory, especially in the French Concession, gave these lanes a particular aspect. Their multitude created a festive atmosphere in the evening, especially in the nineteenth century when the other streets were plunged into darkness at nightfall. Before the introduction of gas and then electricity in the 1880s, these lanterns used oil.

The houses of prostitution were ordinary dwellings that varied according to the type of establishment. The courtesans' houses were organized in two major modes, the collective houses (*dachanghu*) and the individual houses (*zhujia*). A collective house was more likely to be a large Western-style dwelling or a group of Chinese-style dwellings within a *lilong*. It would be set up on the initiative of a male or female manager who would rent a large house and invite courtesans to come and set themselves up. An example will clarify the point: In the spring of 1922, a former musician opened a courtesans' house in the French Concession in what had hitherto been a stock exchange office. The house had fourteen rooms. Each room harbored a "family" consisting of a courtesan, her madam, and her employees. The house drew its new residents from the neighboring settlement, where they had lost their licenses in a draw of lots in December 1921.[2]

In the collective houses (*dachanghu*), the manager (who was most usually the tenant of the premises) provided lodging, board, furniture, and electricity. Expenditure was carefully calculated. Thus, for the consumption of electricity, the number of lanterns and the hours of use were fixed in advance. There was an extra charge for additional consumption.[3] The food was often very ordinary. Famous prostitutes made it a point of honor to order their meals from outside while continuing to pay for their board. Entry into a collective house was obtained through two middlemen, each of whom was paid for his services.[4] The amount of the rent depended on whether an individual was housed upstairs or on the ground floor. It was 40 yuan and 36 yuan, respectively, in 1923.[5] Upstairs rooms had greater value because they offered more peace and quiet and were better isolated. The numbers of courtesans in the collective houses could vary, although on average there would be five or six of them.[6]

For an individual house (*zhujia*), an independent dwelling would be rented. Courtesans who had earned a certain degree of renown would generally leave the collective house in which they had started their working lives and would set up on their own. The most famous of them even rented large individual houses. When this happened, the rent and costs of hiring staff were borne entirely by the courtesan. Dinners would be ordered from outside restaurants. The customers preferred this arrangement, which let them off from having to pay the large tips that were the rule in the collective houses with their numerous employees. The establishments probably did not last long, although there were exceptions. Certain madams trained several "generations" of courtesans whose active life, as we have seen, barely exceeded five to seven years. The older houses would publicize their longevity in press advertisements as evidence of quality.[7]

Interiors

In the *lilong* in which the courtesans' houses were concentrated, each house took up either a "compartment" (*jian*) or a floor (*loumian*).[8] The biggest of them occupied an entire dwelling.[9] Each floor or each compartment housed three to five "families"; a family consisted of a courtesan, her madam, and her employees, each with a room or individual apartment.[10] It was therefore important to give a clear indication of where they were to be found.

Little plaques of lacquered wood with the names of every courtesan present would be hung over the main porch of each establishment.[11]

The dwellings in which the *shuyu* were set up were generally quite huge. However, the space available for each courtesan was smaller in the collective houses (*dachanghu*) than in the individual houses (*zhujia*). The *dachanghu* always had one big room, often the courtesan's room, which could accommodate up to fifteen people.[12] The discretion and intimacy between a courtesan and a customer were ensured by a huge canopied Chinese bed providing for complete isolation. In the 1930s, when the traditional bed fell into disuse and there was greater pressure on living space, the main room was divided into two by a wooden wall. The front room was used as a reception room for gambling and dinners, while the back room was the bedroom.[13]

Peace and discretion within the houses were maintained by compliance with basic unwritten rules. Those who disobeyed these rules would, at best, be regarded as uncouth individuals and, at worst, be thrown out. Access to the rooms was through an entrance with no door but just a curtain that was kept open when the girl was alone and drawn when she had a customer with her. There was an unspoken rule, frequently recalled in the guidebooks, by which a customer was required to turn back if he saw that another customer had preceded him for a visit or a *huatou*. In no circumstance could he disturb the festivities, even if he were a known customer. If he wanted to be sure of meeting a particular courtesan, especially if she was a girl of some renown, then it was best to make a reservation.

There was a code of courtesy expressed by the formal way in which a customer would be greeted on his arrival: He would be given a pipe (later replaced by cigarettes), served tea, and given a towel. When he left, the courtesan would accompany him out of her room up to the staircase. From there onward, he would be escorted to the door by the maidservant because the courtesans had difficulty in moving about with their bound feet. This custom was kept even after the disappearance of bound feet.[14] In the collective houses (*dachanghu*), a known customer would be received, on arrival, in a reception room. There, he would be offered a bowl of tea by the house itself. However, if he had a regular courtesan, she was required to have another bowl of tea brought up to her room as a token of honor.[15] Apart from having the usual "pumpkin seeds," each courtesan's room had plates of fruit.[16] At each change of season (New Year's, the dragon festival, the mid-autumn festival), sweetmeats and special fruits were served.

Once the customer had settled into the courtesan's room, he could smoke, gamble, and dine in the company of friends. This created an often noisy atmosphere, which was one of the features that gave an establishment its standing. The greater the noise and the frequency of social evenings, the greater the reputation of the house. The evenings began to get lively after ten at night when a courtesan, unless she was very much in demand, would return. Each invitee would often get a courtesan to come and enliven the evening. With the added presence of the maidservants who accompanied every courtesan, a table of ten guests would easily mean a group of thirty people.[17] The invitees would leave at two or three in the morning.

At the end of the evening, the host would spend a little more time with the girl in small talk and banter. One author says that, in the privacy of her chamber, the courtesan would sing another repertory where the songs were more ribald.[18] Although I have frequently come across the term (*yinci*), which can be translated as "ribald songs" or "obscene songs," I have been unable to find the smallest trace of any of their texts. In the case of the courtesans, I found only one reference, dating from the years 1920–1930, which probably does not represent the range offered by the courtesans before 1914. The customer did not necessarily stay on. At least, this was the practice before the 1920s. It was up to the courtesan to take the initiative and suggest that he might like to spend the night with her. Conversely, according to the guides and "compasses of the world of gallantry," it was bad form for a customer to ask if he could stay. Even if the girl assented, it meant that she was having her door forced and being made to lose face.[19]

In the more ordinary establishments, the housing conditions for the girls were far less luxurious. The *yao'er* houses were all organized in the same mode: There would be a three-floor building that the managers would partition again to get five or six floors through an extreme compartmentalization. The *yao'er* houses were distinguished by the number of residents, of whom there would be least six and as many as twenty.[20] A 1922 source counted seven houses with a total of eighty-two girls, giving an average of twelve prostitutes per house.[21] As a rule, each girl had her own room. The names of the girls in the establishment were indicated outside by wooden plaques as in the *changsan*. The prostitutes rented a room in a house and shared all their earnings with the manager, except for money collected for banquets.[22] They received two meals of mediocre quality in their rooms.[23]

The pre-1920 *yeji* or *huayanjian* houses were Chinese houses with two levels, of a kind still to be seen in Shanghai. The girls would sit in the lower-level room waiting for customers. When one of them got a customer, she would go into a small room, which was four meters square at most.[24] The *yeji* houses were the ones most discredited by the sources. The commonest adjectives used were "dirty," "small," and "miserable." According to a survey in 1948 of prostitutes in the big houses, when a customer arrived, the girls would be summoned by an electric bell and would present themselves in a state of undress.[25] The *xianrouzhuang* were at a fairly similar level in the manner in which they were packed together. The smallest establishments often had about twenty rooms each, while the largest had about fifty.

Table 9.1. *Size of the courtesans' establishments (1922–1924)*

Number of Prostitutes	International Settlement		French Concession	
	Number	Percentage	Number	Percentage
1	52	21.2	11	12.1
2	59	24.1	18	19.7
3	51	20.8	11	12.1
4	59	24.1	27	29.7
5	13	5.3	12	13.2
6	6	2.5	7	7.7
7	3	1.2	2	2.2
8	1	0.4	2	2.2
9+	1	0.4	1	1.1
Total:	245	100.0	91	100.0

Source: Wang Jimen, *Shanghai liushi nian lai huajie shi, op. cit.*, pp. 186–214.

Each room had a "family" of two to five girls, one madam, and one maid-servant. The names of the girls were posted on the door by order of age (*lao er, lao san*, etc.).[26]

Size and Longevity of the Establishments

The size of the establishments could vary to an extreme degree, but, on the whole, there were more girls to a house as one went down the scale from courtesans to lower-category prostitutes. Among the courtesans, a distinction must be made between the "families" consisting of the madam, the girl or girls, and the servants, and the house itself. In the individual houses (*zhujia*), "family" and "house" exactly overlapped each other. These houses had one or two girls in the nineteenth century and up to three or five in the 1920s. Yet the majority of them were small establishments. In the collective houses, there was sometimes a very large number of girls, but they constituted different "families" being housed by the establishment. In 1923 and 1924, out of eighty-nine requests for permission to open establishments, sixty-seven houses had one to four girls[27] (see Table 9.1). Another source gives an idea of the size of the *changsan* houses.

Most of them had one to four girls. The courtesans' houses remained places where individual relationships between customers and girls were maintained.

It is more difficult to draw a picture of the more common type of establishment. In 1869, according to figures by Dr. Henderson, the houses of prostitution (apart from the courtesans) had an average of six prostitutes.[28] The

Table 9.2. *Size of a group of houses of tolerance in the French Concession (1936)*

Women per House	Number of Houses	Percentage
1–4	5	11.6
5–9	20	46.5
10–14	13	30.3
15–25	5	11.6
Total:	43	100.0

Source: Archives de la direction des services adminis-tratifs, Concession française, dossier 1936 25 MS 1555.

report of the Vice Committee in 1920 reveals an average figure of seven prostitutes per establishment, while in the French Concession in 1936 there were more than ten girls to a house.[29]

In 1922, the seven remaining *yao'er* houses had an average of twelve residents. It is even more difficult to estimate the numbers residing in the other establishments, and all we can do is to cling to the general statistics provided by the different surveys. In the 1940s, the guide agencies (*xiangdaoshe*) often housed more than a dozen girls. Clearly, there was great diversity, but the common establishments generally harbored more girls per house as befitted their role as a sexual outlet. However, it would seem that the very big establishments were few and far between. The case of the Taotao deserves to be described here, because its role as a sex factory symbolizes an important aspect of Shanghai's image.

The Taotao opened as a guide agency (*xiangdaoshe*) before it turned into a house of prostitution. The establishment occupied a huge house that had been partitioned into a multitude of rooms with space for only a bed, a dressing mirror, a chair, and a bucket. The girls called these rooms "pigeon's cages" (*gezilong*). In 1947, there were 84 rooms with 101 girls. To augment its operations, the Taotao built a five-story structure. It was managed by three people, two men and a woman, none of them identified, but it was actually controlled by a madam. The girls who were its residents were not entitled to take customers outside the house under pain of financial sanction. Similarly, although the girls had not been sold to the establishment, the Taotao would require a customer to pay a sum of money (*chujiafei*) when he wished to marry one of them. Every Saturday, the madam assembled all the prostitutes to give them instructions and advice, especially on how to welcome and treat customers.[30]

There were madams renowned for having trained several "generations" of courtesans, but it would appear that the world of prostitution was gen-

Table 9.3. *Fluctuations in the numbers of prostitutes registered in the Laozha district (1947)*

Month	Number	Month	Number
January	156	July	587
February	169	August	324
March	87	September	228
April	139	October	512
May	236	November	303
June	305	December	450

Source: *Shanghai shi jingchaju Laozha fenju sanshiliu niandu niankan* (Annual Report for 1947 of the Laozha police station, Police Bureau of the Municipality of Shanghai), Shanghai, 1948, p. 187.

erally characterized by a relatively high turnover, in the long term as well as the short term. I am unable to quantify this aspect for lack of series corresponding to a sufficiently lengthy period. My impression is based on a number of clues all pointing in the same direction, especially for the 1930s and 1940s where the flows were accelerated. Thus, I would estimate that of the more than 500 courtesans listed in four beauty contests that followed one another from 1917 to 1920, only 75 were seen more than once. Even if the rule of the game was to elect new faces, this rate of appearance is surprisingly low.

The French police archives reveal major fluctuations from one month to another. In a period of six and a half years, the number of houses listed was never constant for more than two or three months in succession.[31] Furthermore, applications for opening new houses poured in all the time. In February 1924 alone, the municipal police granted sixty-eight new licenses.[32] In July 1923, they received twenty-one applications in eleven days. It must be acknowledged, however, that this movement was related to the abolitionist policy of the Shanghai Municipal Council. It is suggested by incomplete sources that, between April 1932 and June 1939, there were ninety-eight applications made to open houses in the French Concession.[33] Finally in 1947, a report by the Laozha police station whose jurisdiction covered the "golden circle" of prostitution showed major variations in the numbers of prostitutes listed every month, as can be seen in Table 9.3.[34] These variations might even be explained by corresponding variations in police vigilance, but there is no reason to believe that the differences could have occurred with such irregularity. These variations were caused by the mobility in space and time of the houses of prostitution. A possible conclusion is that, in every period, there was a very high turnover of houses of prostitution and therefore of prostitutes.

The Turnover Rate for the Girls

The question of staff turnover does not really arise for the middle and lower category of houses of prostitution, which individually often harbored fairly large numbers of girls. In the case of the courtesans' houses, where there was only one to three girls per establishment, the question of turnover has to be formulated differently. It took the form of transfers from one house to another for those who hired themselves out to a madam.

The turnover was related above all to the conditions in which the women had entered prostitution. In the common establishments (*yeji, xian-rouzhuang, xianshuimei*, etc.), the girls could have four different types of status: slaves (*taoren*), pledged girls (*baozhang*), indebted girls (*huoji*), and free girls (*zijia*).[35] These differences in status have already been seen among the courtesans, but, while the terms had the same meaning, they did not have the same implications for those concerned in terms of working conditions and fate. For the slave prostitutes, there was no way out. They were condemned to their fate until illness or age made them "unfit for consumption" or until a customer, generally from the underprivileged sections of society, agreed to marry them. The pledged prostitutes were women placed in a brothel for a specified period of time in return for a sum of money. We have seen in Chapter 7 that the individuals who placed these girls belonged to a very wide variety of categories, including family, friends, and kidnappers.

It is hard to give precise figures on the proportion of the population of prostitutes represented by this group of slaves or, in the case of pledged women, virtual slaves. The available figures are all more or less subjective and even fanciful. It seems to me to be erroneous to assert that 80% of the prostitutes were slaves.[36] Even if, as can be seen in the world of working women, forms of quasi-servitude emerged in the 1930s under the influence of the secret societies, the proportion of girls sold or pledged probably did not amount to more than half. A figure of one-third for the proportion of girls sold is probably closer to reality, but it is at best an approximate figure. The archives of the 1940s revealed a massive reduction in the size of this category. The police charge sheets against arrested prostitutes most usually speak of the girls sharing their earnings with the madam in varying proportions, but the girls appear to have had full rights over their own person. It can be concluded either that earlier estimates had been exaggerated or that a qualitative change had come about with the war – especially with the Civil War, which brought tens of thousands of extremely destitute women into Shanghai and created a huge pool of labor.

The *huoji* prostitutes were women who were indebted to a madam, incapable of repaying her and therefore obliged to make payment with their own person until the sums borrowed had been returned in full. The so-called free prostitutes were girls who had no relationship of dependency with the madam and worked in the house of prostitution on the basis of a mutual income-sharing agreement. The condition of the different types of prostitutes was basically different. The last two categories enjoyed a great deal of freedom. The *huoji* had to work several nights – that is, two to four nights a week. They could go home and were not obliged to reside in the house on the other nights. The free prostitutes did what they liked and received customers as they wished. They had no obligation toward the madam except to declare their income and share it according to a fixed mode.[37] By contrast, the pledged prostitutes and slaves were required to prostitute themselves every day and bring home at least one customer for the night.[38]

In the courtesans' houses, the turnover took other forms. Girls who had acquired a certain degree of celebrity would be approached by the madams when they were free – that is, when they had the freedom of their person. Certain madams would readily try to lure them out of their current houses with better offers. In August 1902, a famous courtesan of Tianjin came to live in Shanghai and was immediately contacted by a house. An enterprising madam, Wang Peilan, tried to attract the courtesan to her own establishment with a promise of higher earnings and a 40/60 sharing arrangement to the courtesan's advantage.[39] Changing a house of prostitution always came about at the end of a season. When a courtesan made a change, she would distribute visiting cards with her new address to her habitual customers. In the twentieth century, these cards would be embellished with the girl's photograph.[40] The courtesans used the "specialized" press to announce their change from one house to another.[41] There were directories of the world of gallantry (*qunfangpu*) published at the beginning of each season with lists of courtesans and information about changes of house.[42]

The Customers

The social origin of the men who patronized the houses of prostitution is not as easily identifiable as might be imagined, even for the courtesans' houses. The sources, as in other fields, are singularly concise. In most cases, the persons concerned are designated by the term "customer" (*ke*), which, as might be imagined, leaves wide scope for interpretation. It is by chance, in a press article or an archival annotation, that the professional occupation of a customer appears. For this section, therefore, I have relied on information gleaned from the sources for Shanghai to which I have added information from documents more general in scope.

For those who patronized the courtesans, I have made abundant use of the terms "elites" and "scholars." These are broad, and one might even say vague, social categories that only reflect my difficulty in qualifying the customers with precision. Naturally, it would be fairly safe to assume that the customers were, to a very great extent, merchants and high-level civil servants under both the Empire and the Republic. But a closer look reveals that the picture is not as clear-cut as all that. The documents of the nineteenth century particularly favor the expression "rich merchants and scholar nobles" (*hao shang gui shen*) or "rich merchants" (*jushang dagu*) to designate those who visited the high-class courtesans' houses. Other frequently used terms were "famous scholar" (*mingshi*) and "lord" (*gongzi*).

A meager reference is that given by the information available on marriages by the prostitutes. Taking a former courtesan as a concubine remained the privilege of well-to-do individuals who could maintain large households. Almost all those whom the sources specifically identify by profession are merchants. Qian Lijun married a "rich merchant" although she was in love with another customer, a scholar without fortune. Another married a rice merchant.[43] The profession of government service was represented by a high-level civil servant who spent more than a thousand yuan in one month with the courtesan Jin Bao.[44] Some, however, were not as lucky: A clerk in the *yamen* of the Shanghai *xian* used to visit a courtesan but was too poor to bring her out of the house that employed her. This also happened to a scholar who was a magistrate's assistant (*mu*).[45] Peasants too would occasionally patronize the courtesans' houses, but they were probably rural notables.[46]

This predominant role of the merchant and political elites was not challenged in the twentieth century. In 1911, it was the chief of the Zhabei police who took a courtesan as a concubine.[47] In 1920, a general belonging to the army staff took a partner from this milieu.[48] One of the "four diamonds" (a group of four famous Shanghai courtesans), Jin Xiaobao, married Lu Daguan, director of the legal department of the Shanghai-Wusong army headquarters.[49] Wu Tiecheng, until he was appointed mayor of Shanghai in 1932, was a diligent customer of the *changsan* houses. Seeking discretion and wishing to save time, he took a mistress from this milieu and set her up on Rue Lafayette in the French Concession.[50] A survey among prostitutes in 1948 revealed that most of the customers of the *changsan* were merchants, while those who went to the ordinary prostitutes belonged to the working classes.[51] The courtesans' houses were therefore inaccessible to a wide section of society.

The more common houses of prostitution received a wide variety of customers. It is impossible to establish even an approximate link between certain categories of prostitutes and specific sections of society, regardless of the period considered. In 1889, a tailor and a male servant got into an argument about a prostitute.[52] In the same period, a cart driver was accused of stealing 12 yuan and spending it on five nights in a brothel.[53] In 1872, the *Shen Bao* reported that two brothers had stolen money from a teahouse to settle their debts toward a brothel. Another made off with 500 yuan from a temple.[54] In 1909, a rickshaw puller had 2 yuan stolen from him in a

236 The Space and Economy of Prostitution

huayanjian.[55] In 1910, a low-level office worker in a railway company was arrested for theft in a hotel. He was trying to repay his debts to a house of prostitution.[56] These few examples show that almost every section of society was concerned.

For the twentieth century, the testimony is to a great extent based on impressions. For one writer, the customers of the *yao'er* in the 1920s were shop assistants or "bumpkins" from surrounding towns.[57] In 1910, the three customers arrested in a brawl were identified as a pharmacy salesman, an office worker in the *xian* administration, and a shopkeeper.[58] According to another author, the customers of the *xianrouzhuang* belonged to the middle classes (*zhongdeng jieji*) and were people who paid for sex without leaving any tips.[59] According to the sources, the customers of the *yeji* belonged to the middle and lower levels of society (*zhongxia jieji*) or to a vague category of itinerant vendors and merchants (*fanfu zouzu*).[60] One author who described himself as a member of the petit-bourgeoisie said he would be incapable of patronizing this class of prostitute.[61] On the whole, these statements reflected their authors' prejudices rather than any attempt at analysis, albeit superficial.

Another source of information on the customers of the prostitution houses consists of published work by Chinese and foreign doctors in China's medical journals. In their surveys on the spread of venereal disease, the doctors drew up tables that included their patients' occupations. These sources must be taken with the greatest caution, but they shed interesting light on Chinese society.[62] It might appear to be arbitrary to set up as direct a link as this between prostitution and venereal disease, in this case syphilis. It must be recalled, however, that in China at this time (1920–1949), extra-marital relations and sexual promiscuity were hardly widespread. Most of the patients affected by venereal disease contracted the disease from prostitutes.

Married men were by far the majority of the patients suffering from the highest rates of infection. Marriage, therefore, offered no protection against venereal disease, and the encouragement of early marriage that many commentators recommended was definitely no solution to this problem. A survey shows that workers whose wives lived far from the city in which they were employed were more frequently infected than those whose families were close to them. However, even when they did live close to their families, married men continued to patronize prostitutes.[63] This observation is confirmed by the age of the patients. Few of them were younger than twenty (11.4% to 14.7%).[64] This may indicate that active sexual life began very late in China. This idea is supported by the fact that many of the young patients were congenital sufferers of venereal disease. The most common age group – the mode – consisted of those aged twenty-five to thirty-nine (57% to 62%). In all the surveys, this group is seen with the highest rates of infection. This age group corresponds to the period of the greatest sexual vigor among males. Those in their forties, although less numerous, accounted for nearly a third of the syphilis patients. It is not rare to find patients in their fifties, although in their case there is another factor to be considered – that of untreated illness and natural remission that could give rise to later relapses.[65]

Among the professional categories, two groups were far ahead on the list in terms of numbers and rate of infection. These were the merchants and the soldiers.[66] The lifestyle of the merchants exposed them to the risks of venereal disease. They traveled a great deal and often spent several weeks or even several months outside their city of residence. But this was not the main reason. Patronizing houses of prostitution was a normal part of social life for this group. The merchants would often clinch a deal with a banquet in a brothel or in a restaurant in the company of courtesans or prostitutes. Soldiers too patronized prostitutes in this way, but for different reasons. During the Republican period, the warlords had to support undisciplined armies that were constantly on the move from one region to another. Condemned as most of them were to a life of *de facto* celibacy, the soldiers would relieve their tedium with gambling, opium, and prostitutes.

Policemen, military officers, and people from other related professions also appear, again with high rates of infection. Many of them had taken leave in order to obtain treatment, thus contributing to a reduction in police efficiency. Just below this category came the itinerant vendors, illicit vendors, servants, and craftsmen. Professionals (namely lawyers, jurists, doctors, and the like), teachers, low-level civil servants, and students were the smallest group among the syphilitics with, moreover, the lowest rates of infection. The surveys include an "all-inclusive" category ("persons of no occupation") ranging from vagabonds to unemployed persons and beggars and sometimes housewives. The coolies, who are often mentioned in my sources as customers of the *yeji* or *huayanjian*, did not represent a major proportion of infected individuals, although their rate of infection was particularly high. Their low wages probably meant that they could not make frequent visits to prostitutes but once they caught an illness, they had no means to obtain treatment.

Proprietors and Madams

The houses of prostitution were managed more often by madams than by men. A police census in the Laozha district in 1947 found that the brothel proprietors comprised 256 women and 9 men.[67] This is a category about which information is extremely scanty. In the nineteenth century, these nevertheless essential figures in the world of prostitution were but very rarely referred to in the sources, even the literary ones, except in relation to the subject of marriage. It was not until the turn of the century, especially in the novels written in the *Wu* dialect, that the character of the madam came to the foreground. She began to assume the more explicit features of a greedy exploiter, constantly dissatisfied with the work of the girls under her authority.[68] This is the view that was conveyed by every form of popular literature – the literature of the "butterflies and mandarin ducks"[69] – up to 1949, and it is the view that the Communists took up after their victory.

The presence of women at the head of the courtesans' houses may seem surprising in the Chinese context, and even at a more general level. In the West, prostitution is associated with the men who dominated this milieu, laying down the rules and inflicting punishment on recalcitrant individuals. However, the reality was far more complex and shifting. Marie-Erica Benabou has shown that the houses of prostitution in eighteenth-century France were controlled by women who were not mere figureheads. They wielded real power within their establishments in which men were in the background.[70] In the following century, studied by Alain Corbin, it was still women who generally managed the houses of tolerance, but the hierarchy of power was far more complex.[71] In China, these figures were designated by explicit terms of derision. The madam was called a *baomu* (literally, "mother goose") while her husband and partner was a *gui* or *guinu* (an untranslatable term, literally meaning "tortoise" or "slave tortoise" and generally designating the male proprietor or manager of a brothel), about whom more will be said later.

The role of the madam was twofold. She was the boss of the house or, where the courtesans were concerned, of a "family" established, most usually, in a collective house (*dachanghu*). This meant that she had practically every power over the life of the girl who was her possession, whether purchased, pledged, or hired. A hired girl, if she became discontented, could sometimes change madams at the end of a season. In the courtesans' houses, the madam fulfilled a major role in the choice of customers. It was she who would assess a new customer and determine his social status, discreetly questioning other customers and acquaintances from the world of prostitution about his professional status, companions in leisure, and so on, in order to ascertain the state of his fortune.[72]

The madam was also a trafficker in human beings. We have seen that the courtesans did not remain very long in the trade. They came in very young but had to get out quickly, before they lost their beauty and charms and ended up in the more disreputable houses. The madam was therefore forced to renew her staff. Whenever a girl managed to get married, the madam would purchase another girl. Sometimes she would have already acquired a little girl who had been trained in the house and was going to take over from the one who was leaving. The archives and the press mention many cases of minors under fifteen found by the police in establishments of prostitution. The madam would see to it that girls she had purchased or who were pledged to her received singing and music lessons. Madams also taught them the art of makeup, hair styling, and dressing as well as ways to treat customers.

Men were also present, although they were in the background. It was the men who often were, in a proportion that cannot be precisely estimated, the organizers of the collective houses (*dachanghu*). They sometimes came from circles closely related to that of prostitution. In 1922, a major establishment was opened in the French Concession by a former musician.[73] Men also appeared very often in the role of the *guinu*. They were most often the partners of the madams, whether as husbands or otherwise. The *guinu* are rarely referred to in the general literature on prostitution. The term appears from time to time in the guides and "compasses," but the authors hardly attached any special importance to them. This is somewhat paradoxical because the *guinu* played a major role in maintaining order and discipline in the houses.

The presence of a man in a house of prostitution provided an assurance of some security in the event of attacks by ruffians from outside or violence on the part of customers. The *guinu* were responsible for collecting money from defaulting customers. They had also a money-lending function: They would lend money to the prostitutes in the house or in other establishments. The *guinu* had an ambiguous status with the madams. They sometimes appeared as legitimate husbands. However, they are more frequently referred to as male partners. This is an interesting point. Up to the 1920s and even thereafter, there was no such thing as a marriage certificate to sanction marriage in China. The social recognition of marriage was established by a family ceremony with devotions to the ancestral tablet, followed by a banquet. Public recognition was conferred on the new couple. Now the Chinese language has a term (*pin*) to designate persons living together without being married, and this is the expression most frequently used with respect to the *guinu* and also with respect to the prostitutes' lovers in both the nineteenth and the twentieth centuries.

Chinese society made a clear distinction, in the absence of formal marriage certificates, between legitimate alliances and those that were considered to be not legitimate. The world of prostitution was characterized by an instability of mores where both men and women changed partners. This is not surprising given the nature of this milieu, but it does shed light on a possibly wider section of society. The press reports mention many cases of unmarried partnerships in court cases involving the poorer classes. No excessively bold conclusions should be drawn here because more details would be needed to support any argument. However, there is a similarity between this form of behavior and that of the lower classes in the French cities in the nineteenth century.[74]

The social origin of the proprietors was fairly wide-ranging, although the few precise details that are available relate to the years 1946 to 1949. According to Wang Tao's writings, certain madams themselves came from the world of prostitution. They had been courtesans before retiring to the back of the stage and recruiting young girls who replaced them in the task of entertaining customers. Sai Jinhua, a famous courtesan who had been married several times, was able to uphold the reputation of her house in Shanghai, Tianjin, and Peking by associating personal qualities with the presence of young girls whom she personally recruited for the pleasure of her customers. Some of the madams were former maidservants who had collected sufficient capital to set themselves up. Others came to this activity almost by chance because difficult circumstances had forced them to prostitute their own daughters or else because they had got hold of young, isolated girls, in many cases orphans, whom they were able to turn into "money trees."

Many of these madams were women living alone, having come from the small professions that enabled women without husbands (spinsters, widows, etc.) to survive in traditional China. They included hairdressers, traveling salesmen for sundry women's articles, matchmakers, footbinders, and so on. In twentieth-century Shanghai, with the explosion of the market of prostitution, there was a great increase in the number of madams and a widening of the range of social classes from which these madams and the owners of prostitution houses came. Although the madam's profession seems to have been dominated by single and relatively older women, those mentioned in the police reports were often married and living with their husbands. The consequences of the Civil War, especially galloping inflation, led merchants in difficult straits or those who had been ruined to turn to the world of prostitution. In 1946, a proprietor who was questioned for ill treatment said that, having lost his job as a professional shoemaker, he had turned to unauthorized shoe-repairing near the Great World establishment. He then began renting rooms at 3,000 yuan a day to five girls who had come to Shanghai looking for work.[75] A former cafe owner and wine merchant also went into the sex trade.[76] In 1947, a female proprietor explained that she and her husband were hosiery merchants who had been forced by inflation to change their trade.[77]

There were always more women than men according to the following table, but my data are very incomplete. This category tended to get younger in the 1930s. While the women in this field were most frequently of mature age, there were increasing numbers of young women.[78] Table 9.4 shows that half of the thirty-seven persons arrested were under age thirty-five. Once again, the information is too fragmentary to draw any definitive conclusions. The distribution by geographical origin of the thirty-seven persons arrested shows that the proprietors came from provinces neighboring Shanghai. Jiangnan (southern Jiangsu) and Zhejiang were almost equally placed. Within these provinces, there was a clear superiority of certain areas, such as Shaoxing-Ningbo, which were traditionally areas of emigration toward

Table 9.4. *Age, sex, and origin by* xian *of managers of houses of prostitution arrested between 1946 and 1948*

Province	Xian	Age	Sex	Province	Xian	Age	Sex
Jiangbei	Yancheng	25	F	Zhejiang	Haining	36	—
Jiangbei	Yangzhou	26	—	Zhejiang	Hangzhou	35	F
Jiangbei	Yangzhou	28	F	Zhejiang	Hangzhou	46	—
Jiangnan	Nanhui	46	F	Zhejiang	Ningbo	24	—
Jiangnan	Nanxiang	45	F	Zhejiang	Ningbo	26	—
Jiangnan	Suzhou	19	—	Zhejiang	Ningbo	26	F
Jiangnan	Suzhou	29	—	Zhejiang	Qingjiang	29	F
Jiangnan	Suzhou	29	—	Zhejiang	Qingjiang	30	M
Jiangnan	Suzhou	36	—	Zhejiang	Shaoxing	22	—
Jiangnan	Suzhou	42	—	Zhejiang	Shaoxing	29	M
Jiangnan	Wuxi	24	—	Zhejiang	Shaoxing	35	—
Jiangnan	Wuxi	25	—	Zhejiang	Shaoxing	42	M
Jiangnan	Wuxi	42	—	Zhejiang	Shaoxing	42	—
Jiangnan	Zhenjiang	46	M	Zhejiang	Shaoxing	47	—
Shanghai	—	34	—	Zhejiang	Yangzhou	42	—
Shanghai	Pudong	25	—	—	—	42	F
Shanghai	Pudong	25	—	—	—	44	F
Shanghai	Pudong	27	—	—	—	60	—
				—	Guangyou	35	M

Source: Police files, archives of the Police Bureau, 1945–1949.

Shanghai, and Suzhou-Wuxi, the two major cities of Jiangsu closest to Shanghai.

To run a house of prostitution, the madam and the manager had to be protected by a member of the secret societies. This is an assertion that I have often found in the sources of the 1920s. It is also an assertion made by every Chinese historian. Similarly, many works support the idea that the secret societies controlled prostitution and even that they acted as its final arbiter or *Deus ex machina*. There can be no doubt that these assertions have some basis in reality, but they do need to be moderated and clarified. It must be stated first of all that it is very difficult to establish this point clearly because none of the sources makes any irrefutable reference to the way in which this control was exercised. The secret societies worked by an orally expressed code and an informal organization. Secret societies did acquire enormous power and influence in twentieth-century Shanghai, especially after 1927, but this does not mean (and I am personally very skeptical in the matter) that a similar situation prevailed before 1927. There is therefore a risk of distortion in projecting a recent image on a more complex and different reality that existed several decades earlier.

For the nineteenth century, the sources yield relatively little information on these aspects. Wang Tao mentions the existence of layabouts (*wulaizi*) who carried out a protection racket against the houses of prostitution, but there is no way of asserting that this was a regular practice organized by a secret society. Furthermore, I have noted a shift in the meaning attached to an expression, *chengtou*. In Wang's time it referred to the bribe paid to the police for protection against layabouts. In the twentieth century it came to mean money obtained through a protection racket organized by members of the secret societies. The more contemporary sources often refer to an establishment's need to find a "pillar" (*kaoshan*, literally a "mountain of support"; or *houtai*, "rear base"), namely, a local gang leader who would take action in the event of disputes between houses or of violence by customers and external gangs. He would also act as an intermediary with the police of the district.

Prostitution was not, strictly speaking, organized by the secret societies. These societies had an extremely decentralized structure with a succession of levels (formally known as "generations" that depended on their date of entry into the society). A given level had no direct power over its immediately lower level. It was therefore a cluster system wherein a disciple had only one godfather but could have several disciples himself, and so on down the line. The houses of prostitution would obtain the patronage of the head of a gang of the district or street belonging to the lower levels of the secret society. Ultimately, it was the Green Gang (*Qingbang*) that became Shanghai's dominant organization through the wealth that it derived from the opium traffic.[80] The bosses of the houses of prostitution, or the *guinu*, had to be introduced to a leader who would ensure their protection. They themselves sometimes, and even frequently, became members of secret societies.[81] The money collected through this racket, after successive deductions, ultimately reached the leaders of the secret society. Despite their real influence, the prevailing impression is one of a flexible and decentralized organization characterized by a succession of steps.

The Maidservants

The houses of courtesans and prostitution employed large numbers of staff. Each member of this staff had a specific function in the organization of the work. Among the courtesans, there were first of all the maidservants (*ajie* or *niangyi*) with numerous responsibilities that varied with age. A single courtesan could have several maidservants, depending on her fame. These maidservants could easily be distinguished from the courtesans by their clothes, which were generally far more simple.

The younger maidservants generally wore no makeup and had two plaits or a pigtail. Their primary task was to help the courtesans in their day-to-day life – that is, help them to carry out their daily toilet, do up their hair, and dress them. They would also be in attendance when the courtesan went out or received customers in her rooms. Most frequently, they brought customers the *pipa* and the water pipe (or opium pipe).

The maidservants also acted as substitutes for the courtesan when she was still too young to receive customers. This was one way of compensating for the sexual expectations of customers who sometimes wanted more than a courtesan's wit and her artistic charms. According to one author, it was rare for girls of more than thirteen or fourteen not to have been deflowered, willingly or not, by the individuals (waiters, actors, and customers) who gravitated around this milieu.[82] In the nineteenth century, the maidservants were often girls of eleven or twelve. However, after 1911 and to an even greater extent after the prohibitory measures promulgated in the settlements, this job was taken over by girls of over fifteen or sixteen.[83]

Beyond their role as substitute, the maidservants were often prostitutes in their own right.[84] Of course, they were at a lower level than their mistresses and were not considered to be courtesans, but they could have regular customers. The practice of patronizing maidservants brought certain advantages. The first was that their favors cost far less than those of a courtesan. They did not have to be approached by a game of seduction, with presents, banquets, and the rest. It was enough to agree on a price. They could also negotiate a share of the income of the house by fulfilling a sort of "target-related contract" – that is, by getting their customers to organize a certain number of *huatou* fixed in agreement with the madam (generally thirty per season).

A second ancillary advantage was the sexual accessibility of the maidservants. For customers who wished to enjoy a courtesan's charms but were unable to spend enough money to win her favors or were quite simply in a hurry, maidservants furnished the requisite sexual services without any of the corresponding difficulties. Besides, unlike the courtesans, the maidservants were free in their movements. This made it easier to invite them out and organize meetings in hotels to escape surveillance by the madam.[85] Nevertheless, the maidservants had to return every evening to their establishment. We therefore must take account of this reality when seeking to determine the number of prostitutes, because the maidservants are never presented as such in the official census figures. The fact, however, is that the conversion of the maidservants into fully-practicing prostitutes was a late phenomenon (that came about after 1915). It is never mentioned in the nineteenth-century sources.

The maidservants had another essential function: keeping a watch over the courtesans to whom they were attached. Indeed, the maidservants were recruited by the madams to whom they sometimes got indebted at the very outset.[86] Thus, the maidservants were the madams' eyes and ears on the activities and contacts of the courtesans. The madams feared the loss of their source of income or premature damage to it. In other words, they would seek to prevent young courtesans from being deflowered without their consent or from eloping with a customer. Similarly, they would try to prevent secret meetings with a customer or a lover where they might lose money.[87] The maidservants therefore accompanied the courtesans wherever they went, listened in on their conversations with customers, kept a watch on their behavior, moods, and so on, and faithfully reported any suspicious behavior to the madam.

The Musicians and House Staff

The musicians formed a group closely related to the world of theater and prostitution. Inasmuch as there was no difference in repertory [the same melodies were played in the theater (the *shuchang*), the teahouses, and the courtesans' houses], the musicians were interchangeable and could pass from one institution to another. The *shuyu* houses had no official musicians, and the courtesans provided their own accompaniment on the *pipa*. Sometimes, at a customer's request, musicians would be engaged for a specific outing. Again, as we have seen above, the *shuyu* who came to a *shuchang* would sing to the accompaniment of musicians from the establishment.[88] In the *changsan* houses, on the contrary, it was normal to have a musician or even an orchestra to accompany a courtesan in the establishment or when she went out. Similarly, the houses of the Cantonese courtesans also maintained an orchestra of four or five musicians. In the collective houses (*dachanghu*), the orchestra was often shared.[89]

Up to 1874–1875, the courtesans would sing *kunqu*, a form of opera that was predominant in the lower Yangzi. The *kunqu* was replaced by the Peking Opera, which led to a decline in the activities of the musicians. Around 1890, the courtesans would accompany themselves on the *pipa* or, more rarely, on the *erhu* (a two-string violin). The musicians tried to stop this development by opposing to the training of the courtesans in the *pipa* and the *huqin* and by teaching them only to sing. In 1923, they held a sort of general assembly in a teahouse and adopted a resolution to this effect.[90] This was but a pious wish for they were in no position to prevent the dissemination of instrumental techniques, especially by courtesans who were themselves already trained in these instruments. At the beginning of the twentieth century, a very small number of houses continued to employ permanent musicians.[91]

In the collective houses (*dachanghu*) in which several courtesans were resident, the staff consisted of two categories. One category included, first of all, the waiters, called *huoji*, *xiangbang*, or *waichang*, whose main task was to receive customers on the ground floor and offer them tea and some sweetmeats. In the bigger houses, they procured supplies and also kept watch against layabouts in the evening. These employees were paid by the owner or proprietor of the premises.[92] Another group, consisting of one or two individuals per courtesan, were in attendance inside the chambers and also provided conveyance for the courtesans when they went out (in sedan chairs or later in rickshaws). Like the servant girls, they also had a role of keeping watch on the actions and gestures of the courtesans and their customers. In the nineteenth century, the lower-level staff was housed in the establishment itself, which provided them with a bare minimum: a bed and a table. The rest was at their expense.[93] Thereafter, they were lodged outside the house, but in the same area.

The second category of staff consisted of cooks responsible for feeding the staff of the house and preparing dinners ordered by customers. In fact, only the collective houses (*dachanghu*) had their own kitchens. The others had dinners brought in from outside. This category of staff does not call for any particular observations. It must be noted, however, that the cooks, like everybody else, joined in this remarkable phenomenon of the circulation of money and exploitation of the courtesans. At each change of season (*jie*), the cooks prepared a special dinner (*sicai*) and sent it to each courtesan, who would then be obliged to invite a customer to pay for the pleasure of dining with her.

The sources indicate that after 1925 the ancillary staff became smaller in the courtesans' houses. The presence of large numbers of employees was not as necessary as in the past. First of all, in order to escape the prohibitory policies of the Shanghai Municipal Council, the houses were forced either to move or else to become clandestine establishments, a condition calling for greater discretion. Secondly, the courtesans began to melt into the ranks of prostitution even if they were seen as high-class prostitutes. They therefore no longer needed all the logistical backup hitherto entailed by the organization of dinners in their chambers. Thereafter, everything came from outside, and the hotels became a favorite place for gambling, inviting girls, and even organizing dinners.[94] This said, there can be no doubt that prostitution continued to support a fairly large number of people up to the war. In 1939, the police carried out 176 raids on 70 *yeji* houses. They arrested 90 proprietors or managers and 1,568 employees. However, the guide agencies (*xiangdaoshe*) provided fewer opportunities for ancillary employment: 51 police raids led to the arrest of 91 proprietors and 118 employees.[95] It is not possible to make any projection on this basis, but these figures confirm the range of the jobs created by prostitution.

It was shown in the last chapter that the houses of prostitution were perfectly well integrated into Shanghai's urban fabric. They took over whole blocks of dwellings that they adapted to their requirements, but few elements set them apart from their surroundings. Apart from the courtesans' signboards and nameplates, there were no external signs pointing to the presence of the brothels. Their interior layout varied according to the level of the establishment. In the courtesans' houses, the emphasis was generally placed on the creation of a comfortable and even luxurious environment that would imitate the interiors of the houses of the elites and give a customer the impression of a convivial place, with no distinctive signs of its true function. Nothing was done to create any particular atmosphere likely to tickle the customer's libido. The ordinary houses did not offer the luxury of the courtesans' houses but they, too, were sober in their interior layout, which, as it turned out, was designed purely for sexual consumption.

The study of these houses of prostitution also confirms the great instability of this milieu and the fact that their residents were being constantly replaced. Even if the prostitutes were the object of repeated transactions from one house to another, we have seen that the majority of them did not remain all their lives in the trade. In one way or another they found a way out. The fact that the houses were short-lived reinforces this interpretation. The trade of the madam or brothel proprietors was, in many cases, as transient as that of the prostitute. The status of the girls themselves, when they entered the houses, differed greatly. Even if some of the prostitutes were practically enslaved (sold or pledged), a good number of them had fairly great or even total freedom of movement. The courtesans changed house according to demand and according to their own reputation, although it is impossible, given the available sources, to assess this mobility.

Shanghai's houses of prostitution, especially the courtesans' establishments, appear to have been real business undertakings, relying on a highly sophisticated organization and a well-defined division of labor. They represented a sector, admittedly a special one, of the leisure industry and directly generated a fairly large number of jobs. The collective houses (*dachanghu*) constituted the most complete mode of organization, with several strata of employees; but even in the common establishments, where the services were less elaborate, a prostitute could provide several individuals with a means of livelihood. Although the notion of "family" is quite illusory, there can be no doubt that, from an economic point of view, the set of individuals living off the work of a prostitute formed a clear entity linked together by the same interests (except those of the prostitute herself, who had come into the trade against her will). A system of this kind could only add to the pressure and surveillance applied by the various employees against the girls, because the subsistence of each employee depended on the efficient functioning of the house.

If there was one exception to male domination in the public sphere, it was really in the world of prostitution. Women were massively present here not only as prostitutes but also as proprietors of houses and as madams. This is an interesting phenomenon in the Chinese context because it tends to show that even in this field, where it might have been imagined that there was a greater intermingling of the sexes, the barrier of separation remained well established. It is not that men were absent – the traffickers, local gang leaders, *guinu*, and managers did belong to the male sex – but that they were unquestionably in the background. The courtesans' houses and the small establishments of ordinary prostitution were all directed by women. I do not know if this phenomenon must be attributed to the moral and ideological barrier of separation between the sexes or to the very low esteem attached to any man who made a living as a procurer. Both factors played a role, although a reading of the press suggests that the latter explanation is more relevant. Up to 1949, the administration of prostitution remained the business of women.

10
The Economy of Sex

In Shanghai, prostitution gave rise to a relatively complex economic system characterized by very subtle modalities of monetary circulation. It is in the world of the courtesans that we find the most sophisticated forms of organization, and this sophistication was linked to the diversity of services and employees. In the other types of establishment, the relationship between sex and money was more univocal and direct, although there were also ancillary forms of expenditure. From the nineteenth century up to 1949, the economy of sex tended to get simplified owing to the disappearance of certain categories of staff and services, but also because of the growing commercialization of this milieu, especially that of the courtesans, and because of the blatant predominance of the money factor. None can question that money had always been at the heart of the sex trade, but the venal dimension was very skillfully concealed by a complicated cycle of the circulation of money. After the First World War, money very crudely became the mainspring of the relationship between a prostitute and her customer.

This chapter deals with the entire economy of sex, regardless of the establishments concerned. Naturally I shall make distinctions between the elaborate organization of the courtesans' houses and the more direct ways by which earnings were distributed in the other establishments. At the very outset it must be stated that my data on the courtesans' houses cover the entire period under study while my data on the latter category are limited to the twentieth century. Prior research on this subject has been based on literary sources that, as I have already said with respect to courtesans, can hardly be used for anything but to illustrate a proposition, certainly not to establish it.[1] The first part of this chapter shall deal with the overheads of the establishments. It will be followed by a description of the earnings and the way in which they were shared. The incomes of the prostitutes themselves and of the servants shall be dealt with separately.

Overhead

The costs borne by the owners of the houses of prostitution naturally varied according to the category of the establishment. The main expense was the rent. Most of the houses of prostitution were set up in dwellings rented from people generally unconnected with the activity that took place in their premises. The Vice Committee report for 1919 notes that, on an average, the rents paid by the houses of prostitution were higher than those paid by ordinary trading establishments.[2] I have only one reference to the amounts paid as rents in the nineteenth century, where a courtesan's house was renting out premises from a foreigner for 60 yuan a month.[3] Up until 1925, the rent was always paid in advance for an entire season, namely, every four months. Thereafter, it appears that a system of monthly rental payments was laid down.[4] In the 1920s, the courtesans paid 36 to 40 yuan to rent out a room in a collective house (*dachanghu*). In the French Concession, the amount paid as rent by the houses of prostitution was chosen, in 1936, as one of the criteria of classification under three categories.[5] For the first-category establishments (nine out of forty-three), the rents paid ranged from 50 yuan to 197 yuan.[6] These were apparently courtesan houses. Because a collective house generally housed at least five or six courtesans, the rent paid by the manager was largely covered by the sums paid by the residents. In the municipal classification, there were twenty-three establishments in the second category and eleven in the third. The rents paid by the second category ranged from 28 yuan to 78 yuan, and those paid by the lower category ranged from 23 yuan to 52 yuan.[7]

Not much capital was needed to set up a house of courtesans or a house of prostitution. All that was needed was a little money to hire or purchase a girl and some furniture. The courtesans were bought, taken in pledge, or hired. The amount paid for the hire depended on the reputation of the girl. Less was paid for beginners and for courtesans who had not yet been deflowered. A 1923 source indicates that the average was in the region of 60 to 70 yuan per season. The amounts mentioned by this source for girls taken in pledge – 6,000 to 7,000 yuan for a period of six to seven years[8] – appear to be far higher than those reported in the police archives and in the press. This would have been a considerable investment at a time when a little girl could be bought for far less. Moreover, I have never come across a case where a girl was pledged for a period as lengthy as this. In general, it was three to four years.

It was also common practice to rent furniture from merchants rather than to purchase it.[9] Renting had the advantage of providing for greater mobility in the event of a refusal to extend a lease, an enforced change of residence, or the departure of a courtesan. In 1899, a madam made an official declaration of the theft of her furniture assessed at 290 yuan.[10] Around 1930–1940, 500 to 600 yuan were needed to furnish a room. On the other hand, it cost 2,000 yuan to set up an individual courtesan's house (*zhujia*).[11] In the lower-class establishments, the furnishings were reduced to the barest minimum and did not represent any significant cost. This explains the fact that, in the 1940s, many small merchants and artisans who had been ruined turned to this more lucrative business. Before the introduction of electricity, the houses were lit with oil lamps. Because a fair amount of lighting was needed, the consumption of oil was high. The houses of prostitution used about 150 liters of oil per day, not to mention the 5,000 to 6,000 candles that were used for ceremonial purposes.[12] The salaries of the staff were small and supplemented by the tips that they routinely obtained from the customers.

In the French Concession, the courtesans' houses and brothels had to take out a license and pay a fee every quarter. The amount of the fee is not known for the first ten years of the concession's existence. Table 10.1 shows the changes in the amount of taxes that had to be paid by the brothels and courtesans' houses from 1920 to 1943. Each house in the former category had to pay a monthly tax that appears to have increased regularly at the beginning of the 1920s, at a time when a large number of establishments set up shop in the concession in order to escape the abolitionist policy of the Shanghai Municipal Council. The following period, from 1925 to 1930, appears to have been relatively stable. There were new and milder increases from 1931 onward. Eight years later, the houses were classified under three categories and subjected to a new tax structure that remained unchanged up to 1941, when inflation led the authorities of the concession to double their rates.

The courtesans' houses were taxed far less than the brothels. Indeed, even allowing for the fact that each girl had to take out a license in addition to the fee paid by the establishment, the total amount paid to the administration was smaller than in the case of the ordinary houses of prostitution because it was a quarterly fee. In 1933, a house with five courtesans paid 30 yuan per month as against 54 yuan for a brothel. Even in 1943, it was only when a courtesan's house had at least seven residents that its annual tax burden went slightly above that of a first-category brothel. I have not found any conflict pitting these houses of tolerance against the authorities except occasionally, in situations of crisis, and then it was for reasons whose relevance is not easy to determine. This was the case, for example, in December 1931 at a time when the region had been suffering, since the summer, from the effects of one of the greatest floods in the history of the Yangzi.[13]

In the International Settlement, a license fee was paid only under the policy of abolition, between 1920 and 1924. Besides, the amount was rather symbolic (1 to 2 yuan). When the Shanghai Municipal Council granted recognition to the singsong girl houses, a licensing system was set up. Only the establishments were taxed, regardless of the number of singsong girls.[14] Around 1940, this fee went up to 30–40 yuan per season and was paid by the manager of the house, who passed on this expenditure to the courtesans in the establishment.[15]

The final item of expenditure was food. The girls were generally provided

Table 10.1. *Changes in the cost of licenses for the houses of tolerance in the French Concession*

Year	Houses of Tolerance	Courtesans	Houses of Courtesans
1920	10/month	—	—
1921	15/month	—	—
1922	20/month	—	—
1923	25/month	—	—
1924	—/month	—	—
1925	—/month	—	—
1926	—/month	—	—
1927	30/month	—	—
1928	30/month	—	—
1929	30/month	—	—
1930	30/month	—	—
1931	40/month	—	—
1932	—/month	10	10
1933	54/month	15	15
1934	56/month	15	15
1935	56/month	15	15
1936	56/month	15	15
1937	56/month	15	15

Year	Houses of Tolerance			Courtesans	Houses of Courtesans
	Third Category	Second Category	First Category		
1938	56/mooth	—	—	15	15
1939	56/month	84	112	15	15
1940	56/month	84	112	15	15
1941	112/month	168	224	—	—
1942	112/month	168	224	30/month	30/month
1943	—	—	—	20/month	30/month

Sources: Archives de la direction des services administratifs, secrétariat, Concession française, Archives municipales de Shanghai, dossiers 1933 25 MS 1554.1; 1936 25 MS 1555; 26 MS 1591.21.

with accommodations and board by the house that employed them. I have no data on this subject before the 1940s apart from statements to the effect that the food, even in the courtesans' houses, was rather poor. In the other categories of establishments, the madam provided only two meals a day, and meat was served only occasionally. After the Sino-Japanese War, the prostitutes preferred to buy their meals in the small local restaurants, and they negotiated better cost-sharing arrangements with their madams.[16] The amounts of money needed to set up and run the houses of prostitution could therefore vary to a very great extent. But the sums were not great when compared with the incomes earned by the madams and the managers of the establishments. This will be seen in the part that follows.

Cost of Services and the Income of the Courtesans' Houses

The courtesans' houses, which provided a great variety of services, derived their income from different avenues, even it was always from the customer that the money came (see Figure 10.1). In the houses of prostitution, it was the cost of the sexual transaction – regardless of whether it was a short encounter or the night spent with the customer – that yielded almost all the takings.

In the case of the *changsan-shuyu*, we might begin by taking a look at the invitations to go out (*tangchai*) for which the fees were dragged downward by competition among the different groups of courtesans. In the nineteen century, it cost 3 yuan to invite a girl "of age" and 1 or 2 yuan to invite a girl who was still a virgin, unless two virgins went out together.[17] At the beginning of the century, Wang Peilan, a famous courtesan, is said to have decided to bring down the prices, which she felt were discouraging customers, in order to accept a larger number of invitations per evening.[18] In 1901, invitations to go out cost only 2 yuan.[19] Because the money paid for outside invitations came to the courtesans, it was in their interest to accept a large number of invitations every evening. The prices dropped further around 1913–1914, when they were about 1 yuan for a courtesan "of age" and 0.5 yuan for a young girl.[20] The houses would halve the price for customers who sent out large numbers (many dozens) of invitations in one season.[21] The *yao'er* charged 2 yuan for each outing. They kept the fee at this level until they went out of existence.[22]

The courtesans' houses, and even some of the houses in the intermediate categories, drew most of their income from the dinners, banquets, and gambling parties organized by the customers. Although there was no fixed rule, the houses would expect a regular customer to organize six or seven *huatou* per season – that is, an equivalent number of dinners and/or gambling sessions.[23] In the collective houses (*dachanghu*), there was a competition between the courtesans to obtain the largest number of *huatou*.[24] The cost of the dinners or gambling parties followed price trends, but it is not always easy to get a clear picture of the situation: The houses continued to use the term *huatou* as a unit of account (equivalent to 12 yuan), and this could give the impression that prices did not vary. In fact, a dinner priced at 24 yuan in the 1930s was counted by the houses of prostitution as two *huatou*.

Holding dinners in the houses of prostitution was one of the preliminary conditions for the recognition by the courtesans of good customers on whom they would be willing to bestow their favors. In most cases, a cus-

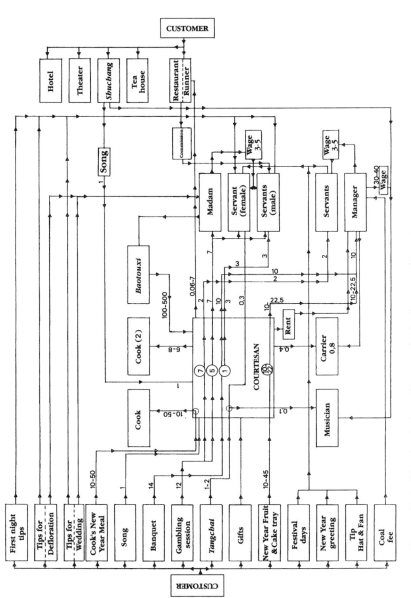

Figure 10.1. The circulation of money in the houses of courtesans.

tomer would invite three, four, or six friends to share an evening with him. For a birthday, it was not infrequent for more people to be invited. The importance given to the number of dinners organized varied according to the nature of the establishments. The collective houses (*dachanghu*) had the advantage here inasmuch as the dishes were prepared by the house cook. Conversely, the individual courtesans (*zhujia*) preferred gambling sessions, with the meals being ordered from outside restaurants.

The price of a dinner around 1860 was 12 yuan. At the turn of the century, the *Youxibao* ("The Journal of Leisure") announced a rise to 13 yuan following the increase in the cost of coal and rice.[25] After the Second World War, the cost went up to 18 yuan, including 8 yuan for tips.[26] However, a writer in 1922 mentions a figure of 14 yuan, including 4 yuan for tips.[27] It is hardly conceivable that the prices would have differed from one establishment to another. The prices were fixed collectively, and changes were duly announced in the press (the small newspapers). The cost probably fluctuated and increased more sharply at certain periods, such as during the First World War. Finally, the "internal" distribution of this fee changed. Up to 1925, it included a part corresponding to tips. Thereafter, the system of tips lost its rationale, although they were always demanded. A guide states that the price was 24 yuan in the 1930s.[28] In 1940, it returned to 20 yuan.[29]

Apart from the regular dinners that they had to organize in order to be well regarded by the courtesan, the customers were solicited on special days when the house, to avoid losing face, needed a customer to organize a *huatou*. First of all, there were the three traditional festivals: *duanwujie* (the Dragon Festival), *qiuzhongjie* (the Mid-Autumn Festival), and the New Year. These days were marked by gifts given to the customers when they were to pay their bill for the season: *pipa* (a sort of small apricot) and glutinous rice puddings (*jueshu*) for the Dragon Festival, "moon cakes" and apples at the Mid-Autumn Festival, New Year's cakes and oranges at the turn of the year.[30] The customers had to tip the waiters 2 to 4 yuan, or even 10 yuan.[31] Apart from these three dates, there were numerous opportunities: the girl's birthday, *qingmingjie* (the commemoration of the dead), *lixia* (the summer solstice), *dongzhi* (the winter solstice), *xuanjuan* (the festival of the city god), and the two ceremonies marking the beginning and end of a season.[32] The courtesans worked actively to inveigle their customers, especially those with whom they had regular relationships.

The New Year, traditionally a time when all accounts were settled and when all debts had to be paid, was more than all other festivals the time when the life of the houses of prostitution reached a high point. For the first fifteen days of the year, the houses offered their customers dishes of fruit, cakes, ham, chicken, and fish (*kai guopan*). The customer, however, was required not to partake of the fish, which was a symbol of prosperity.[33] Although there was no explicitly stated fee, the customer gave "whatever he could." The amount was about 10 yuan in the nineteenth century. This price followed trends in the cost of living. It varied from 12 to 24 yuan around 1920 and 20 to 45 yuan in the following decade, but could have been even more (up to 100 yuan) in the luxury establishments.[34] Naturally, a customer could avoid coming to the houses during this period, but then he would seem to be miserly. The proceeds from the New Year's fruit dish were shared half and half between the girl and the manager.[35]

Gambling (which was officially prohibited in the houses of prostitution) was also an essential source of income. Each game, or rather each session (which included several games), was charged a fixed rate of 12 yuan. The game most played was mahjong (*majiang*), a sort of domino game with four players, that is still widely played in China today, especially in the south. Under the influence of Westerners, card games, especially poker, were added after 1911. A session of poker brought together more players (up to seven) and cost twice as much – 24 yuan – as the mahjong sessions.[36] The fees for gambling sessions changed less than for the dinners. In 1940, they still cost the same.[37] The houses earned fairly large profits from gambling. Inveterate gamblers would easily spend up to 100 yuan in an evening. The houses of prostitution were patronized by professional players who sometimes worked in groups. They would pick on a naive customer not yet versed in the ways of these establishments and join together to fleece him.[38] A guide in the 1930s warned customers against these conartists.[39]

Unlike the dinners, which were at the host's expense, each participant in a gambling session paid his share of the costs. When a customer sent out invitations to friends to play in a courtesan's house, he was not always sure that they would be available or willing to play. To cope with this eventuality and avert loss, the houses instituted a system of tickets to be purchased by the invitees. Even those who were present but did not wish to play had to buy a ticket. These tickets cost 3 yuan each and compensated for the absence of a player who would be replaced by one of the courtesans or would be added to the 12 yuan collected from the other players present.[40] This method was particularly clever because it forced each invitee to participate, even if he were absent.

A system of this kind could work only because it was based on a very subtle game of "face." A customer's friends could not refuse to participate for fear of bringing him into discredit and being paid the same discourtesy at a later stage. This mechanism had the effect of creating obligations to friends because it subsequently became necessary to accept their invitations. Once an individual got caught in this system, he would be stuck in it through fear of permanently losing face, and he could even be drawn into becoming a regular albeit unwilling patron of the courtesans' houses. In the 1930s, this system was still in existence and the cost of a ticket had gone up to 6 yuan. A customer could even take skillful advantage of the ticket system by inviting about twelve friends to cover the 24 yuan paid for the game. The author who made this observation added, however, that one could not always be sure that every friend invited would come and also that the houses of prostitution would not be pleased to see such a large number of participants because that would only add to the overhead.[41]

The expenditure directly related to sex was not necessarily heavy. The customers could offer gifts to the courtesans whom they patronized, but there was no norm or timetable to be complied with. However, the customer had certain moral obligations: For instance, he had to ask a courtesan to sing two operatic songs on her birthday and on certain festivals; for this he had to pay her 2 yuan.[42] The girl's attitude was decisive, especially with respect to the frequency with which the customer organized the *huatou* in her establishment. When for it a customer was allowed to spend the night with a courtesan for the first time, he had to pay a fairly large tip of 3 or 4 yuan at least or up to 12 yuan around 1911. Ten years later, this figure went up to 30–40 yuan.[43] Increasingly, the customers deemed this expenditure to be unnecessary and irksome when all that was required to avoid these extra costs was to go to a hotel.[44] A customer could also reserve a girl to himself by fully paying for all the *huatou* that she was committed to organizing for an entire season. In this case, other customers might invite her out, but they would no longer be received at her place.[45] It was also possible to hire an ordinary prostitute by the month or season.

It is difficult to estimate the amounts spent by customers in the houses of prostitution. One newspaper reports that, at the beginning of 1901, a customer spent 72 yuan in a period of ten days on twelve invitations to go out (24 yuan), two dinners (24 yuan), and two gambling parties (24 yuan).[46] In 1924, a silk merchant with friends spent 950 yuan in an evening.[47] The courtesans expected a minimum recompense from a customer. This payment varied according to the period. In the 1930s, an individual would have to spend 300 to 400 yuan in a season in order to be considered as a good customer and be well treated.[48] This amounted to about 100 yuan per month, which meant that the courtesans were effectively out of the reach of a large part of the male population. To take but a few examples, a factory worker earned no more than 10 to 20 yuan per month. The salary of a police officer was not more than 30 to 40 yuan.[49] And even the mayor of the municipality of Shanghai, who had the highest salary in the local administration, officially earned no more than 450 yuan a month.

Expenditure related to prostitution in Shanghai represented considerable sums of money. Only an approximate estimation of the amounts involved can be made for want of sources such as ledger books of the establishments concerned and registers of customers, such as those found, for example, in Japan.[50] For the courtesans alone, one author estimated in 1923 that, at a rate of two invitations per day for the 1,100 *changsan* and one *huatou* per day for 10% of them, the daily turnover should have been about

4,500 yuan, giving 130,000 to 140,000 yuan per month.[51] This is a low estimate in my view. An average of four outings per day does not seem unlikely.[52] This itself would correspond to 4,500 yuan per day. Similarly for the *huatou*, assuming a low figure of only one *huatou* per day for half of them, the earnings would have amounted to 6,600 yuan. This means that more than 300,000 yuan would have been put into circulation every month at the beginning of the 1920s, not counting subsidiary expenditures in the form of gifts and various tips. Another observer even estimated the courtesans' monthly turnover at 800,000 yuan.[53]

As for the other prostitutes, whose numbers are barely known, if we assume that there were two customers per prostitute per day for a population of 20,000 prostitutes, we get a total of more then 3.5 million yuan per month.[54] These figures are admittedly constructions based on random data and comprising a major element of subjectivity. I give them for what they are worth. The sex trade in Shanghai around 1920 generated a turnover of probably more than 4 million yuan per month. It was a horn of plenty providing a livelihood to large numbers of people and numerous businesses. It also helped finance the activities of the secret societies that were the "patrons" of this activity.[55]

The Prostitutes' Income

The question of the prostitutes' income as such is almost impossible to separate from its context. For the courtesans, we must first of all estimate an individual's total takings and then make a precise reconstruction of the various amounts deducted from the total. It is also necessary to take account of the form of organization of the houses (the *dachanghu* or *zhujia*) and the position of the girl in relation to her madam. The testimony available to me does not make a clear distinction between the house, the family, and the girl herself. Finally, the sources are sometimes self-contradictory on the modes and proportions by which the earnings were shared. In the case of the ordinary prostitutes, the problem appears to be simpler. The income of the girls depended on the category to which they belonged and especially on their status (whether free, pledged, or practically slaves). Although the sources are not unanimous (because they reflect a complex and shifting reality), it is nevertheless possible to shed light on this essential dimension.

In the collective houses (*dachanghu*), the courtesans were hired or, in other words, although this is implicit, they made a sort of contract with an establishment that undertook, for a whole season, to pay them a "flat salary" (*baotouxi*). Beginners (courtesans who were still virgins) received 100 yuan, while others could earn up to 300 to 400 yuan.[56] Another source indicates a sum of 60 to 70 yuan per season.[57] Furthermore, the courtesans shared the income derived from the *huatou* with the owner on a 65/35 or

70/30 basis. They could negotiate a higher rate, but then they had to pay a larger share of the staff overheads. Furthermore, the risk was greater. Indeed, the courtesans undertook at the outset to organize a specified number of *huatou* (100 to 200 in a season). If they did not attain these targets, they had to pay the house out of their own money in proportion to the shortfall of *huatou*.[58]

A few details are available on this relatively complex mode of sharing. For each dinner that that they organized (14 yuan in the 1920s), the courtesans paid 10 yuan back to the manager. The profit was fairly substantial for a dinner that would cost the manager barely 4 or 5 yuan, including staff costs.[59] The balance, namely 4 yuan for tips, was shared with the courtesan's own servants, and the courtesan received only 1 yuan.[60] In the course of a season, the manager of a house could pocket a fairly substantial amount if the courtesan organized the agreed amount of *huatou*. About 30 dinners (a low figure) earned 300 yuan for the house. A reverse mode of apportionment was applied to income earned from the gambling sessions. The manager took nothing. Of the 12 yuan paid for a session, 7 yuan went to the courtesan while the balance was distributed as tips among her servants (3 yuan) and the manager's servants (2 yuan).[61] If no other customer came to play during the season, the courtesan nevertheless had to pay the manager 12 yuan for six hypothetical sessions, namely, the minimum required from a resident of the house.[62] In the individual courtesan houses (*zhujia*), the girl received 5 yuan for each *huatou* while the rest went to the madam and to the employees.[63]

The invitations to go out (*tangchai*) were a major source of income for the courtesans, even if they shared part of it with those who accompanied them (maidservants, musicians, etc.). Some girls made 50 to 60 outings every evening, but most of them had to be satisfied with smaller figures. I have no information with which to determine an average, but even a reasonable assumption of about ten outings would correspond to a sum of 10 yuan per day or 300 yuan per month around 1920 and even more in the prior period, when each outing cost 2 or 3 yuan. The courtesans therefore did not belong to the economically least privileged classes even if the income differences within their group were fairly wide. One author estimates that, in 1940, a famous courtesan was earning an average of 1,000 yuan per season, while the others were within a fairly wide income bracket ranging from 100–200 yuan to 500–600 yuan.[64]

The Management of the Houses

In the collective houses, the largest share of the proceeds generally went to the manager. Their reapportionment among the courtesans and employees took place only at the end of the season, when accounts were closed, or at the end of each month for certain items of expenditure. However, because there were daily living expenses to be paid for, the system was designed so that a part of the money was immediately recycled. Thus, the courtesans kept the income earned from gambling while their servants (maidservants and waiters) received their share of tips immediately. By contrast, the manager's employees received their share only at the end of the season. If the courtesan was unable to pay the manager for board and lodging, she immediately had to yield her place to another. In particular, if she was on an upper floor, which was the most coveted position, then she was required to move to the ground floor. Debts could be carried over from one season to the next.

Among the courtesans, it was the accountant who made the daily rounds of the chambers to make immediate collection of the sums due for the previous day's operations (dinners and invitations to go out), even if the customers only paid them at the end of the season. The accounts were all entered in a ledger book stamped with the accountant's seal.[65] In the big houses of prostitution, it was again an accountant who drew up daily accounts for each girl. Among the *yao'er*, when one of the waiters cried *shang zhang* (bring the accounts), the maidservants would immediately go to the accountant and record all the invitations accepted by their mistresses on the previous day. Each prostitute had a little notebook in which her accounts were written down and then copied into the ledger book of the establishment.[66]

The economy of the courtesans' houses was based entirely on trust, inasmuch as the sums due from the customers were collected only at the end of the season. This explains the precautions taken by the courtesans and the somewhat complicated route that preceded entry to their houses. In particular, the courtesans preferred that a new customer should be introduced to them by a known and reliable customer. Each customer therefore had an account in the establishments that he visited frequently. His name and address were recorded in a ledger book in which the accountant noted down the amount of the expenses made in the course of the season for outside invitations, dinners, and gambling sessions. At the end of the season, the house would draw up a detailed bill and the customer would send for it through a servant or have it brought to him with the last invitation at the end of the season.[67] The payment was made in cash and usually brought by a servant who also took a commission on each yuan paid.[68]

However, the system was not perfect. Some customers shirked their responsibilities through bad faith or because of financial problems. The means of applying pressure available to the courtesans were limited. However, because they were considered to be business establishments, the houses of prostitution could ultimately appeal to the local authorities. A certain Xie Juncai had a bitter experience in this respect. When he refused to pay a debt of 450 yuan to the courtesan Lu Rongquan, she took him to court. His denials notwithstanding, the magistrate sentenced him to receive 50 bamboo strokes, spend five days in prison, and, of course, repay his debt to Lu.[69] When locally well-known members of the gentry were involved, the courtesans would bring their reputations into play by threatening to publicize the names of the defaulters in the small newspapers. This method emerged only at the end of the 1890s. However, it did not always give the expected result. One customer who found his name and address publicized in this way soundly thrashed the maidservant whom the courtesan sent to his house to collect the sum due.[70] As for temporary residents of Shanghai, there was no way to pursue them if they left the city without settling their debts. It was the courtesan then who had to bear the expenses incurred by the manager of the collective house.[71]

The Circulation of Money

The economy of prostitution in Shanghai was characterized by a constant circulation of money related to the presence of a large number of actors, each taking his or her share of the cake. Each category of staff had its own niche where it collected its share of the money put into circulation in the houses.

The employees of the houses, namely those of the courtesans and the managers, were of course the main beneficiaries. The waiters received 3 yuan per month around 1890, a sum that was the same 30 years later.[72] In fact, the logic of the system was such that they drew the essential part of their income from the tips that were automatically collected from the customers. This can be seen as an incentive system. The employees were strongly encouraged to be attentive to customers in order to get them to be more generous. Their fate was linked to the degree of success enjoyed by the courtesan. Thus, they could exert heavy pressure and lay down conditions regarding the girls' relationships with her customers. The collective houses remunerated their staff for each *huatou* organized and, at the end of the season, gave them a share of the total amount of tips received. The courtesans' staff received their share at each operation. In the individual courtesans' houses (*zhujia*), the waiters got nothing from the dinners served in the house but took a commission on orders to restaurants (15%) and to the wine merchants (20%).[73] Finally, the maidservants and other servants (*xiangbang*) of the courtesan collected 3 mao for each outing (for which the fee was about 1 yuan in the 1920s).[74]

The case of the maidservants deserves to be examined separately. They earned a monthly salary (3 yuan in the 1890s, 5 yuan around 1940) in addition to their share of tips, which ranged from 10% to 20% depending on the houses.[75] As was seen above, the rise in the age of these girls in the twentieth century, especially after the First World War, contributed to their becoming full-fledged prostitutes. The madams often hired several maidservants who thus became "secondary" prostitutes, while it was the courtesan who brought the house its fame.[76] This system made it possible to satisfy the sexual demand of a proportion of a courtesan's customers, and these customers could sometimes be numerous. The courtesan would then reserve her favors for her best customers. In this case, the maidservants were remunerated on the basis of a percentage of the "family" earnings. The division was calculated by a system of shares (*fen*). One share was equivalent to 30 *huatou*. If these 30 *huatou* had been organized during the season, the girl would receive 10% of the earnings. However, it was only after the 31st *huatou* that this share was actually paid to her.[77]

Another category on the payroll of prostitution was that of the sedan chair carriers who were later replaced by the rickshaw pullers, the horse carriage drivers, and the automobile drivers. Those of them who were permanently employed by the house received a meager salary. In the New Year, the courtesans gave them a symbolic sum of money known as the "shoe bonus" (*caoxietian*).[78] Those who carried the customers collected a sort of commission. When their occasional or permanent employer was in the company of a courtesan or friends, they had to wait until the end of the festivities. They were paid for the trip by the customer; but because they had to be at hand, they were also paid for their meals. It was the houses that paid them this money, which was taken out of the tips taken from the customer. The procedure was somewhat complicated: The customer issued a note bearing his and the carriers' names, which he then handed over to the establishment. On the next day, the carriers could come and collect their due. The cost of this remuneration (*jiaofanzhang*: literally "the sedan chair carriers' rice") was shared equally between the courtesan and the manager.[79]

The fee was 400 wen (4 mao) in the nineteenth century. Its mode had undergone changes before the appearance of other forms of transport. The rickshaw pullers received only half of this sum (earlier, two carriers had been required to carry one chair). The horse carriage drivers continued to collect 3 mao as compared with 2 mao for the rickshaw pullers.[80] The fee thereafter increased slightly from 4 to 8 mao, especially for the more prestigious forms of employment, such as that of the automobile drivers and also for a new category, the bodyguards, who received the same remuneration.[81] Furthermore, to simplify the system of notes, one courtesan's house introduced copper tokens in 1913 inscribed with the name and address of the establishment as well as the characters *jiaofanzhang*. The other houses followed suit, producing copper tokens of all sizes and shapes. In the beginning, they were manufactured by the houses themselves and then by the tobacco shops and the native-style banks. Around 1920, they were replaced by printed paper tickets bearing the names of the courtesans' houses. Interestingly, this fictitious form of currency was used as normal change by businesses in the courtesans' district.[82]

Debts and Conflicts Over Money

At the beginning of their careers, when they had to set up a wardrobe or quite simply cope with unexpected expenses (such as those incurred by illness) or expenditures related to their lifestyles (opium), the girls would often become indebted to the houses. Naturally, the higher they were situated in the prostitutes' hierarchy, the more money was needed. Apart from the virtual slaves, the freedom enjoyed by the girls was quite relative given the spiral of debt in which they were caught. Indebtedness was often imposed at the very outset on the courtesans and on the *yao'er* because of their need to take an "installation" loan (*daidang*). The amount of the loan varied from 200 to 500 yuan among the *changsan* and varied from 100 to 300 yuan among the *yao'er*.[83] For the other prostitutes, the amounts borrowed were not very great. However, given the very high rates of interest charged by the owners of the houses, it was necessary to repay the debt very quickly or else become completely bound to the establishment. The available information indicates that these rates of interest were quite variable. In the 1890s, the rate was 40% to 50% per annum.[84]

The prostitutes such as the *changsan* and the *yao'er* sometimes also got indebted to the house employees, such as the maidservants, waiters, and so on.[85] They would resort to this means when they could not obtain money from their madam. In general, loans of this kind, where the terms were even worse, created a situation of multiple dependency from which it was difficult to escape. The courtesans were sometimes victims of blackmail and threats from maidservants who would try to get more money out of them. They would force the courtesan to receive one customer rather than another, and they would put up obstacles against excessively close relationships that might arise between a girl and a customer, especially if the customer was not a generous one.[86] More rarely, the courtesans turned to the native-style banks of Shanxi. I have found only one reference to such a practice in the sources.[87]

Individuals apparently external to the houses of prostitution also lent money, either to the courtesans or to the establishments themselves. The *Shen Bao* reports two disputes in this respect. In one case, two individuals had lent 650 yuan to a prostitute, probably a courtesan, who then left the house in which she had been residing. The two individuals claimed to be relatives of the woman in question. Be that as it may, it was the *guinu* (the madam's male partner) whom they approached. The *guinu* defended himself first of all by accusing his creditors of racketeering. The court ordered the *guinu* to repay his creditors according to a specific timetable.[88] In another case, it was a prostitute and her maidservant who were implicated by a man to whom they owed 250 yuan. The prostitute undertook to repay the debt within ten days.[89] The courtesans also borrowed money to gain freedom from their madam. One girl who had taken 500 yuan from two *guinu* two years earlier in order to get married (*congliang*) did not pay her debt. Unable to locate the girl, the two creditors took the madam to court.[90]

Money disputes, which sometimes came before the courts, provide fleeting glimpses of the financial practices of the houses of prostitution and the way in which they functioned. In 1899, a madam brought a complaint before the Mixed Court against her male employee whom she accused of theft and the abduction of her thirteen-year-old daughter. Having had to go to Hangzhou to settle some business, the madam had left the premises and left the girl in the care of Zhang Azeng, who had been taken into her employment seven months earlier. On her return ten days later, she found the house closed. All the articles in the establishment had vanished, and the girl had flown. Zhang, when arrested by the police, had a different statement to make. He had been hired as a waiter and had recommended two prostitutes to the madam. These prostitutes had then gotten married and not paid their rent, the sum of which (265 yuan) had already been advanced to them by Zhang. In the madam's absence, the rent collector had come several times for his due. Zhang had therefore taken the money from the sale of one of the prostitutes to pay the collector. This affair is not very clear. Obviously, Zhang was not a mere waiter. He is sometimes referred to as a *guinu*. His explanation is highly tangled. There was undoubtedly some truth in Zhang's statement, but he probably hoped to obtain payment by stealing the property of the brothel and extorting money out of the madam for the return of her daughter. The judges sentenced Zhang to 500 bamboo strokes.[91]

The Economy of the Houses of Prostitution

In the *yao'er* houses, the principle was similar to that of the *changsan*, although it was less sophisticated. The first courtesy visit (*zhuang ganshi*) cost 1 yuan. In return, the customer was served fruit, watermelon seeds, and tea. The following visits were free unless fruit was served again.[92] The *yao'er* accepted outside calls, for which they charged 2 yuan. When the *changsan* lowered their fee to 2 yuan and then to 1 yuan, the *yao'er* were less in demand. In fact, already many of them lacked the smallest modicum of musical training with which to entertain customers when they went out. Dinners in the *yao'er* houses cost the same as in the *changsan* houses, namely 12 yuan. The cost of the gambling sessions was also the same.

However, the earnings were apportioned differently. Of the 12 yuan paid for a gambling party, 3 yuan went to the waiters as tips while the balance was shared equally between the manager of the house and the girl. For the dinners, 2 yuan went to the waiters and 10 yuan went to the manager for the price of the food. Whatever the number of guests, the house always set the table for eight. As in the case of the *changsan*, these fees were doubled during the festivals that marked each change of season.[93] These houses also went in for the custom of the New Year's tray, which cost barely 12 yuan. The price of the dinners rose with the cost of living. Among the *xian-rouzhuang*, at the end of the 1930s, a dinner cost 16 yuan. The practice of the *huatou* was not indispensable. The customers knew that it was enough to pay to sleep with a prostitute.[94]

What placed the *yao'er* in the prostitute's category was the fact that they were obliged to receive the customers who visited them. The first night cost 6 yuan, of which the girl received only 2 yuan. The waiters of the manager and of the girl each received 1 yuan, and the manager received 2 yuan. Thereafter, the customer paid the girl only the cost of the night.[95] She would often encourage the customer to order fruit, cakes, rice soup, and so on.[96] The *xianrouzhuang* kept a similar system, but the fee was slightly higher, from 5 to 10 yuan a night, while a short encounter (the criterion was the amount of time spent) cost 3 yuan. However, in the case of "goods from a good family" (*renjiahuo*), namely a woman who was a casual prostitute, the cost could rise to 20 to 30 yuan and a short encounter could cost 3 to 5 yuan. The small newspapers published very concise advertisements on the fees: *ju san xiao wu* ("[one] short encounter, three [yuan], [one] night, five [yuan]").[97]

The cost in the lower-class establishments depended on the quality of the girls. An article in 1872 states that 200 wen was enough for a short encounter in a *huayanjian*.[98] In 1879, a customer spent five nights for 12 yuan in an establishment that has not been identified and three nights for 10 yuan in a *huayanjian*, thus paying about 2.5 and 3.5 yuan per night, respectively.[99] Among the *yeji* prostitutes, there was no fixed fee, although there was a scale. Around 1919–1920, those girls who worked individually were asking for 3 to 10 yuan, the prettiest girls being the most expensive. It was up to the customer to bargain over the price.[100] Among the ordinary *yeji*, a night cost 3 to 5 yuan. In addition, the cost also depended on the time of day. If a customer took a girl after midnight, he paid only 1 yuan to spend the night with her.[101] The *yeji* also worked by day and in the evening, receiving customers for short encounters. The cost was 1 to 2 yuan.[102] These fees appear to be fairly similar to those of the Canton establishments where, around 1926, and depending on the category of the house, a short encounter would cost from 6–8 mao to 1.2 yuan and a night would cost 2.2 to 3.5 yuan.[103]

A customer could also hire a girl (a *yeji* or *xianrouzhuang*) by the month in order to have her exclusively to himself. This would cost 30 to 200 yuan, depending on the girl's beauty and the frequency of their meetings.[104] Half of the amount had to be paid in advance, and the customer would pay 1 yuan whenever he came to see her.[105] The lowest fees were among those whom I would call the "rejects" of prostitution, namely the *dingpeng*. The price of a short encounter was 2 to 5 mao, while a night cost hardly more than 1 or 1.2 yuan.[106] The *dingpeng* were similar to the lowest-category

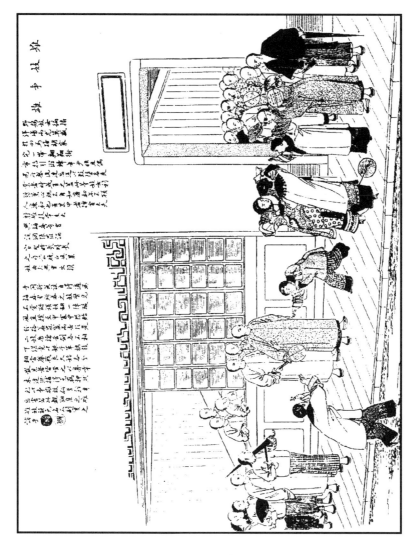

Plate 12. Two *yeji* quarreling in the street.

prostitutes of Tianjin whom the municipal government classified under five levels in 1929. The girls of the third category earned hardly more than 1 to 4 mao per day, while their wretched sisters in the fifth category received only 7 fen to 3 mao.[107]

The various editions of the Shanghai guidebooks show that the fees remained fairly stable from the beginning of the century up to the 1930s. Inflation that began at the end of this period gradually found expression in the cost of the services rendered by the prostitutes, especially after the war. In 1946, the guide agencies were charging 2,000 yuan per hour for the company of a girl. A short encounter would cost 20,000 to 30,000 yuan.[108] Subsequently, the galloping inflation that hit Shanghai pushed fees up to spectacular levels. In 1947, the cost of a short encounter varied from 100,000 to 200,000 yuan.[109] The major establishments like the Taotao had a different fee structure depending on the "quality" of the girls. In 1947, a short encounter with a first-category (*toudeng*) prostitute cost 300,000 yuan, while a second category (*erdeng*) prostitute cost only 200,000 yuan (or 18 dollars) and a third category prostitute cost 160,000 yuan. For one night, the prices were, respectively, 500,000 and 300,000 yuan. A girl's company for fifteen minutes cost 2 to 3 American dollars – that is, 20,000 to 30,000 yuan.[110]

In 1948, prices continued to curve upward: a night in a hotel cost a million to 1,500,000 yuan.[111] Certain prostitutes or madams also tried to shield themselves against the effects of inflation by making foreign customers, especially American soldiers, pay in dollars. In June 1948, in a quarrel between a girl and a madam, it was revealed that the cost of a night was 8 dollars. An American medical report states that the cost of a short encounter was 4 dollars in March 1948.[112] The mode of division between the prostitute and the madam depended on the currency in which payment was received. The girls also solicited in hotels with the complicity of hotel servants who routinely pocketed a commission of 30%.[113] Between 1945 and 1949, the amount of commission could be greater and could even reach 70%. This trade was a real windfall for the minor employees in the hotels. In two different cases, hotel servants who had introduced a prostitute to a customer received 700,000 yuan out of the million paid to the girl.[114] When questioned by the police, one of them said that this sum had been divided between two hotel boys and the two floor attendants. This was the second time that they had been acting as middlemen. On the first occasion, they had taken only 60%.[115] It was found that the same rate of commission was being collected in a similar case involving two hotel employees.[116]

The police archives contain information on the incomes of the houses of prostitution and the way in which they were divided between the girls and the madams. In the 1920s, earnings among the "free" *yeji* (*huoji* or *zijia*) were divided on a 40/60 or 30/70 basis; and among the higher-class sections of the *xianrouzhuang* the earnings were divided on a 40/60 basis, with the girls taking the bigger share.[117] In the most common mode of sharing followed between 1945 and 1949, half of the amount was taken by the girl and the other half by the madam. The prostitutes often paid for their own clothing, food, and medical expenses.[118] In one other case, the medical expenses were paid for by the establishment.[119] The madam generally provided only the room in which the girls received their customers. There were other combinations, but these generally entailed a greater percentage for the house. One establishment that served food took up to 60% of the girl's earnings.[120] The proportion of girls residing in the house and of those living outside is impossible to determine. These data are confirmed by a questionnaire that was given to 500 prostitutes by the municipal dispensary in 1948. The predominant modes of sharing were actually *duizhe* (50/50) or *siliu* (40/60).[121] The Taotao, which housed more than a hundred girls in 1947, took 10% of their earnings as staff overhead, and the balance was shared equally between the girls and the establishment. The establishment provided lodging and two meals a day.[122] The girls were, on the whole, free to go out with a customer. All that the madam did was to note these outside encounters in the accounts and include them in the income of thc house.[123]

The earnings were shared at regular intervals whose frequency depended on the establishment. In certain houses, few in number, the sharing was done on a daily basis.[124] Many preferred a method of weekly sharing, but there are also cases where the sharing was done every ten days or every two weeks.[125] At the Taotao, Shanghai's biggest house of prostitution, the earnings were shared every two days.[126] Unlike the common practice among the courtesans, the houses of prostitution lent little or no money at all to their residents.[127] Those who did grant loans or advance money applied variable rates of interest. One source indicates an interest of 2 or 3 mao; but the basis of the calculation is not given, nor is the duration of the loan.[128] If the amount was based on 1 yuan, then the rate of interest was 20% to 30%. The Taotao lent money at rates that, depending on the source, were set at 20% or 40%. Here again, the precise basis on which these rates were being applied is not given.[129]

Depending on the category to which they belonged, the girls of the Taotao spent 60,000 to 100,000 yuan per month in 1947.[130] In addition to these costs, there were laundry expenses and costs of visits to the doctor, amounting in all to 80,000 yuan per month.[131] A prostitute in another establishment estimated her food expenses at 40,000 to 50,000 yuan per month.[132] When questioned about their earnings, 76% of a sample of 500 prostitutes felt that they were earning an average or above-average income.[133] Of these, 107 said that their business was doing well, while 273 considered that their level of activity was ordinary and only 81 felt that things were going badly. However, none of them said that it was impossible to live on the income earned from prostitution.[134]

Money lies at the heart of prostitution. This is an obvious fact in every age and in every society. However, the link between money and prostitution can take many forms. In this respect, China provides an example that has hardly any equivalent in the contemporary world. While ordinary prostitution did not display any outstandingly specific characteristics, the institution of the courtesan gave rise to a remarkably subtle and complex type of sex economy that the observers of the age did not really know in every detail and whose reconstruction has raised at times insuperable problems of interpretation for the historian. The houses of prostitution and the courtesans' houses were real economic entities that, in the case of the most luxurious and biggest houses, called for a certain capacity for management. This capacity, which was not within the reach of every madam, may explain the existence of the collective houses (*dachanghu*) that took charge of the essential aspects of the logistics on which the activities of the courtesans were based. The sex trade handled large sums of money and was one of the most important sectors of the leisure industry.

The very elaborate mechanisms at work in the circulation of money are undoubtedly among the most fascinating aspects of the economy of the courtesan houses. Although the source of income was unique (the customer), the redistribution among the various categories living off the earnings of prostitution took place through circuits that are seen to be simple when considered category by category, but are extremely complex when taken as a whole. These categories thus prevented the emergence of a direct venal link and the degradation of the customer/courtesan relationship through money. The subtlety of the system was related, first, to the commissions and tips taken in varying proportions by the employees and the individuals (couriers, bearers, and musicians) who gravitated around the courtesans. It was related, second, to the timetable of distribution by which each category (courtesan, waiters, musicians, etc.) received the sums needed for subsistence according to need while, at the same time, the managers obtained a definite advantage through the volume of money that they kept until the distribution at the end of a season.

The courtesans' houses did not derive the essential part of their income from prostitution. Prostitution was supposed to represent only a minor part of their takings. This description has given only the formal and identifiable items of the sums paid by the customers. If this description is to be a full one, the account of expenditures related to sexuality would have to include all the various gifts, some of them very expensive, that were made to the courtesans. However, that would not radically modify my initial observation. Gambling parties, dinners, and, on a more secondary basis, invitations to go out and the musical performances requested by the customers made it possible to collect larger sums of money than those that could have been provided by the sex trade alone. This fact emphasizes the role of the courtesans' houses as places of entertainment and conviviality for the elites and not simply as a sexual outlet, even if this aspect gradually came to prevail in the twentieth century. Patronizing courtesans was a central feature of the lifestyle and social status of the elites.

A major point highlighted in this study relates to the income of the prostitutes. Almost all the literature on this subject by writers of the period and, more particularly, works by historians today, especially Chinese historians, depict and denounce the extreme exploitation of which the prostitutes were the victims. The madams are shown as unscrupulous creatures who grabbed the largest share of the prostitutes' income, if not all of it. The reality that appears in these sources calls for a revision of this portrait. In the courtesans' houses, the girls ultimately kept a small part of the sums that they brought to the establishment in which they resided. They nevertheless earned an income far greater than that which could be earned by other active women, and even by many male workers. It is true that this situation could vary according to the status (free, hired, or pledged) at their time of entry into prostitution. Besides, my sources do not make a clear distinction between the girl's income and that of the "family." Nevertheless, this income gave them the possibility of living in style and enjoying conditions far better than the average.

In the ordinary establishments, there were also modalities of income sharing between prostitutes and madams that, in various degrees, were to the advantage of the prostitutes. It is true that here again we must take account of the status of the girls, especially because my information relates essentially to the 1940s. The earnings were probably shared in a more unequal fashion during the first decades of the twentieth century, even though two accounts from the 1920s and 1930s mention rates of apportionment similar to those of the Civil War period. One might ask if this would deny the notion of exploitation. From the economic point of view, the expression hardly has any meaning. There can be no doubt that the madams and a whole range of individuals lived off the work of the prostitutes. Nevertheless, the concept of exploitation cannot acquire full significance unless it is made to include not only the financial relationships between madams and prostitutes but also all the other dimensions studied in the previous chapters, especially the conditions of entry of women into the trade and the treatment received during their term of activity as prostitutes. Finally, the question is a moral rather than an economic one. In the 1940s, a majority of the prostitutes themselves felt that they were earning an adequate income. Their fear rather was that their activity might be prohibited by the authorities.

Part 4
Abortive Attempts to Regulate
Prostitution in Shanghai

11
Disease Prevention and the Policing of Morality (1860–1914)

The development of a system for the administrative regulation of prostitution in Shanghai was linked to many factors. In the foreign settlements, it drew inspiration chiefly from currents of thinking that had contributed in Europe to the establishment of various systems of health inspection for prostitutes in the major cities and in the ports. However, in Shanghai this development and the modes of control implemented had essentially local roots. And, in the case of the Chinese authorities, it was not so much the health dimension as the view that "morality" was being endangered by changes in the practices of prostitution that prompted their interest in the prostitutes and made them lay down policies of control that were implemented in unequal measure.

Rules and Regulations

When Westerners settled in Shanghai at the end of the 1840s, prostitution was concentrated in the Walled City and in the junks along the Huangpu, and it does not seem to have been a cause of special concern to the municipal authorities until the end of the 1870s. In fact, prostitution was practiced in houses that did not disturb everyday life in any way. A document from 1865 for the guidance of policemen in the French Concession makes no mention whatsoever of prostitution, whether under the heading of "breaches of the peace" or that of "misdemeanors."[1] This shows that prostitution was not a subject of concern for the police during this period. As late as 1893, the chief of the municipal police force was still noting that the houses "rarely give cause for serious action to be taken against them."[2] From the viewpoint of public order and morality, prostitution in the brothels was not a source of harm. Nevertheless, following complaints by residents, the authorities of the concession did prohibit the "junk boats of prostitution."[3]

An 1881 handbook for policemen in the International Settlement defined the act of prostitution in these terms: "Every common prostitute who shall loiter in the public roads for the purpose of prostitution or solicitation, to the annoyance of any inhabitant or passenger, or who shall be indecently dressed or behave indecently."[4] The only real concern was to prevent prostitution from flowing over into the street where it could be visible to all and constitute a nuisance. The houses of prostitution were also required to identify themselves without ambiguity. Article 23 of the "Regulations on the Police and the Public Roads" (the earliest edition of these regulations is dated 1889) stipulated that the houses of tolerance had to be identified by a "lantern" placed above the entrance that opened onto the public road. The prostitutes were not allowed to stand and wait on the public road alone or in groups. Nor could they indulge in inappropriate talk.[5]

These provisions were not modified in the 1903 edition. In 1907, however, a new article (24) was introduced. It prohibited "accosting passers-by on the public road for immoral purposes, soliciting their custom or making advances to them from indoors by words, signs, gestures or in any other way whatsoever." This addition shows that there was a change in the practices of prostitution and that the authorities were trying to nip it in the bud. It would also seem that, apart from taking over the streets, the prostitutes were using more aggressive attitudes to attract customers: "it is forbidden to deliberately expose oneself, even indoors, in an attitude or dress likely to offend the modesty of others."[6] The municipal police were particularly vigilant and stern. Repeated violation of the regulations was punished by closure of the house. The Shanghai Municipal Council wanted to bring all these houses together in one area in order to control them more efficiently and move them away from the main roads of the settlement. It tried to get the various consulates to intervene accordingly with their respective nationals. However, the attitude of the consular corps (the nationals of a country were bound solely by its own laws) meant that no collective action could be taken.[7] Any measures taken were occasional and temporary.[8]

Although it was not yet committed to the policy of setting up districts reserved for prostitution, the Conseil Municipal strove to keep certain major roads, such as the boulevard des Deux-Républiques, free by prohibiting houses of prostitution in these areas.[9] Up until 1925, it was impossible even to set up a massage parlor or a prostitution house in the residential western part of the concession.[10] The authorities were also concerned over the lodging houses, known in Shanghai as "tenants' homes," which provided lodging for an entire mobile population and fostered prostitution. In 1908, a regulation forbade the owners of these establishments to carry out activities related to prostitution. They were not allowed to receive "accompanied women of ill-repute" or provide lodging for less than one night.[11]

The main concern of the authorities was to prevent flagrant breaches of "morality." They were particularly vigorous in the fight against soliciting on the public roads. They responded to requests by representatives of the Chinese administration so long as these requests did not go against the interests of the foreign community, but they did not commit themselves with great conviction. Under pressure from an institution for the rescue of prostitutes, the Door of Hope (see Chapter 14), the Shanghai Municipal Council in 1909 prohibited the presence of minors under fifteen in brothels, theaters, and taverns.[12] Basically, the foreign municipal authorities wanted to limit themselves to a minimum level of regulation. However, there was a distinction between the two settlements. The French Conseil Municipal considered prostitution to be an inevitable activity and tried to obtain revenues from it, while the Shanghai Municipal Council preferred a policy of tolerating a trade with which it wanted to have the least possible contact.

The Birth of the Regulationist Discourse

When the question of controlling prostitution was first raised explicitly in Shanghai, the physicians who initiated the debate themselves acknowledged that neither this activity nor the extent of venereal disease had reached an exceptionally high level. And yet, the question of prostitution and venereal disease did give rise to lengthy polemics and to a hesitant policy leading to intervention by the "state." This intervention took the form of an attempt to bring prostitution under a system of health regulation.[13]

Certain points need to be recalled before these policies are referred to. While it is clear that the development of local conditions played a decisive role in the approach taken by these doctors (and thereafter by the municipal authorities), it must nevertheless be stressed that their attitude was substantially conditioned by the regulationist discourse then dominant in Europe. In Europe and especially in France, the nineteenth century was a period when the control of prostitution very probably reached its high point. Many pointers show, moreover, that this development was part of a more general trend toward a deterioration in the status of women. The literary and artistic work of this period is marked by a pronounced element of misogyny.[14] The French experience, which was followed in many countries on the European continent,[15] is relevant here because a part of Shanghai was under French jurisdiction; Alain Corbin has made a masterly study of the French system.[16]

In July 1868, the French ambassador in Peking wrote a letter to the Conseil Municipal drawing its attention to the condition of the houses of prostitution in the French Concession. He asked the local authorities to exercise strict surveillance and especially to bring prostitutes under a system of medical checks of the kind practiced in Europe.[17] The concession at the time was home to a far greater number of houses of prostitution than the International Settlement. At the same time, its police force was notoriously inadequate for an efficient system of control to be implemented.[18]

Brawls, scuffles, and disorders caused by the presence of soldiers and sailors were a daily occurrence in the concession.[19]

Following the ambassador's letter, the Conseil Municipal appointed a three-man commission under the chairmanship of Dr. Massais, the official doctor of the concession. A year later, the commission gave a report to the council, which examined it on June 19, 1869 and then forwarded it to Dr. Henderson, the health officer of the Shanghai Municipal Council of the International Settlement. The members of the commission noted that it was impossible to make every Chinese prostitute living in the concession undergo the checks being urged by the French ambassador. The inadequacy of the police force – which had about fifty men – and the lack of a health department made any initiative in this direction meaningless.[20] The commission therefore proposed to limit the system of registration and medical checks to prostitutes visited by foreigners.[21] No specific policy seems to have been adopted, pending perhaps the reactions of the Shanghai Municipal Council.

Although the point cannot be established with certainty, it would appear that these first steps toward the establishment of regulations on prostitution at least had contributed to the thinking and work of Dr. Henderson in the International Settlement.[22] In August 1869, Dr. Henderson, who was concerned by the consequences of venereal disease contracted by policemen, recommended the recruitment of a doctor to visit the houses of prostitution and detect infected girls by means of a general external examination. Although three doctors were appointed one after another to this task, the checks were fruitless and the treatment center set up in 1869 was closed a year later for lack of patients.[23] This short-lived experience, which saw the beginnings of a regulatory policy, went unnoticed and provoked no discussion within the foreign community in Shanghai.

Edward Henderson, however, continued to harbor a measure of disquiet over the problem of venereal disease. His fears were based on the fact that Shanghai, as a port, received a very large number of sailors and more generally a large transient population. Furthermore, the foreign community consisted essentially of young bachelors.[24] This approach to the question led Henderson, with the support of the Shanghai Municipal Council, to attempt a precise investigation of the reality of prostitution in Shanghai in order to prepare the ground for regulatory measures that he thought were indispensable to preserving the future of public health in Shanghai.

The results of this inquiry were published in 1871 in a document entitled *A Report on Prostitution in Shanghai; Drawn up for the "Council for the Foreign Community of Shanghai."*[25] This is one of the rare works that show some method in their approach to prostitution in Shanghai at the end of the nineteenth century, although it bears no comparison – alas – with Parent-Duchatelet's work on the city of Paris. Henderson painted a general portrait of the world of prostitution, made a diagnosis of the physical state of the girls and the range of venereal diseases prevalent, and then laid down the basic principles of a project to control this milieu. He noted that most of the prostitutes were patronized by a purely Chinese clientele and "therefore form no item in the calculation of any supervision scheme which has for its object the protection of foreigners only."[26]

The foreign prostitutes, who were a small group of about a dozen individuals, were also excluded from the project on the grounds that they supposedly were more hygienic in their habits.[27] This view was undoubtedly based on the fact that the number of foreign prostitutes was small, but it was also thoroughly discriminatory and reflected the unwillingness of these doctors to have Western women, even prostitutes, treated in the same way as Chinese women. The surveillance was therefore limited for the time being to those Chinese prostitutes who were patronized by foreigners. They alone were seen to constitute a special breeding ground for venereal disease.[28] Edward Henderson's project planned for the registration and checking of 223 women in 62 houses according to his own statistics. The prostitutes were to be subjected to regular examinations, and, in the event of infection, they were to be compulsorily detained in hospital. The expenditure resulting from these regulations, especially the expenditure entailed by the establishment of a lock hospital, was to be covered by a special tax. Henderson insisted that, in regulating Chinese prostitutes in Shanghai, it was necessary to reject any measures that might "fall short of this arbitrary exercise of power.[29] This severe policy explains the fact that the health controls had to be selective. It was seen to be impossible, with the meager medical and police resources available to the International Settlement, to extend such a policy to all the Chinese prostitutes.

It would seem that the Shanghai Municipal Council was indeed poorly equipped for such an undertaking.[30] In 1872, it gave instructions for the construction of a lock hospital for prostitutes in Fuzhou Road. In the following year it put down a sum of 2,000 taels for the operation of this lock hospital. During the same period, in the French Concession, the authorities proceeded as planned with the registration of the girls and laid down a system of compulsory medical checks. However, the French Conseil Municipal initially refused to associate itself with the building of the lock hospital.[31] The establishment of the lock hospital in the International Settlement was suspended in the summer of 1873.[32] It would be unnecessary here to go into the details of the various polemics and discussions that accompanied the preparation of the Henderson project.[33] It is enough to note that the foreign community in the International Settlement did not feel the need for a system that entailed yet another financial burden. The doctors who organized the discussion were divided on the effects to be expected from the medical checks on the girls. Moral considerations hindered the project inasmuch as intervention by the authorities in the realm of prostitution was seen as being somewhat tantamount to legitimizing prostitution. Further-more, there was no existing legal basis for levying a tax on brothels and prostitutes.[34] Lastly, if we add a fear of protests on the part of the Chinese authorities and the difficulties of cooperating with the French Concession, we can understand why the project did not win any real consensus within the foreign community.

In the winter of 1874–1875, the project was launched again, although in a very confused and disorganized fashion. In October 1874, the Conseil Municipal finally acquiesced in the idea of collaborating in a common lock hospital but sought assurances about its operation (with regard to the compulsory detention of infected prostitutes).[35] This requirement came up against the smallness and inadequacy of the premises. The planned collab-oration was again adjourned. The question of the lock hospital was revived in 1876 by Vice-Admiral Ryder, Commander-in-Chief of the British fleet in Asia, who pointed to the positive results of the Contagious Diseases Act in England as well as in the British Crown territories (of Hong Kong and Singapore).[36] The meeting of ratepayers of the Shanghai Municipal Council, most of whom were British, was sensitive to these arguments. Dr. Henderson was again asked to draw up a precise plan together with his counterpart in the French Concession, Dr. Pichon. The project was adopted at the end of an extraordinary meeting on July 26, 1876. After some months of preparation, the lock hospital that was jointly financed by the authori-ties of the two settlements was opened on January 1, 1877.[37]

The debate on the suitability of the lock hospital, however, was not over, as can be seen from statements by residents during the general meeting of ratepayers in March 1877. It was stirred up again two years later by Dr. Jamieson, an influential individual in the local medical community and a strong partisan, like Dr. Henderson, of a policy of controlling prostitution. He noted, however, that after two years the lock hospital had not brought any of the expected improvement. This, he said, was because of lack of resources but also because the project had been only partially implemented (infected girls were not being confined). Jamieson did not convince those at the ratepayers' meeting[38]; but his conclusions were identical to those of the Conseil Municipal, which temporarily stopped participating in the lock hospital at the end of 1879.[39] In 1886, Henderson himself drew up a negative balance sheet of the activity of the lock hospital. However, he attributed this result more to the paucity of the resources used than to the philosophy itself of the project.[40] Nor was it impossible that his conclu-sions were a local reflection of the failure and final repeal of the Conta-gious Diseases Act in England after a vigorous movement led by Josephine Butler.[41]

Despite these various forms of criticism, the Shanghai Municipal Council did not abandon its regulationist policy and renewed the subsidy to the lock hospital from year to year. In 1910 and 1911, the budget of the French Concession was still showing a sum of 600 taels for the lock hospital under the heading of "allocations and donations."[42] Although doubts had taken hold, the lock hospital appeared to be a lesser evil to the authorities and to the general meeting of ratepayers, which maintained the principle of the lock hospital. The medical examination of the prostitutes was conducted in this establishment until 1900 when it was integrated into the new Isolation Hospital.[43] Its premises were then put on sale, but the medical checks continued to be held there until 1920 when a new abolitionist movement began in Shanghai.[44]

The debate on the appropriateness of medical checks for prostitutes soon came to an end. First of all, the discussions had been limited to a small number of individuals and conducted within a well-demarcated framework. The contending viewpoints were those expressed among the Western ratepayers, namely the group of individuals forming the electoral base of the SMC.[45] They spoke during the annual general meeting, staying within the confines of this group. The debates of the meeting on this topic were not published in the *Municipal Gazette* but were recorded in minutes that were published separately. There was no public debate on the subject during this period, except for an exchange of letters between Henderson and Jamieson in 1879 in the *North China Herald*. And the newspaper soon closed the debate on so trivial a subject. The views of the Chinese, both the official authorities and representative organizations, such as the guilds, were not expressed in this discussion.

Outside the Shanghai Municipal Council and the general meeting of ratepayers, there were some attempts made by Protestant religious organizations to oppose the regulation of prostitution.[46] These organizations had little influence during this period, and their initiatives brought no response from the foreign and Chinese communities. The Protestant activists were a small minority within a population consisting essentially of traders, often unmarried, who rarely stayed very long in Shanghai. There did not yet exist a diversified foreign community in which the Protestant activists could find the channels of public opinion through which they could promote their cause as they had done in England.

The Working of the Lock Hospital

The lock hospital began to function on January 1, 1877. It had the financial support of the authorities of both settlements, and it also received the proceeds of a sort of tax levied by the police on the prostitutes. The sources are ambiguous, but it would appear that it was the girls and not the houses of prostitution that paid this monthly tax, which was initially set at 2.5 yuan and then reduced to 2 yuan some months later.[47] The Shanghai Municipal Council and the Conseil Municipal shared this income, which was used especially to pay the doctors responsible for carrying out checks and providing treatment. For his services, Dr. Pichon received 600 taels a year, a large sum at the time.[48]

The lock hospital did not have any outstanding success with the prostitutes, notwithstanding the assertions of its directors. Certain houses refused to submit to the medical checks and preferred to close shop or even leave the settlements. The prostitutes who stayed were resigned, and came in small groups: There were three girls on 24 February, thirteen on 26 February, and so on. By the end of the year, sixty-eight prostitutes from seventeen houses had been registered. Others came but were refused registration because they were infected. Henderson was optimistic: "So far as the prejudices of the women against the system are concerned, they are now satisfactorily overcome – or indeed if they ever constituted a real difficulty."[49] There can be no doubt, however, that for the prostitutes this was a traumatic experience. It was inconceivable for a Chinese woman to expose herself in a naked state and was even more difficult for her to allow a man, albeit a doctor, to see her private parts even if she was sick or suffering. Thus, care during childbirth was administered exclusively by women. There had been a similar reaction in Europe, where the prostitutes had unanimously rejected medical checks as a violation of their very being, in which the inspectors treated them as mere rows of cattle without showing the least consideration for their dignity.[50]

The pace at which the doctors in charge of the lock hospital carried out their examinations was not excessive, despite the growing number of girls who came to the lock hospital. Even at the end of the century, the numbers of prostitutes registered bore no comparison with those being treated by doctors in France or Italy. In Paris, a doctor would examine up to 400 girls per day.[51] The efficiency of the medical checks therefore may be doubted. In Shanghai, the examination was performed in principle by the two doctors officially appointed by the settlements, but we cannot be absolutely certain of this. In 1879, according to the administrative rules of the French Concession, there was a doctor in charge of treatment for the entire municipal staff, assisted by a male nurse "who was also an inspector of morality."[52] Table 11.1 shows major variations in the numbers of people registered as well as of "new requests." If the last two years are not counted, the number of girls registered represents (on average) half, or an even far smaller proportion in certain years, of the prostitutes patronized by foreigners. The policy therefore did not meet with any resounding success, especially because the girls do not seem to have come forward spontaneously and because there was a high rate of renewal of the prostitutes registered. From 1890 onward, the policy of surveillance became considerably stricter with the adoption of a policy to isolate infected girls and show greater severity against clandestine prostitution. Thereafter, most of the "new requests" actually came from

Table 11.1. *Number of prostitutes registered at the lock hospital (1877–1899)*

Year	Registered	Requests	Total	Admitted	Rejected	Percentage	Departures
1877	68	17	85				
1878	106	21	127		12	57	
1879	116	58	174	36	22	38	26
1880	132	98	230	53	45	46	40
1881	137	91	228	45	46	51	
1882	117	57	174	39	18	32	
1883	114	119	233	32	55	46	
1884	111	55	166	26	29	53	
1885	104	49	153	30	19	39	
1886	80	46	126	16	30	65	
1887	87	114	201	30	84	74	
1888	78	48	126	15	33	69	
1889	123	109	232	67	42	39	
1890	110	95	205	57	38	40	
1891	115	45	160	31	14	31	
1892	111	37	148		1	3	
1893	117	25	142			0	
1894	117	41	158		5	12	
1895	128	34	162		25	74	
1896	145		145				
1897	141	29	170		9	31	
1898	182						
1899	223						

Sources: Shanghai Municipal Council, *Report for the Year 1877*, p. 35; *Report for the Year 1878*, p. 47; *Report for the Year 1879*, p. 66; *Report for the Year 1880*, p. 64; *Compte rendu de la gestion pour l'exercice 1880*, pp. 16–17; *Compte rendu de la gestion pour l'exercice 1881*, p. 8; *Compte rendu de la gestion pour l'exercice 1882*, p. 19; *Compte rendu de la gestion pour l'exercice 1883*, p. 21; *Compte rendu de la gestion pour l'exercice 1884*, p. 19; *Compte rendu de la gestion pour l'exercice 1885*, p. 26; *Compte rendu de la gestion pour l'exercice 1886*, p. 3; *Compte rendu de la gestion pour l'exercice 1887*, p. 3; *Compte rendu de la gestion pour l'exercice 1888*, p. 4; *Compte rendu de la gestion pour l'exercice 1889*, p. 2; *Compte rendu de la gestion pour l'exercice 1890*, p. 5; *Compte rendu de la gestion pour l'exercice 1891*, p. 3; *Compte rendu de la gestion pour l'exercice 1892*, p. 7; *Compte rendu de la gestion pour l'exercice 1893*, p. 3; *Compte rendu de la gestion pour l'exercice 1894*, p. 4; *Compte rendu de la gestion pour l'exercice 1895*, p. 3; *Compte rendu de la gestion pour l'exercice 1897*, p. 144; *Compte rendu de la gestion pour l'exercice 1898*, p. 129; *Compte rendu de la gestion pour l'exercice 1899*, p. 223.

clandestine prostitutes arrested by the police and sent automatically to the lock hospital.

The doctors had no doubt at all about the efficiency of the system. They noted a drop in the cases of illnesses detected, even though greater numbers of prostitutes were being examined.[53] The experiment had to continue: "The question of the lock hospital, which has been debated for so long, now appears to have been settled for I do not believe that it is possible to question the real gains made by public health through this institution whose benefits are becoming clearer day by day."[54] The drop in the number of registered prostitutes in certain years was attributed to the strictness of the checks.[55] In reality, a large number of the girls joined the ranks of the clandestine prostitution or returned to brothels patronized by Chinese.[56]

According to the doctors, the prostitutes now seemed to appreciate the system because it was protecting their health.[57] The reality, however, tends to contradict this view. The Chinese prostitutes were conscious of the discrimination against them and complained that the foreign houses of prostitution, especially the Japanese brothels, were not being subjected to medical inspection. They pinned the authorities down to their own logic by saying that this failure to check the foreign prostitutes was exposing the Chinese girls to a health hazard. The doctors supported this argument, but the Western and Japanese prostitutes continued to escape medical surveillance.

The system was therefore defective, and the doctors, who were aware of this, made constant efforts to improve it and make it mirror the systems established in the major cities of Europe. The question of sequesterting infected girls comes up several times in their reports. They regretted the absence of "compulsory sequestration."[58] Through repeated pressure, they finally managed to strengthen the system. In 1890, the Shanghai Municipal Council purchased new premises adjoining the lock hospital. From then on, girls who had "submitted" as well as clandestine prostitutes were sequestered when medical checks showed them to be infected by venereal disease.[59] The efficiency of the system, once again, cannot be doubted: "We shall continue our policy of sequestration until the girls are fully cured . . . and we have proof of the effectiveness of this policy from the impartial testimony of several doctors from several warships." While venereal disease continued to wreak havoc, the fault for this was attributed to the clandestine prostitutes who were as yet "far too numerous" and who had to be repressed with greater severity.[60]

Unlike their colleagues in Europe, the Western doctors in charge of the lock hospital did not prepare any statistics, even of a cursory nature, on the venereal infections of the prostitutes. This explains the vagueness of the arguments presented by partisans and critics of the lock hospital in the 1870s and 1880s. All that is available is very general information from the annual reports of the medical departments of the two settlements on the proportion of infected individuals among the girls examined. Between 1879 and 1899, this proportion varied greatly – between 3% and 22% – from one year to another, but there is no way of knowing whether the variations reflected changes in reality or in medical practice. For lack of scientifically reliable blood tests (such as the Wasserman or Kahn tests), which were not used in China up to the twentieth century, the identification of infection depended as much on the competence of the doctor as on chance. Furthermore, the girls soon learned various ways to conceal their illness. The rate of venereal infection given in Table 11.1 appears to be very low as compared with that detected among prostitutes in Europe in the same period or in China a little later. All that need be said here is that these figures were very probably an understatement.

At the turn of the century, the lock hospital was closed and replaced by the isolation hospital. The question then is whether the authorities managed to achieve their goals. The last set of statistics tends to show that almost all the Chinese prostitutes patronized by foreigners, namely a group of 200 to 250 girls according to all the sources, were duly registered and underwent medical checks. This workload exceeded the capacities of the lock hospital and doctors, who made this fact known to the authorities.[61] This is perhaps one of the reasons why the lock hospital was transferred to the isolation hospital. After 1900, it is impossible to track the evolution of this policy. The sources fall silent. Neither in the budget nor in the report on the medical department is any mention made of checks on prostitutes.

Prostitution and Tax Policy

In addition to the medical inspection tax, the authorities of the settlements made the brothels pay licensing fees for permission to open their establishments. This is an issue that brought condemnation from observers of the time and especially from present-day Chinese historians of Shanghai and the settlements who are unanimous in accusing the foreign municipal authorities of having financed their activities through the brazen exploitation of the prostitutes.[62]

The International Settlement had a hesitant policy in this respect. The powers of the Shanghai Municipal Council were defined by the Land Regulations drawn up in 1845 with the agreement of the Chinese authorities. They could not be modified without assent from the consular corps.[63] One of the articles of the Regulations (Article 34) gave the authorities the power to regulate establishments of public entertainment through the allocation of licenses. Nevertheless, the only establishments concerned were the theaters, music halls, circuses, billiard parlors, and bars. The houses of prostitution were not included in the list of classified establishments. In 1898, Article 34 of the Regulations was revised to include the brothels. Nevertheless, fearing the reaction of public opinion, the Shanghai Municipal Council did not implement this new provision. The issue remained pending until 1905 when a committee of residents demanded the strict application of the rules. But here again, the Shanghai Municipal Council held back. Its reluctance was based on a desire first, in its own words, to avoid a conflict with the Chinese authorities and, second – this was very probably the primary reason – to avert a public debate on a problem that it had every reason to keep within its exclusive domain and thus prevent any challenge to its policies.[64]

In the French Concession, the authorities had no misgivings in the matter. From the very outset they sought to gain revenues from all the different business activities carried out in their territory. It is true that there were few possibilities available to the French in their small bit of land, wedged between the Chinese city with its 300,000 inhabitants and the International Settlement where most the foreigners were settled and where economic activity was prospering at a rapid pace.[65] They explored every avenue and, as the local Anglo-American press pointed out, they were willing, for example, to derive benefit from vice-related activities. This is an image that the French Concession found impossible to shed, even up till the eve of its retrocession to the Chinese authorities, and it is an image that can be found in much of the literature today.[66] The question is whether it corresponds to reality. How was prostitution regulated in the concession, and what revenues did the authorities derive from it?

The houses of prostitution were subjected, like all other classified establishments, to the payment of a licensing fee. The collection of the tax was left to the police: ". . . the taxes on the gaming houses, the brothels, boats, etc. were essentially variable. In fact, they were set more or less arbitrarily by the police officers responsible for collection and (this is not surprising) they were collected or reported to have been collected with extreme difficulty."[67] In 1862, the French authorities had envisaged a system of farming out taxes but had soon changed their minds.[68] For want of access to the French archives in Shanghai, I have been unable to find any documents on the rate at which this tax was levied and its modalities in the nineteenth century. In 1893, the chief of the municipal police said that there were slightly more than 200 houses of prostitution in the concession.[69] This figure, when related to the fiscal earnings for the same year, gives an average taxation rate of 24 taels per year per house, or 2 taels per month. This figure corresponds approximately to the rate applied to houses of entertainment in the International Settlement.

Table 11.2 assembles the data available on the revenues derived by the French Conseil Municipal from prostitution from 1862 to 1911.[70] It can be seen that the French Concession received a very substantial part of its resources from "vice"-related activities. More than 42% was derived from prostitution. In 1865–1866, there was a sudden drop that is inexplicable for lack of sources. The explanation could lie in the substantial departures of population from Shanghai after the defeat of the Taiping in 1864 and the resulting slump that affected the entire business of prostitution at the time.

The authorities compensated for this loss by imposing higher taxes on the gambling establishments, which accounted for more than half of their revenues in 1865–1866.[71] The respite was short-lived, however, because the

Table 11.2. *Tax revenues derived from prostitution in the French Concession*

Fiscal Year	Total Receipts	Houses of Prostitution	Percentage of Receipts (houses of prostitution)	Opium Parlors	Percentage of Receipts (opium parlors)
1862–1863	20,378	8,582	42.1	3,999	19.6
1863–1864	—	—	—	—	—
1865–1866	27,945	2,853	10.2	2,492	8.9
1866–1867	91,938	5,029	5.5	3,078	3.3
1867–1868	82,252	7,855	9.5	3,693	4.5
1868–1869	86,504	—	—	—	—
1869–1870	82,935	6,007	7.2	3,718	4.5
1873–1874	—	6,899	—	3,200	—
1874–1875	84,850	6,287	7.4	3,636	4.3
1880	110,816	7,000	6.3	6,222	5.6
1881	115,209	7,278	6.3	7,842	6.8
1882	110,810	6,970	6.3	7,800	7.0
1883	122,681	6,598	5.4	7,438	6.1
1884	107,665	5,237	4.9	6,317	5.9
1885	110,884	4,780	4.3	6,177	5.6
1886	129,975	4,837	3.7	6,473	5.0
1887	172,771	5,434	3.1	7,953	4.6
1888	159,159	5,713	3.6	8,022	5.0
1889	136,891	5,186	3.8	7,897	5.8
1890	138,478	5,239	3.8	8,370	6.0
1891	160,829	5,140	3.2	8,450	5.3
1892	140,109	5,175	3.7	7,821	5.6
1893	147,623	4,980	3.4	7,677	5.2
1894	150,319	5,133	3.4	7,894	5.3
1895	154,167	5,040	3.3	8,297	5.4
1896	—	—	—	—	—
1897	179,505	5,580	3.1	8,610	4.8
1898	196,638	4,551	2.3	8,302	4.2
1899	214,098	3,491	1.6	8,042	3.8
1900	274,929	3,292	1.2	7,958	2.9
1901	321,803	3,440	1.1	8,186	2.5
1902	343,347	4,060	1.2	8,721	2.5
1903	375,072	4,409	1.2	8,959	2.4
1904	1,014,550	4,754	0.5	9,430	0.9
1905	456,351	4,798	1.1	9,863	2.2
1906	520,553	4,908	0.9	10,421	2.0
1907	557,021	4,777	0.9	19,900	3.6
1908	577,168	4,640	0.8	29,440	5.1
1909	639,074	4,600	0.7	47,853	7.5
1910	581,442	4,510	0.8	14,585	2.5
1911	592,217	4,789	0.8	21,725	3.7

Sources: The sources consulted for this table are the budgets published in the *Comptes rendus* for the years indicated – except for 1862–1863, for which the information is taken from the *North China Herald*, 2 May 1863, p. 71.

concession was forced to close these establishments under pressure from the French ambassador in Peking.[72] The International Settlement had adopted a similar measure six months earlier, but the French Consul-General had allowed the gambling houses to remain in order to maintain the balance of the municipal finances.[73] To compensate for the lost income, the meeting of property owners decided to create several surtaxes, including one on the houses of tolerance, and this explains the leap in income for 1866–1867.[74] However, it can be seen that, from this time onward, there was a constant reduction in the volume of this income as a percentage of the total revenues of the municipality. From about 10% in 1865–1868, it fell to 5% in 1883 and 3% in 1887. It was only 1% in 1901 and amounted to an average of 0.8% up to 1911. Whatever moral judgment may be made about the collection of a tax on prostitution by the authorities of the French Concession, it is clear that they did not live off the work of prostitutes and their exploitation. The criticism expressed by the Anglo-American press of the time and taken up by present-day historians, as well as the judgments of Chinese historians, which have never been verified by a study of the sources, appear to me to be baseless. This does not rule out the fact that special attention was paid to the revenues earned from prostitution, as is attested to by the police archives.[75]

The Chinese Authorities and "Morality"

It is quite difficult to get a definite picture of the position of the Chinese authorities toward prostitution. This is because of an almost total absence of official sources. The general newspapers, which constitute one of the essential sources of this book, came on the scene only in 1872 with the founding of the *Shen Bao*. It is the requests made by the Chinese authorities to the municipal councils of the settlements that provide indirect knowledge of their attitude.

The junk boats and houses of prostitution had a very old presence in Shanghai as attested to by nineteenth-century sources. Nothing in the documents that I have read suggests that the authorities had adopted repressive policies toward them in the past. There is little reason to imagine that they might have been opposed to an activity that was perfectly integrated into the Chinese social fabric and was not reproved as such by the civil servants. The only formal relationship between these establishments and the administration, as in the case of the businesses and the artisans' shops in the city, lay in the collection of a tax. The documents corresponding to this tax are probably the only existing source on prostitution in the Walled City in the nineteenth century, assuming of course that such documents have been preserved.

The imperial administration did not intervene in the regular functioning of prostitution except to settle disputes over money, punish acts of violence, and punish the traffickers in human beings. Prostitution in its usual recognized forms was not a cause of concern for the mandarins. However, the opening of the settlements, with the flow of population that it caused and the great increase in the number of economic activities that developed therein, led to a modification of the forms of prostitution and, more generally, to a growing presence of women in a more diversified range of jobs.[76] This change was perceived by the authorities as a source of disorder, and they strove in vain to remedy the situation.

The increasing immigration of Chinese prostitutes into the settlements, from the 1860s onward, caused a degree of unease among the Chinese mandarins. They watched with displeasure as prostitution grew in an area over which they had no power and that, moreover, was occupied by foreigners. In November 1870, the circuit intendant (*daotai*) ordered the closure of all the brothels in the International Settlement. This was but a pious wish, because he had no way to enforce this decision. In his report, Dr. Henderson also notes that the Chinese magistrate of the Mixed Court preferred to ignore the presence of the houses of prostitution in the settlement. The circuit intendant's order therefore seems to have been a rather symbolic step.[77] In 1883, the *xian* magistrate published a statement in the press announcing the imminent closure of the houses of tolerance in the French Concession. This attempt came up against the opposition of the municipal police in the concession.[78]

What is even more significant is the attention paid to activities that were more clearly related to prostitution and considered by the Chinese civil servants to be unacceptable forms of the sex trade. In 1871, the circuit intendant prohibited the presence of women in the temples. This measure was in fact aimed against prostitutes who went regularly to burn incense in the Longhua pagoda.[79] Similarly, in August 1880, the circuit intendant recalled (this means that the prohibition had already been promulgated) that it was forbidden to employ women in teahouses and opium parlors. Some of them were said to have behaved indecently and sung obscene songs in these places.[80] The Chinese authorities renewed their prohibition in 1881.[81] This time, the Shanghai Municipal Council accepted the Chinese request and ordered its police to enforce the prohibition in the settlement. However, because the prohibition was not applied in the French Concession, the Shanghai Municipal Council was forced to rescind its decision.

The Chinese authorities were powerless to stem a phenomenon that was related to the growing externalization of prostitution. Theirs was a rearguard battle that especially reveals the prejudices of the local officials. The courtesans paid regular visits, without coming up against any official hindrance, to the centers of entertainment where they invited their customers, namely, members of the local scholar and merchant elites. By contrast, once the ordinary prostitutes began to do the same thing, the authorities tried to prohibit their presence.[82] In 1891, the Chinese authorities made another approach to the settlements. The French Conseil Municipal promulgated an ordinance instructing the police to "put a stop to the abuses that fostered the entry of women into the opium parlors."[83] The Shanghai Municipal Council had already adopted a similar measure on its territory.[84] The recruitment of young women as waitresses was indeed a new practice in the establishments concerned (*huayanjian*). It had arisen in the 1860s and was aimed at attracting customers.[85] The prohibition was made public by posters in Chinese. It does not appear to have been strictly applied. This point is also borne out by the press. In 1900, it was reported that the Conseil Municipal had been obliged to call the chief of the municipal police to order and ask him to ensure stricter compliance with the ordinance of 1891.[86] The prohibition was inserted in the regulation on opium parlors (Article 5) in 1907.[87]

The new forms of prostitution – such as that of the *maisons de rendezvous* (*taiji*), which received young women of good family (*liang jia*) – angered the Chinese local authorities. These establishments were accused of sending honest women to satisfy the appetites of debauched youths. Here, the authorities were worried about a phenomenon that fostered a form of sexual permissiveness. The houses of prostitution were the accepted places for venal sexuality. By contrast, the *maisons de rendez-vous* introduced an element of moral disorder and a risk of destruction of the family in that it made it easier for women to escape from family surveillance and establish adulterous relationships. The authorities prohibited these houses throughout the city under pain of severe punishment.[88]

The Chinese authorities were concerned by all that pertained to the presence of women in the public space. This presence brought into question the traditional social order characterized by the confinement of the female sex within the family. Only the prostitutes escaped this rule, but they themselves were confined within a very specific institution, the brothel, which was the only acceptable place for informal contacts between the two sexes. The arrival of women in places that were hitherto reserved for men, such as theaters, taverns, and teahouses, aroused fears because of the promiscuity that it implied in the eyes of the authorities. This change in behavior was seen by the mandarins as a form of deviance from the "classical" forms of prostitution, forms that had never disturbed them in the past. Prohibitions were laid down, although they were poorly applied, as we shall see, in the area under Chinese jurisdiction as well as in the settlements.

The policies of regulating prostitution in Shanghai failed because they were unable to surmount two obstacles proper to the city. The first obstacle was the division of the city into three administrative entities that were separated and even rival, with sharply divergent views on social control and public health. The Conseil Municipal was firmly convinced about tolerating prostitution, provided that it caused no public scandal. It concerned itself solely with the tax revenues that prostitution could bring to it. At the other end of the scale, the Shanghai Municipal Council was more sensitive to the puritanical values of a majority of the local Anglo-American community, while at the same time displaying a degree of indulgence. The two foreign administrations, however, because of the doctors present in the settlements, were influenced by the major currents of thought in Europe at this time. But even here, their divergent ways of looking at the issue reduced the effectiveness of their means of implementing a regulationist policy. As for the Chinese authorities, they had hardly any conception of public health and of the danger of venereal disease. It was the moral dimension that came to the fore when they defined the policies on prostitution that they adopted or whose adoption they sought.

The second obstacle related to the special composition of the population and the nature of the relationships between the municipal administrations and their populations. The settlements, which were originally designed to receive only foreigners, were massively populated by Chinese residents following the Taiping Revolt. The Shanghai Municipal Council and the Conseil Municipal had to take account of this situation when defining local policy. Thus, even though they were tempted to adopt measures for policing morality similar to those applied in the West, they were forced to come to terms with a society whose culture offered little purchase to the health and moral concerns of the foreign residents and to their desire to control the prostitutes. It may even be supposed that this approach was negatively perceived, such was the extent to which the practical implications of the medical inspection of girls went against Chinese ways of looking at these matters. Although we should allow for the limited numbers of staff available to the foreign administrations in Shanghai, the fact that they restricted the scope of their action to prostitutes visited by foreigners resulted also from their awareness of the cultural factor. The spirit of regulationism and the phobia about venereal disease found no corresponding echo within the Chinese population.

To emphasize Shanghai's specific character is not to imply by any means that, in another context, these attempts to adopt a regulationist policy might have succeeded. Research done to date on the policies implemented in France, England, Italy, and Germany has shown the limits and the failure of these policies. In this respect, therefore, Shanghai's experience was not particularly innovative in terms of either discourse or practice, although it sheds light on a specific characteristic that has been discussed elsewhere in this book: the absence in China of a any real moral condemnation of the phenomenon of prostitution and of any concern over the effects of venereal diseases, which nevertheless were extremely widespread at this time. China in the nineteenth century was still deeply rooted in a tradition of tolerance and even acceptance of prostitution. It was only from 1919 onward that this tradition came to be challenged under the combined effect in Shanghai of active campaigns by Protestant organizations and above all of the numerous debates on the status of women that sprang up in the wake of the May 4th Movement.

12
The Abolitionist Movement in Shanghai (1915–1925)

On the eve of the First World War, Shanghai became one of Asia's chief metropolitan cities. The settlements were now beginning to contain a huge Chinese population and a substantial foreign community. Prostitution had grown without stopping during the previous decades and reached a level that brought protests from a section of the foreign residents. The Shanghai Municipal Council continued to exert limited control over Chinese prostitutes who received foreign customers while the Conseil Municipal applied a more stringent policy of registering all the houses of tolerance. In both cases, this regulationist policy was very limited – at a time when prostitution had grown to unprecedented proportions.

Faced with the impotence or unwillingness of the authorities, several organizations attempted to seek the abolition of all regulation in the matter and the total elimination of prostitution in Shanghai. The polemics that these groups provoked and the policies that were adopted gave the Shanghai Municipal Council an opportunity to try and broaden its means of control. At the same time, the abolitionist groups worked actively to prevent their efforts from being diverted in this way. Unlike in the previous century, the debate was public, although to a limited extent, and provoked contradictory views within the Chinese and foreign communities. The French Concession stayed aloof from this debate, which it deemed to be misplaced and undoubtedly pointless. It even benefited from the geographical movement of prostitution activities set in motion by the abolitionist policy of the Shanghai Municipal Council.

The Emergence of the Abolitionist Movement in Shanghai

At the beginning of the First World War, the foreign community comprised several thousands of individuals, many of them long-standing residents.[1] It was structured in a large variety of (cultural, religious, sports, and other) organizations and associations and set the tone for what was now a cosmopolitan city. It was in this very novel context that several religious associations, all of them Protestant, strove to mobilize both Chinese and foreign public opinion to put an end to the houses of prostitution in the International Settlement. This movement grew in all likelihood as a reaction to the phenomenal growth of prostitution in Shanghai and especially the massive presence of prostitutes in the streets. However, the prime inspiration came from elsewhere. It came from the United States, where, from the years 1905–1910 onward, religious groups had undertaken a vigorous crusade against the major social evils of alcoholism and prostitution.[2]

In November 1916, a petition signed by 678 women was sent by the Shanghai Women's Temperance Union demanding the closure of the houses of prostitution and the severe repression of soliciting in the streets.[3] A very similar petition had been presented some years earlier (around summer–autumn 1910) by another women's group, the American Women's Club.[4] The Shanghai Municipal Council had not responded to that petition. This time, after some skirmishing, informal contacts related to specific demands made by various groups to the authorities led to the emergence of a current of public opinion and, a year later, to the establishment of a first group of associations. On May 16, 1918, about thirty individuals met at the Royal Asiatic Society at the invitation of the Shanghai Missionary Society and heard several speakers broach the topic of prostitution. The participants decided to form a Committee on Moral Improvement, which immediately elected an executive bureau of eleven. Protestant missionaries made up approximately half of the members of this bureau.[5]

In May 1918, several participating associations sent identically phrased letters to the Shanghai Municipal Council, asking for the establishment of an inquiry commission on moral conditions in the settlement.[6] This strategy drew inspiration very specifically from that of Protestant groups in the United States. The Shanghai Municipal Council responded by inviting the organizations to bring together all interested parties and form a representative committee, which would discuss this issue. It emphasized the need first of all to deal with the subject from a practical viewpoint, as distinct from a religious and moral one, with the goal of making constructive proposals to the authorities. The Shanghai Municipal Council warned those in charge of the associations against excessive zeal in as delicate a field as this one.[7]

The municipal authorities were clearly very reluctant to commit themselves to the process proposed by the associations. In fact, they tried to skirt their responsibilities in the matter by asking the associations to act as private bodies in making their inquiries and reflecting on the problem of prostitution. The Protestant associations, however, took the Shanghai Municipal Council at its word, and a month later (June 26, 1918) they set up the Shanghai Moral Welfare Committee representing seventeen local religious and philanthropic associations.[8] The new committee decided outright to prepare a publicity campaign for the autumn and asked the Shanghai Municipal Council to adopt a number of measures, especially relating to venereal disease (making it compulsory to disclose illness and publish a warning, in the *Municipal Gazette*, on the dangers of these diseases and the addresses of treatment centers) and to the curbing of soliciting and indecent activities.[9] The Shanghai Municipal Council rejected all these demands.[10]

During the summer, the committee continued to organize and define its tasks. It organized talks and lectures within member associations.[11] On October 21, 1918, on the eve of the publicity campaign that they were planning to launch, it published the founding document of the association entitled "Present Aim of the Moral Welfare Committee": "Our ideal and aim is the abolition of every form of commercialized vice in Shanghai." The goal was clearly defined: It was not limited to discussing and reflecting on the problem of prostitution in Shanghai. The committee set itself squarely within the context of a resolutely abolitionist logic. It intended to make this fact known and take every possible step to achieve its ends. Through the fight against prostitution, it was also the associated scourges of gambling, alcohol, opium, and extravagance that were the targets. The committee furthermore proposed two immediate steps, the elimination of the term "brothel" from Article 34 of the Land Regulations and an end to the medical examination of prostitutes by municipal agents.[12]

In its reply, the Shanghai Municipal Council waxed ironical about the possible impact of a revision of Article 34 on the business of prostitution, inasmuch as the article was not being applied in any case. Basically, the authorities thought it undesirable to eliminate the houses of prostitution, which ensured a certain spatial segregation of this activity. On the question of medical checks, the explanation of the municipal authorities was not without piquancy. They said that the Shanghai Municipal Council delivered no health certificates but only ensured that the girls were duly registered and made to undergo medical checks. The authorities preferred to ignore the fact that the prostitutes used their health registration cards as official certificates of good health in order to attract customers. The committee's demands very rightly touched on the two central points of the regulatory system that had been set up with a great deal of difficulty in the nineteenth century and that the Shanghai Municipal Council intended to keep out of the domain of public debate.[13]

The Polemics on "Morals" and "Practice"

The relationship between the authorities and the abolitionist movement soon took a polemical turn with the effective launching of the publicity campaign of the committee. The first document was widely distributed: It was sent to all residents of Shanghai whose names could be found in the Hong List, the directory of foreign companies in Shanghai. The committee took care to send the document only to adult males representing these companies.[14] The Shanghai Municipal Council severely condemned the campaign, which it deemed to be "ill-conceived," and felt that it did not deal with the issue "in an appropriate way" as it had itself recommended. It found it scandalous that the pamphlet should be sent to individuals having nothing to do with prostitution and felt that the whole subject was likely to shock people. The Shanghai Municipal Council asked for an end to the campaign and told the committee that the question of prostitution had to be looked at from a practical point of view.[15]

The letter from the Shanghai Municipal Council had the effect of a bucket of cold water. The committee said it was amazed by the peremptory tone of the authorities and criticized them for having taken no specific action on prostitution since the previous summer. The committee leaders also said they could not accept the Shanghai Municipal Council's distinction between a "practical" point of view and a "moral" point of view: Prostitution and its evils would find their "most practical solution" in a "essentially religious and moral" atmosphere. They therefore felt that their moral approach to the problem was entirely legitimate.[16] The Shanghai Municipal Council accused the leaders of the committee of being unaware of the extent of the harm that they had caused. The publicity campaign had prompted many written and verbal protests and created a great deal of resentment in a large section of the foreign community. While acknowledging the good faith of the authors of the pamphlet, the municipal authorities felt that their proposals were unrealistic because daily practical experience showed that the abolition of prostitution could not be obtained by the promulgation of rules and regulations. The Shanghai Municipal Council made it apparent that it preferred a comprehensive system (which had never been achieved) to regulate prostitution in the settlement. While it was aware of the contradictory views on prostitution being advanced in Western countries, the Shanghai Municipal Council maintained that the committee, in its reforming zeal, was not paying sufficient attention to the nature and complexity of the phenomenon. It rejected the committee's demands.[17]

The Shanghai Municipal Council very clearly saw the risks of an official inquiry that it feared would confirm the committee's arguments. There was a possibility that an official report might convince a majority of the ratepayers of the validity of the committee's proposals, whereas its pamphlets and projects were limited to the realm of private initiative. The strategy of the Shanghai Municipal Council, which continued to favor the status quo, therefore was to prevent the activities of the committee from acquiring any official character. At the same time, it sought to unburden itself of certain tasks by transferring them to private organizations such as the Door of Hope – a charitable organization devoted to the rescue of prostitutes – which it proposed to entrust with the work of visiting the houses of prostitution with official financial assistance.[18]

Unlike the debate in 1870–1880 on the appropriateness of the lock hospital, which took place within a very closed circle – limited to the doctors and the members of the ratepayers assembly – the polemics on the appropriateness of eliminating prostitution and on the means to do so were reported to some extent in the local press and in the official gazette. The debate was short-lived. It provided no new or specific information on the Chinese or Shanghai situation. The arguments put forward were hardly different from those used during the same period in the West.[19] Furthermore, there was limited participation by the residents in the debate initiated by the committee, at least in public via the press. There was a degree of embarrassment about prostitution, a phenomenon that the majority preferred to ignore and not to discuss in public.

The Establishment of the Vice Committee

At the meeting of April 9, 1919, a draft resolution was indeed submitted to the ratepayers, seeking to set up an official commission of inquiry on prostitution in Shanghai. This draft does not seem to have provoked any discussion according to the minutes of the debate published in the municipal gazette. Mr. Alfred J. Walker noted that the committee and the Shanghai Municipal Council were agreed in deeming prostitution to be a "social evil" and that it was a delicate and difficult subject to broach. The resolution was adopted without difficulty. The two parties were favorable to the establishment of an inquiry commission that would bring better results and provide a new opportunity for a policy of reform.[20]

The "Vice Committee" (this is the name given to the inquiry commission in all the documents of the period) was therefore given the task of carrying out a survey on prostitution in the settlement, preparing a report and making proposals to the next general meeting. To ensure impartiality, the new organization was formed by nine members chosen as follows: Three were appointed by the Shanghai Municipal Council and three by the committee; the remaining three members were chosen in common by the first six members.[21] Two of the members were women. The Vice Committee held twenty-two meetings. It would appear that the essential part of the information collected was obtained from hearings of "witnesses" (of whom there were twenty-five). There were no details given about their identity and occupation, but they included a number of directors of municipal departments (police and health), officials of the charitable organizations (Door of Hope, Shanghai Anti-Kidnapping Society), and missionaries.

The Vice Committee therefore based its findings on administrative reports and on residents' letters that had been called for in the *Municipal Gazette*. The opinions of "representative Chinese" were obtained through the General Chamber of Commerce. By contrast, although this point cannot be proved, the members of the inquiry teams do not seem to have made any "field surveys."[22] The report, which is analyzed below, shows a very superficial knowledge of the world of prostitution. This is not wholly surprising inasmuch as the lines of research chosen gave priority to the quantitative dimension of the problem (namely, the number of houses and prostitutes, modes of control, condition of venereal diseases, and the possibilities of treatment). Nowhere is it apparent that there was any real desire to penetrate this world – that is, obtain information from within on the condition of the women and on prostitutional practices or on the traffic in women and the recruitment of prostitutes.

After a year of deliberations, the Vice Committee handed in its report.[23] The members were unanimous: The right policy to be followed was to eliminate the houses of prostitution in the settlement. The Committee recommended the application of Article 34 of the Land Regulations to register all brothels, followed by the withdrawal of licenses through the successive drawing of lots over a period of five years. The licenses would be allotted only to establishments in business as of 31 December 1919, with the number of girls being limited to ten per house. The police were to be responsible for noting down the names of the brothel owners, the girls present, and the landlords of the buildings and land in a register. The landlords were to be specifically informed of the use to which their property was being put. The Vice Committee also took up one of the Moral Welfare Committee's demands, namely, the ending of medical checks on prostitutes. The only limits placed on the functioning of the brothels was the prohibition of soliciting under pain of withdrawal of license, the prohibition of alcoholic drinks, and the requirement that notices be put up inside the brothel indicating the addresses of the nearest police station and VD center. The members of the Vice Committee acknowledged their inability to make any estimation whatsoever of the prevalence of venereal disease in Shanghai. At the same time, they recommended that statistics be prepared by the health service and that venereal disease clinics be opened in several places in the city.

The Vice Committee was aware of the limits of its work and results, and it even tended to be apologetic: "Your committee has made no heroic recommendations." It acknowledged the limits of the municipal authorities in the matter of prostitution, especially in the settlement where several nations were represented. However, its members felt that they had approached the problem of prostitution sufficiently to enable the creation of policies to reduce this phenomenon, especially the institution of the house of prostitution. The impression given by the report is that the mountain had labored to bring forth a mouse. Given the heated debate that had accompanied the initiative of the Moral Welfare Committee and the goals that the inquiry commission had set for itself, the result was rather meager. For the historian, this is all the more frustrating because this was one of the very rare surveys made of the world of prostitution by the authorities. Leaving aside the fact that the period was a different one, this report is hardly any more enlightening than the Henderson report of 1871.

The nature of the recommendations provides a measure of the investigators' blindness to the reality of prostitution in Shanghai. The main goal chosen was that of eliminating the brothels even if it was ultimately stated in the report that prostitution could not be made to disappear through an act of Parliament. The reasons for the phenomenon of prostitution as also the "sources of the supply," the functioning of the institution, and the condition of the girls were completely sidetracked. The steps recommended to help prostitutes after the closure of the brothels were more in the nature of pious wishes than a clear policy of reintegration. Besides, no thought was given to ways of exerting some degree of control over the inevitable phenomenon of clandestine prostitution (which, as it turned out, was not mentioned).

On the whole, the recommendations of the Vice Committee rather precisely overlapped the demands that the Moral Welfare Committee had made as early as in the autumn of 1918. The authorities clearly understood this fact when they replied to the Vice Committee's opinions point by point. The Shanghai Municipal Council expressed agreement with all the minor points (prohibition of soliciting, alcohol, misleading publicity, etc.) but declared its opposition to the central recommendations of the report, namely, the elimination of brothels and of medical checks. It argued that such a decision was inappropriate because it would result in a transfer of the brothels to the neighboring settlement or into the Chinese city without any possibility of control, the growth of a large number of clandestine houses, which would be difficult to suppress even with an increase in the police force, and an increase in outdoor soliciting. The Shanghai Municipal Council also defended the principle of medical surveillance, which it believed played a role in the maintenance of public health. However, it did not reject the idea of the application of Article 34, which would enable the authorities to exert greater control over the houses.[24]

Clearly, the thrust of the Vice Committee's report was not that expected by the authorities, but they did try to make it serve their interests and their goal of establishing a comprehensive system of regulation. This point was expressed even more clearly by its representative, E. C. Pearce, before the ratepayers meeting: "We are in whole-hearted agreement with the licensing of brothels with a view to their regulation . . . [but] we consider their total elimination as inadvisable. . . . I must emphasize that we do not believe in licensing of brothels to secure their elimination as contrasted with their regulation." The Reverend Isaac Mason, who defended the Vice Committee standpoint, expressed satisfaction with the official recognition of the existence of brothels by the authorities while wondering somewhat ingenuously about the absence of repression against these brothels. He added: "You cannot put down all moral laxity by legislation, but we can by such power as exists, or may be obtained by this meeting, oppose, attack and destroy the commercialized vice evil as has been done in other cities and countries."[25]

The Polemics on the Abolition of the Houses of Prostitution

Despite the opposition of the Shanghai Municipal Council, the ratepayers' meeting adopted the report in its entirety and asked that its recommendations be implemented.[26] This was but the start of a long struggle between local authorities and the Moral Welfare Committee (renamed League in December 1920 and hereinafter called MWL), because, the authorities were to implement the policy of prohibiting brothels to the letter while deliberately refraining from any serious attempt to curb clandestine prostitution and greatly watering down the system of prohibition at the request of certain sectors of the Chinese population.

In a municipal notification dated May 13, 1920, the Shanghai Municipal Council made it obligatory for the houses of prostitution to register with the police. The license assigned to the brothel owners and prostitutes was nontransferable. The departure of a girl before the date of expiry of her license could not be compensated for by the recruitment of another girl. Any change had to be notified to the police. Gambling, alcohol, opium, disorderly behavior, and soliciting were prohibited, and no girl could be held against her will. The nameplate that was given, the text of the rules, and the addresses of the nearest police station and treatment center had to be posted up inside the brothel. The brothel had to maintain proper levels of hygiene and open its doors at all times to police, health, and tax officials.[27] In fact, these provisions were never complied with.

Registration, which began on May 24, was to have been completed on June 14. However, the scale of the task (more than 1,700 houses were concerned, and not all of them knew about the new regulations[28]) forced the Shanghai Municipal Council to adopt more forceful measures. On June 7, by which date only a small number of proprietors had registered their names of their own accord, the authorities decided to send out teams of policemen to note down the brothels in their areas of jurisdiction.[29] The deadline was postponed to June 30, which was a sign of the difficulties experienced in accomplishing this task.[30] By the beginning of the summer, the registration had been completed. The police continued, however, to make routine checks on the addresses and the numbers of girls declared in each house.[31] The registers could be consulted by all the ratepayers.[32] The action of the abolitionists in Shanghai had a small but unmistakably totalitarian flavor to it.

At the beginning of the autumn, the Shanghai Municipal Council announced the date of the first draw by lots: December 21, 1920.[33] The draw took place four days later than planned. It was preceded by an information campaign among the residents of the brothels by the police and through the press.[34] The meeting took place in the town hall in the presence of about a hundred individuals (mostly women) belonging to the "profession." These were essentially brothel managers and madams.[35] The draw was done with a drum of the kind used today in some major lotteries, with 884 tickets corresponding to the number of houses officially registered being placed in the drum. By the end of the afternoon, the names of 174 establishments had been drawn. The list was published in the municipal gazette and in the Chinese press for the information of the public. The houses had three months in which to bring their activities to an end.[36]

The brothels continued to be eliminated with a new draw every year. The second draw, which was organized on December 6, 1921, took place under the same conditions. Again, 139 houses had to close down before March 31, 1922.[37] Two police officers were assigned full time to the job of seeing to it that the brothels chosen by lot did really close shop. By the end of 1921, 218 establishments had been officially closed, but the number of violations of the licensing rules (a majority of them concerned clandestine establishments) was 239. The police noted that prostitution was becoming geographically more spread out in the settlement but admitted that they were incapable of stemming the phenomenon.[38] The successive draws led above all to migratory movements by prostitutes throughout the city and to the growth of clandestine prostitution in the settlement.

The Moral Welfare League nevertheless did not suspend its crusade against "vice," and in particular it demanded explanations concerning the terms of the police report of 1921.[39] The authorities confirmed the closure of the brothels but emphasized that the former occupants were continuing to do business on a private basis (which was not an offense) and were beyond any form of control. The task of the police was therefore strictly limited to applying the licensing rules in the settlement. The fewer licenses there were, the less able were the police to control prostitution and its evils.[40] The MWL militants were embittered by the official attitude of deliberate obstinacy and even disdain. They believed that a policy of eliminating the brothels was bound to bring about a drop in this activity.[41]

Veiled accusations on the part of the MWL did not shake the faith of the municipal authorities in the soundness of their approach. They confirmed the observations of the police that prostitutional activities were on the rise in the different districts of the settlement and regretted the fact that a policy of spatial segregation of prostitution had not been preferred. The Shanghai Municipal Council claimed to be "deeply concerned" about this state of affairs but felt that it did not have the means to counter it. The police were required only to see to the application of the law, namely, the closure of the brothels after each draw. The Shanghai Municipal Council asserted that it was not possible to do any more and observed that to take up a contrary viewpoint was to refuse to see "the real facts of the case." It urged the MWL to approach the police directly.[42] At this point, the exchange of correspondence on the subject practically came to an end.[43] The MWL nevertheless continued to remind the authorities constantly of their duties and sought to broaden the scope of the struggle against prostitution, especially by having women prohibited from entering bars and taverns. The Shanghai Municipal Council rejected this proposal, which would have amounted to a formal prohibition of dancing by women in any place of public entertainment. The SMC, which was already greatly restricted by the ratepayers' decision on the houses of prostitution, had little stomach for waging a struggle on all fronts.[44]

The MWL was also very active on the ground, disseminating its message and mobilizing the population, especially the foreigners, around its activities. My partial data on this activity reveal much determination to heighten the awareness of large sections of the public, even if the result was not always up to the ambitions of the activists.[45] In 1922, the MWL covered twenty-two associations (Americans, British, Chinese, and Japanese) led by American citizens. It had ten thousand members, but it is not stated whether this figure corresponds to the total membership of the twenty-two associations or to MWL's own activists.[46] It organized lectures in English for very varied audiences generally having links with missionary circles (such as the YMCA or Nanyang College). In all, 2,500 individuals, including 650 Chinese, attended these lectures.[47] These people represented only a very small proportion of the foreign population, and an even smaller proportion of the Chinese population. The use of English set up a linguistic barrier that immediately eliminated practically the entire Chinese population.

This said, the MWL made every effort to reach a wider proportion of the residents by sending out publications. These included first of all its own publications, of which some 23,520 copies were printed and distributed among businessmen, students, and professional groups. The report of the Vice Committee was distributed in Chinese (2,500 copies), as were two other documents, "Brief History and Program of the Moral Welfare League" and "Simple Sex Education in the Home" (15,000 and 10,000 copies respectively in Chinese, and 8,000 and 5,000 copies respectively in English). The distribution of the English-language publications raised no problems, but that of the Chinese versions came up against a lack of distribution channels within local society, notwithstanding attempts to contact Chinese journalists and publishers.[48]

The Effects of Closure on Prostitution

The closure of the houses of prostitution had unexpected consequences, as can be understood from the exchange of correspondence between the MWL and the authorities. The planned timetable was scrupulously followed. The first draw eliminated 174 houses out of the 972 listed in the final census of 1920. The second draw, which took place on December 6, 1921, eliminated 139 houses out of 559.[49] In December 1922, there were only 343 establishments left, 114 of which were drawn. A year later, in the last draw, the number of houses left fell to 196, half of which were drawn by lot and had to close shop on March 31, 1924. The last group had the deadline extended to the end of the year.[50] In all, some 300 girls were still licensed to exercise their profession.[51]

The reaction of the houses of prostitution to the policy of abolition was far from being uniform. It varied according to the categories of establishment, even if the primary concern of all was to find a way of staying in business. Their solution to this problem took two main forms: going into clandestinity and moving out of the International Settlement. Houses whose names were drawn by lot had no choice but to become clandestine if they wished to remain in the settlement. It is difficult to form an opinion on the reality of the closure because those houses that "closed" may very well have set themselves up elsewhere as shall be seen below. One statistic deserves a closer look: In 1920, the police delivered 1,771 licenses, whereas only 972 houses remained in existence at the time of the first draw. This difference means that nearly 800 establishments had disappeared spontaneously between the time of the registration and the day of the draw. While some of them had closed, there can be no doubt that the majority had chosen clandestinity. Moreover, those whose names were drawn did not all comply with the decision to close. An inquiry in August 1922 on 140 licenses withdrawn in the third draw in December 1921 (requiring closure on March 31, 1922) showed that about half (48.5%) of the houses concerned had closed while the rest had continued to function through illegal transfers of licenses.[52]

The mobility of the houses and their residents was indeed very high. The police reports for the period following the first draw emphasize the very fluid nature of this world, an aspect that confounded the police officials. They would find that a license-holder had vanished along with his or her girls without leaving any address even though they had permission to operate and had not been drawn in any lot. In May 1921, the police informed the tax office that they were unable to locate sixty-two license-holders.[53] Between 1920 and 1923, the authorities revoked a total of 115 licenses for this reason. This figure does not include those whose premises had been destroyed (7) and those who had moved into the French Concession (8) or had died (4). It must be added that certain landlords did throw out their tenants when they learned of the use that was being made of their premises.[54] To these figures, which account for about half of the difference seen further above, we must add the number of licenses withdrawn for infringement of the rules (37).[55]

The police also noted frequent transfers of licenses from one house to another or from one girl to another. This was a form of semiclandestinity for which a high price could be negotiated (450 yuan for an establishment license).[56] All these practices that undoubtedly reflected real mobility and turnover in the world of prostitution were also a sign of adaptation to the novel circumstances created by the policy of abolition. Many establishments tried to escape the rigors of regulation by closing before the expiry of their license and setting themselves up elsewhere in the city. The police were not hoodwinked but were unable to curb these movements. They suppressed all cases of clandestine houses discovered by their agents or reported to them by the MWL.[57]

When a clandestine house was discovered, its premises were automatically closed. The madam would be fined and the girls released or sent to a charitable institution.[58] The punishments for prostitutes not declared by the establishments were not truly deterrent in nature. Even in the lower-category houses, five yuan – the usual amount of the fine – was no more than the price of a night with a prostitute.[59] The police and the judges were sometimes trapped by the regulations. A house that a Cantonese woman had opened without a license was discovered by the police. The madam and four girls were brought before the Mixed Court, which was incapable of pronouncing judgment because all four girls asserted that the woman accused of procuring was not a madam. Although they shared the same premises, each girl claimed to be working independently.[60] The skill with which these prostitutes were able to defend themselves highlights one of the flaws in the regulations adopted by the Shanghai Municipal Council.[61]

Closure also led to the appearance or development of new forms of prostitution. The use of hotels, which was not new, became a widespread practice. Those prostitutes who came to set themselves up in the International Settlement but could no longer get licenses because the total number had been frozen at the December 31, 1919 level took up hotel rooms. Despite a prohibitory ruling, the police noted an increase in this phenomenon among all the prostitutes.[62]

Establishments moving away from the International Settlement went primarily to the French Concession and to a lesser extent to Hongkou and the Walled City. All the observers confirmed this phenomenon, which was accompanied by a diversification of the forms of prostitution.[63] The attitude of the French Municipality was particularly unambiguous. It held aloof from the debates that racked the International Settlement before 1920 and seems to have been spared the pressure that the MWL put on the Shanghai Municipal Council. Neither in the documents of the MWL nor in those of the Conseil Municipal have I been able to find the smallest mention of any contact or exchange of conflicting standpoints. In its 1922 report, the MWL referred to the movement of brothels into the neighboring settlement and noted several times that this would require cooperation with the French authorities, a subject about which it had no specific plan of action. In 1924, it would seem that matters were still at the same point.[64]

The fact nevertheless remains that the authorities were unable to totally escape the dynamics of the situation set in motion by the MWL and the Shanghai Municipal Council, the latter unwillingly. At a time when the abolitionist policy had been adopted by the ratepayers assembly and caused a migration of the prostitutes, the Chinese councilors in the Conseil Municipal asked the Consul what his intentions were and what steps he was planning to take to prevent the coming of new houses of prostitution. The French Consul-General, who was the *de jure* and *de facto* head of the concession, declared that the Conseil Municipal had no intention of increasing the number of licenses granted and that it would not accept the establishment of brothels from the International Settlement on its territory. He said that the reports circulating on this subject were but rumors to be scotched.[65] Some months later, the Consul disclosed his intention to carry out a census of the houses of tolerance and gradually eliminate them by drawing lots every three months over a period of five years.[66]

The resemblance with what was being done in the neighboring settlement was obviously not fortuitous. It was the expression of a desire, on the part of the French, not to be misjudged in the domain of public morality especially because, ever since the nineteenth century, the French Concession had had the reputation of being a cesspool of vice. The Conseil Municipal took the same view. However, these declarations had no effect. On the contrary, the French Concession received a growing number of establishments fleeing the severity of the law in the neighboring settlement.[67] While the registration of the houses was being completed, the police in the Shanghai Municipal Council noted that many *yeji* houses had refused to take out licenses and had gone into the area under French jurisdiction. One group of courtesans, whose establishments had been unable to obtain licenses owing to their proximity to the schools, made the move *en bloc*.[68]

Despite the declarations of the French authorities, increasing numbers of houses of prostitution came to this area that was not encumbered by any prohibitory measure. They were sure that the Conseil Municipal would ultimately recognize their presence and give them licenses. Their expectations were not unfounded. In May 1922, the authorities, noting the increasing number of clandestine establishments in the concession, decided to give out about a hundred licenses, specifying the areas in which the houses could be set up. In the eyes of the municipal authorities, this form of recognition, which enabled them to exercise a certain degree of surveillance, was preferable to the kind of situation developing in the International Settlement.[69] The press broadly confirmed this phenomenon of transfer, which shows that the policy of abolition in no way changed the condition of the girls who remained in a state of submission to their madams.[70]

The authorities of the French Concession made every effort to preserve a good image in the eyes of local public opinion. In reply to a letter from the MWL in 1923, inquiring about the number of licenses granted in the concession since the introduction of the abolitionist policy of the Shanghai Municipal Council, the Conseil Municipal stated that the number of licenses had remained constant, at about 195 in 1922 and 1923. The Conseil Municipal denied the rumor spread by the police of the International Settlement that more than a thousand licenses had been handed out. The documents provided by the municipal police tend to confirm these assertions.[71] However, they need be modulated. First, I have no data for the years 1920 and 1921 when a very large number of establishments "disappeared" from the police registers of the Shanghai Municipal Council. Again, the French administration kept separate records for the houses of tolerance and the singsong girl (courtesan) houses, although both these categories were really establishments of prostitution. Now the lists that I have consulted for 1923 and 1924 show a high influx of new applications from the singsong girl houses that undoubtedly came from the neighboring settlement.[72] The French Concession thus seems to have carried out a selective policy of receiving prostitutes, favoring the courtesan houses (*changsan*), which are the ones that received the hundred licenses mentioned above.[73]

The *realpolitik* of the Conseil Municipal in the matter of prostitution drew protests. In May 1924, a group of residents asked the authorities to abolish prostitution in the concession. They pointed out that the houses were opening in hitherto residential areas where new housing was being built.[74] This was also the line of reasoning that the Federation of Commerce (*Shangye lianhehui*) of the concession developed behind a number of ostensibly moral arguments.[75] Some months later, the Federation of Commerce asked the Consul to increase the number of police rounds to ensure law and order.[76] In 1924, the Federation renewed its demand for the prohibition of the installation of prostitutes in the concession. These protests were specific and had no effect on the policy of tolerance of the French authorities.

One of the problems that arose concerned the fate of the prostitutes. Nothing was done for the social reintegration of the girls when their establishments closed. The MWL stated that the task of taking charge of these prostitutes was rather better performed by organizations such as the Door of Hope and the Foreign Women's Home and that no pressure had been put on them to carry out this task themselves. Besides, the MWL deemed it more important to diminish the "organizing and advertising powers" of the houses and reduce the number of new victims than to save women already reduced to the state of wrecks.[77] It is true that in many cases the notion of saving these women was illusory inasmuch as they were often prisoners of their madams.

The Reaction of Chinese Public Opinion

Unlike what happened in the nineteenth century with respect to health checks on prostitutes, the policy of abolition of the brothels in the 1920s aroused many contradictory reactions among the Chinese population. To a good extent, these reactions resulted from the fact that the debate was conducted partially in public through the press. It must also be noted that the goals of this policy were far more ambitious than those of the health checks and directly affected the daily life of the Chinese. Finally, there now existed a body of Chinese public opinion, hinging on different groups and organizations that expressed their views without hesitation and took standpoints on any official decisions that closely affected them. However, we cannot fail to be struck by the differences in tone and the contradictions that characterized the Chinese discourse. It must be added that there was only one category that really expressed itself: This was the category of the merchants.

The registration of the higher category of houses of prostitution, the *changsan*, patronized by the local elites, led to a protest movement. A group of merchants meeting in restaurants, teahouses, cafes, and so on, asked the General Chamber of Commerce to intervene with the Shanghai Municipal Council in order to support a demand for a dispensatory status for the courtesans. The merchants' group approved the policy of regulation but regretted the fact that there was no classification of houses, especially of the courtesans' houses. They invoked the essential role of these establishments in Chinese social and economic life and their irreplaceable role as meeting places *par excellence* for the merchants. The group asserted that the girls were artistes and not prostitutes.[78] Behind this facade of reasoning, the merchants' group was seeking above all to defend its economic interests, which were being affected by the closure and shifting of the houses.

A lawyer well known in Shanghai circles, Lemière, also became the courtesans' spokesman with the authorities. He emphasized the major role of these artistes and their establishments, which were a center of business activity, and testified to their high moral character. Their disappearance would not only remove a favorite meeting place for merchants and create discontent but also bring about the decline of a whole range of craft activities (jewelry-making, embroidery, shoe-making, and the like.). Either that or they would have to move elsewhere. In any case, it meant a loss of tax income for the authorities of the concession.[79] Everyone supported the repeal of the policy of the registration of the courtesans' houses.

The General Chamber of Commerce agreed to support the merchants' request and wrote accordingly to the Shanghai Municipal Council. The latter turned down the Chamber on the grounds that it had no choice but to implement the decision of the ratepayers' assembly, even if it disagreed with it. However, the Shanghai Municipal Council felt that while the courtesans were also prostitutes, establishments that were *bona fide* places of musical entertainment employing singers did not need to take out licenses.[80] The Shanghai Municipal Council clearly showed its reluctance over the policy of abolition and indicated that it was ready to make an exception even if the distinction between *bona fide* singsong establishments and the others was based on no specific criterion. Besides, four years later, they were to embark upon a change in the regulations. In 1920, this could not be done for fear of the protests that would inevitably be aroused.

The letter from the General Chamber of Commerce to the Shanghai Municipal Council raised an outcry of indignation from several personalities in the business world who were scandalized that the Chamber should intervene on behalf of prostitutes, even if they were disguised under the name of singsong girls. They called for explanations from those responsible. At the same time, they announced the creation of a Society for the Abolition of Prostitution (*Feichanghui*), but nothing seems to have come of it.[81] Only two of the signatories to the letter were mentioned by the newspaper that reported it. They were Zhao Nangong and Wang Wuwei, both from the middle levels of the business world. In this respect, their intervention was a symptom of a more widespread attitude among the small Chinese merchants who supported an abolitionist policy without, however, clearly expressing the reasons for their disapproval. As for the General Federation of Street Unions (*Shanghai ge lu shangjie zong lianhehui*), which also approached the Shanghai Municipal Council, its letters were a bundle of varied and contradictory arguments. The Federation above all stressed the point that the fundamental causes of prostitution (poverty and the weakness of the Chinese economy) had not disappeared and that it was necessary also to wage the battle at this level.[82] As shall be seen below, the merchants were not opposed to the principle of prostitution as much as they were hostile to the nuisance that it caused in certain districts and roads.

In November 1923, several Chinese personalities led by Yao Gonggue (the only individual named by the newspaper) sent a long letter to the Shanghai Municipal Council, inviting it to adopt policies complementing the policy of abolition. They noted that, instead of being confined to certain districts as in the past, prostitution had become geographically more dispersed in the city, causing all manner of inconvenience to decent people. These personalities regretted the fact that the debate about the abolitionist policy had been limited to vain polemics about morality, whereas it should have enabled a search (*yanjiu*) for a concrete solution to the problems raised. Drawing a parallel with the opium smokers, they said that it was not enough to close the establishments but that it was necessary also to change habits and cut off the sources of supply. Conditions therefore had to be created for the social reintegration of the prostitutes. Otherwise they would continue the same activity underground.[83]

The Chinese press, which was not hostile to the idea of eliminating the houses of prostitution, tended to take an increasingly critical attitude.[84] We have already seen that it echoed the view of various groups that criticized the inconsistency of the Shanghai Municipal Council. The *Shen Bao* reproduced an editorial from the *Dalubao* (*The Continent*) condemning the policy of abolishing the brothels as a total failure and citing the negative effects already referred to by others. The editorial condemned the general hypocrisy involved in prohibiting houses under various moral pretexts while avoiding a genuine public debate in the press and thus preventing youth from being informed of the reality of prostitution. The end result of all this, said the editorial, was the spread of prostitution to every area, where it was in full view of all children.[85]

There were unmistakable contradictions between the different standpoints of the spokesmen for the Chinese population. As among the Westerners, there were those who were for and those who were against, but with one major difference. It was only exceptionally that the debate took a moral dimension. The considerations in each camp were essentially practical. Those who backed regulations conferring official recognition on the courtesans sought above all to defend their economic interests. Conversely, a portion of the merchants, sometimes in the same districts, were opposed to the resumption of an activity that attracted not only rich customers but also all sorts of ruffians. Their trade derived no direct profit from the activity of prostitution, and so they generally preferred that these houses, which did not add to the reputation of their areas, should disappear.[86]

Except in the case of the merchants, the complaints were most often motivated by the nuisance created by prostitution once it spread over the city. The Chinese implicitly had the idea of a spatial segregation of prostitution. In the settlements, this idea, while accepted, was brought into question by the effects of the policy of abolition. The frequent coming and going of customers as well as the variety of noises (music, cries, brawls, etc.) emanating from the brothels upset the day-to-day life of the districts concerned. Not to mention the fact that, as in the French Concession, the prostitutes who came in large numbers looking for premises came into competition with the merchants and other residents and pushed rents up significantly while bringing little new business to the shopkeepers of the area.[87] It would not be an exaggeration in my view to say that there was a gradual increase in awareness of the negative effects of the abolition of the houses of prostitution. Within the foreign community, the absence of further public reaction, except on the part of the MWL, would point to a similar development.

The corollary of this change in public opinion was the failure of the MWL when it made another attempt to obtain an official assessment of the policy of abolition.

An End to Polemics and a Return to Tolerance

When the five-year program came to an end, the MWL asked the police commissioners for their opinion on the success of the policy of abolition. The police chief's reply was a fine piece of casuistry: Nothing could be said on the subject of success because "no statement has ever been made as to precisely what object the council's suppressive measures were designed to accomplish." He pointed out that if it was a matter of abolishing the houses of prostitution in the legal sense of the term, then these houses had effectively ceased to exist. As for the phenomenon of prostitution, his judgment was final: "But if the aim of the council was the abolition of *prostitutes* or the suppression of *prostitution*, or the improvement of *public morality*, then, of course, the measures adopted by them [Shanghai Municipal Council] . . . have been a failure."[88] He thought it impossible to say to what extent the present state of prostitution in the settlement was the result of abolitionist policies or a development related to other factors.[89] The MWL was not satisfied with this explanation. It wanted a clear-cut response to the debate that it had initiated and that the authorities had evaded. It asked the Shanghai Municipal Council to appoint a new commission to assess the results of the five-year program for the elimination of the houses of prostitution. The MWL suggested the creation of a commission comprising the different sections of local society, including Chinese representatives.[90]

It must be acknowledged that the authorities had displayed a certain stubbornness in resisting the application of a decision that they had not approved. They clearly had no wish to be trapped now, as they had been five years earlier, by the proposals of an official inquiry commission. They also felt that it was far too early to draw conclusions and consider new policies. The Shanghai Municipal Council therefore politely suggested that the MWL set up an inquiry commission of its own, capable of working without restriction. It no longer wanted to hear of any official inquiry commission whose conclusions, to go by past experience, would purely and simply repeat the MWL's original demands.[91] No resolution was presented to the ratepayers' assembly – a sign of a weakening of the positions of the MWL and of a change in opinion in the foreign community, which noted that the abolition of the brothels had not resolved the problem of prostitution in Shanghai. After 1924, my sources no longer mention the MWL.

The failure of the abolitionist movement led the Shanghai Municipal Council to restore official recognition to prostitution in a roundabout way. Of course, the measure adopted was discriminatory. It applied only to the courtesans. But, in choosing this category alone (and thus meeting the demands of several groups within the Chinese population) and by introducing a new classification, that of the singsong girls – a designation that fooled nobody – the Shanghai Municipal Council opened a breach in the strictness of the policy of abolition while at the same time sparing itself a debate on the issue.[92] It is worth noting that the MWL did not react publicly to the Shanghai Municipal Council's decision – unless this silence pertains to the nature of the sources. Similarly, prostitution does not seem to have been the subject of any further debate in the ratepayers' general meeting in 1924 or in the years that followed.

The abolitionist policy implemented by the Shanghai Municipal Council had hardly ever had any chances of success. In itself, an undertaking of this kind had all the odds stacked against it and was bound to create numerous difficulties. In the context of Shanghai, it was a utopian project. In a city divided into three separate, if not rival, administrations, the suppression of prostitution came up against indifference and a lack of willingness to cooperate. In this respect, the attitude of the MWL appears to be have been fairly inconsistent. Logically speaking, it should have approached the French and Chinese authorities in Shanghai as well and asked them to apply a policy similar to that of the Shanghai Municipal Council. As we have seen, it seems to have done nothing of the kind in the case of the French Concession. As for the Chinese authorities, the MWL asked them to prohibit the presence of girls under fifteen in bars and generally ban the activity of the hostesses who pushed customers to consume alcohol and prostituted themselves.[93]

More than in the previously described experience of health regulation and inspection, the abolitionist movement in Shanghai reveals the gulf between the two communities, the Chinese and the foreigners, that lived together in Shanghai. Perhaps the distinctions among the foreign residents need to be further sharpened. Let us look briefly at the basic idea of an opposition between a narrow view of the problem of prostitution, based on moral and religious standards, that a militant section of the foreign community attempted to foster, and the more pragmatic view, admittedly marked by contradictions but singularly tolerant, that predominated within the Chinese population.

The Protestant activists of the MWL were imbued with sincere faith and a praiseworthy desire to change the world for the better. In Shanghai, their concerns and projects found an echo in the presence of a large Anglo-American community whose majority was responsive to a way of thinking that emphasized the defense of public morality. Furthermore, already in that period, the flow of information was sufficient to make Shanghai's foreign residents aware of similar campaigns being conducted in the United States against the same "social evils." There was therefore a fertile soil that could have permitted the emergence of an operation whose origin was purely private. The Shanghai Municipal Council was thus trapped by a discourse that it could not explicitly reject. On the contrary, it had to clearly assert its attachment to the values defended by the MWL while trying to maintain a course toward a pragmatic if hypocritical policy toward prostitution.

Despite its reluctance and shilly-shallying, the Shanghai Municipal Council was caught in the logic of the abolitionist discourse. The MWL was able to win over the greater part of foreign public opinion (which itself reflected the views of a small minority of the population) and impose a fundamental decision on the territory of the International Settlement that overwhelmingly transformed the landscape of prostitution and led to unexpected changes. The policy of abolition ended in a failure that contributed to the disappearance of the MWL from the local political scene and to a return, with the agreement of the authorities, to a state of *de facto* tolerance of prostitutional activities. It appeared to be difficult, even with greater administrative and policing means, to implement a process of eliminating the houses of prostitution when no such provisions existed in the other parts of the city, especially in the French Concession. This experience, however, underlines the formidable capacity of a small and highly militant group to impose its views in an important issue by taking advantage of a political system where power was concentrated in the hands of a minority.

The ultimate failure of the abolitionist project was above all the failure of this mode of thinking among the Chinese community. In the United States, the abolitionist campaigns had been well received because they echoed the sentiments of a population that largely shared their puritanical values and they found channels of transmission within this population. Shanghai's Chinese residents were indifferent to a debate that hardly resonated within their own culture. Even if some groups or individuals expressed opinions on the matter, there was no major degree of mobilization to support the project or to thwart it. The voices that were heard were those of the merchants, concerned with their own interests, and the philanthropists who were already committed to specific action on behalf of the disinherited, especially the female victims of kidnapping (see Chapter 7). Although the May 4, 1919 movement paved the way for a debate on the condition of the prostitutes, the Chinese press barely participated in the discussion on the appropriateness of abolition even if the magazines did publish many articles on the problem of prostitution.[94]

The abolitionist movement of 1920–1925 was an artificial experience imposed willy-nilly by a foreign administration on a Chinese society that neither understood nor accepted it. The many forms of evasion employed by the houses of prostitution points to their remarkable ability to adapt to the new conditions to which they were subjected. This adaptation was above all a response to a demand that had not varied, and it paid no heed to the discourse and the policies of policing. The daily life of the Chinese population was not altered by the attempts of the municipal authorities to inflect its direction. The force of the *habitus* and of the culture were undeniably superior to the pressures exerted, in contradictory fashion, by the artisans of the campaign to abolish a phenomenon – namely prostitution – that was profoundly rooted in Chinese social practice.

13

The Nationalists and Regulationism Chinese-Style (1927–1949)

The last two decades of the Republic were marked by a gradual return to regulationism, notwithstanding abolitionist inclinations on the part of the Nationalist regime in its early days, along with pressure in this direction from the League of Nations. At the national as well as local levels, the advent of the Guomindang heralded the establishment of modern institutions of governance seeking to transform China into a country that was powerful, rich, and respected. Shanghai thus, for the first time, was endowed in its Chinese sector with a unified municipal administration placed under the tutelage of the central authorities.[1] At the international level, the main actor was the League of Nations, which, since its inception, had inherited the concern of Western governments about the white slave trade. After paying almost exclusive attention to Europe and America, the League of Nations began, after 1929, to look more closely at the Far East.

The Sino-Japanese War and the occupation of Shanghai by the Japanese army once again altered the basic facts of the problem. The authorities of the three municipal zones (Chinese, French, and International) were placed one after the other and in varying degrees under the tutelage of the Japanese army. The Japanese military authorities had an ambivalent attitude toward prostitution that made them hesitate between elimination and regulation. However, their plans for control came up against the inefficiency and corruption of the new Chinese municipal authorities, as well as the legal limits of the Land Regulations to which the English and American members of the Shanghai Municipal Council unfailingly drew their attention. The business of prostitution declined during this period, but this development was related more to general living conditions (curfews, the internal blockade, and electricity cuts) than to official action.

It was only after the Japanese defeat that the Nationalist Government revived its links with Shanghai and its numerous problems. Prostitution, which underwent extraordinary growth, was one of the social problems to which the new authorities tried to furnish an answer. The context was radically different. The settlements had disappeared and the Chinese administration now governed the entire city. The influx of refugees caused by the Sino-Japanese War continued during the Civil War, and many women

came to swell the ranks of prostitution. From the very outset, the municipal government directed its efforts toward a policy of regulation along with
medical checks with the ultimate aim of totally eliminating prostitution
from the city. The victory of the Chinese Communist Party left it with no
time to achieve this goal, and it was the new authorities that were to inherit
the task of actually implementing this last stage.

The Nationalists and Prostitution: Phase I (1927–1937)

The policy of the Nationalist regime toward prostitution was singularly
lacking in clarity and transparency. Despite abolitionist inclinations, the
central government did not adopt the means to carry out its policy of controlling prostitution and, more generally, of suppressing all traffic related to
this activity. Even if it can be assumed that the fight against prostitution was
not a priority of the new regime, the extreme attention that it paid to the
development of modern military and police forces should nevertheless have
yielded some indirect results in this area.[2] This clearly did not happen. On
the contrary, it was not rare for policemen to protect illegal activity in
exchange for bribes. It would be quite difficult to find any trace of an active
policy against prostitution in either the central or the municipal sources
(whether archival documents or public documents) from this period.

The question of the abolition of prostitution is reported to have been
debated at the Second Congress of the Guomindang in Nanking in August
1928.[3] The press reports do not confirm this point, which is mentioned in
several sources.[4] However, it is an established fact that the Nanking municipality, the capital of the country, an ancient and famous center of prostitution – especially under the Ming Dynasty (1368–1644) – decided to set an
example and put out an order banning all the city's brothels. This policy was
part of a more general movement to prohibit and suppress activities
deemed to be "negative" (such as gambling, fortune telling by cards, etc.).
The municipal notification was dated 30 July 1928.[5] At the same time, the
national government sent a circular to the local authorities, in paticular to
the governments of the big cities, asking them to eliminate all taxes on prostitution, either encourage prostitutes to change their profession or expel
them from the brothels, and create shelters or businesses that could take in
the girls.[6] However, the timing and modalities of application were left to
the initiative of the local authorities.[7]

The Nationalist Government's policy was not publicly debated. A com-
mentator writing shortly after the decision to prohibit prostitution shed
some light on the government's motives: "They are acting on the conviction that prostitution is, to say the least, a disgrace to womanhood, a blight
on national vitality, and a thorn in the side of our ideals of equality and
justice."[8] Here indeed are the essential factors that determined the attitude
of the Guomindang. The emancipation of women was an issue widely

debated in China since the May 4, 1919 movement. Many Nationalist leaders belonged to that generation, and it is therefore not surprising that the new government took up this theme even though it actually did little about it. Prostitution was also perceived as being harmful to the nation's vitality. This was another essential theme of this period when the Nationalist Government sought to mobilize every resource to restore China's power and dignity. Prostitution was seen as a blemish that had to be erased. In addition, the abolition of prostitution was in line with the ideals of justice and equality that the leaders of the Guomindang proclaimed and to which many of them sincerely adhered.

The Chinese municipality of Shanghai followed the example of Nanking. This can be explained by the presence in Shanghai of municipal leaders who had close ties with the central government and faithfully followed the instructions sent to them. In addition, they aimed to make their sector a model area comparable or even superior to the foreign settlements, with the avowed purpose of obtaining the return of these settlements by proving that a Chinese administration was quite capable of managing a metropolis like Shanghai.[9] Prostitution was not a major issue for the authorities inasmuch as it was concentrated in the settlements. The annual police reports made no mention of prostitution except to state that its practice was prohibited in the territory of the municipality.[10] The League of Nations Commission of Inquiry into the Traffic in Women and Children in the Far East incorporated the statements of the Chinese authorities in its report.[11]

A former police officer in the French Concession, Joseph Hsieh, confirmed that there really were prostitutes in the sector under Chinese jurisdiction. There is no reason to doubt his statement. It is supported by other sources as far as foreign prostitutes are concerned. Nevertheless, I believe that this prostitution was peripheral to that of the settlements, and that it was oriented toward the settlements and quantitatively small. The police of the Chinese municipality had no reason to conceal this aspect of things in their regular reports on their operations in the illegal opium dens and gambling houses. In 1945–1948, when there were no longer any administrative barriers between the different parts of the city, prostitution continued to be concentrated in the former settlements while the outer districts, according to the police reports, were largely free of it (see Chapter 8).[12]

The Chinese municipality tried to broaden its field of action to include the foreign settlements and started negotiations, which proved to be abortive, with the French municipal council and the Shanghai Municipal Council with a view to setting up a system of medical checks for prostitutes. On 30 June 1930, the Health Bureau sent a letter to the Conseil Municipal and the Chinese Ratepayers Association in the International Settlement, suggesting that they take measures to gradually restrict prostitution and especially that they set up a system of medial checks for girls.[13] In his reply, the director of the health and assistance department in the French Concession said he agreed with his colleague's observations but all the same rather disdainfully turned down the Chinese proposal.[14]

The French doctor had decided to close the chapter of the lock hospital that had been set up between 1876 and 1900, when the French authorities had demanded greater strictness. He did so without concerning himself with the views of the interested parties or of the Chinese residents in general. During this period, neither the level of education nor the lack of a system of registration of births, marriages, and deaths hindered the performance of medical checks on prostitutes. In fact, although the times had indeed changed and although the French authorities might worry about protests on the part of Chinese public opinion, the essential reason for their reluctance lay in the fact that they did not wish to be implicated in a difficult task that concerned only the Chinese population. The other reason was that they did not wish to cooperate with the new Chinese municipal institutions and especially with the Chinese Health Bureau, which the foreigners held in low esteem.[15] The Shanghai Municipal Council, which had already had its own fingers burnt, also gave a negative reply.[16]

In the French Concession, up to 1943 when the territory was returned to the Chinese authorities, the municipal council continued to exert the same control, if slightly reinforced, relying on a police force that was not wholly above suspicion. In fact, this police force seems to have acted as it wished, provoking protests from the brothel owners, who were the victims of what they deemed to be arbitrary fines and arrests of staff. In February 1929, they organized themselves in an Association of Houses of Tolerance (*Pingkang tongshanhui*) that planned to bring together all the brothels in the concession, lay down uniform rules of presence on the public roads, and defend their interests against the police. The association also sent a letter to the Consul General to complain about racketeering by the police. This letter led the director of the General Secretariat to ask the chief of the municipal police for explanations.[17]

In this document, which was strictly reserved for internal circulation, the director very frankly spelled out the desire of the French authorities to preserve the houses of prostitution: "The regular and irregular actions of the General Secretariat and of the police should not stop them from continuing to earn a living and should not force them to go elsewhere to the detriment of the public finances. . . . At a time when we are trying to make the singsong girls [courtesans] come back to the concession, there should not be any unfortunate rumors about the activities of our departments towards the establishments of pleasure."[18] The chief of the police force was asked to prevent unqualified individuals from hindering the regular functioning of the houses.[19] The police suspected the leaders of the association of trying to derive profit through the fees collected from the houses and the prostitutes.[20] The police tended to consider this practice as a form of racketeering, although it does not seem to have been prohibited.[21]

It would appear that the association worked at least until 1932 and continued to complain to the police, especially about the mass arrests of prostitutes in the streets. According to the association, these arrests were causing economic difficulties, especially after the Sino-Japanese conflict in the winter of 1931–1932. It asked the police to respect the tacit agreement under which the association could operate without being either formally recognized or prohibited. The director of the General Secretariat as well as the chief of the municipal police received the representatives of the association, but these meetings seem to have been fruitless because of the intransigence of the police departments.[22] The sources are silent after 1932. In the following years, soliciting in public became a widespread practice and applications to open new houses became increasingly rare.[23]

In 1932, the authorities of the concession introduced a new policy designed to control the prostitutes more efficiently. In May, the French municipal council decided to establish a system of compulsory medical checks for all prostitutes. Within two years, it implemented the policy demanded by Hu Hongji, director of the Health Bureau in the municipal government of Shanghai. I have no information on the reasons for this change in orientation, which I discovered from the press.[24] The check was organized once every two weeks and entailed the collection of a tax of 1.5 yuan that was paid by the establishment.[25] Furthermore, following a proposal by the Health Bureau, the prostitutes were routinely vaccinated against cholera and smallpox.[26] The sources are far too scanty for any judgment to be made, but we may question the efficiency of this system in the 1930s.

In the International Settlement, the Shanghai Municipal Council too maintained its attitude of 1925 following the official abolition of the brothels. Only the "singsong girls" were officially recognized, although not as prostitutes.[27] The establishments managed and patronized by foreign residents enjoyed *de facto* toleration on the pretext that it was difficult to establish proof of their activity (the customers refused to testify and, in many cases, the police would not go to the spot on the grounds that they were in Chinese territory).[28] Whatever suppression of prostitution was carried out concerned soliciting in public and the opening of illegal houses of prostitution. The number of brothel owners brought before the Mixed Court for disobeying the rules dropped constantly between 1920 and 1925 when abolition was implemented. The number of irregularities detected fell from 296 to 160. In the years that followed, it continued to fall (122, 7, 64, 29) until it went through another upward curve, but in a zigzag.[29]

The Nationalists, the League of Nations, and the "Yellow Slave Trade"

The traffic in women and children for prostitution had a profoundly emotional effect on public opinion in all Western countries at the beginning of the twentieth century. The issue of the white slave trade (because this is how this traffic was designated) came to be very widely debated by the press, by public opinion, and in government circles over the years. On this subject, there is an area of myth that very considerably shrouds the underlying reality. Nevertheless, starting with the 1900s, the governments of Western countries took the question very seriously and initiated surveys to try to apprehend the reality of the phenomenon. The police reports point to a flow of women to foreign countries even though, as Alain Corbin has shown, for example, in the case of France, there was no real international "market in women" but only an outward extension of activities affected by the decline of brothels in France and more generally in Western Europe.[30] Several international congresses met to debate this question. They drafted international conventions (1904 and 1910) on the elimination of the traffic in women that were signed by many countries.[31] China did sign these agreements but took none of the steps called for.

The individual actions of the different European countries were taken up by the League of Nations. In June 1921, it held its first international conference in Geneva on the white slave trade. The conference adopted an international convention that was proposed to member countries for ratification.[32] On January 14 in the following year a consultative committee was set up to study the traffic in women and children. The task of this committee was to pinpoint trade circuits, identify individuals implicated in this traffic, and devise ways and means to put an end to it.[33] Through this committee, the League of Nations strove to encourage the countries concerned to bar the circulation of women for purposes of prostitution and especially to abolish the brothels. The activity of the League of Nations committee produced a considerable mass of documents on the practices of prostitution in various European countries and on the modes of their regulation.

Throughout the 1920s, the work of the League of Nations covered Europe and America. The League of Nations made regular checks through annual questionnaires on the development of the situation in these regions. In 1923, the survey was extended to the eastern colonies of the European countries and to certain countries in the Far East. The Chinese central authorities, who were then considerably weakened by rivalries and clashes between the warlords, nevertheless reacted positively to the requests of the League of Nations. They sent out orders to the local governments asking them to collect information on the condition of prostitution in China. The governor of Jiangsu and the *xian* magistrate of Shanghai asked the cities under their jurisdiction for detailed reports. The information collected in 1923 by the Chinese authorities was used by a group of experts of the League of Nations to prepare a report not only on China but on the entire Far East. This report was classified as "strictly confidential" and, despite its serious weaknesses and its many gaps, provides a rare view of prostitution in China.[34] During this very same period, the Chinese national assembly conducted a brief and inconclusive debate on the feasibility of abolishing prostitution.[35]

In 1929, the League of Nations decided to broaden the field of its investigations to the traffic in women in the Far East. A five-man mission therefore spent several months traveling to every major port likely to harbor traffickers.[36] In China, the commission went to Canton, Shanghai, and Tianjin at the end of the spring of 1931. It was received by the highest state officials, including Chiang Kai-shek, as well as various local administrative bodies. In Shanghai, its stay was organized by the secretary of the Shanghai Medical Association and by former members of the 1919 "Vice Committee." The commission held interviews with the political leaders of the three municipal administrations, the officials of the municipal services concerned with prostitution, and private organizations involved in providing aid to prostitutes.[37]

The preliminary report of the commission was drawn up by Carol Pindor. The document was finalized in several plenary meetings held by the commission when its delegates returned to Geneva. It was a voluminous work but still leaves the reader unsatisfied.[38] In the end, very little is learned about Shanghai itself. The commission accepted the Chinese government's statements to the effect that prostitution had disappeared from the municipality.[39] This was also the case with the settlements for which the members of the inquiry team were unable even to provide precise figures on the state of prostitution. It seems that the authorities of the French Concession refused to furnish whatever information they possessed. The members of the commission noted the absence of sustained links between the three municipal administrations of Shanghai and did not go beyond making a mild appeal for cooperation.[40] It is clear that whenever the commission looked into the basic aspects of the problem, it generally chose to uncritically adopt the official view, especially that of the Chinese authorities, even though the opinions actually expressed were probably more diversified. On a subject as important to their mission as the traffic in women and the conditions of the prostitutes, the inquiry team displayed much naiveté.[41]

Its work nevertheless demonstrated that the trade in women, as it existed in the Far East, was above all a Chinese problem.[42] The international trade in Chinese women was but a simple extension of the huge traffic that existed inside the country. The Chinese authorities, who were vigilant about their country's image abroad, ordered the Chinese delegate to the League of Nations to ask for the removal, from the final report, of maps showing China's central role in the "yellow slave trade."[43] All the same, the inquiry commission's trip to the Far East led China to try to comply with the agreements of 1904 and 1910 and the convention of 1921. In 1933, the Nationalist Government expressed its desire to comply with the conventions by designating the Ministry of Interior as the "central authority" in the matter.[44] This in no way changed the situation on the ground where control remained in the hands of the municipality.

It is through the gaps in the Chinese government's answers to the League of Nations' questionnaires that light is thrown on the reality of the situation, revealing the way in which the problem of prostitution was perceived by the Nationalists and their desire to project a positive image of the country. Their discourse was quite contradictory and hypocritical. According to the Chinese government, the instructions given in the 1928 circular had ordered a police inquiry to determine the status of the prostitutes. If they had come to the profession through poverty, they were to be helped to change their line of work; if they had been forced into it, they were to be turned over to charitable institutions. The major difficulty of rehabilitation lay in finding them jobs and housing and improving their moral and mental "standards." While acknowledging the usefulness of providing them with professional training, the Chinese authorities felt that the best solution was still marriage.[45]

The kind of work envisaged for the rehabilitation of the prostitutes was limited to embroidery, painting, cooking, and light but artistic crafts. The prostitutes were considered to be unsuited to manual work and to the kind of group discipline entailed in factory work. It was therefore not easy to find professions in which they could be happy, and some preferred to return to prostitution.[46] In the part of the questionnaire dealing with venereal disease, the Chinese government went so far as to assert that its health services were providing the population with information and urging sick persons to get treatment, that the cost of treatment was very low owing to public subsidies, and that the prostitutes, when registered, were being medically monitored and treated almost free of charge until total recovery.[47] Finally, they said that the girls were quite free to change their profession: All they had to do was to go to a police station or approach a policeman in the street, and they would be taken to a charitable organization.[48]

It is clear that many of the replies were total fabrications and had been made in bad faith. At the same time they underlined a desire (already noted) on the part of the Chinese government to be seen as a modern country on the world stage. But what is more to the point here is the picture that the authorities had of the prostitutes and, by extension, of Chinese women. The authorities did not entertain the illusion that the prostitutes might be able to turn to other activities. They probably were not wrong, but it is symptomatic of a certain mindset that they gave preference, in professional training, to typically female kinds of activity that would be more useful in a household than as a genuine way to earn a living.[49] The Chinese government did not consider prostitutes to be responsible individuals. The only way out of prostitution was through segregation, whether in a real sense (for example, by automatic placement in a charitable institution) or symbolically by marriage. A woman could not be the master of her destiny, and even less so in the case of the prostitutes who were doubly despised and remained mere objects of transaction.

In 1937, the League of Nations Committee on the Traffic in Women sent out a new questionnaire on developments in the field of prostitution since 1931.[50] The Chinese government confirmed that it had not adopted any new regulations since the visit by the inquiry commission, nor had it modified its policy. At the same time, it claimed that the strict implementation of existing policies was making the work of the traffickers more difficult. It noted an improvement in the collaboration between the Chinese police services and the other authorities (the foreign settlements) and, above all, between them and the private organizations.[51] The Chinese government refrained from informing the committee that the regulation of prostitution had been restored in the Chinese capital and dissimulated the fact that there was a very persistent traffic in women.

The report of the Far Eastern inquiry commission, which revealed the existence of real trading circuits procuring supplies for the houses of prostitution, led the League of Nations to set up a system of coordinated action among the different Asian countries. In October 1936, it convened a "conference of central authorities" that met in Bandung (Indonesia) on February 2, 1937.[52] The Chinese government sent its consular representatives in Java as well as five delegates.[53] In defense of their country's abolitionist policy, these representatives said that it was foreigners who were responsible for the international traffic in Chinese women.[54]

This meant, according to the Chinese delegation, that it was important above all to appoint a liaison officer based in Shanghai to facilitate cooperation between the different authorities.[55] The idea was taken up and recast in the more elaborate form of a liaison office aimed at coordinating action among the different Asian governments.[56] After the conference, negotiations on the creation of this Far Eastern bureau continued, but the Sino-Japanese conflict finally came in the way of the project.[57] While the Far East did have what could be called a real "yellow slave traffic," the majority of whose victims were Chinese women who were kidnapped, seduced, and sent on to destinations that they had not chosen, the Chinese government was practically never involved in the efforts of the League of Nations to put an end to it. Two types of explanation can be put forward for this attitude. First of all, the "export" of Chinese women abroad was but a small and even marginal aspect of the huge "market in women" that existed in China. Second, the Chinese authorities did not wish their country to be seen as the epicenter of the traffic in women in the Far East at a time when they wished to project the image of a country on the road to rapid modernization. The strategy they adopted therefore was one of concealment and of passing on some of the responsibility to the foreign powers.

Prostitution during the Japanese Occupation

In November 1937, after three months of hard fighting, the Chinese army was no longer capable of standing up to superior Japanese forces and had to withdraw to the interior of the country, abandoning Shanghai to the enemy troops. The districts of the former Chinese municipality were occupied and placed under the control of the Japanese army. However, the army did not wish to take direct responsibility for the management of the city, which it entrusted to a collaborationist Chinese municipal government (*Dadao zhengfu*) that controlled only a part of it.[58] In fact, the new authorities did little more than collect taxes without really ensuring law and order, especially in the so-called "extra-settlement road area."[59] It was only in October 1938 that a real municipal government was set up under the leadership of Fu Xiao'an and then, after his assassination in 1940, Chen Gongbo. The settlements, owing to their neutral status, were not occupied and formed an island of security and relative prosperity. This privileged situation came to an end with the attack on Pearl Harbor in December 1941. The two settlements came under Japanese control, both *de jure* and *de facto*. The final act was played in 1943 with the return of the settlements to the collaborationist municipal authorities under the pressure of the Japanese army.

It is extremely difficult to trace the development of prostitution during this period. The press, a major source of information on this subject devoted itself almost exclusively to political issues. At the end of 1937, certain newspapers like the *Shen Bao* left Shanghai. However, they returned in the following year, when they took up a highly militant standpoint. Severe economic difficulties considerably reduced the number of pages published, leading to the complete disappearance of the sections devoted to miscellany. Furthermore, after 1941, the entire press came under Japanese censorship. As for the archives on this particularly sensitive period of Chinese history, I have been granted only a glimpse of their contents.

Prostitution was not a source of major disquiet for the authorities during the early years of occupation. The wartime conditions, which led to the departure of a section of the upper strata, caused a certain slump in this activity, in the same way as at the end of the 1860s. Major changes took place in the former Chinese municipality where there was no longer any genuine authority. The puppet government was unable to get hold of the records of the municipal government, which were being held for safekeeping by the French Concession. It was therefore no longer able to raise taxes. Hence, pending a reconstruction of the tax system, it showed leniency toward "vice"-related traffic. Thus, numerous illegal establishments (gambling houses, houses of prostitution, and opium dens) sprang up again in the Walled City and (this was a new phenomenon) in the Western districts of Shanghai, namely, the "extra-settlement road" area.[60]

The transformation of the outlying and hitherto exclusively residential districts of this area was related to the fact that policing authority, under Chinese pressure and with the support of the Japanese military forces, had been partially transferred to the Chinese collaborationist authorities.[61] "Huxi" (western Shanghai) very soon became a synonym for gambling, prostitution, and opium. A large number of establishments were set up in this area with the complicity of the Chinese authorities who derived financial benefit therefrom. The Shanghai Municipal Council, which in theory was jointly responsible for law and order in Huxi, protested but remained impotent.[62] This area became part of what came to be known in common parlance as the "badlands"; and it was only in 1941, when the Japanese authority decided to restrict these activities throughout the city, that the Chinese authorities began to close down a proportion of the establishments in this sector.[63]

In that part of the International Settlement (Honkou and Yangshupu) that was under their control and beyond the authority of the Shanghai Municipal Council, the Japanese were lax or else encouraged private initiative seeking to compensate for the inefficiency of the municipal administration. In 1941, an organization known as the "Ping Hong Welfare Association," with its offices at 679 Jukong Road outside the settlement, proposed to register all the houses of prostitution to the north of the River Suzhou – that is, in Zhabei and Hongkou, where there was a concentration especially of establishments patronized by foreigners (sailors, soldiers, etc.).[64] The Association, which claimed to act with the support of the Japanese naval authorities, published a press notification on September 15, announcing the beginning of a registration procedure. In fact, it later transpired that the Japanese navy had no official links with the Association but that it was in favor of a system of surveillance of the prostitutes.[65] Given the degree of control exerted by the Japanese military authorities in these districts, it is difficult to believe that they did not tacitly approve the action of the Association and were not repeating what they had done in 1932 when they tried to obtain the creation of a settlement in Zhabei with the support of "spontaneous" local organizations.[66]

The Shanghai Municipal Council was powerless against the Japanese military authorities. It sent a courteous letter to the naval headquarters indicating its interest in this private initiative to control prostitution but recalling that a project of this kind would require a fairly large and above all honest group of inspectors if the door was not to be opened to corruption and racketeering.[67] In fact, the Ping Hong Welfare Association came to nothing. It did not live up to the expectations of the Japanese army, which was worried primarily about the effects of prostitution-related venereal disease. Thus, encouraged by the Japanese army, a Shanghai Prevention Committee (*Shanghai fangyi weiyuanhui*) was formed and immediately started looking into the problems related to prostitution.

The committee adopted an extremely stern resolution asking for the elimination of prostitution to the greatest extent possible, by the use of force if necessary. The brothel owners were to be summoned and urged to change their business.[68]

The committee considered instituting a system for the regulation of prostitution with the establishments being brought together in a single district, the setting up of medical surveillance, and the suppression of "undeclared" prostitution. A propaganda campaign was launched to warn the population of the risks of venereal diseases and promote the rectification of sexual morality. The document that I have consulted (dated December 1941) cannot be used to date the foundation of the committee. The fact that the committee asked the representative of the Chinese municipality to report on his work suggests that it had been in existence for a while. According to the Chinese delegate, the police undertook to register the houses (twenty-two on the day of the meeting), established a system of medical checks, and set up a center to receive prostitutes in Hongkou. This was deemed to be still quite insufficient by the Vice President, who admonished the Chinese municipality and asked it to put an end to prostitution.[69]

Having failed to eliminate prostitution, as required by the project, the Japanese turned to a system of strict controls, which, however, was worn down by the resistance of the Anglo-American members of the Shanghai Municipal Council and by the inefficiency and corruption of the Chinese municipal administration. Venereal disease – a common preoccupation for armies – was again the cause of this new attempt at regulation as can be seen from a long letter by the Chief of Police of the International Settlement, Mr. Tabata, who recalled precedents in this respect (the 1914–1918 War and the case of foreign soldiers in Shanghai in 1927). Mr. Tabata called for the setting up of a special district (whose boundaries he demarcated), the registration of all prostitutes, and the carrying out of medical checks on them.[70] The regulations that he envisaged covered every category of female employment that he included under prostitution: singsong girls, dance hostesses, masseuses, waitresses, and other similar professions (storytellers, bathhouse attendants, etc.).[71]

The health department, which was dominated by the British, put forward legal and medical arguments against the Japanese project. Medical checks were seen to be useful only if they were extremely strict, but this entailed a very high cost that would have to be passed on to the establishments of prostitution because the administration could not bear expenditure on such a scale. If the cost was indeed passed on in this way, the houses of prostitution would react by going into a state of illegality. This would mean a total failure of the plan for surveillance. It was therefore necessary to be resigned to the situation or, in the euphemistic words of the health department: "We might have to be satisfied with a certain amount of limited control in practice." From a moral viewpoint, the secretariat felt that registration, spatial segregation, and the prohibition of soliciting would be quite sufficient. Furthermore, the municipal lawyer, R. J. Bryan, consulted on the legality of the regulation, confirmed that Article 34 of the Land Regulations did not allow dancers, waitresses, singsong girls, and so on, to be subjected to a licensing procedure. Only establishments could be licensed and not individuals.[72]

The resistance of the Anglo-American members of the Shanghai Municipal Council did not discourage Umemoto, the new chief of police, who proposed an immediate measure by which the association mentioned above would be able to control the houses of prostitution under police supervision to the north of the Suzhou River while control over the area to the south of the river would be postponed to a later date, as and when circumstances allowed it. The Japanese were primarily concerned by the northern area in which their civilian and military community was concentrated. The Anglo-Americans showed the same reluctance toward the idea of indirect control and said that they preferred surveillance by the police and the health services. However, they were not hostile to the creation of a spontaneous association of brothel owners with a view to self-regulation. On the question of spatial segregation, they pointed out that the land acquisition powers of the Shanghai Municipal Council were limited to the field of sanitation and that the proprietors and residents might oppose such a step.[73]

The Anglo-American members of the Shanghai Municipal Council had clearly not changed their point of view since 1920. Thomas Beesly, deputy secretary of the Shanghai Municipal Council, wrote a letter to Umemoto confirming the refusal of the authorities to set up a red-light district.[74] The Anglo-Americans continued to prefer a general regulation of the brothels by the police without any spatial segregation, accompanied by a system of medical surveillance. This was the thrust of the regulation finally adopted in October 1942. The new system of surveillance, which appeared to be very severe, obliged all houses of prostitution to register with the police. This was a direct acknowledgment of the fact that the previous measures, exhortations, and modes of indirect control had barely had any effect or had remained a dead letter. What was new was the set of measures designed to restrict the spread of venereal disease. Apart from imposing a compulsory weekly check on the prostitutes, the plan laid down that the establishment had to bear the cost of medical care and made it compulsory for customers to leave a record of their personal details (name, address, and resident's card number) to ensure medical follow-up in the event of any illness that they might contract or transmit.[75] In the context of Shanghai, we may doubt that these provisions were really applied.

The measures adopted by the authorities were hardly efficient if we go by the police statistics. Barely a few thousand girls were registered. Their real numbers, despite the crisis that Shanghai was going through, could not have been as small. Prostitution therefore continued to be practiced essentially in illegal establishments. In March 1943, the police departments again approached the secretariat of the Shanghai Municipal Council to get all the known illegal houses shifted to a single district, which would be placed under the responsibility of a private undertaking. The project this time was of a different type. It was proposed by a Chinese resident covering for two Japanese residents. He proposed to use two pieces of land located to the north of Hongkou and to the west of Yangshupu and turn them into a prostitution and shopping center. His plan was to set up several two-story buildings equipped with a medical center, sick rooms, baths, entertainment halls, restaurants, various shops, and even firefighting and anti-air-raid equipment.[76]

The scale of the investment envisaged shows how profitable prostitution was as an economic activity. It is worth noting that the author of the project intended to give prostitution the form of a modern diversified enterprise with managers, employees, and a rational organization. It would have been a sort of sex mart before its time. The project was symptomatic of the growing commercialization of prostitution in Shanghai. It was examined by the police and health departments as well as by the secretariat. The secretariat did not seem to have been hostile to the idea, whereas the health officer, who was Japanese, asked for a delay pending additional information and further reflection.[77] No other steps were taken until the liberation of Shanghai in August 1945.[78]

The Nationalists and Prostitution: Phase II (1945–1949)

No sooner had they returned to Shanghai than the Chinese authorities got down to the task of restoring law and order, which had been greatly compromised by the activities of the Japanese and the corruption of collaborationist municipal governments. This task was all the more urgent because natural calamities and especially clashes between the Nationalist army and the Communist troops brought successive waves of thousands of refugees into Shanghai, most of them completely destitute. They swelled the ranks of the wretched and were housed at best in the slums that sprang up throughout the city. Many of them lived a hand-to-mouth existence through petty manual jobs or simply by begging. As for the women, both married and single, their wretched lot often meant entry into prostitution.

Among the authorities, there was a feeling of urgency prompted by an increase in deviant behavior in every field, from which those in authority were far from immune. Life in Shanghai was particularly difficult at this time. Economic activity resumed slowly, most of the factories were still closed, and inflation continued to rise. The different official institutions were vying with one another to take over Japanese property, and corruption was rife in the economic and social spheres. At the same time, there was also an atmosphere of liberation after the weight of years of occupation, with the return of a large and generally well-to-do section of the population, which had followed the Nationalist Government into internal exile. This group brought in fortunes amassed during the war or gained through the victory. Large quantities of money circulated in Shanghai. They formed a contrast with the extreme poverty of a portion of the population. In this context of instability, prostitution underwent a genuine explosion, which aroused concern among the authorities.

As soon as it had settled down, the Police Bureau (*jingchaju*) made efforts to bring in a provisional regulation (*Shanghai shi jingchaju guanli changji zanxing banfa*) that, at least by intent, went beyond a mere administrative control of prostitution. The regulation naturally stipulated the compulsory registration of houses and girls, specifying that it was formally forbidden for an establishment to house a girl who had come to prostitution by force, by deceit, as the result of a sale, or if she was sick. Gambling was prohibited, and so was noisy behavior. Prostitution had to be practiced exclusively in the establishment. The prostitutes were not allowed to accompany a customer to a hotel. Finally the regulation instituted a mode of sharing, even if it was illusory, based on the services and amenities provided by the house.[79]

The Police Bureau also proposed a plan for the "reorganization" (*zhengli*) of prostitution. Its main principles were laid down in the regulations subsequently adopted by the municipal government. The first principle was that of the conversion of undeclared prostitutes into public prostitutes (*hua si wei gong*), namely, the authorization of prostitution, which went together with a registration and census-taking procedure designed to pave the way for a gradual reduction in the number of prostitutes. The second principle was that of the administrative simplification of the dozen or so terms covering the operation of various types of establishments that were not really different from one another in any way (*hua fan wei jian*). The number of categories was now reduced to three, all of which were called "houses of prostitution" (*jiyuan*). The last principle was that of concentrating the houses in a single place (*hua ling wei zheng*) far from the main city area and prohibiting the practice of soliciting.[80]

Pending an official decision, the police managed the situation on a day-to-day basis, without any law to which they could refer, working according to the rules and regulations drawn up by the collaborationist government.[81] The varied and multitudinous nature of prostitution nevertheless was a source of disquiet that pushed the police to try to establish regulations in all directions. In particular, the police proposed a set of regulations to control the singsong girls, dance hostesses, and waitresses, who were all suspected of indulging in prostitution. The mayor gave his approval but nevertheless asked that separate regulations be drawn up for each category.[82] The Police Bureau also demanded the elimination of establishments – such as the massage parlors and the guide agencies (*xiangdaoshe*) – that practiced prostitution under cover of respectable activities, and they demanded that these establishments be converted into aboveboard establishments.[83]

In January 1946, the municipal government approved the draft regulations on prostitution presented by the Police Bureau.[84] Following this decision, which was confirmed a little later by the Municipal Council, the chief of police, Xuan Tiewu, asked that all qualified persons and organizations be convened to reflect on means to eliminate prostitution and draw up a timetable.[85] The mayor therefore laid down two principles of action for the offices concerned – the regulation of prostitution (*hua si wei gong*) for the police and the establishment of a mobile medical team for the Health Bureau (see below) – and asked them to draw up regulations.[86]

After a relatively long period, namely five months, two sets of regulations were finally promulgated on December 11, 1946. The first document (*Shanghai shi jingchaju zhengli changji shishi banfa*) defined the principles and steps for the control of prostitution. It took up the clauses set forth in the reorganization plan presented in autumn 1945 by the Police Bureau (see above). The second document consisted of the regulations themselves (*Shanghai shi jingchaju zhengli changji shishi banfa*). It must be noted at the outset that the title of the document indicates the intentions of the authorities. What they wanted above all was a method (*banfa*) and not a set of regulations (*guize, guizhang, tiaoli*) in the strict sense of the word, the goal of which was to manage (*guanli*) prostitution. The document (Article 2) defined a prostitute as a woman whose (professional) business was to carry out a trade in sex (*mai yin wei ye zhi funü*). The novel features of the law lay in the clauses protecting the girls – for example, rules prohibiting ill treatment and making it illegal to force a girl to have sexual relations if she was more than four months pregnant or had given birth less than three months earlier or was suffering from venereal disease. The protection of the health of the prostitutes had to be guaranteed by the compulsory use of articles of personal hygiene and of condoms by the customers.[87]

The new regulations laid down by the municipality represented a form of progress inasmuch as they sought to establish certain minimum rules for the protection of the prostitutes. Nevertheless, as in the previous documents, they stressed above all the administrative control of prostitutes and of the houses of prostitution, the maintenance of law and order, and the preservation of public health. The fate of the girls was not a central preoccupation of the rules, which defined no criteria (even if their application had been difficult or even illusory) of working conditions, housing, medical care, the drawing up of contracts, payment, and so on. These points, however, had been considered in the initial drafts of 1945 (see above). This document was supplemented by a text common to the police and health services (*Shanghai shi jingchaju weishengju changji jianyan hezuo banfa*) instituting a system of medical checks.[88]

The houses of prostitution and their residents were required to declare themselves to the authorities before June 30, 1947. This date was subsequently postponed to December 31.[89] The registration of the prostitutes and of the houses continued in fits and starts as can be seen from the official statistics. By the end of 1946, before the implementation of the new regulations, the number of girls registered was 8,000. After the new regulations, whose ultimate purpose was to reduce the number of prostitutes, it seems that the girls became alarmed as they had done in 1920. They preferred to get themselves taken off the registers under various pretexts (illness, return to the village, etc.) and practice their trade clandestinely. In December 1947, there were no more than 3,000 girls registered. The police reacted by making numerous mass arrests, which raised the number of registered persons to 10,000 in June 1948.[90] The mayor allowed a new extension of the deadline for registration to December 31, 1948.[91]

The chief of police, Xuan Tiewu, became impatient with the successive postponements of the final date, which went against the policy of "officializing" prostitution (*hua si wei gong*). The spread of prostitution in the city was such that it was no longer possible to count on police repression alone to eliminate it. He recommended going on to the next step, namely, that of spatial segregation (*hua ling wei zhen*) according to the class of establishment. Brothels of the first category were to be concentrated in a few streets and lanes where they had been set up since the beginning of the century. As for the second- and third-category establishments, which were far too numerous to be grouped in the same area, Xuan Tiewu proposed to suspend the issue of new licenses and asked existing establishments to close down upon the expiry of their current licenses.[92] He was counting on a sort of spontaneous elimination of licensed establishments without raising the question of illegal houses, which already represented three-quarters of the activity of prostitution in this period.

At the end of 1948, Xuan Tiewu's successor, Yu Shuping, noted that his departments were incapable of coping with the expansion and constant turnover of prostitution in the city. He therefore asked the mayor yet again to postpone the deadline to December 31, 1949 so that the work of registration could be continued. Unlike his predecessor, Yu no longer aimed to stem the flow and gradually reduce it. He planned to register both those who had escaped police vigilance and those who spontaneously requested registration.[93] Clearly, the Shanghai police, which were already under great pressure to carry out a host of tasks (dealing with petty delinquency and criminality, taking a census of the population, managing social conflicts, fighting against the Communist Party, etc.), was powerless in the face of a phenomenon as widespread as prostitution. This was especially true because, as we shall see, they devoted only a small portion of their time to this problem and came up against the resistance not only of the girls but also of the customers.

The effectiveness of the system for the control of prostitution depended primarily on the efficient organization of the police services. Now it would seem that the definition of a clear division of work and the dissemination of information did not keep pace with reform. In May 1946, the Jing'ansi police station was still asking headquarters for the name of the section in charge of prostitution.[94] The Police Bureau established a "morality section" (*zhengsuke*) responsible for generally keeping track of the policy of regulation. However, effective control fell to the district police stations, which sent policemen out from time to time to ascertain that the regulations were being properly applied.[95] The policemen visited fifteen to twenty-five establishments one after the other, spending five to ten minutes in each establishment, which meant that all they could do was to carry out simple checks of licenses. Even in the famous Taotao establishment, which housed more than a hundred prostitutes, the policemen did not stay more than ten minutes.[96]

The work of the police came up against both the multiform nature of prostitution and the resistance of the girls and their customers. Ever since the 1920s, the hotels had become the favorite places of prostitution despite prohibition by the authorities. The police regularly inspected the hotels, but their inspections did not reveal anything unusual.[97] Cases of procuring in hotels were sometimes brought to their notice through denunciatory letters.[98] Certain establishments appear very frequently in the police reports and in requests for investigation by the chief of police – for example, the *Shenzhou lüguan* ("China Hotel").[99] The most efficient method therefore was that of police raids, but such raids aroused protests on the part of other customers who would be disturbed by the noise, not to mention those who questioned the right of policemen to break into their rooms. The press frequently reported cases of indignation, and the municipal councilors themselves criticized such methods and asked for a greater respect for the freedom of individuals (*renmin ziyou*).[100]

Resistance on the part of the customers could take an even more violent turn. Two policemen on an inspection round, who had arrested two undeclared prostitutes in the act of soliciting in public and were taking them to the police station, were immediately surrounded by about a hundred Chinese soldiers who jostled and threatened them. The policemen had to blow their whistles a few times to bring colleagues, along with American military policemen, to their rescue. The two girls took advantage of the brawl to escape by car in the company of a soldier.[101] The policemen were sometimes heavy-handed as in the case of two trainees who, instigated by their colleagues, shaved the heads of two prostitutes caught red-handed in the act of soliciting. This scene provoked strong disapproval on the part of the inhabitants of the district.[102] These two incidents point to a current of sympathy among the inhabitants toward the prostitutes as individuals (which did not belie a condemnation of the phenomenon or of the nuisance that it caused) and also reveal a certain hostility toward the police.

The policy of regulation and of reducing prostitution envisaged by the Police Bureau gave rise to an attempt on the part of the brothel owners to organize themselves. This to some extent recalls the attempts made by a similar group in the French Concession in 1929 or under the Japanese during the war. On November 14, 1945, a group of brothel owners met to organize a preparatory committee for an "association of prostitutes of the municipality of Shanghai" (*Shanghai shi huanü lianyihui choubei weiyuanhui*). In fact, it was a genuine professional association (*Huanü yule tongye gonghui*) that the organizers were planning in the documents that they sent to the Bureau of Social Affairs in December asking for official recognition. They specified that the association had existed before 1945 and that it had revived itself on the occasion of a questionnaire distributed by the Laozha district police station.[103]

The arrival of this letter clearly embarrassed the Bureau of Social Affairs, which replied in March that the prevailing regulations would not permit the existence of the proposed association.[104] The organizers, however, were received by a departmental head in the bureau who forwarded the request to the police for their opinion. In June, while still waiting for an official answer, the association again approached the authorities, reiterating its desire to eliminate bad elements (*buliang fenzi*) from the milieu and help the police achieve greater efficiency in their control over the houses of prostitution. The police evaded the issue by replying that the matter did not come under their jurisdiction, while the Bureau of Social Affairs felt there was a risk that the establishment of such an association might strengthen the legal position of the houses and form an obstacle to the official policy of reducing prostitution.[105] On October 1, 1946, the police decided to invite the representatives of the different institutions mentioned in the letter of the Bureau of Social Affairs so that a common position could be adopted. The various institutions were united against the association, which does not seem to have continued with its projects.[106] As in the previous case of the French Concession, this was an initiative designed actually to enable a few individuals to establish a sort of monopoly of control over prostitution. It did not correspond to any genuine mobilization of the brothel owners, who constituted a socially and geographically fragmented milieu whose ranks were in a state of constant renewal.

The decision to regulate prostitution by keeping only three categories, all with the same designation (*jiyuan*), also led to a movement of protest on the part of the courtesans (*shuyu*) who, as in 1920, asserted that they were not prostitutes and that they were selling only their art. They came together in a Federation of *Shuyu* (*Shuyu lianyihui*), which wrote to the mayor and asked him for a dispensation from registration and health checks. They proposed the establishment of a special license along with a rule that would provide for the prohibition of prostitution and for the severe punishment of offenders.[107] The new chief of police, Yu Shuping, recalled that the term *shuyu* (singsong girl) had been restored in an artificial manner by the authorities of the settlements (see Chapter 12), but that this had not changed anything in reality. Under the new classification, the *shuyu* houses had become first-category establishments. However, they were really houses of prostitution that had to submit to the same regulations as the others.[108]

The police planned to begin reducing the number of prostitutes as soon as they had completed the process of registration. Unlike in the previous experience, the authorities were conscious of the need to plan for institutions to receive and rehabilitate prostitutes. According to an undated document (from 1946), the Bureau of Social Affairs planned to create an aid association (*jiujihui*) or a shelter for women (*funü jiaoyangsuo*). At the same time, it rejected a proposal of cooperation by a private association.[109] In June 1947, the situation was therefore at the same point while the police began to round up girls whose houses were closing down. The municipal council had planned to convert the premises of the winter shelters (*bihansuo*) normally used for the homeless, but there was only one such shelter available in Taixing Road, and its capacity was limited.[110] Ultimately, this site proved to be quite unsuitable. In September, when a first group of eighty undeclared prostitutes who had been arrested were brought there, the police complained about the smallness of the premises. Those in charge of the center refused to take more of them, especially because the presence of these women brought them a great deal of trouble. Their job was to receive women without means or families who had not given themselves up to prostitution – or who had deliberately given up this activity. This was not the case of the girls dispatched to them by the police. These were girls who either escaped while on their way to the shelter or immediately began discussing ways of escaping with their neighbors. What was even more serious was that groups of accomplices and friends, both ruffians and soldiers, would break into the center to free these girls.[111]

The Police Bureau thus practiced a policy of locking up prostitutes. Of course its resources were limited and the arrests covered only undeclared prostitutes. However, it is clear that the purpose of the project was to lock up all the prostitutes until they were reformed or, better still, married. This is a constant feature in the attitude of the Chinese authorities toward single women: A woman was not deemed to have the status of an individual responsible for her actions and her life. In the case of prostitutes, it is possible in part to understand the concern of authorities who felt that if they were not confined in some measure, the girls would return to street-walking because they had no other way of earning a living or because they would be forced to it by their madams. Nevertheless, this is not the only explanation. The establishment, traditionally dominated by men in China, could not conceive of the idea of women existing alone, without any ties. A woman had to have a point of anchorage – that is, a father, a husband, a family, or even a brothel. For want of resources, the Shanghai police were unable to resolve the dilemma of how to shelter the prostitutes. In November 1946, the health and police bureaus proposed that the mayor should create a reception center with two thousand places, where the girls could be interned for one to two years depending on their conduct.[112] Lack of money prevented this project from being carried out.

The attitude of the Chinese authorities toward prostitution in the twentieth century can be distinguished from that of the bureaucrats of the Empire before 1911. However, the break was not a clear-cut one. While the language used was radically different, the action that flowed therefrom was far more ambivalent. When they took power in 1927, the Nationalists believed themselves to be invested with a mission to redeem the Chinese nation. They wished to eliminate the ills that had weakened it and perverted its nature. Prostitution was undoubtedly not at the forefront of their concerns. However, it was in the name of modernity that the new authorities dealt with this problem. The health dimension of prostitution was undoubtedly present – it is regularly mentioned – but it was not the mainspring of Nationalist policy. China was "the sick man of Asia," but it was its soul rather than its body that was stricken. From this viewpoint, prostitution was seen as a blot on the dignity of China. It distorted the image of a country that wished to regain its place in the comity of nations and be seen as a modern and substantial power. The Nationalists did not seriously get down to the task of eliminating or even reducing prostitution. They chose the more convenient path of dissimulation for external consumption while at the same time catering to internal consumption with timorous directives that they did not specifically follow up.

In the continuum of abolition and regulation by the Nationalists, the Japanese occupation was but an interruption of no real significance. The Japanese army did not follow the same logic as the preceding foreign administrations or the Chinese authorities. Although the same ingredients were to be found, the Japanese policy toward prostitution was quite simply an import. In Shanghai, the Japanese sought to implement administrative and health controls to which Japanese prostitutes had been subjected for decades.[113] This episode sheds light on certain constant features such as the refusal on the part of the Anglo-American members of the Shanghai Municipal Council to set up restrictive systems of surveillance that would infringe on individual freedom. Similarly, the efforts made to set up forms of control came up against the incapacity and disorganization of the puppet municipal authorities and their urgent need for resources. The Japanese army therefore could not count on any reliable channels to implement its policies. This is probably the reason for its interest in proposals from private individuals and associations.

The return of the Nationalists to power in Shanghai in 1945 opened new prospects. The municipal government administered the entire city, which became a major center of the political and economic power of the Guomindang. The postwar context was radically different from that of the Nanking Decade (1927–1937): It was a time of unprecedented economic crisis, inflation, and civil war. Shanghai society was profoundly affected by the upheavals of the regime and by the deterioration of the economic situation. The influxes of population from the countryside and from the surrounding cities pushed thousands of women into conditions of precariousness and extreme poverty. Prostitution underwent exponential growth and escaped the means of control available to the authorities. The authorities nevertheless adopted a voluntarist and rational approach. They sought to register the prostitutes, bring them together, and treat them before reducing their numbers.

This constituted a challenge in the social climate of this period, especially because the municipal administration did not have the resources – whether human or financial – that corresponded to its goals. The task was disproportionate and could not be dealt with by mere administrative means. The reduction of the phenomenon of prostitution in Shanghai required efforts in two directions: a return to peace and economic stability and a tremendous task of education. Without these two conditions, which were definitely beyond the scope of the municipal government, administrative pressure would be but a meager palliative without any real effect. The Chinese authorities, however, were trapped in an illusory regulationist logic, at the very time when countries most fiercely attached to this system, like France, were deciding to abandon it. The Communist authorities that came to power in 1949 did not go in for such an undertaking. They waited for the return to stability to bring about a spontaneous elimination of prostitution before vigorously tackling its vestiges.[114]

14
Institutions for the Rescue of the Prostitutes (1880–1949)

Providing assistance to prostitutes in order to bring them "out of hell" (*tiaochu huokang*) was never a major concern of the administration and the abolitionist associations in their struggle to curb this activity in Shanghai. The municipal authorities in every period preferred rather to manage prostitution. Even when they embarked on a policy of elimination, their efforts to rehabilitate the prostitutes or, even more simply, to protect them never went beyond the stage of pious intentions. As for the abolitionist associations, the rescue of "fallen women" was secondary to their agenda, whose main purpose was to do away with the breeding ground of vice that was the brothel and thus, as they saw it, prevent the entry of new victims into the sex market. In general, the "rescue" (*jiuji*) of prostitutes, a theme that dominated all thinking on prostitution in the magazines, especially the women's magazines, remained an abstraction. Nowhere in China, not even in Shanghai (where many feminine and even feminist organizations came into existence), was there any vigorous and sustained movement to help prostitutes who wished to escape their fate.

The nineteenth-century sources are hardly eloquent on the ways by which women could leave the world of prostitution. The method most frequently mentioned is that of "redemption" (*congliang*) – that is, marriage with a customer (see Chapters 2 and 5). The silence of the sources is ultimately a faithful reflection of a lack of action. In Shanghai, there was no organization concerned exclusively with the fate of the prostitutes, although the city did have several charitable institutions. Public opinion – that is, the thin segment of local society that dominated political and economic life – did not attach any particular importance to this matter. The elites patronized the high-class houses and painted a particularly idealized picture of this milieu. They did not visit the common establishments that housed low-level prostitution, where the condition of the women was less enviable than that of the courtesan. In either case, this was prostitution in an enclosed environment. It hardly ever spilled over into the street.

In the nineteenth century, the only charitable institutions in existence were general-purpose ones. China has a long tradition of assistance to the underprivileged sections of society. It was one of the expressions, in the life of society, of the Confucian values from which the Chinese elites drew inspiration.[1] The charitable associations had been created by scholars and then increasingly by merchants. The latter came together in organizations based primarily on regional solidarity, guilds (*huiguan, gongsuo*), and native-place associations (*tongxianghui*) that played a crucial role in maintaining local identities in the Chinese cities. Coming from more or less distant regions, isolated within a community of "strangers" (namely, the city in which they resided for their work), these "internal immigrants" found a home and a place of fellowship in their respective guilds (even if it was sometimes a very exclusive place) where they could meet, get their bearings, and be of some consequence as a group. These organizations also furnished a large number of individual services (providing assistance to the destitute, returning coffins to native places, etc.) as well as services for the group (making tax claims, obtaining official recognition, etc.). At the same time, they assumed responsibility for an increasing share of urban services.[2]

In Shanghai, there were thus several institutions, some of them very old, that devoted themselves to the most destitute sections and more generally to rescuing human lives. One of the best-known associations was the orphanage (*yuyingtang*) founded in 1710, which received abandoned babies. These associations do not really concern us here.[3] In the middle of the century, there were also two benevolent institutions in the Walled City, one to the south and the other to the north. Both had the same purpose: assisting aged persons, procuring coffins and places in cemeteries for destitutes, providing clothing and firewood in winter, and so on.[4] These two institutions may have taken in ex-prostitutes reduced to poverty by the fading of their beauty. However, this was only a very marginal aspect of their activity. None of my sources mention any other institutions that might have helped prostitutes, even on an exceptional basis.

It was only after 1900 that two organizations appeared one after the other. Their inspiration and mode of action were very different. They devoted their efforts to combating the traffic in women and rescuing prostitutes. The Door of Hope (*Jiliangsuo*) founded by Protestant missionaries took in both prostitutes who had escaped from brothels and minors discovered by the police. The goal of the Shanghai Anti-Kidnapping Society (*Zhonggui furu jiuji zonghui*), which was created by a group of well-known philanthropist merchants from the powerful Shaoxing–Ningbo community, was one of prevention. Its workers sought to detect women and children in transit areas such as docks and stations who might be victims of such traffic. The combined action of these two associations was unable to prevent or even limit the huge trade in women linked to prostitution. However, it helped release thousands of individuals from an unenviable fate and helped some of them to return to their families. It must be added at the very outset that these two associations formed part of a system that, regardless of its founders' wholly generous motives, did help support the system of the segregation of Chinese women.

Rescuing Bodies and Souls: The Door of Hope

In 1900, while traveling, as was her habit, in a rickshaw to the institution where she taught English, a young American missionary witnessed a scene that was to transform her life. On the pavement, a very young girl was trying to escape from a woman of ripe years who was dragging her along by the hair. The loud cries that came from the young girl (who was a bondservant or *beinü*) did not appear to move the surrounding crowd. This scene made the missionary – Cornelia Bonnel – decide to do whatever was in her power to save these wretched victims.[5] Her vocation led her to join five other missionaries with whom she founded a refuge for bondservants and formed a fund-raising committee for helping prostitutes.[6] With the little money that she had, a few donations, and tremendous determination, Cornelia Bonnel converted a house lent to her free of charge by a Chinese pastor into a refuge for prostitutes.[7] In 1902, the committee joined the National Florence Crittenton Association for Rescue Work and took the name of the Shanghai Florence Crittenton Home.[8] The name "Door of Hope" already used before 1905 became official only after the group separated from the Florence Crittenton Association in 1906.[9]

The house containing the refuge was located in the northeast of Shanghai, in a lane off Seward Road, a district well away from the traditional areas of prostitution. The nearest area of prostitution was Hongkou, which was patronized mainly by foreign sailors. The missionaries' good intentions were hardly rewarded in the earliest years. Few girls came spontaneously to the refuge. In 1902, an agreement with the Mixed Court and the circuit intendant (*daotai*) of Shanghai allowed the committee to receive girls brought before the courts. However, their numbers remained modest. The work of the committee was still poorly known, especially by prostitutes. However, it aroused the interest of a group of members of the Chinese gentry (not identified by name in any of my sources) with whom negotiations began in 1904 to find premises near the areas of prostitution in order to help prostitutes escape.[10] In the following year, these members of the gentry decided to rent out a room at 181 Fuzhou Road, an active district par excellence, in order to create what was known as a receiving home for prostitutes.[11] A huge electrical signboard announced *Yesu Neng Jiuren* (Jesus Saves) while a flag that pushed well into the street gave the Chinese name of the institution (*jiliangsuo*).

The Door of Hope fell victim to its own success. It soon became impossible to keep all the prostitutes who came to the receiving home. The premises were too small and the environment was hardly favorable to the reeducation of young girls. The refuge on Seward Road was not enough.

The missionaries who were in charge of it wished to separate girls who had been "saved in time" from those who "had been less fortunate." They emphasized the difficulties faced by the Door of Hope with some of the inmates. In 1904, the purchase of a neighboring house (Seward Road) brought together the youngest of the girls and made for a greater measure of discipline.[12] But these new premises were soon saturated. In 1908, more spacious premises were rented in Zhejiang Road.[13] These premises contained both (a) the "first-year home" where those who were assured of remaining were placed for at least one year and (b) the "industrial home," which received inmates who did not leave at the end of the first year. The "industrial home," provided a place of work and a job by which long-term inmates could earn some money while reducing the financial burden on the Door of Hope.[14] The acute problem of premises was only resolved in 1913 with the construction of a new, very spacious building on land acquired in Jiangwan for the children's refuge (see below).[15]

In 1909, the group of gentry who had financed the receiving center withdrew. They stopped providing financial assistance. The reports give no information on the reasons for this suspension.[16] In fact, there was disagreement about the missionaries' evangelical activities and the decision of the Door of Hope to get its inmates married, as far as possible, to Christians.[17] The receiving home opened in 1913 in a bylane off Nanking Road. The premises on Fuzhou Road, along with other dwellings, had been destroyed by the Shanghai Municipal Council so that a market could be set up.[18] Although Nanking Road was a place of active prostitution, the missionaries were not satisfied with the new layout, which was not sufficiently visible. In 1919, they were able to acquire new premises on Fuzhou Road, where the receiving home remained until its closure under Japanese occupation.[19]

The Door of Hope frequently faced major crises resulting from the armed conflicts that affected Shanghai and the surrounding region. In 1924, fighting between warlords for the control of the metropolis forced the missionaries to gather all their inmates together in the children's refuge on Brenan Road.[20] The Northern Expedition in 1927 had the same effect.[21] The change of residence entailed a whole convoy of carriages and carts conveying girls, children, and equipment. In 1932, heavy fighting caused by the Japanese attack prompted similar safety measures. Each time they moved, they would later have to make the same journey in reverse. By chance, the Jiangwan premises, which lay in one of the main battle zones, was spared. During the second Japanese aggression in August 1937, the Door of Hope was forced to abandon its premises permanently because they had been completely burned down, and it had to distribute its inmates between two sites in the two settlements.[22] The missionaries continued their work until 1941, when some of them were interned in Japanese camps. The others left Shanghai. The Chinese staff continued their work for a while, but the collapse of the finances of the Door of Hope led to its closure during the war.[23]

In the beginning, the Door of Hope was served by a very small staff: Cornelia Bonnel was helped by a preacher and a Chinese servant.[24] In 1903, Minnie Morris joined the small group on Seward Road. Every year, new members joined the committee, but not all took a direct part in the work of the two homes. As and when the numbers of inmates grew and the premises became diversified, the Door of Hope recruited staff. In 1905, there were fifteen persons in all. The first-year home housed missionaries, two teachers, two assistants, and one professional instructor.[25] The number of resident missionaries continued to grow. There were six in 1909 and seven in 1910, with fourteen Chinese assistants.[26] In March 1930, the various homes were under the responsibility of sixteen missionaries. The number of Chinese assistants, most of them former inmates, is not given. The staff of the Door of Hope was exclusively female except for the watchmen and porters.

Funding for the Door of Hope came essentially from donations.[27] Some of them were fixed, coming for example from life members' cards, monthly subscriptions, and annual donations. Most, however, were occasional donations. In one year, the Door of Hope received 460 donations.[28] Christmas was a time for special donations that were listed separately. In all, donations yielded 50% to 65% of the association's income.[29] The Door of Hope also received large sums on a one-time basis, such as the Wong Kwe-sung funds (1,090 yuan), the Christian Herald Fund (4,545 yuan), and the Chinkiang Famine Relief Fund (10,000 yuan). The Chinese share in the donations was small. In the first four years, the committee of gentry that financed the receiving home in Fuzhou Road handed out 1,200 to 1,700 taels, sums not accounted for in the general budget. Thereafter, contributions from foreign residents were ten times greater than those of the Chinese. The authorities also provided support (through fines received by the Mixed Court). Finally, the sale of articles made by the inmates brought in some money, although it was far from sufficient to generate funds internally. To this we must add various forms of income (rents from properties in Jiangwan, sums paid to particular inmates, etc.).

The most important expenditure was related, as can be seen, to the inmates' upkeep. Food and clothing took up a growing portion of the budget. The share went from 0.3% in 1901 to an average of 25% after 1908. The wages of the Chinese and foreign staff also amounted to a substantial but uneven proportion of expenditure. The Door of Hope did not directly pay salaries to all the missionaries who were supposed to come under their parent organizations. Starting in 1928 (or perhaps earlier, as I do not have figures for 1910 to 1928), a new heading known as "partial support of missionaries" appeared in the accounts. This section could cover additional salaries. The Door of Hope also had to cope with increasing maintenance expenses due to the extension of its premises and the purchase of new equipment (furniture). Rents for premises and money spent to pay taxes were not a heavy burden except in 1928 and 1929. Finally, there were items of small-scale expenditure in certain years for marriages and funerals. This expenditure was actually a constant item but was probably incorporated into other sections of the budget.

By 1935, the Door of Hope had received more than 4,000 young girls and more than 5,500 children, most of them girls.[30] One author relates that in 1941, more than 12,000 people had come to its premises.[31] A good proportion of the prostitutes (and bondservants) did not remain very long in the Door of Hope. The new inmates were routinely placed in the receiving home. They stayed there until a way could be found to make sure that there was no risk of their returning to prostitution or until a decision had been taken by the courts. It is only after this stage that they were transferred to other homes. In twenty-five years, more than half (53.5%) left the receiving home before they could be settled in another home. However, this proportion tended to diminish with the years. As the number of girls received went up, it became increasingly difficult to search for their original families. Yet, most of those who left before being transferred to another home (1,315 of them) were indeed entrusted to their families (parents or near relatives, husbands, and even friends). The rest (79) were handed over to the authorities (police, Mixed Court) and were either returned to their "owners" (these cases were fairly rare) or entrusted to another benevolent institution or sent to their home villages when their families could not make the trip to Shanghai. Some (13) soon found jobs, while others ran away (15).[32]

Those who had nobody to receive them were admitted to the first-year home (1,141) or to homes for children (552). Of the approximately 1,500 inmates of the first-year home, a little more than 400 remained in the Door of Hope, where they were sent to the industrial home. Some of them were kept as assistants in the homes generally after being put through a school. All the others found a way out through marriage (125), a return to their families (155), escape (42), studies (30), employment (13), and being sent to the Mixed Court (24). Death also took a heavy toll (80).[33] At the end of this year, only 10% of those who had come in remained. Once again, there was a disparity between the number of those transferred to the industrial home (411) and the real numbers of inmates in this home (774). The difference resulted from the transfer of girls from the children's shelters. Marriage accounted for the greatest number of departures (251) followed by transfer to a school (47), a return to the family (43), and placement with an employer (20). Deaths, escapes, and cases of girls sent back to the authorities accounted for the remainder (36). The overall balance does not exactly correspond to the numbers counted between 1908 and 1925 (411).

Certain conclusions can be drawn from these figures. First of all, the Door of Hope made every effort to send the girls back as soon as possible to their families as understood in the broadest sense of the term. This was their first priority. This was the most logical solution and probably the one that corresponded most to the wishes of the concerned parties themselves. Second in the list of priorities came marriage. This option concerned long-term inmates. It corresponded to the traditional social belief in China concerning the feminine condition, according to which a woman could not remain without ties. This aspect of matters will be discussed below. Employment, which was supposed to result from the professional training given to the girls ultimately, was of little importance as a factor. It is an illusion, in the social context of this period, especially up to the 1920s, to imagine that the girls would find employment and be capable of fending for themselves. Chinese women hardly had any solution other than that of marriage or prostitution.

The question is where these prostitutes came from. The ambition of the Door of Hope was to draw girls who had been forced into prostitution. There can be no doubt, from the viewpoint of the missionaries, that the large majority of the prostitutes were in this condition against their will and that most of them would seize the very first opportunity to escape. In fact, as the reputation of the Door of Hope grew, so did the number of prostitutes who took refuge with it. Two factors prevented prostitutes from escaping. First of all, the matrons, madams, and the staff of the houses of prostitution exerted strict surveillance over their deeds and gestures. The prostitutes represented a form of capital, a "money tree" (*yaoqianshu*), which could not be allowed to escape until they had yielded the maximum returns (see Chapter 9). Second, even when they were dissatisfied with their status, the prostitutes were hardly in any mood to revolt. They were often very young, completely isolated in the city, without family or resources of their own. Many of them were pledged and felt obliged to assume some sort of moral responsibility for the money paid to their parents. As most of the testimony shows, it is only when they suffered ill treatment and genuine physical violence that they buckled under and took flight. The majority of them stayed.

In the early years, most of the new inmates came from police arrests: "A large majority of cases received were police cases."[34] In 1905, thirty-three prostitutes and nine bondservants were thus brought in by the police.[35] The Mixed Court routinely sent in minors under fifteen as well as other prostitutes who said that they wished to give up their trade or escape from their madams. In the first five years, half of the approximately 140 girls that were received came in this way. In 1927, 90% of the new inmates were minors sent by the courts.[36] In general, it was the authorities of the International Settlement who sent the largest number of girls. The Mixed Court of the French Concession sent only a few. In the 1930s, the Bureau of Social Affairs of the Chinese Municipality also began to have recourse to the Door of Hope to place certain bondservants.[37] Again, the Door of Hope sometimes indirectly saved prostitutes after receiving anonymous letters (there were more than 200 such cases in 1905). Such letters would be the result of collusion between a girl and a willing customer. The Door of Hope always had these cases verified by the police.[38]

I have no information on the reaction of the houses of prostitution to the fact that the Door of Hope was established in Fuzhou Road. Those in charge of the Door of Hope felt that the presence of the receiving center in the very middle of the prostitution area would lead the brothel owners to treat the girls less harshly for fear that they might escape.[39] In 1906, when six prostitutes found refuge all together in the receiving center, a crowd of ruffians, madams, and other members of the underworld came to demonstrate in front of the establishment and throw stones at its windows: "Foochow Road is ablaze with the ire of brothel owners". The owner had to call the police to disperse the mob and provide protection for the center. Two policemen were left to stand guard for a few days.[40] According to testimony by prostitutes who escaped, the brothel owners spread rumors to the effect that the Door of Hope was a place where girls were imprisoned, ill treated, made to undergo special medical treatment, and so on.[41] The hostility was real but remained unspoken.

When they arrived at the Door of Hope, the prostitutes were often in a wretched physical condition.[42] Many were suffering from advanced stages of venereal disease. Those girls who were very sick were routinely sent to the missionary hospitals, where they were given free treatment.[43] In addition, a volunteer doctor came twice a week to examine the inmates and treat the mildest cases.[44] In 1921, the Door of Hope finally acquired premises in Zhabei where it set up a sanatorium, a sort of internal nursing home that avoided their transfer to a hospital where it was the regular practice for certain inmates to escape once they had been restored to health.[45] Sometimes, the missionaries received prostitutes only in the last stages of illness, only to see them die. In thirty-five years, 167 inmates died of their illnesses. From this number, we must of course subtract the deaths of newborn infants and children received in poor physical condition (about fifty of them). This nevertheless gives a figure of about a hundred young girls who died as a result of illness or ill treatment in the houses of prostitution.

The period of stay could vary. The Door of Hope made every effort, with the help of the police, to locate the families of the inmates and send the girls back to their parents, husbands, or close relatives. A good third of the 3,217 girls received in the course of thirty-five years thus went back to their families after spending a few weeks to a few months with the Door of Hope. Sometimes, the members of the family in question would turn out to be persons who had pledged the girl to an establishment of prostitution. These individuals would be admonished and made to promise never to repeat their deed or else face legal punishment. Certain families tried to recover their daughters against the will of the Door of Hope and went so far as to take action in the courts and threaten the missionaries.[46] The Mixed Court generally decided in favor of the Door of Hope. More rarely, as in 1912, a kidnapping operation was organized with the complicity of foreign residents.[47]

The fact, however, is that the Door of Hope did participate in the confinement of women. The missionaries who directed the organization were undoubtedly aware of the state of Chinese society, which did not permit women to have an independent role. However, although there was a great amount of social change from 1900 to 1935 and even up to 1941, the practices of the Door of Hope did not vary. So long as the girls were in the receiving center, the prostitutes could leave when they wished, provided that the right conditions (family, employment, other institutions) were present. Those who remained, whether minors or majors, were automatically placed in the first-year home for a minimum stay of one year. The only way for them to leave was to return to their families, get married, or be placed in a family or with an employer.[48] Therefore, if a woman were to leave the brothel, it did not mean that she would gain her freedom. The institution played the role of a transit space prior to permanent reintegration into society through very traditional channels: return to the family, marriage, or, secondarily, employment.[49]

The Door of Hope assumed the task not only of pulling the prostitutes out of their fate but of giving them tools to prepare for their reintegration into society. Three main bases of action can be singled out in the training imparted to them: literacy teaching, professional training, and religious education. Daily life was organized on identical lines in all the homes. The girls rose at 7:30 A.M. After breakfast, they would devote their time to basic learning, namely, the study of Chinese ideograms. This teaching was complemented by courses in arithmetic and hygiene. Between these two courses, one hour was devoted to religious education.[50] A frugal lunch was served at midday. From 1:00 P.M. to 4:30 P.M., from Monday to Friday, the inmates would be instructed in a number of manual arts such as sewing, embroidery, and cooking. The purpose of this training was to give young girls knowledge that they could use later on to earn a living. Dinner was served early, around 5:30 P.M., according to the Chinese custom. A prayer session was organized every evening at 7:00 P.M. The lights had to be out at 9:00 P.M.[51]

The role of manual work was not only to impart professional training but also to reeducate ex-prostitutes in the virtues of work and give them the feeling of being in charge of their own lives and of being useful and capable of carrying out productive work. After 1949, the Chinese Communists used the same methods, but in a more intensive mode, to reeducate the prostitutes interned in rehabilitation centers. The other purpose of manual work was to provide income for the Door of Hope. The inmates produced embroidered handkerchiefs, socks for babies or for bound feet, fan boxes, and so on. They made brides' trousseaux to order and also manufactured dolls.[52] The income earned from this activity never amounted to more than a small proportion of the funds available to the Door of Hope, which nevertheless was thereby able to legitimate its activity. The inmates were not just maintained, but contributed actively to their own upkeep.

With fewer departures than arrivals, the numbers grew, and this meant that new resources had to be found. The industrial home provided employment to long-term inmates. It was in fact a huge clothing workshop. In 1906, it received twenty-one girls. It received about fifty from 1908 to 1912, between sixty and seventy in the following decade, and nearly ninety up to 1935. The demand was very great. As soon as a job became vacant following a departure, a new girl would be brought in from the first-year home.[53] The girls worked from 9:00 A.M. to 4:30 P.M. The industrial home was not self-sufficient. However, the income that it generated was sufficient to cover the costs of feeding the girls and paying them a modest salary of 1.75 to 3 yuan per month.[54] The inmates could thus put aside small sums of money in anticipation of marriage or purchase small articles that they might wish to have.[55] The brightest inmates could hope to study in the missionary schools. A rough count for 1901 to 1935 shows that there were ninety of these girls. Some of them became nurses or teachers. Those who preferred to stay or had not found a husband were kept on by the Door of Hope as assistants or teachers in the children's shelter.[56]

Religious education was an essential dimension of the rescue work of the missionaries. They cannot be accused of fanaticism. Tremendous conviction was needed to carry out a task as thankless and poorly esteemed as this, a task moreover that no Chinese association had ever undertaken in Shanghai. Every day, as we have seen, the inmates had to attend a course devoted to catechism and the reading of religious texts. On Friday afternoons, there would be a regular service with the participation of visiting missionaries or Chinese Christian women who would give sermons to the young girls.[57] Some were sent to Bible classes and missionary schools. At regular intervals, conversions would be announced (there were twenty-five baptisms in 1906).[58] Religious education was omnipresent and, although they denied it, the missionaries of the Door of Hope did all they could to bring their inmates to "a Christian way of life."[59] During their stay in the Door of Hope, most of the inmates converted to Christianity.[60]

The reeducation of the prostitutes was not an easy task. As I have pointed out earlier, those in charge of the Door of Hope sought to separate the youngest girls from the older ones who had spent longer periods in the world of prostitution and were therefore more deeply affected. The missionaries felt that readaptation could sometimes be laborious

Table 14.1. *Fate of the inmates of the Door of Hope (1901–1925)*

Year	Marriage	Returned to Family	Escape	Death	Entrusted to Official Organs
1901	1	—	—	—	1
1902	5	—	—	—	2
1903	11	4	—	3	5
1904	13	11	3	8	4
1905	22	5	12	2	10
1906	21	4	10	4	13
1907	30	7	11	7	8
1908	22	123	8	6	19
1909	31	82	7	6	10
1910	26	97	2	9	23
1911	18	92	7	6	13
1912	15	69	7	11	15
1913	35	100	10	3	21
1914	34	49	4	7	16
1915	26	61	7	4	—
1916	20	54	3	4	—
1917	24	60	4	11	1
1918	41	51	4	10	1
1919	—	—	—	—	—
1920	29	56	1	17	—
1921	28	76	3	7	—
1922	25	90	1	5	—
1923	71	102	—	11	—
1924	60	109	—	14	—
1925	79	94	—	12	—
Total:	687	1,396	104	167	162

because the girls (especially those who had come to the Door of Hope through a court decision and not of their own free will) would have retained "bad habits" from past experience. The homes often had "stormy days." The most recalcitrant inmates received special attention, and the idea was even envisaged of creating a special shelter far from the city.[61] The Door of Hope was unable to carry out this project, which probably was not really justified.

The most recalcitrant girls (104 of them in thirty-five years) chose to run away, but they were sometimes found and brought back to the home. They were brought before the assembly of missionaries and fellow inmates, who helped them in the task of heart-searching to find the causes of their deeds and mend their ways.[62] There is an undeniably striking similarity between this method and the one used by the Communist cadres after 1949. The content of the message was different, but the presiding logic was the same: the application of group pressure, making rebels feel guilty, the practice of owning up to faults in public, and the transformation of the soul – or consciousness as the case may be. Those in charge of the Door of Hope did not forgive serious infringements of group discipline.[63]

Like the Chinese, they felt that marriage was the best solution – by far preferable to professional training, which could not ensure sufficient means to protect against the possibility of "backsliding" by the girls.[64] It could be argued, given the number of prostitutes pledged to the brothels, that the existence of a husband or a family was not an absolute guarantee either. However, the missionaries placed themselves within the context of a Chinese form of reasoning and reproduced the dominant social model. Between 1900 and 1935, 687 young women were married under the auspices of the Door of Hope, namely, 40% of the girls (2,284) who remained in any one of its homes after the initial one-year stay in the receiving home.[65] The modalities were carefully regulated. Marriage applications were filed in the homes or received by mail. The marriage agreement was concluded, according to custom, by a go-between. At the home, it was generally one of the foreign missionaries who played this role. For the suitor, the go-between would be a friend or a parent.

The annual reports give some idea of the candidates for marriage. A majority were peasants, mainly natives of regions surrounding Shanghai, especially after the settlement of refuges in Jiangwan.[66] In all likelihood, they belonged to the least privileged sections, those groups in which young men found it difficult to get married because they were not very good matches. These peasants did not ask too many questions about the antecedents of the inmates of the Door of Hope who were in good health and had been transformed by their stay into good housewives.[67] For these peasants, this was an opportunity to make an inexpensive marriage and thus continue the family line as required by tradition. Among the other categories most frequently mentioned, there were the Protestant ministers.[68] They too were not very desirable matches in the eyes of Chinese families. Marrying an inmate of the Door of Hope was one way in which a minister could perform a good deed in keeping with his vocation. These other categories also included Chinese physicians, tailors, and so on.[69]

These marriages were concluded without regard to the viewpoint of the concerned parties, although a girl could indeed turn down a suitor if he did not really please her. However, they did not really have any choice, unless they wanted to remain in a home. We can imagine that the missionaries made every effort to convince the inmates of the worth of the match being presented to them. According to the 1909 report, out of the total number of people married in that year, ten had managed to set up happy homes. The other matches had been less successful but were deemed to be "good," namely healthy from a moral viewpoint.[70] The former inmates did not all lose all contact with the Door of Hope. Some of them returned regularly to visit the missionaries, especially when they could come as proud mothers with children. Others returned in more tragic circumstances as refugees, during the wars that ravaged the surrounding countryside in the 1920s.[71]

Preventive Action: The Shanghai Anti-Kidnapping Society

As I have noted in the introduction to this chapter, before the twentieth century, there was no specifically Chinese organization that took an interest in the rescue of prostitutes. Those that did emerge displayed little inclination in this respect. It would be worthwhile to look at the reasons for this absence. I shall return to this question later. While they did nothing to rescue girls engaged in prostitution, the Chinese elites made efforts further up the line to prevent the traffic in human beings whose primary victims were women and also – although with a different purpose – boys. The organization that committed itself to this ambitious undertaking was founded by one of Shanghai's most influential communities, the Zhejiang natives, especially from the Shaoxing–Ningbo region. This was an initiative by merchants and cannot easily be explained. The sources that I have consulted do not include the founding documents of the organization, and I have found no explanation coming from the merchants themselves for this initiative.[72]

What is even more intriguing is the group that took this initiative. The Shaoxing–Ningbo natives were concerned about the traffic in women, but probably less so than other communities close to Shanghai. There did exist a group of Ningbo prostitutes, but it was relatively small. As we have seen in Chapter 7, the traffic concerned all the women of Jiangsu, who were sold in Shanghai as well as in more remote provinces. This said, it was not in any parochial spirit that these merchants organized themselves. Their initiative formed part of a trend that was already well underway and had seen the emergence, in the major urban centers, of benevolent institutions and activities conducted by the merchant elites and directed toward the entire population. Perhaps this must be seen also as part of the impulse provided by the 1911 revolution, which led certain groups to combat phenomena that symbolized China's backwardness.

In November 1912, several members of the board of directors of the Shaoxing native-place association (*Shaoxing lühu tongxianghui*) took the initiative to set up an association to come to the aid of women and children who had been victims of kidnapping. This association, called the *Zhongguo furu jiuji zonghui* (General Association for the Rescue of the Women and Children of China), was known in the local English-language press by an absolutely different but more explicit name: the Shanghai Anti-Kidnapping Society (AKS). Its head office was in the building that housed the native-place association.[73] The first general assembly meeting of the AKS was held on February 7, 1913 in the general Chamber of Commerce.[74]

The members present elected a board of thirty-three directors headed by a weighty triumvirate: Wang Yiting, Yu Xiaqing, and Xu Qianlin.[75]

The AKS sent a letter to the foreign and Chinese local authorities asking for official recognition. Their permission was indeed indispensable for the para-police tasks that the association was planning to carry out. The association also acquired means of action. A former Buddhist temple (*Jiangwan yufosi*) was rented out at Jiangwan and entirely refurbished so that it could receive women and children. The AKS took out a twenty-year lease, thus setting its sights at the very outset on the long term. The association also recruited its first inspectors.[76] The board met every month to review the situation. There were also extraordinary assembly meetings that could be convened on the initiative of the chairman or of one-third of the members. The organization of the AKS was almost a model of the type of voluntary association existing in Western countries. It was in any case based on principles that were quite democratic in their form.

The association was financed by voluntary contributions from the directors and by fund-raising from the merchant community. The association had a fairly wide base because in 1914, at the election of the second board of directors, more than 2,000 individuals took part in the vote.[77] Throughout its existence, the association remained an organization dominated by the merchants. In 1935, it was led by a group of leading citizens. In addition to Wang Yiting, the group included Wang Xiaolai, Wang Binyan, Xu Shiying, and even Du Yuesheng, leader of the Green Gang (*Qingbang*).[78]

I have been able to find only a few details on the finances of the AKS. Besides, it is not easy to reconstruct a clearly set-out budget inasmuch as accounts were kept for each category of currency received (tael, yuan, foreign money, Chinese copper coins, and foreign copper coins). For the second half of 1914, the AKS collected 14,252 yuan. The first half of 1915 brought in about 9,814 yuan. This amounts to a total annual income of more than 24,000 yuan, which was a sum substantially equivalent to the budget of the Door of Hope organization during the same period (22,000 yuan in 1910).[79] Although, in principle, it relied on a community of merchants that greatly outnumbered the donors of the Door of Hope, the AKS nevertheless did not have a bigger income. In 1925, its budget went up to 70,000 yuan. But the biggest share of this amount, 60,000 yuan, was provided by about fifty members of the board of directors. Contributions from outside therefore remained at a relatively low level. In 1936, the budget was still 60,000 yuan.[80]

The relations of the AKS with the authorities were fairly good, as can be seen from the presence of the most important local personalities at the functions organized by the association. In 1920, the association organized a big reception at the inauguration of its new premises in Jiangwan. More than 10,000 people were present and watched various singing and theatrical performances, some of them presented by the residents of the association.[81] In the following year, for the eighth anniversary of the AKS, 3,000 individuals came in reply to the invitation of the association.[82] The AKS was considered to be an institution that was representative in its field of action. The Interior Ministry, through the *xian* magistrate, asked for information that the Chinese government could use in filling out the questionnaires of the League of Nations.[83] The coming to power of the Nationalists in 1927 had only a limited impact. Like all the other benevolent associations, the AKS was the target of an attempted takeover by the new municipality, especially the Bureau of Social Affairs.[84] The new dispensation did not change the mode of operation of the AKS, which was already extremely strict about the way in which persons to whom they had given shelter could leave.[85]

In 1915, the AKS had four inspectors. Their duties were difficult and sometimes dangerous. They had to be vigilant and not let traffickers get past them, but, at the same time, they could inform the police only when they were convinced that there really had been a kidnapping. They had to avoid making demands on the policemen and avoid disturbing or alarming other travelers unnecessarily. Given the very dense human traffic that characterized Shanghai, they had all the odds stacked against them in their task, even if it was relatively easy up to the beginning of the 1920s to single out girls and young women, because not many of them were likely to be traveling alone. The inspectors worked from 8:00 A.M. to 8:00 P.M. – that is, during the hours that saw most of the movement by travelers in the railway stations and wharves. The AKS set up a system of incentives and punishments. Promotion and monetary rewards were given according to the number of cases discovered and traffickers arrested. At the same time, no mistakes could be made. After three errors, an inspector was automatically dismissed.[86]

The inspectors of the AKS were officially accredited to the police services and the navigation companies. Their work consisted in visiting all ships that dropped anchor in Shanghai or that were about to leave the city. They also monitored the wharves and the railway stations. Among the mass of travelers, they had to single out men (or rather women) of doubtful aspect, either in physical appearance (in the case of girls who had been beaten or drugged) or in numbers (one trafficker was arrested with nineteen children[87]). If they saw something unusual, they had to keep a closer watch on the group they had identified to make sure that there had really been a kidnapping and then inform the police. The inspectors had no powers to make arrests, and for this purpose they had to rely on the authorities.[88] By around 1927, the inspectors of the AKS had rescued more than 2,000 women and children through their intervention.[89]

The AKS also took action when approaches were made to it from the other direction. It frequently received requests from families who had lost all trace of their members. These families sometimes approached the police or the local authorities; but very often it was toward the AKS that they turned, seeking either direct action or intervention with the authorities. In the former case, the families would approach the AKS because they felt that the association was more likely than the police to find the missing person. In the latter case, it was because they thought it more likely that their request would be taken into consideration. But one of the essential reasons was that the AKS was seen as an extension of the guild or native-place association. It was therefore to the association that they went most naturally in the same way as they might approach it in order to settle a dispute with a rival or with the administration. It was a form of automatic behavior – a *habitus*, to use Bourdieu's expression. It was not rare for a native of one region or another to approach the AKS of his own accord and inform it about the presence, in a house of prostitution, of a kidnapped "compatriot" who had asked him to help her and inform her family about her fate (see Chapter 7).

The efficiency of the AKS depended on the work of its inspectors in Shanghai as well as on the contacts that it made outside the city, especially when trying to find girls who had been sent afar, toward the northern and northeastern provinces (see Chapter 7). The articles of the association stated that branches could be set up with the permission of the AKS.[90] The local sections of the association were set up through the interprovincial links that existed between the guilds or the native-place associations (*tongxianghui*) of Shaoxing–Ningbo in the different cities of China. Thus, in Fengtian (the old name for Liaoning in Manchuria) in May 1915, Harbin in 1919, and in Heilongjiang, it was from the guilds representing Zhejiang that these associations originated. The role of community links is undeniable. The creation of these sections was a response to the need to be represented in areas in which many girls kidnapped from around Shanghai had become stranded. The AKS was also present in Dalian (August 1915), Yingkou, Hankou in Hubei, and Hangzhou and Wuxing in Zhejiang.[91]

The AKS also approached the various local authorities: police departments, Japanese consuls, *xian* magistrates, and so on. In February 1915, the association took up the case of a girl who had been kidnapped and taken to Xinshi in Manchuria with the Japanese Consul in Shanghai. The consul forwarded the request to his counterpart in Manchuria and to the Japanese police there.[92] The cases in which the police were approached are too numerous to be all cited here. The applications covered the entire eastern part of the Chinese territory, from Changchun in Manchuria to Xiantou (Swatow) in Guangdong, including Shanghai, Tianjin, Qingdao, Fuzhou, and so on. Conversely, the police from outer regions approached the AKS when they could not identify parents of victims.[93] The AKS provided a unique recourse because it had investigators in all the major cities serving as hubs for the female trade, and it took charge of the job of rescuing and repatriating the victims.

The reception center was managed by a director, appointed by the board for one year, along with the two wardens (a man and a woman) who assisted him.[94] The directors of the AKS closely monitored the work of the center and had no qualms about dismissing inefficient staff (an example is given below). Life in the center was austere and harder than that in the Door of Hope. Inmates had to rise at 6:00 A.M. (in winter, they were allowed an extra half-hour of sleep). After breakfast, which was served an hour later, the inmates got down to work or attended classes. There was a break for lunch, served at midday sharp. Dinner was served at 6:00 P.M. The afternoon was also devoted to work or study. By 9:00 P.M., everybody had to be in bed.[95] The center had a primary school for the youngest girls. The others were trained in different forms of manual work in an ordinary workshop (*putong gongyi*) as well as in Western and Chinese pharmacology.[96] Moral education classes were also held every week.[97]

The house rules emphasized compliance with the principles of hygiene (with respect to water, clothing, and sheets). In the event of illness, the inmates were transferred to a sick house to avoid the risk of contagion. Patients were treated in the center itself except in the more serious cases when they were treated in Chinese hospitals. The inmates were also routinely vaccinated by the health department of the Shanghai Municipal Council.[98] However, these strict rules were not always followed, perhaps because of the increase in the number of inmates. In 1928, an inspection by the Bureau of Social Affairs revealed the fact that many children were sick. The Bureau asked the association to keep a watch over the risks of infection.[99] Two years later, an inspection visit by the Health Bureau noted even more serious faults. The AKS gave the managers one month to put things right in the reception center. Two months later, a second inspection visit noted the same faults. The association dismissed the three main persons in charge and appointed new managers.[100]

The period of stay depended on the girl's age. Girls under sixteen remained in the center up to their sixteenth birthday if no one came forward to claim them. For young girls above this age or women without husbands, the stay was limited to one year. At the end of this period, they were put up for marriage. Twice a year, in the spring and in the autumn, the AKS would post notices outside its premises with photographs and brief details (name, age, native province) of those inmates who were eligible to leave the center. Candidates wishing to marry these girls had to fill out a form that would be scrutinized by the managers of the center and then by a member of the AKS.[101] Apart from giving a guarantee that he had a fixed job, a suitor had to promise not to ill-treat his wife, take concubines, or sell his wife, on the understanding that if he were to break his promise, and if the AKS were to learn of it, the marriage would be declared null and void and the authorities would be immediately informed.[102] In 1935, the AKS adopted an even more active approach to publicize the names of the inmates that it put up for marriage. Not only were their photos and short details of their life posted up outside the premises as in the past, but the association went in for more extensive forms of advertising, probably through the press.

In most of the cases, the children and women received in the center were sent back to their families. The families in principle had to pay a sum of money to compensate for costs of stay with the AKS. In fact, only a minority were able to pay, and the association (which did not really have any money-making vocation) did not enforce this rule, leaving it to the families to make a financial contribution if they thought fit to do so. Moreover, the AKS itself sent its agents to accompany some of the inmates to their homes when their families were unable to send any one to Shanghai. In 1915, out of 216 persons received, 90 were taken back by a member of their family while 53 were accompanied by an AKS agent.[103]

For obvious financial reasons, the AKS tried to find the families of the victims as soon as possible, thus seeking to avoid an excessive increase in the number of inmates. Every new arrival was announced in the press along with a photograph of the young girl or child concerned.[104] In three years (1913–1916), the association rescued 890 individuals, 342 of whom became inmates.[105] In 1921, the AKS housed 392 inmates.[106] As in the case of the Door of Hope, the numbers tended to increase with time, even though the system was designed to obtain the departure of as many as possible. In 1931, the Jiangwan center received more than 400 inmates. Four years later, the numbers went up to 938, including more than 200 children.[107] It is not easy to assess the overall impact of the AKS. In 1936, it claimed to have rescued very precisely 10,233 individuals since it had been set up.[108]

The task of rescuing and rehabilitating the prostitutes was also undertaken in varying degrees by other organizations whose ambitions were more limited. Some of these organizations, which sprang up especially at the time of the abolitionist movement in the International Settlement, had only an ephemeral or even a purely formal existence. The details that I have gathered on these groups are even more disparate than my information on the Door of Hope and the AKS. The silence of the sources points to the fairly widespread indifference in which all the associations conducted their action, and this indifference is even truer with regard to the "small" organizations. This probably indicates the limits of their resources and the little impact made by their activities.

There is no indication of any specifically Chinese initiative that bore genuine fruit.[109] There were a few attempts made during the abolitionist movement, but their trail is soon lost. In June 1920, a group of about ten individuals founded a Society for Assistance to Prostitutes (*Jinü jiujihui*), whose offices were on Fuzhou Road in one of the main lanes (*Tongxingli*) with a concentration of houses of prostitution. The society even appointed representatives for each city (Nanking, Hangzhou, Peking, Zhenjiang, Suzhou, Wuxi, Tianjin, and Hankou) where it intended to develop its activities. The goal of the society was to provide assistance to prostitutes and enable them to get out of their predicament. This assistance was to be obtained by fund-raising activities among all professional and business organizations (*tuanti*).[110] I have no further details on this organization, which the press never again mentioned and about which I have found no reference anywhere else.[111]

Most of the activities undertaken to combat prostitution or help prostitutes flowed from the initiative of missionaries and of religious groups with which Chinese and foreigners were associated. This can be seen, for example, from an inquiry conducted by Protestant missions in China in 1922.[112] Shelters were opened by Chinese volunteers in certain cities, such as Kaifeng, Hankou, or Si'anfu. Such shelters were also opened by the police as in Peking.[113] Elsewhere, it was indifference that prevailed. According to the directory of religious missions in China, the Door of Hope came up, in its early days, against the prejudices and reticence of the Chinese (especially the authorities) toward such an undertaking.[114] Although this is the only testimony of its kind and was probably itself affected by prejudice, it reinforces the idea that the Chinese felt a certain degree of unease about any contact with prostitutes outside the normal client–prostitute relationship. A methodical and exhaustive study of the *Shen Bao* from 1895 to 1927, made by a young Taiwan historian, has not revealed the existence in Shanghai of organizations other than those mentioned in this study.[115] There was no real mobilization against prostitution or to rescue prostitutes even on the part of Chinese women and their organizations. The Association of Shanghai Women (*Shanghai funühui*), founded in December 1920, limited itself to supporting the Moral Welfare League's abolitionist campaign without taking any specific action of its own.[116]

The example of Shanghai illustrates the very different approaches adopted by the Western missionaries and by the Chinese regarding the issue of assistance to prostitutes. Their discourse in this respect was quite eloquent. The former emphasized the religious dimension of their action and the exemplary character of certain particular cases of "redemption." It is true that the goal was to move the reader so that he or she might make a contribution to the cause being supported by the Door of Hope. However, their work included a dimension of religious proselytizing (linked to the view that everything happened by the grace of God) and of the moral education of society. The Chinese elites had a more pragmatic approach, although it too was based on an ethic. Their concerns were centered on the individuals rescued: their age, geographical origin and (even if this was imprecisely stated) social origin, circumstances of kidnapping, and modalities of rescue. Here, there was no divine intervention but rather an interplay of *tongxiang* networks. For the missionaries, it was a matter of combating an evil related to human nature; but for those who initiated the AKS, it was a social reality, a social problem that they had to try to resolve.

In these different activities, each of the organizations concerned worked with the greatest autonomy. There was no coordination or contact between these institutions, even those closest to each other. My certainty on this point is based on a reading of my admittedly imperfect sources. This lack of coordination and contact is not surprising, nor was it necessarily harmful. In many respects, these different organizations played a complementary role. This state of affairs highlights the cruel absence of the State in China, even at the local level. The disinherited and fringe sections of the population could count only on themselves and on the assistance that a few private benevolent institutions tried to bring to them. In this context, the prostitutes had little chance of being given consideration by the Chinese urban elites who supported these different initiatives and were keen to have their names associated with socially prestigious forms of charitable work. Because assistance to prostitutes did not come under this category, the task of rescuing the girls ultimately fell to organizations whose primary vocation – evangelism – lay in a realm that was diametrically opposite to the world of prostitution.

Conclusion

In one century (1849–1949), Shanghai experienced the effects of a powerful process of modernization that radically transformed its physical structure as well as the composition and lifestyles of the local population. This accelerated change affected and altered every field of life – economic, social, and cultural. Prostitution, through its particular function in society, was very intimately bound up with these changes. In adapting to them, it faithfully reflected the development of the city. Prostitution, to a greater extent than in the West, had an important and even central place in Chinese society as a result of the spatial and social segregation of women. With the vast majority excluded from the public domain, women were represented on the social scene by the prostitutes, who formed a small but diversified group.

The nature of prostitution and its functions changed singularly during this period. This change can be expressed by two complementary terms: *sexualization* and *commercialization*. There appears to be a measure of paradox in the fact of singling out these two notions with respect to a group of women whose calling was precisely to furnish sexual services in return for remuneration. The paradox, however, does not exist. At a time when wives were confined to their apartments and were often poorly educated and totally isolated, the courtesans formed a distinct class of women whose company was sought after by the male members of the elite for their artistic talents and wit and, of course, for sexual gratification. The transformation of the elites, combined with the gradual if measured emancipation of women within Chinese society, led to the collapse of this arrangement. The world of the courtesans – a milieu itself consisting of several strata – gradually became homogeneous and uniform, leaving only one group, the *changsan*. The scholar elites, whose influence was dominant in the sphere of values, were supplanted by more numerous and varied categories of merchants less imbued with classical culture. Although they were concerned with appearances and wished to display their social status by visiting the "hetaerae," these new customers nevertheless did not attach as much importance as their predecessors to the "spiritual" dimension. From being admired and respected sources of entertainment, the courtesans became mere "high-class prostitutes."

The same process was at work among all the groups of prostitutes, although its implications differed. The first point to be emphasized is the remarkable increase in the supply of prostitution after the First World War. This was an increase not just in numbers but also in the range of quality. The variety of places of prostitution grew. It ranged from the low-class brothels and their ever-changing types to the massage parlors and dance halls. Although these establishments cannot all be placed at the same level, they all did form part of the phenomenon of prostitution. Nevertheless, the fact that the space of prostitution came to harbor a multitude of forms should not conceal the main constant that underlay the transformation, namely, the fact that the milieu was becoming uniform. Here, the qualitative change did not result from a reversal of a function as in the case of the courtesans (the link between sex and money had always formed part of common prostitution) but resulted instead from novel modes of vending sex characterized by a greater presence outdoors and the increased circulation of the prostitutes.

As the landscape of prostitution was redrawn, the way in which it was perceived by society changed. It would not be an exaggeration, in referring to the discourse of the elites on prostitution, to speak of "dominant values." In the nineteenth century, their view of this milieu, inherited from a long tradition of extolment of the courtesans by the scholars, came to prevail in the current media, namely personal narratives, the novel, and the theater. This was a positive discourse, univocal but fallacious, that concealed a far more diversified reality. Among the population, the prostitute's trade did not confer an enviable status, and few families would wish such a fate for their female progeny. Still, the frequency of marriages between prostitutes and members of the poorer classes indicates the relative tolerance of society toward these "fallen" girls. The explosion of the phenomenon of prostitution in Shanghai and the changes in the nature of the social classes helped erase the favorable view conveyed by earlier writings. They gave rise to a different image of prostitution, one in which it was seen as a social problem (a carrier of disease, ruin, moral dissipation, etc.) and, later, as a symbol of the subordination of women. In the 1920s, there was no one left to sing the praises of the courtesans or prostitutes. The scholars had been dethroned by the bureaucrats, the specialists in the social sciences, the journalists, and the abolitionist militants.

However, the change in the way in which the phenomenon of prostitution was perceived within society did not present any fundamental challenge to the existence of prostitution. The abortive experience of regulationism in the nineteenth century revealed the limits of any action whose original impulse came from a foreign authority lacking the means to relay it to the Chinese population. After the Second World War, the presence of a large and predominantly Anglo-American foreign community enabled the development of an abolitionist movement whose goals, however, were only partially achieved. Even if we allow for the inherent difficulties of such an undertaking in a city that was divided into three, the essential unsurmounted obstacle was the indifference – whether it was apathy or tolerance – of the Chinese community, a majority of which was unconcerned by the religious principles on which the abolitionists' action was based. In the eyes of Chinese public opinion, the debate on prostitution in the 1920s and its progress hinged on the question of the feminine condition rather than the condition of the prostitutes themselves. No form or structure of intervention (in terms of rescue or repression) emerged from this theoretical discussion, which was conducted by men and women who appear to have been ill informed of the realities of prostitution.

Prostitution may not provide explanations or keys to an understanding of China's social evolution, especially in Shanghai, but it does offer a mirror of change. In the nineteenth century, Chinese society was marked by an extreme degree of segregation in which the public sphere was reserved for men. This segregation created two distinct and complementary groups of women, namely, the wives and the prostitutes/courtesans. These two groups occupied different spaces, the home and the house of prostitution, each of them equally circumscribed. Only the courtesans had a wider field of action, although it was carefully limited. Economic modernization and the rise in living standards led to new demands. Schools were opened to girls. Factories recruited female workers who had greater dexterity than the men but earned lower wages. The leisure industry was on the lookout for more comely faces from the female species in order to please a predominantly male clientele. There were other signs of the growing participation of women in economic and social life. This was only the beginning of a long march toward emancipation. The modernization that was taking place broke the mold within which courtesans had found their *raison d'être*. It reduced prostitution to a strictly commercial exchange as in the West. What continued to distinguish China in the contemporary period was the important role that prostitution continued to play in the daily life of men.

On the question of sexuality, prostitution sheds little light. Of course, the fact that men could assiduously visit prostitutes (as an ordinary act of social life) points to the absence of any of the unease, embarrassment, or shame that is attached to this activity in the West. In this respect, the Chinese enjoyed a degree of moral liberty that had no equivalent in Judeo-Christian culture. The fact remains, however, that this freedom was reserved for men, whether single or married. The wives had hardly any say in the matter although the husbands' freedom gradually came to be curtailed by abolitionist campaigns and feminist demands. Despite the relative liberty that men enjoyed in the matter of mores, sexuality in China remained a taboo subject that was routinely passed over in various writings on prostitution. There are few exceptions, and these do not give a clear picture of how individuals fulfilled their sexual lives or how they lived them. The fragments of information that have been assembled in this study are far too disparate to provide material for any interpretation, especially in historical perspective.

There is no real contradiction between this apparent liberty and the silence of the sources. Sexuality was perceived as being a normal and natural dimension of the life of individuals, but it was relegated to the most private space. The rules of etiquette and Confucian ethics prohibited its public expression even in the form of written works. This silence can be interpreted as a form of "social" inhibition that nevertheless did not affect the perception of sexuality as a natural act of life. In Shanghai, the concealment of this aspect of things in the sources was counterbalanced by the growing externalization of sexuality that could be seen not only in the visible presence of prostitutes soliciting in the street but also in the proliferation of various media (the press advertisements vaunting the merits of anti-venereal clinics and remedies as well as virility-boosting items were the main examples of these) that played a role in a sexualization of daily life. Of course, we are still far from the eroticized consumer society of the West today, but there can be no doubt that there was a foretaste of it in pre-1949 Shanghai.

It is commonplace to state that women were reduced to a state of submission in Chinese society. However, prostitution emphasized the precarious condition of women. It highlighted the harsh consequences of any absence of social legitimacy outside marriage and the family in an underdeveloped society where the State was singularly absent. It is not that the phenomenon of prostitution was peculiar to China – it can be found practically in every latitude and in every age – but that, in this country, it fed on a huge, many-sided traffic in which the central object of transaction consisted of women and little girls. We might argue over the definition of "slavery," which refers to differing historical experiences. Nevertheless, the fact is that slavery, essentially that of women, is a reality that was widespread in pre-1949 China. Whether they were victims of professional criminals, uncaring relatives, parents who had plumbed the depths of poverty, chance circumstances, or violent abduction, these women were sold, hired, and pledged, sometimes to a succession of "owners," changing hands like common merchandise. The prostitutes were the most numerous and most conspicuous group in this huge market in women. To them, we must add the bondservants (*beinü*), concubines, hired workers, and others.

The authorities reacted with concern to the female trade under the Empire and the Republic. However, despite laws that were at times severe, they did not really adopt the means to efficiently combat this practice of trafficking. In Shanghai, the task of tracking down the traffickers was left to a private association, the Anti-Kidnapping Society. The police of course did not remain idle, but there was no coordinated and sustained effort to combat this scourge. Furthermore, Shanghai was only one of the centers of the huge trade in women. It was a hub for "exports" to Manchuria and Fujian as well as for supply of local brothels. Despite the proven existence of trafficking, especially in the circles of prostitution, there was no specifically Chinese institution that took an interest in the fate of women forced to sell their bodies in the establishments of pleasure. The only initiative in this field, that of the Door of Hope, came from the efforts of Westerners, namely, Protestants and missionaries.

This absence may be interpreted as the sign of a certain degree of unease about a group that was tolerated and even accepted in its particular social function but that prompted feelings of distaste. The impression one gets is that, in China, it was only through their sexual function in a customer–girl relationship that the prostitutes could be considered as suitable company, but that there was some unease about "treating them" as prostitutes in order to help them get out of their condition. This perhaps also results from the fact that they generally found ways to be reintegrated into society. This said, the prostitutes nevertheless appear as deviants who did not conform to the standards of good behavior followed by decent women and whose fate was deemed to be uncertain until and unless they found a man who would agree to marry them. In this respect, there was one constant element in the way in which the different institutions that had to deal with prostitutes (or single women or slaves) under the Empire, the Republic, and the Communist regime apprehended the problem of reintegration into society: Marriage was seen as the only reliable way out. Failing this, the only other solution was the one taken by the Communist leaders after 1949 when they sent the prostitutes far from the cities into areas where all they could do was work. Women on the loose, without any ties, had no place in Chinese society.

In China, there is a series of images, clichés, and even myths attached to prostitution that this study has sought to verify, challenge, or show to be false. All these projections result from various distortions, the main one of which is the lack of any critical approach to the sources that have conveyed them. The information available on prostitution and sexuality in East Asia far too often belongs to the realm of approximation. In the contemporary period, the distortions have been accentuated by the politically biased research of Chinese historians wishing to condemn a phenomenon that is perceived solely from the viewpoint of exploitation. Even if this viewpoint needs to be accounted for and elucidated, it corresponds to only one dimension of a multifaceted phenomenon. A strictly economic approach would not necessarily be capable of establishing "legal proof of exploitation." The question is how to determine whether or not a female worker drawing silk threads barehanded from vats of boiling water for a wage of 8 to 10 yuan a month was more exploited than a prostitute selling her charms for 2 to 3 yuan per encounter. Once we set aside moral considerations (according to which it is more shameful to be a prostitute than to work in a factory) and look at the matter from a purely economic viewpoint, the whole question obviously becomes irrelevant.

To assess the condition of the prostitute, other variables need to be introduced. Of these, the chief one is unquestionably the status under which a woman practiced this activity. Was she free, hired, pledged, or sold? Did she have any other alternative? It is those who had lost their freedom who were naturally in the most difficult situation. It would appear that in the nineteenth century, a very large proportion of the prostitutes were in a state of servitude that was temporary (when they were pledged or hired) or permanent (when they were sold). The effects of official repression and the adoption of new penal codes, and especially changes in the forms of prostitution and in the conditions in which this market was supplied, led to a decline in servitude and to greater individual autonomy for the prostitutes.

Another dimension that must be taken into account is that of the extreme heterogeneity of this milieu and the constant turnover of its members. The idea of associating the courtesans with the wretched girls who officiated in the opium dens and the "junk boats of tolerance" is unimaginable. They belonged to two different worlds, even if their activities were related. It would be like identifying a retailer with a wholesaler. The idea of a "hierarchy" is tempting in this respect. There was undoubtedly a gradation between different levels of prostitution. However, the term "hierarchy" is far too reminiscent of a strict and somewhat unchanging order of things. The reality, on the contrary, reveals an interweaving and overlapping of different forms of prostitution between which it is difficult to draw clear boundaries. It might be more appropriate to say that there was a continuum of groups with ill-defined contours whose configuration corresponded to a series of circles intersecting at certain points rather than to a pyramid. With time, some of these circles (such as the *ersan* or the *shuyu*) were totally absorbed while new circles emerged at the fringes or from the core of the original circles.

Even in China, it was rare for prostitution to be a condition that lasted for an entire lifetime. All the indications given in this study show that the overwhelming majority of the prostitutes were young girls rarely aged over thirty. They therefore necessarily and naturally looked for ways to become reintegrated into society even if some of them did not manage to do so or fell by the wayside before they could attain their goal (through illness, suicide, or murder). Those who did make an exit very probably continued to bear the marks of this painful experience, which had rarely come of their own choice. While the population and the authorities might have perceived an unbridled expansion of prostitution in Shanghai, especially after the First

World War, this was a view that only partially corresponded to reality. Barring the exceptional period of the Civil War, the number of prostitutes remained relatively constant in relation to the resident population. By contrast, there was a considerable increase in the visibility of the prostitutes. Their presence in the city, which, in the nineteenth century, had been limited to the brothels and to certain districts, gradually extended into the more business-oriented areas. This came about with the invasion of the streets, which, more than any other factor, conditioned the new image of prostitution as a constant vortex of proliferation.

Despite intervention by the local authorities and initiatives on the part of active minorities, such as Protestant organizations, prostitution was never seen as a major social problem in Shanghai. The authorities of the concessions took an interest in them, as in the great European cities, seeking to control and regulate the phenomenon rather than eliminate it. Even in the most active phase of the elimination of prostitution, between 1920 and 1924 in the International Settlement, the Shanghai Municipal Council markedly dragged its feet over any strict application of the policy of prohibition that had been adopted under pressure from the abolitionist organizations. During the same period, although there was an outpouring of articles on prostitution in the press, and especially in the women's' magazines, no link can be perceived between what was happening in the settlement and the general and rather abstract debates of the time on the elimination of prostitution. Chinese public opinion displayed great tolerance toward prostitution as a social phenomenon, even if, individually, the prostitutes could be a source of unpleasantness. The Chinese authorities, despite the problems of public health posed by the high prevalence of venereal disease, were not much more sensitive to this issue, except perhaps in 1945–1949.

The causes of the exaggerated growth of prostitution that characterized twentieth-century Shanghai must not really be sought in the poverty of the countryside, the attraction exerted by the opulence of the cities, the cynical greed of the merchants of human flesh, or a supposed hankering after sexual pleasure on the part of debauched elites as is claimed by both the press of the period and Chinese historians today. At best, these factors only aggravated the phenomenon. Prostitution is a constant in human societies that results above all from a combination of natural and cultural factors. Arguments from nature (referring to the male libido) do not furnish an explanation. No act in a man's life (including the most essential ones of drinking and eating) is free from some cultural conditioning. There is therefore nothing that is inevitable, invariable, or "natural" in the demand that calls forth prostitution in human societies. Only the primary sexual act is an act of nature, not the conditions under which it is performed. Prostitution arises out of an inequality between sexes marked by a cultural imprint that has placed women in a condition of subordination, an imprint from which mankind is barely beginning to emerge. The state of prostitution in

Shanghai in the nineteenth to twentieth centuries was but another expression of a culture that denied women any recognition of their rights, integrity, and dignity. As an object of transaction, women were never really protected by any institution (family, marriage, or the State) from the risk of falling into the "world of flowers." The totalitarian regime that asserted its sway over Chinese society after 1949 proclaimed its will to sweep away every last vestige of feudalism. None can deny the progress that has been accomplished. Yet today's reality, especially the resurgence of prostitution in forms that reproduce earlier practices, shows that this digression is now coming to an end without having achieved any profound transformation of the status of women.

Notes

Note: *SB*: *Shen Bao*

Introduction

1. Louis Chevalier, *Classes laborieuses et classes dangereuses*, Paris, L.G.F., 1978 (1st ed., 1958), New York, H. Ferting, 1973 (translation).
2. Alain Corbin, *Les filles de noce. Misère sexuelle et prostitution (XIXᵉ–XXᵉ siècle)*, Paris, Flammarion (coll. Champs), 1982 (1st ed., Aubier-Montaigne, 1978).
3. The Chinese-administered parts of the city were not truly unified until 1927 when the Nationalists set up the municipal government of Shanghai: cf. Christian Henriot, *Shanghai 1927–1937. Municipal Power, Locality, and Modernization*, Berkeley, University of California Press, 1993.
4. A good introduction to the history of homosexuality in China can be found in Bret Hinsch, *Passion of the Cut Sleeve. The Male Homosexual Tradition in China*, Berkeley, University of California Press, 1990.
5. Christian Henriot, "'La fermeture': The Abolition of Prostitution in Shanghai, 1949–1958," *The China Quarterly*, December 1995, pp. 148–167.
6. "Villes et société urbaine en Chine aux XIXᵉ–XXᵉ siècles," *Historiens et géographes*, No. 340, 1993, pp. 217–232. On the historiography of prostitution in the Western world; cf. Chapter 1 of my *Docteur d'État* thesis.
7. Jean Chesneaux, *Le mouvement ouvrier chinois de 1919 à 1927*, Paris, Mouton, 1962; Marie-Claire Bergère, *La bourgeoisie chinoise et la révolution de 1911*, Paris, Mouton, 1968; Mark Elvin, "The Gentry Democracy in Shanghai, 1905–1914," unpublished dissertation, Cambridge University, 1967; Emily Honig, *Strangers and Sisters: Women in the Shanghai Cotton Mills, 1919–1949*, Stanford, Stanford University Press, 1986; Alain Roux, *Grèves et politique à Shanghai. Les désillusions (1927–1932)*, Paris, Éditions de l'EHESS, 1995, and *Le Shanghai ouvrier des années trente. Coolies, gangsters et syndicalistes*, Paris, L'Harmattan (collection "Chemins de la mémoire"), 1993; Elizabeth Perry, *Shanghai on Strike*, Stanford, Stanford University Press, 1993.
8. Alain Corbin, *Women for Hire. Prostitution and Sexuality in France after 1850*, Cambridge, MA, Harvard University Press, 1990, pp. vii–viii. The following is a list of works consulted on the history of sexuality and prostitution in the West: G.S. Rousseau and Roy Porter, *Sexual Underworlds of the Enlightenment*, Charlotte, University of North Carolina Press, 1988; Stevens Marcus, *The Other Victorians. A Study of Sexuality and Pornography in Mid-Nineteenth-Century England*, New York, Basic Books, 1964; Jacques Poumarède and Jean-Pierre Royer (textes réunis par), *Droit, histoire and sexualité*, Lille, L'espace

juridique, 1987, or the study by Claude Quetel, *Le mal de Naples. Histoire de la syphilis*, Paris, Seghers, 1986; Fernando Henriques, *Love in Action: The Sociology of Sex*, London, Panther Books, 1959, and *Prostitution and Society: A Survey*, London, Macgibbon and Kee, 1962; Vern L. Bullough, *The History of Prostitution*, New York, University Books, 1964; Vern Bullough and Bonnie Bullough, *Prostitution, an Illustrated History*, New York, Crown Publishers, 1978, and *Women and Prostitution*, New York, Prometheus Books, 1987; Regina Schulte, *Sperrbezirke: Tugendhaftigkeit und Prostitution in der bürgerlichen Welt*, Frankfurt/am Main, Syndikat, 1979; Richard J. Evans, "Prostitution, State and Society in Imperial Germany," *Past and Present*, no. 70, 1976, pp. 106–126; Ana Maria Atondo, "La prostitution and la condition féminine à Mexico (1521–1821)," unpublished dissertation, Université Paris I, 1987; Jacques Rossiaud, *La prostitution médiévale*, Paris, Flammarion, 1988; Leah Lydia Otis, *Prostitution in Medieval Society*, Chicago, University of Chicago Press, 1985; Marie-Erica Benabou, *La prostitution and la police des moeurs au XVIIIe siècle*, Paris, Perrin, 1987; Jill Harsin, *Policing Prostitution in Nineteenth-Century Paris*, Princeton, Princeton University Press, 1985; Elizabeth Ann Weston, "Prostitution in Paris in the Later Nineteenth Century," unpublished dissertation, State University of New York at Buffalo, 1979; Laure Adler, *La vie quotidienne dans les maisons closes, 1830–1930*, Paris, Hachette, 1990; Mary Gibson, *Prostitution and the State in Italy, 1860–1915*, New Brunswick, Rutgers University Press, 1986; Jacques Termau, *Maisons closes de province: l'amour vénal au temps du réglementarisme à partir d'une étude du Maine-Anjou*, Le Mans, Cénomane, 1986; Francis Ronsin, "Les prostituées de Rambervilliers," *Revue d'histoire moderne and contemporaine*, no. 34, janvier–mars 1987, pp. 138–153; *Prostitution in the Victorian Age. Debates on the Issue from 19th Century Journals*, Westmead, Gregg International Publishers, Ltd., 1973; Paul MacHugh, *Prostitution and Victorian Social Reform*, New York, St. Martin's, 1980; Judith Walkowitz, *Prostitution and Victorian Society: Women, Class, and the State*, Cambridge, Cambridge University Press, 1980; Frances Finnegan, *Poverty and Prostitution. A Study of Victorian Prostitutes in York*, Cambridge, Cambridge University Press, 1979; Marion S. Goldman, *Gold Diggers and Silver Miners: Prostitution and Social Life on the Comstock Lode*, Ann Arbor, University of Michigan Press, 1981; Anne M. Butler, *Daughters of Joy, Sisters of Misery. Prostitutes in the American West, 1865–1890*, Urbana, University of Illinois Press, 1985; Jacqueline Barnhard, *The Fail but Frail: Prostitution in San Francisco, 1849–1900*, Reno, University of Nevada Press, 1986; David Pivar, *Purity Crusade, Sexual Morality, and Social Control, 1868–1900*, Westport, CT, Greenwood Press, 1973; Mark T. Connelly, *The Response to Prostitution in the Progressive Era*, Chapel Hill, University of North Carolina Press, 1980; Ruth Rosen, *The Lost Sisterhood: Prostitution in America, 1900–1918*, Baltimore, Johns Hopkins University Press, 1982.

9. Nor have historians shown any greater curiosity about prostitution in Japan. Apart from books of an anecdotal flavor, there is no solid work in any Western language except for: De Becker, *The Nightless City*, London, Probsthain and Co., 1906 (1st ed., 1899); Liza Crihfield, "The Institution of the Geisha in Modern Japanese Society," doctoral thesis, Stanford University, 1978, which is sociological rather than historical in its thrust; and the recent work by Cecilia Segawa Seigle, *Yoshiwara. The Glittering World of the Japanese Courtesan*, Honolulu: University of Hawaii Press, 1993.

10. Pierre Dufour (a pseudonym of Paul Lacroix), *Histoire de la prostitution chez tous les peuples du monde depuis l'antiquité la plus reculée jusqu'à nos jours*, Paris, Seré, 1851–1853; Félix Regnault, *L'évolution de la prostitution*, Paris, Flammarion, 1906; William W. Sanger, *The History of Prostitution: Its Extent, Causes, and Effects Throughout the World*, New York, The Medical Publishing Co., 1910; James Marchant, *The Master Problem*, London, Stanley Paul & Co., 1917; Joseph MacCabe, *The Story of the World's Oldest Profession. Prostitution in the Ancient, Medieval and Modern Worlds*, Girard, KS, Haldeman-Julius Publications, 1932.

11. Charles-Ernest Martin, "Étude sur la prostitution en Chine," *Union médicale*, 2e série, vol. IX, no. 25, 1872, pp. 25, 401–408; no. 26, pp. 29, 465–474; Maxime Durand-Fardel, "La prostitution et la condition des femmes en Chine," *Union médicale*, 3e série, vol. XXI, no. 60, 1876, pp. 68, 810; no. 64, pp. 73, 869; no. 67, pp. 905–906; no. 73, pp. 84, 993 (published as an offprint: *La vie irrégulière et la condition des femmes en Chine*, Paris, Germer-Baillère, 1876).

12. Maurice Jametel, *La Chine inconnue*, Paris, Imprimerie de l'art, 1884.

13. See the introduction to Gustaaf Schlegel, *Le vendeur d'huile qui seul possède la Reine-de-beauté, ou splendeurs et misères des courtisanes chinoises*, Paris/Leyden, Brill et Maisonneuve, 1877 and, by the same author, *Histoire de la prostitution en Chine*, Rouen, 1880.

14. (Mrs.) Archibald MacKirdy and W. N. Willis, *The White Slave Market*, London, Stanley Paul and Co., 1912; Ernest A. Bell, *Fighting the Traffic in Young Girls or War on the White Slave Traffic*, 1930; Henry Champley, *The Road to Shanghai. White Slave Traffic in Asia*, London, John Long, Ltd., 1934; Joseph Crad, *Traders in Women: A Comprehensive Survey of "White Slavery,"* London, John Long, Ltd., 1940.

15. George R. Scott, *Far Eastern Sex Life: An Anthropological, Ethnological and Sociological Study of the Love Relations, Marriage Rites and Home Life of the Oriental Peoples*, London, Gerald C. Swan, 1970 (1st ed., 1943).

16. Robert Van Gulik, *Sexual Life in Ancient China*, Leiden, E. J. Brill 1961.

17. Robert Van Gulik, *Erotic Colour Prints of the Ming Period*, Tokyo, n.pub., 1951.

18. John Byron, *Portrait of a Chinese Paradise: Erotica and Sexual Customs of the Late Qing Period*, London, Quartet Books, 1987.

19. Howard S. Levy, "Record of the Gay Quarters," *Orient/West*, vol. VIII, no. 5, September–October 1963, pp. 121–128; no. 6, November–December 1963, pp. 115–122; vol. IX, no. 1, January–February 1964, pp. 103–110; "T'ang Women of Pleasure," *Sinologica*, vol. VIII, no. 2, 1965, pp. 89–113; "The Gay Quarters of Ch'ang-an," *Orient/West*, vol. VII, no. 9, Sept. 1962, pp. 93–105; *A Feast of Mist and Flowers: The Gay Quarters of Nanking at the End of the Ming*, Yokohama, 1966; *The Illusory Flame*, Tokyo, Kenkyusha, 1962. Howard Levy is also known for his historical study of the practice of binding the feet of Chinese women, *Chinese Footbinding: The History of a Curious Erotic Custom*, New York, Bell Publishing Company, 1966.

20. Arthur Waley, "The Green Bower Collection" (1957), in *The Secret History of the Mongols and Other Pieces*, New York, Barnes & Noble, 1967, pp. 89–107; Robert des Rotours, *Courtisanes à la fin des T'ang entre circa 789 et le 8 January 881: Pei-li tche (Anecdotes du quartier du Nord) par Souen K'i*, Paris, Presses Universitaires de France, 1968.

21. James H. Willey, "A Study of Chinese Prostitution," M.A. dissertation, University of Chicago, 1929.

22. Sue Gronewold, *Beautiful Merchandise. Prostitution in China, 1860–1936,* New York, Haworth Press, 1982 (Women's (XXX) History series no. 1).

23. A fuller list would include Kerrie L. MacPherson, "State Medicine and the Experiment of the Lock Hospital," *A Wilderness of Marshes. The Origins of Public Health in Shanghai, 1843–1893,* Oxford, Oxford University Press, 1987, pp. 213–258; Norman Miners, "The State Regulation of Prostitution, 1857–1941," *Hong Kong under Imperial Rule,* Hong Kong/London, Oxford University Press, East Asian Historical Monographs, 1987, pp. 191–206. However, these two studies examine the question of prostitution solely from the viewpoint of regulationism and action by the authorities.

24. He Wannan and Yang Jiezeng, *Shanghai changji gaizao shihua* ("A Short History of the Re-education of Prostitutes in Shanghai"), Shanghai, Sanlian shudian, 1988; *Beijing fengbi jiyuan jishi* ("The True Story of the Closure of the Houses of Prostitution in Peking"), Beijing, Zhongguo heping chubanshe, 1988; Ma Weigang, *Jinchang jindu* ("The Abolition of Prostitution and Gambling"), Beijing, Jinguan jiaoyu chubanshe, 1993.

25. Tang Weikang, "Shili yangchang de changji" ("The Prostitutes of the 'Foreigners' District"), in Tang Weikang et al., *Shanghai yishi* ("Shanghai Anecdotes"), Shanghai, Wenhua chubanshe, 1987, pp. 261–274; *Jiu Shanghai de yan du chang* ("Prostitution, Gambling and Opium in Old Shanghai"), Shanghai shi wenshiguan bian, Shanghai, Baijia chubanshe, 1988; Sun Guoqun, *Jiu Shanghai changji mishi* ("Secret History of Prostitution in Old Shanghai"), Henan, Henan renmin chubanshe, 1988.

26. Xue Liyong, "Ming-Qing shiqi de Shanghai changji" ("Prostitution in Shanghai in Ming-Qing Times"), in *Jiu Shanghai de yan du chang,* pp. 150–158; Ping Jinya, "Jiu Shanghai de changji" ("Prostitutes in Old Shanghai"), in *Jiu Shanghai de yan du chang,* pp. 159–171; Xie Wuyi, "Minchu Shanghai changji yi pie" ("A Glance at Prostitution in Shanghai at the Beginning of the Republic"), in *Jiu Shanghai de yan du chang,* pp. 172–175; Zhao Zhiyan, "Zhengjiu changji de cishan jigou – Jiliangsuo" ("A Charitable Organization Rescuing Prostitutes – the Door of Hope") *in Jiu Shanghai de yan du chang,* pp. 176–178.

27. Renate Scherer, *Das System der chinesischen Prostitution dargestellt am Beispiel Shanghais in der Zeit von 1840 bis 1949,* Inaugural dissertation, Freie Universität Berlin, 1983, Berlin, Papyrus-Druck, 1986.

28. Gail Hershatter, "The Hierarchy of Shanghai Prostitution, 1870–1949," *Modern China,* vol. XV, no. 4, October 1989, pp. 463–498; "Prostitution and the Market in Early Twentieth-Century Shanghai," in Rubie S. Watson and Patricia Buckley Ebrey, *Marriage and Inequality in Chinese Society,* Berkeley, University of California Press, 1991, pp. 256–285; "Courtesans and Streetwalkers: The Changing Discourse on Shanghai Prostitution, 1890–1949," *Journal of the History of Sexuality,* vol. III, no. 2, pp. 245–269; "Regulating Sex in Shanghai. The Reform of Prostitution in 1920 and 1951," in Frederic Wakeman and Wen-hsin Yeh, *Shanghai Sojourners,* Berkeley, University of California Press, 1992, pp. 145–185; "Modernizing Sex, Sexing Modernity: Prostitution in Early Twentieth-Century Shanghai," in Christina Gilmartin et al., *Engendering China. Women, Culture, and the State,* Cambridge, MA, Harvard University Press, 1994, pp. 147–174.

29. Wolfram Eberhard, *Guilt and Sin in Traditional China,* Berkeley, University of California Press, 1967.

30. Sue Gronewold has devoted her recently completed dissertation to this institution. Sue Groneworld, "The Door of Hope," unpublished dissertation.

Chapter 1

1. Gail Hershatter, "The Hierarchy of Shanghai Prostitution, 1870–1949," *Modern China*, vol. XV, no. 4, October 1989, pp. 463–498.
2. Cf. Ping-ti Ho, *The Ladder of Success in Imperial China. Aspects of Social Mobility, 1368–1911*, New York, Columbia University Press, 1962; and Chang Chung-li, *The Chinese Gentry*, Seattle, University of Washington Press, 1962.
3. Etienne Balazs, *La bureaucratie céleste*, Paris, Gallimard (collection NRF), 1968.
4. The circuit intendant was the civil servant in charge of the *xian* (district) or prefecture. In the big cities like Shanghai or Hankou, he became the *de facto* representative of State authority for the entire city, although his function could not be likened to that of a mayor. On the role and function of the circuit intendant in Shanghai, cf. Leung Yüen-Sang, *The Shanghai Taotai: Linkage Man in a Changing Society, 1843–1890*, Honolulu, University of Hawaii Press, 1990. There are many references to this figure in William T. Rowe, *Hankow: Commerce and Society in a Chinese City, 1796–1889*, inf.; *id., Hankow. Conflict and Community in a Chinese City, 1796–1895*. To place the position of the circuit intendant in the context of the imperial administration, cf. T'ung-tsu Chü, *Local Government in China under the Ch'ing*, Stanford, Stanford University Press, 1962; and John R. Watt, *The District Magistrate in Late Imperial China*, New York, Columbia University Press, 1972.
5. Yüen-sang Leung, *The Shanghai Taotai*, 1990, p. 125.
6. William T. Rowe, *Hankow: Commerce and Society in a Chinese City, 1796–1889*, Stanford, Stanford University Press, 1984; *Hankow. Conflict and Community in a Chinese City, 1796–1895*, Stanford, Stanford University Press, 1989.
7. Yüen-sang Leung, *The Shanghai Taotai*, p. 162.
8. William T. Rowe, *Hankow. Conflict and Community in a Chinese City, 1796–1895*, p. 92.
9. Wang Tao, *Songbin suohua* ("Idle Talk on the Riverside"), Shanghai, n.pub., n.d., p. 202; Tang Weikang, "Shili yangchang de changji" ("The Prostitutes of the Foreigners' District"), in Tang Weikang et al., *Shanghai yishi* ("Shanghai Anecdotes"), Shanghai, Wenhua chubanshe, 1987, p. 265.
10. Robert des Rotours, *Courtisanes à la fin des T'ang entre circa 789 et le 8 janvier 881: Pei-li tche (Anecdotes of the Northern District) by Souen K'i*; Howard S. Levy, "Record of the Gay Quarters"; *id.,* "Tang Women of Pleasure"; "The Gay Quarters of Ch'ang-an"; *ibid., A Feast of Mist and Flowers: The Gay Quarters of Nanking at the End of the Ming*, Yokohama, 1966; *id., Banqiao zaji* ("Various Notes on the Wooden Bridge"); *id., The Illusory Flame*; Arthur Waley, "The Green Bower Collection."
11. "*Mai yi bu mai shen*" or "*Mai zui* (mouth) *bu mai shen*."
12. Wang Tao, *Songbin suohua*, p. 202.
13. Paul Cohen, *Between Tradition and Modernity. Wang T'ao and Reform in Late Ch'ing China*, Cambridge, MA: Harvard University Press, 1974. Wang Tao's works have been very useful in depicting the world of the courtesans in the mid-nineteenth century. Wang was known above all for his writings in favor

of reform at the end of the Qing dynasty. This was the main theme of Paul Cohen's work from which the unconventional aspects of Wang's private life have been practically expunged. Wang came in 1848 to Shanghai, where his father was employed as a teacher. A year later, upon his father's death, he became head of the family, having already won the title of *xiucai*. In the following year, he lost his first wife. From then on until 1862, he worked as an editor for the London Missionary Society Press. Wang was suspected of having links with the Taiping and was forced to flee to Hong Kong, where he began to express his ideas on reform. It was only in 1884 that he returned permanently to Shanghai. He seems to have stayed there for brief spells in between. Wang was a regular customer of courtesans during all his life. This is not something exceptional. His diary reveals that he often went out carousing with friends. In Shanghai, he was an assiduous patron of these establishments, even when he returned at the age of fifty-five in 1884. His second wife tried to dissuade him from such activities, and she regularly sent an old servant to remind him of his duties. In a letter to a friend, he wrote at the age of 60: "All my life, I have been rather a Bohemian, fond of girls and wine, and even today I am always in the garden and other resorts here in Shanghai. This has always seemed to me a perfectly normal recreation and not the sort of thing a man has to hide from other people." Paul Cohen, *Between Tradition and Modernity*, pp. 8, 13–15, 47, 181, 293.

14. Yu Baosheng (pseudonym of Wang Tao), *Haizou yeyou fulu* ("Addenda to Tales of Libertinage at the Seaside"), Shanghai, Hanwen yuanshusi, 1929, I, p. 7; Wang Tao, *Songbin suohua*, p. 201.

15. I have made extensive use of Wang Tao's writings for this period, especially Yu Baosheng, *Haizou yeyou lu* ("Tales of Libertinage at the Seaside), Shanghai, Hanwen yuanshusi, (1870) 1929; *id.*, *Haizou yeyou fulu, op. cit.*; *id.*, *Haizou yeyou yulu* ("Tales of Libertinage at the Seaside (continued)"), Shanghai, Hanwen yuanshusi, 1929; Yu Baosheng, *Huaguo jutan* ("Chat on the [Theater of the] World of Flowers"), Shanghai, Hanwen yuanshusi (1878), 1929. In the first volume of *Haizou yeyou*, all the years referred to are between 1846 and 1853. The second, *fulu*, covers a wider range, from 1853 to 1878; however, most of the the years referred to are 1860–1861. The last volume, *yulu*, covers the years 1864–1875. *Huaguo jutan* relates to the years 1860–1876.

16. *Shanghai lanyou zhinan* ("A Sightseeing Guide to Shanghai"), Shanghai, Zhonghua tushu jicheng gongsi, 1923, p. 1.

17. Yu Baosheng, *Haizou yeyou fulu*, I, p. 5.

18. "Demi-Monde of Shanghai (The)," *China Medical Journal*, vol. XXXVII, no. 9, 1923, p. 783; Tang Weikang, "Shili yangchang de changji" ("The Prostitutes of the 'Foreigners' District"), in Tang Weikang et al., *Shanghai yishi* ("Shanghai Anecdotes"), p. 266.

19. Yu Baosheng, *Haizou yeyou fulu*, I, p. 7.

20. Wang Tao, *Songbin suohua*, p. 202.

21. Wang Tao, *Songbin suohua*, p. 201.

22. Yu Baosheng, *Haizou yeyou fulu*, II, p. 1.

23. Wang Tao, *Songbin suohua*, p. 201.

24. *Shanghai zhinan* ("Guide to Shanghai: A Chinese Directory of the Port"), Shanghai, Shangwu yinshuguan (1st ed., 1909), 1919, V, p. 18.

25. "Demi-Monde of Shanghai (The)," *China Medical Journal*, vol. XXXVII, no. 9, 1923, p. 784.

26. Yu Baosheng, *Haizou yeyou fulu*, II, p. 1; see also *SB*, 5 May 1872.
27. Wang Jimen, *Shanghai liushi nian lai huajie shi* ("Sixty Years of History of the World of Flowers in Shanghai"), Shanghai, Shixin shuju, 1922, p. 6.
28. *Shanghai lanyou zhinan*, p. 1; *Lao Shanghai* ("Old Shanghai"), Shanghai, n.pub., n.d., p. 122; Wang Jimen, *Shanghai liushi nian lai huajie shi*, pp.186–214. See also Tang Weikang, "Shili yangchang de changji," p. 264; and Xie Wuyi, "Minchu Shanghai changji yi pie" ("A Glance at Prostitution in Shanghai at the Beginning of the Republic"), in *Jiu Shanghai de yan du chang* ("Prostitution, Gambling and Opium in Old Shanghai"), Shanghai shi wenshiguan bian, Shanghai, Baijia chubanshe, 1988, pp. 172–173.
29. Chen Wuwo, *Lao Shanghai san shi nian jianwen* ("Thirty Years of Sights and Sounds of Old Shanghai"), Shanghai, Dadong shuju, 1928, p. 37.
30. Yu Baosheng, *Haizou yeyou lu*, *op. cit.*; *id.*, *Haizou yeyou fulu*, *op. cit.*; *id.*, *Haizou yeyou yulu*, *op. cit.*; *Huaguo jutan*, *op. cit.*
31. Bryna Goodman, *Native Place, City, and Nation: Regional Networks and Identities in Shanghai, 1853–1937*, Berkeley, University of California Press, 1995.
32. Wang Jimen, *Shanghai liushi nian lai huajie shi*, p. 9.
33. Xu Ke (ed.), *Qing bai lei chao* ("The Hundred Categories of the Qing"), Shanghai, 1920, "changji lei," p. 15.
34. Yu Baosheng, *Haizou yeyou fulu*, III, p. 4; Wang Tao, *Songbin suohua*, p. 105.
35. Xu Ke (ed.), *Qing bai lei chao*, p. 31.
36. *Shanghai lanyou zhinan*, p. 4.
37. I have examined seventeen applications filed between 5 and 16 July 1923, from the Archives de la direction des services administratifs, Concession française, Archives municipales de Shanghai, dossier 1934 25 MS 1554.2, "Maisons de chanteuses – Demandes de licence" [1922–1924].
38. I have included data from *Songbin suohua* concerning fourteen courtesans. In this book, Wang Tao refers to some fifty girls.
39. Yu Baosheng, *Huaguo jutan*, I, p. 3.
40. The notion of a "good family" (*liang jia*) must be taken in the broad sense of the term. It does not refer to any particular socioeconomic category. In the legal sense, good families were the contrary of "base" or "mean" (*jianmin*), a term denoting an inferior legal status applied to only certain population groups, among them the prostitutes, up to the eighteenth century. Cf. Harry Hansson, "Regional Outcast Groups in Late Imperial China," doctoral thesis, Harvard University, 1988; on adopted daughters, see Rubie S. Watson, "Concubines and Maids: Servitude and Kin Status in the Hong Kong Region, 1900–1940," in Rubie S. Watson and Patricia Buckley Ebrey, *Marriage and Inequality in Chinese Society*, Berkeley, University of California Press, 1991; Maria Jaschok, *Concubines and Bondservants. The Social History of a Chinese Custom*, London, Zed Books, 1989.
41. Yu Baosheng, *Huaguo jutan*, I, p. 7.
42. Jean Duval, "Les aventures révélatrices d'un dandy amoureux: étude d'un roman en dialecte *wu* de la fin de l'époque Qing, *La tortue à neuf queues*, de Zhang Chunfan," doctoral thesis, Paris, Institut national des langues et civilisations orientales, 1975, p. 99.
43. Mu zhen shan ren, *Qinglou meng* ("The Dream of the Green Bower" [Courtesans' House]), Hengyang, Yuelu shushe [1878–1884], reprinted 1988;

Han Bangqing, *Haishang hualie zhuan* ("Chronicle of Flowers on the Sea"), Taibei, Wenhua tushu gongsi [1892], reprinted 1984; Chi xian shu shi shi, *Haishang fanhua meng: san ji* ("Luxuriant Dream in Shanghai: Three Collections"), n.p., Jinbu shuju, 1916; Chi xian shu shi shi, *Xu haishang fanhua meng. san ji* ("Luxuriant Dream in Shanghai (continued)"), n.p., n.pub., n.d.; Jean Duval, "Les aventures révélatrices d'un dandy amoureux," *op. cit.*

44. Gustaaf Schlegel, "Préface," *Le vendeur d'huile qui seul possède la reine-de-beauté, ou Splendeur and misères des courtisanes chinoises*, Paris/Leyden, Brill et Maisonneuve, 1877, pp. ix–x.

45. Yu Baosheng, *Huaguo jutan*, I, p. 2.

46. Wang Jimen, *Shanghai liushi nian lai huajie shi*, pp. 156–157.

47. *Haishang yeyou beilan* ("Omnium of Licentiousness in Shanghai"), Shanghai, n.pub. 1891, III, p. 14.

48. *Shanghai lanyou zhinan*, p. 6.

49. *Hua Bao* ("The Flowers"), 18 September 1926.

50. Wang Shunu, *Zhongguo changji shi* ("History of Prostitution in China"), Shanghai, Shenghuo shudian, 1934 (reprinted, Taibei, 1971), p. 286; Haishang juewusheng (pseud.), *Jinü de shenghuo* ("The Life of the Prostitutes"), Shanghai, Chunmin shudian, 1940, p. 8.

51. Wang Tao, *Songbin suohua*, p. 107.

52. Wang Tao, *Songbin suohua*, p. 118.

53. *Shanghai shenmi zhinan* ("Secret Guide to Shanghai"), Shanghai, Datong tushushe jianyin, n.d., p. 9.

54. Wang Dingjiu, *Shanghai guwen* ("Guide to Shanghai"), Shanghai, Zhongyang shudian, 1934, p. 662.

55. The expression *da chawei* is untranslatable. It refers to the practice of taking tea around a table in the company of women or friends. To render it by "going on a round" would not accurately reflect the spirit of these visits.

56. Zhang Qiugu, *Piao du baibi daguan* ("An Overview of the Evils of Gambling and Whoring"), Shanghai, Qiugu chubanbu, 1920, I, p. 4; *Shanghai lanyou zhinan*, p. 5.

57. Haishang juewusheng (pseudonym), *Jinü de shenghuo*, pp. 130–131.

58. *Shanghai shenmi zhinan*, p. 4; Haishang juewusheng (pseudonym), *Jinü de shenghuo*, p. 22.

59. Chen Wuwo, *Lao Shanghai san shi nian jianwen*, pp. 72–74.

60. Cf. *Xiaolinbao* ("A Thousand Smiles"), 6 July 1902.

61. *Haishang yeyou beilan*, IV, p. 8.

62. Wang Jimen, *Shanghai liushi nian lai huajie shi*, p. 150.

63. Door of Hope and Children's Refuge Mission. China, *Annual Report*, 1910, p. 10.

64. I use this notion of "places of entertainment" deliberately, in order to express the change that occurred in the behavior of the Chinese elites in their leisure activities from the First World War onward. There had been major changes since the arrival of the Westerners, but, in my view, the traditional forms of behavior endured. The date 1914–1915 is probably quite arbitrary. There was no clear-cut and sharp break in this continuous process of social transformation in Shanghai. However, rather than 1911, a date that is far too political and not very relevant as a milestone, I would choose 1914–1915 because it correponds to the beginning of a fantastic leap forward in the local economy and to the emergence of new social classes that were the vectors of modern-

ization. See Marie-Claire Bergere, *The Golden Age of the Chinese Bourgeoisie*, Cambidge: Cambridge University Pres, 1989.

65. In 1919, a Shanghai guide listed 162 teahouses. Ten years later (in 1928), one writer was able to count no more than 68 of them. *Shanghai zhinan*, V, pp. 12–14; Wu Chenglian, *Jiu Shanghai chaguan jiulou* ("The Taverns and Tea-Houses of Old Shanghai"), Shanghai, Huadong shifan daxue chubanshe, 1989, p. 12.
66. The others were *Jiangnan diyilou, Haishang yipinlou, Ronghua fuguilou, Pinyulou, Pinshenglou*. Chen Wuwo, *Lao Shanghai san shi nian jianwen*, I, p. 52.
67. Wang Jimen, *Shanghai liushi nian lai huajie shi*, p. 6.
68. *Shanghai zhinan*, V, p. 18.
69. Chi Zhicheng, "Hu you mengying lu" ("Notes and Sights from a Journey to Shanghai"), *Dang'an yu lishi*, no. 1, 1989, p. 2. This is a first hand account by a Chinese scholar settled in Taiwan, who recounted his experiences in Shanghai when he journeyed there in September 1891.
70. Cf. *Xiaolinbao* ("A Thousand Smiles"), 2 April 1901. On the small newspapers, see the next chapter.
71. *Haishang yeyou beilan*, IV, p. 12; Wang Jimen, *Shanghai liushi nian lai huajie shi*, p. 6.
72. *Shanghai lanyou zhinan*, p. 4.
73. Wang Tao, *Songbin suohua*, p. 202.
74. *Shanghai lanyou zhinan*, p. 5.
75. Wang Tao, *Songbin suohua*, p. 202.
76. Chi Zhicheng, "Hu you mengying lu," p. 2.
77. Yu Baosheng, *Haizou yeyou fulu*, I, p. 2.
78. *Haishang yeyou beilan*, I, p. 13.
79. Wang Jimen, *Shanghai liushi nian lai huajie shi*, p. 145. The story is probably exaggerated. It is difficult to see how the courtesan in question could have responded to the 670 invitations from two rivals in a course of a single theatrical performance.
80. Chi Zhicheng, "Hu you mengying lu," p. 3.
81. *Haishang yeyou beilan*, III, p. 9.
82. *Haishang yeyou beilan*, III, p. 4; Wang Jimen, *Shanghai liushi nian lai huajie shi*, p. 11.
83. *Haishang yeyou beilan*, III, p. 8.
84. *Haishang yeyou beilan*, I, p. 14.
85. *Haishang yeyou beilan*, III, p. 6. These games could have unfortunate consequences for certain customers when they reached an advanced stage of inebriation or torpor. When a customer got drunk or drowsy, the courtesans would lightly shake a little silver box containing whole nutmeg seeds, causing a slight rolling sound that would awaken the customer.
86. In 1918, more than 70 corporations still conducted their exchanges in 27 teahouses of the city. This practice continued until 1949. We can imagine the extent to which the teahouses were a happy hunting ground for the courtesans and prostitutes. Wu Chenglian, *Jiu Shanghai chaguan jiulou*, pp. 58 and 60.
87. Wang Tao, *Haizou yeyou fulu*, I, p. 3.
88. Wu Chenglian, *Jiu Shanghai chaguan jiulou*, pp. 27 and 31.
89. Chi Zhicheng, "Hu you mengying lu," p. 3.
90. Wang Tao, *Haizou yeyou fulu*, I, p. 3.

91. The sedan chair was gradually replaced by the rickshaw, which came in at the end of the century, and by horse-drawn carriages, which offered greater comfort. These two modes of transport dominated the urban space up to the end of the first decade of the twentieth century. They themselves, and especially the horse-drawn carriages, were challenged by the appearance of modern means of transport: the tramways (1908), automobiles, and buses (1924). Chang Ying-hwa, "The Internal Structure of Chinese Cities, 1920's and 1930's: An Ecological Approach," doctoral thesis, Princeton University, 1982, p. 202.
92. Wang Jimen, *Shanghai liushi nian lai huajie shi*, p. 101.

Chapter 2

1. The expression *xiangfen*, which I have interpreted as "perfume and powder," is a conventional term used to designate the courtesans in writings prior to the twentieth century. The courtesans and the prostitutes were always designated by metaphorical expressions. It was after 1914–1915 that the terms *jinü, changji* (prostitute), and *jiyuan* (brothel) came into common use in references to the phenomenon of prostitution.
2. *Haishang yeyou beilan* ("Omnium of Licentiousness in Shanghai"), Shanghai, n.pub., 1891, III, p. 14.
3. Eberhard, Wolfram, "What Is Beautiful in a Chinese Woman," *Moral and Social Values of the Chinese: Collected Essays*, Taibei, Cheng Wen Publishing Co., 1971, pp. 294–295.
4. *Dianshizhai huabao* ("Studio Pictorial Newspaper"), Shanghai, 1884–1898, reprint. Guangzhou, Guangzhou renmin chubanshe, 1983, 44 vol. The *Dianshizhai huabao* has been studied by Fritz Van Briessen, *Shanghai-Bildzeitung 1884–1898: eine Illustrierte aus dem China des ausgehenden 19. Jahrhunderts*, Zurich/Freiburg, 1977.
5. *Haishang yeyou beilan, op. cit.*, III, p. 10.
6. Alain Corbin, *Les filles de noce. Misère sexuelle and prostitution (XIXe–XXe siècle)*, Paris, Flammarion (coll. Champs), 1982 (1st ed., Aubier-Montaigne, 1978), p. 108.
7. Jean Duval, "Les aventures révélatrices d'un dandy amoureux: Étude d'un roman en dialecte Wu de la fin de l'époque Qing, *La Tortue à neuf queues*, de Zhang Chunfan," doctoral thesis, Paris, Institut national des langues et civilisations orientales, 1975, pp. 99 and 109.
8. *Shanghai lanyou zhinan* ("A Sightseeing Guide to Shanghai"), Shanghai, Zhonghua tushu jicheng gongsi, 1923, pp. 37–38.
9. See the doctoral thesis by Jr-lien Tsao, "Remembering Suzhou. Urbanism in Late Imperial China," University of California, 1992.
10. Wang Jimen, *Shanghai liushi nian lai huajie shi* ("Sixty Years of History of the World of Flowers in Shanghai"), Shanghai, Shixin shuju, 1922, p. 151.
11. Frances J., Heath, "Review of Eight Years' Work in China in a Gynecological Out-Patient Clinic," *China Medical Journal*, vol. 39, 1925, pp. 701–705.
12. *Shanghai lanyou zhinan, op. cit.*, p. 30; Haishang juewusheng (pseudonym), *Jinü de shenghuo* ("The Life of the Prostitutes"), Shanghai, Chunmin shudian, 1940, p. 48.
13. Jin Buhuan, *Chunjiang huayue hen* ("Recollections of the Good Old Times"), Xianggang, Tianwentai baoshe, 1962, p. 28.

14. *Shanghai shenmi zhinan* ("Secret Guide to Shanghai"), Shanghai, Datong tushushe jianyin, n.d., p. 13.
15. Yu Baosheng (pseudonym of Wang Tao), *Huaguo jutan, op. cit.*, I, pp. 2 and 5. In the 1880s, the annual salary of civil servants ranged from 33 to 180 taels. This income, however, was supplemented by various sources that pushed the average income of officeholders to around 5,000 taels a year. At the Jiangnan Arsenal in Shanghai, a director earned a monthly salary of 200 taels, a chief accountant earned 80 taels, and a work inspector earned 26 taels. At the turn of the century, the rate between the tael and the yuan was around 0.73 tael for one yuan. Chang Chung-li, *The Income of the Chinese Gentry*, Seattle, University of Washington Press, 1962, p. 42 and pp. 12–13; Christine Cornet, *Etat et entreprises en Chine aux XIXe–XXe siècles. Le chantier naval de Jiangnan, 1865–1937*, Paris, Arguments, 1997, pp. 32–33.
16. Zhang Qiugu, *Piao du bai bi daguan, op. cit.*, I, p. 17; *Shanghai lanyou zhinan, op. cit.*, p. 5.
17. *Shanghai shenmi zhinan, op. cit.*, p. 13.
18. *Shanghai lanyou zhinan, op. cit.*, p. 5.
19. *Haishang yeyou beilan, op. cit.*, I, p. 5.
20. Haishang juewusheng (pseudonym), *Jinü de shenghuo, op. cit.*, pp. 116–117.
21. Robert Van Gulik, *Sexual Life in Ancient China*, Leiden, E. J. Brill, 1961; translation *La vie sexuelle dans la Chine ancienne*, Paris, Gallimard, 1971, pp. 2–3 and 412.
22. Yu Baosheng (pseudonym of Wang Tao), *Huaguo jutan, op. cit.*, I, p. 8.
23. *Haishang yeyou beilan, op. cit.*, III, p. 14.
24. *Haishang yeyou beilan, op. cit.*, III, p. 16.
25. *Haishang yeyou beilan, op. cit.*, IV, p. 2; *SB*, 4 September 1872.
26. Jin Buhuan, *Chunjiang huayue hen, op. cit.*, p. 23.
27. *Hua Bao* ("The Flowers"), 6 September 1926.
28. The year was divided into three four-month seasons marked out by three festivals: the New Year, the Dragon Festival (*duanwujie*), and the Mid-Autumn Festival (*zhongqiujie*).
29. Wang Dingjiu, *Shanghai guwen* ("Guide to Shanghai"), Shanghai, Zhongyang shudian, 1934, p. 666.
30. Christian Henriot, "Medicine, V.D., and Prostitution in Pre-Revolutionary China," *Social History of Medicine*, Oxford University, vol. V, no. 1, 1992, pp. 95–120.
31. *Haishang yeyou beilan, op. cit.*, III, p. 14.
32. *Hua Bao* ("The Flowers"), 18 September 1926.
33. Haishang juewusheng (pseudonym), *Jinü de shenghuo, op. cit.*, p. 110.
34. Zhang Qiugu, *Piao du bai bi daguan, op. cit.*, I, p. 19.
35. *Shanghai lanyou zhinan, op. cit.*, p. 6; Preston J., Maxwell, "On Criminal Abortion in China," *China Medical Journal*, vol. 42, 1928, pp. 12–19.
36. Haishang juewusheng (pseudonym), *Jinü de shenghuo, op. cit.*, pp. 90–91.
37. *Hua Bao* ("The Flowers"), 6 September 1926.
38. Wang Dingjiu, *Shanghai menjing, op. cit.*, chapter entitled "piao," p. 7; Haishang juewusheng (pseudonym), *Jinü de shenghuo, op. cit.*, p. 109.
39. *Haishang yeyou beilan, op. cit.*, I, p. 13.
40. Wang Jimen, *Shanghai liushi nian lai huajie shi, op. cit.*, pp. 137–140.
41. Yu Baosheng [pseudonym of Wang Tao], *Haizou yeyou lu, op. cit.*, I, p. 5.
42. Yu Baosheng [pseudonym of Wang Tao], *Huaguo jutan, op. cit.*, II, p. 12.

43. Yu Baosheng [pseudonym of Wang Tao], *Huaguo jutan, op. cit.*, I, p. 2.
44. *SB*, 5 May 1872.
45. Wang Jimen, *Shanghai liushi nian lai huajie shi, op. cit.*, p. 156.
46. *Shanghai lanyou zhinan, op. cit.*, p. 33.
47. Zhang Qiugu, *Piao du bai bi daguan, op. cit.*, I, p. 20; *Shanghai lanyou zhinan, op. cit.*, p. 5.
48. Jin Buhuan, *Chunjiang huayue hen, op. cit.*, pp. 42–43.
49. Wang Tao, *Songbin suohua, op. cit.*, p. 121.
50. *SB*, 4 June 1872.
51. Yu Baosheng (pseudonym of Wang Tao), *Huaguo jutan, op. cit.*, I, p. 13; *SB*, 20 January 1879.
52. Yu Baosheng (pseudonym of Wang Tao), *Huaguo jutan, op. cit.*, II, p. 10.
53. Wang Tao, *Songbin suohua, op. cit.*, p. 119.
54. Yu Baosheng [pseudonym of Wang Tao], *Huaguo jutan, op. cit.*, I, p. 13; II, p. 6.
55. Wang Tao, *Songbin suohua, op. cit.*, p. 119.
56. Yu Baosheng [pseudonym of Wang Tao], *Huaguo jutan, op. cit.*, I, pp. 6 and 20; II, pp. 3, 6, 11, and 12.
57. Cf. Bram Dijkstra, "The Cult of Invalidism," *Idols of Perversity. Fantasies of Feminine Evil in Fin-de-Siècle Culture*, Oxford, Oxford University Press, 1986.
58. Yu Baosheng (pseudonym of Wang Tao), *Huaguo jutan, op. cit.*, I, p. 11.
59. Yu Baosheng (pseudonym of Wang Tao), *Huaguo jutan, op. cit.*, I, p. 8.
60. *SB*, 8 June 1872.
61. *SB*, 21 June 1872.
62. *SB*, 9 December 1873.
63. *SB*, 14 June 1872; 14 February 1899.
64. Wang Jimen, *Shanghai liushi nian lai huajie shi, op. cit.*, p. 158.
65. *SB,* 10 May 1919.
66. Wang Jimen, *Shanghai liushi nian lai huajie shi, op. cit.*, p. 159.
67. *SB,* 29 December 1919.
68. *SB*, 24, 25, 27, and 28 March 1921.
69. Wang Jimen, *Shanghai liushi nian lai huajie shi, op. cit.*, p. 156.
70. Wang Jimen, *Shanghai liushi nian lai huajie shi, op. cit.*, pp. 156–157.
71. Wang Jimen, *Shanghai liushi nian lai huajie shi, op. cit.*, p. 158.
72. Examples of this literature can be found in Wang Jimen, *Shanghai liushi nian lai huajie shi, op. cit.*, pp. 99–139; Zhang Zhongjiang, *Jinü yu wenxue* ("Prostitutes and Literature"), Taibei, Kang Naixin chubanshe, 1969 (1st ed., 1966), *Lidai jinü yu shige* ("The Famous Prostitutes of History and Poetry"), Taibei, Zhiquan chubanshe; Wang Suxin, *Zhongguo lidai mingji shihua* ("Short History of Famous Prostitutes in Chinese History"), Taibei, Xinzhuang, 1972; Wei Shaochang, *Li Boyuan yanjiu ziliao* ("Research Materials on Li Boyuan"), Shanghai, Guji chubanshe, 1980, pp. 513–518.
73. Xu Ke (ed.), *Qing bai lei chao* ("The Hundred Categories of the Qing"), Shanghai, 1920, "changji lei," p. 1.
74. Wang Tao, *Songbin suohua, op. cit.*, p. 118.
75. Yu Baosheng (pseudonym of Wang Tao), *Haizou yeyou fulu, op. cit.*, II, p. 1.
76. Xu Ke (ed.), *Qing bai lei chao, op. cit.*, "changji lei," p. 2; Wang Tao, *Songbin suohua, op. cit.*, pp. 97, 102, and 109; Yu Baosheng (pseudonym of Wang Tao), *Haizou yeyou fulu, op. cit.*, III, p. 1.
77. Wang Jimen, *Shanghai liushi nian lai huajie shi, op. cit.*, p. 77.

78. *Shanghai lanyou zhinan, op. cit.*, p. 16; Lin Zhen, *Shanghai zhinan* ("Guide to Shanghai"), Shanghai, Shangwu yinshuguan, 1930, p. 16.
79. Wang Jimen, *Shanghai liushi nian lai huajie shi, op. cit.*, pp. 79–80.
80. Wang Jimen, *Shanghai liushi nian lai huajie shi, op. cit.*, pp. 81–82.
81. *Lao shanghai* ("Old Shanghai"), Shanghai, n.pub., n.d., pp. 26–27.
82. *Shanghai lanyou zhinan, op. cit.*, p. 1.
83. Wang Jimen, *Shanghai liushi nian lai huajie shi, op. cit.*, p. 85.
84. Yu Baosheng (pseudonym of Wang Tao), *Haizou yeyou fulu, op. cit.*, III, p. 7.
85. Cf. *Huaguo ribao* ("The Kingdom of Flowers Daily"), November 1920.
86. *Huaguo ribao* ("The Kingdom of Flowers Daily"), 4 December 1920.
87. Wang Tao, *Songbin suohua, op. cit.*, p. 109.
88. Christian, Henriot, "Le nouveau journalisme politique chinois (1895–1911: Shanghai–Hong Kong)," *Chine. Cahiers d'études chinoises*, Paris, INALCO, 1981, no. 1, pp. 5–80.
89. Wang Jimen, *Shanghai liushi nian lai huajie shi, op. cit.*, p. 132.
90. Wei Shaochang, *Li Boyuan yanjiu ziliao, op. cit.*, p. 5.
91. Lin Ruiming, *Wan Qing qianze xiaoshuo de lishi yiyi* ("Historical Significance in Late Ch'ing Fiction of Social Critique"), Taipei, Guoli Taiwan daxue chuban, 1980, p. 35.
92. Cf. *Xiaolin bao*, 11 August 1902.
93. Chen Wuwo, *Lao Shanghai san shi nian jianwen* ("Thirty Years of Sights and Sounds of Old Shanghai"), Shanghai, Dadong shuju, 1928, pp. 75–76.
94. Cf. *Xiaolin bao*, 11 August 1902.
95. Chen Wuwo, *Lao Shanghai san shi nian jianwen, op. cit.*, pp. 72–74.
96. *Hua Bao* ("The Flowers"), 25 and 28 August 1926.
97. *Huaguo ribao* ("The Kingdom of Flowers Daily"), December 1920.
98. Cf. *Haishang yeyou beilan, op. cit.*; *Haishang qinglou lejing tushuo* ("The Delights of Shanghai's Green Chambers in Words and Illustrations"), *Haishang qinglou tuji* ("Illustrated Notes on Shanghai's Green Chambers"), Shanghai, Yingzhou xinzui shuwu, 1892, 4 vols.; Zhang Qiugu, *Piao du bai bi daguan, op. cit.*; Haishang juewusheng (pseudonym), *Jinü de shenghuo* ("The Life of the Prostitutes"), Shanghai, Chunmin shudian, 1940.
99. *Shanghai zhinan* ("Guide to Shanghai: A Chinese Directory of the Port"), Shanghai, Shangwu yinshuguan, 1909 (1st ed.), 1919, 1920, 1923, 1925, 1926, 1930; *Shanghai lanyou zhinan* ("A Sightseeing Guide to Shanghai"), Shanghai, Zhonghua tushu jicheng gongsi, 1923; Lin Zhen, *Shanghai zhinan* ("Guide to Shanghai"), Shanghai, Shangwu yinshuguan, 1930; Wang Dingjiu, *Shanghai menjing* ("Gateway to Shanghai"), Shanghai, Zhongyang shudian, 1932 (reprint 1937); Shen Bojing, *Shanghai shi zhinan* ("Guide to the Municipality of Shanghai"), Shanghai, Zhonghua shuju, 1933; Wang Dingjiu, *Shanghai guwen* ("Guide to Shanghai"), Shanghai, Zhongyang shudian, 1934; *Da Shanghai zhinan* ("Guide to Greater Shanghai"), Shanghai, Zhonghua shuju, 1936; Xu Wancheng, *Shanghai zhinan* ("Guide to Shanghai"), Shanghai, Guoguang shudian, n.d.; Leng Shengwu, *Zuixin Shanghai zhinan* ("New Guide to Shanghai"), Shanghai, Shanghai wenhua yanjiushe, 1946; Liu Peiqian (ed.), *Da Shanghai zhinan* ("Guide to Greater Shanghai"), Shanghai, Dongnan wenhua fuwushe, 1947; Lu Jialiang, *Shanghai shouce* ("Pocket Guide to Shanghai"), Shanghai, Zhonghu shuju, 1949; *Shanghai shenmi zhinan* ("Secret Guide to Shanghai"), Shanghai, Datong tushushe jianyin, n.d.; (in English) *All About Shanghai and Environs*, Shanghai, China Press, 1935; *Shanghai's*

Commercial and Shopping Pocket Guide, Shanghai, Kwang Hsueh Publishing House, [1936]; *Guide to Shanghai*, Shanghai, American Express Co., Mercury Press, 1940; *Guide to Shanghai 1941*, n.p., n.pub., n.d.

Chapter 3

1. Gail Hershatter, "The Hierarchy of Shanghai Prostitution, 1870–1949," *Modern China*, vol. XV, no. 4, October 1989, p. 494.
2. Yu Baosheng, *Haizou yeyou lu*, I, p. 3.
3. *Haishang yeyou beilan* ("Omnium of Licentiousness in Shanghai"), Shanghai, n.pub., 1891, I, p. 1.
4. Xu Ke (ed.), *Qing bai lei chao* ("The Hundred Categories of the Qing"), Shanghai, 1920, p. 25.
5. Yu Baosheng, *Haizou yeyou fulu*, I, p. 2; *Shanghai lanyou zhinan* ("A Sight-seeing Guide to Shanghai"), Shanghai, Zhonghua tushu jicheng gongsi, 1923, chapter entitled "Yeyou xuzhi," p. 8.
6. *Shanghai shenmi zhinan* ("Secret Guide to Shanghai"), Shanghai, Datong tushushe jianyin, n.d., p. 25.
7. Yu Baosheng, *Haizou yeyou lu*, I, p. 4; Xue Liyong, "Ming-Qing shiqi de Shanghai changji" ("Prostitution in Shanghai in Ming-Qing times"), in *Jiu shanghai de yan du chang* ("Prostitution, Gambling and Opium in Old Shanghai"), Shanghai shi wenshiguan bian, Shanghai, Baijia chubanshe, 1988, p. 153.
8. Yu Baosheng, *Haizou yeyou lu*, I, p. 4; *Haishang yeyou beilan*, I, p. 2.
9. Yu Baosheng, *Haizou yeyou lu*, I, p. 4.
10. Yu Baosheng, *Haizou yeyou lu*, I, p. 2.
11. Yu Baosheng, *Haizou yeyou fulu*, II, p. 4.
12. Yu Baosheng, *Haizou yeyou fulu*, I, p. 2.
13. *SB*, 5 September 1899.
14. Yu Baosheng, *Haizou yeyou lu*, III, p. 5.
15. William Rowe, *Hankou. Conflict and Community in a Chinese City, 1796–1895*, Stanford, Stanford University Press, 1990, pp. 216–244.
16. Yu Baosheng, *Haizou yeyou lu*, III, p. 5.
17. Bryna Goodman, *Native Place, City, and Nation: Regional Networks and Identities in Shanghai, 1853–1937*, Berkeley, University of California Press, 1995, Chapter 2, "Foreign Imperialism, Immigration and Disorder," pp. 47–83.
18. Rowe makes explicit reference to Louis Chevalier's work, although he is very cautious, and with good reason, about transposing the notion of "dangerous classes" to the Chinese cities of the nineteenth century. A reading of the Shanghai press and the so-called denunciation (*qianze xiaoshuo*) literature, which was essentially a product of Shanghai, does not support the idea of any perception of a threat from the working classes in Shanghai. The work of William Rowe and Bryna Goodman emphasizes the tremendous capacity of the traditional organizations for integration and social control (*huiguan, gongsuo*). William Rowe, *Hankou. Conflict and Community in a Chinese City*; Bryna, Goodman, *op. cit.*
19. Lynda C. Johnson, "The Decline of Soochow and Rise of Shanghai: A Study in the Economic Morphology of Urban Change, 1756–1894," doctoral thesis, University of California, Santa Cruz, 1986, p. 99.

20. Yu Baosheng, *Haizou yeyou lu*, I, p. 2.
21. Yu Baosheng, *Haizou yeyou lu*, I, p. 2; III, p. 2.
22. Ch.-B. Maybon and Jean Fredet, *Histoire de la Concession française de Changhai*, pp. 264 and 291; Financial statements in the annual reports of the municipal administration of the Concession, *Compte rendu de la gestion pour l'exercice* 1863/1864–1864/1865, Conseil d'administration municipal de la Concession française, Shanghai, The China Printing Co.
23. Yu Baosheng, *Haizou yeyou lu*, I, p. 3.
24. Yu Baosheng, *Haizou yeyou lu*, II, p. 4.
25. Xu Ke (ed.), *Qing bai lei chao*, p. 27.
26. Yu Baosheng, *Haizou yeyou fulu*, I, p. 2.
27. Yu Baosheng, *Haizou yeyou lu*, II, p. 4.
28. Chi Zhicheng, "Hu you mengying lu" ("Dream Shadows of a Journey to Shanghai"), *Dang'an yu lishi*, no. 1, 1989, p. 4.
29. *SB*, 11 October 1899.
30. Xu Ke (ed.), *Qing bai lei chao*, pp. 29–30.
31. Yu Baosheng, *Haizou yeyou fulu*, I, p. 2.
32. *SB*, 3 February 1873.
33. Yu Baosheng, *Haizou yeyou lu*, I, p. 3.
34. Yu Baosheng, *Haizou yeyou lu*, I, p. 5.
35. Yu Baosheng, *Haizou yeyou fulu*, II, p. 4.
36. Gail Hershatter, "The Hierarchy of Shanghai Prostitution," pp. 471–473; Gail Hershatter, "Prostitution and the Market in Early Twentieth-Century Shanghai," in Rubie S. Watson and Patricia Buckley Ebrey, *Marriage and Inequality in Chinese Society*, Berkeley, University of California Press, 1991, pp. 263–264.
37. Wang Dingjiu, *Shanghai guwen* ("Guide to Shanghai"), Shanghai, Zhongyang shudian, 1934, p. 674.
38. Jin Buhuan, *Chunjiang huayue hen* ("Recollections of the Good Old Times"), Xianggang, Tianwentai baoshe, 1962, p. 166.
39. Haishang juewusheng (pseudonym), *Jinü de shenghuo* ("The Life of the Prostitutes"), Shanghai, Chunmin shudian, 1940, p. 161.
40. Jin Buhuan, *Chunjiang huayue hen*, p. 166; Wang Dingjiu, *Shanghai guwen*, p. 674.
41. Yu Baosheng, *Haizou yeyou lu*, III, p. 2.
42. *Shanghai zhinan* ("Guide to Shanghai: A Chinese Directory of the Port"), Shanghai, Shangwu yinshuguan, 1st ed., 1909; 1919, V, p. 20.
43. *Shanghai zhinan*, V, p. 20.
44. Wang Dingjiu, *Shanghai guwen*, p. 675.
45. Haishang juewusheng (pseudonym), *Jinü de shenghuo*, p. 160.
46. Wang Jimen, *Shanghai liushi nian lai huajie shi* ("Sixty Years of the History of the World of Flowers in Shanghai"), Shanghai, Shixin shuju, 1922, p. 25.
47. "Demi-monde of Shanghai (The)," *China Medical Journal*, vol. 37, no. 9, 1923, pp. 787–788.
48. *Shanghai lanyou zhinan* ("A Sightseeing Guide to Shanghai"), Shanghai, Zhonghua tushu jicheng gongsi, 1923, p. 1; Wang Jimen, *Shanghai liushi nian lai huajie shi*, p. 21.
49. This was the case especially with *Shanghai shenmi zhinan* and Wang Dingjiu, *Shanghai guwen*, who made no distinction between the *yao'er* and the *xianrouzhuang*. *Shanghai shenmi zhinan*, p. 23; Wang Dingjiu, *Shanghai guwen*,

p. 667; Wang Dingjiu, *Shanghai menjing* ("Gateway to Shanghai"), Shanghai, Zhongyang shudian, 1932, (revised edition, 1937), chapter entitled "piao," p. 20; Haishang juewusheng, *Jinü de shenghuo*, p. 149.

50. *Shanghai lanyou zhinan*, chapter entitled "yeyou xuzhi," p. 7; Haishang juewusheng, *Jinü de shenghuo*, p. 150.

51. Zhang Qiugu, *Piao du bai bi daguan*, II, pp. 2–3.

52. *Shanghai shenmi zhinan*, p. 27.

53. Zhang Qiugu, *Piao du bai bi daguan*, II, pp. 2–3.

54. *Shanghai lanyou zhinan*, chapter entitled "yeyou xuzhi," p. 7.

55. *Shanghai lanyou zhinan*, chapter entitled "yeyou xuzhi," p. 8.

56. Wang Dingjiu, *Shanghai menjing*, chapter entitled "piao," pp. 27–28.

57. Lu Dafang, *Shanghai tan yijiu lu* ("Reminiscences of the Shanghai Bund"), Taibei, Shijie shuju, 1980, p. 7. The term does not bear any particular meaning that can be rendered in a translation.

58. *Shanghai shenmi zhinan*, p. 47; Wang Dingjiu, *Shanghai guwen*, p. 669.

59. Jin Buhuan, *Chunjiang huayue hen*, p. 124.

60. *Shanghai shenmi zhinan*, p. 48.

61. The term *yeji* itself, which does not appear even in a work on prostitution published in 1891, was applied to all unattached workers who were not linked to a particular company (rickshaw and cart pullers, boatmen, etc.). There is another set of ideograms pronounced *yaji* ("elegant hen"), which was a homophonous deformation of the Shanghai dialect and a more stylish way of designating this group. In my opinion, it was toward the end of the 1930s that the expression *yaji* began to be used. *Shanghai zhinan*, V, p. 19b.; Wang Jimen, *Shanghai liushi nian lai huajie shi*, p. 23.

62. *Shanghai zhinan*, V, p. 20.

63. Wang Dingjiu, *Shanghai guwen*, 1934, p. 672; Zhang Qiugu, *Piao du bai bi daguan*, IV, p. 1. On the definition of *tangpai*, Ping Jinya, "Jiu Shanghai de changji" ("Prostitutes in Old Shanghai"), in *Jiu shanghai de yan du chang* ("Prostitution, Gambling and Opium in Old Shanghai"), Shanghai shi wenshiguan bian, Shanghai, Baijia chubanshe, 1988, p. 164.

64. Haishang juewusheng (pseudonym), *Jinü de shenghuo*, p. 164.

65. Zhang Qiugu, *Piao du bai bi daguan*, III, p. 6.

66. Lu Dafang, *Shanghai tan yijiu lu*, pp. 11–12.

67. Ji Longsheng, *Da Shanghai* ("Greater Shanghai"), Taibei, Nanfang zazhi chubanshe [1942], p. 103.

68. Jin Buhuan, *Chunjiang huayue hen*, pp. 178–179.

69. "Prostitution Problem in Shanghai [The]," p. 8.

70. Report, 31 October 1945, Police Archives, Municipality of Shanghai (1945–1949), file 011-4-173: January 1946–July 1948.

71. Undated letter and reply sheet from the police station, 26 August 1946, Police Archives, Municipality of Shanghai (1945–1949), file 011-4-173.

72. Lu Dafang, *Shanghai tan yijiu lu*, p. 13.

73. Zhang Qiugu, *Piao du bai bi daguan*, III, p. 8.

74. *Shanghai zhinan*, V, p. 20.

75. *Shanghai lanyou zhinan*, chapter entitled "yeyou xuzhi," p. 11.

76. "Demi-monde of Shanghai (The)," p. 787.

77. *Dianshizhai huabao* ("Studio Pictorial Newspaper"), Shanghai 1884–1898, reprint. Guangzhou, Guangzhou renmin chubanshe, 1983, 44 vols.

78. *Report for the Year 1909*, p. 54; *Report for the Year 1910*, p. 51; *Report for the*

Year 1911, p. 49; *Report for the Year 1912*, p. 45; *Report for the Year 1914*, p. 50A; *Report for the Year 1915*, p. 43A; *Report for the Year 1916*, p. 41A; *Report for the Year 1917*, p. 43A; *Report for the Year 1918*, p. 47A. I do not have any data for 1919 and 1920 or for 1931 and 1932.

79. Letter from the Consul-General of France, 12 April 1916, correspondance politique and commerciale (NS), 1897–1918, NS280, Concession française de Shanghai, XXIII, archives diplomatiques, pièces 134–138.

80. Shanghai Municipal Council, *Report for the Year 1920*, Shanghai, Kelly & Walsh, p. 70A; *Report for the Year 1922*, p. 72A; *Report for the Year 1923*, p. 41; *Report for the Year 1924*, p. 48; *Report for the Year 1925*, p. 42.

81. *SB*, 25 May 1922.

82. Mary N. Gamewell, *Gateway to China: Pictures of Shanghai*, New York, n.pub., 1916, p. 45.

83. *SB*, 9 September 1899.

84. *SB*, 22 May 1899.

85. *SB*, 21 December 1909; 25 January 1909.

86. *SB*, 28 November 1919.

87. *Shanghai zhinan*, V, p. 19b; Ji Longsheng, *Da Shanghai* ("Greater Shanghai"), Taibei, Nanfang zazhi chubanshe [1942], p. 30.

88. Mary N. Gamewell, *Gateway to China*, p. 48. Also quoted in Emily Honig, *Strangers and Sisters: Women in the Shanghai Cotton Mills, 1919–1949*, Stanford, Stanford University Press, 1986, p. 21.

89. *SB*, 8 September 1899; 16 January 1909; 21 January 1909; 25 December 1909; 16 July 1919; 27 July 1919; 29 July 1919; 19 August 1919; 1 September 1919; 6 October 1919; 21 October 1919; 10 November 1919; 12 November 1919; 13 November 1919; 18 November 1919; 20 November 1919; 28 November 1919; 27 December 1919; 20 January 1920; 23 July 1920; 26 July 1920.

90. *SB*, 7 October 1909.

91. *SB*, 24 June 1910.

92. Zhang Qiugu, *Piao du bai bi daguan* ("An Overview of the Evils of Gambling and Whoring"), Shanghai, Qiugu chubanbu, 1920, III, p. 6; *Shanghai lanyou zhinan*, Chapter "yeyou xuzhi," p. 9.

93. Wang Jimen, *Shanghai liushi nian lai huajie shi*, p. 24.

94. *SB*, 27 January 1924.

95. Letter from a resident, 22 October 1923, archives de la Direction des services administratifs, Concession française, dossier 1936 MS 1555.

96. Letter from a resident, 30 June 1931, archives de la Direction des services administratifs, Concession française, dossier 1936 MS 1555.

97. *SB*, 2 August 1923.

98. *SB*, 22 May 1899.

99. *SB*, 8 September 1899.

100. *SB*, 13 January 1899.

101. Letter from the chief of police, 17 September 1914, archives de la Direction des services administratifs, Concession française, dossier 1936 MS 1555.

102. Letter from a resident, archives de la Direction des services administratifs, Concession française, dossier 1936 MS 1555.

103. Memorandum from the chief of police, undated [1915–1920], archives de la Direction des services administratifs, Concession française, dossier 1936 MS 1555.

104. Letter from the Association *Pingkang tongshanhui*, 19 March 1929, archives

de la Direction des services administratifs, Concession française, dossier 1936 MS 1555.

105. Wang Jimen, *Shanghai liushi nian lai huajie shi*, p. 134.
106. Wang Dingjiu, *Shanghai guwen*, 1934, p. 674.
107. Cf. the informative article by Huang Kewu, "Cong Shen Bao yiyao guanggao kan min chu Shanghai de yiliao wenhua yu shehui shenghuo, 1912–1926" ("The Medical Culture and Social Life in Shanghai: A Study Based on the Medicine Advertisements in *Shen Pao*, 1912–1926"), *Jindaishi yanjiusuo jikan* ("Bulletin of the Institute of Modern History, Academia Sinica"), vol. XVII, part II, 1988, pp. 141–194.

Chapter 4

1. *Shanghai shenmi zhinan* ("Secret Guide to Shanghai"), Shanghai, Datong tushushe jianyin, n.d., p. 57.
2. Tian Xiaode, "Shenmi de anmoyuan" ("The Secret Massage Parlours"), in Yuan Shike et al., *Shanghai fengqing* ("Shanghai Romance"), n.p., Lantian shubao zazhishe, n.d., p. 2.
3. Wang Dingjiu, *Shanghai menjing* ("Gateway to Shanghai"), Shanghai, Zhongyang shudian, 1932 (revised edition 1937), chapter entitled "wan de menjing," p. 7.
4. Tian Xiaode, "Shenmi de anmoyuan," p. 2.
5. Ordonnances consulaires, 1873–1942, Archives diplomatiques françaises, Nantes.
6. Tian Xiaode, "Shenmi de anmoyuan," p. 2.
7. Ji Longsheng, *Da Shanghai* ("Greater Shanghai"), Taibei, Nanfang zazhi chubanshe [1942], p. 107.
8. Tian Xiaode, "Shenmi de anmoyuan," p. 2.
9. Wang Dingjiu, *Shanghai menjing*, chapter entitled "wan de menjing," p. 7.
10. Wang Dingjiu, *Shanghai menjing*, chapter entitled "wan de menjing," p. 4.
11. *Shanghai shenmi zhinan*, p. 58.
12. Jin Buhuan, *Chunjiang huayue hen* ("Recollections of the Good Old Times"), Xianggang, Tianwentai baoshe, 1962, p. 177.
13. Ji Longsheng, *Da Shanghai*, p. 107. The average daily wage of a male worker in the 1930s was 0.75–1.0 yuan.
14. Tian Xiaode, "Shenmi de anmoyuan," p. 3; Wang Dingjiu, *Shanghai menjing*, chapter entitled "wan de menjing," p. 8.
15. Wang Dingjiu, *Shanghai menjing*, chapter entitled "wan de menjing," p. 6.
16. "Règlement sur les établissements de bains, d'hydrothérapie et/ou de massages," 30 July 1932, ordonnances consulaires, 1873–1942, Archives diplomatiques françaises, Nantes.
17. Xia Lingen, *Jiu Shanghai sanbai liushi hang* ("The 360 Trades of Old Shanghai"), Shanghai, Huadong shifan daxue chubanshe, 1989, p. 46.
18. Emily Honig, *Strangers and Sisters: Women in the Shanghai Cotton Mills, 1919–1949*, Stanford, Stanford University Press, 1986, pp. 148–151.
19. Xia Lingen, *Jiu Shanghai sanbai liushi hang*, p. 45.
20. Lu Dafang, *Shanghai tan yijiu lu* ("Reminiscences of the Shanghai Bund"), Taibei, Shijie shuju, 1980, p. 52.

21. Interview with a waitress 2, Lu He, *Zhongguo funü shenghuo xiezhen*, pp. 93–96.
22. Paul, Cressey, *Taxi-Dance Hall*, Chicago, University of Chicago Press, 1932.
23. Jin Buhuan, *Chunjiang huayue hen*, pp. 62–63.
24. Wu Shenyuan, *Shanghai zui zao de zhong zhong* ("For the First Time in Shanghai"), Shanghai, Huadong shifan daxue chubanshe, 1989, p. 119.
25. Jin Buhuan, *Chunjiang huayue hen*, pp. 102–103. On the effects of the Japanese occupation, especially on the social fabric of the city, see Christian Henriot, " 'Einsame Insel.' Shanghai unter Japanischer Herrschaft, 1937–1945," in Marlene Hiller, Eberhard Jäckel, and Jürgen Rohwer, *Städte im 2. Weltkrieg. Ein internationaler Vergleich*, Essen, Klartext, 1991, pp. 28–46.
26. *North China Herald*, 4 August 1928, p. 201.
27. Articles 1, 3, 4, 5, 7, 9, "Shanghai shi gong'an ju dengji tiaowuchang wunü yingye guize" ("Regulation of the Public Security Bureau of the Municipality of Shanghai on the Registration of the Activities of the Dancing Halls [Professionnal] Dancers"), in Shen Bojing, *Shanghai shi zhinan* ("Guide to the Municipality of Shanghai"), Shanghai, Zhonghua shuju, 1933, pp. 159–161.
28. *Xinwenbao* ("The News"), 31 October 1934.
29. *Minbao* ("People's Newspaper"), 31 October 1934.
30. *Xinwenbao*, 2 November 1934.
31. *Zhongyang ribao* ("Central Daily"), 3 November 1934; 5 November 1934.
32. *Xinwenbao*, 6 November 1934.
33. *China Times* [?], December 1934.
34. *Shanghai Morning Post*, 18 December 1934.
35. I have found no information about the state of public opinion on the dancing halls during this period. However, in 1942 and 1944 a leading women's journal, *Funü zazhi*, published two documents calling for the closure of the dancing halls, which were accused of fostering sexual promiscuity, corrupting youth, and even causing the ruin of households. Liu Yang, "Wunü shenghuo yu tiaowu wenti" ("The Life of the Taxi-Dancers and the Question of Dancing"), *Funü zazhi* ("The Ladies' Journal"), vol. III, no. 10, 1942, pp. 41–45; Sha Ni, "Wuchang de cun jin" ("Maintaining of the Prohibition on Dancing"), *Funü zazhi* ("The Ladies' Journal"), vol. 4, 1944, p. 13.
36. "Provisional Regulation of the Police Bureau of the Municipality of Shanghai on the Administration of the Taxi-Dancers" (*Shanghai shi jingchaju guanli wunü zanxing guize*), Police Archives, Municipality of Shanghai (1945–1949), Shanghai Municipal Archives, file 1-4-125.
37. "Provisional Regulation of the Police Bureau of the Municipality of Shanghai on the Administration of the Waitresses" (*Shanghai shi jingchaju guanli nüzhaodai zanxing guize*), Police Archives, Municipality of Shanghai (1945–1949), file 1-4-125.
38. Fan Xipin, "Shanghai wuchao an qinli ji" ("Personal Notes on the Protest Movement of the Taxi-Dancers in Shanghai"), *Shanghai wenshi ziliao* ("Materials on the History and Culture of Shanghai"), no. 12, 1979, pp. 190–199.
39. *SB*, 1 February 1948; 2 February 1948.
40. *SB*, 3 February 1948.
41. *SB*, 1 February 1948; 2 February 1948.
42. *SB*, 3 February 1948; 4 February 1948. I do not share Emily Honig's interpretation of the nature of the taxi dancers' protest movement. First of all, their

strike action could have only a limited effect, economically and above all politically. Economically, they could not stop working for long and could hardly
count on the solidarity and support of the population. Politically, they were dispersed in a large number of establishments. They were unorganized and, unlike
the female workers, did not represent a real force. Besides, the movement was
undeniably orchestrated by the owners of the dancing halls, seeking above all
to defend their own interests, and the supervisors (*daban*), who used the taxi
dancers as a shield. Emily Honig, *Strangers and Sisters: Women in the Shanghai Cotton Mills, 1919–1949*, Stanford, Stanford University Press, 1986, p. 239.
43. *SB*, 13 February 1948.
44. *SB*, 5 February 1948.
45. Letter from the Union of Coffee-Houses, 25 September 1948, Police Archives,
    Municipality of Shanghai (1945–1949), file 011-4-161: August 1947–July 1949;
    police report, undated [September 1946], Police Archives, Municipality of
    Shanghai (1945–1949), dossier 011-4-176: August 1946–May 1948.
46. *Shanghai shi jingchaju Laozha fenju sanshiliu niandu niankan* ("Annual
    Report for the Year 1947 for the Laozha Police Station, Police Bureau of the
    Municipality of Shanghai"), Shanghai, n.pub., 1948.
47. Shen Bojing, *Shanghai shi zhinan*, p. 159; Wang Dingjiu, *Shanghai menjing*,
    chapter entitled "Wan de menjing," p. 9.
48. *Shanghai shi nianjian* ("Yearbook of the Municipality of Shanghai"),
    Shanghai, Shanghai huadong tongxunshe, 1947, p. M9; *Shanghai shi jingchaju
    sanshiwu nian tongji nianbao* ("Annual Statistical Report 1946 of the Police
    Bureau of the Municipality of Shanghai"), Shanghai, Shanghai shi shi zhengfu
    jingchaju, 1947.
49. Wang Dingjiu, *Shanghai menjing*, chapter entitled, "Wan de menjing," p. 12.
50. League of Nations, Traffic in Women and Children, Conference of Central
    Authorities in Eastern Countries, *Minutes of Meetings*, Geneva, document no.
    C-476.M.318.1937.IV, 1937, p. 34. These figures are also mentioned in a press
    article, "Prostitution Problem in Shanghai [The]," *The China Critic*, XVII, 1,
    April 1937, p. 8.
51. *Shanghai shi nianjian*, p. M9; *Shanghai shi jingchaju sanshiwu nian tongji
    nianbao*.
52. Emily Honig quotes the correspondent of the International Labour Office and
    gives a figure of 6,000 demonstrators, an estimate that I have found nowhere
    in the local press. This is also the figure mentioned in a recent article on this
    demonstration published in China. Emily Honig, *Strangers and Sisters*, p. 239;
    Fan Xipin, "Shanghai wuchaoan qinliji" ("Personal Notes on the Protest Move-
    ment of the Taxi Dancers in Shanghai"), *Wenshi ziliao* ("Historical and Liter-
    ary Materials"), Shanghai, no. 12, 1979, pp. 190–199. On the total number of
    dancers, Emily Honig also mentions a figure of 10,000 for their strike move-
    ment. This estimate appears to be excessive and relies on a questionable
    source. Emily Honig, *Strangers and Sisters*, p. 38.
53. Xia Lingen, *Jiu Shanghai sanbai liushi hang*, p. 40.
54. Wang Dingjiu, *Shanghai menjing*, chapter entitled "Wan de menjing," p. 12.
55. "The life of a taxi-dancer is . . . like prostitution, it is an employment which can
    be of short duration." Paul Cressey, *Taxi-Dance Hall*, p. 84.
56. League of Nations, Traffic in Women and Children, Conference of Central
    Authorities in Eastern Countries, *Minutes of Meetings*, Geneva, document no.
    C-476.M.318.1937.IV, 1937, p. 34.

57. The statistical data in this part are taken from *Shanghai shi jingchaju sanshiwu nian tongji nianbao* ("Annual Statistical Report for 1946 of the Police Bureau of the Municipality of Shanghai"), Shanghai, Shanghai shi shi zhengfu jingchaju, 1947, p. 078.
58. *Xinwanbao*, 26 May 1934.
59. Jin Buhuan, *Chunjiang huayue hen*, p. 63.
60. *North China Herald*, 26 July 1933, p. 136; 27 July 1933, p. 125.
61. Lu Dafang, *Shanghai tan yijiu lu*, p. 31; Jin Buhuan, *Chunjiang huayue hen*, p. 98.
62. Wang Dingjiu, *Shanghai menjing*, chapter entitled "Wan de menjing," pp. 10, 15.
63. *Shanghai shenmi zhinan*, p. 65.
64. Jin Buhuan, *Chunjiang huayue hen*, p. 63.
65. Lu Dafang, *Shanghai tan yijiu lu*, pp. 32–33.
66. Jin Buhuan, *Chunjiang huayue hen*, pp. 90–91.
67. *Shanghai shenmi zhinan*, pp. 67–68.
68. Press article (no reference), Police Archives, Municipality of Shanghai (1945–1949), file 011-4-180.
69. Press article 2, no reference, Police Archives, Municipality of Shanghai (1945–1949), file 011-4-180.
70. Jin Buhuan, *Chunjiang huayue hen*, p. 63.
71. Jin Buhuan, *Chunjiang huayue hen*, p. 100.
72. *Shanghai shenmi zhinan*, p. 68.
73. Anonymous letter, Police Archives, Municipality of Shanghai (1945–1949), file 011-4-180.
74. Directive from the Mayor, 29 August 1946, Police Archives, Municipality of Shanghai (1945–1949), file 011-4-180.
75. Official Record of Questioning, 19 September 1946, Police Archives, Municipality of Shanghai (1945–1949), file 011-4-180.
76. Press article 3, no reference, Police Archives, Municipality of Shanghai (1945–1949), file 011-4-180.
77. Letter from the Police Bureau, 2 September 1946, Police Archives, Municipality of Shanghai (1945–1949), file 011-4-180.
78. Directive from the Police Bureau, 7 August 1946; Letter from the Police Bureau, 20 August 1946; Letter from Headquarters, 5 September 1946, Police Archives, Municipality of Shanghai (1945–1949), file 011-4-180.
79. Letter of 14 August 1946, Police Archives, Municipality of Shanghai (1945–1949), file 011-4-180.
80. Letter from the Police Bureau, 20 August 1946; police station reports, Police Archives, Municipality of Shanghai (1945–1949), file 011-4-180.
81. Letter from the Association of the Employees of the Dance Halls of the Municipality of Shanghai (*Shanghai shi wuting congyeyuan xiehui*), 13 August 1946, Police Archives, Municipality of Shanghai (1945–1949), file 011-4-180; press article 1, no reference, Police Archives, Municipality of Shanghai (1945–1949), file 011-4-180; letter of the Social Affairs Bureau, 6 August 1946, Police Archives, Municipality of Shanghai (1945–1949), file 011-4-180.
82. Letter from the Mayor, 22 August 1946; Letter from the Police Bureau, 2 September 1946, Police Archives, Municipality of Shanghai (1945–1949), file 011-4-180.

83. Directive from the Mayor, 29 August 1946; Letter from the Police Bureau, 5 September 1946, Police Archives, Municipality of Shanghai (1945–1949), file 011-4-180.
84. Letter dated 17 August 1946 and negative reply by the police: Police Archives, Municipality of Shanghai (1945–1949), file 011-4-180.
85. Investigation Report, 17 September 1946; investigation report, 23 September 1946, Police Archives, Municipality of Shanghai (1945–1949), file 011-4-180.
86. Paul Cressey's analysis of the three forces underlying the development of leisure activities in Chicago, which is valid for all the great modern cities, could easily be applied here: "The insistent human demand for stimulation, the growth of commercialized recreation, the growing tendency to promiscuity in the relations of sexes." Paul Cressey, *Taxi-Dance Hall*, p. xiii.

Chapter 5

1. Edward Henderson, *A Report on Prostitution in Shanghai*, Shanghai, n.pub., 1871, p. 11.
2. Tang Weikang, "Shili yangchang de changji" ("The Prostitutes of the Foreigners' District), in Tang Weikang et al., *Shanghai yishi* ("Shanghai Anecdotes"), Shanghai, Wenhua chubanshe, 1987, p. 270.
3. Chen Yuanqi, "Yongxianzhai biji" ("Notes from the Studio of Idleness"), in *Biji xiaoshuo daguan* ("Overview of the Literature of Personal Notes"), in *Biji xiaoshuo daguan*, Taibei, Xinxing shuju, reprint, 1962, part 1, vol. 3, p. 2730.
4. I have obtained this figure by adding Henderson's data to the number of *shuyu/changsan* (500) and the prostitutes of the common brothels (1,500). It is a simple approximation that takes account of the fact that a section of the prostitutes of the Chinese zone were probably included in the figures of the French Concession inasmuch as a good many establishments were located close to the Northern and Eastern Gates and the small Eastern Gate, all of which adjoined the territory under French administration.
5. It appears that the article was published in 1915. It is quoted in *Lao shanghai*, p. 122, in "Demi-monde of Shanghai (The)," *China Medical Journal*, vol. 37, no. 9, 1923, pp. 785–788, and by two Chinese historians: Tang Weikang, "Shili yangchang de changji" ("The Prostitutes of the Foreigners' District") in Tang Weikang et al., *Shanghai yishi* ("Shanghai Anecdotes"), Shanghai, Wenhua chubanshe, 1987, p. 264; and Ping Jinya, "Jiu Shanghai de changji" ("Prostitutes in Old Shanghai"), in *Jiu shanghai de yan du chang* ("Prostitution, Gambling and Opium in Old Shanghai"), Shanghai, Baijia chubanshe, 1988, p. 159. The same data are attributed to another journal, *Xinren* ("New Man"), vol. II, no. 2 (August), published in 1919, quoted by a third historian, Xie Wuyi, "Minchu Shanghai changji yi pie" ("A Quick Look at Prostitution in Shanghai at the Beginning of the Republic"), in *Jiu Shanghai de yan du chang*, pp. 172–173.
6. At best, the total was 7,821, and I do not know how the author arrived at a figure of 9,791. This is only one example of a host of counting errors. With none of my sources have I been able to arrive at the same totals as the authors – even though I have used their own figures.
7. Shanghai Municipal Council, *Report for the Year 1920*, Shanghai, Kelly & Walsh, p. 254A; *Report for the Year 1921*, p. 45C; relevé des Maisons de tolérance, Archives de la Direction des services administratifs, Concession

française, dossier 1936 25 MS 1555, "Nature des dossiers and documents," [1883–1942].

8. The figure of 60,000 given by Gail Hershatter for 1920 does not seem to correspond to any precise original source. Willey does not give this information. Yi Feng's article is the only one to cite this figure (60,141), without giving its source. It was also taken up by Wang Shunu, who gives a detailed breakdown, the total of which (65,766) greatly exceeds his initial figures. I would attach little credibility to the figure of 60,000 because, given that the method used to enumerate the houses of prostitution in 1920 yielded a figure of 20,000 girls, it is unlikely that two out of every three prostitutes escaped the net. Gail Hershatter, "The Hierarchy of Shanghai Prostitution, 1870–1949," *Modern China*, vol. 15, no. 4, October 1989, p. 466; *id.*, "Prostitution and the Market in Early Twentieth-Century Shanghai," in Rubie S. Watson and Patricia Buckley Ebrey, *Marriage and Inequality in Chinese Society*, Berkeley, University of California Press, 1991, p. 265; Wang Shunu, *Zhongguo changji shi* ("A History of Prostitution in China"), Shanghai, Shenghuo shudian, 1934, p. 331.

9. Feng Dja-chien [Feng Zhajian], "Prostitution in Shanghai," M.A. thesis, Shanghai College Library, 1929, pp. 195, 202 (quoted by Daniel Lai, "Syphillis and Prostitution in Kiangsu," *China Medical Journal*, no. 44, 1930, p. 559).

10. Zuili tuitangsheng (pseudonym), "Shanghai zhi ji" ("The Prostitutes of Shanghai"), *Xin Shanghai* ("New Shanghai"), no. 12, April 1926, p. 36.

11. Police report, 10 September 1936, archives de la Direction des services administratifs, Concession française, dossier 1936 no. 25 MS 1555 "Nature des dossiers and documents" [1883–1942]; Service d'hygiène and d'assistance, rapport imprimé de présentation du service, 1933, Archives diplomatiques, Nantes, carton no. 39.

12. The figure for 1931 comes from two concordant sources: first, an undated memorandum, archives de la Direction des services administratifs, Concession française; second, dossier 1936, no. 25, MS 1555, "Nature des dossiers and documents" [1883–1942]; League of Nations, Commission of Inquiry into Traffic in Women and Children in the East, *Report to the Council*, Geneva, document no. C.849.M.393.1932.IV, pp. 143–145. The latter document is cited in "Prostitution Problem in Shanghai [The]," *The China Critic*, vol. XVII, no. 1, April 1937, p. 7.

13. Luo Qiong, "Changji zai zhongguo" ("The Prostitutes in China"), *Funü shenghuo* ("Women's Life"), vol. I, no. 6, December 1935, p. 37.

14. League of Nations, Commission of Inquiry into Traffic in Women and Children in the East, *Report to the Council*, Geneva, document no. C.849.M.393.1932.IV, pp. 143–145.

15. League of Nations, Traffic in Women and Children, Conference of Central Authorities in Eastern Countries, *Minutes of Meetings*, Geneva, document no. C-476.M.318.1937.IV, 1937, p. 11; "Prostitution Problem in Shanghai [The]," p. 7.

16. League of Nations, Traffic in Women and Children, Conference of Central Authorities in Eastern Countries, *Minutes of Meetings*, Geneva, document no. C-476.M.318.1937.IV, 1937, p. 33; *Shanghai shi tongji [di'er ci] buchong cailiao* ("Second Supplement to the Statistics of the Municipality of Shanghai"), Shanghai, Shanghai difang xiehui, 1936, p. 127.

17. League of Nations, Commission of Inquiry into Traffic in Women and Children in the East, *Report to the Council*, Geneva, document no. C.849.M.393.1932.IV,

pp. 143–145; Shanghai Municipal Council, *Report for the Year 1939*, Shanghai, Kelly & Walsh, p. 223.

18. The reports are cited in Yu Wei, "Shanghai changji wu bai ge an diaocha" ("A Study of 500 Prostitutes in Shanghai"), *Shizheng pinglun* ("The Municipal Affairs Weekly"), vol. 10, no. 9/10, p. 10.

19. Yu Wei, "Shanghai changji wu bai ge an diaocha," p. 10.

20. He Wannan and Yang Jiezeng, *Shanghai changji gaizao shihua* ("A Short History of the Re-education of Prostitutes in Shanghai"), Shanghai, Sanlian shudian, 1988, p. 4.

21. Zou Yiren, *Jiu shanghai renkou bianqian de yanjiu* ("A Study of the Development of the Population of Old Shanghai"), Shanghai, Renmin chubanshe, 1980, pp. 122–123.

22. Shanghai Municipal Council, *Report for the Year 1920*, Shanghai, Kelly & Walsh, p. 253A. I have given these figures as an indication because these calculations are not only of little value but appear to have been badly done inasmuch as they are based on a population of 665,000 inhabitants, whereas the census of the Shanghai Municipal Council itself gave a figure of 783,146 in 1920. Zou Yiren, *Jiu shanghai renkou bianqian de yanjiu*, p. 90.

23. On the methodological problems raised by these calculations, cf. Christian Henriot, "La prostitution à Shanghai aux xixe–xxe siècles (1849–1958)," doctoral thesis (doctorat d'État), Paris, École des hautes études en sciences sociales, Chapter 10.

24. Sue Gronewold, *Beautiful Merchandise. Prostitution in China, 1860–1936*, New York, Haworth Press, 1982, p. 71; Emily Honig, *Strangers and Sisters: Women in the Shanghai Cotton Mills, 1919–1949*, Stanford, Stanford University Press, 1986, p. 71; and "The Politics of Prejudice: Subei People in Republican-Era Shanghai," *Modern China*, vol. 15, no. 3, July 1989, p. 251; Gail Hershatter, "The Hierarchy of Shanghai Prostitution, 1870–1949," *Modern China*, vol. 15, no. 4, October 1989, p. 472.

25. Emily Honig, *Creating Chinese Ethnicity. Subei People in Shanghai, 1850–1980*, New Haven, Yale University Press, 1993; *id.*, "Pride and Prejudice: Subei People in Contemporary Shanghai," in Perry Link, Richard Madsen, and Paul Pikovitch. *Unofficial China. Popular Culture and Thought in the People's Republic of China*, Boulder, Westview Press, 1989, pp. 138–155; *id.*, "The Politics of Prejudice: Subei People in Republican-Era Shanghai," *op. cit.*

26. Yu Wei, "Shanghai changji wu bai ge an diaocha," p. 12.

27. He Wannan, Yang Jiezeng, *Shanghai changji gaizao shihua, op. cit.*, p. 64.

28. Yu Wei, "Shanghai changji wu bai ge an diaocha," pp. 12–13.

29. Lu Feiyun, Zhang Zhongru, "Shanghai jiefang chuqi de jinü gaizao gongzuo" ("The Reform of Prostitutes in the Early Liberation Period of Shanghai), in *Shehuixue wenji* ("A Collection of Sociological Texts"), Shanghai, Shanghai shi shehuixue xuehui bian, 1083, p. 134.

30. Yu Wei, "Shanghai changji wu bai ge an diaocha," p. 12.

31. There is an error in the figures. The percentage of girls from working-class families was stated as 50% in the Chinese version of the article in 1949. This gives a total of 123%. It is impossible to find the real figures. Yu Wei, "Shanghai changji wu bai ge an diaocha," p. 13; Yu Wei and Wong Amos, "A Study of 500 Prostitutes in Shanghai," *The International Journal of Sexology*, vol. II, no. 4, May 1949, p. 237.

32. Sue Gronewold, *Beautiful Merchandise. Prostitution in China, 1860–1936*, New York, Haworth Press, 1982, p. 44.
33. Cf. Sun Guoqun, *Jiu Shanghai changji mishi* ("A Secret History of Prostitution in Old Shanghai"), Henan, Henan renmin chubanshe, 1988, in particular, pp. 4–21.
34. He Wannan and Yang Jiezeng, *Shanghai changji gaizao shihua, op. cit.*, pp. 2–3.
35. This is an article that was published in 1937 and reprinted in an expanded form in a work in 1961. My reference is to the latter document. Davis Kingsley, "The Sociology of Prostitution," *American Sociological Review*, vol. II, October 1937, pp. 744–755; *id.*, "Prostitution," in Robert K. Merton and Robert A. Nisbet (eds.), *Contemporary Social Problems*, New York, Harcourt, Brace and World, 1961, pp. 262–288.
36. He Wannan and Yang Jiezeng, *Shanghai changji gaizao shihua, op. cit.*, p. 62.
37. Procès-verbal d'interrogatoire, 15 April 1948, Police Archives, Municipality of Shanghai (1945–1949), file 011-4-163.
38. *SB*, 21 January 1930.
39. Police report, 17 October 1946, Police Archives, Municipality of Shanghai (1945–1949), file 011-4-176, August 1946–May 1948.
40. Police report, 17 October 1946, Police Archives, Municipality of Shanghai (1945–1949), file 011-4-163.
41. Interrogation Report, 29 September 1947, Police Archives, Municipality of Shanghai (1945–1949), file 011-4-176.
42. Police report (three prostitutes), 17 October 1946, Police Archives, Municipality of Shanghai (1945–1949), file 011-4-163.
43. Yu Wei, "Shanghai changji wu bai ge an diaocha," p. 12.
44. Yu Wei, "Shanghai changji wu bai ge an diaocha," p. 13.
45. *SB*, 6 September 1872.
46. *SB*, 13 January 1879.
47. *SB*, 4 October 1920; 10 October 1920.
48. *SB*, 20 December 1909.
49. *SB*, 1 June 1909; 24 June 1909; 10 August 1909 (DH); 4 January 1919; 8 January 1919; 22 May 1919; 23 May 1919 (DH); 21 June 1919 (DH); 4 July 1919 (DH); 9 July 1919 (DH); 11 February 1920 (DH); 23 March 1920 (DH); 10 April 1920 (DH); 17 June 1920 (DH); 24 July 1920 (DH); 14 February 1921; 16 September 1921 (DH).
50. The term *guinu* ("slave-tortoise") was a pejorative term used by the press and the authorities to designate the husband or male companion of the brothel owner. The role of the *guinu* is explained in Chapter 9.
51. *SB*, 8 November 1899.
52. *SB*, 26 February 1909.
53. *SB*, 6 October 1879; 9 October 1879.
54. *SB*, 29 November 1910.
55. *SB*, 29 February 1909; 6 March 1909; 17 October 1910.
56. *SB*, 25 February 1922.
57. *SB*, 9 February 1909.
58. *SB*, 21 November 1879.
59. *SB*, 26 June 1899.

60. *SB*, 20 February 1899.
61. *SB*, 9 March 1889; 20 January 1899; 14 July 1899; 29 November 1899; 3 December 1899; 13 November 1899.
62. *SB*, 4 July 1899.
63. *SB*, 19 September 1899; 8 November 1899; 16 November 1899.
64. *SB*, 2 April 1874; 13 December 1899.
65. *SB*, 21 November 1879; 8 November 1899; 26 June 1899; 26 February 1909; 29 November 1910; 3 February 1921.
66. *SB*, 20 April 1910.
67. *SB*, 4 March 1899.
68. Alain Corbin, *Les filles de noce. Misère sexuelle and prostitution (19ᵉ–20ᵉ siècle)*, Paris, Flammarion (coll. Champs), 1982 (1st ed., Aubier-Montaigne, 1978), pp. 78–79.

Chapter 6

1. Yu Baosheng [pseudonym of Wang Tao], *Haizou yeyou lu* ("Notes of a Libertine on the Seaside"), Shanghai, Hanwen yuanshusi, [1878] 1929, I, p. 2.
2. *Shanghai shenmi zhinan* ("Secret Guide to Shanghai"), Shanghai, Datong tushushe jianyin, s.d., pp. 49–50.
3. Jin Buhuan, *Chunjiang huayue hen* ("Recollections of the Good Old Times"), Xianggang, Tianwentai baoshe, 1962, pp. 123, 127.
4. Robert Van Gulik, *Erotic Colour Prints of the Ming period*, Tokyo, n.pub., 1951; John, Byron, *Portrait of a Chinese Paradise: Erotica and Sexual Customs of the Late Qing Period*, London, Quartet Books, 1987.
5. Jin Buhuan, *Chunjiang huayue hen*, p. 126.
6. Earlier dynasties produced many erotic – I would call them pornographic – novels describing the sexual behavior of the Chinese. The information found in these novels cannot be taken literally, but they help shed light on an aspect of private life that remained tightly concealed during the Qing period. *Nuages et pluie au palais des Han*, erotic novel translated by Christine Kontler, Arles, Éditions Philippe Picquier, 1988; *Du rouge au gynécée: roman érotique de la dynastie Ming*, translated by Martin Maurey, Arles, Éditions Philippe Picquier, 1989; *Belle de candeur. Zhulin yeshi. Roman érotique de la dynastie Ming*, translated by Christine Kontler, Arles, Éditions Philippe Picquier, 1987; *Jéou-p'ou-t'ouan ou la Chair comme tapis de prière*, novel by Li Yu, translated by Pierre Klossowski, Paris, Pauvert, 1962.
7. Haishang juewusheng (pseudonym), *Jinü de shenghuo* ("The Life of the Prostitutes"), Shanghai, Chunmin shudian, 1940, p. 167.
8. *North China Herald*, 25 June 1941, p. 498.
9. Undated report, Police Archives, Municipality of Shanghai (1945–1949), file 011-4-261, January 1946–December 1946.
10. Ji Longsheng, *Da Shanghai* ("Greater Shanghai"), Taibei, Nanfang zazhi chubanshe, [1942], p. 151.
11. Jin Buhuan, *Chunjiang huayue hen*, pp. 83, 121–122, 172.
12. Jin Buhuan, *Chunjiang huayue hen*, pp. 154–155, 157.
13. Wei Xue, "Nüren yu gou" ("Women and Dogs"), in Yuan Shike et al., *Shanghai fengqing* ("Shanghai Romance"), Shanghai, Lantian shubao zazhishe, [1948], p. 6.

14. Yu Wei and Wong Amos, "A Study of 500 Prostitutes in Shanghai," *The International Journal of Sexology*, vol. II, no. 4, May 1949, p. 238.
15. Police report, April 1948, Police Archives (1945–1949), file 011-4-163, "Qudi jiyuan an" ("Cases of the Closure of Houses of Prostitution").
16. Letter from a prostitute, undated, Police Archives (1945–1949), file 011-4-263, October 1947.
17. Christian Henriot, "Medicine, V.D., and Prostitution in Pre-Revolutionary China," *Social History of Medicine*, Oxford University, vol. V, no. 1, 1992, pp. 95–120.
18. Anne W. Fearn, *My Days of Strength: An American Woman Doctor's Forty Years in China*, New York, Harper & Brothers Publishers, 1939, p. 59.
19. See report drawn up in 1937 by Chester N. Frazier, "The Prevention and Control of Syphilis," *China Medical Journal*, vol. LI, January 1937, pp. 1043–1046.
20. Lien-teh Wu, "The Problem of Venereal Diseases in China," *China Medical Journal*, vol. XLI, January 1927, p. 30.
21. "Commercialized Vice in China," *National Medical Journal*, vol. VIII, no. 3, September 1922, p. 197.
22. W. W. Peter, "Fighting Venereal Disease Openly," *China Medical Journal*, vol. XXXV, January 1921, pp. 62, 64.
23. Shanghai Municipal Council, *Report for the Year 1922*, pp. 308–309A.
24. Shanghai Municipal Council, *Report for the Year 1923*, pp. 123–124.
25. Shanghai Municipal Council, *Report for the Year 1924*, p. 148; *Report for the Year 1925*, p. 134.
26. Shanghai Municipal Council, *Report for the Year 1934*, p. 137; *Report for the Year 1937*, p. 153.
27. *Le Journal de Shanghai*, 4 June 1931.
28. Report of 23 November 1934, Archives diplomatiques, Nantes, carton no. 39.
29. *Yewu baogao* ("Annual Report"), Shanghai, Shanghai tebie shi weishengju bian, Shanghai, 1941, pp. 1, 19; *Yewu baogao* ("Annual Report"), Shanghai, Shanghai tebie shi weishengju bian, 1942.
30. Letters from the Health Bureau, 14 February 1946, Police Archives (1945–1949), file 011-4-269; 19 February 1946, Police Archives (1945–1949), file 011-4-261.
31. Regulations on the organization of the dispensary, 5 February 1948, Police Archives (1945–1949), file 011-4-269.
32. Order by the Health Bureau, October 1946; Letter from the Health Bureau, 1 May 1948, Police Archives (1945–1949), file 011-4-269.
33. "Changji jianyan buzou shuoming" ("Instructions on the Procedure for Examining Prostitutes"), Police Archives (1945–1949), file 011-4-269.
34. Public Security Bureau document, October 1946, Police Archives (1945–1949), file 011-4-269.
35. Letter from the Health Bureau, 2 December 1946, Police Archives (1945–1949), file 1-10-246: May 1946–January 1949; Letter from the Mayor, 8 December 1947, Police Archives (1945–1949), file 6-19-666.
36. Public Security Bureau document, 18 February 1946, Police Archives (1945–1949), file 011-4-269.
37. Police report, 30 January 1948, Police Archives (1945–1949), file 011-4-161, August 1947–July 1949.

38. Letter from the Health Bureau, 30 October 1946, Police Archives (1945–1949), file 011-4-269.
39. Letter from the Mayor, 15 June 1946; 12 August 1946; Health Bureau project, undated; Letter from the Bureau, 6 August 1946, Police Archives (1945–1949), file 011-4-261.
40. Yu Wei, "Jin chang yu xingbing fangzhi" ("The Prohibition of Prostitution and the Prevention of Venereal Diseases"), *Shizheng pinglun* ("Journal of Municipal Affairs"), vol. IX, no. 9/10, 1948, p. 18.
41. Letters from the Health Bureau, 27 September 1946; 22 October 1946, Police Archives (1945–1949), file 011-4-269.
42. Frances J. Heath, "Review of Eight Years' Work in China in a Gynecologica Out-patient Clinic," *China Medical Journal*, vol. 39, 1925, pp. 701–703.
43. L. F. Heimburger, "The Incidence of Syphilis at the Shantung Christian University Dispensary," *China Medical Journal*, vol. 41, June 1927, p. 548.
44. Between 1927 and 1933, Shanghai had 4,681 traditional physicians and 596 doctors trained in Western methods. Huang Kewu, "Cong Shen Bao yiyao guanggao kan min chu Shanghai de yiliao wenhua yu shehui shenghuo, 1912–1926" ("The Medical Culture and Social Life in Shanghai: A Study Based on the Medicine Advertisements in *Shen Pao*, 1912–1926"), *Jindaishi yanjiusuo jikan* (Bulletin of the Institute of Modern History, Academia Sinica), 1988, vol. XVII, part 2, p. 149.
45. K. C. Wong and Wu Lien-teh, *History of Chinese Medicine*, Tientsin, Tientsin Press, 1932, pp. 218–219; L. F. Heimburger, "The Incidence of Syphilis at the Shantung Christian University Dispensary," *China Medical Journal*, vol. XLI, June 1927, p. 548.
46. These two medicines owed their rather peculiar names to the number of experiments carried out by their inventor, one Doctor Ehrlich of Frankfurt. Claude Quetel, *Le mal de Naples. Histoire de la syphilis*, Paris, Seghers, 1986, p. 178.
47. Wu Lien-teh, "The Problem of Venereal Diseases in China," *China Medical Journal*, vol. 41, January 1927, p. 34.
48. *SB*, publicity, 15 August 1928.
49. Ji Longsheng, *Da Shanghai*, p. 111.
50. Huang Kewu, "Cong Shen Bao yiyao guanggao kan min chu Shanghai de yiliao wenhua yu shehui shenghuo, 1912–1926," pp. 141–194.
51. Huang Kewu, "Cong Shen Bao yiyao guanggao kan min chu Shanghai de yiliao wenhua yu shehui shenghuo, 1912–1926," pp. 162–163, 168, 180.
52. Cf. *SB*, 12 September 1899.
53. Archives of the Secretariat, International Settlement (Secretariat, Shanghai Municipal Council) (1920–1924), Shanghai Municipal Archives, 3-00445, file 1486, part 3, Secretariat (SMC), "Prostitution: Brothels, Withdrawal of Licences, 1920–1924."
54. The other newpapers consulted: (undated [April 1930]) are: *Xiaoxiao da mimi* ("Secrets Big and Small"), *Liyuan gongbao* ("The Player"), *Qiongbao* ("The Jade"), *Xiaoribao* ("The Small Daily"), *Shanghaitan* ("The Shanghai Bund"), *Que'ersideng* ("The Charleston"), *Da Shanghai* ("Greater Shanghai"), *Qingsi* ("The Thread of Feeling"), *Lingbao* ("The Bell"), *Shangsheng* ("The Voice of Trade"), *Fu'ermosi* (?).
55. Huang Kewu, "Cong Shen Bao yiyao guanggao kan min chu Shanghai de yiliao wenhua yu shehui shenghuo, 1912–1926," pp. 162, 173, and 182–183.

56. Ji Longsheng, *Da Shanghai*, p. 111.
57. Cf. *Shanghai zhinan* ("Guide to Shanghai: A Chinese Directory of the Port"), Shanghai, Shangwu yinshuguan (1st ed., 1909), 1919, V, p. 19.
58. Yu Wei, "Shanghai changji wu bai ge an diaocha" ("A Survey of Five Hundred Prostitutes in Shanghai"), *Shizheng pinglun* ("The Municipal Affairs Weekly"), vol. X, no. 9/10, 1948, p. 13.
59. Shanghai Municipal Council, *Report for the Year 1923*, p. 125.
60. The table has two additional columns, one for patients infected with two venereal diseases simultaneously and the other for those suffering from various unidentified maladies.
61. "Report on the Control and Treatment of Venereal Disease in Shanghai," *China Medical Journal*, Supplement, vol. 38, January 1924, pp. 19–21.
62. Yu Wei, "Jin chang yu xingbing fangzhi," p. 17.
63. Joshua S. Horn, *Away with All Pests. An English Surgeon in People's China: 1954–1969*, London, New York, Monthly Review Press, 1971, p. 92; Judith Banister, *China's Changing Population*, Stanford, Stanford University Press, 1987, pp. 53–54.
64. "Xingbing he jiyuan" ("Venereal Diseases and the Brothels"), *Wenhuibao*, 25 November 1951, p. 72.
65. Daniel Lai, "Syphilis and Prostitution in Kiangsu," *China Medical Journal*, no. 44, 1930, pp. 559–560.
66. Yu Wei, "Shanghai changji wu bai ge an diaocha," p. 13.
67. Yu Wei, "Shanghai changji wu bai ge an diaocha," p. 13.
68. Yu Wei, "Jin chang yu xingbing fangzhi," p. 18.
69. Letter from the Health Bureau, 30 October 1946, Police Archives (1945–1949), file 011-4-269.
70. He Wannan, Yang Jiezeng, *Shanghai changji gaizao shihua*, p. 73.
71. Daniel Lai, "Incidence of Syphilis among Prostitutes and Cabaret Hostesses in Tsingtao," *Chinese Medical Journal*, vol. 66, July 1948, pp. 389–390.
72. L. W. Chu and C. H. Huang, "Gonorrhea among Prostitutes," [Peking], *China Medical Journal*, vol. 66, June 1948, pp. 312–318.
73. *Xing bing zai Zhongguo* ("Venereal Diseases in China"), Beijing, Beijing shiyue wenyi chubanshe, 1990, p. 4.
74. Letters from the Health Bureau, 22 November 1947; 2 July 1948, Police Archives (1945–1949), file 011-4-269.
75. Police report, undated, Police Archives (1945–1949), file 011-4-263, October 1947.
76. Interrogation of a Prostitute, 18 October 1947, Police Archives (1945–1949), file 011-4-263, October 1947.
77. Interrogation of a Prostitute, 15 June 1948, Police Archives (1945–1949), file 011-4-269.
78. Letter from the Health Bureau, 2 December 1946, Police Archives (1945–1949), file 1-10-246, May 1946–January 1949.
79. Yu Wei, "Jin chang yu xingbing fangzhi," p. 18.
80. *SB*, 14 October 1899.
81. *SB*, 29 September 1909.
82. *SB*, 2 April 1921.
83. *SB*, 20 April 1924.
84. *Dagongbao* ("L'impartial"), 24 November 1951; 28 December 1951.
85. He Wannan, Yang Jiezeng, *Shanghai changji gaizao shihua*, p. 69.

86. He Wannan, Yang Jiezeng, *Shanghai changji gaizao shihua*, pp. 69 and 76.
87. *SB*, 24 December 1889.
88. *SB*, 8/8/1872.
89. *SB*, 30 October 1879.
90. *SB*, 21 June 1909.
91. *SB*, 12 October 1920.
92. *SB*, 22 July 1923; 9 July 1923; 21 March 1924.
93. *SB*, 22 February 1899.
94. *SB*, 4 June 1910.
95. *SB*, 6 December 1910.
96. *SB*, 23 September 1899; 19 October 1899.
97. *Compte rendu de la gestion pour l'exercice 1893*, Conseil d'administration municipale de la Concession française, Shanghai, Imprimerie Fonseca et Silva, 1894, p. 7.
98. *SB*, 27 June 1879.
99. *SB*, 25 February 1899; 27 February 1899.
100. *SB*, 6 December 1899.
101. *SB*, 8 October 1919.
102. *SB*, 29 January 1920.
103. Archives of the *Zhongguo jiuji fu ru zonghui* (Anti-Kidnapping Society), Municipal Archives of Shanghai, file 113-1-12/13, p. 197.
104. *SB*, 30 April 1879.
105. *SB*, 26 June 1899.
106. *SB*, 1 December 1899.
107. *SB*, 2 May 1910; 11 September 1910.
108. *SB*, 1 December 1899.
109. *SB*, 21 June 1909.
110. *SB*, 4 June 1910; 10 November 1922; 18 May 1923; 24 May 1923; 22 July 1923; 21 March 1924.
111. *SB*, 4 May 1910.
112. *SB*, 6 December 1910; 30 January 1923.
113. *SB*, 12 October 1921.
114. *SB*, 6 July 1924.
115. It must be noted, however, that the prostitutes were not the only group to be concerned with violence. There were frequent references made in the press, during the 1920s, to acts of violence against women. The most frequent cases involved rape (almost one every day), violence and rape perpetrated on bondservants (*beinü*), cases of battered women, and kidnapped women and children.
116. *SB*, 14 December 1879; a similar case is reported in *SB*, 11 July 1879.
117. *SB*, 16 April 1879.
118. *SB*, 11 July 1909; 12 September 1899; 12 October 1899.
119. *SB*, 24 October 1910; 27 December 1910; 17 June 1910; 28 February 1909; 25 February 1922.
120. *SB*, 25 March 1909.
121. *SB*, 21 December 1921.
122. *SB*, 15 December 1938.
123. *SB*, 6 January 1924.
124. *SB*, 10 January 1910.

125. *SB*, 16 September 1899.
126. *SB*, 12 September 1899.
127. *SB*, 12 October 1899.
128. *SB*, 4 November 1899; 9 November 1899.
129. The physical punishments inflicted by the Chinese police were extremely violent. This is how an English resident of Shanghai described the inflicting of a sentence of 200 strokes on a group of "vagabonds": ". . . they were severely stripped, and stretched on a large stone in the pavement by four of these lictor-model men in tall black feathered caps. Held by the feet and hands, they then received between the shoulders about fifty blows with two bundles of rods, inflicted alternately by two of these policemen. . . . This castigation laid open the flesh in many places, and to prevent mortification, a wholesome rubbing of salt into the wounds, of course, added not a little to the painfulness of the punishment. The salting over, the policemen were changed, and two fresh hands . . . began to lay on blows upon the thighs, to the number of forty, with the broad splint of bamboo, nearly three inches in width and about four feet in length: forty blows given, the hands were changed, and each fresh couple appeared to lay on with increased energy, until the legs of the prisoners, from which the skin started, at the first score of blows, were beaten well nigh mincemeat by the time the number had reached two hundred." ("Punishment of the Canton and Fuhkeen Vagabonds," *North China Herald*, 31 August 1850.)
130. *SB*, 28 February 1909.
131. *SB*, 25 February 1922.
132. *SB*, 22 September 1923.
133. Yu Baosheng [pseudonym of Wang Tao], *Haizou yeyou lu*, III, p. 5.
134. *Haishang yeyou beilan* (Omnium of Licentiousness in Shanghai), Shanghai, n.pub., 1891, II, p. 13.
135. *SB*, 17 June 1879.
136. *SB*, 7 February 1889.
137. *SB*, 1 October 1899.
138. *SB*, 6 January 1920; 28 March 1920; 4 April 1920.
139. *SB*, 22 September 1923.
140. *SB*, 25 February 1922.
141. *SB*, 26 June 1920.
142. *Haishang yeyou beilan*, II, p. 10.
143. *SB*, 26 December 1899.
144. *SB*, 15 December 1899.
145. *SB*, 2 August 1910.
146. *SB*, 14 January 1910; 15 January 1910; 5 March 1910; 18 March 1910; 28 November 1910.
147. *SB*, 19 January 1899.
148. *SB*, 19 May 1909.
149. *SB*, 17 July 1910.
150. *SB*, 29 December 1910.
151. *SB*, 13 March 1909.
152. *SB*, 18 October 1924.
153. *SB*, 11 July 1909.
154. *SB*, 14 August 1909.

155. *SB*, 30 April 1910.
156. *SB*, 6 September 1920.
157. *North China Herald*, 29 January 1941; 23 July 1941.
158. *SB*, 24 May 1909.
159. *SB*, 11 July 1879.
160. *SB*, 29 May 1920.
161. Christian Henriot, "Modern Medicine, V.D., and Prostitution in Pre-Revolutionary China," *op. cit.*
162. *SB*, 30 November 1938.

Chapter 7

1. James L. Watson, "Transactions in People: The Chinese Market in Slaves, Servants and Heirs," in James L. Watson (ed.), *Asian and African Systems of Slavery*, Berkeley, University of California Press, 1980, p. 223.
2. Slavery was officially abolished only in 1906 with the reform of the Qing code. However, certain quasi-legal forms of slavery persisted, especially the practice of having "adopted daughters" (*beinü* or *muitsai*), who were real bondservants. It was only in 1936 that the Nationalist Government adopted a law prohibiting this practice: League of Nations, Traffic in Women and Children, Conference of Central Authorities in Eastern Countries, *Minutes of Meetings*, Geneva, document no. C-476.M.318.1937.IV, 1937, p. 12; F. Oldt, "Purity Campaign in Canton," *China Medical Journal*, vol. XIIIL, September 1923, p. 777; Norman Miners, *Hong Kong under Imperial Rule*, Hong Kong/London, Oxford University Press, in particular the excellent chapters "The Abolition of the *Mui Tsai* System, 1917 to 1924" and "The Abolition of the *Mui Tsai* System, 1925 to 1941," pp. 153–190. On slavery and its abolition in China, see Marinus Jan Meijer, "Slavery at the End of the Ch'ing Dynasty," in J. Cohen, Chen-Chang Fu-mei, and R. Edwards, *Essays on China's Legal Tradition*, Princeton, Princeton University Press, 1980, pp. 327–358; James L. Watson, "Transactions in People: The Chinese Market in Slaves, Servants and Heirs," *op. cit., id.*, "Chattel Slavery in Chinese Peasant Society: A Comparative Analysis," *Ethnology*, no. 15, October 1976, pp. 361–375.
3. Sue Gronewold, *Beautiful Merchandise. Prostitution in China, 1860–1936*, New York, Haworth Press, 1982, p. 12.
4. Emily Honig, *Strangers and Sisters: Women in the Shanghai Cotton Mills, 1919–1949*, Stanford, Stanford University Press, 1986, pp. 181 and 186.
5. Emily Honig, *Strangers and Sisters*, pp. 83, 103, and 151.
6. Gail Hershatter, "The Hierarchy of Shanghai Prostitution, 1870–1949," *Modern China*, vol. XV, no. 4, October 1989, pp. 477–478.
7. Gail Hershatter, "Prostitution and the Market in Early Twentieth-Century Shanghai," in Rubie S. Watson and Patricia Buckley Ebrey, *Marriage and Inequality in Chinese Society*, Berkeley, University of California Press, 1991, pp. 266–267.
8. *North China Herald*, 1 March 1870, p. 147.
9. "Women Slavery in Shanghai," reported by *China Recorder*, 22 June 1891, p. 293.
10. "Famine and Civil War in China," *Chinese Recorder*, vol. 61, no. 6, June 1930, pp. 339–347.

11. Report with Regard to the Traffic in Women and Children, Conf/Orient/25 (4 February 1937), Archives of the League of Nations, file no. R3047, p. 2.

12. *Shanghai shi tongji [di'er ci] buchong cailiao* ("Second Supplement to the Statistics of the Municipality of Shanghai"), Shanghai, Shanghai difang xiehui, 1936, p. 127.

13. League of Nations, Commission of Enquiry into Traffic in Women and Children in the East, *Report to the Council*, New York, 1933, p. 91.

14. I would contest the idea of a formalized division of labor as presented by Joseph Hsieh (Xue Gengxin), a former police official in the French Conces-sion. His accounts mention three personalities belonging to the police of the settlements who are supposed to have controlled a vast organization running the traffic in women and children. One of them is supposed to have had a "retinue" of 5,000 individuals. This seems to me to be lacking in credibility, unless the notion of "retinue" or "followers" is interpreted in the sense that I have suggested further below. Xue Gengxin, "Jindai shanghai de liumang" ("The Gangsters of Shanghai in the Modern Period"), *Shanghai wenshi ziliao xuanji*, no. 3, 1980, p. 173.

15. *SB*, 25 May 1899.

16. *SB*, 19 December 1909.

17. *North China Herald*, 1 June 1912.

18. Archives of the *Zhongguo jiuji fu ru zonghui* (Anti-Kidnapping Society), Municipal Archives of Shanghai, file 113-1-2: 1936, p. 13.

19. *SB*, 28 October 1921.

20. *SB*, 20 February 1919; *SB*, 14 August 1923.

21. *SB*, 14 December 1921.

22. *Minguo ribao* ("The Republican"), 27 May 1927.

23. *SB*, 24 April 1930.

24. Alain Roux, *Le Shanghai ouvrier des années trente. Coolies, gangsters et syndicalistes*, Paris, L'Harmattan, 1993, pp. 217–218.

25. *SB*, 9/5/1872; "Notes and Queries," *The China Review*, vol. XVI, no. 2, September–October 1887, p. 125.

26. Police Archives. International Settlement (1920–1924): file 3-00445: file 1486, part 3, Secretariat (SMC), "Prostitution, Brothels, Withdrawal of Licences, 1920–1924."

27. Yen Ching-yüeh, *A Study of Crime in Peiping*, Yenching University, series C, no. 20, December 1929, p. 11.

28. Report with Regard to the Traffic in Women and Children, Conf. Orient/25, (4 February 1937), Archives of the League of Nations, file no. R3047, p. 6.

29. Archives of the *Zhongguo jiuji fu ru zonghui*, file 113-1-9.

30. Report with Regard to the Traffic in Women and Children, Conf/Orient/25, (4 February 1937), Archives of the League of Nations, file no. R3047.

31. Report with Regard to the Traffic in Women and Children, Conf/Orient/25 (4 February 1937), Archives of the League of Nations, file no. R3047, p. 6.

32. Archives of the *Zhongguo jiuji fu ru zonghui*, file 113-1-2: 1936. On the activ-ities of the Anti-Kidnapping Society, a private organization dedicated to the rescue of kidnapped women; see Chapter 14.

33. The few old women who appear in the data were not involved in prostitution. They were poor women sent to the AKS by various institutions. However, there can be no doubt whatsoever that those in the 30–36 age group had really been kidnapped.

34. E.H. Parker, "A Journey into North Szech'uan," *The China Review*, vol. X, no. 6, May–June 1882, p. 375.
35. The definitions of Jiangnan and Jiangbei are variable. In this book, I use these terms in a strictly geographical sense to cover Southern Jiangsu and Northern Jiangsu, respectively. Although the historian must necessarily adopt this definition, the boundary between the two parts of Jiangsu did not have any real existence as can be seen from the work of Emily Honig. Nevertheless, whereas in the case of contemporary observers, subjectivity might have prevailed over geographical considerations, I have limited myself to geography in order to properly apportion that which should belong to Jiangnan or to Jiangbei, respectively. This said, the inclusion of the Northern parts of Zhejiang in what is called Jiangnan has further bolstered my arguments on the predominance of the women of this region (Jiangnan).
  On this subject, see Emily Honig, *Creating Chinese Ethnicity. Subei People in Shanghai, 1850–1980*, New Haven, Yale University Press, 1993; Lynda C. Johnson et al. (eds.), *Cities of Jiangnan in Imperial China*, New York, SUNY Press, 1994, "Preface"; and Antonia Finnane, "The Origins of Prejudice: The Malintegration of Subei in Late Imperial China," *Comparative Studies in Society and History*, vol. XXXV, no. 2, April 1993, pp. 211–237.
36. Bryan Martin, *The Green Gang in Shanghai. Politics and Organized Crime, 1919–1937*, Berkeley, University of California Press, 1996.
37. Report with Regard to the Traffic in Women and Children, Conf-Orient/25 (4 February 1937), Archives of the League of Nations, file no. R3047, p. 4.
38. Archives of the *Zhongguo jiuji fu ru zonghui*, file 113-1-4, p. 94 [1926]; see another case in 1923, *SB*, 6 July 1923.
39. *SB*, 26 May 1930.
40. *SB*, 20 November 1930.
41. Emily Honig, *Strangers and Sisters*, p. 181.
42. *SB*, 16 November 1909; 17 September 1910.
43. Archives of the *Zhongguo jiuji fu ru zonghui*, file 113-1-2: 1936, [1920 report], p. 112.
44. *North China Herald*, 1 March 1924.
45. "Famine and Civil War in China," *Chinese Recorder*, vol. 61, no. 6, June 1930, p. 339.
46. Of the 82 women whose fate is known, 63 (77%) were sold and 17 (23%) were pledged.
47. *SB*, 8 June 1879.
48. *SB*, 17 March 1899.
49. Archives of the *Zhongguo jiuji fu ru zonghui* (Anti-Kidnapping Society), file 113-1-2: 1936, [1920 report], p. 116.
50. *SB*, 26 November 1899.
51. *SB*, 2 December 1910.
52. *SB*, 27 June 1922.
53. *SB*, 2 June 1909; 23 January 1909.
54. *SB*, 11 September 1910.
55. *SB*, 28 October 1921.
56. *SB*, 9 December 1910; 21 January 1920; 1 January 1921.
57. *SB*, 13 January 1909.
58. Archives of the *Zhongguo jiuji fu ru zonghui*, file 113-1-2: 1936, [1920 report], pp. 112–113.

59. *SB*, 13 October 1909.
60. Archives of the *Zhongguo jiuji fu ru zonghui*, file 113-1-2: 1936, [1920 report], p. 110.
61. Archives of the *Zhongguo jiuji fu ru zonghui*, file 113-1-2: 1936, [1920 report], p. 122.
62. Archives of the *Zhongguo jiuji fu ru zonghui*, file 113-1-4, p. 11 (1928).
63. Archives of the *Zhongguo jiuji fu ru zonghui*, file 113-1-4, p. 21 (1925).
64. *SB*, 12 April 1919.
65. Archives of the *Zhongguo jiuji fu ru zonghui*, file 113-1-4, p. 86 [1926].
66. *SB*, 28 October 1910; another similar case in *SB*, 8 October 1924.
67. Archives of the *Zhongguo jiuji fu ru zonghui*, file 113-1-2: 1936, [1920 report], p. 111.
68. *SB*, 7 January 1924; 24 October 1938.
69. *SB*, 20 February 1919; 7 November 1920.
70. *SB*, 11 January 1924.
71. Archives of the *Zhongguo jiuji fu ru zonghui*, file 113-1-4, p. 79 [1926].
72. *SB*, 13 February 1940.
73. Archives of the *Zhongguo jiuji fu ru zonghui*, file 113-1-12/13, p. 116.
74. Report with Regard to the Traffic in Women and Children, Conf. Orient/25, (4 February 1937), Archives of the League of Nations, file no. R3047, p. 2; Archives of the *Zhongguo jiuji fu ru zonghui*, file 113-1-12/13, p. 65, p. 135.
75. *Compte rendu de la gestion pour l'exercice 1911*, Conseil d'administration municipale de la concession française, 1912, p. 163.
76. *SB*, 8 June 1879.
77. *SB*, 16 April 1899.
78. *SB*, 17 March 1899.
79. *SB*, 19 January 1899.
80. *SB*, 16 November 1909.
81. William Alford, "Arsenic and Old Laws: Looking Anew at Criminal Justice in Late Imperial China," *California Law Review*, 1984, vol. 72, no. 6, December 1984, pp. 1180–1255, and Shuzo Shiya, "Criminal Procedure in the Qing Dynasty," *Memoirs of the Toyo Bunko*, 1976, no. 34, pp. 1–137.
82. *SB*, 25 February 1909.
83. *SB*, 2 May 1909.
84. *SB*, 8 May 1909.
85. *SB*, 4 January 1909.
86. *SB*, 27 November 1910.
87. *SB*, 9 June 1920.
88. *SB*, 14 December 1921.
89. *SB*, 11 January 1924.
90. *SB*, 17 July 1920.
91. Archives of the *Zhongguo jiuji fu ru zonghui*, file 113-1-9.
92. *SB*, 20 March 1899; 24 March 1923.
93. *SB*, 3 July 1922; 4 May 1923; 9 July 1924.
94. *SB*, 28 October 1921; 14 December 1921.
95. *SB*, 3 July 1922.
96. *SB*, 16 November 1909.
97. *SB*, 28 January 1909.
98. *SB*, 16 February 1909.

99. *SB*, 26 May 1899; 13 June 1899.
100. *SB*, 17 November 1909.
101. *SB*, 9 September 1910.
102. *SB*, 25 June 1879.
103. *SB*, 4 September 1909.
104. *SB*, 14 December 1921.
105. *SB*, 20 March 1899.
106. *SB*, 15 June 1921.
107. *SB*, 17 November 1911.
108. Archives of the *Zhongguo jiuji fu ru zonghui*, file 113-1-4, p. 86 [1926].
109. *SB*, 11 April 1920.
110. Archives of the *Zhongguo jiuji fu ru zonghui*, file 113-1-4, p. 50 (1927).
111. Archives of the *Zhongguo jiuji fu ru zonghui*, file 113-1-4, p. 79 [1926].
112. *SB*, 7 January 1924.
113. For example, the case of a hairdresser's daughter: Archives of the *Zhongguo jiuji fu ru zonghui*, file 113-1-2: 1936 [1920 report], p. 112; for other examples of girls being rescued as a result of letters, *ibid.*, p. 115; *SB*, 28 October 1921; Archives of the *Zhongguo jiuji fu ru zonghui*, file 113-1-4, p. 94 [1926], p. 109.
114. For the charcoal merchant's wife, cf. Archives of the *Zhongguo jiuji fu ru zonghui*, file 113-1-2: 1936 [1920 report], p. 114.
115. *SB*, 1 January. 1921; 18 July 1921.
116. Archives of the *Zhongguo jiuji fu ru zonghui*, file 113-1-4, p. 75 (1926).
117. Archives of the *Zhongguo jiuji fu ru zonghui*, file 113-1-4, p. 107 [1926].
118. Archives of the *Zhongguo jiuji fu ru zonghui*, file 113-1-4, p. 31 (1927).
119. Archives of the *Zhongguo jiuji fu ru zonghui*, file 113-1-4, p. 50 (1927); see also other cases in file 113-1-4, pp. 94 (1926) and p. 107.
120. Archives of the *Zhongguo jiuji fu ru zonghui*, file 2-113-1 (1927).
121. Archives of the *Zhongguo jiuji fu ru zonghui*, file 2-311-1 [1928]; file 113-1-4, p. 14 [1928]; see also file 113-1-4, p. 79 [1926].
122. Archives of the *Zhongguo jiuji fu ru zonghui*, file 2-311-1 [1927–1928]; see also other cases in file 113-1-4, p. 86 [1926] and p. 91 (1926).
123. Archives of the *Zhongguo jiuji fu ru zonghui*, file 2-311-1 [1927–1928].
124. Archives of the *Zhongguo jiuji fu ru zonghui*, file 113-1-4, p. 126 [1926].
125. *Funü yuebao* ("The Women's Weekly"), vol. II, no. 3, 10 April 1936, pp. 47–48.
126. Cf. Sue Gronewold, for whom the exodus of poor women from the countryside was among the causes of a demographic imbalance affecting the institution of marriage. Sue Gronewold, *Beautiful Merchandise*, New York, Haworth Press, 1982, p. 47.
127. *China News Analysis*, no. 1426, 1 January 1991, p. 6.
128. Wu Ruting, "Guaimai funü ertong fanzui xianzhuang chutan" ("Preliminary Inquiry into Offenses of Traffic in Women and Children"), *Gong'an ribao* ("Public Security Daily"), 22 February 1991.
129. "Sihong xian jiji jiejiu 'longzhongniao'" ("Sihong *Xian* Provides Active Help to the 'Caged Birds'"), *Gong'an ribao* ("Public Security Daily"), 8 February 1991.
130. "Yancheng yinyou rongliu qiangpo funü Mayyin fanzui" ("Crimes of Illegal Restraint and Forced Prostitution [must be] Severely Punished"), *Fazhi ribao* ("Legality Daily"), 23 January 1991.

Chapter 8

1. Zhang Zhiying, "Jingshen wenming zhi hua zai huileli shengkai" ("The Flowers of a Spiritual Civilization are Blooming in *Huileli*"), *Xinmin wanbao* ("New People") 28 September 1989.
2. Described in Chapter 12 of my thesis.
3. Paul A. Cohen, *Between Tradition and Modernity. Wang T'ao and Reform in Late Ch'ing China*, Cambridge, MA, Harvard University Press, 1974.
4. Yu Baosheng [pseudonym of Wang Tao], *Haizou yeyou lu* ("Notes of a Libertine on the Seaside"), Shanghai, Hanwen yuanshusi [1878], 1929.
5. Yu Baosheng [pseudonym of Wang Tao], *Haizou yeyou lu, op. cit.*, vol. I, pp. 1–5, vol. III, pp. 1–3.
6. For the former source, I had the opportunity to consult two files of archives of the Shanghai Municipal Council. One of them was precisely about the last three draws. I have completed this list with those published in the Chinese press after each draw. Archives of the Secretariat, International Settlement (Secretariat, Shanghai Municipal Council) (1920–1924), Shanghai Municipal Archives, files 3-00445: File 1486, part 3, Secretariat (SMC), "Prostitution, Brothels, Withdrawal of Licences, 1920–1924"; 4-2428: File 147/1; 4-2429: File 147/2; *SB*, 22 December 1920; 7 December 1921; 6 December 1922; 7 December 1923; Wang Jimen, *Shanghai liushi nian lai huajie shi* ("Sixty Years of the History of the World of Flowers in Shanghai"), Shanghai, Shixin shuju, 1922.
7. "Liste des maisons de tolérance au 30 March 1925," archives de la Direction des services administratifs, Secrétariat, Concession française, Archives municipales de Shanghai, dossier no. 25 MS 1555.
8. Ordonnances consulaires, 1873–1942, Archives diplomatiques françaises, Consulat général de Shanghai, Nantes.
9. "Liste des maisons de tolérance enregistrées sur la Concession française," archives de la Direction des services administratifs, Concession française, dossier no. 25 MS 1555.
10. *Shanghai xianzhi* ("Local Gazette of the *Xian* of Shanghai"), Shanghai, Nanyuan zhiju, 1871 (reprint, Taibei, Chengwen chubanshe, 1970); *Shanghai xian xuzhi* ("Supplement to the Local Gazette of the *Xian* de Shanghai"), Shanghai, 1918 (reprint, Taibei, Chengwen chubanshe, 1970).
11. *Shanghai shi hanghao lutu lu* ("Shanghai Street Directory"), Shanghai, Free Trading Co., 1939 (C.I.) and 1941 (C.F.); *Shanghai shi hanghao lutu lu* ("Shanghai Street Directory"), Shanghai, Free Trading Co., 1947.
12. *Shanghai zhinan* ("Guide to Shanghai: A Chinese Directory of the Port"), Shanghai, Shangwu yinshuguan (1st ed., 1909), 1919, 1920, 1923, 1925, 1926, 1930.
13. Xue Liyong, "Ming-Qing shiqi de Shanghai changji" ("Prostitution in Shanghai in Ming-Qing Times"), in *Jiu Shanghai de yan du chang* ("Prostitution, Gambling and Opium in Old Shanghai"), Shanghai shi wenshiguan bian, Shanghai, Baijia chubanshe, 1988, pp. 150–153.
14. Lynda C. Johnson, "The Decline of Soochow and Rise of Shanghai," *op. cit.*, pp. 146–147.
15. Lynda C. Johnson, "The Decline of Soochow and Rise of Shanghai," *op. cit.*, pp. 345–352.
16. Yu Baosheng [pseudonym of Wang Tao], *Haizou yeyou lu, op. cit.*, I, pp. 1–2.
17. Yu Baosheng [pseudonym of Wang Tao], *Haizou yeyou lu, op. cit.*, I, p. 3.

18. Yu Baosheng [pseudonym of Wang Tao], *Haizou yeyou lu, op. cit.*, I, p. 2, and III, p. 2.
19. Yu Baosheng [pseudonym of Wang Tao], *Haizou yeyou lu, op. cit.*, I, p. 1.
20. Wang Jimen, *Shanghai liushi nian lai huajie shi, op. cit.*, p. 1.
21. Lynda C. Johnson, "The Decline of Soochow and Rise of Shanghai," *op. cit.*, p. 189; On the Small Sword Rebellion in Shanghai, cf. Bryna Goodman, *Native Place, City, and Nation: Regional Networks and Identities in Shanghai, 1853–1937*, Berkeley, University of California Press, 1995, pp. 72–83.
22. Lynda C. Johnson, "The Decline of Soochow and Rise of Shanghai," *op. cit.*, p. 274.
23. In the Walled City, the number of residents rose from 250,000–300,000 to about 500,000 in 1862 and nearly 750,000 in 1863. A large group, numbering 150,000, settled in the boats near Hongkou (20,000 of them), the International Settlement (70,000), and the Walled City (60,000). In the International Settlement and the the French Concession, the population reached 250,000 and 80,000, respectively, at the high point of the crisis. Lynda C. Johnson, "The Decline of Soochow and Rise of Shanghai," *op. cit.*, pp. 275–277, 307, and 316.
24. Lynda C. Johnson "The Decline of Soochow and Rise of Shanghai," *op. cit.*, p. 325.
25. Yu Baosheng [pseudonym of Wang Tao], *Haizou yeyou fulu, op. cit.*, I, p. 2.
26. Wang Jimen, *Shanghai liushi nian lai huajie shi, op. cit.*, p. 2; Tang Weikang, "Shili yangchang de changji," *op. cit.*, pp. 266–267.
27. Yu Baosheng [pseudonym of Wang Tao], *Haizou yeyou lu, op. cit.*, III, p. 3.
28. Lynda C. Johnson, "The Decline of Soochow and Rise of Shanghai," *op. cit.*, pp. 177 and pp. 294–295.
29. Yu Baosheng [pseudonym of Wang Tao], *Haizou yeyou fulu, op. cit.*, I, p. 2.
30. Yu Baosheng [pseudonym of Wang Tao], *Haizou yeyou lu, op. cit.*, III, p. 2.
31. See Alain Roux, *Le Shanghai ouvrier des années trente*, Paris, L'Harmattan, 1993, Chapter V, pp. 213–256.
32. Shanghai Municipal Council, *Report for the Year 1920*, Shanghai, Kelly & Walsh, 1921, p. 253A.
33. Yu Wei, "Shanghai changji wu bai ge an diaocha" ("A Study of 500 Prostitutes in Shanghai"), *Shizheng pinglun* ("The Municipal Affairs Weekly"), vol. X, no. 9/10, 1948, p. 13.
34. Tang Weikang, "Shili yangchang de changji," *op. cit.*, p. 267; Wang Jimen, *Shanghai liushi nian lai huajie shi, op. cit.*
35. All I have are very limited statistics, but they confirm this shift. For the month of July 1923 alone, 76 girls put in applications for licenses. From August to October, 33 houses obtained licenses to work in the concession. Finally, a report in February 1924 reveals that there were 68 new brothels. See: Demandes de licences (maisons de tolérance), archives de la Direction des services administratifs, Concession française, dossier no. 25 MS 1554.2.
36. *Shanghai shenmi zhinan* ("Secret Guide to Shanghai"), Shanghai, Datong tushushe jianyin, n.d., p. 23; Xu Ke (ed.), *Qing bai lei chao* ("The Hundred Categories of the Qing"), Shanghai, 1920, p. 25.
37. *Shanghai zhinan, op. cit.*, V, p. 19.
38. *Shanghai zhinan, op. cit.*, V, p. 19.
39. Lu Dafang, *Shanghai tan yijiu lu* ("Reminiscences of the Shanghai Bund"), Taibei, Shijie shuju, 1980, pp. 1–4.

40. *Shanghai zhinan, op. cit.,* V, p. 19.
41. *Shanghai zhinan, op. cit.,* V, p. 19.
42. The "Trenches" area is referred to by Marcel E. Grancher, *Shanghai: Roman Colonial,* Toulouse, Ed. S.T.A.E.L., 1945, p. 180.
43. *Shanghai zhinan, op. cit.,* V, p. 20.
44. *Shanghai zhinan, op. cit.,* V, pp. 18–19.
45. On the structure of the *lilong,* cf. contemporary works by Pierre Clément, Françoise Ged, and Wan Qi, "Transformations de l'habitat à Shanghai," rapport de recherche, Institut français d'architecture, Paris, 1988.
46. Police memorandum (following a complaint by shopkeepers), undated [1914–1921], archives de la Direction des services administratifs, Concession française, dossier no. 25 MS 1555.
47. This breakdown is based on information from *Shanghai zhinan, op. cit.,* V, pp. 1–13.

Chapter 9

1. In earlier times, the brothels could be recognized by their outer shutters, which were painted green – hence the name "green chamber" or "green bower" (*qinglou*) usually given to them in Chinese literature. Cf. Arthur Waley, "The Green Bower Collection" [1957], in *The Secret History of the Mongols and Other Pieces,* New York, Barnes & Noble, 1967, pp. 89–107.
2. Wang Jimen, *Shanghai liushi nian lai huajie shi, op. cit.,* p. 12.
3. Wang Jimen, *Shanghai liushi nian lai huajie shi, op. cit.,* p. 13.
4. Wang Jimen, *Shanghai liushi nian lai huajie shi, op. cit.,* p. 13.
5. *Shanghai lanyou zhinan* ("A Sightseeing Guide to Shanghai"), Shanghai, Zhonghua tushu jicheng gongsi, 1923, p. 2.
6. *Shanghai shenmi zhinan* ("Secret Guide to Shanghai"), Shanghai, Datong tushushe jianyin, n.d., p. 3.
7. *Huaguo ribao* ("The Kingdom of Flowers Daily"), 30 November 1920; Wang Jimen, *Shanghai liushi nian lai huajie shi, op. cit.,* pp. 142–143.
8. Anonymous letter, 27 September 1935, note on tax revenue from the houses of tolerance, n.d., archives de la Direction des services administratifs, Secrétariat, Concession française, Archives municipales de Shanghai, dossier 1936 25 MS 1555 "Nature des dossiers and documents" [1883–1942].
9. Haishang juewusheng (pseudonym), *Jinü de shenghuo, op. cit.,* p. 20.
10. Haishang juewusheng (pseudonym), *Jinü de shenghuo, op. cit.,* p. 20.
11. Xu Ke (ed.), *Qing bai lei chao* ("The Hundred Categories of the Qing"), Shanghai, 1920, p. 21.
12. Wang Tao, *Songbin suohua* ("Idle Talk on the Riverside") Shanghai, n.pub., n.d., p. 201.
13. *Shanghai shenmi zhinan, op. cit.,* p. 1.
14. Haishang juewusheng (pseudonym), *Jinü de shenghuo, op. cit.,* pp. 34–35.
15. *Haishang yeyou beilan, op. cit.,* II, p. 2.
16. A French traveler has this description of the abundant variety of dainties offered to customers in the courtesans' houses: ". . . heaped up on plates, pyramids of preserved fruits, dates, oranges, plums, dried pears and peaches . . . , saucers full of pumpkin seeds." Maurice Jametel, *La Chine inconnue,* Paris, Imprimerie de l'Art, 1884, p. 231.

17. Jin Buhuan, *Chunjiang huayue hen* ("Recollections of the Good Old Times"), Xianggang, Tianwentai baoshe, 1962, pp. 18–19.
18. Jin Buhuan, *Chunjiang huayue hen, op. cit.*, p. 22.
19. Jin Buhuan, *Chunjiang huayue hen, op. cit.*, p. 26.
20. *Shanghai shenmi zhinan, op. cit.*, p. 26.
21. Wang Jimen, *Shanghai liushi nian lai huajie shi, op. cit.*, pp. 213–214.
22. *Shanghai shenmi zhinan, op. cit.*, p. 26.
23. Wang Jimen, *Shanghai liushi nian lai huajie shi, op. cit.*, p. 21; *Shanghai shenmi zhinan, op. cit.*, p. 26.
24. He Wannan and Yang Jieceng, *Shanghai changji gaizao shihua* ("A Short History of the Re-Education of Prostitutes in Shanghai"), Shanghai, Sanlian shudian, 1988, p. 219.
25. Yu Wei, "Shanghai changji wu bai ge an diaocha," *op. cit.*, p. 13.
26. Wang Dingjiu, *Shanghai menjing*, 1932 (reprint 1937), p. 20; Haishang juewusheng (pseudonym), *Jinü de shenghuo, op. cit.*, pp. 148–149.
27. Analysis of 21 applications for authorization from 5 to 16 July 1923; "État du mouvement des maisons de tolérance pendant le mois de février 1924," archives de la Direction des services administratifs, Secrétariat, Concession française, Archives municipales de Shanghai, dossier 1934 25 MS 1554.2, "Maisons de chanteuses – demandes de licence" [1922–1924].
28. Edward Henderson, *A Report on Prostitution in Shanghai*, Shanghai, n.pub., 1871, p. 11.
29. Shanghai Municipal Council, *Report for the Year 1920*, Shanghai, Kelly & Walsh, pp. 253–254A; League of Nations, Commission of Inquiry into Traffic in Women and Children in the East, *Report to the Council*, Geneva, document no. C.849.M.393.1932.IV, pp. 143–145; police report, 10 September 1936, archives de la Direction des services administratifs, Concession française, dossier 1936 25 MS 1555, "Nature des dossiers and documents" [1883–1942].
30. Police report, undated, Police Archives, Municipality of Shanghai (*Shanghai shi jingchaju*) 1945–1949, Shanghai Municipal Archives, file 011-4-263, October 1947.
31. Police report, archives de la Direction des services administratifs, Concession française, dossier 1936 25 MS 1555, "Nature des dossiers and documents" [1883–1942].
32. "État du mouvement des maisons de tolérance pendant le mois de February 1924"; analysis of 21 applications for authorization from 5 to 16 July 1923, archives de la Direction des services administratifs, Concession française, dossier 1934 25 MS 1554.2, "Maisons de chanteuses – demandes de licence" [1922–1924].
33. Analysis of consular ordinances, 1932–1939, Archives diplomatiques françaises, Consulat général de Shanghai, Nantes.
34. *Shanghai shi jingchaju Laozha fenju sanshiliu niandu niankan* ("Annual Report for 1947 of the Laozha Police Station, Police Bureau of the Municipality of Shanghai"), Shanghai, n.pub., 1948, p. 187.
35. Ji Longsheng, *Da Shanghai* ("Greater Shanghai"), Taibei, Nanfang zazhi chubanshe [1942], p. 110.
36. Sue Gronewold, *Beautiful Merchandise. Prostitution in China, 1860–1936*, New York, Haworth Press, 1982, p. 34.
37. Wang Jimen, *Shanghai liushi nian lai huajie shi, op. cit.*, p. 24.
38. Wang Dingjiu, *Shanghai guwen, op. cit.*, p. 669.

39. *Xiaolinbao* ("A Thousand Smiles"), 4 August 1902.
40. Jin Buhuan, *Chunjiang huayue hen*, *op. cit.*, p. 15.
41. Cf. *Xiaolinbao* ("A Thousand Smiles"), 2 April 1901.
42. They came in the shape of little booklets, 12 × 7 cm, that could easily be slipped into a pocket. Jin Buhuan, *Chunjiang huayue hen*, *op. cit.*, p. 33.
43. Yu Baosheng [pseudonym of Wang Tao], *Huaguo jutan*, *op. cit.*, II, p. 10; Wang Tao, *Songbin suohua*, *op. cit.*, p. 109.
44. Yu Baosheng [pseudonym of Wang Tao], *Huaguo jutan*, *op. cit.*, II, p. 9.
45. Wang Tao, *Songbin suohua*, *op. cit.*, p. 109; *SB*, 5 April 1873.
46. Wang Tao, *Songbin suohua*, *op. cit.*, p. 121.
47. Wang Jimen, *Shanghai liushi nian lai huajie shi*, *op. cit.*, p. 151.
48. Wang Jimen, *Shanghai liushi nian lai huajie shi*, *op. cit.*, p. 156.
49. Jin Buhuan, *Chunjiang huayue hen*, *op. cit.*, p. 3.
50. Jin Buhuan, *Chunjiang huayue hen*, *op. cit.*, p. 36.
51. Yu Wei, "Shanghai changji wu bai ge an diaocha," *op. cit.*, p. 13.
52. *SB*, 21 March 1889.
53. *SB*, 27 March 1879.
54. *SB*, 13 October 1872.
55. *SB*, 21 May 1909.
56. *SB*, 15 October 1910.
57. *Shanghai lanyou zhinan*, *op. cit.*, p. 7.
58. *SB*, 29 December 1910.
59. Haishang juewusheng (pseudonym), *Jinü de shenghuo*, *op. cit.*, p. 152.
60. Wang Dingjiu, *Shanghai guwen*, *op. cit.*, p. 672.
61. Jin Buhuan, *Chunjiang huayue hen*, *op. cit.*, p. 150.
62. For a critical discussion of the nature and quality of these sources, see my article: Christian Henriot, "Medicine, V.D., and Prostitution in Pre-Revolutionary China," *Social History of Medicine*, Oxford University, vol. V, no. 1, 1992, pp. 95–120.
63. J. H. Korns, "An Examination of Domestic Servants for Communicable Diseases," *China Medical Journal*, vol. 34, November 1920, pp. 624–629; *id.*, "Further Statistics on Communicable Diseases among Domestic Servants," *China Medical Journal*, vol. 35, July 1921, pp. 382–384.
64. The figures within brackets give the minimum and maximum percentages found in the surveys.
65. R. H. R. Sia, "Routine Wassermann Tests on 502 In-patients," *China Medical Journal*, vol. XXXV, January 1921, pp. 39–43; J. H. Snell, "Report of Routine Wassermann Tests at Soochow Hospital for One Year," *China Medical Journal*, vol. XXXV, January 1921, pp. 36–39; *id.*, "Report of 3000 Routine Wassermann Tests at the Soochow Hospital," *China Medical Journal*, vol. 43, December 1930, pp. 1238–1241; L. F. Heimburger, "The Incidence of Syphilis at the Shantung Christian University Dispensary," *China Medical Journal*, vol. 41, June 1927, pp. 541–550; Daniel Lai and Suchen Wang-Lai, "Incidence of Syphilis Among the Chinese Soldiers at Swatow," *China Medical Journal*, vol. 42, August 1928, pp. 557–567; *id.*, "Incidence of Syphilis among Chinese Civilian Patients in Swatow District," *China Medical Journal*, vol. 43, January 1929, pp. 22–27.
66. The sources used for this paragraph and the next one are: J. H Korns, "An Examination of Domestic Servants for Communicable Diseases," *China Medical Journal*, vol. XXXIV, November 1920, pp. 624–629; *id.*, "Further

Statistics on Communicable Diseases among Domestic Servants," *China Medical Journal*, vol. XXXV, July 1921, p. 382–384; R. H. R. Sia, "Routine Wassermann Tests on 502 Inpatients," *China Medical Journal*, vol. XXXV, January 1921, pp. 39–43; J. H. Snell, "Report of Routine Wassermann Tests at Soochow Hospital for One Year," *China Medical Journal*, vol. XXXV, January 1921, pp. 36–39; E. T. H. Tsen, "The Prevalence of Syphilis in Peking," *National Medical Journal*, vol. VI, 1921, p. 156; Ernest Tso, "Statistics of Communicable Diseases Among Hospital Employees in Peking," *China Medical Journal*, vol. XXXVII, March–April 1923, p. 226–230; F. Oldt, "Purity Campaign in Canton," *China Medical Journal*, vol. XXXVII, September 1923, pp. 776–782; L. F. Heimburger, "The Incidence of Syphilis at the Shantung Christian University Dispensary," *China Medical Journal*, vol. XLI, June 1927, pp. 541–550; Daniel Lai and Suchen Wang-Lai, "Incidence of Syphilis among the Chinese Soldiers at Swatow," *China Medical Journal*, vol. XLII, August 1928, pp. 557–567; id., "Incidence of Syphilis among Chinese Civilian Patients in Swatow District," *China Medical Journal*, vol. XLIII, January 1929, pp. 22–27; J. H. Snell, "Report of 3000 Routine Wassermann Tests at the Soochow Hospital," *China Medical Journal*, vol. XLIII, December 1930, pp. 1238–1241.

67. *Shanghai shi jingchaju Laozha fenju sanshiliu niandu niankan* ("Annual Report for 1947 of the Laozha Police Station, Police Bureau of the Municipality of Shanghai"), Shanghai, n.pub., 1948, p. 195.

68. The facts support this picture: In 1926, a girl from Shaoxing who had been sold to a house of prostitution in Fuzhou was unable to get herself purchased by a customer who offered the madam 2,000 yuan. The madam was unwilling to let the prostitute go for less than 3,000 yuan. Archives of the *Zhongguo jiuji fu ru zonghui* (Anti-Kidnapping Society), file 113-1-4, p. 75 (1927).

69. For a discussion on this literature, see the excellent work by Perry Link, *Mandarin Ducks and Butterflies: Popular Fiction in Early 20th Century Chinese Cities*, Berkeley, University of California Press, 1981, and Wei Shaochang, *Yuanyang hudie pai yanjiu ziliao* ("Research Materials on the School of Mandarin Ducks and Butterflies"), Shanghai, Wenyi chubanshe, 1962.

70. Marie-Erica Benabou, *La prostitution et la police des moeurs au XVIIIᵉ siècle*, Paris, Perrin, 1987.

71. Alain Corbin, *Les filles de noce. Misère sexuelle and prostitution (19ᵉ–20ᵉ siècle)*, Paris, Flammarion (coll. Champs), 1982 (1st ed., Aubier-Montaigne, 1978).

72. *Shanghai lanyou zhinan, op. cit.*, p. 13.

73. Wang Jimen, *Shanghai liushi nian lai huajie shi, op. cit.*, p. 12.

74. I am referring, of course, among others to the work of Louis Chevalier, *Classes laborieuses and classes dangereuses*, Paris, L.G.F., 1978.

75. Police report, 17 October 1946, Police Archives (1945–1949), file 011-4-176, August 1946–May 1948.

76. Record of Interrogation, undated [1946], Police Archives (1945–1949), file 011-4-176, August 1946–May 1948.

77. Record of Interrogation, 26 February 1947, Police Archives (1945–1949), file 011-4-163, "Qudi jiyuan an" ("Cases of Closure of Houses of Prostitution").

78. Haishang juewusheng (pseudonym), *Jinü de shenghuo, op. cit.*, p. 19.

79. The sources for this section are police archives of the police bureau, 1945–1949.

80. On the secret societies in Shanghai, the reference work is, without question,

Bryan Martin, "*The Green Gang in Shangai. Politics and Organized Crime, 1919–1937,* Berkeley, University of California Press, 1996. Cf also the article by Fan Songfu, "Shanghai banghui neimu" ("The Corridors of Shanghai's Secret Societies"), *Wenshi ziliao xuanji* ("Selection of Historical and Literary Materials"), vol. 1980, pp. 150–178; Xue Gengxin, "Jindai Shanghai hei shehui jianwen" ("Some Rumors about the Secret Societies of Shanghai"), in *Jiu Shanghai de yan du chang,* pp. 179–195; Dai Xuanzhi, "Qingbang de Yuanliu" ("The Sources of the Green Gang"), *Shihuo yuekan* ("Material Life"), vol. III, no. 4, July 1973, pp. 172–177; and above all the work by Bryan G. Martin, "Warlords and Gangsters: The Opium Traffic in Shanghai and the Creation of the Three Prosperities Company," paper prepared for the Asian Studies Association of Australia, sixth national conference, 11–16 May 1986; *id.*, "Tu Yuèh-sheng and Labour Control in Shanghai: The Case of the French Tramways Union, 1928–1932," *Papers in Far Eastern History*, 32, September 1985, Australian National University, pp. 99–132. The central figure in this world, Du Yuesheng, is the subject of several biographical works that sometimes refer to the prostitutes but say nothing about the links between the two worlds: Y. C. Wang, "Tu Yueh-sheng (1891–1951): A Tentative Biography," *Journal of Asian Studies*, no. 6, May 1967, pp. 433–455; Yang Wei, *Du yuesheng waizhuan* ("Unauthorized Biography of Du Yuesheng"), Taibei, Xin Qiye shijie chubanshe, 1984; Zhang jungu, *Du Yuesheng zhuan* ("A Biography of Du Yuesheng") [according to the memoirs of Lu Jingshi], Taibei, Zhuanji wenxue zazishe, 1986, 4 vols.; Wang benhu, *Minguo jiaofu Du Yuesheng* ("The Master of the Secret Societies, Du Yuesheng"), Taibei, yeqiang chubanshe, 1990.

81. He Wannan and Yang Jieceng, *Shanghai changji gaizao shihua, op. cit.,* pp. 17–18.
82. *Haishang yeyou beilan, op. cit.,* I, p. 6.
83. Zhang Qiugu, *Piao du bai bi daguan* ("An Overview of Gambling and Whoring"), Shanghai, n.pub., 1920, I, p. 7; Wang Jimen, *Shanghai liushi nian lai huajie shi, op. cit.,* p. 9; *Shanghai lanyou zhinan, op. cit.,* p. 14.
84. The expression *dadi* was applied to those of them who went in for prostitution: *dadi dajie* or *dadi niangyi*. *Shanghai zhinan, op. cit.,* V, p. 19.
85. Jin Buhuan, *Chunjiang huayue hen, op. cit.,* p. 10.
86. *Haishang yeyou beilan, op. cit.,* I, p. 6.
87. *Haishang yeyou beilan, op. cit.,* I, p. 13.
88. When they were employed by the *shuchang,* the musicians received no fixed remuneration. They shared the takings from the show presented at each change of season with the owner of the establishment. When they were hired on a permanent basis, the musicians received a salary of 30 to 40 yuan. When on the job, they took one *mao* out of the payment for each outside invitation. *Shanghai lanyou zhinan, op. cit.,* p. 5; Wang Jimen, *Shanghai liushi nian lai huajie shi, op. cit.,* p. 13.
89. In a small classical formation of four musicians, the instruments represented were the flute, the lute, the panpipe, and the drum. *Haishang yeyou beilan, op. cit.,* II, p. 6; *Shanghai zhinan, op. cit.,* V, p. 19b.
90. *Shanghai lanyou zhinan, op. cit.,* p. 6.
91. Wang Jimen, *Shanghai liushi nian lai huajie shi, op. cit.,* p. 13.
92. Wang Jimen, *Shanghai liushi nian lai huajie shi, op. cit.,* p. 13.
93. *Haishang yeyou beilan, op. cit.,* I, p. 3.
94. *Shanghai shenmi zhinan, op. cit.,* pp. 17–18.

95. Shanghai Municipal Council, *Report for the Year 1939*, Shanghai, Kelly & Walsh, 1940, p. 223.

Chapter 10

1. Sue Gronewold's work is particularly weak in this respect. The data on the economy of prostitution are the result of a compilation that does not take account of the chronology and of the types of prostitutes. In addition, the author has introduced distortions in converting her figures into U.S. dollars. Sue Gronewold, *Beautiful Merchandise. Prostitution in China, 1860–1936*, New York, Haworth Press, 1982, pp. 10–11 and 15.
2. "Report of the Special Vice Committee," Shanghai Municipal Council, *Report for the Year 1920*, Shanghai, Kelly & Walsh, 1921, p. 253A.
3. *SB*, 4 May 1899.
4. *Shanghai shenmi zhinan* ("Secret Guide to Shanghai"), Shanghai, Datong tushushe jianyin, n.d., p. 3.
5. "Liste des maisons de tolérance enregistrées sur la Concession française," archives de la Direction des services administratifs, Secrétariat, Concession française, file no. 25 MS 1555.
6. The distribution was as follows: 50, 60, 62, 74, 80, 112, 120, 120, 197 yuan.
7. Second category: 28, 28, 28, 28, 30, 31, 42, 50, 50, 50, 50, 50, 54, 55, 57, 57, 59, 62, 62, 66, 77, 78, 78 yuan; third category: 23, 28, 38, 38, 38, 38, 38, 38, 52 yuan.
8. *Shanghai lanyou zhinan* ("A Sightseeing Guide to Shanghai"), Shanghai, Zhonghua tushu jicheng gongsi, 1923, p. 13.
9. *Shanghai shenmi zhinan, op. cit.*, p. 2.
10. *SB*, 4 May 1899.
11. *Shanghai shenmi zhinan, op. cit.*, p. 4; Haishang juewusheng (pseudonym), *Jinü de shenghuo* ("The Life of the Prostitutes"), Shanghai, Chunmin shudian, 1940, p. 19.
12. Yu Baosheng [pseudonym of Wang Tao], *Haizou yeyou fulu* ("Addenda to Notes of a Libertine on the Seaside"), Shanghai, Hanwen yuanshusi, 1929, I, p. 4.
13. Letter of 20 January 1932 and reply from the Secretariat, 22 January 1932, archives de la Direction des services administratifs, Concession française, dossier 1936 25 MS 1555 "Nature des dossiers and documents" [1883–1942]; undated letter, file 1933 25 MS 1554.1, "Maisons de chanteuses – règlements" [1923–1943].
14. *Shanghai shenmi zhinan, op. cit.*, p. 6.
15. Haishang juewusheng (pseudonym), *Jinü de shenghuo, op. cit.*, p. 26.
16. Questioning of prostitutes, 18 October 1947, Police Archives, Municipality of Shanghai (*Shanghai shi jingchaju*), 1945–1949, Municipal Archives of Shanghai, file 011-4-263, October 1947.
17. *Shanghai lanyou zhinan, op. cit.*, p. 4.
18. Wang Jimen, *Shanghai liushi nian lai huajie shi, op. cit.*, p. 10.
19. *Xiaolinbao* ("A Thousand Smiles"), 26 April 1901.
20. *Shanghai lanyou zhinan, op. cit.*, p. 4.
21. *Shanghai zhinan* ("Guide to Shanghai: A Chinese Directory of the Port"), Shanghai, Shangwu yinshuguan (1st ed., 1909), 1919, V, p. 19.
22. Haishang juewusheng (pseudonym), *Jinü de shenghuo, op. cit.*, p. 12.

23. Zhang Qiugu, *Piao du bai bi daguan, op. cit.*, I, p. 1; *Shanghai lanyou zhinan, op. cit.*, p. 1.
24. Wang Jimen, *Shanghai liushi nian lai huajie shi, op. cit.*, p. 13.
25. Chen Wuwo, *Lao Shanghai san shi nian jianwen* ("Thirty Years of Sights and Sounds of Old Shanghai"), Shanghai, Dadong shuju, 1928; Shanghai, Zhonghua tushu jicheng gongsi, 1923, p. 78.
26. *Shanghai zhinan, op. cit.*, V, p. 18b.
27. Wang Jimen, *Shanghai liushi nian lai huajie shi, op. cit.*, p. 17.
28. *Shanghai shenmi zhinan, op. cit.*, p. 10.
29. Haishang juewusheng (pseudonym), *Jinü de shenghuo, op. cit.*, pp. 101–102.
30. *Haishang yeyou beilan, op. cit.*, III, p. 1; *Shanghai lanyou zhinan, op. cit.*, p. 2.
31. Zhang Qiugu, *Piao du bai bi daguan, op. cit.*, I, p. 10.
32. There were two ceremonies, one at the beginning and the other at the end of each season. They were respectively called *kaizhang lutou* ("opening the accounts") and *shouzhang lutou* ("settling the accounts"). *Shanghai zhinan, op. cit.*, V, p. 19.
33. Haishang juewusheng (pseudonym), *Jinü de shenghuo, op. cit.*, p. 16.
34. *Hua Bao* ("The Flowers"), 6 September 1926; *Shanghai shenmi zhinan, op. cit.*, p. 21; Haishang juewusheng (pseudonym), *Jinü de shenghuo, op. cit.*, p. 9.
35. Wang Jimen, *Shanghai liushi nian lai huajie shi, op. cit.*, p. 18.
36. Zhang Qiugu, *Piao du bai bi daguan, op. cit.*, I, p. 14.
37. Haishang juewesheng (pseudonym), *Jinü de shenghuo, op. cit.*, pp. 101–102.
38. In 1901, the police discovered a group of eight professional players. They had won a tidy sum of 6,000 yuan by making arrangements with certain manageresses of brothels where customers might be found in search of gambling partners. *Xiaolinbao* ("A Thousand Smiles"), 4 August 1902.
39. Wang Dingjiu, *Shanghai guwen* ("Guide de Shanghai"), Shanghai, Zhongyang shudian, 1934, p. 665.
40. Wang Jimen, *Shanghai liushi nian lai huajie shi, op. cit.*, p. 17; *Shanghai shenmi zhinan, op. cit.*, p. 12.
41. *Shanghai shenmi zhinan, op. cit.*, p. 10.
42. *Shanghai zhinan, op. cit.*, p. 19; Wang Dingjiu, *Shanghai guwen, op. cit.*, p. 663.
43. Wang Jimen, *Shanghai liushi nian lai huajie shi, op. cit.*, p. 15.
44. *Hua Bao* ("The Flowers"), 3 September 1926.
45. Haishang juewusheng (pseudonym), *Jinü de shenghuo, op. cit.*, p. 103.
46. *Xiaolinbao* ("A Thousand Smiles"), 26 April 1901.
47. *SB*, 6 January 1924.
48. Wang Dingjiu, *Shanghai guwen, op. cit.*, p. 665.
49. In 1930, the average annual income of eighty-five families (with an average of five members) of post office employees amounted to 574 yuan and that of a hundred working-class families (with four members) was 461 yuan. Herbert D. Lamson, *Social Pathology in China: A Source Book for the Study of Livelihood, Health and the Family*, Shanghai, Commercial Press, 1935, pp. 50–51.
50. De Becker, *The Nightless City*, London, Probsthain and Co., 1906 (1st ed., 1899), pp. 81–83.
51. *Shanghai lanyou zhinan, op. cit.*, p. 10.
52. 750 girls with two outings (1,500), 200 with five (1,000), 100 with ten (1,000), 50 with twenty (1,000). Total: 4,500 outings.
53. Wang Jimen, *Shanghai liushi nian lai huajie shi, op. cit.*, p. 142.

54. Estimating the average daily earning (from short encounters and nights) at 3 yuan.
55. By way of a comparison, the revenue of the Shanghai government in 1927–1928 and 1928–1929 was 3.4 and 4.4 million yuan, respectively. Christian Henriot, *Shanghai, 1927–1937; Municipal Power, Locality, and Modernization*, Berkeley: The University of California Press, 1993, pp. 141–142.
56. Haishang juewusheng (pseudonym), *Jinü de shenghuo, op. cit.*, p. 23; Wang Jimen, *Shanghai liushi nian lai huajie shi, op. cit.*, p. 15.
57. *Shanghai lanyou zhinan, op. cit.*, p. 13.
58. Haishang juewusheng (pseudonym), *Jinü de shenghuo, op. cit.*, p. 23; Wang Jimen, *Shanghai liushi nian lai huajie shi, op. cit.*, p. 15.
59. Wang Jimen, *Shanghai liushi nian lai huajie shi, op. cit.*, p. 15.
60. Wang Jimen, *Shanghai liushi nian lai huajie shi, op. cit.*, p. 17.
61. Wang Jimen, *Shanghai liushi nian lai huajie shi, op. cit.*, p. 17.
62. *Shanghai shenmi zhinan, op. cit.*, p. 7.
63. Haishang juewusheng (pseudonym), *Jinü de shenghuo, op. cit.*, pp. 27–28.
64. Haishang juewusheng (pseudonym), *Jinü de shenghuo, op. cit.*, p. 64.
65. Wang Jimen, *Shanghai liushi nian lai huajie shi, op. cit.*, p. 17.
66. *Haishang yeyou beilan, op. cit.*, II, p. 6.
67. Haishang juewusheng (pseudonym), *Jinü de shenghuo, op. cit.*, p. 61.
68. Haishang juewusheng (pseudonym), *Jinü de shenghuo, op. cit.*, p. 64.
69. *SB*, 19 December 1910.
70. Chen Wuwo, *Lao Shanghai san shi nian jianwen* ("Thirty Years of Sights and Sounds of Old Shanghai"), Shanghai, Dadong shuju, 1928, p. 77.
71. *Shanghai shenmi zhinan, op. cit.*, p. 4.
72. *Haishang yeyou beilan* ("Omnium of Licentiousness in Shanghai"), Shanghai, n.pub., 1891, I, p. 3; Wang Jimen, *Shanghai liushi nian lai huajie shi* ("Sixty Years of the History of the World of Flowers in Shanghai"), Shanghai, Shixin shuju, 1922, pp. 13 and 20.
73. Wang Jimen, *Shanghai liushi nian lai huajie shi, op. cit.*, p. 20.
74. Wang Jimen, *Shanghai liushi nian lai huajie shi, op. cit.*, p. 15.
75. Haishang juewusheng (pseudonym), *Jinü de shenghuo, op. cit.*, pp. 27–28.
76. Jin Buhuan, *Chunjiang huayue hen* ("Recollections of the Good Old Times"), Xianggang, Tianwentai baoshe, 1962, p. 15.
77. Haishang juewusheng (pseudonym), *Jinü de shenghuo, op. cit.*, pp. 25 and 30.
78. Haishang juewusheng (pseudonym), *Jinü de shenghuo, op. cit.*, p. 16.
79. Wang Jimen, *Shanghai liushi nian lai huajie shi, op. cit.*, p. 18.
80. *Shanghai zhinan, op. cit.*, V, p. 19b; Wang Jimen, *Shanghai liushi nian lai huajie shi, op. cit.*, p. 11.
81. *Shanghai shenmi zhinan, op. cit.*, p. 12; Haishang juewusheng (pseudonym), *Jinü de shenghuo, op. cit.*, p. 12.
82. Wang Jimen, *Shanghai liushi nian lai huajie shi, op. cit.*, p. 11; Haishang juewusheng (pseudonym), *Jinü de shenghuo, op. cit.*, p. 13.
83. *Haishang yeyou beilan, op. cit.*, II, p. 16.
84. *Haishang yeyou beilan, op. cit.*, II, p. 7.
85. Haishang juewusheng (pseudonym), *Jinü de shenghuo, op. cit.*, p. 27.
86. *Shanghai lanyou zhinan* ("A Sightseeing Guide to Shanghai"), Shanghai, Zhonghua tushu jicheng gongsi, 1923, p. 14.
87. *Haishang yeyou beilan, op. cit.*, III, p. 7.
88. *SB*, 18 September 1899; 27 September 1899.

89. *SB*, 20 October 1899.
90. *SB*, 17 December 1899.
91. *SB*, 4 May 1899.
92. *Shanghai zhinan*, 1919, V, p. 19b.
93. Wang Jimen, *Shanghai liushi nian lai huajie shi, op. cit.*, p. 21; *Shanghai shenmi zhinan* ("Secret Guide to Shanghai"), Shanghai, Datong tushushe jianyin, n.d., p. 29.
94. Haishang juewusheng (pseudonym), *Jinü de shenghuo, op. cit.*, p. 155.
95. A practice that gave rise to the expression *liu diedao* ("a tumble for six [yuan]"). Wang Jimen, *Shanghai liushi nian lai huajie shi, op. cit.*, p. 21.
96. Zhang Qiugu, *Piao du bai bi daguan, op. cit.*, II, p. 4.
97. Jin Buhuan, *Chunjiang huayue hen, op. cit.*, p. 126.
98. *SB*, 4 September 1872.
99. *SB*, 27 March 1879.
100. *Shanghai shenmi zhinan, op. cit.*, p. 52; Zhang Qiugu, *Piao du bai bi daguan, op. cit.*, III, pp. 3–4.
101. Zhang Qiugu, *Piao du bai bi daguan, op. cit.*, III, p. 6; Wang Dingjiu, *Shanghai guwen*, 1934, *op. cit.*, p. 672.
102. Zhang Qiugu, *Piao du bai bi daguan, op. cit.*, III, p. 6.
103. Wang Shunu, *Zhongguo changji shi* ("A History of Prostitution in China"), Shanghai, Shenghuo shudian, 1934, p. 334.
104. Zhang Qiugu, *Piao du bai bi daguan, op. cit.*, III, p. 2; *Shanghai shenmi zhinan, op. cit.*, p. 49.
105. Zhang Qiugu, *Piao du bai bi daguan, op. cit.*, IV, p. 2.
106. Haishang juewusheng (pseudonym), *Jinü de shenghuo, op. cit.*, p. 172; *Shanghai lanyou zhinan, op. cit.*, pp. 2 and 11.
107. Gail Hershatter, *The Workers of Tianjin, 1900–1949*, Stanford, Stanford University Press, p. 190.
108. Undated letter [August 1946], Police Archives of the Municipality of Shanghai (1945–1949), file 011-4-173, January 1946–July 1948.
109. Dong Li brothel, report, 20 October [1947], Police Archives of the Municipality of Shanghai (1945–1949), file 011-4-259, August 1946–October 1946, p. 707.
110. Letter from a prostitute, undated; interrogation of prostitute, 18 October 1947, Police Archives of the Municipality of Shanghai (1945–1949), file 011-4-263, October 1947.
111. The Hotel Cangzhou Case, 17 February 1948, report, 20 October [1947]; The Hotel Yangzi Case, 17 February 1948, Police Archives of the Municipality of Shanghai (1945–1949), file 011-4-176, August 1946–May 1948.
112. Complaint by the prostitute Hou Huangyin, 14 June 1948, Police Archives of the Municipality of Shanghai (1945–1949), file 011-4-161, August 1947–July 1949; medical report, 31 March 1948, file 011-4-269.
113. *Shanghai shenmi zhinan, op. cit.*, p. 49.
114. The Hotel Cangzhou Case, 17 February 1948; the Hotel Yangzi Case, 17 February 1948, report, 20 October [1947], Police Archives of the Municipality of Shanghai (1945–1949), file 011-4-176, August 1946–May 1948.
115. The Hotel Cangzhou Case, 17 February 1948, report, 20 October [1947], Police Archives of the Municipality of Shanghai (1945–1949), file 011-4-176, August 1946–May 1948.
116. The Hotel Yangzi Case, 17 February 1948, Police Archives of the Municipality of Shanghai (1945–1949), file 011-4-176, August 1946–May 1948.

117. Wang Jimen, *Shanghai liushi nian lai huajie shi, op. cit.*, p. 24; Lu Dafang, *Shanghai tan yijiu lu* ("Reminiscences of the Shanghai Bund"), Taibei, Shijie shuju, 1980, p. 41.

118. Cases of the Tangyu, Qian'e, Xu Liu brothels, report, 20 October [1947], Police Archives of the Municipality of Shanghai (1945–1949), file 011-4-259, August 1946–October 1946, pp. 601, 617, and 709; testimony by the prostitute, the Hotel Cangzhou Case, 17 February 1948, file 011-4-176, August 1946–May 1948; record of interrogation (three prostitutes), 26 February 1947; interrogation of madam, 10 June 1948; record of interrogation (three girls), 15 April 1948, file 011-4-163, "Qudi jiyuan an" ("Cases of Closure of Houses of Prostitution").

119. Dong Li brothel, report, 20 October [1947], Police Archives of the Municipality of Shanghai (1945–1949), file 011-4-259, August 1946–October 1946, p. 707.

120. Laoying brothel, report, 20 October [1947], Police Archives of the Municipality of Shanghai (1945–1949), file 011-4-259, August 1946–October 1946, p. 703.

121. Yu Wei, "Shanghai changji wu bai ge an diaocha" ("A Study of 500 Prostitutes in Shanghai"), *Shizheng pinglun* ("The Municipal Affairs Weekly"), vol. X, no. 9/10, p. 13.

122. Police report, undated, Police Archives of the Municipality of Shanghai (1945–1949), file 011-4-263, October 1947.

123. Laoying brothel, report, 20 October [1947], Police Archives of the Municipality of Shanghai (1945–1949), file 011-4-259, August 1946–October 1946, p. 703; Case of Zhang Jingyu, Xu Liu brothels, report, 20 October [1947], Police Archives of the Municipality of Shanghai (1945–1949), file 011-4-259, August 1946–October 1946, p. 617 and p. 709.

124. Case of Zhang Jingyu, report, 20 October [1947], Police Archives of the Municipality of Shanghai (1945–1949), file 011-4-259, August 1946–October 1946, p. 617.

125. Xu Liu brothel, report, 20 October [1947], Police Archives of the Municipality of Shanghai (1945–1949), file 011-4-259, August 1946–October 1946, p. 709; Dong Li brothel, report, 20 October [1947], file 011-4-259, p. 707; Tangyu and Qian'e brothels, report, 20 October [1947], file 011-4-259, pp. 601 and 617; questioning of madam, 10 June 1948, file 011-4-163, "Qudi jiyuan an" ("Cases of Closure of Houses of Prostitution"); Taotao, letter from a prostitute, undated, file 011-4-263, October 1947.

126. Police report, undated, Police Archives of the Municipality of Shanghai (1945–1949), file 011-4-263, October 1947.

127. Case of Zhang Jingyu, Laoying brothel, report, 20 October [1947], Police Archives of the Municipality of Shanghai (1945–1949), file 011-4-259, August 1946–October 1946, pp. 617 and 703.

128. Liu Xu brothel, report, 20 October [1947], Police Archives of the Municipality of Shanghai (1945–1949), file 011-4-259, August 1946–October 1946, p. 709.

129. Letter from a prostitute, undated; interrogation of prostitute, 18 October 1947, Police Archives of the Municipality of Shanghai (1945–1949), file 011-4-263, October 1947.

130. Police report, Police Archives of the Municipality of Shanghai (1945–1949), file 011-4-263, October 1947.

131. Interrogation of a prostitute, 18 October 1947, Police Archives of the Municipality of Shanghai (1945–1949), file 011-4-263, October 1947.

132. Tangyu brothel, report, 20 October [1947], Police Archives of the Municipality of Shanghai (1945–1949), file 011-4-259, August 1946–October 1946.

133. Yu Wei, "Shanghai changji wu bai ge an diaocha," *op. cit.*, p. 13.
134. Yu Wei and Wong Amos, "A Study of 500 Prostitutes in Shanghai," *International Journal of Sexology*, vol. II, no. 4, May 1949, p. 238.

Chapter 11

1. *Police municipale à Shanghai*, Shanghai, Kelly & Walsh, 1865, p. 14.
2. *Compte rendu de la gestion pour l'exercice 1893*, Conseil d'administration municipale de la Concession française, Shanghai, The China Printing Co., p. 7.
3. Ch.-B Maybon and Jean Fredet, *Histoire de la Concession française de Changhai*, Paris, Plon, 1929, p. 291.
4. *Rules and Regulations for the Guidance of the Action of the Shanghai Municipal Force*, Shanghai, "Celestial Empire" Office, 1881.
5. *Règlement municipal de police et de voirie*, Shanghai, Imprimerie de la presse orientale, 1889.
6. *Règlement municipal de police et de voirie*, Shanghai, Imprimerie de la presse orientale, 1907.
7. Shanghai Municipal Council, *Report for the Year 1904*, pp. 69–71.
8. In 1906, the United States, where the prevailing mood was in favor of abolition, decided to set up a law court in Shanghai and take action against the eight brothels known as "American houses." In fact, these establishments managed to change their "nationality" by various stratagems, and none of them was closed by a decision of the court. Anne W. Fearn, *My Days of Strength: An American Woman Doctor's Forty Years in China*, New York, Harper & Brothers Publishers, 1939, pp. 160–162; Rhoads Murphey, *Shanghai: Key to Modern China*, Cambridge, MA: Harvard University Press, 1953, pp. 7–8.
9. Session of the Conseil Municipal on 28 September 1914, *Compte rendu de la gestion pour l'exercice 1914, op. cit.*
10. Letter from the chief of police, 6 March 1925, archives de la Direction des services administratifs, Concession française, file 1936 25 MS 1555, "Nature des dossiers et documents" [1883–1942].
11. Letter from the chief of police Mallet to the consul-general, 22 May 1908, Archives diplomatiques, Nantes, carton no. 70R; "Règlement sur les hôtels et maisons de loueurs indigènes," in *Règlements municipaux*, Shanghai, Kelly & Walsh, 1910.
12. *Shen Bao*, 21 February 1909.
13. "State Medicine and the Experiment of the Lock Hospital," Kerrie L. MacPherson, *A Wilderness of Marshes. The Origins of Public Health in Shanghai, 1843–1893*, Oxford, Oxford University Press, 1987, pp. 213–258. MacPherson's use of the notion of "State" with regard to the action of the Shanghai Municipal Council in the medical inspection of the prostitutes is inappropriate in my opinion. The Shanghai Municipal Council was a municipal institution independent of any "State" unlike incidentally the Municipal Council of the French Concession, which was entirely dependent on the French consul-general.
14. See the fascinating book by Bram Dijkstra, *Idols of Perversity. Fantasies of Feminine Evil in Fin-de-Siècle Culture*, Oxford, Oxford University Press, 1986.
15. See Abraham Flexner, *La prostitution en Europe*, Paris, 1919 (*Prostitution in Europe*, New York, The Century Co., 1914]; Richard J. Evans, "Prostitution,

State and Society in Imperial Germany," *Past and Present*, no. 70, 1976, pp. 106–126; Mary Gibson, *Prostitution and the State in Italy, 1860–1915*, New Brunswick, NJ, Rutgers University Press, 1986.

16. Alain Corbin, *Les filles de noce. Misère sexuelle and prostitution (19ᵉ–20ᵉ siècle)*, Paris, Flammarion (coll. Champs), 1982 (1st ed., Aubier-Montaigne, 1978), pp. 13–36.

17. *Compte rendu de la gestion pour l'exercice 1867–1868, op. cit.*, p. 21.

18. Around 1865, the French police force consisted of only about fifty Europeans assisted by varying numbers of Chinese. The figure went up to 72 in 1880, 99 in 1890, 143 in 1900, and 459 in 1910. By comparison, the police of Shanghai Municipal Council had 245 men already in 1883. Ch.-B. Maybon and Jean Fredet, *Histoire de la Concession française de Changhai, op. cit.*, p. 335; minutes de la séance de la Commission d'administration municipale, 27 September 1897, ordonnances consulaires, vol. XLVIII (1873–1900), archives diplomatiques françaises, Consulat général de Shanghai, Nantes; *Compte rendu de la gestion pour l'exercice 1869–1870, op. cit.*, p. 55; "Rapport de la garde," *Compte rendu de la gestion pour l'exercice* 1880, *op. cit.*, p. 11; *Compte rendu de la gestion pour l'exercice 1890, 1900, 1910*.

19. Ch.-B. Maybon and Jean Fredet, *Histoire de la Concession française de Changhai, op. cit.*, p. 274.

20. *Règlement administratif*, Shanghai, Kelly & Walsh, 1872.

21. *Compte rendu de la gestion pour l'exercice 1869–1870, op. cit.*, p. 4.

22. On this point, I would contest MacPherson's chronology in *A Wilderness of Marshes. The Origins of Public Health in Shanghai, 1843–1893, op. cit.*, pp. 220–221.

23. Edward Henderson, *A Report on Prostitution in Shanghai*, Shanghai, n.pub., 1871, p. 18.

24. Edward Henderson, *A Report on Prostitution in Shanghai, op. cit.*, pp. 3–4.

25. Edward Henderson, *A Report on Prostitution in Shanghai, op. cit.*, pp. 3–4.

26. Edward Henderson, *A Report on Prostitution in Shanghai, op. cit.*, p. 12.

27. Edward Henderson, *A Report on Prostitution in Shanghai, op. cit.*, p. 18.

28. In Jiaozhou (Shandong), in 1897, the German authorities went much further in the matter of race discrimination by setting up a system of brothels reserved to foreigners (and therefore barred to the Chinese) and vice versa. Wolfgang Uwe Eckart, *Deutsche Ärtzte in China, 1897–1914. Medizin als Kulturmission im zweiten deutschen Kaiserreich*, Stuttgart, Gustav Fischer Verlag, 1989, pp. 33 and 52.

29. Edward Henderson, *A Report on Prostitution in Shanghai, op. cit.*, p. 28.

30. Kerric MacPherson, *A Wilderness of Marshes. The Origins of Public Health in Shanghai, 1843–1893, op. cit.*, p. 227.

31. Kerric MacPherson, *A Wilderness of Marshes. The Origins of Public Health in Shanghai, 1843–1893, op. cit.*, p. 230.

32. Kerric MacPherson, *A Wilderness of Marshes. The Origins of Public Health in Shanghai, 1843–1893, op. cit.*, pp. 230–231.

33. On these aspects, see MacPherson's detailed research in *A Wilderness of Marshes. The Origins of Public Health in Shanghai, 1843–1893, op. cit.* The following paragraphs are based to a great extent on this study.

34. Shanghai Municipal Council, *Report for the Year 1874*, p. 71; *Report for the Year 1880*, p. 34.

35. *Compte rendu de la gestion pour l'exercice 1874–1875, op. cit.*, p. 24.

36. Shanghai Municipal Council, *Report for the Year 1876*, pp. 22–37.
37. Kerric MacPherson, *A Wilderness of Marshes. The Origins of Public Health in Shanghai, 1843–1893*, op. cit., p. 235.
38. Shanghai Municipal Council, *Report for the Year 1879*, p. 33; Kerric MacPherson, *A Wilderness of Marshes. The Origins of Public Health in Shanghai, 1843–1893*, op. cit., pp. 244–249.
39. Shanghai Municipal Council, *Report for the Year 1880*, p. 67; *Compte rendu de la gestion pour l'exercice 1880, op. cit.*, pp. 10 and 16.
40. Kerric MacPherson, *A Wilderness of Marshes. The Origins of Public Health in Shanghai, 1843–1893*, op. cit., pp. 254–257.
41. *Prostitution in the Victorian Age. Debates on the Issue from 19th Century Journals, op. cit.*; Paul MacHugh, *Prostitution and Victorian Social Reform, op. cit.* Regarding Josephine Butler, see Moberly E. Bell, *Josephine Butler*, Constable, 1963, and Joseph Williamson, *Josephine Butler. The Forgotten Saint*, Leighton Buzzard, Faith Press, 1977.
42. *Compte rendu de la gestion pour l'exercice 1910* and *Compte rendu de la gestion pour l'exercice 1910, op. cit.*
43. In 1920, 195 girls were officially entered in the registers of the dispensary. Shanghai Municipal Council, *Report for the Year 1920*, p. 253A.
44. MacPherson, *A Wilderness of Marshes. The Origins of Public Health in Shanghai, 1843–1893*, op. cit., p. 257.
45. The political regime of the International Settlement has been called a "businessmen's plutocracy," where the right to vote was restricted to Westerners whose property was worth at least 500 taels or who paid a total annual rent of at least 500 taels. Katherin B. Meyer, "Splitting Apart: The Shanghai Treaty Port in Transition, 1914–1921," doctoral thesis, Temple University, 1985, p. 3; Richard Feetham, *Report of the Hon. Mr. Justice Feetham, C.M.G., to the Shanghai Municipal Council, Shanghai North China Daily News and Herald*, 1921, p. 80.
46. *The Chinese Recorder*, vol. 19, no. 7, July 1888, p. 346; *Compte rendu de la gestion pour l'exercice 1888, op. cit.*, p. 14; *Compte rendu de la gestion pour l'exercice 1889, op. cit.*, p. 24; Shanghai Municipal Council, *Report for the Year 1920*, p. 253A.
47. Shanghai Municipal Council, *Report for the Year 1877*, p. 20; *Report for the Year 1881*, "Watch Committee Report."
48. *Compte rendu de la gestion pour l'exercice 1880*, p. 16; Shanghai Municipal Council, *Report for the Year 1884*, "Watch Matters."
49. Shanghai Municipal Council, *Report for the Year 1877*, p. 35.
50. Alain Corbin, *Les filles de noce. op. cit.*, pp. 134–135; Mary Gibson, *Prostitution and the State in Italy, op. cit.*, p. 190.
51. Alain Corbin, *Les filles de noce., op. cit.*, p. 138.
52. *Règlement administratif*, 1879, p. 31.
53. Shanghai Municipal Council, *Report for the Year 1878*, p. 47; *Report for the Year 1878*, p. 66; *Report for the Year 1880*, p. 64.
54. *Compte rendu de la gestion pour l'exercice 1880*, p. 16.
55. *Compte rendu de la gestion pour l'exercice 1882*, p. 19.
56. *Compte rendu de la gestion pour l'exercice 1886*, p. 3.
57. Shanghai Municipal Council, *Report for the Year 1878*, p. 47; *Compte rendu de la gestion pour l'exercice 1880*, p. 17; Shanghai Municipal Council, *Report for the Year 1879*, p. 66.

58. *Compte rendu de la gestion pour l'exercice 1883*, p. 21; *Compte rendu de la gestion pour l'exercice 1884*, p. 19.
59. *Compte rendu de la gestion pour l'exercice 1890*, p. 5.
60. *Compte rendu de la gestion pour l'exercice 1891*, p. 3; *Compte rendu de la gestion pour l'exercice 1895*, p. 3; *Compte rendu de la gestion pour l'exercice 1886*, p. 3; *Compte rendu de la gestion pour l'exercice 1890*, p. 5; *Compte rendu de la gestion pour l'exercice 1892*, p. 7.
61. *Compte rendu de la gestion pour l'exercice 1898*, p. 129; *Compte rendu de la gestion pour l'exercice 1899*, p. 125.
62. Sun Guoqun, *Jiu shanghai changji mishi* ("A Secret History of Prostitution in Old Shanghai"), Henan, Henan renmin chubanshe, 1988, p. 20; Ping Jinya, "Jiu Shanghai de changji" ("The Prostitutes in Old Shanghai"), in *Jiu shanghai de yan du chang* ("Prostitution, Gambling and Opium in Old Shanghai"), Shanghai shi wenshiguan bian, Shanghai, Baijia chubanshe, 1988, p. 169.
63. Richard Feetham, *Report of the Hon. Mr. Justice Feetham, op. cit.*, pp. 54–62.
64. *The Chinese Recorder*, 5 June 1905, p. 308; Shanghai Municipal Council, *Report for the Year 1920*, pp. 252–253A.
65. Lynda C. Johnson, "The Decline of Soochow and Rise of Shanghai: A Study in the Economic Morphology of Urban Change, 1756–1894," doctoral thesis, University of California, Santa Cruz, 1986, pp. 186–188.
66. Michael Sinclair, "The French Settlement of Shanghai on the Eve of the Revolution of 1911," *op. cit.*, pp. 144, 243, 371; Rhoads Murphey, *Shanghai: Key to Modern China, op. cit.*, p. 19.
67. Ch.-B. Maybon and Jean Fredet, *Histoire de la Concession française de Changhai, op. cit.*, p. 261.
68. Ch.-B. Maybon and Jean Fredet, *Histoire de la Concession française de Changhai, op. cit.*, pp. 258–261 and p. 264.
69. *Compte rendu de la gestion pour l'exercice 1893*, p. 7.
70. Between 1874–1875 and 1880, the French Concession changed its fiscal year from 1 April to 31 March to a period corresponding to the calendar year. Because I do not have the complete series of the *Comptes rendus*, I do not know when this change came into effect.
71. *Compte rendu de la gestion pour l'exercice 1865–1866*; *North China Herald*, 2 May 1863, p. 71.
72. Ch.-B. Maybon and Jean Fredet, *Histoire de la Concession française de Shanghai, op. cit.*, pp. 292–296 and 310–315.
73. Archives diplomatiques, Correspondance consulaire and commerciale, tome VIII, pièces 090 and 095; *Compte rendu de la gestion pour l'exercice 1866–1867*, p. 10.
74. Archives diplomatiques, Correspondance consulaire and commerciale, tome VIII, pièce 140.
75. Letter from the chief of police, 30 May 1883, archives de la Direction des services administratifs, file 1936 25 MS 1555 "Nature des dossiers et documents" [1883–1942].
76. The range of jobs available to women in the Chinese cities was very limited. They could be employed above all as domestic servants and amahs. They could also work in rather discredited professions as waitresses, clothes menders, or peddlers. The change that had begun with the arrival of the Westerners was as yet modest and slow. But it was to bring in irreversible transformations in the socioprofessional structure of the local population.

77. Edward Henderson, *A Report on Prostitution in Shanghai*, op. cit., pp. 9–11.
78. Letter from the chief of police, 30 May 1883, archives de la Direction des services administratifs, file 1936 25 MS 1555 "Nature des dossiers et documents" [1883–1942].
79. *North China Daily News*, 21 April 1871.
80. Shanghai Municipal Council, *Report for the Year 1880*, p. 58.
81. Shanghai Municipal Council, *Report for the Year 1887*, p. 58.
82. Wu Chenglian, *Jiu Shanghai chaguan jiulou* ("The Taverns and Tea Houses of Old Shanghai"), Shanghai, Huadong shifan daxue chubanshe, 1989, pp. 23–25.
83. Ordonnance no. 120 du 10 June 1891, archives diplomatiques (Nantes), ordonnances consulaires, vol. 47.
84. *Compte rendu de la gestion pour l'exercice 1891*, p. 30.
85. Literally, "Chambers of Smoke and Flowers." The term *yan* actually referred to opium and *hua* referred to the prostitutes. It is a revealing fact that the use of the term did not become entrenched before the 1880s. That the authors hesitate beween *huayan* and *yanhua* is an indication of the novelty of this type of establishment.
86. *Compte rendu de la gestion pour l'exercice 1900*, p. 51.
87. "Règlement sur les fumeries d'opium," archives diplomatiques (Nantes), carton 62 (Conseil d'administration de la Concession française).
88. *SB*, 4 November 1899, p. 2.

Chapter 12

1. In 1885, the foreign population reached 3,673. This number doubled by 1900 (6,774), and then again by 1910 (13,536). Between 1920 and 1925, the number of foreign residents went up from 23,307 to 29,997. In the French Concession, the foreign population was insignificant (around 400) up to 1910, for which date I have counted 1,476. The subsequent increase was small (2,405 in 1915, 3,562 in 1920). It was only from 1925 onward – when there were 7,811 residents – that the French Concession experienced a significant growth in its foreign population. Zou Yiren, *Jiu shanghai renkou bianqian de yanjiu* ("A Study of the Development of the Population of Old Shanghai"), Shanghai, Renmin chubanshe, 1980, p. 141.
2. Vern Bullough and Bonnie Bullough, *Women and Prostitution*, New York, Prometheus Books, 1987, pp. 281–282. There is a considerable pool of materials, following the surveys carried out by the various "Vice Committees" of the major American cities, that have not yet been exploited by historians. Until now, the historiography has concentrated on the nineteenth century: David Pivar, *Purity Crusade, Sexual Morality, and Social Control, 1868–1900*, Westport, CT, Greenwood Press, 1973; Marion S. Goldman, *Gold Diggers and Silver Miners: Prostitution and Social Life on the Comstock Lode*, Ann Arbor, University of Michigan Press, 1981; Anne M. Butler, *Daughters of Joy, Sisters of Misery. Prostitutes in the American West, 1865–1890*, Urbana, University of Illinois Press, 1985; Jacqueline Barnhard, *The Fair but Frail: Prostitution in San Francisco, 1849–1900*, Reno, University of Nevada Press, 1986. Regarding the twentieth century, see *The Response to Prostitution in the Progressive Era*, Chapel Hill, University of North Carolina Press, 1980; and Ruth Rosen, *The

Lost Sisterhood: Prostitution in America, 1900–1918, Baltimore, Johns Hopkins University Press, 1982.

3. Some months later, another petition demanded a reduction in the number of drinking establishments. The signatory organizations were the Shanghai Women's Temperance Union, the Union Church Ladies' Society, the Shanghai Free Christian Church, the Committee of the Union Church, the Southern Methodist Mission, and the Men's Total Abstinence League. Société des Nations, *Renseignements concernant la prostitution et la traite des femmes et des enfants dans divers pays et colonies asiatiques*, C.T.E.F. [Experts] 44 (confidentiel), Genève, Imp. de la "Tribune de Génève," [1924], p. 25.

4. Anne W. Fearn, *My Days of Strength: An American Woman Doctor's Forty Years in China*, New York, Harper & Brothers Publishers, 1939, p. 158.

5. Rev. F. Rawlinson, Rev. E. Morgan, Rev. J. W. Crofoot, Rev. K. Fujita, Dr. Margaret A. Polk, Dean A. J. Walker, Mr. and Mrs L. E. Canning, I. Mason, S. K. Tao. *North China Herald*, 25 May 1918.

6. The senders were the Shanghai Women's Temperance Union, Union Church Ladies' Society, Shanghai Missionary Association (comprising the various Protestant churches), King's Daughter Society, Mothers' Union (Shanghai Branch), American Women's Club, and the Men's Total Abstinence League. *Report for the Year 1918*, p. 90B.

7. Shanghai Municipal Council, *Report for the Year 1918*, Shanghai, Kelly & Walsh, 1919, p. 90B.

8. Shanghai Municipal Council, *Report for the Year 1918, op. cit.*, p. 92B.

9. *Ibid.*

10. Letter of 16 August 1918, *Report for the Year 1918, op. cit.*, p. 93B.

11. *Chinese Recorder*, no. 3, 1918, p. 200.

12. "Present Aim of the Moral Welfare Committee," Shanghai Municipal Council, *Report for the Year 1918, op. cit.*, pp. 93–94B.

13. Letter of 18 November 1918, Shanghai Municipal Council, *Report for the Year 1918, op. cit.*, p. 94B.

14. "Shanghai's Moral Welfare – Enthusiastic Meeting at Church House," *North China Herald*, 25 January 1919.

15. Letter of 6 February 1919, *Report for the Year 1919*, p. 242A.

16. Letters of 14 February 1919 and 19 February 1919, Shanghai Municipal Council, *Report for the Year 1919, op. cit.*, pp. 242–243A.

17. Letter of 20 March 1919, Shanghai Municipal Council, *Report for the Year 1919*, pp. 243–244A.

18. Letter of 28 March 1919, Shanghai Municipal Council, *Report for the Year 1919*, p. 245A. The Door of Hope gave a favorable answer. But no further steps seem to have been taken on the proposal of the Shanghai Municipal Council. Letter of 2 April 1919, Shanghai Municipal Council, *Report for the Year 1919*, p. 246A.

19. On these discussions; cf. Christian Henriot, "La prostitution à Shanghai aux xixe–xxe siècle (1849–1958)," doctoral thesis (*doctorat d'État*), Paris, École des hautes études en sciences sociales, chapter III.

20. *Municipal Gazette*, 10 April 1919, p. 137.

21. The members of the "Vice Committee" were Judge Skinner Turner, T. Ibukiyama, and A. Brooke Smith, appointed by the Shanghai Municipal Council; the Reverend Frank Rawlinson, Alice W. Remer, and L. E. Canning, chosen by the Committee; Dorothy M. Henman, S. C. Lin, and W. D. McCallum, selected jointly by the first six members. T. Ibukiyama died and was

replaced in December 1919 by William P. Lambe. *North China Herald*, 22 May 1919, p. 179; Shanghai Municipal Council, *Report for the Year 1919*, p. 246A.

22. *Municipal Gazette*, 11 April 1919, p. 137.
23. "Report of the Special Vice Committee," *Report for the Year 1920*, pp. 252–256A, also published in *The Municipal Gazette*, 19 March 1920 and in the press, *SB*, 19 March 1920; *North China Herald*, 19 March 1920, pp. 83–86.
24. *The Municipal Gazette*, 9 April 1920, pp. 162–164; *SB*, 1 April 1920; *North China Herald*, 1 April 1920, p. 124.
25. *The Municipal Gazette*, 9 April 1920, p. 164.
26. *The Municipal Gazette*, 9 April 1920, p. 162.
27. *The Municipal Gazette*, 9 April 1920, pp. 257–258A; *SB*, 13 May 1920; *North China Herald*, 13 May 1920, pp. 192–193.
28. The "Vice Committee" had counted 633 brothels, whereas the first draw in 1920 had revealed the existence of 972. This count is incomplete because 1,771 licenses were distributed in 1920. This gives an idea of the scale of the phenomenon of prostitution in the French Concession. Shanghai Municipal Council, *Report for the Year 1920*, p. 253A; *Report for the Year 1921*, p. 45C; *SB*, 22 December 1920.
29. *SB*, 24 May 1920; 7 June 1920.
30. *SB*, 10 June 1920; *North China Herald*, 10 June 1920, p. 228.
31. *SB*, 2 July 1920; 16 October 1920.
32. *SB*, 9 September 1920.
33. *SB*, 22 October 1920.
34. *SB*, 8 November 1920.
35. *SB*, 22 December 1920.
36. *North China Herald*, 25 December 1920, p. 875; Shanghai Municipal Council, *Report for the Year 1920*, p. 259A.
37. Correspondence, archives of the secretariat. International Settlement (1920–1924), file 3-00445; *SB*, 28 November 1921.
38. Shanghai Municipal Council, *Report for the Year 1921*, p. 63A.
39. Letter of 24 March 1922, Shanghai Municipal Council, *Report for the Year 1922*, p. 311A.
40. Letter of 4 April 1922, Shanghai Municipal Council, *Report for the Year 1922*, p. 311A.
41. Letter of 26 May 1922, Shanghai Municipal Council, *Report for the Year 1922*, p. 312A.
42. Letter of 16 June 1922, Shanghai Municipal Council, *Report for the Year 1922*, p. 312A.
43. The two parties decided by mutual agreement to publish their correspondence. This was done in the *Municipal Gazette* and in the annual report for 1922. Letter of 22 July 1922, Shanghai Municipal Council, *Report for the Year 1922*, p. 313A; Letter of 4 August 1922, Shanghai Municipal Council, *Report for the Year 1922*, p. 314A; Letters of 8 August 1922 (MWL) and of 9 August 1922 (SMC), Shanghai Municipal Council, *Report for the Year 1922*, p. 314A.
44. Shanghai Municipal Council, *Report for the Year 1922*, pp. 95–96A.
45. These data are taken from the report of the MWL, "Organised Effort Against Organized Vice." The experts of the League of Nations made extensive use of it in their own report in 1924, Société des nations, *Renseignements concernant la prostitution et la traite des femmes et des enfants*, *op. cit.*

46. Société des nations, *Renseignements concernant la prostitution et la traite des femmes and des enfants, op. cit.*, p. 28.
47. *Ibid.*
48. *Ibid.*
49. *SB*, 28 November 1921.
50. Shanghai Municipal Council, *Report for the Year 1922*, p. 36C; *Report for the Year 1923*, p. 29C; letter from the police to the secretariat (17 March 1924), archives of the secretariat, International Settlement, file 3-00445; *SB*, 22 December 1920; 7 December 1921; 6 December 1922; 17 December 1923.
51. *SB*, 17 December 1923; 22 December 1920.
52. Société des nations, *Renseignements concernant la prostitution et la traite des femmes and des enfants, op. cit.*, p. 38.
53. Police report (18 May 1921), archives of the secretariat. International Settlement, file 3-00445.
54. Police report to the secretariat (13 April 1921), archives of the secretariat. International Settlement, file 3-00445.
55. Many of the police reports consulted are in the same file (3-00445) and are dated: 25 November 1920; 4 February 1921; 30 March 1921; 13 April 1921; 18 May 1921; 21 October 1921; 23 March 1922; 4 April 1922; 12 April 1922; 28 April 1922; 19 June 1922; 11 November 1922; 12 November 1922; 6 April 1923; 27 April 1923; 20 May 1923; 7 March 1923; 16 June 1923; 5 July 1923; 3 August 1923; 12 October 1923; 31 October 1923.
56. Police report, "Improper Use of Brothel Licences," 25 November 1920; 30 March 1921, archives of the secretariat. International Settlement, file 3-00445.
57. Société des nations, *Renseignements concernant la prostitution et la traite des femmes and des enfants, op. cit.*, p. 38.
58. *SB*, 2 September 1922; 22 April 1923; 4 January 1924.
59. *SB*, 9 March 1921.
60. *SB*, 13 August 1921.
61. Société des nations, *Renseignements concernant la prostitution et la traite des femmes and des enfants, op. cit.*, p. 38.
62. *SB*, 25 May 1922.
63. Zuili tuitangsheng (pseudonym), "Shanghai zhi ji" ("The Prostitutes of Shanghai"), *Xin Shanghai* ("The New Shanghai"), no. 10, February 1926, pp. 43–48; no. 12, April 1926, pp. 35–41; Jin Buhuan, *Chunjiang huayue hen* ("Recollections of the Good Old Times"), Xianggang, Tianwentai baoshe, 1962, p. 155.
64. Société des nations, *Renseignements concernant la prostitution et la traite des femmes and des enfants, op. cit.*, p. 38.
65. Letters of 22 June 1920 (from the councillors) and 24 June 1920 (from the consul), *SB*, 15 July 1920.
66. *SB*, 8 October 1920.
67. It was at this time, in 1921, that the municipal police set up a vice department that promulgated rules of conduct for the houses of tolerance in the territory of the French Concession. Letters from the Association *Pingkang Tongshanhui* (Association des maisons de tolérance), 19 March 1929; 18 May 1932, archives de la Direction des services administratifs, secrétariat, Concession française, Municipal Archives de Shanghai: file 1936 25 MS 1555, "Nature des dossiers and documents" [1883–1942].
68. *SB*, 2 July 1920.

69. *SB*, 22 May 1922.
70. *SB*, 1 April 1923.
71. Letter from the MWL, 8 December 1923; Letter from the Municipal Council, 8 December 1923, archives de la Direction des services administratifs, Concession française, file 1936 25 MS 1555.
72. Analysis of 21 requests (July 1923); "État du mouvement des maisons de tolérance pendant le mois de février 1924", archives de la Direction des services administratifs, Concession française, file 1934 25 MS 1554.2.
73. *SB*, 8 June 1922.
74. *SB*, 20 May 1924.
75. *SB*, 31 May 1924.
76. *SB*, 10 July 1924.
77. Société des nations, *Renseignements concernant la prostitution et la traite des femmes and des enfants, op. cit.*, p. 38.
78. Letter of 8 June 1920, *SB*, 8 July 1920; Shanghai Municipal Council, *Report for the Year 1920*, p. 259A.
79. Letter of 23 June 1920, *SB*, 8 July 1920. Lemière publicly defended the courtesans by publishing an article that was tellingly entitled: "Sing Song Girl: From a Throne of Glory to a Seat of Ignominy," Shanghai Municipal Council, *Report for the Year 1920*, p. 260A; J. Lemière, "Sing Song Girl: From a Throne of Glory to a Seat of Ignominy," *Chinese Journal of Science and Art*, no. 1, March 1923, pp. 126, 130, 134.
80. Letters of 26 June 1920 and 28 June 1920, *SB*, 8 July 1920; Shanghai Municipal Council, *Report for the Year 1920*, p. 260A.
81. Letter of 8 July 1920, *SB*, 9 July 1920.
82. *SB*, 3 October 1920; 5 October 1920.
83. *SB*, 3 June 1923.
84. Société des nations, *Renseignements concernant la prostitution et la traite des femmes and des enfants, op. cit.*, p. 25.
85. *SB*, 8 March 1924.
86. *SB*, 5 May 1924.
87. *SB*, 31 May 1924.
88. The words in italics were underlined in the original text.
89. Letter of 29 January 1924 (MWL); Letter of 19 February 1924 (police), Shanghai Municipal Council, *Report for the Year 1924*, pp. 178–179.
90. Letter of 2 May 1924, Shanghai Municipal Council, *Report for the Year 1924*, p. 65.
91. Letter of 9 May 1924, Shanghai Municipal Council, *Report for the Year 1924*, p. 65.
92. *SB*, 5 May 1924; 12 June 1924.
93. *SB*, 1 November 1922.
94. This dimension is dealt with in Christian Henriot, "La prostitution à Shanghai aux xixe–xxe siècle," Chapter 17.

Chapter 13

1. Christian Henriot, *Shanghai, 1927–1937, Municipal Power, Locality, and Modernization, op. cit.*
2. On the modernization and the role of the police in Shanghai, see Frederic

Wakeman, Jr., *Policing Shanghai, 1927–1937*, Berkeley, University of California Press, 1994.

3. League of Nations, Traffic in Women and Children, Conference of Central Authorities in Eastern Countries, *Minutes of Meetings*, Geneva, document no. C-476.M.318.1937.IV, 1937, p. 35. The GMD meeting was more precisely the Fifth Plenum of the Central Executive Committee, set up by the Second National Congress of the Guomindang, which met in Nanking from 8 to 14 August. Martin C. Wilbur, *The Nationalist Revolution in China, 1923–1928*, Cambridge, Cambridge University Press, 1983, pp. 185–191.

4. League of Nations, Commission of Inquiry into Traffic in Women and Children in the East, *Report to the Council*, Geneva, document no. C.849.M.393.1932.IV, 1932, pp. 130 and 133; League of Nations, Conference of Central Authorities in Eastern Countries, *Minutes of Meetings, op. cit.*, p. 35.

5. *Shizheng baogao* ("Municipal Gazette"), vol. 1, 1930, p. 44.

6. League of Nations, Conference of Central Authorities in Eastern Countries, *Minutes of Meetings, op. cit.*, p. 35.

7. Nothing further is known about the nature and contents of this document, which does not appear to have ever been made public. Even the members of the League of Nations Commission of Enquiry in the Far East were unable to obtain a copy of it. "Enquiry in the East: Questionnaires to Governments," 5th session, Archives of the League of Nations, file no. R3055; League of Nations, Conference of Central Authorities in Eastern Countries, *Minutes of Meetings, op. cit.*, p. 35.

8. "Browbeating Prostitution," *The China Critic*, Shanghai, no. 16 (13 September 1928), p. 313.

9. Christian Henriot, *Shanghai, 1927–1937. Municipal Power, Locality, and Modernization*.

10. *Shanghai tebie shi gong'anju yewu jiyao, 1927* ("Annual Report of Activity of the Public Security Bureau of the Municipality of Shanghai"), Shanghai, Shanghai shi gong'anju, 1928; *Shanghai shi gong'anju yewu baogao, 1928* ("Annual Report of Activity of the Public Security Bureau of the Municipality of Shanghai"), Shanghai, Shanghai shi gong'anju, 1929; *Shanghai shi gong'anju yewu baogao, 1931–1932* ("Annual Report of Activity of the Public Security Bureau of the Municipality of Shanghai"), Shanghai, Shanghai shi gong'anju, 1932.

11. League of Nations, *Report to the Council, op. cit.*, p. 133.

12. Reports from district police stations (July 1946), Police Archives. Municipality of Shanghai (1945–1949), file no. 011-4-269.

13. Letter of 30 June 1930, archives de la Direction des services administratifs, Concession française, file 1936 25 MS 1555 "Nature des dossiers et documents" [1883–1942].

14. Letter of 4 July 1930, archives de la Direction des services administratifs, Concession française, dossier 1936 25 MS 1555.

15. Christian Henriot, *Shanghai, 1927–1937, op. cit.*, pp. 241–242.

16. Letter of 11 July 1930, League of Nations, *Report to the Council, op. cit.*, p. 159.

17. Letter from the association, 19 March 1929; welfare association "Bing K'ang Dong Zeu Wei" for the houses of tolerance, by-laws, archives de la Direction des services administratifs, Concession française, dossier 1936 25 MS 1555; "Compte-rendu," 13 May 1929, archives de la Direction des services administratifs, Concession française, dossier 1936 25 MS 1555.

18. Letter from the director of administrative services, 16 May 1929, archives de la Direction des services administratifs, Concession française, dossier 1936 25 MS 1555.
19. *Ibid.*
20. Letters from the association, 21 February 1931; 27 April 1932; "Note concernant l'Association des maisons de tolérance," 23 April 1929, archives de la Direction des services administratifs, Concession française, dossier 1936 25 MS 1555.
21. "Compte rendu," 13 May 1929, archives de la Direction des services administratifs, Concession française, dossier 1936 25 MS 1555.
22. Letter from the association, 18 May 1932, archives de la Direction des services administratifs, Concession française, dossier 1936 25 MS 1555.
23. Archives du bureau des travaux publics, Concession française, dossier 166–49, "Travaux publics," 1938–1941.
24. *SB*, 15 May 1932.
25. *SB*, 26 January 1934.
26. *SB*, 5 September 1933.
27. Note from the chief of police dated 1932. League of Nations, *Report to the Council, op. cit.*, pp. 144–145.
28. "Enquiry in the East: Questionnaires to Governments," Archives of the League of Nations, 1930–1931, file no. R3055, 7th session.
29. Shanghai Municipal Council, *Report for the Year 1920*, Shanghai, Kelly & Walsh, p. 70A; *Report for the Year 1922*, p. 72A; *Report for the Year 1923*, p. 41; *Report for the Year 1924*, p. 48; *Report for the Year 1925*, p. 42; *Report for the Year 1929*, pp. 86–87; *Report for the Year 1932*, pp. 124–125; *Report for the Year 1933*, pp. 131–132; *Report for the Year 1934*, pp. 95–96; *Report for the Year 1935*, pp. 123–124; *Report for the Year 1936*, pp. 103–104; *Report for the Year 1937*, p. 113.
30. Alain Corbin, *Les filles de noce. Misère sexuelle and prostitution (XIXᵉ–XXᵉ siècle)*, Paris, Flammarion (coll. Champs), 1982 (1st ed., Aubier-Montaigne, 1978), pp. 412–414 and p. 435.
31. Alain Corbin, *Les filles de noce, op. cit.*, pp. 430–435.
32. Frederick S. Northedge, *The League of Nations: Its Life and Times, 1920–1946*, Leicester, Leicester University Press, 1986, p. 185.
33. *Ibid.*
34. Société des nations, *Renseignements concernant la prostitution et la traite des femmes et des enfants dans divers pays and colonies asiatiques*, C.T.E.F. [Experts] 44 (confidentiel), Genève, Imp. de la "Tribune de Genève," [1924].
35. League of Nations, Conference of Central Authorities in Eastern Countries, *Minutes of Meetings, op. cit.*, p. 35.
36. The Commission of Enquiry in the Far East consisted of three delegates, Bacom Johnson (United States), Carol Pindor (Poland), Alma Sundquist (Sweden), and two assistants, Mr. Von Schmiden (secretary) and Mr. Marshall (stenographer). Letter of acceptance of the commission by the Chinese government, 19 December 1929, "Enquiry in the East: Questionnaires to Governments," Archives of the League of Nations, 1930–1931, file no. R3055.
37. The exact list of persons interviewed is in League of Nations, *Report to the Council, op. cit.*, pp. 496–499. The contents of the interviews are recorded in the files of the commission, which are currently kept in the Archives of the League of Nations in Geneva, "Commission of Inquiry into the Traffic in

Women and Children in the Far East," Archives of the League of Nations, file COL 115-128.

38. League of Nations, *Report to the Council, op. cit.*
39. League of Nations, *Report to the Council, op. cit.*, pp. 130 and 133; "Enquiry in the East: Questionnaires to Governments," Archives of the League of Nations, 7th meeting, 1930–1931, file no. R3055.
40. "Enquiry in the East: Questionnaires to governments," Archives of the League of Nations, 9th session, 1930–1931, file no. R3055.
41. "Enquiry in the East: Questionnaires to Governments," Archives of the League of Nations, 8th session, 1930–1931, file no. R3055.
42. Preliminary report of the Inquiry Commission, "Enquiry in the East: Questionnaires to Governments," Archives of the League of Nations, 1930–1931, file no. R3055. The majority of the Chinese women were dispatched to the various countries of South-East Asia where large Chinese communities were settled.
43. Letter from the Chinese delegate to the League of Nations, 26 December 1932, "Supplementary documentation supplied by governments, 1928–1930," Archives of the League of Nations, file no. R3047.
44. League of Nations, *The Work of the Bandoeng Conference, op. cit.*, p. 9.
45. Questions I.1–4, "Reply of the Chinese Government to the Questionnaire on Measures of Rehabilitation," in "Methods of Rehabilitation, Enquiry: Countries, 1935–1945," Archives of the League of Nations, file no. R4698.
46. Questions I.5–6, *op. cit.*, Archives of the League of Nations, file no. R4698.
47. Questions II.1–3, *op. cit.*, Archives of the League of Nations, file no. R4698.
48. Questions II.7, *op. cit.*, Archives of the League of Nations, file no. R4698.
49. In Hong Kong, in 1935, when the government prohibited the houses of prostitution, the girls were received one by one by the police, who offered them assistance to start a new life. The majority of the girls declined the offer and said they wished to continue the same activity elsewhere in China or in Macao. Norman Miners, "The State Regulation of Prostitution, 1857–1941," in N. Miners, *Hong Kong under Imperial Rule*, Hong Kong/London, Oxford University Press, East Asian Historical Monographs, 1987, p. 204.
50. Replies from the Chinese Government, "Enquiry in the East: Questionnaires to Governments," Archives of the League of Nations, 1930–1931, file no. R3055; League of Nations, Traffic in Women and Children, *Annual Reports*, Archives of the League of Nations, files no. R3042-, 3028-3029, 3049-3050, 3056-3057, 3060-3061, 3063 [1926–1932]; *Annual Reports*, 1932–1946.
51. "Questionnaire," p. 81; reply from the Chinese Government, League of Nations, *Minutes of Meetings, op. cit.*, pp. 85–86; during the conference itself, the delegation also mentioned the same document of 1928 and the instructions of 1932, League of Nations, *The Work of the Bandoeng Conference, op. cit.*, p. 35.
52. League of Nations, Far Eastern Conference, Bandung, "General," Archives of the League of Nations, file no. R4693-4694.
53. League of Nations, Far Eastern Conference, Bandung, "Correspondance with governments, 1937–1939," Archives of the League of Nations, file no. R4695; League of Nations, "Situation of Russian Women Refugees in the Far East, 1937–1939," Archives of the League of Nations, file no. R4692.
54. League of Nations, *The Work of the Bandoeng Conference, op. cit.*, pp. 17 and 27.

55. League of Nations, *The Work of the Bandoeng Conference, op. cit.*, pp. 18–19 and 35.
56. League of Nations, *The Work of the Bandoeng Conference, op. cit.*, p. 19.
57. "League of Nations' Far Eastern Bureau," Archives of the League of Nations, file no. R4708.
58. There is no monograph on Shanghai during the Japanese occupation, except for an old work: Robert W. Barnett, *Economic Shanghai: Hostage to Politics, 1937–1941*, New York, Institute for Pacific Relations, 1941. Some information can be found in the two reference works on collaboration in China: John H. Boyle, *China and Japan at War, 1937–1945: The Politics of Collaboration*, Stanford, Stanford University Press, 1972, and Gerald E. Bunker, *The Peace Conspiracy: Wang Ching-wei and the China War, 1937–1941*, Cambridge, MA, Harvard University Press, 1972, as well as in Christian Henriot, "'Einsame Insel.' Shanghai unter Japanischer Herrschaft, 1937–1945," in Marlene Hiller, Eberhard Jäckel, and Jürgen Rohwer, *Städte im 2. Weltkrieg. Ein internationaler Vergleich*, Essen, Klartext, 1991, pp. 28–46.
59. The "external road" area was an integral part of the Chinese municipal territory, where the Shanghai Municipal Council, in the absence of Chinese municipal authorities before 1927, had built roads over which it exercised policing and tax-collecting prerogatives. The negotiations conducted between 1927 and 1937 had led to an agreement that was never implemented because of Japanese opposition. Richard Feetham, *Report of the Hon. Mr. Justice Feetham, C.M.G., to the Shanghai Municipal Council*, Shanghai, North China Daily News and Herald, 1931, vol. II, part VI, "External Road Area"; Christian Henriot, *Shanghai, 1927–1937. Municipal Power, Locality and Modernization, op. cit.*, p. 139.
60. *SB*, 23 November 1938; 26 January 1940.
61. Christian Henriot, "'Einsame Insel.' Shanghai unter Japanischer Herrschaft, 1937–1945," *op. cit.*; *SB*, 3 February 1940.
62. Apart from the impossibility of directly opposing the collaborationist municipal authorities, who were protected by the Japanese, the Shanghai Municipal Council was also enfeebled by budgetary restrictions that led to numerous resignations by members of the police. *SB*, 30 April 1940.
63. *SB*, 2 April 1940; *North China Herald*, 5 March 1941, p. 489; 26 March 1941, p. 289; 18 June 1941, p. 352.
64. Although I have not been able to establish the existence of any formal link between these two organizations, the name "Ping Hong Welfare Association" is very similar to that of the association (*Pingkang tongshanhui*) that had tried to organize the houses of prostitution in the French Concession some years earlier. The archives that I have consulted have not been able to clarify this matter.
65. "Memorandum to Watch and Health Committees," 21 September 1942, Police Archives (1937–1945), file no. 4-2428.
66. Christian Henriot, *Shanghai, 1927–1937. Municipal Power, Locality, and Modernization, op. cit.*, p. 93.
67. "Memorandum to Watch and Health Committees," 21 September 1942, Police Archives (1937–1945), file no. 4-2428.
68. Letter of 21 December 1941, Police Archives (1937–1945), file no. 12-4-1445.
69. Letter of 21 December 1941, Police Archives (1937–1945), file no. 12-4-1445.
70. Letter of 8 July 1942, Police Archives (1937–1945), file no. 4-2428.

71. Letter of 17 July 1942, Police Archives (1937–1945), file no. 4-2428.
72. Letter of 7 September 1942, Police Archives (1937–1945), file no. 4-2428. The argument is somewhat biased inasmuch as the prostitutes were to be personally required to have licences (*vide infra*).
73. "Minutes of Meeting, Watch and Health Committees," 21 September 1942, Police Archives (1937–1945), file no. 4-2428.
74. Letter from the deputy secretary, 3 October 1942; see also "Minutes of Meeting, Watch and Health Committees," 21 September 1942, Police Archives (1937–1945), file no. 4-2428.
75. Articles in the *Shanghai Times*, 4 October 1942 and 10 October 1942, found in the Police Archives (1937–1945), file no. 4-2428.
76. Lettre from Liu Jie, n.d., Police Archives (1937–1945), file no. 4-2429.
77. Letter from the police, 16 April 1943; Letter from the health department, 7 May 1943, Police Archives (1937–1945), file no. 4-2429.
78. A Chinese journalist writing at the beginning of the 1960s recalled the opening of brothels by the Japanese army outside Shanghai. These were real "meat factories," where the Chinese prostitutes received soldiers (carrying coupons) one after the other. I have not found any other reference to these houses in the press or in other sources. Jin Buhuan, *Chunjiang huayue hen* ("Recollections of the Good Old Times"), Xianggang, Tianwentai baoshe, 1962, p. 135.
79. "*Shanghai shi jingchaju guanli changji zanxing banfa*" (Provisional Regulation for the Management of Prostitutes by the Police Bureau of the Municipality of Shanghai), Police Archives (1945–1949), file 1-4-125.
80. "*Zhengli Shanghai shi changji jihua*" ("Plan for the Reorganization of the Prostitutes in the Municipality of Shanghai"), Police Archives (1945–1949), file 1-4-125; Letter from the Police Bureau to the Mayor, 14 November 1945, Police Archives (1945–1949), file 1-4-125.
81. Letter from the Police Bureau to the Mayor, 24 December 1945, Police Archives (1945–1949), file 1-4-125.
82. Letter from the Police Bureau to the Mayor, 19 October 1945; Letter from the Mayor, 6 November 1945, Police Archives (1945–1949), file 1-4-125.
83. Letter from the Police Bureau to the Mayor, 24 December 1945, Letter from the Mayor, 31 December 1945, Police Archives (1945–1949), file 1-4-125.
84. Letter from the Mayor, 3 January 1946, Police Archives (1945–1949), file 1-4-125.
85. Letter from the Police Bureau to the Mayor, 21 May 1946, Police Archives (1945–1949), file 1-10-246; Letter from the Mayor, 19 June 1946, Police Archives (1945–1949), file 1-10-246.
86. Order by the Mayor, 13 June 1945; *ibid.* 4 July 1946, Police Archives (1945–1949), file 011-4-269.
87. "*Shanghai shi jingchaju zhengli changji shishi banfa*" ("Method to Carry out the Management of the Prostitutes: Police Bureau of the Municipality of Shanghai") and "*Shanghai shi jingchaju guanli changji shishi banfa*" ("Method for the Management of the Prostitutes: Police Bureau of the Municipality of Shanghai"). The text of these two documents can be found in the Police Archives (1945–1949), file 6-9-353.
88. "*Shanghai shi jingchaju weishengju changji jianyan hezuo banfa*" ("Joint Regulation of the Police Bureau and of the Health Bureau of the Municipality of Shanghai on the Medical Surveillance of the Prostitutes"), 31 December 1945, Police Archives (1945–1949), file 1-10-246.

89. Order by the Police Bureau, 28 December 1946, Police Archives (1945–1949), file 1-10-246; Yu Wei, "*Shanghai changji wu bai ge an diaocha*" ("A Study of 500 Prostitutes in Shanghai"), *Shizheng pinglun* ("The Municipal Affairs Weekly"), vol. 10, no. 9/10, p. 10.
90. Yu Wei, "*Shanghai changji wu bai ge an diaocha*," *op. cit.*, p. 10.
91. Note from the Mayor, 19 April 1948, Police Archives (1945–1949), file 1-10-246.
92. Letter from the Police Bureau, 10 March 1948, Police Archives (1945–1949), file 1-10-246.
93. Letter from the Police Bureau, 4 Jan. 1949, Police Archives (1945–1949), file 1-10-246.
94. Letter dated May 1946, Police Archives (1945–1949), file 011-4-259.
95. Yu Wei, "*Jin chang yu xingbing fangzhi*" ("The Prohibition of Prostitution and the Prevention of Venereal Diseases"), *Shizheng pinglun* ("The Municipal Affairs Weekly"), vol. 9, no. 9/10, p. 18.
96. Analysis of the reports found in the Police Archives (1945–1949), file 011-4-178.
97. Police Archives (1945–1949), file 011-4-178.
98. Indignant letter by a foreign resident, 17 October 1947; police report, 12 December 1947, Police Archives (1945–1949), file 011-4-176.
99. Request for an inquiry by Xuan Tiewu, 11 March 1946, Police Archives (1945–1949), file 011-4-162.
100. Police Archives (1945–1949), file 011-4-176. This file also contains newspaper cuttings (*Shen Bao, Xinwenbao*) dated March 1948.
101. Letter of 12 August 1946, Police Archives (1945–1949), file 011-4-264.
102. Note from the chief of the police, 23 April 1946, Police Archives (1945–1949), file 011-4-162.
103. Letter and by-laws of the association, 30 November 1945, Police Archives (1945–1949), file 011-4-260.
104. Letter from the Social Affairs Bureau, 8 March 1946, Police Archives (1945–1949), file 011-4-260.
105. Letter from the association, 29 June 1946, Police Archives (1945–1949), file 011-4-260; Letter from the Police Bureau, 1 August 1946; Letter from the Police Bureau, 3 August 1946, Police Archives (1945–1949), file 011-4-260; Letter from the Social Affairs Bureau, 20 September 1946, Police Archives (1945–1949), file 011-4-260.
106. Letter from the Police Bureau, 29 September 1946; report of the meeting of 1 October, 9 November 1946, Police Archives (1945–1949), file 011-4-260.
107. Letter of June 1948, Police Archives (1945–1949), file 1-10-246.
108. Letter from the Police Bureau, 29 July 1948, Police Archives (1945–1949), file 1-10-246.
109. Letter from the Social Affairs Bureau (1946), Police Archives (1945–1949), file 1-10-246; Letter of 24 September 1946, Police Archives (1945–1949), file 1-10-246.
110. Letter from the Police Bureau to the Mayor, June 1947, Police Archives (1945–1949), file 1-10-246.
111. Letter from the Police Bureau to the Mayor, 25 September 1947, Police Archives (1945–1949), file 1-10-246.
112. Joint letter by the Health Bureau and the Police Bureau, 14 November 1947, Police Archives (1945–1949), file 1-10-246.

113. On checks on prostitutes in the Meiji period, cf. De Becker, *The Nightless City*, London, Probsthain and Co., 1906 (1st ed. 1899), pp. 163–166.

114. Christian Henriot, "La fermeture: The Abolition of Prostitution in Shanghai, 1949–1958," *The China Quarterly*, December 1995, pp. 148–167.

Chapter 14

1. Tsu Yu-yue, *The Spirit of Chinese Philanthropy*, New York, Columbia University Press, 1912; Raymond D., Lum, "Philanthropy and Public Welfare in Late Imperial China," doctoral thesis, Harvard University, 1985.

2. The two best studies to date are those by William T. Rowe, *Hankow: Commerce and Society in a Chinese City, 1796–1889*, Stanford, Stanford University Press, 1984; *Hankow. Conflict and Community in a Chinese City, 1796–1895*, Stanford, Stanford University Press, 1989; and Bryna Goodman, *Native Place, City, and Nation: Regional Networks and Identities in Shanghai, 1853–1937*, Berkeley, The University of California Press, 1995.

3. For a discussion on the orphanages at the end of the Qing period, see Kiche Angela Leung, "L'accueil des enfants abandonnés dans la Chine du bas Yangzi aux XVIIᵉ et XVIIIᵉ siècles," *Études chinoises*, vol. IV, no. 1, spring 1985, pp. 15–54. On the *yuyingtang* of Shanghai, see William C. Milne, *La vie réelle en Chine*, Paris, Hachette, 1858, pp. 50–54; "The Foundling Hospital at Shanghai," *Chinese and Japanese Repository*, 2 January 1865, pp. 37–40, 1 March 1865, pp. 129–136; *Shehui yuekan* ("Monthly Journal of the Bureau of Social Affairs"), vol. I, no. 6, June 1929, pp. 1–13.

4. William C. Milne, *La vie réelle en Chine, op. cit.*, p. 68.

5. Anne W. Fearn, *My Days of Strength: An American Woman Doctor's Forty Years in China*, New York, Harper & Brothers Publishers, 1939, pp. 143–144; "A Tribute of Love," *Chinese Recorder*, no. 40, December 1916, pp. 830–841.

6. "A Tribute of Love," *Chinese Recorder, op. cit.*, p. 831; Anne W. Fearn, *My Days of Strength, op. cit.*, pp. 143–144. The information presented in this part is drawn essentially from the annual reports of the Door of Hope. There is an almost complete collection (1900–1918, 1920–1925, 1927–1935) in the Burkey Missionary Library [MR8-7] in New York. I have not been able to find any trace of the archives of the Door of Hope, which, in all likelihood, remained in Shanghai and may have even been lost or destroyed during the Japanese occupation. Door of Hope and Children's Refuge Mission, China, *Annual Report*, no. 1–25 (1900–1925), no. 27–35 (1927–1935).

7. Door of Hope, *Annual Report*, 1901; *Annual Report*, 1910, pp. 5 and 11.

8. Door of Hope, *Annual Report*, 1902, p. 1; on the National Florence Crittenton Home, see Charlton Edholm, *Traffic in Girls and Florence Crittenton Missions*, Chicago, Women' Temperance Public Association, 1893.

9. The 1905 report is entitled *Annual Report, Shanghai Florence Crittenton Home, known as the Door of Hope*. No information is given on the reasons for the separation. Door of Hope, *Annual Report*, 1906, p. 1.

10. Door of Hope, *Annual Report*, 1921, p. 1.

11. Door of Hope, *Annual Report*, 1904, p. 3; *Annual Report*, 1905, p. 4; *Chinese Recorder*, no. 36: 2 February 1905, p. 98.

12. Door of Hope, *Annual Report*, 1904, p. 2; *Annual Report*, 1905, p. 3.

13. Door of Hope, *Annual Report*, 1921, p. 2.

14. Door of Hope, *Annual Report*, 1906, p. 5.
15. Door of Hope, *Annual Report*, 1913, p. 1.
16. Door of Hope, *Annual Report*, 1909, p. 5.
17. "A Tribute of Love," *Chinese Recorder, op. cit.*, pp. 836–838.
18. Door of Hope, *Annual Report*, 1929, p. 4.
19. Door of Hope, *Annual Report*, 1913, p. 1; *Annual Report*, 1921, p. 3; *SB*, 30 April 1919. Apart from sheltering prostitutes, the Door of Hope also sheltered young girls and babies born to prostitutes during their stay. In 1905, premises were found in Wusong Road; two years later, land was purchased in Jiangwan. The Door of Hope also took over the management of two centers for receiving abandoned children. Door of Hope, *Annual Report*, 1921, p. 1; Door of Hope, *Annual Report*, 1906, p. 6; *Annual Report*, 1909, p. 14; *Annual Report*, 1911, p. 5; Door of Hope, *Annual Report*, 1915, p. 1; *Annual Report*, 1922, p. 10; Door of Hope, *Annual Report*, 1922, p. 10.
20. Door of Hope, *Annual Report*, 1924, pp. 17–18.
21. Door of Hope, *Annual Report*, 1927, p. 12.
22. Xu Wancheng, *Shanghai cishan jiguan gaikuang* ("General State of Charitable Institutions in Shanghai"), Shanghai, Longwen shudian, 1941, p. 18.
23. Zhao Zhiyan, "Zhengjiu changji de cishan jigou – Jiliangsuo" ("A Charitable Organization Saving Prostitutes – the Door of Hope"), in *Jiu shanghai de yan du chang* ("Prostitution, Gambling and Opium in Old Shanghai"), Shanghai shi wenshiguan bian, Shanghai, Baijia chubanshe, 1988, pp. 176–178.
24. Door of Hope, *Annual Report*, 1921, p. 1.
25. Door of Hope, *Annual Report*, 1905, p. 2.
26. Door of Hope, *Annual Report*, 1909, p. 17; *Annual Report*, 1910, p. 5.
27. A detailed examination of the finances of the Door of Hope can be found in Christian Henriot, "La prostitution à Shanghai aux XIXᵉ–XXᵉ siècles (1849–1958)," doctoral thesis (doctorat d'État), Paris, École des hautes études en sciences sociales, Chapter 5.
28. Door of Hope, *Annual Report*, 1924, p. 4.
29. 1901: 93%; 1902: 51%; 1903: 61%; 1904: 63%; 1905: 81%; 1906: 33.5%; 1908: 60%; 1910: 52%; 1928: 60%; 1929: 52%; 1933: 68%; 1935: 67%.
30. The following analysis is based on the tables published in the annual reports for 1901 to 1925 and also on figures gleaned from the pages of the reports themselves. The figures are often inconsistent. The distribution of inmates per shelter does not correspond to the figures of persons entering and leaving the Door of Hope. It was impossible for me to establish the numbers of inmates to the nearest individual. This said, the inconsistencies are minor and do not cast doubt on my presentation.
31. Xu Wancheng, *Shanghai cishan jiguan gaikuang, op. cit.*, p. 18.
32. All these figures have to be revised upward because they do not include the years 1926–1935.
33. The same observation applies here as in note 32.
34. Door of Hope, *Annual Report*, 1904, p. 4.
35. Door of Hope, *Annual Report*, 1905, p. 4.
36. Door of Hope, *Annual Report*, 1905, p. 4; *Annual Report*, 1927, p. 7; see also *Annual Report*, 1933, p. 5.
37. Door of Hope, *Annual Report*, 1933, p. 8.
38. Door of Hope, *Annual Report*, 1905, p. 4; *Annual Report*, 1909, p. 5.
39. Door of Hope, *Annual Report*, 1905, p. 4.

40. Door of Hope, *Annual Report*, 1934, p. 6 (extract from a letter by Cornelia Bonnel in 1906).
41. Door of Hope, *Annual Report*, 1918, pp. 3–4; *Annual Report*, 1929, p. 4.
42. Anne W. Fearn, *My Days of Strength, op. cit.*, pp. 143–144.
43. Door of Hope, *Annual Report*, 1905, p. 3.
44. Door of Hope, *Annual Report*, 1935, p. 13.
45. Door of Hope, *Annual Report*, 1908, p. 8; *Annual Report*, 1922, p. 10; *Annual Report*, 1933, p. 21; *SB*, 8 November 1922.
46. Door of Hope, *Annual Report*, 1933, p. 9.
47. *North China Herald*, 12 October 1912, p. 93; 30 November 1912, p. 578.
48. Door of Hope, *Annual Report*, 1908, p. 8; *Annual Report*, 1929, p. 7.
49. The charitable institutions also assisted the law-enforcement authorities in the punishment of certain offenses commited by women. In 1909, a woman surprised in adultery by her husband was sentenced by the Mixed Court to four months' confinement in the Puyutang, a private institution that usually received women in distress. *SB*, 22 February 1909.
50. Door of Hope, *Annual Report*, 1902, p. 3; *Annual Report*, 1903, p. 2.
51. Door of Hope, *Annual Report*, 1911, p. 20.
52. Door of Hope, *Annual Report*, 1902, p. 3; *Annual Report*, 1903, p. 2.
53. Door of Hope, *Annual Report*, 1923, p. 10.
54. Door of Hope, *Annual Report*, 1906, p. 5; *Annual Report*, 1911, p. 20.
55. Door of Hope, *Annual Report*, 1909, p. 12; *Annual Report*, 1922, p. 10.
56. Door of Hope, *Annual Report*, 1933, p. 12.
57. Door of Hope, *Annual Report*, 1902, p. 3.
58. Door of Hope, *Annual Report*, 1906, p. 4.
59. Door of Hope, *Annual Report*, 1922, p. 8; *Annual Report*, 1929, p. 15.
60. Mary N. Gamewell, *Gateway to China: Pictures of Shanghai*, New York, 1916, p. 192.
61. Door of Hope, *Annual Report*, 1916, p. 7.
62. Door of Hope, *Annual Report*, 1930, p. 6; *Annual Report*, 1934, p. 19.
63. *SB*, 29 December 1922.
64. Door of Hope, *Annual Report*, 1902, p. 3.
65. Door of Hope, *Annual Report*, 1932, p. 16.
66. Door of Hope, *Annual Report*, 1913, p. 5.
67. Door of Hope, *Annual Report*, 1925, p. 6.
68. Door of Hope, *Annual Report*, 1925, p. 16.
69. Door of Hope, *Annual Report*, 1925, p. 6.
70. Door of Hope, *Annual Report*, 1909, p. 12.
71. Door of Hope, *Annual Report*, 1923, p. 16.
72. I have had the good fortune to find a number of archival documents of the Anti-Kidnapping Society in the municipal archives of Shanghai. The collection is unfortunately incomplete and cannot be used to reconstruct the working of this institution in all its details. The list of the documents consulted is given in the bibliography under "Archives of the *Zhongguo furu jiuji zonghui*."
73. *North China Herald*, 31 August 1912.
74. Archives of the *Zhongguo jiuji fu ru zonghui* (Anti-Kidnapping Society), Shanghai Municipal Archives, file no. 113-1-3, p. 3.
75. Wang and Yu were two of the leading figures of the Ningbo guild (*Siming gongsuo*), and they had considerable influence with Shanghai's business elite. Both of them were known for their numerous philanthropic activities.

76. "She hui lu qi" ("Notes on the Foundation of the Association"), *Zhongguo jiujihui yijiu yiwu nian baogao* (1915 report of the Anti-Kidnapping Society), *op. cit.*

77. Archives of the *Zhongguo fu ru jiuji zonghui*, file no. 113-1-2, p. 29.

78. *Funü yuebao* ("Women's Monthly"), vol. 11, no. 7, 1 August 1935, pp. 22–23. The "Green Gang" was implicated in every form of illegal trafficking (opium, gambling), racketeering, and trafficking in women (see Chapter 7).

79. Archives of the *Zhongguo fu ru jiuji zonghui*, file no. 113-1-2, pp. 50–56 and p. 73.

80. Archives of the *Zhongguo fu ru jiuji zonghui*, file no. 113-1-3, p. 3; minutes of the general assembly meeting of 20 October 1935, file no. 113-1-3; file no. 113-1-9, p. 5.

81. *SB*, 10 May 1920.

82. *SB*, 17 June 1921; 20 June 1921.

83. Archives of the *Zhongguo fu ru jiuji zonghui*, file no. 113-1-3.

84. The Bureau of Social Affairs the Shanghai Municipal Government made every effort, up to 1932, to weaken the power and influence of the bourgeoisie by working against its representative institutions (namely, the Chamber of Commerce, the Street Unions, the Merchant Militias, etc.). The charitable associations, which were symbols of the power of the merchants, also came under their purview. However, the attempts made to bring these associations under the control of the Social Affairs Bureau and find out the amount of the state of their finances remained fruitless. Christian Henriot, *Shanghai, 1927–1937. Municipal Power, Locality, and Modernization*, p. 212.

85. Archives of the *Zhongguo fu ru jiuji zonghui*, file no. 113-1-3.

86. Archives of the *Zhongguo fu ru jiuji zonghui*, file no. 113-1-2, p. 9.

87. "Zhongguo furu jiujihui zhengqiu huiyuan gaikuang," *op. cit.*, Archives of the *Zhongguo fu ru jiuji zonghui*, file no. 113-1-3.

88. Archives of the *Zhongguo fu ru jiuji zonghui*, file no. 113-1-2, p. 30.

89. "Zhongguo furu jiujihui zhengqiu huiyuan gaikuang," *op. cit.*, Archives of the *Zhongguo fu ru jiuji zonghui*, file no. 113-1-3.

90. Archives of the *Zhongguo fu ru jiuji zonghui*, file no. 113-1-2, p. 2.

91. Archives of the *Zhongguo fu ru jiuji zonghui*, file no. 113-1-2, pp. 30, 97, and 126; Archives of the *Zhongguo fu ru jiuji zonghui*, file 113-1-9, p. 3.

92. Archives of the *Zhongguo fu ru jiuji zonghui*, file 113-1-2, p. 13; see other cases of approaches to the Japanese authorities, *ibid.*, p. 116 (1920).

93. Archives of the *Zhongguo fu ru jiuji zonghui*, file 113-1-2, p. 14.

94. In 1921, the AKS employed a total of 26 persons, not counting the inspectors. Archives of the *Zhongguo fu ru jiuji zonghui*, file no. 113-1-2, pp. 8 and 127.

95. Archives of the *Zhongguo fu ru jiuji zonghui*, file no. 113-1-2, p. 8.

96. Archives of the *Zhongguo fu ru jiuji zonghui*, file no. 113-1-2, p. 8.

97. Archives of the *Zhongguo fu ru jiuji zonghui*, file no. 113-1-2, p. 9.

98. Archives of the *Zhongguo fu ru jiuji zonghui*, file no. 113-1-2, pp. 9 and 31.

99. Letter from the Social Affairs Bureau of 22 October 1930, Archives of the *Zhongguo fu ru jiuji zonghui*, file no. 113-1-3.

100. Letter from the Social Affairs Bureau of 22 April 1930; letter of the AKS of 14 June 1930, Archives of the *Zhongguo fu ru jiuji zonghui*, file no. 113-1-3.

101. *Funü yuebao* ("Women's Monthly"), vol. XI, no. 7, 1 August 1935, pp. 22–23.

102. *Funü yuebao* ("Women's Monthly"), vol. 11, no. 7, 1 August 1935, pp. 22–23; Archives of the *Zhongguo fu ru jiuji zonghui*, file no. 113-1-2, p. 10.
103. Archives of the *Zhongguo fu ru jiuji zonghui*, file no. 113-1-2, p. 31.
104. Mary N. Gamewell, *Gateway to China, op. cit.*, pp. 211–212.
105. Archives of the *Zhongguo fu ru jiuji zonghui*, file no. 113-1-2, p. 31.
106. *SB*, 20 June 1921.
107. *Funü yuebao* ("Women's Monthly"), vol. XI, no. 7, 1 August 1935, pp. 22–23; minutes of the General Assembly meeting of 20 October 1935, Archives of the *Zhongguo fu ru jiuji zonghui*, file no. 113-1-3.
108. *Zhongguo fu ru jiuji zonghui*, file no. 113-1-9, p. 4.
109. Two foreign institutions also devoted their work to prostitution: the "Foreign Women's Home," whose purpose was to receive foreign (Western) prostitutes, and "Le Bon Pasteur," whose work was directed chiefly toward orphans. But they also worked with "repentant" girls. See Christian Henriot, "La prostitution à Shanghai au XIXe–XXe siècle (1849–1958)," doctoral thesis (doctorat d'État), Paris, École des hautes études en sciences sociales, pp. 285–290.
110. *SB*, 25 June 1920.
111. Ot the three other organizations, two were the Shelter of the Charitable Associations of Zhabei (*Zhabei cishantuan nü liuyangsuo*) and the Shelter for Girls established in the New School for Universal Education (*Xin puyutang nü liuyangsuo*), which was a religious institution. They received only little girls. The third organization, *Qingjietang*, was the oldest and was intended for destitute widows. Wu Ruohua, "Shanghai funü jiuji shiye ying you de gaige" ("The Reform Required by the Activities of Assistance to Women in Shanghai"), *Shehui yuekan* ("Social Affairs Monthly"), vol. 1, no. 2, 1929, pp. 1–8.
112. "Commercialized Vice in China," *National Medical Journal*, vol. 8, no. 3, September 1922, p. 199.
113. Cf. Christian Henriot, "La prostitution à Shanghai au XIXe–XXe siècle (1849–1958)," doctoral thesis (doctorat d'État), Paris, École des hautes études en sciences sociales, pp. 292–293.
114. *China Mission Year Book*, Shanghai, Christian Literary Society for China, 1910, p. 456.
115. Zhu Ruiyue, "Shen bao fanying xia de shanghai shehui bianqian, 1895–1927" ("Social Changes in Shanghai Seen Through the *Shen Bao*"), Master's dissertation, Guoli taiwan daxue, 1990.
116. *SB*, 3 January 1921; 27 February 1923.

Bibliography

A Ying, *Wan Qing xiaoshuo shi* ("History of the Novel at the End of the Qing Period"), Beijing, Renmin chubanshe, 1980 (1st ed., Shanghai, 1937).

Ahern, Emily, "Power and Pollution of Chinese Women," in A. Wolf (ed.), *Studies in Chinese Society*, Stanford, Stanford University Press, 1978, pp. 269–290.

Alabaster, Ernest, *Notes on Chinese Law and Practice Preceding Revision*, Shanghai, Shanghai Mercury, 1906.

Alford, William, "Arsenic and Old Laws: Looking Anew at Criminal Justice in Late Imperial China," *California Law Review*, 1984, vol. 72, no. 6, December 1984, pp. 1180–1255.

All About Shanghai and Environs, Shanghai, China Press, 1935.

American Red Cross China Famine Relief Committee, *Report of the China Famine Relief American Red Cross*, October 1920–September 1921.

"Analyse journalière de la presse chinoise," Concession française, service de police, service politique, 1934–1940, 1946–1947.

Annual Report, Shanghai Municipal Police, Shanghai Municipal Council, 1926–1927.

Archives de la Direction des services administratifs, Secrétariat, Concession française, Archives municipales de Shanghai: 1933 25 MS 1554.1 "Maisons de chanteuses – règlements" [1923–1943]; 1934 25 MS 1554.2 "Maisons de chanteuses – demandes de licence" [1922–1924]; 1935 25 MS 1554 "Maisons de chanteuses – réclamations et durées" [1925–1940]; 1936 25 MS 1555 "Nature des dossiers et documents" [1883–1942]; 26 MS 1591.21 "Maisons de chanteuses – règlements" [1923–1943].

Archives of the League of Nations. Geneva. Files R3028-3029/3042/3049-3050/3056-3057/3060-3061/3063: "Committee on the traffic in women and children, annual reports, 1926–1932"; R3037-3041: "Committee on the traffic in women and children, sessions, 1928–1933"; R3035: "Committee on the traffic in women and children, progress, 1928–1933"; R3036: "The Mui Tsai system in Hong Kong"; R3055: "Enquiry in the East, questionnaires to governments, 1930–1931"; R3061-3063: "Second inquiry, preliminary reports"; R4662: "Second inquiry in the East, governmental committee"; R4665: "The Mui Tsai system in Hong Kong, Shanghai, 1933–1942"; R4669: "Second inquiry in the East, general, 1933–1934"; R4670: "Second inquiry in the East, central authorities, 1932–1939"; R4675, "Second inquiry in the East, report, 1933–1935"; R4676: "Second inquiry in the East, Central authorities, 1933–1935"; R4686-4688: "Countries, 1934–1937"; R4696-4698: "Methods of rehabilitation, enquiry, 1935–1945"; R4691-4692: "Situation of Russian women in the Far East, 1934–1937"; R4693-4694: "Far Eastern Conference, 1937, general, 1934–1937";

R4695, "Far Eastern Conference, 1937, correspondence with governments, 1937–1939"; R4709: "Far Eastern Conference, 1937, Execution and recommendations, 1937–1939"; R4700: "Regional conference concerning the traffic in women and children in the Far East, July 1935"; R4708: "League of Nations' Far Eastern Bureau"; S172: "First inquiry in the traffic of women and children, China, 1921–1926"; S182: "Laws and regulations, China, 1925–1936"; COL 115-128: "Commission of inquiry into the traffic of women and children in the Far East"; Committee on the traffic in women and children, Annual reports, 1932–1946.

Archives de la *Zhongguo jiuji furu zonghui* (Anti-Kidnapping Society), Municipal Archives of Shanghai: 113-1-2 (1936); 113-1-3 (1926–1935); 13-1-4 "Shimin guanyu funü rutong bei xiuguai pianmai he nüedai qingqiu huanzhu jiuji wenti de han" ("Letters concerning requests for help and [economic] assistance made by citizens with respect to kidnapped, sold and ill-treated women and children") (1925–1928); 113-1-6 (1924–1926); 113-1-9; 113-1-12/13 (1926–1936); 113-1-13 (1926–1927); 113-1-17 "huiyi gaishi" ("Assembly Meeting on the Reorganization [of the Society]").

Archives diplomatiques françaises. Paris. Correspondance consulaire et commerciale. Shanghai, 1847–1901. Correspondance politique, 1847–1896. Correspondance politique et commerciale, NS 258–280: Concession de Shanghai, 1863–1917. Questions judiciaires, NS 597–598: Cour mixte de Shanghai, 1901–1902, 1903–1906 – Série E Asie 1918–1940. 31: Situation politique, Shanghai 1918–1922; 59: Concession française de Shanghai, 1918–1922; 231: Shanghai 1924–1928; 336–338: Concession française de Shanghai, 1922–1929; 343: Budgets de la Concession française; 499–501: hygiène, médecins français et hôpitaux; 586: Bulletins mensuels des services de police de la Concession française, 1936–1940; 615: Shanghai (nouvelles des provinces), 1936–1940 – Série E Vichy-Asie 1940–1944. 90: Problèmes posés par la rétrocession de la Concession française, 1940–1944; 137: Concession internationale, 1940–1943; 138: Ville de Shanghai, 1940–1944; 142–144: Concession française de Shanghai: archives du gouvernement de Tchongking à Shanghai, 1940–1944; Bulletins mensuels des services de police, 1940–1941.

Archives diplomatiques françaises. Nantes. Consulat général de France à Shanghai [for want of any classification or inventory of these resources, I have given the numbers of their boxes of origin]. Cartons 29–30, police et garde municipale, 1863–1900; cartons 31–32, conseil municipal, 1865–1900; cartons 36 and 39, hygiène et santé publique; cartons 62–63, conseil d'administration de la Concession française; cartons 68–70, garde municipale (organisation, rapports de police, police des établissements publics, hygiène et santé); carton 75, questions sociales; municipalité française de Shanghai: carton 106, textes fondamentaux; carton 108, budget et taxes; carton 110, règlements municipaux et statistiques; cartons 111 and 112, affaires diverses; carton 113, services municipaux, cadastre; exterritorialité et juridictions chinoises dans la Concession française: cartons 154–155, fonctionnement des cours chinoises; carton 156, cour chinoise; carton 157, divers; carton 158–159, cour spéciale de district dans la Concession internationale, 1930–1935; carton 160, installation de cours chinoises dans la Concession française; carton 161, Cour mixte internationale; carton 162–163, reddition de la Cour mixte internationale; carton 164–168, Cour mixte française; ordonnances consulaires, 1873–1915, 1921–1924, 1926–1942.

Archives of the Social Affairs Bureau (*Shehuiju*), Municipality of Shanghai, 1945–1949, Municipal Archives of Shanghai: 6-9-353, December 1946; 6-19-666, April 1946–December 1947.

Archives of the Bureau of Public Works, Concession française, Municipal Archives of Shanghai: 166-49, public works, 1938–1941.

Archives of the Secretariat, Shanghai Municipal Council (1920–1924), Municipal Archives of Shanghai: 3-00303, file 1362, Part 1, Secretariat, "Russian refugees"; 3-00445, file 1486, part 3, Secretariat (SMC), "Prostitution: Brothels, Withdrawal of Licences, 1920–1924"; 4-2428: file 147/1; 4-2429: file 147/2.

Archives historiques du Bon Pasteur, livres 16; BE 2a (previously livre 18a); BE 4b; BA2/01; *Nos fondations pendant la guerre*; *Bulletin de la congrégation du Bon Pasteur*, 1934–1952.

Balazs, Etienne, *La bureaucratie céleste*, Paris, Gallimard (collection NRF), 1968.

Balme, Harold, "The History of Western Medical Education in China," *China Medical Journal*, vol. 40, no. 8, 1926, pp. 636–650.

Balme, Harold, *China and Modern Medicine. A Study in Medical Missionary Development*, London, United Council for Missionary Education, 1921.

Banister, Judith, *China's Changing Population*, Stanford, Stanford University Press, 1987.

Bao Tianxiao, "Zujie shouhui hou de changji wenti" ("The Problem of Prostitution in the Foreign Settlements after their Retrocession to China"), *Zhonghua yuebao* ("China Monthly"), vol. 6, no. 2, August 1943, pp. 24–26.

Bao Xiaoqun, "Xia Tingzhi he ta de 'Qinglouji'" ("Xia Tingzhi and his Green Bower Collection" [House of Courtesans]), *Wenshi zhishi* ("Literary and Historical Knowledge"), no. 4, 1988, pp. 83–85.

Bao Zubao, *Changji wenti* ("The Question of the Prostitutes"), Shanghai, Nüzi shudian, 1935 (collection Xiandai Zhongguo funü wenti congkan).

Barnett, Robert W., *Economic Shanghai: Hostage to Politics, 1937–1941*, New York, Institute for Pacific Relations, 1941.

Barnhard, Jacqueline, *The Fail but Frail: Prostitution in San Francisco, 1849–1900*, Reno, University of Nevada Press, 1986.

Barret-Ducrocq, Françoise, *L'amour sous Victoria*, Paris, Plon, 1989.

Baulant, M., and Chartier, R., *Les marginaux et les exclus de l'histoire*, Paris, Union générale d'édition, 1979.

Behan, Charlotte, "The Women's Movement and Nationalism in Late Ch'ing China," doctoral thesis, Columbia University, 1976.

Beijing fengbi jiyuan jishi ("The True Story of the Closure of the Houses of Prostitution in Peking"), Beijing, Zhongguo heping chubanshe, 1988.

Bell, Ernest A., *Fighting the Traffic in Young Girls or War on the White Slave Traffic*, n.p., n.pub, 1930.

Bell, Moberly E., *Josephine Butler*, London, Constable, 1963.

Benabou, Marie-Erica, *La prostitution et la police des mœurs au XVIIIe siècle*, Paris, Perrin, 1987.

Berenguer, Françoise, "Le mythe de la femme orientale chez les écrivains voyageurs français de 1806 à 1869," doctoral thesis, Paris, Université Paris III, 1988.

Bergère, Marie-Claire, *La bourgeoisie chinoise et la révolution de 1911*, Paris, Mouton, 1968.

Bergère, Marie-Claire, "Shanghai ou 'l'autre Chine,' 1919–1949," *Annales E.S.C.*, no. 5, September–October 1979, pp. 1039–1068.

Bergère, Marie-Claire, "The Chinese Bourgeoisie, 1911–1937," in *Cambridge*

History of China, vol. 12, *Republican China, 1912–1949*, part. I, Cambridge, Cambridge University Press, 1986, pp. 721–825.

Bergère, Marie-Claire, *The Golden Age of the Chinese Bourgeoisie*, Cambridge, Cambridge University Press, 1989.

Bi Yin, "Changji wenti de jiantao" ("An Examination of the Problem of Prostitution"), *Dongfang zazhi* ("Eastern Miscellany"), vol. 32, no. 17, September 1935, pp. 99–102.

Billingsley, Phil, *Bandits in Republican China*, Stanford, Stanford University Press, 1988.

Biot, Edouard, "Mémoire de la condition des esclaves et des serviteurs gagés en Chine," *Journal asiatique*, vol. 3, no. 3, 1837, pp. 246–299.

Bo Fan, "Changji yu hualiubing" ("The Prostitutes and Syphilis"), *Funü shijie* ("The Ladies' World"), II, 7/8, 1941, p. 40.

Bodde, Derk, and Morris, Clarence, *Law in Imperial China*, Cambridge, MA, Harvard University Press, 1967.

Bonnel, C., *A Story of Love*, followed by "Shadow and Light in Shanghai," Shanghai, Door of Hope, 1921.

Bonnel, C., *Seeking Love*, followed by "Pan Tsu, Precious Pearl," Shanghai, Door of Hope, 1921.

Bonnel, C., *The Fifth Precious*, Shanghai, Methodist Publishing House, 1909.

Boulais, Guy, *Manuel du code chinois*, Variétés sinologiques, no. 55, Shanghai, Imprimerie de la Mission catholique, 1923.

Bowers, John, et al., *Science and Medicine in Twentieth-Century China: Research and Education*, Chicago, University of Chicago Press, 1988.

Boyle, John H., *China and Japan at War, 1937–1945: The Politics of Collaboration*, Stanford, Stanford University Press, 1972.

Briessen, Fritz van, *Shanghai-Bildzeitung 1884–1898: eine Illustrierte aus dem China des ausgehenden 19. Jahrhunderts*, Zürich/Freiburg, Atlantis, 1977.

"Browbeating Prostitution," *The China Critic*, Shanghai, no. 16, 13 September 1928, pp. 313–316.

Bryon, Robert, *An Outline of Chinese Law*, Shanghai, Commercial Press, 1925.

Bullock, Mary B., *An American Transplant: The Rockefeller Foundation and Peking Union Medical College*, Berkeley, University of California Press, 1980.

Bullough, Vern, *The History of Prostitution*, New York, University Books, 1964.

Bullough, Vern, and Elcano Barret W., *Annotated Bibliography of Prostitution*, New York, Garland Publishing, 1976.

Bullough, Vern, and Bullough, Bonnie, *Prostitution, an Illustrated History*, New York, Crown Publishers, 1978.

Bullough, Vern, and Bullough, Bonnie, *Women and Prostitution*, New York, Prometheus Books, 1987.

Bunker, Gerald E., *The Peace Conspiracy: Wang Ching-wei and the China War, 1937–1941*, Cambridge, MA, Harvard University Press, 1972.

Butler, Anne M., *Daughters of Joy, Sisters of Misery. Prostitutes in the American West, 1865–1890*, Urbana, University of Illinois Press, 1985.

Byron, John, *Portrait of a Chinese Paradise: Erotica and Sexual Customs of the Late Qing Period*, London, Quartet Books, 1987.

Central China Famine Relief Committee, *Report and Accounts, 1910–1911*, Shanghai, 1912.

Central China Famine Relief Committee, *Report and Account from October 1, 1911 to June 30, 1912*, Shanghai, 1912.

Champley, Henry, *The Road to Shanghai. White Slave Traffic in Asia*, London, John Long, Ltd., 1934.

Chang Ching-Sheng, *Sex History, China's First Modern Treatise on Sex Education*, (translated by Howard S. Levy), Yokohama, 1967.

Chang Chung-Li, *The Income of the Chinese Gentry*, Seattle, University of Washington Press, 1962.

"Changji jiuji shiye" ("The Work of Aiding Prostitutes"), *Shehui xunbao* ("Society"), Nanjing, no. 5, pp. 18–20.

Changji wenti zhuanti xiaozu yanjiu baogao ("Study Report by the Cell in Charge of Problems of Prostitution"), Taibei, Zhonghua minguo ertong shaonian fazhan cejin weiyuanhui, 1970.

Changji xianxing ji ("Notes on the Present Condition of the Prostitutes"), Shanghai, Zhongwai shuju, 1924.

"Changji yu zhencao" ("Prostitutes and Chastity"), *Funü zazhi* ("The Ladies' Journal"), vol. VI, no. 5, 1920, pp. 1–12.

Chen Chongguang, "Minguo chuqi funü diwei de yanbian" ("Changes in the Status of Women at the Beginning of the Republic"), Master's dissertation, Zhongguo wenhua xueyuan, Taibei, 1972.

Chen Dezheng, "Maiyin shiye zhi jingji de yuanyin" ("The Economic Causes of Prostitution"), *Funü zazhi* ("The Ladies' Journal"), vol. IX, no. 3, 1923, pp. 13–18.

Chen Dongyuan, *Zhongguo funü shenghuoshi* ("History of the Life of Chinese Women"), Shanghai, Shangwu yinshuguan, 1935 (reprint 1937).

Chen K. Fong, "The Diagnosis of Early Syphilis," *China Medical Journal*, vol. 41, January 1927, pp. 36–41.

Chen Wuwo, *Lao shanghai san shi nian jianwen* ("Thirty Years of Sights and Sounds of Old Shanghai"), Shanghai, Dadong shuju, 1928.

Chen Xuan, "Changji wenti" ("The Problem of Prostitution"), *Liumei xuesheng jibao* ("The Chinese Students' Quarterly"), vol. VIII, no. 4, December 1921, pp. 1–38.

Chen Yingshi xiansheng jinian quanji ("A Full Anthology in Commemoration of Mr Chen Yingshi [Qimei]"), n.p., n.pub., n.d., 2 vols.

Chen Yuanqi, "Yongxianzhai biji" ("Notes from the Studio of Idleness"), in *Biji xiaoshuo daguan* ("Overview of the Literature of Personal Notes"), Taibei, Xinxing shuju, reprint, 1962, part 1, vol. 3, pp. 2667–2747.

Chen Zhiyi, "Cong lishi shehui ji falü san fangmian tan changji wenti" ("Discussion of the Problem of Prostitution from the Historical, Social and Legal Viewpoints"), *Funü yuekan* ("Women's Monthly"), vol. VI, no. 6, January 1948, pp. 9–14.

Cheng, Stephen H. L., "*Flowers of Shanghai* and the Late-Ch'ing Courtesan Novel," doctoral thesis, Harvard University, 1979.

Chesneaux, Jean, *Le mouvement ouvrier chinois de 1919 à 1927*, Paris, Mouton, 1962.

Chesney, Kellow, *The Victorian Underworld*, Harmondsworth, Penguin Books, 1974.

Chevalier, Louis, *Classes laborieuses et classes dangereuses*, Paris, L.G.F., 1978 (1st ed., Plon, 1958).

Chi Xian Shu Shi Shi [pseudonym of Sun Yusheng], *Haishang fanhua meng. San ji* ("Luxuriant Dream in Shanghai: Three Anthologies"), Shanghai, Jinbu shuju, 1916.

Chi Xian Shu Shi Shi [Sun Yusheng's pseudonym], *Xu haishang fanhua meng. San ji* ("Sequel to Luxuriant Dream in Shanghai"), Shanghai, n.pub., n.d.

Chi Zhicheng, "Hu you mengying lu" ("Dream Shadows of a Journey to Shanghai"), *Dang'an yu lishi* ("Archives and History"), no. 1, 1989, pp. 1–7.

Chi Zhicheng, "Hu you mengying lu" ("Dream Shadows of a Journey to Shanghai"), Shanghai, Guji chubanshe, 1989 [1893].

China Medical Journal (continuation of *China Medical Missionary Journal*), 1887–1888, 1891, 1892–1895, 1896, 1897–1898, 1913, 1916–1951.

China Mission Year Book, Shanghai, Christian Literary Society for China, 1910, 1911, 1912, 1934–1935.

China Review (The), Shanghai, 1882–1887.

China Weekly Review, Shanghai, weekly (initially *Millard's Review*), 1924–1937.

Chinese Recorder (The), Shanghai, monthly, 1867–1941.

Chinese Recorder Index (The): A Guide to Christian Missions in Asia, 1867–1941, compiled by Kathleen Lodwick, Washington, Delaware, Scholarly Resources, 1986.

Chinese Yearbook (The), Shanghai, The Year Book Company, 1935–1936, 2 vols.; 1936–1937, 2 vols.; 1937, 2 vols. (Nendeln, Klaus Reprint, 1968).

Chou, Eric, *The Dragon and the Phœnix*, New York, 1970.

Chow, Tse-tsung, *The May Fourth Movement. Intellectual Revolution in Modern China*, Cambridge, MA, Harvard University Press, 1960.

Chu Ming Linfang, "Fuzhou deng di anchang huodong qingkuang diaocha" ("An Inquiry into Clandestine Prostitution in Fuzhou and Other Places"), Neibu ziliao, Fujian gong'an zhuanke xuexiao, pp. 13–15.

Chu, L. W., and Huang, C. H., "Gonorrhea Among Prostitutes," *Chinese Medical Journal*, vol. 66, June 1948, pp. 312–318.

Chü, T'ung-tsu, *Law and Society in Traditional China*, Paris-La Hague, Mouton, 1965. (Le monde d'outre-mer – passé et présent).

Chü, T'ung-tsu, *Local Government in China under the Ch'ing*, Stanford, Stanford University Press, 1962.

Chu Wei, "Tan tan feichang de wenti" ("On the Question of the Abolition of Prostitution"), *Funü zazhi* ("The Ladies' Journal"), vol. XIII, no. 12, 1927, pp. 12–16.

Clément, Pierre, Ged, Françoise, and Wan, Q. I. "Transformations de l'habitat à Shanghai," rapport de recherche, Institut français d'architecture, Paris, 1988.

Coble, Parks McL., *The Shanghai Capitalists and the Nationalist Government, 1927–1937*, Cambridge, MA, Harvard University Press, 1980.

Cohen, Paul, *Between Tradition and Modernity. Wang T'ao and Reform in Late Ch'ing China*, Cambridge, MA, Harvard University Press, 1974.

"Commercialized Vice in China," in Stauffer Milton, T., *The Christian Occupation of China*, Shanghai, China Continuation Committee, 1922, pp. 396–397.

"Commercialized Vice in China," *National Medical Journal*, vol. 8, no. 3, September 1922, pp. 191–200.

Committee on Social and Moral Welfare, *To-day's World Problem in Disease Prevention*, Shanghai, Commercial Press, 1925.

Compte rendu de la gestion pour l'exercice, 1863/1864–1869/1870, 1873/1874–1874/1875, 1880–1895, 1897–1924, 1926–1931, Conseil d'administration municipale de la Concession française, Shanghai, The China Printing Co.

"Cong gen chanchu jiyuan zhidu" ("Attack the System of the Houses of Prostitution at the Root"), *Xin zhongguo funü* ("Femmes de Chine nouvelle"), editorial, *Beijing*, no. 6, December 1949, pp. 6–7.

Connelly, Mark T., *The Response to Prostitution in the Progressive Era*, Chapel Hill, University of North Carolina Press, 1980.

Corbin, Alain, *Les filles de noce. Misère sexuelle et prostitution (XIXe–XXe siècles)*, Paris, Flammarion (coll. Champs), 1982 (1st ed., Aubier-Montaigne, 1978).

Corbin, Alain, "Le péril vénérien au début du siècle. Prophylaxie sanitaire et prophylaxie morale," *Recherches*, no. 29, December 1977, pp. 245–283.

Corbin, Alain, "L'hérédo-syphilis ou l'impossible rédemption. Contribution à l'histoire de l'hérédité morbide," *Romantisme, revue du XIXe siècle*, no. 31 ("Sangs"), 1981, pp. 131–149.

Corbin, Alain, "Commercial Sexuality in Nineteenth-Century France: A System of Images and Regulations," *Representation*, vol. 14, spring 1986, pp. 209–219.

Corbin, Alain, "La mauvaise éducation de la prostituée au XIXe siècle," *Bulletin de la société d'histoire moderne*, vol. XXXIV, no. 2, 1987, pp. 8–13.

Corbin, Alain, *Women for Hire. Prostitution and Sexuality in France after 1850*, Cambridge, MA, Harvard University Press, 1990.

Cornet, Christine, *État et entreprises en Chine aux XIXe–XXe siècles. Le chantier naval de Jiangnan, 1865–1937*, Paris, Arguments, 1997.

Crad, Joseph, *Traders in Women: A Comprehensive Survey of "White Slavery,"* London, John Long, Ltd., 1940.

Crawford, Wallace, "Syphilis in West China," *China Medical Journal*, vol. 44, December 1930, pp. 1129–1131.

Cressey, Paul, *Taxi-Dance Hall*, Chicago, University of Chicago Press, 1932.

Crihfield, Liza, "The Institution of the Geisha in Modern Japanese Society," doctoral thesis, Stanford University, 1978.

Customs Gazette, Shanghai, Customs Press, biannual – became *Medical Reports*, Shanghai, Statistical Department of the Inspectorate General, China Imperial Maritime Customs, 1871–1897, 1904–1910.

Dagongbao ("L'impartial"), Shanghai, daily, 1949–1953.

Da qing Huidian ("Laws and Statutes of the Qing"), 1818, 1899 (reprint, 1963), Taibei, Zhongwen shuju, 24 vols.

Da qing lüli huitong xinzuan ("A New Edition of the Laws and Statutes of the Qing"), Yao Yuxiang Beijing, 1873; reprint Taibei, Wenhai chubanshe, 1964, 5 vols.

Da qing lüli ("Code of the Qing"), Wu Tan, 1886 (reprint, Taibei, Chengwen chubanshe, 1965).

Da shanghai zhinan ("Guide to Greater Shanghai"), Shanghai, Dongnan wenhua fuwushe, 1947.

Dai Qiu, "Maiyin de dongji" ("The Factors of Prostitution"), *Funü zazhi* ("The Ladies' Journal"), vol. IX, no. 3, 1923, pp. 22–24.

Dai Xuanzhi, "Qingbang de yuanliu" ("The Sources of the Green Gang"), *Shihuo yuekan* ("Material Life"), vol. 3, no. 4, July 1973, pp. 172–177.

Dao Shou and Wang Jingtao, *Shanghai de xing shichang* ("The Sex Market in Shanghai"), Shanghai, Manli shuju, 1932.

Darwent, C. E., *Shanghai: A Handbook for Travellers and Residents to the Chief Object of Interest in and around the Foreign Settlements and the Native City*, Shanghai, 1920 (reprint, Taibei, 1973).

De Becker, *The Nightless City*, London, Probsthain and Co., 1906 (1st ed., 1899).

"Demi-monde of Shanghai (The)," *China Medical Journal*, vol. 37, no. 9, 1923, pp. 782–788.

Dian Gong (pseudonym), *Shanghai zhi pianshu shijie* ("Illustrated Volume on the Arts of Deception in Shanghai"), n.p., Saoye shanfang (faxing), 1924.

Dianshizhai huabao ("Studio Pictorial Newspaper"), Shanghai, 1884–1898; Reprint. Guangzhou, Guangzhou renmin chubanshe, 1983, 44 vols.

Dijkstra, Bram, *Idols of Perversity. Fantasies of Feminine Evil in Fin-de-Siècle Culture*, Oxford, Oxford University Press, 1986.

Ding Ling, "Qingyunli zhong" ("In Qingyun Lane"), in *Ding Ling xuanji* ("Selected Works of Ding Ling"), 1929, Xianggang, Wenxue chubanshe, n.d., pp. 91–98.

Door of Hope and Children's Refuge Mission. China, *Annual Report*, no. 1–25 (1900–1925), no. 27–35 (1927–1935).

Drucker, Alison, "The Role of the YMCA in the Development of the Chinese Women's Movement, 1890–1927," *Social Service Review*, vol. 53, no. 3, September 1979, pp. 421–440.

Du Shipin (ed.), *Shanghai shi daguan* ("The Magnificent Spectacle of Shanghai"), Shanghai, Zhongguo tushu zazhi gongsi, 1948.

Dufour, Pierre (pseudonym of Paul Lacroix), *Histoire de la prostitution chez tous les peuples du monde depuis l'antiquité la plus reculée jusqu'à nos jours*, Paris, Seré, 1851–1853, 6 vols.

Durand-Fardel, Maxime, "La prostitution et la condition des femmes en Chine," *Union médicale*, 3rd ed., vol. XXI, no. 60, 1876, pp. 68, 810; no. 64, pp. 73, 869; no. 67, pp. 905–906; no. 73, pp. 84, 993 (published separately as *La vie irrégulière et la condition des femmes en Chine*, Paris, Germer-Baillère, 1876).

Durand-Fardel, Maxime, *Les établissements de bienfaisance indigènes et les institutions sanitaires étrangères en Chine*, Paris, J.-B. Baillière, 1882.

Duval, Jean, "Les aventures révélatrices d'un dandy amoureux: Étude d'un roman en dialecte *wu* de la fin de l'époque Qing, *La tortue à neuf queues*, de Zhang Chunfan," doctoral thesis, Paris, Institut national des langues et civilisations orientales, 1975, 2 vols.

Duval, Jean, "The Nine-Tailed Tortoise: Pornography or 'Fiction of Exposure'?," in Dolozelova-Velingerova, M. (ed.), *The Chinese Novel at the Turn of the Century*, Toronto, University of Toronto Press, 1980, pp. 177–188.

Eberhard, Wolfram, *Guilt and Sin in Traditional China*, Berkeley, University of California Press, 1967.

Eberhard, Wolfram, *Moral and Social Values of the Chinese: Collected Essays*, Taibei, Cheng Wen Publishing Co., 1971.

Eberstein, Bernd, *Das chinesische Theater im 20. Jahrhundert*, Wiesbaden, Otto Harrassowitz, Schriften des Instituts für Asienkunde in Hamburg, vol. 45, 1983.

Eckart, Wolfgang Uwe, *Deutsche Ärtzte in China, 1897–1914. Medizin als Kulturmission im zweiten deutschen Kaiserreich*, Stuttgart, Gustav Fischer Verlag, 1989.

Eckart, Wolfgang Uwe, "Editorial," *China Medical Journal*, vol. 34, November 1920, pp. 635–637.

Elvin, Mark, "The Mixed Court of the International Settlement at Shanghai," *Papers on China*, no. 17, Cambridge, MA, Harvard University Press, East Asian Research Center, 1963, pp. 131–159.

Englert, Siegfried, *Materialen zur Stellung der Frau und zur Sexualität im vormodernen China*, Frankfurt, Haag + Herchen, Heidelberger Schriften zur Ostasienkunde, 1980.

Er Shisheng, "Shizhou chunyu" ("Springtime Words on the Islands of Paradise"), in *Yanshi shi er zhong* ("A History of Lewdness in Twelve Tales"), Yu Chensheng, Shanghai, Hanwenyuan shusi, 1929, 8 vols. (reproduction of the 1878 edition) [1841 text on the prostitutes of Ningbo].

Evans, Richard J., "Prostitution, State and Society in Imperial Germany," *Past and Present*, no. 70, 1976, pp. 106–126.

Everett, Ray, "International Traffic in Women and Children," *Journal of Social Hygiene*, no. 13, May 1927, pp. 269–276.

Fan Songfu, "Shanghai banghui neimu" ("The Corridors of Shanghai's Secret Societies"), *Wenshi ziliao xuanji* ("Selection of Historical and Literary Materials"), vol. 31, 1980, pp. 150–178.

Fan Xipin, "Shanghai wuchao'an qinliji" ("Personal Notes on the Protest Movement of the Taxi-Dancers in Shanghai"), *Shanghai wenshi ziliao* ("Historical and Literary Materials"), Shanghai, no. 12, 1979, pp. 190–199.

Fearn, Anne W., *My Days of Strength: An American Woman Doctor's Forty Years in China*, New York, Harper & Brothers Publishers, 1939.

Feetham, Richard, *Report of the Hon. Mr. Justice Feetham, C.M.G., to the Shanghai Municipal Council*, Shanghai, North China Daily News and Herald, 1931, 2 vols.

Fei Peide, "Gongchang wenti zhi jiejue" ("A Solution to the Problem of Official Prostitution"), *Qingnian jinbu* ("The Progress of Youth"), vol. 13, no. 5, May 1918, and *Dongfang zazhi* ("Eastern Miscellany"), vol. 15, no. 10, October 1918, pp. 162–166.

Fei Peide, "Feichang chuyan" ("Superficial Talk on the Abolition of Prostitution"), *Xinwenbao* ("The News"), 19 January 1946.

Feng Demei, "Chengdu shi jinü duoluo yuanyin ji jiuji fang'an" ("The Causes of the Fall of the Prostitutes in Chengdu and Plan of Assistance"), *Shehui kexue xuebao* ("Journal of Social Sciences"), vol. 1, no. 1, 1939.

Feng Dja-Chien [Feng Zhajian], "Prostitution in Shanghai," M.A. thesis, Shanghai College Library, 1929.

Fewsmith, Joseph, *Party, State and Local Elites in Republican China*, Honolulu, University of Hawaii Press, 1985.

Finnane, Antonia, "The Origins of Prejudice: The Malintegration of Subei in Late Imperial China," *Comparative Studies in Society and History*, vol. 35, no. 2, April 1993, pp. 211–237.

Finnegan, Frances, *poverty and Prostitution. A Study of Victorian Prostitutes in York*, Cambridge, Cambridge University Press, 1979.

Flexner, Abraham, *La prostitution en Europe*, Paris, 1919 (*Prostitution in Europe*, New York, The Century Co., 1914).

Foucault, Michel, *Histoire de la sexualité*, Paris, Gallimard, vol. 1, "La volonté de savoir," 1976.

Foundling Hospital at Shanghai (The), *Chinese and Japanese Repository*, 2 January 1865, pp. 37–40; 1 March 1865, pp. 129–136.

Frazier, Chester N., "The Prevention and Control of Syphilis," *Chinese Medical Journal*, vol. 51, January 1937, pp. 1043–1046.

Freudenberg, Michael, *Die Frauenbewegung in China am Ende der Qingdynastie*, Bochum, Brockmeyer (Chinathemen, vol. 20), 1985.

Funü nianjian ("Women's Yearbook"), (Mei Sheng, ed.), Shanghai, Xin wenhua shushe, 1926–1928, 4 vols.

Funü yuebao ("Women's Monthly"), Shanghai, Shanghai funü jiaoyuguan, 1935–1936.

Gamble, Sydney, *Peking: A Social Survey*, New York, Georre H. Doran Co., 1921.

Gamewell, Mary N., *Gateway to China: Pictures of Shanghai*, New York, Fleming H. Revell Co., 1916.

Gao Shan (translator), "Changji zhidu de genben wenti" ("The Fundamental

Problem of the System of Prostitution"), *Funü zazhi* ("The Ladies' Journal"), vol. XI, no. 8, 1925, pp. 1156–1165.

Ge Yuanxu, *Huyou zazi* ("Miscellaneous Notes on a Journey to Shanghai"), 1876, 4 vols., reprinted 1930 with Japanese punctuation, 3 vols. (reprinted Shanghai, Guji chubanshe, 1989).

Gear, H. S., "The Incidence of Venereal Diseases in Hospital Patients in China," *Chinese Medical Journal,* vol. 49, October 1935, pp. 1122–1135.

Gibson, Mary, *Prostitution and the State in Italy, 1860–1915*, New Brunswick, Rutgers University Press, 1986.

Gipoulon, Catherine, "Emergence des femmes en politique en Chine (1898–1927)," in Henriot, Christian (ed.), *La femme en Asie orientale*, Lyon, Université Lyon III/CRREOC, 1988, pp. 7–21.

Goldman, Marion S., *Gold Diggers and Silver Miners: Prostitution and Social Life on the Comstock Lode*, Ann Arbor, University of Michigan Press, 1981.

"Gongchang shi liang zhidu ma?" ("Is Regulated Prostitution a Good System?"), *Funü zazhi* ("The Ladies' Journal"), vol. X, no. 5, 1924, pp. 586–587.

Goodman, Bryna, *Native Place, City, and Nation: Regional Networks and Identities in Shanghai, 1853–1937*, Berkeley, University of California Press, 1995.

Gordon, C. A. (Surgeon Gal), *An Epitome of the Reports of the Medical Officers to the Chinese Imperial Maritime Customs Service (from 1871 to 1882)*, London, Baillière, Tinder and Cox, 1884.

Grancher, Marcel E., *Shanghai: Roman Colonial*, Toulouse, Éditions S.T.A.E.L., 1945.

Gronewold, Sue, *Beautiful Merchandise. Prostitution in China, 1860–1936*, New York, Haworth Press, 1982 (coll. Women History, no. 1).

Gronewold, Sue, "Encountering hope: The Door of Hope Mission in Shanghai and Taipei, 1900–1976 (China, Taiwan)," unpublished dissertation, Columbia University, 1996.

Guide to Shanghai 1941, n.p., n.pub., n.d.

Guide to Shanghai, Shanghai, American Express Co., Mercury Press, 1940.

Guo Chongjie, "Lun suqing changji" ("Discussion on the Elimination of Prostitution"), *Shehui banyuekan* ("Social Affairs Fortnightly"), vol. I, no. 6, 1934, pp. 23–28.

Guo Zhenyi, *Zhongguo funü wenti* ("The Question of Women in China"), Shanghai, Shangwu yinshuguan, 1935.

"Guolian diaocha yuandong fanyun funü de zhenxiang" ("The League of Nations Investigates the True Face of the Traffic in Women in the Far East"), *Nü qingnian yuekan* ("The Young Women's Monthly"), vol. 10, no. 2, 1931, pp. 23–25.

Haishang Juewusheng (pseudonym), *Jinü de shenghuo* ("The Life of the Prostitutes"), Shanghai, Chunmin shudian, 1940.

Haishang qinglou lejing tushuo ("The Delights of Shanghai's Green Chambers in Words and Illustrations"), Shanghai, 1892.

Haishang qinglou tuji ("Illustrated Notes on Shanghai's Green Chambers"), Shanghai, Yingzhou xinzui shuwu, 1892, 4 vols.

Haishang qunfangpu ("Directory of Shanghai's Flowers"), Shanghai, Shenbao guan, 1884.

Haishang yeyou beilan ("Omnium of Licentiousness in Shanghai"), Shanghai, n.pub., 1891.

Han Bangqing, *Haishang hua liezhuan* ("Chronicle of Flowers on the Sea"), Taibei, Wenhua tushu gongsi, 1892 (reprint, Taipei, 1984).

Hansson, Harry, "Regional Outcast Groups in Late Imperial China," Doctoral thesis, Harvard University, 1988.

Harsin, Jill, *Policing Prostitution in Nineteenth-Century Paris*, Princeton, Princeton University Press, 1985.

Hauser, Ernest O., *Blancs et jaunes à Shanghai*, Paris, La Nouvelle Edition, 1945 (coll. Diplomatie et politique internationale).

Hauser, Ernest O., *Shanghai: City for Sale*, New York, Harcourt, Brace and Co., 1940.

He Shizhen, "Ji shanghai gonggong zujie linshi fating" ("Notes on the Provisional Court of Justice of the International Settlement"), *Wenshi ziliao xuanji* ("Selection of Historical and Literary Materials"), no. 4, 1980, pp. 134–147.

He Wannan and Yang Jiezeng, *Shanghai changji gaizao shihua* ("A Short History of the Re-Education of Prostitutes in Shanghai"), Shanghai, Sanlian shudian, 1988.

Heath, Frances J., "Review of Eight Years' Work in China in a Gynecological Out-patient Clinic," *China Medical Journal*, vol. 39, 1925, pp. 701–705.

Hedblom, C. A., "On Disease Incidence in China," *China Medical Journal*, vol. 31, July 1917, pp. 271–283.

Heimburger, L. F., "Dermatology: Recent Advances in Treatment," *China Medical Journal*, vol. 37, February 1923, pp. 220–226.

Heimburger, L. F., "The Incidence of Syphilis at the Shantung Christian University Dispensary," *China Medical Journal*, vol. 41, June 1927, pp. 541–550.

Henderson, Edward, *A Report on Prostitution in Shanghai*, Shanghai, n.pub., 1871.

Henriot, Christian, "Le nouveau journalisme politique chinois (1895–1911: Shanghai–Hong Kong)," *Chine. Cahiers d'études chinoises*, Paris, INALCO, 1981, no. 1, pp. 5–80.

Henriot, Christian, *La femme en Asie orientale*, Lyon, Université Lyon III/CRREOC, 1988.

Henriot, Christian, "Prostitution et 'police des mœurs' à Shanghai aux xixe–xxe siècles," in Henriot, Christian. (ed.), *La femme en Asie orientale*, Lyon, Université Lyon III/CRREOC, 1988, pp. 64–93.

Henriot, Christian, "Municipal Reform in Guomindang China (1927–1937): A First Appraisal," *Republican China*, vol. XV, no. 1, November 1989, pp. 19–38.

Henriot, Christian, "'Einsame Insel.' Shanghai unter Japanischer Herrschaft, 1937–1945," in Hiller, Marlene, Jäckel, Eberhard, and Rohwer, Jürgen, *Städte im 2. Weltkrieg. Ein internationaler Vergleich*, Essen, Klartext, 1991, pp. 28–46.

Henriot, Christian, *Shanghai 1927–1937. Municipal Power, Locality, and Modernization*, Berkeley, University of California Press, 1993.

Henriot, Christian, "Medicine, V. D., and Prostitution in Pre-Revolutionary China," *Social History of Medicine*, Oxford University, vol. V, no. 1, 1992, pp. 95–120.

Henriot, Christian, "La prostitution à Shanghai aux xixe–xxe siècles (1849–1958)," Doctoral thesis (doctorat d'Etat), Paris, École des hautes études en sciences sociales, 3 vols, 1992.

Henriot, Christian, "Villes et société urbaine en Chine aux xixe–xxe siècles," *Historiens et géographes*, no. 340, 1993, pp. 217–232.

Henriques, Fernando, *Love in Action: The Sociology of Sex*, London, Panther Books, 1959.

Henriques, Fernando, *Prostitution and Society: A Survey*, London, Macgibbon and Kee, 1962.

Hershatter, Gail, *The Workers of Tianjin, 1900–1949*, Stanford, Stanford University Press, 1986.

Hershatter, Gail, "The Hierarchy of Shanghai Prostitution, 1870–1949," *Modern China*, vol. 15, no. 4, October 1989, pp. 463–498.

Hershatter, Gail, "Prostitution and the Market in Early Twentieth-Century Shanghai," in Watson, Rubie S., and Buckley Ebrey, Patricia, *Marriage and Inequality in Chinese Society*, Berkeley, University of California Press, 1991, pp. 256–285.

Hershatter, Gail, "Courtesans and Streetwalkers: The Changing Discourse on Shanghai Prostitution, 1890–1949," *Journal of the History of Sexuality*, vol. 3, no. 2, 1992, pp. 245–269.

Hershatter, Gail, "Regulating Sex in Shanghai. The Reform of Prostitution in 1920 and 1951," in Wakeman, Frederic, and Yeh, Wen-hsin, *Shanghai Sojourners*, Berkeley, University of California Press, 1993, pp. 145–185.

Hershatter, Gail, "Modernizing Sex, Sexing Modernity: Prostitution in Early Twentieth-Century Shanghai," in Gilmartin, Christina, et al., *Engendering China. Women, Culture, and the State*, Cambridge, MA, Harvard University Press, 1994, pp. 147–174.

Hershatter, Gail, *Dangerous Pleasures: Prostitution and Modernity in Twentieth Century Shanghai*, Berkeley, University of California Press, 1997.

Hinsch, Bret, *Passion of the Cut Sleeve. The Male Homosexual Tradition in China*, Berkeley, University of California Press, 1990.

Hodges, S. R., "Syphilis as Seen in China," *China Medical Journal*, vol. 21, September 1907, pp. 237–239.

Hong Zhezheng, "Guangzhou shi maiyin huodong de qingkuang pouxi ji duice de tantao" ("An Analysis of the Activities of Prostitution in the Municipality of Guangzhou [Canton] and Reflexion on Steps to Be Taken"), *Faxun* ("Legal News"), Shanghai, "Minzhu yu fazhi" yanjiubu, neibu ziliao, no. 34, 6 August 1988, pp. 1–6.

Honig, Emily, *Strangers and Sisters: Women in the Shanghai Cotton Mills, 1919–1949*, Stanford, Stanford University Press, 1986.

Honig, Emily, *Creating Chinese Ethnicity. Subei People in Shanghai, 1850–1980*, New Haven, Yale University Press, 1993.

Honig, Emily, "The Politics of Prejudice: Subei People in Republican-Era Shanghai," *Modern China*, vol. 15, no. 3, July 1989, pp. 243–274.

Honig, Emily, "Pride and Prejudice: Subei People in Contemporary Shanghai," in Link, Perry, Madsen, Richard, and Pikovitch, Paul, *Unofficial China. Popular Culture and Thought in the People's Republic of China*, Boulder, Westview Press, 1989, pp. 138–155.

Horn, Joshua S., *Away with All Pests. An English Surgeon in People's China: 1954–1969*, London, New York, Monthly Review Press, 1971.

Hou Baotian and Chen Qiongyan, "Nüxing fanzui de xinli tezheng" ("The Psychological Traits of Sexual Delinquents"), *Shehui* ("Society"), no. 6, 1984, pp. 13–15.

Hu chang yanjiu shumu tiyao ("Bibliographical Summary for Research on Prostitution in Shanghai"), in *Shanghai yanjiu ziliao* ("Research Materials on Shanghai"), Shanghai, Shanghai shudian, 1984 (1st ed., Shanghai tongshe, 1936), pp. 578–608.

Hu Huaichen, "Feichang wenti" ("The Question of the Abolition of Prostitution"), *Funü zazhi* ("The Ladies' Journal"), vol. VI, no. 6, 1920, pp. 7–11 (reprinted in Mei Sheng (ed.), *Zhongguo funü wenti taolun ji* ("Collection of Documents on the Feminine Question"), pp. 92–93.

Hu shang xinhua baimei tu ("Etchings of a Hundred New Beauties of Shanghai"), Shanghai, 1884.

Hu Shi, "'Haishang hua liezhuan' shi wuyu wenxue de di yi bu jiezuo" ("The 'Chronicle of Flowers on the Sea' Is the First Work of Literature in the *wu* Dialect"), in *Hu Shi wencun* ("Collection of Works by Hu Shi"), Taibei, Yuandong tushu gongsi, 1953, vol. 3, pp. 488–496.

Hu Shi, "'Haishang hua liezhuan' xu" ("Introduction to the 'Chronicle of Flowers on the Sea'"), in *Haishang hua liezhuan* ("Chronicle of Flowers on the Sea"), Shanghai, Dongya tushuguan, 1935 (1st ed., 1926), pp. 1–35.

Hua Bao ("The Flowers"), Shanghai, July 1926–April 1927.

Hua shijie mingbao ("The World of Flowers"), Shanghai, 2 March 1919.

Huaguo ribao ("The Kingdom of Flowers Daily"), Shanghai, 1920.

Huang Kewu, "Cong Shen Bao yiyao guanggao kan min chu shanghai de yiliao wenhua yu shehui shenghuo, 1912–1926" ("The Medical Cultural and Social Life of Shanghai: A Study Based on Advertisements for Medicines in *Shen Pao*, 1912–1926"), *Jindaishi yanjiusuo jikan* ("Bulletin of the Institute of Modern History, Academia Sinica"), vol. XVII, part 2, 1988, pp. 141–194.

Huang Shi, "Feichang yundong" ("The Movement for the Abolition of Prostitution"), *Xin nüxing* ("New Woman"), vol. II, no. 8, 1928, pp. 795–807.

Huang Shiquan, *Songnan mengying lu* ("Reverie in the South of the River Songjiang"), Shanghai, Guji chubanshe, 1989 [1883].

Huang Wei and Xia Lingen (eds.), *Jindai shanghai diqu fangzhi jingji shiliao xuanji, 1840–1949* ("Selected Materials on Economic History [Taken from] Gazettes of the Shanghai Region in the Modern Period"), Shanghai, Renmin chubanshe (coll. Shanghai ziliao congkan), 1984.

Huashi ("History of the Flowers"), Shanghai, Yueyue xiaoshuoshe, 1907.

Huitu shanghai zazi ("Miscellaneous Notes on Images of Shanghai"), Shanghai, Wenbao shuju, 1905, 4 vols.

Humana, Ch., and Wang, Wu, *Le yin-yang ou l'art d'aimer en Chine*, Paris, Albin Michel, 1973 (translated from the English, *The Yin Yang: The Chinese Way of Love*, New York, 1971).

Hung, William S. H., *Outlines of Modern Chinese Law*, Shanghai, n.pub., 1934.

Hung, William S. H., *International Convention for the Suppression of the Traffic in Women and Children*, Treaty Series no. 26, 1923, London, Stationary Office, 1924.

Ishihara, A., and Levy, H. S., *The Tao of Sex*, Yokohama, Shibundo, 1968 (reprint, New York, 1970).

Jametel, Maurice, *La Chine inconnue*, Paris, Imprimerie de l'Art, 1884.

Jaschok, Maria, *Concubines and Bondservants. The Social History of a Chinese Custom*, London, Zed Books, 1989.

Ji Longsheng, *Da shanghai* ("Greater Shanghai"), Taibei, Nanfang zazhi chubanshe [1942].

Jiang Sihu and Wu Yuanshu, "Shanghai qibai ge qigai de shehui diaocha" ("A Sociological Survey of Seven Hundred Beggars in Shanghai"), Shanghai, Master's dissertation, Hujiang daxue (Sociology), 1933, 2 vols.

Jiang Suzhen and Wang Wanliu, "Taolun dangqian de maiyin xianxiang ji duice" ("Discussion of the Phenomenon of Prostitution and of Steps to Be Taken," Neibu ziliao, n.d., pp. 5–9.

Jin Buhuan, *Chunjiang huayue hen* ("Recollections of the Good Old Times"), Xianggang, Tianwentai baoshe, 1962.

Jiu shanghai de yan du chang ("Prostitution, Gambling and Opium in Old Shanghai"), *Shanghai wenshi* ("History and Literature of Shanghai"), Shanghai, 1989, no. 1, pp. 75–78 and p. 83.

Jiu shanghai de yan du chang ("Prostitution, Gambling and Opium in Old Shanghai"), Shanghai shi wenshiguan bian, Shanghai, Baijia chubanshe, 1988.

Johnson, Lynda C., "The Decline of Soochow and Rise of Shanghai: A Study in the Economic Morphology of Urban Change, 1756–1894," doctoral thesis, University of California, Santa Cruz, 1986.

Johnson, Lynda C., *Cities of Jiangnan in Late Imperial China*, New York, State University of New York Press, 1993.

Jo Tshong-Chan (translator), *Code civil de la République de Chine*, Shanghai, 1930.

Jones, William C., "Studying the Ch'ing Code – The Ta Ch'ing lü li," *American Journal of Comparative Law*, vol. 22, 1974, pp. 330–359.

Kai Shi, "Jingji wenti yu changji" ("Economic Problems and Prostitution"), *Xin nüxing* ("New Woman"), II, 10, 1928, pp. 1163–1165.

Ke Xiangfeng, *Zhongguo pinqiong wenti* ("The Problem of Poverty in China"), Shanghai, Shangwu yinshuguan, 1935 (reprint, Zhengzhong, 1947).

King, G. E., "Kansuh and Its Diseases," *Chinese Medical Journal*, vol. 39, January 1925, pp. 19–22.

Kingsley, Davies, "Prostitution," in Merton, Robert K., and Nisbet, Robert A. (eds.), *Contemporary Social* Problems, New York, Harcourt, Brace and World Inc., 1961, pp. 263–288.

Kingsley, Davies, "The Sociology of Prostitution," *American Sociological Review*, vol. 2, October 1937, pp. 744–755.

Koo, Charles, Dzao, P. V., and Young, M. P., "Wassermann Reports," *China Medical Journal*, vol. 49, October 1929, pp. 1017–1018.

Korns, J. H., "An Examination of Domestic Servants for Communicable Diseases," *China Medical Journal*, vol. 34, November 1920, pp. 624–629.

Korns, J. H., "Further Statistics on Communicable Diseases among Domestic Servants," *China Medical Journal*, vol. 35, 1921, pp. 382–384.

Kotenev, Anatol M., *Shanghai, Its Mixed Court and Council: Material Relation to the History of the Shanghai Municipal Council and the History, Practice and Statistics of the International Mixed Court*, Shanghai, North-China Daily News and Herald, 1925.

Kotenev, Anatol M., *Shanghai, its Municipality and the Chinese: Being the History of the Shanghai Municipal Council and its Relations with the Chinese, the Practice of the International Mixed Court, and the Inauguration of the Shanghai Provincial Court*, Shanghai, North-China Daily News and Herald, 1927.

Kranzler, David H., *Japanese, Nazis and Jews: The Jewish Refugee Community of Shanghai, 1938–1945*, New York, Yeshiva University Press, 1974.

Lai, Dr., "Syphillis and Prostitution in Kiangsu," *China Medical Journal*, vol. 44, 1930, pp. 558–563.

Lai, Daniel, "Incidence of Syphilis among Prostitutes and Cabaret Hostesses in Tsingtao," *Chinese Medical Journal*, vol. 66, July 1948, pp. 389–390.

Lai, Daniel, and Wang-Lai, Suchen, "Incidence of Syphilis among the Chinese Soldiers at Swatow," *China Medical Journal*, vol. 42, August 1928, pp. 557–567.

Lai, Daniel, and Wang-Lai, Suchen, "Incidence of Syphilis among Chinese Civilian

Patients in Swatow District," *China Medical Journal*, vol. 43, January 1929, pp. 22–27.

Lamson, Herbert D., *Social Pathology in China: A Source Book for the Study of Livelihood, Health and the Family*, Shanghai, Commercial Press, 1935.

Lao shanghai ("Old Shanghai"), Shanghai, n.pub., n.d.

League of Nations, Advisory Commission for the Protection and Welfare of Children and Young People, *Digest of the Comments by Private Organizations on the Report of the League of Nations Commission of Inquiry into Traffic in Women and Children in the East*, Geneva, document no. C.F.T.E.613, 1934.

League of Nations, Advisory Commission for the Protection and Welfare of Children and Young People, *Report on the Work of the Commission*, Geneva, 1933–1939.

League of Nations, Advisory Committee on Social Questions, *Enquiry into Measures of Rehabilitation of Prostitutes*, part I, "Prostitutes: Their Early Lives," Geneva, document no. C.218.M.120.1938.IV, 1938; part II, "Social Services and Venereal Diseases," document no. C.6.M.5.1938.IV, 1938; part III & IV, "Methods of Rehabilitation of Adult Prostitutes," document no. C.83.M.43.1939.IV, 1939.

League of Nations, Advisory Committee on Social Questions, *Prevention of Prostitution*, Geneva, document no. C.26.M.26.1943.IV, 1943.

League of Nations, Commission of Enquiry into Traffic in Women and Children in the East, *Report to the Council*, Geneva, 1932, 1933, 1934 (Series of League of Nations Publications).

League of Nations, Traffic in Women and Children, *Concise Study of the Laws and Penalties Relating to Souteneurs*, Geneva, 1931.

League of Nations, Traffic in Women and Children, Conference of Central Authorities in Eastern Countries, *Minutes of Meetings*, Geneva, document no. C-476.M.318.1937.IV, 1937.

League of Nations, Traffic in Women and Children, *Position of Women of Russian Origin in the Far East*, Geneva, document no. A.12.1935.IV.1935.

League of Nations, Traffic in Women and Children, *The Work of the Bandoeng Conference*, Geneva, document no. C.516.M.357.1937.IV, 1938.

Lei Jingjiao, "Shanghai yangshupu renlichefu diaocha" ("A Survey of the Rickshaw-pullers of Yangshupu in Shanghai"), Master's dissertation, n.p., n.d.

Lei Zhusheng, *Haishang huodiyu* ("Living Hell in Shanghai"), Shanghai, Huacheng shuju, 1931, 4 vols.

Lemière, J., "Sing Song Girl: From a Throne of Glory to a Seat of Ignominy," *Chinese Journal of Science and Art*, no. 1, March 1923, pp. 126, 130, and 134.

Leng Shengwu, *Zuixin shanghai zhinan* ("New Guide to Shanghai"), Shanghai, Shanghai wenhua yanjiushe, 1946.

Lennox, William G., *China Medical Journal*, vol. 33, 1919, p. 356, quoted in Lamson, Herbert, *Social Pathology in China*, Shanghai, The Commercial Press Ltd., 1935, p. 354.

Lennox, William G., "Neurosyphilis among the Chinese with Findings in Sixty-Five Cases," *China Medical Journal*, vol. 37, August 1923, pp. 663–671.

Lennox, William G., "A Self-Survey by Mission Hospitals in China," *Chinese Medical Journal*, vol. 46, 1932, pp. 484–534.

Leung, Kiche Angela, "L'accueil des enfants abandonnés dans la Chine du bas Yangzi aux xviie et xviiie siècles," *Études chinoises*, vol. IV, no. 1, spring 1985, pp. 15–54.

Leung Yüen-sang, *The Shanghai Taotai: Linkage Man in a Changing Society,* *1843–1890,* Honolulu, University of Hawaii Press, 1990.

Levy, Howard S., "Record of the Gay Quarters," *Orient/West,* vol. 8, no. 5, September–October 1963, pp. 121–128; no. 6, November–December 1963, pp. 115–122; vol. 9, no. 1, January–February 1964, pp. 103–110.

Levy, Howard S., "T'ang Women of Pleasure," *Sinologica,* vol. VIII, no. 2, 1965, pp. 89–113.

Levy, Howard S., "The Gay Quarters of Ch'ang-an," *Orient/West,* vol. 7, no. 9, September 1962, pp. 93–105.

Levy, Howard S., *Banqiao zaji* ("Miscellaneous Notes from the Wooden Bridge") [1697], Yokohama, n.pub, 1966.

Levy, Howard S., *A Feast of Mist and Flowers: The Gay Quarters of Nanking at the End of the Ming,* translation, Yokohama, n.pub., 1966.

Levy, Howard S., *Chinese Footbinding: The History of a Curious Erotic Custom,* New York, Bell Publishing Company, 1966.

Levy, Howard S., *Chinese Sex Jokes in Traditional Times,* Taibei, The Orient Cultural Service, 1973 (Asian Folklore and Social Life Monographs, vol. 58).

Levy, Howard S., *The Illusory Flame,* Tokyo, Kenkyusha, 1962.

Li Boyuan, *Haishang huodiyu* ("Living Hell in Shanghai"), Shanghai, Wenhua chubanshe, reprint 1956 [1903–1906].

Li Sanwu, "Feichang yundong guanjian" ("Viewpoint on the Abolitionist Movement"), *Funü zazhi* ("The Ladies' Journal"), vol. VI, no. 8, 1920, pp. 7–16 [reprinted in Mei Sheng (ed.), *Zhongguo funü wenti taolun ji* ("Collection of Documents on the Feminine Question"), pp. 75–85].

Li Youning, *Jindai zhongguo nüquan yundong shiliao* ("Materials on the History of the Feminist Movement in Modern China"), Taibei, Zhuanji wenxueshe, 1975.

Li Zilai, "Changji zhidu yu jiating" ("The System of Prostitution and the Family"), *Funü yuekan* ("Women's Monthly"), vol. VI, no. 6, January 1948, pp. 15–17.

Lian Ying canshi. Shanghai huaguo zongtong ("The Tragic Story of Lian Ying, President of the Republic of Flowers"), Shanghai, Shen Queji shuju, 1921.

Lin Li, "Ba youmin changji gaizao cheng xin ren" ("Transform the Prostitutes and the Vagabonds into New Beings"), in *Shanghai jiefang san shi wu nian wenshi ziliao jinian zhuanji* ("Special Issue: Historical and Literary Materials for the 35th Anniversary of the Liberation of Shanghai"), no. 4, 1984, pp. 128–133.

Lin Ruiming, "Wan Qing qianze xiaoshuo de lishi yiyi" ("Historical Significance in Late Ch'ing Fiction of Social Critique"), Taibei, Guoli Taiwan daxue chuban, 1980.

Lin Zhen, *Shanghai zhinan* ("Guide to Shanghai"), Shanghai, Shangwu yinshuguan, 1930.

Link, Perry, *Mandarin Ducks and Butterflies: Popular Fiction in Early 20th Century Chinese Cities,* Berkeley, University of California Press, 1981.

Liu Jie, "Changji wenti yu yousheng yundong" ("The Problem of Prostitution and the Eugenic Movement"), *Dongfang zazhi* ("Eastern Miscellany"), vol. 32, no. 1, January 1935, pp. 49–60.

Liu Peiqian (ed.), *Da shanghai zhinan* ("Guide to Greater Shanghai"), Shanghai, Zhonghua shuju, 1936.

Liu Qingyu and Xu Huifang, "Shanghai nüxingfan de shehui wenti" ("Sociological Analysis of the Delinquents of Shanghai"), *Dalu zazhi* ("Journal of the Continent"), vol. I, no. 4, 1932, pp. 71–93.

Liu Yang, "Wunü shenghuo yu tiaowu wenti" ("The Life of the Taxi-Dancers and the Question of Dancing"), *Funü zazhi* ("The Ladies' Journal"), vol. III, no. 10, 1942, pp. 41–45.

Long Sanli, "Xiandai shijie ge guo de changji wenti ji qi jiejue fangfa" ("The Problem of Prostitution in the World and Its Solutions"), *Dongfang zazhi* ("Eastern Miscellany"), vol. 28, no. 14, July 1931, pp. 25–38.

Lu Dafang, *Shanghai tan yijiu lu* ("Reminiscences of the Shanghai Bund"), Taibei, Shijie shuju, 1980.

Lu Feiyun and Zhang Zhongru, "Shanghai jiefang chuqi de jinü gaizao gongzuo" ("The Reform of Prostitutes in the Early Liberation Period of Shanghai"), in *Shehuixue wenji* ("A Collection of Sociological Texts"), Shanghai, Shanghai shi shehuixue xuehui bian, 1983, pp. 121–136.

Lu Hanbo, "Gongchang ma?" ("Public Prostitution?") *Funü yuekan* ("Women's Monthly"), vol. V, no. 2, November 1946.

Lu He, *Zhongguo funü shenghuo xiezhen* ("True Account of the Life of Chinese Women"), Shanghai, Guangyi shuju, 1934.

Lu Jialiang, *Shanghai shouce* ("Pocket Guide to Shanghai"), Shanghai, Zhonghu shuju, 1949.

Lu Luxi, "Wunü riji zhailu" ("Excerpts from the Diary of a Taxi-Dancer"), *Funü shenghuo* ("Women's Life"), vol. 8, 1935, pp. 155–157.

Lu Wei, "Tiaochu huokang yihou" ("After Coming out of Hell"), *Shanghai funü* ("Shanghai Women"), vol. 1, no. 12, October 1938, pp. 14–15.

Lu Xun, "Qing zhi xiaxie xiaoshuo" ("The Prostitutional Novel and the End of the Qing"), in *Lu Xun quanji* ("The Complete Works of Lu Xun"), Hong Kong, Xianggang wenxue yanjiushe, n.d., vol. 8, pp. 215–226.

Lu Xun, "Shanghai wen yi zhi yi pie" ("A Look at the Arts and Literature in Shanghai"), in *Lu Xun quanji* ("The Complete Works of Lu Xun"), Hong Kong, Xianggang wenxue yanjiushe, n.d., vol. 8, pp. 228–241.

Lu Yizhuang, "Changji zhidu yanjiu" ("Inquiry into the System of Prostitution"), Peking (unconsulted thesis).

Lucas, Ann Elissa, *Chinese Medical Modernization. Comparative Policy Continuities, 1930s–1980s*, New York, Praeger, 1982.

Lum, Raymond D., "Philanthropy and Public Welfare in Late Imperial China," doctoral thesis, Harvard University, 1985.

Luo Qiong, "Changji zai Zhongguo" ("The Prostitutes in China"), *Funü shenghuo* ("Women's Life"), vol. I, no. 6, December 1935, pp. 34–40.

Ma Shunwei, "Shanghai bangpiao diaocha" ("A Study of Kidnappings in Shanghai"), Master's dissertation (sociology), n.p., n.d.

Ma Weigang (ed.), *Jin chang jin du* ("The Repression of Prostitution and Narcotics"), Beijing, Jinguan jiaoyu chubanshe, 1993.

MacCartney, J. L., "Chinese Military Medicine," *U.S. Naval Medical Bulletin*, vol. 25, no. 4, October 1927, pp. 783–816.

MacHugh, Paul, *Prostitution and Victorian Social Reform*, New York, St. Martin's, 1980.

MacKirdy, Archibald (Mrs.), and Willis, W. N., *The White Slave Market*, London, Stanley Paul and Co., 1912.

MacPherson, Kerrie L., *A Wilderness of Marshes. The Origins of Public Health in Shanghai, 1843–1893*, Oxford, Oxford University Press, 1987.

Mai Qianzeng, "Beiping changji diaocha" ("Inquiry into the Prostitutes of Peking"), *Shehui xuejie* ("World of Sociology"), no. 5, 1931, pp. 105–146.

Mann, Susan, "Widows in the Kinship, Class and Community Structures of Qing

Dynasty China," *The Journal of Asian Studies*, vol. 46, no. 1, February 1987, pp. 37–56.

Marcus, Stevens, *The Other Victorians. A Study of Sexuality and Pornography in Mid-Nineteenth-Century England*, New York, Basic Books, 1964.

Martin, Bryan, "Tu Yüëh-sheng and Labour Control in Shanghai: The Case of the French Tramways Union, 1928–1932," *Papers in Far Eastern History*, 32, September 1985, Australian National University, pp. 99–132.

Martin, Bryan, "Warlords and Gangsters: The Opium Traffic in Shanghai and the Creation of the Three Prosperities Company," paper prepared for the Asian Studies Association of Australia, Sixth national conference, 11–16 May 1986, 31 pp.

Martin, Bryan, *The Green Gang in Shanghai. Politics and Organized Crime, 1919–1937*, Berkeley, University of California Press, 1996.

Martin, Charles Ernest, "Étude sur la prostitution en Chine," *Union médicale*, 2nd ed., vol. IX, no. 251872, pp. 25, 401–408; no. 26, pp. 29, 465–474.

Maxwell, J. L., "Some Notes on Syphilis among the Chinese," *China Medical Journal*, vol. 27, 1913, pp. 379–383.

Maxwell, J. L., "A Century of Medical Missions in China," *China Medical Journal*, vol. 39, 1925, pp. 636–650.

Maxwell, J. L., *Diseases of China*, Shanghai, 1930 (1st ed., with W. H. Jefferys, Philadelphia, 1910).

Maxwell, Preston J., "On Criminal Abortion in China," *The China Medical Journal*, vol. 42, 1928, pp. 12–19.

Maybon, Ch.-B., and Fredet, Jean, *Histoire de la Concession française de Changhai*, Paris, Plon, 1929.

Medical Reports, China Imperial Maritime Customs, Shanghai, Statistical Department of the Inspectorate General, 1878 (succeeded the *Customs Gazette*).

Mei Sheng (ed.), *Zhongguo funü wenti taolun ji* ("Collected Documents on Discussions on the Question of Chinese Women"), Shanghai, Xin wenhua shushe, 1926.

Meijer, Marinus Jan, "Slavery at the End of the Ch'ing Dynasty," in Cohen, J., Chen-Chang Fu-mei, and Edwards, R., *Essays on China's Legal Tradition*, Princeton, Princeton University Press, 1980, pp. 327–358.

Meijer, Marinus Jan, *The Introduction of Modern Criminal Law in China*, Batavia, De Unie, 1949.

Meyer, Katherin B., "Splitting Apart: The Shanghai Treaty Port in Transition, 1914–1921," doctoral thesis, Temple University, 1985.

Miller, G. E., *Shanghai, Paradise of Adventurers*, Shanghai, Modern Book Co., 1937.

Milne, William C., *La vie réelle en Chine*, Paris, Hachette, 1858 (translated from the English *Life in China: Fourteen Years Among the Chinese*, London).

Miners, Norman, "The State Regulation of Prostitution, 1857–1941," in *Hong Kong under Imperial Rule*, Hong Kong/London, Oxford University Press, East Asian Historical Monographs, 1987, pp. 191–206.

Ming (pseudonym), "Nanjing jinchang cheng le wenti" ("The Prohibition of Prostitution in Nanking Raises Problems"), *Pangguan xunkan* ("Obliques"), Nanjing, no. 11, 1933, pp. 2–4.

Mu Ji, "Changji" ("Prostitute"), in Mei Sheng (ed.), *Zhongguo funü wenti taolun ji* ("Collection of Documents on the Female Question"), Shanghai, Xin wenhua shushe, 1926, pp. 85–93.

Mu Zhen Shan Ren [pseudonym of Yu Da or Yu Yinxiang], *Qinglou meng* ("The Dream in the Green Bower [Courtisans' House]"), Hengyang, Yuelu shushe, 1988 (1st ed., 1878).

Murphey, Rhoads, *Shanghai: Key to Modern China*, Cambridge, MA, Harvard University Press, 1953.

Nagler, E. M., "The Problem of Food and Shelter for Refugees in Shanghai," *China Quarterly*, 3, 1937–1938, pp. 67–70.

National Medical Journal of China, 1915–1931.

Ng, Vivian W., "Ch'ing Law Concerning the Insane: An Historical Survey," *Ch'ing-shih wen-t'i*, no. 4, 1980, pp. 55–89.

Ng, Vivian W., "Ideology and Sexuality: Rape Laws in Qing China," *Journal of Asian Studies*, vol. 46, no. 1, February 1987, pp. 57–70.

North China Daily News, Shanghai, daily, 1866–1871.

North China Herald, Shanghai, 1850–1864, 1895, 1898, 1912, 1918–1921, 1925, 1928–1929, 1931–1932, 1940–1941.

Northedge, Frederick S., *The League of Nations: Its Life and Times, 1920–1946*, Leicester, Leicester University Press, 1986.

Nü qingnian yuekan ("The Young Women's Journal"), [journal of the Y.W.C.A.], Shanghai, 1934–1937.

Nüsheng ("Women's Voice"), Shanghai, 1932–1948.

Nüzi mimi shi ("Secret History of Women"), n.p., n.pub., n.d.

O'Callaghan, S., *The Yellow Slave Trade: A Survey of the Traffic in Women and Children in the East*, London, Blond, 1968.

Oldt, F., "Purity Campaign in Canton," *China Medical Journal*, vol. 37, September 1923, pp. 776–782.

Otis, Leah Lydia, *Prostitution in Medieval Society*, Chicago, University of Chicago Press, 1985.

Parker, E. H., "A Journey into North Szech'uan," *The China Review*, vol. X, no. 6, May–June 1882, pp. 365–384.

Peking United International Famine Relief Committee, *North China Famine of 1920–1921, with Special Reference to the West Chihli Area*, Peking, 1922.

People's Tribune, Hankou, weekly, 1931–1937.

Perry, Elizabeth, *Shanghai on Strike*, Stanford, Stanford University Press, 1993.

Peter, W. W., "Fighting Venereal Disease Openly," *China Medical Journal*, vol. 35, January 1921, pp. 61–66.

Peters, Ernest W., *Shanghai Policeman*, London, Rich and Cowan, 1937.

Pfister, M. O., "Syphilis in China," *China Medical Journal*, vol. 44, February 1930, p. 191.

Philastre, P.-L.-F., *Le Code annamite, nouvelle traduction comprenant les commentaires officiels du Code, traduits pour la première fois, de nombreuses annotations extraites des commentaires du Code chinois*, Paris, E. Leroux, 1876, 2 vols.; 2nd ed., 1909 (reprint, Taibei, Chengwen chubanshe, 1967).

Ping Jinya, "Jiu shanghai de changji" ("Prostitutes in Old Shanghai"), in *Jiu shanghai de yan du chang* ("Prostitution, Gambling and Opium in Old Shanghai"), Shanghai shi wenshiguan bian, Shanghai, Baijia chubanshe, 1988, pp. 159–171.

Ping Shuyi, "Haishang qing lou" ("The Green Chambers of Shanghai"), *Shanghai huabao* ("Illustrated Journal of Shanghai"), no. 5, 1989, pp. 30–31.

Pivar, David, *Purity Crusade, Sexual Morality, and Social Control, 1868–1900,* Westport, CT, Greenwood Press, 1973.

Police Archives (*Shanghai tebie shi jingchaju*), Special Municipality de Shanghai, 1937–1945: 1-4-125: August 1941; 1-62-44: "Fenghua yingye tongji biao" ("Statistical Table of Prostitution" [26 September 1942]); R2-82: January 1944; 12-4-1445: Police Report (13 August 1941), 1st half-year of 1941; (from January 1943), 2nd half-year 1941, sent to the Mayor of Shanghai: statistics on the houses of prostitution, gambling, and opium.

Police Archives (*Shanghai shi jingchaju*), Municipality of Shanghai, 1945–1949, Municipal Archives of Shanghai: 1-4-125; 1-10-246: May 1946–January 1949; 011-4-80: August 1946–October 1948; 011-4-161: August 1947–July 1949; 011-4-162: "Qudi jiyuan an" ("Cases of Closure of Prostitution Houses"), January 1946–July 1948; 011-4-163: "Qudi jiyuan an" ("Cases of Closure of Prostitution Houses"); 011-4-170: "Qudi jinü la ke an" ("Cases of Soliciting in the Street"), February 1946–May 1948; 011-4-171: "Jinü bu zhao guiding jianyan shenti an" ("Cases of Non-Compliance with the Regulations Concerning Health Checks on Prostitutes"), December 1947–May 1948; 011-4-172; 011-4-173: January 1946–July 1948; 011-4-174; 011-4-175: December 1946–November 1948; 011-4-176: August 1946–May 1948; 011-4-178: July 1947–October 1948; 011-4-180: August 1946–October 1948; 011-4-259: August 1946–October 1946; 011-4-260: March 1947–April 1948; 011-4-261: January 1946–December 1946; 011-4-263: October 1947; 011-4-264; 011-4-266: October 1945–February 1948; 011-4-269; 011-4-270: December 1946–December 1948.

Police municipale à Shanghai, Shanghai, Kelly & Walsh, 1865.

Poumarède, Jacques, and Royer, Jean-Pierre, *Droit, histoire et sexualité,* Lille, L'espace juridique, 1987.

Poumarède, Jacques, and Royer, Jean-Pierre, "[The] Prevention and Control of Syphilis. A Problem of Adequate Treatment," *Chinese Medical Journal,* vol. 51, June 1937, pp. 1043–1046.

Poumarède, Jacques, and Royer, Jean-Pierre, *Prostitution in the Victorian Age. Debates on the Issue from 19th Century Journals,* Westmead, Gregg International Publishers Ltd., 1973.

Poumarède, Jacques, and Royer, Jean-Pierre, "Prostitution Problem in Shanghai [The]," *The China Critic,* vol. XVII, no. 1, April 1937, pp. 7–9.

Pulleyblank, E. G., "The Origins and Nature of Chattel Slavery in China," *Journal of the Economic and Social History of the Orient,* vol. 1, 1958, pp. 184–220.

Qian Chengxu, *Zhan hou shanghai zhi gong shang ge ye* ("Industry and Commerce in Shanghai after the War"), Shanghai, Zhongguo jingji yanjiuhui, 1940.

Qian Shengke, *Qing hong bang zhi heimu* ("The Secret Story of the 'Green Gang' the 'Red Gang'"), Shanghai, Qian Shengke heimu faxingsuo, in *Mimi shehui congkan,* 2nd series, vol. 4.

Qian Shengke, *Shanghai heimu huibian* ("The Mysteries of Shanghai"), Shanghai, Zhentan yanjiuhui, 1929, 4 vols., vols. 2 and 4.

Qian Xuantong, "Heimushu" ("The Books of the Black Curtain"), in Wei Shaochang, *Yuanyang hudie pai yanjiu ziliao* ("Research Materials on the School of Mandarin Ducks and Butterflies"), Shanghai, Wenyi chubanshe, 1962, pp. 44–46.

Qian Yiwei, "Changji de chansheng he jiuji" ("The Training and Rescue of Prostitutes"), *Funü shijie* ("The Ladies' World"), vol. II, no. 6, 1941, pp. 20–21.

Qiao Feng, "Feichang de genben wenti" ("The Fundamental Problem of the Abolition of Prostitution"), *Funü zazhi* ("The Ladies' Journal"), vol. IX, no. 3, 1923, pp. 6–8.

Qiao Feng, "Qinglou ji" "Notes on the Green Bower [Courtesans' House]," in *Xiangyan congshu* ("Collection [of the World] of Beautics"), published by Zhang Tinghua, Shanghai, Guoxue fulunshe, [1909–1911], 80 vols. [document from the Yuan dynasty].

Qiao Feng, "Quanguo yi nian jiejiu wanming funü ertong" ("Ten Thousand Women and Children Have Been Rescued This Year Throughout the Country"), *Renmin ribao* ("The People's Daily"), 30 December 1990.

Quetel, Claude, *Le mal de Naples. Histoire de la syphilis*, Paris, Seghers, 1986.

Rapport annuel 1940, Service de police, Concession française, n.p., n.pub.

Reckless, Walter C., *Vice in Chicago*, Chicago, University of Chicago Press, 1933.

Règlement administratif, Shanghai, Kelly & Walsh, 1872, 1879.

Règlement municipal de police et de voirie, Shanghai, Imprimerie de la presse orientale, 1889, 1907.

"Report on the Control and Treatment of Venereal Disease in Shanghai," *China Medical Journal*, Supplement, vol. 38, January 1924, pp. 1–29.

Rosen, Ruth, *The Lost Sisterhood: Prostitution in America, 1900–1918*, Baltimore, Johns Hopkins University Press, 1982.

Rossiaud, Jacques, *La prostitution médiévale*, Paris, Flammarion, 1988.

Rotours, Robert des, *Courtisanes à la fin des T'ang entre circa 789 et le 8 January 881: Pei-li tche (Anecdotes du quartier du Nord) par Souen K'i*, Paris, Presses universitaires de France, 1968.

Rousseau, G. S., and Porter, Roy, *Sexual Underworlds of the Enlightenment*, Charlotte, The University of North Carolina Press, 1988.

Roux, Alain, "Ouvriers et ouvrières de Shanghai à l'époque du Guomindang, 1927–1949," doctoral (doctorat d'État) thesis, Université Paris-1, Panthéon-Sorbonne, 1991.

Roux, Alain, *Le Shanghai ouvrier des années trente. Coolies, gangsters et syndicalistes*, Paris, L'Harmattan, 1993.

Rowe, William T., "The Qingbang and Collaboration Under the Japanese, 1939–1945," *Modern China*, vol. 8, no. 4, 1982, pp. 491–499.

Rowe, William T., "Urban Control in Late Imperial China: The Pao-chia System in Hankow," in Vogel J. A., and Rowe W. T., *Perspectives on a Changing China: Essays in Honor of Prof. Martin C. Wilbur*, Boulder, Westview Press, 1979, pp. 89–112.

Rowe, William T., *Hankow: Commerce and Society in a Chinese City, 1796–1889*, Stanford, Stanford University Press, 1984.

Rowe, William T., *Hankow. Conflict and Community in a Chinese City, 1796–1895*, Stanford, Stanford University Press, 1989.

Rules and Regulations for the Guidance of the Action of the Shanghai Municipal Force, Shanghai, "Celestial Empire" Office, 1881.

Scherer, Renate, *Das System der chinesischen Prostitution dargestellt am Beispiel Shanghais in der Zeit von 1840 bis 1949*, Inaugural dissertation, Freie Universität Berlin, 1983, Berlin, Papyrus-Druck, 1986.

Schlegel, Gustaaf, *Histoire de la prostitution en Chine*, Rouen, J. Lemonnyer, 1880 (translated from the Dutch *Iets over de prostitutie in China*, Batavia, Lange, 1866).

Schlegel, Gustaaf, *Le vendeur d'huile qui seul possède la reine-de-beauté, ou splendeurs et misères des courtisanes chinoises*, Paris/Leyden, Brill et Maisonneuve, 1877.

Schon, Jenny, *Frauen in China: Eine Studie über die gesellschaftliche Stellung der chinesischen Frau vor 1949*, Bochum, Brockmeyer, 1982.

Schulte, Regina, *Sperrbezirke: Tugendhaftigkeit und Prostitution in der bürgerlichen Welt*, Frankfurt am Main, Syndikat, 1979.

Scott, George R., *Far Eastern Sex Life: An Anthropological, Ethnological and Sociological Study of the Love Relations, Marriage Rites and Home Life of the Oriental Peoples*, London, Gerald C. Swan, 1970 (1st ed., 1943).

Se Lu, "Changji zhidu shikao" ("Historical Study of the System of Prostitution"), *Funü zazhi* ("The Ladies' Journal"), vol. VI, no. 9, pp. 1–8.

Service d'hygiène et d'assistance, Rapport imprimé de présentation du service, 1933, Archives diplomatiques, Nantes, carton no. 39.

Sha Ni, "Wuchang de cun jin" ("The Keeping of the Prohibition on Dancing"), *Funü zazhi* ("The Ladies' Journal"), vol. 5, no. 4, 1944, p. 13.

Shang Sidi, *Shanghai dili jianhua* ("A Short Description of the Geography of Shanghai"), Shanghai, Renmin chubanshe, 1974.

Shang Yiren, "Jinü da shourong mulu ji" ("Personal Testimony on the Great Raid on Prostitutes"), *Shanghai tan* ("The Bund"), May 1989, no. 29, pp. 18–21.

Shanghai difang ziliao ("Local Materials on Shanghai"), Shanghai, Municipal Library of Shanghai, neibu cankao, 1963, Volume on Western authors; 1964, Volume on Chinese works.

Shanghai fengsu zaji ("Notes on the Customs of Shanghai"), Shanghai, Shanghai xintuo gufen youxian gongsi, 1932.

Shanghai funü ("Shanghai Women"), Shanghai, Shanghai funüshe, vol. 1, no. 1; vol. 3, no. 2, 1938–May 1939.

Shanghai jiye wenti ("The Problem of Prostitution in Shanghai"), Shanghai, Shanghai jindehui pilu lunwen, no. 2, 1919.

Shanghai lanyou zhinan ("A Sightseeing Guide to Shanghai"), Shanghai, Zhonghua tushu jicheng gongsi, 1923.

Shanghai Municipal Council, *Report for the Year*, Shanghai, Kelly & Walsh, 1872–1881, 1883–1885, 1887–1904, 1907–1910, 1921–1940.

Shanghai pinyan baihua tu ("Hundred Portraits of Courtesans of Shanghai"), Shanghai, 1884, 5 vols.

Shanghai shenghuo, Shanghai, Lianhua guanggaoshe, vols. 1–5, March 1937–December 1941.

Shanghai shenmi zhinan ("Secret Guide to Shanghai"), Shanghai, Datong tushushe jianyin, n.d., 2 vols.

Shanghai shi ershijiu niandu suiyue hukou shumu tongjibiao ("Monthly Statistics of the Population of Shanghai, 1940"), Shanghai shizheng gongbao ("Official Journal of the Municipality of Shanghai"), 1941.

Shanghai shi gong'anju yewu baogao ("Annual Report of the Public Security Bureau of the Municipality of Shanghai"), Shanghai, Shanghai shi gong'anju, 1928–1929.

Shanghai shi hanghao lutu lu ("Shanghai Street Directory"), Shanghai, The Free Trading Co. Ltd., 1939–1941, 1947.

Shanghai shi jiedao tu ("Map of Shanghai Roads"), Shanghai, Shanghai dixueshe chuban, 1949.

Shanghai shi jingchaju fagui huibian ("Collection of Laws and Regulations of the Police of the Municipality of Shanghai"), Shanghai, Shanghai shi jingchaju, no. 1, March 1947, 5 vols.

Shanghai shi jingchaju gongzuo baogao ("Annual Report on the Work of the Police Bureau of the Municipality of Shanghai"), Shanghai, Shanghai shi jingchaju, September 1945–March 1946, September 1945–August 1946, 4 vols.

Shanghai shi jingchaju laozha fenju sanshiliu niandu niankan ("Annual Report for the Year 1947 of the Laozha Police Station, Police Bureau of the Municipality of Shanghai"), Shanghai, n. pub., 1948, 5 vols.

Shanghai shi jingchaju sanshiwu nian tongji nianbao ("Annual Statistical Report for 1946 of the Police Bureau of the Municipality of Shanghai"), Shanghai, Shanghai shi shi zhengfu jingchaju, 1947.

Shanghai shi jingchaju sanshiliu nian tongji nianbao ("Annual Statistical Report for 1947 of the Police Bureau of the Municipality of Shanghai"), Shanghai, Shanghai shi shi zhengfu jingchaju, 1948.

Shanghai shi nianjian ("Shanghai Municipality Yearbook"), Shanghai, Shanghai shi tongzhiguan, 1935, 2 vols.; 1936, 2 vols.; 1937, 2 vols.

Shanghai shi nianjian ("Shanghai Municipality Yearbook"), Shanghai, Zhonghua shuju, 1946; Shanghai huadong tongxunshe, 1947.

Shanghai shi shehui tongji gaiyao ("Compendium of Statistics of the Municipality of Shanghai"), Shanghai, Shanghai shi shehuiju, 1935.

Shanghai shi shehuiju gongzuo baogao ("Report of Activity of the Social Affairs Bureau of the Municipality of Shanghai"), Shanghai, Shanghai shi shehuiju, 1946, 4 vols.; 1947, 4 vols.

Shanghai shi shehuiju xingzheng tongji ("Administrative Statistics of the Social Affairs Bureau of the Municipality of Shanghai"), Shanghai, Shanghai shi shehuiju, May 1948, 4 vols.

Shanghai shi shehuiju yewu baogao ("Annual Report of Activity of the Social Affairs Bureau of the Municipality of Shanghai"), Shanghai, Shanghai shi shehuiju, 1931, 1932.

Shanghai shi tongji ("Statistics of the Municipality of Shanghai"), Shanghai, Shanghai difang xiehui, 1933, 2 vols.

Shanghai shi tongji [di'er ci] buchong cailiao ("Second Supplement to Statistics of the Municipality of Shanghai"), Shanghai, Shanghai difang xiehui, 1936.

Shanghai shi tongzhiguan qikan ("Journal of the Compilation Bureau of the Municipality of Shanghai"), Shanghai, vol. 1, no. 1; vol. 2, no. 4, June 1933–March 1935.

Shanghai shi weishengju san nian lai gongzuo gaikuang ("Report on Work [Done by] the Health Bureau of the Municipality of Shanghai for the Past Three Years"), Shanghai, n.pub., [1949].

"Shanghai shuyu de fuhuo" ("The Resurrection of the Courtesans of Shanghai"), *Funü zazhi* ("The Ladies' Journal"), vol. X, no. 7, 1924, pp. 1067–1068.

Shanghai subei nanmin jiuji baogao ("Report on Assistance to Refugees from Subei in Shanghai"), Shanghai, Subei nanmin jiujihui shanghai banshichu bian, 1947.

Shanghai tebie shi gong'anju yewu jiyao ("Annual Report of Activity of the Public Security Bureau of the Municipality of Shanghai"), Shanghai, Shanghai shi gong'anju, 1927–1928.

Shanghai wenshi ziliao ("Selected Materials on the History and Culture of Shanghai"), Zhongguo renmin zhengzhi xiehui Shanghai shi weiyuanhui wenshi ziliao gongzuo weiyuanhui bian, Shanghai, Renmin chubanshe, quarterly.

Shanghai xian xuzhi ("Supplement to the Local Gazette of the *Xian* of Shanghai"), 1918 (reprint, Taibei, Chengwen chubanshe, 1970).

"Shanghai xian zai qing dai" ("The *Xian* of Shanghai under the Qing"), *Shanghai shi tongzhiguan qikan* ("Journal of the Bureau of Compilation of the Municipality of Shanghai"), vol. 2, no. 2, 1936.

Shanghai xianzhi ("Local Gazette of the *Xian* of Shanghai"), Shanghai, Nanyuan zhiju, 1871 (reprint, Taibei, Chengwen chubanshe, 4 vols.).

Shanghai yanjiu ziliao ("Research Materials on Shanghai"), Shanghai, Shanghai tongshe, 1936 (reprint, Taibei, Zhongguo chubanshe, 1973; revised edition, Shanghai, Shanghai shudian, 1984).

Shanghai yanjiu ziliao xuji ("Supplement to Research Materials on Shanghai"), Shanghai, Shanghai tongshe, 1939 (reprint, Shanghai, Shanghai shudian, 1984).

Shanghai zhinan ("Guide to Shanghai: A Chinese Directory of the Port"), Shanghai, Shangwu yinshuguan, 1st ed., 1909; 1919; 1920; 1923; 1925; 1926; 1930.

Shanghai zhinan ("Guide to Shanghai"), Shanghai, Guoguang shudian, n.d.

Shanghai's Commercial and Shopping Pocket Guide, Shanghai, Kwang Hsueh Publishing House, [1936].

Shao Yi, "Lun changji zhi you bai hai er wu yi li" ("The Prostitutes Cause a Hundred Evils and Bring No Benefit"), *Funü shibao* ("Women's Journal"), no. 5, December 1911, pp. 6–8.

Shehui ban yuekan ("Social [Affairs] Fortnightly"), Shanghai, Shanghai shi shehuiju, biweekly.

Shehui diaocha huikan ("Journal of Social Inquiry"), Beiping, Beiping tebieshi shehuiju, vol. I, 1930.

Shehui yuekan ("Monthly Journal of the Bureau of Social Affairs"), Shanghai, monthly, January 1929–January 1932.

Shehui zhi hua ("Flowers of Society"), Shanghai, vol. I, no. 15, 1924, pp. 7–8 (advertisements).

Shen Bao ("The Shanghai Times"), Shanghai, daily, 1872–1949 (abbreviated as *SB*).

Shen Bao nianjian ("*Shen Bao* Yearbook"), Shanghai, Shen Bao, 1933–1937.

Shen Bao zhoukan ("Weekly Supplement of the *Shen Bao*"), Shanghai, weekly, January 1936–December 1937.

Shen Bojing, *Shanghai shi zhinan* ("Guide to the Municipality of Shanghai"), Shanghai, Zhonghua shuju, 1933.

Shen Shuzhen, "Hu shang ni she jinü xuexiao lun" ("Discussion on the Plan to Create a School for Prostitutes"), *Funü shibao* ("Women's Journal"), no. 7, 1912, pp. 45–47.

Shenjiang mingsheng tushuo ("Famous Places of Shanghai in Words and Etchings"), Shanghai, 1884, 2 vols.

Shi Bao ("The Times"), Shanghai, daily, 1909–1937.

Shidai funü ("Women of the Age"), Zhangjiakou (Kalgan), no. 1, July 1949.

"Shijie renlei de chiru" ("The Shame of All of Mankind"), *Funü zazhi* ("The Ladies' Journal"), vol. IX, no. 3, pp. 2–5.

Shiya Shuzo, "Criminal Procedure in the Qing Dynasty," *Memoirs of the Toyo Bunka*, 1976, no. 34, pp. 1–137.

Shizheng pinglun ("Journal of Municipal Affairs"), Shanghai, vol. 8, nos. 1–10, vol. 9, nos. 1–11, October 1945–April 1949.

Sia, R. H. R., "Routine Wassermann Tests on 502 In-patients," *China Medical Journal*, vol. 35, January 1921, pp. 39–43.

"Sihong xian jiji jiejiu 'longzhongniao' " ("The *Xian* of Sihong Has Actively Aided 'Caged Birds' "), *Gong'an ribao* ("The Public Security Daily"), 8 February 1991.

Sinclair, Michael, "The French Settlement of Shanghai on the Eve of the Revolution of 1911," doctoral thesis, Stanford University, 1973.

Skinner, J. E., "Kahn Precipitation Test for Syphilis," *China Medical Journal*, vol. 41, no. 12, December 1927, pp. 1004–1006.

Skinner, William G., *The City in Late Imperial China*, Stanford, Stanford University Press, 1977.

Snell, J. H., "Report of Routine Wassermann Tests at Soochow Hospital for One Year," *China Medical Journal*, vol. 35, January 1921, pp. 36–39.

Snell, J. H., "Report of 3000 Routine Wassermann Tests at the Soochow Hospital," *China Medical Journal*, vol. 43, December 1929, pp. 1238–1241.

Snell, J. H., "[The] Social Evil in China," *China Medical Journal*, vol. 38, June 1924, pp. 488–494.

Société des nations, Conférence diplomatique pour la répression de la traite des femmes majeures et des enfants, *Convention internationale relative à la répression de la traite des femmes majeures*, Geneva, document no. C.590.M.276.1933.IV, 1933.

Société des nations, *Renseignements concernant la prostitution et la traite des femmes et des enfants dans divers pays et colonies asiatiques*, C.T.E.F. [Experts] 44 (confidentiel), Geneva, Imprimerie de la "Tribune de Genève," [1924].

Traite des femmes et des enfants. "Réponse du gouvernement chinois," in *Réponse des gouvernements au questionnaire publié par le secrétériat*, Geneva, document no. 12/13716/11622, 1921, 41 vols.

Song Haibo, "Guaimai funü ertong fanzui de falü wenti" ("The Legal Problems Relating to Cases of Traffic in Women and Children"), *Fazhi ribao* ("Legality Daily"), 1 April 1991.

Stauffer, Milton T., *The Christian Occupation of China*, Shanghai, China Continuation Committee, 1922.

Strand, David, *Rickshaw Beijing: City People and Politics in the 1920s*, Berkeley, University of California Press, 1989.

Sun Dingwo, *Changji yu falü* ("The Prostitute and the Law"), Taibei, Minzhong wenhua chubanshe, 1980.

Sun Guoqun, "Lun jiu shanghai changji zhidu de fazhan ji qi tedian" ("On the Development of the System of Prostitution in Old Shanghai and its Characteristics"), in *Shanghai yanjiu luncong* ("Collection of Research Work on Shanghai"), no. 4, Shanghai shi difang zhi bangongshi, Shanghai, Shanghai shehui kexueyuan chubanshe, 1989, pp. 210–224.

Sun Guoqun, *Jiu shanghai changji mishi* ("A Secret History of Prostitution in Old Shanghai"), Henan, Henan renmin chubanshe, 1988.

Ta Tsing Leu Li, *Being the Fundamental Laws and Selection from the Supplementary Statutes of the Penal Code of China*, translated by Staunton, George T., London, 1810 (reprint, Taibei, 1966).

Tang Weikang, "Shili yangchang de changji" ("The Prostitutes of the 'Foreigners' District'," in Tang Weikang et al., *Shanghai yishi* ("Shanghai Anecdotes"), Shanghai, Wenhua chubanshe, 1987, pp. 261–274.

Tang Weikang et al., *Shanghai yishi* ("Shanghai Anecdotes"), Shanghai, Wenhua chubanshe, 1987.

Tang Youfeng, *Xin shanghai* ("New Shanghai"), Shanghai, Shanghai yinshuguan, 1931.

Tao Juyin, *Gudao jianwen: kangzhan shiqi de shanghai* ("Sounds and Sights from an Isolated Island: Shanghai During the War of Resistance Against Japan"), Shanghai, Renmin chubanshe, 1979.

Thin, G., *On the Early History of Syphilis in China*, Shanghai, 1868.

Tian Di, "Sichang yu gongchang de libi" ("The Advantages and Disadvantages of Public Prostitution and Clandestine Prostitution"), *Funü zazhi* ("The Ladies' Journal"), vol. X, no. 8, 1924, pp. 1264–1272.

Tian Xiaode, "Shenmi de anmoyuan" ("The Secret Massage Parlours"), in Yuan Shike et al., *Shanghai fengqing* ("Shanghai Distractions"), Shanghai, Lantian shubao zazhishe [1948], pp. 2–6.

"Traffic in Women Problem for China," *The Transpacific*, Tokyo, 28 March 1935, p. 15.

Tsang, M. L., "The Importance of Venereal Disease Clinics, with a Report of 400 Cases from St. Luke's Genito-Urinary Clinic, Shanghai," *National Medical Journal*, vol. 10, June 1925, pp. 172–187.

Tsao, Jr-lien, "Remembering Suzhou. Urbanism in Late Imperial China," doctoral thesis, University of California, 1992.

Tsen, E. T. H., "The Prevalence of Syphilis in Peking," *National Medical Journal*, vol. 6, 1920, p. 156.

Tso, Ernest, "Statistics of Communicable Diseases among Hospital Employees in Peking," *China Medical Journal*, vol. 37, March–April 1923, pp. 226–230.

Tsu Yu-yue, *The Spirit of Chinese Philanthropy*, New York, Columbia University Press, 1912.

Tu Jiyuan, "Pan Hannian tongzhi he shanghai de gaizao" ("Comrade Pan Hannian and the Reform of Shanghai"), *Wenshi ziliao xuanji* ("Selection of Historical and Literary Materials on Shanghai"), no. 4, 1982, pp. 104–106.

Tui Tangsheng, "Shanghai changji zhi cheyu wenti" ("The Problem of the Transportation of Prostitutes"), *Xin shanghai* ("The New Shanghai"), vol. 2, no. 4, January 1927, pp. 65–67.

Tun Min, "Changji he zhenjie" ("Prostitutes and Chastity"), *Funü zazhi* ("The Ladies' Journal"), vol. IX, no. 3, 1923, pp. 19–21.

Tyau, E. S., "The Incidence of Skin Diseases in Shanghai," *National Medical Journal*, vol. 9, 1924, p. 75.

Van Gulik, Robert, *Erotic Colour Prints of the Ming Period*, Tokyo, n.pub., 1951 (reprint, Taibei, n.d.).

Van Gulik, Robert, *Sexual Life in Ancient China*, Leiden, E. J. Brill, 1961 (*La vie sexuelle dans la Chine ancienne*, Paris, TEL Gallimard, 1971).

Vignettes from the Chinese. Lithographs from Shanghai in the Late Nineteenth Century, edited and translated by Cohn, Don J., Hong Kong, The Chinese University of Hong Kong, Renditions paperbacks, 1987.

Wakeman, Frederic, Jr., *Policing Shanghai, 1927–1937*, Berkeley, University of California Press, 1994.

Waley, Arthur, "The Green Bower Collection" [1957], in *The Secret History of the Mongols and Other Pieces*, New York, Barnes & Noble Inc., 1967, pp. 89–107.

Walkowitz, Judith, *Prostitution and Victorian Society: Women, Class, and the State*, Cambridge, Cambridge University Press, 1980.

Wang Benhu, *Minguo jiaofu Du Yuesheng* ("The Master of the Secret Societies, Du Yuesheng"), Taibei, Yeqiang chubanshe, 1990.

Wang Dingjiu, *Shanghai guwen* ("A Guide to Shanghai"), Shanghai, Zhongyang shudian, 1934.

Wang Dingjiu, *Shanghai menjing* ("Gateway to Shanghai"), Shanghai, Zhongyang shudian, 1932 (reprint, 1937).

Wang Fuxiang et al., *Shehui de ling yi mian: Xinjiapo changji diaocha* ("Another Face of Society: Inquiry into the Prostitutes of Singapore"), Singapore, Yunnan shuju, 1970.

Wang Houze, *Shanghai baojian* ("Precious Mirror of Shanghai"), Shanghai, Shijie shuju, 1925.

Wang Jimen, *Shanghai liushi nian lai huajie shi* ("Sixty Years of the History of the World of Flowers in Shanghai"), Shanghai, Shixin shuju, 1922.

Wang Jingtao, *Shanghai de xing shichang* ("The Sex Market in Shanghai"), Shanghai, Manli shuju, 1932.

Wang Nanping, "Jiangbei nongcun shikuang" ("The Real Situation of the Villages of Jiangbei"), in Qian Jiaju, *Zhongguo nongcun jingji lunwenji* ("Collection of Essays on Village Economy in China"), Shanghai, Zhonghua shuju, 1936, pp. 610–619.

Wang Shijie, "Zhongguo nubei zhidu" ("The Legal Existence of Slavery in the History of China"), *Shehui kexue jikan* ("Social Science Quarterly"), vol. 3, no. 3, April–June 1925, pp. 302–328.

Wang Shubi, *Shanghai heimu yi qian zhong* ("The Thousand Mysteries of Shanghai"), Shanghai, Chunming shudian, 1939, 2 vols.

Wang Shunu, *Zhongguo changji shi* ("A History of Prostitution in China"), Shanghai, Shenghuo shudian, 1934.

Wang Suxin, *Zhongguo lidai mingji shihua* ("Short History of Famous Prostitutes in Chinese History"), Taibei, Xinzhuang, 1972.

Wang Tao, *Songbin suohua* ("Idle Talk on the Riverside") Shanghai, n.pub., n.d.

Wang Tao, *Yinru zazhi* ("Miscellaneous Notes from the Seaside"), Shanghai, Gujichubanshe, 1989 (1st ed., 1870).

Wang Xinyuan, "Hualiubing bu zu chi" ("Venereal Diseases Are Not Shameful"), *Xin shanghai* ("The New Shanghai"), vol. 2, no. 9, June 1927, pp. 95–103.

Wang, Y. C., "Tu Yueh-sheng (1891–1951): A Tentative Biography," *Journal of Asian Studies*, no. 6, May 1967, pp. 433–455.

Wang Zhongxian, *Shanghai suyu tushuo yi ce* ("Illustrated Book of Sayings from Shanghai"), Shanghai, Shanghai shehui chubanshe, 1935 (reprint, Lixing chubanshe, 1948).

Watson, James L., "Chattel Slavery in Chinese Peasant Society: A Comparative Analysis," *Ethnology*, no. 15, October 1976, pp. 361–375.

Watson, James L., "Transactions in People: The Chinese Market in Slaves, Servants and Heirs," in Watson, James L. (ed.), *Asian and African Systems of Slavery*, Berkeley, University of California Press, 1980, pp. 223–250.

Watson, Rubie S., "Concubines and Maids: Servitude and Kin Status in the Hong Kong Region, 1900–1940," in Watson, Rubie S., and Buckley Ebrey, Patricia, *Marriage and Inequality in Chinese Society*, Berkeley, University of California Press, 1991, pp. 231–255.

Watson, Rubie S., "The Named and the Nameless: Gender and Person in Chinese Society," *American Ethnologist*, vol. 13, no. 4, November 1984, pp. 619–631.

Watt, John R., *The District Magistrate in Late Imperial China,* New York, Columbia University Press, 1972.

Wei Shaochang, *Li Boyuan yanjiu ziliao* ("Research Materials on Li Boyuan"), Shanghai, Guji chubanshe, 1980.

Wei Shaochang, *Yuanyang hudie pai yanjiu ziliao* ("Research Materials on the School of Mandarin Ducks and Butterflies"), Shanghai, Wenyi chubanshe, 1962.

Wei Xue, "Nüren yu gou" ("Women and Dogs"), in Yuan Shike et al., *Shanghai fengqing* ("Shanghai Romance"), Shanghai, Lantian shubao zazhishe, [1948], p. 6.

Wenhuibao, Shanghai, daily, 1949–1952.

Weston, Elizabeth Ann, "Prostitution in Paris in the Later Nineteenth Century," doctoral thesis, State University of New York at Buffalo, 1979.

Wilbur, Martin C., *The Nationalist Revolution in China, 1923–1928*, Cambridge, Cambridge University Press, 1983.

Willey, James H., "A Study of Chinese Prostitution," master's dissertation, University of Chicago, 1929.

Williamson, Joseph, *Josephine Butler. The Forgotten Saint*, Leighton Buzzard, Faith Press, 1977.

Wilson, Carol C., *Chinatown Quest*, Stanford, Stanford University Press, 1950 (1st ed., 1931).

Wolf, Arthur, *Marriage and Adoption in China, 1845–1945*, Stanford, Stanford University Press, 1980.

Wolfe, Barnard, *The Daily Life of a Chinese Courtesan Climbing up a Tricky Ladder*, Hong Kong, Learner's Bookstore, 1980.

Wollock, W., "Shanghai de changji wenti" ("The Problem of the Prostitutes in Shanghai"), *Dangdai* ·("Present Age"), vol. I, no. 2, 1929, pp. 223–229.

Wong, K. C., "The Social Evil in China," *China Medical Journal*, vol. 34, November 1920, pp. 630–634.

Wong, K. C., and Wu, Lien-teh, *History of Chinese Medicine*, Tientsin, Tientsin Press 1932.

Wou, Chan-cheng, *L'Érotologie de la Chine: Tradition chinoise de l'érotisme*, translated by F. Albertini, Paris, J. J. Pauvert, 1963.

Wu Chenglian, *Jiu shanghai chaguan jiulou* ("The Taverns and Tea Houses of Old Shanghai"), Shanghai, Huadong shifan daxue chubanshe, 1989.

Wu Guifang, "*Haishang hua liezhuan* de 'shixie jijia'" ("The *Chronicle of the Flowers on the Sea* and the True Description of the Brothels"), *Dang'an yu lishi* ("Archives and History"), no. 3, 1987, pp. 93–97.

Wu Jing, "Maiyin zhi shehuixue de kaocha" ("Sociological Study of Prostitution"), translated from the Japanese, *Funü zazhi* ("The Ladies' Journal"), vol. IX, no. 3, 1923, pp. 25–41.

Wu Jun-yi, *Qing mo shanghai zujie shehui* ("The Society of the Settlements in Shanghai at the End of the Qing"), Taibei, Wenshizhe chubanshe, 1978.

Wu Lien-teh, "The Problem of Venereal Diseases in China," *China Medical Journal*, vol. 41, January 1927, pp. 28–36.

Wu Ruohua, "Shanghai funü jiuji shiye ying you de gaige" ("The Reform Required by the Activities of Assistance to Women in Shanghai"), *Shehui yuekan* ("Social Affairs Monthly"), vol. I, no. 2, 1929, pp. 1–8.

Wu Ruting, "Guaimai funü ertong fanzui xianzhuang chutan" ("Preliminary Inquiry into Offenses of Traffic in Women and Children"), *Gong'an ribao* ("The Public Security Daily"), 22 February 1991.

Wu Shenyuan, *Shanghai zui zao de zhong zhong* ("For the First Time in Shanghai"), Shanghai, Huadong shifan daxue chubanshe, 1989.

Wuli Kanhuake (pseudonym of Qian Xinbo, *Zhenzheng lao Lin Daiyu* ("The True Lin Daiyu"), Shanghai, Guomin tushuguan, 1919.

Xia Lingen, *Jiu shanghai sanbai liushi hang* ("The 360 Trades of Old Shanghai"), Shanghai, Huadong shifan daxue chubanshe, 1989.

Xiangyan congshu ("Collection [of the World] of Beauties"), Zhang Tinghua, Shanghai, Guoxue fulunshe, [1909–1911], 80 vols.

Xiaolinbao ("A Thousand Smiles"), Shanghai, periodical, 1902.

Xie Kang, *Maiyin zhidu yu Taiwan changji wenti* ("The Sex Trade and the Problem of Prostitution in Taiwan"), Taibei, Dafeng chubanshe, 1972.

Xie Wuyi, "Minchu shanghai changji yi pie" ("A Quick Look at Prostitution in Shanghai at the Beginning of the Republic"), in *Jiu shanghai de yan du chang* ("Prostitution, Gambling and Opium in Old Shanghai"), Shanghai shi wenshiguan bian, Shanghai, Baijia chubanshe, 1988, pp. 172–175.

Xin nüxing ("New Woman"), vol. I, nos. 2, 8, August 1927; vol. II, nos. 2, 11, November 1927.

Xin shanghai ("New Shanghai"), Shanghai, monthly, May 1925–September 1927.

Xin wenhua ("New Culture"), vol. I, no. 6, Shanghai.

Xing Taozuo, "Lunluo tu" ("Pictures of Downfall"), *Funü yuekan* ("Women's Monthly"), vol. VI, no. 6, January 1948, pp. 25–27.

Xingbing zai Zhongguo ("Venereal Disease in China"), Beijing, Beijing shiyue wenyi chubanshe, 1990.

Xinminbao ("The New People"), 1949–1956.

Xinwen ribao ("The News"), Shanghai, daily, 1951.

Xixi shanren, *Wumen huafang lu* ("Story of the Brothels of Suzhou"), in *Yanshi shi er zhong* ("History of Lasciviousness in Twelve Tales"), Yu Chensheng, Shanghai, Hanwenyuan shusi, 1929, 8 vols. (reproduction of the edition of 1878).

Xu Guang, "Zhongguo changji yange gailun" ("General Presentation of the Development of Prostitution in China"), *Funü zazhi* ("The Ladies' Journal"), vol. V, no. 7, 1944, pp. 8–9.

Xu Ke (ed.), *Qing bai lei chao* ("The Hundred Categories of the Qing"), Shanghai, Shangwu yinshuguan, 1920, 8 vols. (1st ed., 1917).

Xu Ruoping, "Zhongguo changji shihua" ("Abridged History of Prostitution in China"), *Funü yuekan* ("Women's Monthly"), vol. VI, no. 6, January 1948, pp. 22–24.

Xu Wancheng, *Shanghai cishan jiguan gaikuang* ("General State of Charitable Institutions in Shanghai"), Shanghai, Longwen shudian, 1941.

Xu Yasheng, "Changji yu shehui" ("Prostitutes and Society"), *Funü zazhi* ("The Ladies' Journal"), vol. XVI, no. 6, 1930, pp. 16–27.

Xu Yuzhai, "Shanghai zaji" ("Miscellaneous Notes on Shanghai"), in *Xu Yuzhai zixupu* ("Autobiography of Xu Yuzhai"), [Shanghai], Xiangshan-xushixiao, n.d.

Xue Gengxin, "Jindai shanghai de liumang" ("The Gangsters of Shanghai in the Modern Period"), *Shanghai wenshi ziliao xuanji*, no. 3, 1980, pp. 160–178.

Xue Gengxin, "Jindai shanghai hei shehui jianwen" ("Some Rumors about the Secret Societies of Shanghai"), in *Jiu shanghai de yan du chang* ("Prostitution, Gambling, and Opium in Old Shanghai"), Shanghai shi wenshiguan bian, Shanghai, Baijia chubanshe, 1988, pp. 179–195.

Xue Liyong, "Ming-Qing shiqi de shanghai changji" ("Prostitution in Shanghai in Ming-Qing Times"), in *Jiu shanghai de yan du chang* ("Prostitution, Gambling, and Opium in Old Shanghai"), Shanghai shi wenshiguan bian, Shanghai, Baijia chubanshe, 1988, pp. 150–158.

Yamata, Kiku, *Vies de geisha*, Paris, Gallimard, 1934 (6th ed.).

Yan Guoyi, "Feichang wenti de zhongyao" ("On the Importance of Prohibiting Prostitution"), *Funü zazhi* ("The Ladies' Journal"), vol. IX, no. 5, 1923, pp. 28–29.

Yan Jingyao, "Beiping fanzui zhi shehui fenxi" ("Social Anlaysis of Crime in Peking"), *Shehui xuejie* ("The Sociological World"), no. 2, 1929, pp. 33–77.

Yan Zhijun, "Jinü de zui" ("The crime of the Prostitutes"), *Xin nüxing* ("New Woman"), vol. IV, no. 4, 1929, p. 485.

Yang Huifu, "Shanghai ertong fanzui wenti yanjiu dagang" ("General Draft of a Study of Juvenile Delinquency in Shanghai"), thesis, Hujiang University (sociology), 1942.

Yang Wei, *Du Yuesheng waizhuan* ("Unauthorized Biography of Du Yuesheng"), Taibei, Xin qiye shijie chubanshe, 1984.

Yanshi shi er zhong ("History of Lasciviousness in Twelve Tales"), published by Yu Chensheng, Shanghai, Hanwenyuan shusi, 1929, 8 vols. (reproduction of 1878 ed.).

Yen Ching-yüeh, "Crime in Relation to Social Change in China," doctoral thesis, University of Chicago, 1934.

Yen Ching-Yüeh, *A Study of Crime in Peiping*, Yenching University, series C, no. 20, December 1929.

Yewu baogao ("Activity Report"), Shanghai, Shanghai tebie shi weishengju bian, Shanghai, 1941, 1942.

Yi Feng, "Changji wenti yanjiu" ("Research on the Problem of the Prostitutes"), *Funü gongmin yuekan* ("Women Citizens' Monthly"), February 1933, pp. 31–44.

Yi jiu ba qi. Shanghai dang'an shiye nianjian ("Yearbook of Activities of Shanghai Archives 1987"), Shanghai, Shanghai shi dang'anju bian, 1988.

You Xiong, "Changji weisheng de qudi" ("The Abolition of Health Controls on Prostitutes"), *Funü zazhi* ("The Ladies' Journal"), vol. IX, no. 3, 1923, pp. 42–44.

Young, Luke C. P., "The Kahn Reaction Test for Syphilis," *China Medical Journal*, vol. 41, December 1927, pp. 999–1004.

Yu Baosheng [pseudonym of Wang Tao], *Haizou yeyou fulu* ("Addenda to Notes of a Libertine on the Seaside"), Shanghai, Hanwen yuanshusi, 1929 (1st ed., 1878).

Yu Baosheng [pseudonym of Wang Tao], *Haizou yeyou lu* ("Notes of a Libertine on the Seaside"), Shanghai, Hanwen yuanshusi [1860], 1929 (1st ed., 1878).

Yu Baosheng [pseudonym of Wang Tao], *Haizou yeyou yulu* ("A Sequel to Notes of a Libertine on the Seaside – Continued"), Shanghai, Hanwen yuanshusi, 1929 (1st ed., 1878).

Yu Baosheng [pseudonym of Wang Tao], *Huaguo jutan* ("Talks about the Theater of the World of Flowers"), Shanghai, Hanwen yuanshusi [1878], 1929.

Yü Chüan Chang, "The Chinese Judiciary," *The Chinese Political and Social Science Review*, vol. III, no. 1, March 1918, pp. 1–25.

Yu Lan (translation), "Changji fan lun" ("Lengthy Words on Prostitution"), *Funü yuekan* ("Women's Monthly"), vol. VI, no. 6, January 1948, pp. 18–21.

Yu Wei, "Jin chang yu xingbing fangzhi" ("The Prohibition of Prostitution and the Prevention of Venereal Diseases"), *Shizheng pinglun* ("The Municipal Affairs Weekly"), vol. 9, no. 9/10, pp. 17–18.

Yu Wei, "Shanghai changji wu bai ge an diaocha" ("A Study of 500 Prostitutes in Shanghai"), *Shizheng pinglun* ("The Municipal Affairs Weekly"), vol. 10, no. 9/10, pp. 10–14.

Yu Wei and Wong, Amos, "A Study of 500 Prostitutes in Shanghai," *The International Journal of Sexology*, vol. II, no. 4, May 1949, pp. 234–238.

Yuan Shike et al., *Shanghai fengqing* ("Shanghai Romance"), Shanghai, Lantian shubao zazhishe, [1948].

Zhang Jungu, "*Du Yuesheng zhuan*" ("Biography of Du Yuesheng"), Taibei, Zhuanji wenxue chubanshe, 1967–1969, 4 vols.

Zhang Qiugu, *Piao du baibi daguan* ("An Overview of the Evils of Gambling and Whoring"), Shanghai, Qiugu chubanbu, 1920, 2 vols.

Zhang Shaowei, "Jingshi kaichang yihou" ("After the Legislation on Prostitution in the Capital [Nanking]"), *Pangguan xunkan* ("Obliques"), Nanjing, no. 22, 11 June 1933, pp. 14–21.

Zhang Zhiying, "Jingshen wenming zhi hua zai Huileli sheng kai" ("The Flowers of a Spiritual Civilization Are Blooming in Huileli"), *Xinmin wanbao* ("New People"), Shanghai, 28 September 1989, p. 4.

Zhang Zhiyun, *Shanghai shi fenqu lilong xiangtu* ("Detailed Map of the Streets of Shanghai by District"), Shanghai, Xinzhong yudi xueshe, 1947, 2 vols.

Zhang Zhongjiang, *Jinü yu wenxue* "("Prostitutes and Literature"), Taibei, Kang Naixin chubanshe, 1969 [1st ed., 1966, *Lidai jinü yu shige* ("The Famous Prostitutes of History and Poetry"), Zhiquan chubanshe].

Zhao Fengjie, "Zhongguo funü zai falü shang zhi diwei bupian" ("Further Study of the Legal Status of Chinese Women"), *Shehui kexue* ("The Social Sciences"), vol. I, no. 4, July 1936, pp. 1099–1142.

Zhao Qingzhen, *Qinglou xiaoming lu* ("Yearbook of the Green Chamber"), Shanghai, Guoxue fulunshe, 1910, 4 vols.

Zhao Zhiyan, "Zhengjiu changji de cishan jigou – Jiliangsuo" ("A Charitable Organization Saving Prostitutes – the Door of Hope"), in *Jiu shanghai de yan du chang* ("Prostitution, Gambling and Opium in Old Shanghai"), Shanghai shi wenshiguan bian, Shanghai, Baijia chubanshe, 1988, pp. 176–178.

Zheng Hecheng, "Anguo xian yaoshi diaocha" ("A Survey of the Market for Medicine in the *Xian* of Anguo"), *Shehui kexue zazhi* ("Social Sciences Journal"), vol. 3, no. 1, March 1932, pp. 118–124.

Zheng Yisheng, *Jing-Hu baojian* ("Peking-Shanghai"), Shanghai, Zhongguo gongshang fuwushe, 1949.

Zhong Mi, "Zai lun 'heimu'" ("New Discussion on Literature of the 'Black Curtain'"), in Wei Shaochang *Yuanyang hudie pai yanjiu ziliao* ("Research Materials on the School of Mandarin Ducks and Butterflies"), Shanghai, Wenyi chubanshe, 1962, pp. 76–83.

Zhong Yan, "Feichang shijian de wo jian" ("My Viewpoint on the Abolition of Prostitution"), *Funü zazhi* ("The Ladies' Journal"), vol. XIII, no. 12, 1927, pp. 16–19.

Zhongguo jiuji furu zonghui, *Chajiu fu ru bei guai waibu an* ("Cases of Inquiry and of Assistance to Women and Children Kidnapped and Taken Out of Shanghai"), [Shanghai], n.pub., 1928.

Zhonghua minguo fagui da quan ("Compendium of Laws and Regulations of the Chinese Republic"), Shanghai, Shangwu yinshuguan, 1936.

Zhou Gucheng, *Zhongguo shehui zhi bianhua* ("Social Changes in China"), Shanghai, Xin shengming shuju, 1932.

Zhou Yinjun, Yang Jiezeng, and Xue Suzhen, "Xin shehui ba gui biancheng ren: shanghai gaizao changji shihua" ("The New Society Transforms Demons into Human Beings: A Short History of the Rehabilitation of Prostitutes of Shanghai"), *Shehui* ("Society"), no. 1, October 1981, pp. 46–51.

Zhu Ruiyue, "Shen bao fanying xia de shanghai shehui bianqian, 1895–1927"

("Social Changes in Shanghai Seen Through the *Shen Bao*"), Master's thesis, Guoli taiwan daxue, 1990.

Zhu Zhenxin, "Lun changji wenti" ("On Prostitution"), *Funü zazhi* ("The Ladies' Journal"), vol. IX, no. 3, 1923, pp. 9–12.

Zhu Zhongfan, "Riben feichang wenti" ("The Abolition of Prostitution in Japan"), *Funü zazhi* ("The Ladies' Journal"), vol. XVII, no. 9, 1931, pp. 25–29.

Zi Fang, "Jin chang lun" ("Discussion on the Abolition of Prostitution"), *Funü shijie* (The Ladies' World), vol. II, no. 7–8, 1941, p. 15.

Zou Yiren, *Jiu shanghai renkou bianqian de yanjiu* ("A Study of the Development of the Population of Old Shanghai"), Shanghai, Renmin chubanshe, 1980.

Zuili Tuitangsheng (pseudonym), "Shanghai zhi ji" ("The Prostitutes of Shanghai"), *Xin shanghai* ("New Shanghai"), no. 10, February 1926, pp. 43–48; no. 12, April 1926, pp. 35–41.

Index

photography, 48, 100, 106, 351
physical appearance of courtesans, 29,
47–50
pipa, 24, 25, 29, 31, 38, 243, 244
pledged women, 33, 191, 199, 233, 238,
246, 249, 269, 340, 357, 359
police, 89, 131, 318; raids, 245, 329;
sanitary controls, 276; registration of
prostitutes, 104, 116, 123, 145, 232,
284, 298–309, 328–31; repression
against soliciting, 89–90, 94, 315;
surveillance, 95–6, 112, 140, 150,
273–4, 324; traffic in women, 168,
191, 195; and protection of
prostitutes, 152, 156, 327
poverty, 29, 187, 326, 333, 357
pregnancy, 55
press, 67–8, 94, 139, 154, 159, 238, 254,
307, 313, 321
prison, 153, 155, 156, 192, 198
Protestants, 92, 104, 290, 291, 292, 309,
335, 352, 360
Public Health Bureau, 144, 145–7, 150,
314, 350
Public Security Bureau, 104, 119
punishments, 95

Qingbang. See Green Gang
Qingliange, 42, 93

race course, 43, 207, 215
rape, 188, 190, 192
recruitment of prostitutes, 128–9, 165–7
refugees, 88, 89, 99, 104, 107, 108, 191,
207, 208, 312, 325, 346
regulationism, 275–9, 289, 355
relatives, 32, 187
religious societies. *See* Protestants and
missionaries
restaurants, 34, 36, 37, 42–3, 46, 63, 83,
88, 206, 224, 237, 251, 325
riots, 106
ruffians, 134, 154, 155, 156, 159, 341
Russians, 99, 100, 101, 108, 140, 142,
158, 219, 239

scholars. *See* literati
school, 31, 64
secret societies, 109, 154, 159, 169, 172,
233, 241–2, 257, 341. *See also* Green
Gang
seduction, 56
sexual culture, 21, 138

sexual education, 9
sexual relations, 35, 50, 53, 54, 140–1
sexuality, 52–6, 113, 139–41, 356–7, 358
Shanghai Municipal Council, 85, 86, 87,
100, 118, 119, 120, 142, 146, 147, 202,
215, 218, 232, 245, 250, 274, 275, 276,
277, 278, 279, 282, 283, 287, 288, 289,
291, 292–5, 312, 314, 316, 322, 324,
325, 360
Shenbao, 48, 60, 63, 80, 87, 91, 93, 162,
175, 185, 235, 262, 286, 307, 321, 352
shuchang, 24, 36, 37, 38–40, 41, 244
shuyu, 23, 25, 86, 207, 209, 215, 228, 244,
252, 331
siju, 77, 97, 116
social origin: of courtesans, 28–9; of
prostitutes, 125, 179, 181; of
traffickers in women, 172–4; of
managers of brothel houses, 239–40;
of customers, 234–5
soldiers, 237. *See also* army
soliciting, 91–5, 98, 135, 274, 274, 297,
298, 316, 329, 357
songs, 22, 24, 29, 31, 38, 41, 65, 229, 238,
256, 287
sterility, 146
students, 89, 90, 104, 105, 107, 118, 237
suicide, 61–2, 134, 153
Suzhou, 22, 25, 26, 27, 82, 88, 204, 206,
240
syphilis, 90, 95, 148–52, 161, 237

taiji, 78, 116, 209
tangming, 76, 77
taxes, 250, 283–6
taxi dancers, 89, 99, 107–8, 116, 162,
323, 324
tea houses, 36, 37, 40, 42–3, 42, 93, 102,
169, 171, 224, 287, 288
theater, 25, 37, 38, 40–2, 58, 63, 275,
288
tongxianghui. See native-place
associations
traffic in women: over long distance,
171, 183–5; and legislation, 192, 198,
199, 357; and courts, 191–4; and
sale price, 182–3; in East Asia, 318,
320
traffickers, 172–4, 185–7, 320, 348, 357

underground prostitution, 116, 281,
282
unemployment, 126, 136, 166

DATE DUE

MAY 3 2004	
NOV 3 0 2007	
129095278	